Stretching along the west coast of southern Africa, Namibia is a country of extremes. The harsh climate, arid grasslands and barren deserts are like no other part of Africa. It's also a hauntingly beautiful country with wide horizons and big skies, which offer a feeling of unconfined space. Wildlife still roams freely in the vast wildernesses, while some people retain traditional lifestyles that haven't changed for thousands of years.

The country's most dominant feature is the brooding and desolate Namib Desert, where the highest sand dunes in the world march determinedly towards the sea in a dune field 300 km wide. An essential experience is to climb one of Sossusvlei's dunes at sunrise and watch as the sun changes them into incredible shades of peach and orange. In the south, the Fish River Canyon is a 300-million-year-old gash in the earth forcing the river to wind tortuously through the towering sandstone rocks. To the north are the stony, parched plains of Damaraland and Kaokoland, which harbour free-roaming rhino and elephant and some unusual rock formations. Also in this region, the fabulous Etosha National Park has a network of waterholes that give life to a staggering number of animals, while birdwatchers should head to the lush perennial rivers along the splendidly green Caprivi Strip.

Being a place of wide open spaces, there are plenty of opportunities for adventure throughout Namibia. You can try quad biking or sandboarding in the giant sand dunes, mountainous multi-day hikes or gentle rambles around a guest farm, and if the sky is your thing, ballooning or skydiving. On water there are leisurely canoe trips on the Kunene and Orange rivers, or coastal cruises to spot sea life; while the cool Benguela Current creates a perfect environment for angling and deep-sea fishing.

Windhoek and Swakopmund are worth a visit for their charming laid-back atmospheres, modern amenities and excellent infrastructure. You can learn about Namibia's colonial history and the country's rise to independence from the museums, monuments and architecture, and then enjoy a German *bröchten* roll with your coffee or a fine Namibian steak with a frosty Windhoek beer.

THIS PAGE Skeleton Coast extreme driving
PREVIOUS PAGE Etosha waterhole

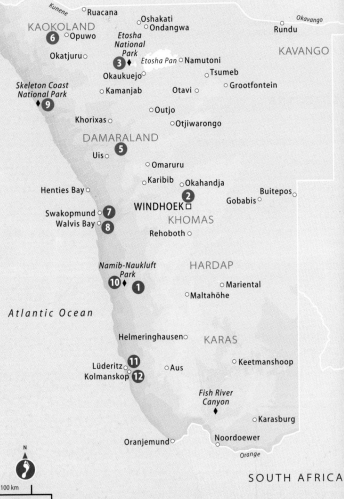

ANGOLA

Kunene
Ruacana
KAOKOLAND
6 Opuwo
Okatjuru

Oshakati
Ondangwa
Etosha
National
Park
3 ♦ *Etosha Pan* Namutoni
Okaukuejo
Kamanjab
Tsumeb
Otavi
Grootfontein

Okavango
Rundu
KAVANGO

Skeleton Coast
National Park
♦ **9**

Outjo

Khorixas
Otjiwarongo

DAMARALAND
5
Uis

Omaruru

Karibib
Okahandja

Henties Bay
WINDHOEK □ **2**
Gobabis
Buitepos

Swakopmund **7**
KHOMAS
Walvis Bay **8**

Rehoboth

Namib-Naukluft
Park
10 ♦ **1**
HARDAP
Mariental
Maltahöhe

Atlantic Ocean

Helmeringhausen
KARAS
Keetmanshoop

Lüderitz **11**
Kolmanskop **12**
Aus

Fish River Canyon ♦
Karasburg

Oranjemund
Noordoewer
Orange

N

100 km
100 miles

SOUTH AFRICA

Don't miss...

See colour maps at end of book

Katimo
Mulilo ○

APRIVI **4**

○ Ngoma
Bridge

BOTSWANA

1 Adventure activities ▶▶ page 4
Experience an adrenaline rush in the dunes by
quad biking or sandboarding.

2 Windhoek ▶▶ page 48
Enjoy a hearty meat feast with a cold Namibian lager
at the legendary Joe's Beerhouse.

3 Etosha National Park ▶▶ page 119
View a full range of African animals at the shimmering
white Etosha Pan.

4 Caprivi Strip ▶▶ page 152
Seek out birds in the well-watered parks along the
confluences of scenic rivers.

5 Damaraland ▶▶ page 176
Visit the Twyfelfontein rock paintings and see desert
elephants on the gravel plains.

6 Kaokoland ▶▶ page 192
Meet the Himba and search for desert rhino in a vast
stony wilderness.

7 Swakopmund ▶▶ page 224
Explore this characterful and attractive seaside town
between desert and ocean.

8 Walvis Bay ▶▶ page 241
Take to the ocean on a cruise or kayak to see the birdlife
and seal colonies.

9 Skeleton Coast National Park ▶▶ page 272
Drive along this harsh strip of wild coastline pounded by
the unforgiving Atlantic.

10 Namib-Naukluft Park ▶▶ page 291
Marvel at the the world's largest sand dunes.

11 Lüderitz ▶▶ page 343
Admire the German architecture and eat oysters at this
quirky fishing port.

12 Kolmanskop ▶▶ page 350
Scramble through this old diamond mining ghost town
which is being swallowed up by shifting dunes.

Itineraries for Namibia

Namibia is well geared up for tourism with well-organized activities and experiences, and quality accommodation and restaurants. It has a good network of (mainly gravel) roads, making it a an ideal self-drive destination and allowing great flexibility and freedom. However, if you're not confident about driving yourself, tour operators offer scheduled and tailor-made itineraries to even the remotest corners of the country. There's also the option of taking charter flights, which cuts travelling times down considerably, although the lodges and camps that have airstrips are usually in the luxury bracket so fly-in safaris tend to be expensive. While the official tourist hot spots are spread all over the map, the kilometres that separate them are far from lackluster; the seemingly endless landscapes provide plenty of distractions along the way. But beware of being too ambitious in your agenda as distances are significant; rather than cram in too much, try to arrange stops of two to four days in each region to fully appreciate what there is on offer.

ITINERARY ONE: 2 weeks
Desert and ocean highlights

Windhoek, the usual point of arrival, is an attractive city to wander around and easily warrants a day at the beginning or end of your trip. From Windhoek head north through Okahandja, Otjiwarongo and the 'Triangle' towns to Etosha National Park, which warrants at least three nights staying at the park's camps or the private lodges around the edge. Then head west to Damaraland to explore the extraordinary scenery, and you can approach the coast via the Skeleton Coast National Park or

Himba women, Kaokoland

Abandoned house, Kolmanskop Ghost Town

the shorter route via the Dorob National Park (formerly the West Coast Recreation Area) and stop off to see the seals at Cape Cross. How long you stay in Swakopmund rather depends on what you want to do, but at least two days is recommended to enjoy the atmosphere of this quirky seaside town and the numerous activities on offer. Head inland again to the vast Namib-Naukluft Park to explore the region

TRAVEL TIP
Depending on time and budget, mix it up a little; it's possible to combine fly-in safaris to the more out-of-the-way destinations with an organized or self-drive tour to easier destinations such as Etosha, Swakopmund and the Namib-Naukluft Park.

Cape Cross Seal Reserve

around Sesriem and most certainly watch a sunrise melt over the giant dunes at Sossusvlei. Then head south to the coast at Lüderitz, stopping to see Duwisib Castle, the desert horses near Aus, and the ghost town of Kolmanskop. Further south make your way to Hobas at the top of the Fish River Canyon for the spectacular views, and perhaps allow a night to relax at the /Ai-/Ais Hot Springs Spa at the bottom of the canyon.

TRAVEL TIP
Many South African car hire companies in Cape Town and Johannesburg permit vehicles to be taken into Namibia, which allows a choice of extended itineraries between the two countries.

Swakopmund

ITINERARY TWO: 4 weeks or more
Wilderness and adventure

Those with more time can get right off the beaten track in the extreme northwest of Namibia where you'll experience the thirstlands of Kaokoland and possibly track desert elephant and rhino and meet the Himba; one of the last nomadic, herding peoples in southern Africa. This is a remote and adventurous region but navigable if you're in a fully equipped vehicle and are confident about driving; it's especially rewarding if you're prepared to camp beneath the magnificent skies. If you are en route to Zimbabwe, Botswana or Zambia you will be able to experience the Caprivi Strip in Namibia's extreme northeast where there are game-filled forests and rivers that are markedly different to the arid deserts and plains in the rest of the country. If you enjoy hiking allow time to explore Namibia's wilderness on foot; there are plenty of challenging options, such as the five-day Fish River Canyon Trail. Alternatively, a few days on a guest or game farm makes for a relaxing couple of days perhaps at the end of your holiday where there may be interesting wildlife encounters or horse riding and farm tours.

TRAVEL TIP

From where the Caprivi Strip ends in the eastern tip of Namibia, it's only a short hop over the border to southern African highlights such as the Victoria Falls or Botswana's Okavango Delta and Chobe National Park.

Sandboarding

Kaokoland

Fish River Canyon

x

Contents

↘ iii **Introduction**
v Don't miss ...
vi Itineraries

↘ 3 **Essentials**
4 Planning your trip
9 Getting to Namibia
12 Transport in Namibia
21 Where to stay in Namibia
25 Food and drink in Namibia
28 Entertainment in Namibia
29 Shopping in Namibia
32 Essentials A-Z

↘ 45 **Windhoek & Central Namibia**
48 Windhoek
86 Around Windhoek
96 East to Botswana

↘ 103 **Etosha & the Northeast**
106 Otjiwarongo and around
119 Etosha National Park
130 The Triangle
142 Bushmanland and Kavango
152 Caprivi

↘ 173 **The Northwest &**
the Far North
176 Damaraland
192 Kaokoland
208 Far North

↘ 221 **The Coast &**
Namib-Naukluft
224 Swakopmund and around
267 Skeleton Coast
280 The Hinterland
291 Namib-Naukluft Park

↘ 313 **The South**
316 Windhoek to Keetmanshoop
331 Keetmanshoop and around
343 Lüderitz and around
358 The Far South and
    Fish River Canyon

↘ 375 **Background**
376 History of Namibia
391 Modern Namibia
393 Economy
395 Culture
397 Land and environment

↘ 409 **Footnotes**
410 Useful words and phrases
411 Index
415 Advertisers' index
416 Credits

Contents

4 Planning your trip
4 When to go to Namibia
4 What to do in Namibia
7 Going on safari

9 Getting to Namibia
9 Air
10 Road

12 Transport in Namibia
13 Air
14 Rail
14 Road

21 Where to stay in Namibia

25 Food and drink in Namibia

28 Entertainment in Namibia

29 Shopping in Namibia

32 Essentials A-Z

Footprint features

5 Packing for Namibia
8 Game-viewing rules
11 Border crossings
16 Intercape timetable
19 Driving tips
23 Price codes
26 Braai recipies
30 Responsible travel
in Namibia

Essentials

Planning your trip

When to go to Namibia

Namibia can be visited all year round as the climate is continually warm and dry. The average temperature in winter (May to September) is 18-25°C, though the summer months (December to March) can be brutal with the average temperature of 35°C often creeping into the 40°s; this may not be the best time to visit for those who struggle with the heat. Temperatures along the coast are cooled by the Benguela Current and are comfortable all year round; in summer there is a mass exodus from the interior to the cooler coastal resorts, such as Swakopmund.

With 300 days of sunshine per year, Namibia is definitely a sunny country, and the central, southern and coastal areas constitute some of the most arid landscapes south of the Sahara. As with all desert regions, days are hot while nights are generally cool. In winter months, particularly July, nights get very cold and there are frosts. Most of the countryside is totally unrecognizable after the rains, which mostly fall between February and March, as the landscape is green and full of unusual flowering plants. While there have been exceptional years of heavy rain (2006, for example, when the town of Mariental had to be evacuated after it was flooded), on normal years there's so little rain it shouldn't hamper any visit. The average annual rainfall varies from as little as 50 mm along the coast to a more generous 350 mm in the central interior and 700 mm in the well-watered Caprivi Strip. The only issue is that the dry riverbeds that criss-cross the dirt roads fill with water and, after heavy rain, roads in rural areas can be closed to saloon cars for several days. The rainy season is not the best time for wildlife watching because the animals do not have to rely on waterholes, so the game is more dispersed. However, birdwatching is best after the rains, because the numerous flooded depressions attract migrant species.

July and August are fairly busy months for tourism as they coincide with the European (especially German) school holidays. More of a factor, however, is the long South African summer holiday (December and January) when Namibia becomes a playground for outdoorsy South Africans. Be sure to book your accommodation and car hire well in advance during these periods. ➤➤ See also Climate, page 397.

What to do in Namibia

Ballooning
With virtually year-round clear blue skies and warm sunshine, Namibia is an ideal place to go ballooning. A 1-hr trip over the desert at Sossusvlei is a favourite with many people, and there is also the option of a balloon ride near Swakopmund.

The only drawback is the expense – a 1-hr trip costs more than US$400 per person (champagne breakfast included) but few people complain once they are airborne and see the first rays of the dawn sun bathe the vast desert in incredible light.

Packing for Namibia

Before you leave home, send yourself an email to a web-based account with details of passport, driving licence, credit cards and travel insurance numbers. Be sure that someone at home also has access to this information.

A backpack or travelpack (a hybrid backpack/suitcase) rather than a rigid suitcase covers most eventualities and survives the rigours of travel. Hikers will need a smaller and sturdier pack. A lock for your luggage is strongly advised – there are cases of pilfering by airport baggage handlers the world over.

Everybody has their own list, but a good rule of thumb when packing is to take half the clothes you think you'll need and twice the money. Laundry services are generally cheap and speedy in Namibia and you shouldn't need to bring too many clothes. Bear in mind, though, night-time temperatures in winter can get very low and deserts are very cold at night; by the coast it can get very windy. Light cotton clothing is best, with a fleece for

evenings and a raincoat for wet weather. On safari expect to get dirty, particularly during the dry season when dust can be a problem – sensitive equipment such as laptops and cameras should be looked after carefully. During the day you will need a hat, sunglasses and high-factor suncream. Footwear should be airy; sandals or canvas trainers are ideal. Hikers will need comfortable walking boots that have been worn in. Those going on camping safaris will need a towel, torch and a sleeping bag, though a sleeping sheet may be enough in the warmer months. If driving yourself, the car hire companies rent out all camping equipment with the vehicles; it is best to pre-arrange this and check that the camping gear you want is in stock.

Virtually anything you require is available to buy in Namibia, but outside Windhoek and Swakopmund the choice reduces dramatically, and outside the larger towns it dwindles to essentials only.

Birdwatching

With a wide range of habitats from coastal wetlands or savannahs to riverine forest, Namibia is home to 706 recorded species of bird. Of these, 14 species are near endemic including the white-tailed shrike, Carp's black tit, Hartlaub's francolin and Ruppell's korhaan. Birdwatchers should head for the parks and reserves along the Caprivi Strip (which has the highest concentration of birds in the whole country) and also to Walvis Bay Lagoon (one of the most important coastal wetlands in Africa) where pelicans

and flamingos are common. The sandy coastal flats are also the breeding ground of the endangered Damara tern, while the nearby dunes are home to the Gray's lark and the dune lark. These last 3 species are endemic to Namibia.

Canoeing

Whether it's a casual 30-min paddle or a fully fledged expedition, a canoe trip on one of Namibia's perennial rivers is great fun. Perhaps the most popular is a 4- or 5-day trip along the Orange River, which marks the border with South Africa.

Spending a few days floating down the river either in your canoe (winter) or submerged alongside it (summer) is a fabulous way to unwind from the rigours of the road and admire the silent desert wilderness beyond the riverbanks.

Sea kayaking is available on the Walvis Bay Lagoon and is ideal for birdwatching or getting close to seals and dolphins.

Fishing

Extremely popular with Namibians, fishing trips can be organized either from Walvis Bay, Henties Bay or Swakopmund. The cold, clean waters of the southern Atlantic provide rich feeding grounds for a wide range of species including kabeljou, West Coast steenbras, snoek, yellow tail, mackerel and shark. There are hundreds of regulations restricting location, season, methods, species and catch sizes, so the best option is to go with a tour operator. Trips include permits, fishing gear and bait as well as lunch and refreshments. In the Caprivi Strip, many of the lodges offer river angling and the prize species in this region is the tiger fish.

Hiking

Walking in the bush is an excellent way of getting a close look at Namibia's diverse flora and fauna, and whether you walk for an hour or a day, you are sure to see something new and interesting. Most parks and many guest farms have well-marked trails suitable for inexperienced walkers, though hiking should not be attempted during the hot summer months.

For the experienced hiker there is the challenge of the multi-day Fish River Canyon (see page 366), and Naukluft hiking trails (see page 300), which both require high levels of fitness. For those not wishing to get too serious, there are rewarding day hikes at the Waterberg Plateau Park (see page 112), Daan Viljoen (see page 86) and easy marked-out trails around many of the guest farms.

Horse riding

Namibia Horse Safari Company, T0814-703384, www.namibiahorsesafari.com, offers the 400-km Namib Desert Ride, which is one of the toughest trails in the world. The route runs from the Khomas Hochland across the plains of the Namib-Naukluft Park, ending on the beach in Swakopmund 12 days later. There are also a number of 4-day rides available. For the less experienced, **Okakambe Trails**, T064-402799, near Swakopmund, offers 2-hr sunset and moonlight rides into the desert. **Desert Homestead and Horse Trails**, T063-683103, www.deserthomestead-namibia.com, near Sesriem, offers scenic/game rides and overnight horseback safaris where mobile camps are set up in the desert. There are also plenty of opportunities on the privately owned guest farms, where sunrise rides usually include breakfast, and sunset rides include sundowners such as gin and tonics and the like.

Quad biking

A number of lodges and guest farms offer quad biking around their properties to admire the scenery; usually no previous experience is needed. The most popular trails are in the dune field outside of Swakopmund (see page 260). Guided trips, for both the adrenaline seeker and the complete novice, cover 35-50 km, and follow the crests of the dunes where there are some very steep ascents and descents.

Sandboarding

The Namib Desert is famous for its giant dunes and there's no better way to conquer them than by zooming down on a traditional Swakopmund sandboard, or carving up the dune on a snowboard adapted for sand. The beauty is that sand is not abrasive, and you can board in shorts and T-shirts. The worst that can happen is that you walk away covered in sand. No experience is necessary; it's exhilarating and lots of fun.

Scenic flights

Flights vary from 1½-hr trips along the coast to see seal colonies and inaccessible wrecks, to all-day safaris to northern Namibia that include landings and 4WD adventures. From the air you can clearly see Namibia's deserts, dried up riverbeds, moonscapes, rock formations, mountains and gravel plains. There is a handful of scenic flight companies in Swakopmund (see page 261), and for those lucky enough to be able to afford an air safari around the country, the air-taxi services will fly you to the lodges over incredible landscapes.

Skydiving

Jumps at Swakopmund (see page 262) normally take place after the morning fog has lifted. You board a small plane for a 35-min scenic flight before being strapped to your instructor and shuffling to the open door. At 3500 m you tumble into the sky for a mind-blowing 30-second free-fall at around 220 kph – a totally exhilarating experience. Then the parachute opens and you float to the ground enjoying the breathtaking desert scenery.

Going on safari

One of the main reasons for going to Namibia is to see the wonderful wildlife in splendid African landscapes, and there are a number of parks, reserves and conservation areas around the country. Some are owned by the government (such as the wonderful Etosha National Park, which is home to most animals that visitors expect to see on an African safari), and some are privately owned. Additionally, Namibia has species that roam outside the fences of designated areas – most famously the desert-adapted elephant and black rhino in the northwest, which are perhaps Namibia's most special and sought-after wildlife encounters.

Namibia has the advantage of being a good self-drive destination, and those in hired cars can get to Etosha and many of the more popular wildlife areas fairly easily. By contrast, some of the more remote parks are so challenging that 4WDs may be essential and driving in a convoy of at least two vehicles is recommended in case of an accident or breakdown. As the majority of game viewing is undertaken independently and visitors are largely left to their own devices, it is a good idea to buy some wildlife identification books to keep in your car. Driving around endlessly searching for animals is not the best way to spot many of these creatures. While speed limits are often 40 kph, the optimum speed for game viewing by car is around 15 kph. Drives can be broken up by stops at waterholes, picnic sites and hides. Time spent around a waterhole with your engine switched off gives you an opportunity to listen to the sounds of the bush and experience the rhythms of

Game-viewing rules

- Keep on the well-marked roads and tracks; off-road driving is harmful because smoke, oil and destruction of the grass layer cause soil erosion.

- Do not drive through closed roads or park areas. It is mandatory to enter and exit the parks through the authorized gates.

- For your own safety, stay in your vehicle at all times. Your vehicle serves as a blind or hide, since animals will not usually identify it with humans. In all the parks that are visited by car, it is forbidden to leave the vehicle except in designated places, such as picnic sites or walking trails.

- Stick to the parks' opening hours; it is usually forbidden to drive from dusk to dawn unless you are granted special authorization. At night you are requested to stay at your lodge or campsite.

- Never harass the animals. Make as little noise as possible; do not flash lights or make sudden movements to scare them away; never try and attract the animals' attention by calling out or whistling.

- Never chase the animals and always let them pass unhindered; they always have right of way.

- Do not feed the animals; the food you provide might make them ill. Worse still, once animals such as elephants

learn that food is available from humans they can become aggressive and dangerous when looking for more and will eventually have to be shot.

- If camping at night in the parks, ensure that the animals cannot gain access to any food you are carrying.

- Do not throw any litter, including used matches or cigarette butts; this increases the fire risk in the dry season and some animals will eat whatever they find.

- Do not disturb other visitors. They have the same right as you to enjoy nature. If you discover a stopped vehicle and you want to check what they are looking at, never hinder their sight or stop within their photographic field. If there is no room for another car, wait patiently for a car to leave. If there is a group of vehicles, most drivers will take it in turns to occupy the prime viewing spot.

- Always turn the engine off when you are watching game up close.

- Do not drive too fast; the speed limit is usually 40 kph. Speeding damages road surfaces, increases noise and raises the risk of running over animals.

- Wild animals are dangerous; despite their beauty their reactions are unpredictable. Don't expose yourself to unnecessary risks; excessive confidence can lead to severe accidents.

nature as game moves to and from the water. The best time of day to spot animals on a vehicle safari is early in the morning and late in the afternoon, as many animals sleep through the intense midday heat. Animals can most easily be seen during the dry season when the lack of surface water forces them to congregate around rivers and waterholes. However, the rainy seasons are when the animals are in the best condition after feeding on the new shoots, and there are chances of seeing breeding displays and young animals. The disadvantage of the wet season is that the thicker vegetation and the wider availability of water mean that the wildlife is more spread out and more difficult to spot; also, driving conditions are harder as none of the park roads are paved.

Most parks are only open to visitors during daylight hours; the camp leaflets provide details of seasonal changes. It is important to plan your game-viewing drive so that you can start at first light and return before the camp gates shut just before dark. For other tips, see box, opposite.

Organizing a safari

The alternative to self-driving is to book an organized safari with one of the safari companies that operate from Windhoek and Swakopmund (see tour operators in the relative sections). Rates include guides, transport, accommodation, meals and park entry fees. Trip duration varies enormously from a three-day excursion to visit a specific park or region, to a two-week fully escorted tour of the country. Tour operators offer basically the same safari but at different prices, reflecting the mode of transport and standard of accommodation. For example, you could choose a three-day safari from Windhoek to Etosha National Park and the options would be flying or driving, then either camping (the companies provide the equipment), staying in mid-range park accommodation, or a top-end luxury lodge. Everyone is likely to have the same sort of game-viewing experiences, but the level of comfort depends how much you spend; compare prices and itineraries carefully.

Getting to Namibia

Air

Scheduled international flights to Namibia arrive at **Hosea Kutako International Airport (HKIA)** ① *45 km east of Windhoek on the B6 road to Gobabis, T062-295 5600, www.airports.com.na*. Most charter, private and **Air Namibia** domestic services fly into **Windhoek – Eros Airport (ERS)** ① *Aviation Rd, off Rehobother Road (B1), 5 km south of the city, T061-295 5501, www.airports.com.na.* ⇥ *For airport information, see page 48.*

From Europe

The only direct flights from Europe are with **Air Namibia** (www.airnamibia. com) which offers daily nine-hour flights from Frankfurt to Windhoek. Seats are particularly popular in July and August, which is the high season for German visitors; book as far ahead as you can. From all other European destinations the option is to first travel to Frankfurt.

Alternatively by far the most frequent services to Namibia are via South Africa, and most European carriers fly to Johannesburg's OR Tambo International Airport, from where it is a one-hour flight to Windhoek. Carriers include **South African Airways** (www.flysaa.com), **British Airways** (www.britishairways.com), **Air France** (www.airfrance.com) and **KLM** (www.klm.com), to name but a few. Indirect flights from other airlines can also be good value: **Kenya Airways** (www.kenyaairways.com) flies from London to Johannesburg via Nairobi, and **Emirates** (www.emirates.com) flies to Johannesburg via Dubai from just about anywhere else in the world. Once in South Africa, the final hop to Windhoek is with either **Air Namibia**, **British Airways** or **South African Airways**.

Jetlag is not usually an issue if flying from Europe to South Africa or Namibia as there is only a minimal time difference, and most flights are overnight.

From North America
There are no direct flights from North America to Namibia. It is usual to fly via London or another European city, or Dubai, to Johannesburg. Alternatively, **Delta** (www.delta.com) and **South African Airways** have flights from New York to Johannesburg on a code-share agreement.

From Australia, New Zealand and Asia
There are no direct flights from Australia, New Zealand or Asia to Namibia, but again a number of indirect routes go via Johannesburg. Between them **Qantas** (www.qantas.com.au) and **South African Airways**, on a code-share agreement, fly between Perth and Sydney and Johannesburg. From Australia and New Zealand, **Emirates** (www.emirates.com) flies via Dubai, **Malaysia Airlines** (www.malaysiaairlines.com) via Kuala Lumpur, and **Singapore Airlines** (www.singaporeair.com) via Singapore. **Cathay Pacific** (www.cathaypacific.com) flies to Johannesburg from Hong Kong.

From Africa
Air Namibia flies to and from Windhoek and Johannesburg, Maun in Botswana, Victoria Falls and Harare in Zimbabwe, Lusaka in Zambia, and Luanda in Angola.

There are at least 18 direct daily flights between Johannesburg's OR Tambo International Airport and Windhoek's Hosea Kutako International Airport with either **Air Namibia**, **British Airways** or **South African Airways**. There are links in Johannesburg with just about every African airline.

Road

Namibia shares borders with South Africa, Botswana, Zambia and Angola. Although Namibia does not share a border with Zimbabwe, it is close and easily accessible, and many visitors combine a trip to northern Namibia with a visit to the Victoria Falls. You need to cross at the Ngoma Bridge border at the extreme east of the Caprivi Strip into Botswana, from where it is just an hour's drive along the very top of Botswana's Chobe National Park to Kasane and the border with Zimbabwe. Border crossings vary from little more than a farm gate and a simple check point with limited opening hours, to modern buildings on major highways which are open 24 hours. All customs, immigration and vehicle formalities are efficient and

Border crossings

Namibia–South Africa
Mata Mata, page 320
Ariamsvlei–Nakop, page 362
Noordoewer–Vioolsdrif, page 362
Sendelingsdrift, page 360

Namibia-Botswana
Buitepos–Mamuno, page 99
Dobe, page 144
Mohembo, page 158
Ngoma Bridge, page 164

Namibia–Zimbabwe
Kazungula, page 164

Namibia-Zambia
Kazungula, page 165
Wenela–Sesheke, page 165

Namibia-Angola
Ruacana–Calueque, page 202
Oshikango–Santa Clara, page 216

reasonably quick. Border crossings are detailed in the relevant chapters. The most important thing to remember is the time difference. Namibian daylight saving time begins at 0200 on the first Sunday of April, and ends at 0200 on the first Sunday in September. Opening and closing times on the Namibian side of borders could be an hour earlier than those on the opposite side, as none of the neighbouring counties have daylight saving time.

Bus

The only bus company with cross-border services is **Intercape** ① *main office opposite the railway station off Bahnhof St, Windhoek, T061-227847, or contact reservations in South Africa T+27 (0)21-380 4400, www.intercape.co.za*, one of the principal South African long-distance coach companies. The routes are Cape Town in South Africa to Livingstone in Zambia (it can also drop clients on the Zambian side of the Victoria Falls border with Zimbabwe) via Namibia; and Windhoek to Upington in South Africa's Northern Cape province. There are also **Intercape** services within Namibia between Windhoek and Swakopmund and Walvis Bay; and Windhoek and Oshikango. Each service stops at any town of reasonable size en route. The buses are comfortable with air-conditioning, reclining seats and a toilet, and some show videos and serve tea and biscuits. They stop at large petrol stations for lengthy breaks where you can buy refreshments and stretch your legs. ▶▶ *For Intercape timetable, see pages 16-17.*

Car

If in a private car, you must have a registration document, a letter of authorization from the registered owner (if the vehicle is not owned by the driver) and a driving licence in English with a photograph. If in a foreign-registered vehicle, you'll need a Carnet de Passages issued by a body in your own country or in the country of origin of the vehicle (in the UK, the RAC issues these). If driving a hire car from

South Africa, you need a letter of permission from the car hire company to take a vehicle out of the country and a 'ZA' sticker which has to be stuck on the car whilst in Namibia. Likewise you will need a 'NA' sticker if taking a hire car from Namibia into a neighbouring country; the car hire companies will provide these or they are available from Automobile Association (AA) shops. Cross-border charges apply to all vehicles and are N$220 for a car and N$140 for a trailer. Fees are paid in Namibian dollars, South African rand or US dollars cash; be sure to have the correct amount as there is not always change. ▸▸ *For car hire, see page 15.*

Overland trucks

Overland truck safaris are a popular and economical way of exploring Africa by road. They demand a little more fortitude and adventurous spirit from the traveller, but the compensation is usually the camaraderie and friendships that result from what is invariably a real adventure. The standard three-week overland route most commercial trucks take through southern Africa (in either direction) is from Cape Town up to Swakopmund via the Fish River Canyon and Sesriem for the Namib-Naukluft Park. The first weekend is usually spent in Swakopmund to enjoy the activities before heading north to the Etosha National Park via Damaraland, then into Botswana to visit the Okavango Delta and Chobe National Park and finishing in either Victoria Falls in Zimbabwe or Livingstone in Zambia to enjoy the activities around the Victoria Falls. This three-week trip can be combined with another three weeks to or from Nairobi via Zambia, Malawi, Tanzania and Zanzibar, and finishing in Kenya. Again the circuit continues with a two-week route into Uganda to see the mountain gorillas via some of the Kenyan national parks. There are several overland companies and there are departures along the circuit almost weekly from Cape Town, Livingstone/Victoria Falls and Nairobi throughout the year. Some also pick-up/drop off in Windhoek and Swakopmund on this circuit.

Overland truck operators

Acacia Africa, www.acacia-africa.com
African Trails, www.africantrails.co.uk
Africa Travel Co, www.africatravelco.com
Dragoman, www.dragoman.com

Exodus, www.exodus.co.uk
G Adventures, www.gadventures.com
Oasis Overland, www.oasisoverland.co.uk
Tucan Travel, www.tucantravel.com

Transport in Namibia

Namibia is a big country and there are some vast distances between sights through remote terrain. It does, however, have an excellent road network and, because of these remote locations, a very well-developed air service with almost 300 airstrips around the country. The public transport system, on the other hand, is very limited and, compared to other African countries whose roads are pumping with buses and shared vehicles, Namibia has only a few lonely buses travelling along the main arteries. For the visitor, the best choices of exploring Namibia are on a tour, by expensive air safari, or to self-drive.

Domestic flights

Flying is the quickest way to get around Namibia and most destinations are within a two-hour flight of each other. Try to get a window seat to fully enjoy the landscape. **Air Namibia** serves all the regional centres and has regular flights to Lüderitz, Oranjemund and Walvis Bay in the west and south of the country from Windhoek's **Hosea Kutako International Airport** (see page 48). Flights to Katima Mulilo, Rundu and Ondangwa in the north of the country go from Windhoek's **Eros Airport** (see page 50). Prices vary but expect to pay in the region of N$1300-1600 for a one-way flight between Windhoek and Lüderitz, for example.

Charter flights

There are a number of small companies offering short scenic flights over the dunes, along the Skeleton Coast, out to the Kalahari for a 'Bushman experience', or to Opuwo to visit the Himba. Most charter planes in Namibia are Cessna 210s, which can carry a pilot and five passengers. The advantages of these planes are that the wings are above the windows allowing a better view, they are fast over long distances and hardy enough to land on dirt runways. In the past, flights only attracted the top end of the tourism market, but today seeing the Namibian landscapes from the air is considered an unmissable highlight, and short scenic flights can work out at a reasonable price for a group of four or five people (a two-hour sightseeing flight from Swakopmund over Sossusvlei and back costs about N$2300 per person if there are four people in the plane). If there are only two of you, the companies will endeavour to find other people to fill the plane. The Sossusvlei trip is the most popular of the scenic flights and the planes invariably fill up.

If you have more cash to splash, tour operators can organize multi-day fly-in safaris to remote regions, game parks and private guest farms and lodges. They are expensive but a more comfortable and quicker alternative to long road trips, and there is a good network of airstrips and daily flights. Cross-border destinations like Victoria Falls or the Okavango Delta in Botswana can be added in. Tour operators will build flights into a safari and tailor a trip to suit your interests, or you can liaise with the charter companies directly. ►► *See tour operators in Windhoek, page 77, and Swakopmund page 262.*

Charter companies

The **Dune Hopper**, www.dunehopper.com, is a daily air taxi that runs a service from Windhoek and Swakopmund to several lodges in the Sesriem/Sossusvlei area in the Namib-Naukluft Park. Reservations can be made through the website, or book through **Nature Friend Safaris** in Windhoek (see below).

Atlantic Aviation, Swakopmund, T064-404749, www.flyinnamibia.com.
Desert Air, Windhoek, T061-228101, www.desertair.com.na.
Namibia Commercial Aviation, Windhoek, T061-223562, www.nca.com.na.
NatureFriend Safaris, Windhoek, T061-234793, www.naturefriendsafaris.com.

Pleasure Flights and Safaris, Swakopmund, T064-404500, www.pleasureflights.com.na.
Scenic Air, Windhoek, T061-249268, www.scenic-air.com.
Skeleton Coast Safaris, Windhoek, T061-224248, www.skeletoncoastsafaris.com.

Westair Wings Charters, Windhoek, T061-221091, www.westwing.com.na.
Wings over Africa, Windhoek, T061-255001; Swakopmund, T064-403720, www.flyinafrica.com.

Rail

Few tourists use the Namibian railway service, TransNamib, because it is slow and serves few centres of interest to visitors. The passenger trains that do run, however, are very cheap and have comfortable airline-style seats in air-conditioned carriages. DVDs are shown and there are vending machines for snacks and drinks. Most services depart in the early evening and arrive at their destination the following morning. Trains stop everywhere along the way (thus their slow progress) and, given their main use is freight haulage, there can be a good deal of noise and shunting, often in the early hours of the morning. For details contact **TransNamib Starline Passenger Services** ⓘ *central reservations: Windhoek railway station, accessed from Bahnhof St at the northern end of Mandume Ndemufayo St, T061-298 1111, www.transnamib.com.na.*

Luxury trains

TransNamib also runs a far more appealing overnight luxury service from Windhoek to Swakopmund once a week, the **Desert Express** ⓘ *reservations: Windhoek railway station, T061-298 2600, www.transnamib.com.na, Mon-Fri 0800-1700.* It departs Windhoek every Friday at 1130 (1230 in summer) and includes a late-afternoon stop at a game farm for a game drive with sundowner, and dinner in the on-board **Welwitschia Restaurant** before spending the night on the train. After breakfast, there is a dune excursion before arriving in Swakopmund at 1000. The return journey leaves Swakopmund every Saturday at 1430 and the itinerary runs in reverse.

The seven-day **Swakopmund and Etosha Holiday** has several departures throughout the year. The itinerary includes visits to Okahandja, Walvis Bay, Swakopmund and Otjiwarongo, as well as a two-night side-trip to Etosha National Park. ⏭ *For further details of luxury train services, see Windhoek Transport, page 84.*

Road

Bus

Namibia's long-distance buses are more comfortable and much quicker than the trains, but are still very limited in terms of destinations. Intercape (see Getting there, page 50) runs the cross-border routes between Windhoek and Cape Town (stopping at Rehoboth, Mariental, Keetmanshoop, Grünau and the Voolsdrif border); it also runs between Windhoek and Upington in South Africa via Rehoboth, Mariental,

Keetmanshoop, Grünau, Karasburg and the Ariamsvlei border; and Windhoek and Livingstone (Victoria Falls) in Zambia via Okahandja, Otjiwarongo, Otavi, Tsumeb, Grootfontein, Rundu, Bagani, Kongola and Katima Mulilo. The final route is within Namibia between Windhoek and Oshikango via Okahandja, Otjiwarongo, Otavi, Tsumeb, Omuthiya, Ondangwa, Ongwediva and Oshakati. ▶▶ See Intercape timetable, page 16.

There are daily shuttle services using micro/sprinter buses between Windhoek and Swakopmund (four hours) and Walvis Bay (4½ hours). Expect to pay in the region of N$250 one way to Swakopmund, and N$270 one way to Walvis Bay; there are discounts for children under 12. On the way they stop at Okahandja, Karibib, Usakos and the other towns on the B2 road. Check the websites for pick-up and drop-off places; most are in large car parks in the centre of the towns, and for a small extra fee they will pick up/drop off from your hotel. ▶▶ For details of companies and schedules see Windhoek Transport, see page 80.

Car

Car hire Namibia has 5450 km of paved roads and 37,000 km of gravel roads. Many visitors drive themselves around the country as a more affordable alternative to organized tours or expensive flights. There is a good choice of car hire companies, particularly in Windhoek (see page 82), which can arrange vehicles with roof-tent, kitchen and cooking equipment, tools, first-aid kit, jerry cans, extra fuel tanks, bedding, fridge, lights, and every other piece of equipment you might need. Depending on your itinerary, some 4WDs are equipped with long-distance (140 litre) fuel tanks, which are worth asking about. Many of the companies also hire out campervans and motorhomes, and all will arrange to meet you with the vehicle at either of Windhoek's airports or at your accommodation in Windhoek.

The best rates are available if you book a few months in advance. If you leave car hire until you arrive in Namibia you may find it more difficult to find something suitable and the rates will be higher. It is worth comparing several companies before committing yourself. Shop around on the internet for a company that offers good service and is clear about what is and is not included in the price. Try to get a car that is no more than two years old. Also get a full list of all equipment included and check it is complete when you pick up the car. Additionally if you are taking a vehicle over the border (South Africa, Botswana, Zimbabwe and Zambia), ensure you have the relevant paperwork and the company has provided an 'NA' sticker for the car. Finally, talk through your planned itinerary with your car hire company. They are the experts when it comes to driving in Namibia and can advise on road conditions and what type of vehicle you'll need. A 2WD car will cost in the region of N$400-600 per day; a minibus that seats eight to 12 people (for families and groups) will cost N$1000-1300 per day, depending on the season and length of hire; a 4WD (necessary if travelling to remote areas) will cost N$800-1100 depending on whether a roof-tent and camping equipment is included; while a fully equipped campervan will cost N$800-1200 depending on whether it sleeps two or four and if it has 4WD.

When collecting your vehicle, as well as checking it for bumps and scratches it is worth taking 10 minutes to familiarize yourself with it. Check the spare tyre

Intercape timetable

Upington–Windhoek (Namibian time) Tue, Thu, Fri, Sun

	Arrive	Depart		Arrive	Depart
Upington		1930	Keetmanshoop	0125	0140
Ariamsvlei border	2000	2100	Mariental	0350	0355
Karasburg	2210	2215	Rehoboth	0535	0540
Grünau	2320	2325	Windhoek	0630	

Windhoek–Upington (Namibian time) Mon, Wed, Fri, Sun

	Arrive	Depart		Arrive	Depart
Windhoek		1700	Grünau	0030	0035
Rehoboth	1800	1805	Karasburg	0100	0105
Mariental	1945	1950	Ariamsvlei border	0230	0330
Keetmanshoop	2235	2305	Upington	0730	

Windhoek–Cape Town (Namibian time) Mon, Wed, Fri, Sun

	Arrive	Depart		Arrive	Depart
Windhoek		1700	Vanrhynsdorp	0915	0920
Rehoboth	1800	1805	Klawer	0950	1020
Mariental	1945	1950	Clanwilliam	1050	1055
Keetmanshoop	2235	2350	Citrusdal	1125	1130
Grünau	0030	0035	Piketberg	1235	1255
Vioolsdrif border	0210	0310	Moorreesburg	1325	1330
Steinkopf	0600	0605	Malmesbury	1350	1355
Springbok	0625	0630	Bellville	1430	1435
Garies	0745	0750	Cape Town	1505	

Cape Town–Windhoek (Namibian time) Tue, Thu, Fri, Sun

	Arrive	Depart		Arrive	Depart
Cape Town		1000	Garies	1700	1705
Bellville	1025	1030	Springbok	1825	1830
Malmesbury	1125	1130	Steinkopf	1900	1920
Moorreesburg	1200	1205	Vioolsdrif border	1905	2005
Piketberg	1230	1235	Grünau	2220	2225
Citrusdal	1340	1345	Keetmanshoop	0040	0100
Clanwilliam	1410	1415	Mariental	0330	0335
Klawer	1445	1510	Rehoboth	0510	0515
Vanrhynsdorp	1530	1535	Windhoek	0625	

Oshikango–Windhoek Mon, Tue, Thu, Fri, Sun

	Arrive	Depart		Arrive	Depart
Oshikango		1900	Tsumeb	0015	0045
Oshakati	1915	1930	Otavi	0125	0130
Ongwediva	1940	1950	Otjiwarongo	0240	0300
Ondangwa	2020	2030	Okahandja	0450	0500
Omuthiya	2130	2140	Windhoek	0600	

Windhoek–Oshikango Mon, Wed, Thu, Fri, Sun

	Arrive	Depart		Arrive	Depart
Windhoek		1800	Omuthiya	0300	0310
Okahandja	1900	1905	Ondangwa	0410	0420
Otjiwarongo	2130	2145	Ongwediva	0445	0450
Otavi	2245	2250	Oshakati	0500	0515
Tsumeb	2335	2355	Oshikango	0520	

Victoria Falls–Windhoek (Namibian time) Wed, Fri, Sun

	Arrive	Depart		Arrive	Depart
Livingstone		1100	Grootfontein	2345	2350
Wenela border post	1400	1500	Tsumeb	0030	0035
Katima Mulilo	1515	1530	Otavi	0115	0120
Kongola	1710	1715	Otjiwarongo	0230	0235
Bagani	1915	1920	Okahandja	0415	0420
Rundu	2030	2050	Windhoek	0600	

Windhoek–Victoria Falls (Namibian time) Mon, Wed, Fri

	Arrive	Depart		Arrive	Depart
Windhoek		1300	Rundu	2205	2220
Okahandja	1400	1405	Bagani	0130	0145
Otjiwarongo	1630	1645	Kongola	0345	0350
Otavi	1745	1750	Katima Mulilo	0550	0630
Tsumeb	1835	1840	Livingstone	1000	
Grootfontein	1910	1915			

(two are preferable) and how to use it. Is there a puncture repair kit and a pump? Do you know how to use them? What sort of fuel does it take? Do you have sufficient clearance for the terrain you are planning to cross? You don't want to be discovering a problem for the first time in an emergency, in the middle of nowhere.

Drivers must be at least 23 years of age (some companies stipulate 25) and need to have a driver's licence in English with a photograph, passport and credit card to hire a car in Namibia. For drivers accustomed to European roads, the traffic is virtually non-existent, but the roads are not without their dangers (see box, opposite). Third-party insurance is included in the hire price but drivers are advised to take out extra insurance for 100% collision damage and loss waiver. The dangers of unexpected people/animals, poor roads and bad driving are considerable and the dangers of driving at night cannot be over-emphasized.

Buying your own car   If you plan to stay in the country for a while, buying your own car may be a sensible option. With the dry climate, most cars will be free from rust but, with the great distances to be travelled and rough gravel roads, even young cars may become tired and scratched. Windhoek (or, better still, Johannesburg or Cape Town) is the best place to buy or sell. In Windhoek, dealerships are concentrated around the John Meinert Street and Independence Avenue junction. Check the local press for private sales. Be sure to discuss the possibility of selling back to your dealer. Alternatively, if you are going to be spending several weeks or months in southern Africa consider buying a car on a buy-back scheme. There are companies that will sell you a car and sign a contract to buy it back at an agreed price once you have finished with it. Work out the costs, though, and compare them to long-term car hire. Sometimes the price difference is minimal and with the buy-back scheme you don't get the back-up of a car hire company in case of emergency. The following websites are useful: www.drivesouthafrica.co.za and www.driveafrica.co.za.

Driving   Driving is on the left side of the road and speed limits are 60-80 kph in built-up areas, 80-90 kph on gravel roads, and 120 kph on tar roads. By law, you must wear a seat belt in the front and back seats at all times and have your driving licence and passport available for inspection. The police are very strict on drink-driving, and checkpoints and speed traps with on-the-spot fines are employed. The distances to be travelled are massive, and must be done during daylight hours, so plan your overnight stops carefully. Away from the tarred highways, Namibia has an excellent network of gravel roads through some beautiful scenery, but if you intend to drive through some of the more remote regions, it is worth being prepared. If driving way off the beaten track, go in a group of at least two vehicles and remember that mobile phone coverage is limited in remote areas. When looking at a map of Namibia, remember all roads off the main highways are gravel, and although maintained regularly by the big yellow graders seen all over the country, driving on gravel takes a bit of skill and care. This surface can be very slippery, especially if driving at speed, and there have been some serious accidents involving tourists in the past. When a car goes too fast on gravel, slight bends in the road cause the vehicle to slide, and over-correction by the driver can cause an accident or roll.

Driving tips

- Because of the great distances in Namibia, plan shorter travel routes and stay an extra night from time to time.
- Bear in mind that only 40% of Namibian roads are tarred. The remaining 60% are gravel roads.
- Depending on the appearance of the roads they are subdivided into B, C and D roads. B-roads are tarred and C-roads are wide and relatively well-prepared gravel roads. D-roads can usually only be accessed with a high-clearance vehicle and in some cases a 4WD.
- Driving in Namibia is on the left. Long distances, especially on lonely gravel roads, require a high degree of concentration, especially if you are used to driving on the opposite side of the road as you easily start drifting to the right. Oncoming traffic often appears out of the blue.
- Busy gravel roads often develop corrugations roads as the sand and gravel are compacted by the frequent traffic. Driving on corrugated gravel roads calls for slow and cautious driving.
- Glaring sunlight, heat haze and dust makes assessing distances very imprecise. Driving with your headlights enables oncoming traffic to see you more easily.
- Make sure you arrive at your accommodation or campsite before dusk, as this is when wildlife often strays onto the road and dust and light from the sunset increases the risk of accidents.
- Always make sure that the fuel tank has enough diesel/petrol and that there are two spare tyres.
- Always carry sufficient drinking water.

Also many of the gravel roads have quite a high camber so exercise caution when overtaking or passing an oncoming vehicle and watch that the car does not slide down to the edge of the road. In dusty conditions it is a good idea to put on your headlights so other road users can see you more easily. Although mostly tarred, the 'salt' roads along the coast can also be slippery, especially in the dense fog. Their foundation is gypsum from the desert which is soaked with brine, turning it into a surface as hard and smooth as tar. Also watch out for animals: kudu, springbok and warthog often graze along the side of the road and can leap in front of your car without warning. Bear in mind that roads may become impassable during heavy rain as the dried up riverbeds that cross the roads fill with water and you may have to turn back and take another route.

Be sure you have enough fuel to cover the distance you are planning to travel; there are often no petrol stations between towns. Also, not all petrol stations accept credit cards or have an ATM, so budget sufficient cash for fuel as part of your day-to-day needs. On the whole, petrol stations are modern and efficient, often with a shop and takeaway attached to them. An attendant will fill up your car while you fill up on provisions; a small tip is expected for efficient service, which includes cleaning windscreens and checking oil, water and tyre pressure. Finally it also goes without saying that you should ensure you have enough drinking water in the vehicle to cover your entire journey.

4WD driving Southern Africans are great outdoors types and 4WD driving is a hugely popular pastime, but this is something few overseas visitors may have tried. Good 4WD companies are not going to look too favourably on hiring out their cars to complete novices. Consider doing a course in 4WD driving in your home country, or at least buy a book, which greatly enhances confidence in driving around remote regions. A good basic mechanical knowledge is also useful in the event that you break down in the middle of nowhere. Once in Namibia, **Be Local** ① *T061-305795, www.be-local.com*, offers two-hour 'Drive Namibia' courses on getting to know your 4WD, which you can arrange for after you've picked up your vehicle and before setting off. This teaches the correct application of high and low range gears, use of hub and differential locks and practical use of equipment such as high-lift jacks, changing tyres, etc. The company also rents out mobile phones and SIM cards as well as satellite phones, which have emergency numbers programmed into them, and GPSs with detailed coordinates for Namibia. Many car hire companies also now rent out satellite phones and GPSs; both are definitely worth considering if you are heading for Kaokoland or Bushmanland.

Hitchhiking

Hitching is not recommended, simply because the distances in Namibia are vast, there are few people, and consequently few vehicles. Hitchhikers may have some very long waits in the hot sun at the side of the road. It is a risky method of travelling, particularly if you are alone. If you do decide to give it a try, it is a good idea to walk or take a taxi to the edge of town (perhaps the last petrol station on the main road) and start hitching from there. As a general rule, a sign stating your destination is a good idea, as is standing at a junction or fuel station in full view, so that your hosts can give you a once over from close range before committing and have time to brake safely. Be sure to take food and plenty of liquids with you.

Mountain bike and motorbike

Some of the lodges and guest farms offer leisurely scenic trails on their properties, but for more serious mountain bikers **Mountain Bike Namibia** ① *T064-402078, www.mountainbikenamibia.com*, offers more challenging terrain on guided tours from eight to 18 days. They take in all the attractions, including the towns, and accommodation is either camping or in guest farms.

Probably the only European bikers you will see will be bearded, tanned, trans-Africa adventurers, but for the tourist with a motorbike licence and experience at handling gravel roads it is possible to go on a guided motorbike tour of Namibia. Try **Gravel Travel** ① *T061-257053, www.gravel-travel.com*, or **Africa Motion Tours** ① *T061-237258, www.africamotiontours.com*.

Shared taxi

In the absence of a public transport network, entrepreneurs have stepped in with vehicles of greater or lesser safety, size and comfort. They are almost without exception serving the non-white market and run from town centre to town centre rather than to the tourist spots. Prices average about N$50 per 100 km, but check out what your fellow travellers are paying and agree to pay exactly that amount, on arrival.

Maps

The best map and travel guide store in the UK is **Stanfords** ① *12-14 Long Acre, Covent Garden, London WC2 9LP, T0207-8361321, www.stanfords.co.uk,* with another branch in Bristol. In South Africa, the **Map Studio** ① *T+27(0)21-462 4360, www.mapstudio.co.za,* produces a wide range of maps of southern Africa. The **Namibia Tourist Board** (NTB) produces a very good road map highlighting all the minor roads and road numbers. This is available from all their offices and very usefully it can also be downloaded: www.map-of-namibia.com.

Where to stay in Namibia

It is a requirement for every hotel, lodge, guest farm, campsite and backpacker hostel to be graded and registered by tourism inspectors to ensure minimum standards are met and that the establishment deserves the right to be registered with the **Namibia Tourist Board** (NTB) and promoted to tourists. If they don't meet the standards, establishments are not permitted to operate. Of course this does not mean that every place is well run or has modern facilities, but generally speaking the quality of the tourism establishments in Namibia in every price bracket is very good. These vary from top-of-the-range game lodges and tented camps for US$300-1000 per couple per day; mid-range safari lodges and hotels with self-contained air-conditioned double rooms for US$100-200; to simple guesthouses and B&Bs for US$40-100 for a double room; and dorm beds or camping for under US$20 per person per day. Hotels in the towns and cities usually keep the same rates year-round, but safari lodges have seasonal rates depending on weather and periods of popularity of overseas (especially European) visitors. Generally, there are reasonable discounts for children and most places offer family accommodation. Reservations, especially in the parks, should be made well in advance if possible, particularly during the southern African school holidays, the longest of which is in December and January. You will be able to book the majority of places online.

Backpacker hostels

Apart from camping, backpacker hostels provide the cheapest accommodation in Namibia. However, they are only found in Windhoek and Swakopmund. A bed in a dormitory will cost as little as US$12 a night. Some also have budget double rooms with or without bathrooms, while others have space to pitch a tent in the garden. You can usually expect a self-catering kitchen, hot showers, a TV/DVD room and internet access/Wi-Fi. Many hostels also have bars and offer meals or nightly *braais*, plus a garden and a swimming pool. Most hostels are a good source of travel information and many act as booking agents for local activities, budget safaris and car hire.

Camping and caravan parks

For visitors on a limited budget who wish to see as much of the country as possible, camping and using the money saved on hotels towards hiring a car is a great option.

Thanks to its climate, camping is hugely popular in Namibia with both domestic and South African tourists. There are good facilities at many parks, most guest farms have their own private campsites and there are some excellent community-run sites scattered around the country. In the most popular parks, such as Etosha, campsites get booked up months in advance, so if you are in Namibia during the school holidays (see page 36) don't automatically assume there will be space. Expect to pay US$8-15 per person for camping and, as with the **NWR** campsites, the charges may be for a 'site' that can take several people and not per person, which sometimes works out expensive for just two people.

Even the most basic site will have a clean washblock, many with electric points, lighting and hot water. At some resorts, such as those in Etosha, there is the added excitement of the presence of wildlife, despite the fact that the campsites are fenced. Smaller mammals such as jackals, mongooses and honey badgers regularly make their way through the fences on night-time raids of the rubbish bins and there have been many an occasion when a saucepan or shoe has been scurried away. Many campsites will also have self-catering rooms, of varying quality and facilities, ranging from a single room with a couple of beds to chalets with several rooms and fully equipped kitchens. Be sure to stock up on provisions in the supermarkets and bottle stores of the major towns. Officially bush or free camping in Namibia is illegal, although in extremely isolated spots, campers can get away with it. Nevertheless it's recommended to camp in formal campsites whenever possible.

If you don't want to carry it with you, camping equipment such as lightweight tents, sleeping bags, ground mats, gas lights, stoves and cooking equipment, etc, can be bought in Windhoek and Swakopmund; look for **Cymot** (www.cymot.com) in particular. The cooking side of camping can be the most awkward for overseas visitors; however, many car hire companies have vehicles with everything you need from bulky items such as tables, chairs and cool boxes to small items such as cooking utensils and towels. If cost is no concern you can hire one with a built-in refrigerator, water tank, solar-heated portable shower, roof-tents, long-range fuel tanks and all the smaller items necessary for a successful and safe journey into the bush. Pre-book car hire and camping equipment before your arrival in Namibia, which will enable you to head straight off from the airport, not wasting a minute in town.
▶▶ *For camping shops to hire or buy equipment, see page 74.*

Guest farms and ranches

If you are coming from Europe, it is easy to be misled by the word 'farm'. In fact, most Namibian farms are vast tracts of land, typically as large as 10,000 ha (10 km by 10 km) used predominantly for livestock farming. Namibia has hundreds of guest farms (*gästefarm* in German) all over the country that offer accommodation, good country food and relaxation in a tranquil, rural setting. Some were established by farmers simply to make easy money from passing tourists, while others, hard hit by drought, looked at it as a lifeline for survival. Activities might include farm tours, hiking and horse riding. While guest farms also usually have some game such as springbok, gemsbok and warthog, the 'game drives' offered will tend to be scenic, rather than wild, experiences.

Price codes

Where to stay

$$$$	over US$300	$$$	US$151-300
$$	US$75-150	$	under US$75

Unless otherwise stated, prices refer to the cost of a double room including tax.

Restaurants

$$$	over US$25	$$	US$10-25	$	under US$10

Prices refer to the cost of a main course with either a soft drink, a glass of wine or a beer.

A game farm or ranch on the other hand will usually have been especially stocked with wild game such as elephant, rhino, the carnivorous cats and the antelope on which they feed. Here the emphasis will be on game-viewing drives and possibly guided hikes in the bush, offering a first-hand view of the bush, the 'spoor' (footprints and droppings) and the animals themselves. A stay at a good game ranch does not come cheap but is well worth the expense for the unique experience it offers visitors.

Most guest farms and game ranches cater for a limited number of visitors and provide an intimate, personable service. Overall they offer a superb opportunity to experience the bush first hand, with guides who know their land and everything that lives on it intimately, so aim to spend at least a couple of nights to enjoy the hospitality and experience.

Finally, many farms offer not only regular tourist accommodation and activities, but also hunting. Hunting common antelope for meat is common practice in southern Africa, but trophy hunting (and in some instances canned hunting, meaning the customer is guaranteed a kill by the simple expedient of the hosts capturing the animal and releasing it into an area where the hunter can take a shot at it) is also big business in Namibia. There is a proactive lobby in Namibia supporting the benefits of hunting, sometimes citing it as a culling control in areas where there are problems with over-populations of animals, and in some cases citing it as contributing to the tourism revenue to the country. However, we believe that most of our readers would prefer not to be in the situation of sharing a dinner table at a guest farm with a hunter who has specifically come to Namibia to shoot and kill a leopard, cheetah, buffalo or elephant (for sport), and wherever possible have refrained from listing the establishments that offer this activity.

Guesthouses

These vary from a small hotel-type establishment with 10-20 rooms to a B&B in someone's home with just three or four rooms, and are generally found in Windhoek, Swakopmund and the towns of the central and southern regions. Standards obviously vary enormously; much of what you'll get has to do with the character of the owners and the location of the homes. Guesthouses generally offer en suite twin/double rooms, sometimes with Wi-Fi and DSTV, and often have a small swimming pool with an outdoor *braai* area for guests to use. A hearty cooked breakfast is usually included in the rates which will range from US$40-100 per double room. Guesthouses do not usually have bars or restaurants, although there may be a small fridge in your room and it may also be possible to arrange an evening meal by calling ahead. Smaller than your average hotel, guesthouses tend to offer a more personal service which some people enjoy; while others prefer the relative anonymity of a hotel where they can come and go unnoticed.

Hotels and lodges

Every medium-sized town has at least one small hotel that falls into the two- to three-star category, offering basic, clean rooms, a restaurant serving three meals a day and a bar – often the only comfortable bar and restaurant in town. Although some tend to be aimed at local business travellers and may be characterless buildings, they nevertheless represent good value and rates will generally range from US$40-100 per double room and usually include a full cooked breakfast. For such places it is not usually necessary to book in advance, although during school holidays it is possible that places en route to Etosha and in Swakopmund may get busy. The more upmarket hotels in the cities and towns provide good service and international standards, and vary from boutique hotels with stylish interiors to more anonymous chain hotels, such as the South African managed **Protea Hotels**. Most have several public areas, restaurants and bars that are almost always open to non-guests, and maybe a gym and swimming pool. For these you can expect to pay in the region of US$100-200 per double room. Under **NTB's** grading system, a hotel must have at least 20 rooms, whilst a hotel pension must have at least 10 but not more than 20, and to be called a lodge or resort, the establishment has to be located in a rural area or within a natural environment and must have at least five guest rooms, a dining room or restaurant, and provide recreational activities.

National parks accommodation

ⓘ *Namibia Wildlife Resorts (NWR), www.nwr.com.na. Reservations offices: Erkrath Building, Independence Av, Windhoek, T061-285 7200, Mon-Fri 0800-1500; Bismarck St, Swakopmund, T064-402172, Mon-Fri 0900-1630; Pinnacle Building, (beneath the Cape Town Tourist Office), Burg St, Cape Town, South Africa, T+27(0)21-422 3761.*

While the Ministry of Environment and Tourism (MET) manages the national parks and reserves, **Namibia Wildlife Resorts** (NWR) is responsible for management of the accommodation at most of them. The majority of the larger parks, like Etosha National Park and Waterberg Plateau Park, have resorts where the accommodation is a mix of chalets or bungalows with two to six beds (most but not all are self-catering) and well-serviced campsites, and have facilities such as a restaurant and swimming pool. Reservations can be made up to 18 months in advance and payment must be made in full if the accommodation is to be taken up less than 25 days from the date of the reservation. Visitors from overseas can organize their accommodation by phone, email or online through the website, and pay in advance with a credit card (worth considering, particularly for Etosha, if you are going to be in Namibia during school holidays). Entry fees into the parks are paid separately at the entrance gates on arrival.

In most cases the camps are located in beautiful positions and the accommodation is clean and in good working order, although some are in need of minor repair. Others, such as Popa Falls (see page 154) have been recently upgraded by NWR and are now more akin to a lodge than a typical park resort; and then there are the former self-catering chalets in Etosha, which are now upmarket units with rates that include breakfast in the restaurant and in some cases dinner too (see page 124). Chalets and bungalows start at US$100-150 for a double/twin unit to US$150-250 for a four-bed unit. The upgraded accommodation in Etosha costs considerably more.

Food and drink in Namibia

Food

The staple diet for most black Namibians is a stiff maize porridge known as *pap*, served with a stew. *Pap* tends to be rather bland, but the accompanying stews can be tasty. Carnivores heading to Namibia should lick their lips as meat is plentiful, excellent and very cheap (by European standards). One of the first local terms you are likely to learn will be '*braai*', which quite simply means barbecue. The *braai* is incredibly popular, part of the Namibian way of life, and every campsite, self-catering accommodation, picnic spot and lay-by has a *braai* pit. Given the excellent range of meat available, learning how to cook good food on a *braai* is an art that needs to be mastered quickly, especially if you are self-catering. Supermarkets and butchers sell a wide range of steaks, sausages, ribs and choice cuts (the *sosaties* are delicious). For details (and recipes) see box, page 26. Local game specialities are also recommended and you may encounter these if staying at guest or game farms. Another Namibian favourite is *biltong*, a heavily salted and sun-dried meat that is very moreish and a perfect snack on the road. Fresh fruit and vegetables can be hard to find in smaller towns, so vegetarians should stock up when they can. For example, a supermarket in a northern town may only get a delivery of fresh fruit and vegetables (usually imported from South Africa) once a week, so if you happen to visit on delivery day there will be a good selection but hardly anything will be left at the end of the week.

Drink

Namibia's tap water is safe to drink, though does have rather a metallic taste due to the treatments used. Bottled water is widely available as are a number of good brands of soft drinks and juices, many are part of the Ceres or Liquifruit range imported from the fruit-growing regions of South Africa. Another popular drink is *rooibos* (or red bush) tea – a caffeine-free tea with a smoky flavour, usually served with sugar or honey, which is grown in the Cederberg Mountains in South Africa.

The beer in Namibia is excellent, as you would expect given the German heritage. The prize-winning **Windhoek Lager** is made with mineral water and is very tasty. Other locally brewed beer is **Tafel**, and South African **Castle** lager and **Black Label** are also common. A 330 ml bottle costs around US$2 from a bottle store and not

Braai recipes

One of the first local terms you are likely to learn in Namibia will be 'braai', which translates as 'roast' in Afrikaans and loosely means barbecue. It serves as a verb when describing how food is cooked and a noun when describing the cooking equipment, meaning a grill over an open fire. The *braai* is incredibly popular and part of the fun of eating in Namibia.

Once you have established a core of heat using firelighters and wood or charcoal (charcoal is more eco-friendly and less smoky but wood makes for a wonderful fire), wrap up potatoes, sweet potatoes, squash, butternut, etc, in heavy-duty foil and cook them in the coals for an hour or so. Set aside a good piece of meat, with a sauce and a cold beer, and you will be living the Namibian dream. A common indication of the ideal heat of a *braai* is to hold your hand over the coals and count to 10. If you have to pull your hand back before 10 it's too hot, and later than 10 then it's not hot enough.

An extension of the *braai* is the *potjie* (pronounced 'poy-kee'), literally a cast-iron pot with legs that sits on top of coals. The word means 'little-pot' in Afrikaans, and it is thought to originate from the Voortrekkers who hooked the pots under their wagons, and then heated them up again over the fire at night after adding ingredients collected during the day. Once in Namibia you can buy *potjies* (in varying sizes) from local supermarkets, branches of the camping and outdoor shop **Cymot** (see page 75) and even some petrol stations sell them. They are wonderfully simple to use. Just brown your meat and throw in any vegetables and leftover meat, together with fruit, dried fruit, stock, chutney and herbs and leave the pot to simmer away on the coals. Once prepared, apart from occasionally replenishing the coals, the dish requires no attention whatsoever. Allow to cook slowly so that all the flavours blend. A chicken *potjie* might take up to two hours to cook, lamb two to three, and oxtail perhaps six hours to reach its best. Most Namibian bookstores will have sections devoted to *braai* and *potjiekos* ('kos' is food in Afrikaans) recipe books.

Namibian braai recipes
Butternut soup
1 small butternut cut in 2-cm squares
1 tsp ginger, ground (crushed if fresh)
1 tsp salt
1 tsp curry powder
1 cup cream or milk

Cover butternut with water and boil, together with all ingredients except cream, until soft. Mash. Return to the heat for a couple of minutes, add cream and allow to heat through.

Chicken potjie (serves two)
500 g chicken
oil
1 onion, chopped
1 clove garlic, crushed
carrots, diced
sweet potatoes, cubed
celery
dried peaches
1 cup white wine, ½ cup water
seasoning

Fry the chicken with oil, onion and garlic until brown. Add (in order) layers of carrots, sweet potato, celery, peaches and seasoning, pour in the wine and stock, cover and leave to simmer gently for one hour. Do not stir, the layering is important. Serve with rice. This dish has long been the local method of using up whatever leftovers and produce is available, so be bold and experiment with your own *potjie*.

Ratatouille (serves two)
1 onion, chopped
1 green pepper, chopped
1 clove garlic, crushed
oil
small carrot, diced
1 tin chopped tomatoes
1 courgette, sliced
salt and seasoning

Fry onion, pepper and garlic until soft, add the rest and simmer until tender (you may have to add a little water).

Quick braai sauce/marinade
½ cup ketchup
¼ cup Worcester sauce
1 tbsp chutney
1 tsp mustard powder
½ cup vinegar
1 tbsp oil
1 clove garlic, crushed
1 tbsp sugar
½ cup cream

Mix all the ingredients together and simmer for five minutes; use as a marinade for any meat dish.

Cowboy dampers
250 g self-raising flour
1 tsp baking powder
pinch salt
little water
30 g margarine

Work all the ingredients into a sticky dough. Whittle a stick (multi-pronged if you want) to get a clean end. Wrap a fingerful around the end of the stick and bake over the fire. Serve with jam as a simple dessert, or with savouries (see potato fillings, below) as a starter.

Stuffed potatoes
Wrap clean potatoes in foil (shiny side in to reflect the heat) and cook deep in the coals of the fire for one hour. Remove the potato and upwrap; scoop out some of the flesh and replace with your favourite filling. For example: tuna and mayonnaise mixed with a shredded carrot, onion, curry powder, paprika and lemon juice; ham cubes and cottage cheese with black pepper; home-made sour cream (lemon juice and long-life cream) mixed with tinned oysters or mussels and black pepper; fish (preferably smoked) mixed with cocktail sauce and lemon juice.

Stuffed butternut
Slice the butternut in half lengthways and scoop out the seeds. Then fill the cavities with blanched and chopped spinach, feta cheese, butter and parsley. Wrap in foil and *braai* on the coals for 40 minutes – you'll know the butternuts are cooked when the sides squash in easily.

much more in most bars. Wine is plentiful and cheap given that it is all imported from South Africa, and even bottle stores in rural areas offer a good selection. The Afrikaner influence means that low-grade brandy is available everywhere (ask for a *Klipdrift* and coke – 'klippies and coke' – in a bar and see how you go).

You will have no problem finding a bottle store (*drank-winkel* in Afrikaans) in every town and they open Monday to Saturday 0900-1800. You are unable to buy alcohol from shops in the evening and it is illegal for them to sell alcohol on a Sunday (but okay for restaurants or bars). Bottle stores sell all types of booze, while supermarkets are only permitted to stock wine. Most bottle stores and supermarkets also sell ice for you to fill your cool box, as well as firewood for your *braai*.

Eating out

Food and drink is good value in Namibia and an evening meal with wine in a reasonable restaurant can cost less than US$40 for two people, and you can be pretty much assured of good food and large portions. Restaurants tend to have menus revolving around steak, chicken and schnitzel, plus good, fresh seafood by the coast, although vegetarians may have limited choice. Quality and service vary of course, depending on where you are. Small-town restaurants tend to serve fairly simple meals focusing on standard meat-and-two-veg dishes, while town restaurants are often part of a mediocre chain. However, it's a different story in Windhoek and Swakopmund where an excellent variety of restaurants represent every kind of international cuisine as well as and a good choice of quality South African wine. Informal family restaurants are open all day from breakfast to late at night. The more formal specialist restaurants are generally open for lunch 1200-1500 and dinner from 1800. Kitchens usually close about 2200 but earlier in the smaller towns, where some may not open on one or two days a week (usually Sunday or Monday).

Costs can be brought down by making your own food either at campsites or in self-catering accommodation. Food in supermarkets is considerably cheaper than, say, in Europe, especially meat, beer and wine. There are several large supermarket chains in Namibia such as **Pick 'n' Pay** and **Shoprite**, which also feature extensive counters for takeaways like chicken and chips, pizzas and sandwiches, which are worth stopping at to pick up a cheap meal as a picnic while driving or to reheat in the microwave at your self-catering accommodation later. Namibia's petrol stations almost all invariably have a shop for snacks such as hot pies and perhaps filled rolls and muffins.

Entertainment in Namibia

Bars and clubs

Although Windhoek and Swakopmund have a few bars and a couple of nightclubs, on the whole, Namibia is not the place to come for nightlife and you will be surprised at how quiet towns become at night. In most places, the action is restricted to a few hotel bars which only really get going at weekends and on major holidays. On these evenings you'll mingle with beer-bellied farmers in their trademark khaki shorts and shirts and *vellies* (leather boots) speaking in English, Afrikaans and German.

Cinema

Only Windhoek and Swakopmund have cinemas that show international releases. The main cinema in Windhoek, Ster-Kinekor (see page 73) has seven screens and is located in the Maerua Mall; the tiny cinema in Swakopmund is the Atlanta (two screens) at the Swakopmund Hotel and Entertainment Centre (see page 256).

Performing arts

The main venues for performing arts like theatre, concerts and dance are in Windhoek. These include the National Theatre of Namibia (see page 73), the Franco-Namibian Cultural Centre (see page 84) and the Warehouse Theatre (see page 73).

Shopping in Namibia

African art and crafts vary in quality and can be surprisingly expensive in Namibia. Sculptures, baskets, ceramics and other souvenirs start as curios sold at roadside stalls but as the craftsmanship improves and they are sold in formal curio shops, these products become increasingly pricey. Nevertheless there are a number of regional handicraft centres and excellent craft and curio shops in Windhoek and Swakopmund. Probably the best in the country is the Namibia Craft Centre in Windhoek (see page 75), which is literally a one-stop-shop for just about all the curios produced in Namibia including carvings, pottery, baskets, leatherwork, jewellery and paintings. Items are sourced directly from the producers to make sure rural people have an outlet for their crafts and receive an adequate income.

Elsewhere, the San (Bushmen) of the northeast produce colourful and intricate beadwork; baskets, woodcarving and pots are produced in the Kavango and Caprivi regions; and in the northwest, centred on Opuwo and Epupa, you can buy the intricately designed jewellery made by the Himba.

Other items unique to Namibia include the wool and leather of Namibia's hardy, desert-reared karakul sheep which is both woven into clothing and carpets, often with attractive local and animal designs, and made into leather items such as bags, belts, wallets, etc; the trade name is Namibia Karakul Leathers (NAKARA). There are furriers and tanneries in Windhoek and Swakopmund, and weavers in Dordabis and Karabib. Other locally produced goods are leather shoes. Every farmer, tour guide and hiker in the country will wear his *vellies* – boots made from kudu or gemsbok leather which are durable and comfortable.

Namibia is of course a good place to buy diamonds at a good price. Each retailer is a member of the Jewellery Association of Namibia, a programme sponsored by the Diamond Trading Company and the Diamond Board of Namibia. There are a number of jewellers in Windhoek and Swakopmund, and designs are very contemporary. Remember the four Cs: cut, colour, clarity and carat. Only buy diamonds from a licensed dealer, as it is illegal to buy uncut or not polished diamonds in Namibia.
➤ *For VAT refunds, see page 40.*

Responsible travel in Namibia

Since the early 1990s there has been a phenomenal growth in tourism that promotes and supports the conservation of natural environments and is also fair and equitable to local communities. Namibia was the first country in the world to incorporate environmental protection into its constitution when it gained independence in 1990. More than 20% of the country falls within protected conservation areas in the parks and reserves and, with the 2010 declaration of the Dorob National Park, Namibia became the first and only country in the world to have its entire coastline protected in a national park. Additionally many community-based tourism options provide real monetary and social benefits to local communities, and many Namibian tour operators, guest farms and lodges fund conservation and community projects through fees taken from tourists. Well worth supporting, we try to highlight these in the book.

10 ways to be a responsible traveller

There are some aspects of travel that you have to accept are going to have an impact, but try to balance the negatives with positives by following these guidelines:

Cut your emissions Plan an itinerary that minimizes carbon emissions whenever possible. This might involve hiring a bike or booking a walking or canoeing tour rather than one that relies on vehicle transport. See also carbon offset programmes, below.

Check the small print Choose travel operators that abide by a responsible travel policy (it will usually be detailed on their website). Visit www.responsibletravel.com.

Keep it local If travelling independently, try to use public transport, stay in locally owned accommodation, eat in local restaurants, buy local produce and hire local guides.

Cut out waste Take biodegradable soap and shampoo and leave excess packaging, particularly plastic, at home.

Get in touch Find out if there are any local schools, charities or voluntary conservation organizations that you could include in your itinerary. If appropriate, take along some useful gifts or supplies. For a list of projects that could benefit from your support, see www.stuffyourrucksack.com.

Learn the lingo Practise some local words, even if it's just to say 'hello', 'thank you' and 'goodbye'. See page 410 for useful words and phrases.

Respect local customs and beliefs When meeting cultural groups in Namibia such as the Himba or San (Bushmen), interaction should remain sensitive, sympathetic and polite at all times – visit with a guide; take an interest in learning about their lifestyles and share information about your own; and don't push Western values or ideals. Don't treat people as part of the landscape and always ask permission before taking photographs – including your wildlife tour guide. Remember to honour any promises you've made to send photographs.

Take only photos Resist the temptation to buy souvenirs made from animals or plants. Not only is it illegal to import or export many wildlife souvenirs, but their uncontrolled collection supports poaching and can have a devastating impact on local populations, upsetting the natural balance of entire ecosystems. CITES (www.cites.org) bans international trade in around 900 species of animals and plants, and controls trade in a further 33,000 species. Several organizations, including WWF, TRAFFIC and the Smithsonian Institution have formed the Coalition Against Wildlife Trafficking (www.cawtglobal.org).

Use water wisely Water is a precious commodity in Namibia and it is very important not to waste it: take a shower instead of a bath; don't let the tap run while brushing your teeth; and only wash vehicles at official car washes.

Don't interfere Avoid disturbing wildlife, damaging habitats or interfering with natural behaviour by feeding wild animals, getting too close or being too noisy. Leave plants and shells where you find them.

Code green for hikers and campers

- Take biodegradable soap, shampoo and toilet paper, long-lasting lithium batteries and plastic bags for packing out all rubbish and unused food.
- Use a water filter instead of buying bottled water.
- Keep to trails to avoid erosion and trampling vegetation. Don't take short cuts, especially in arid deserts where plants may take years to recover.
- Always use a formal campsite; it is illegal to 'free' camp in Namibia.
- When you build a fire to *braai*, use a purpose-built fireplace (*braai* pit)

whenever possible. Allow the fire to burn down to a fine ash which can be raked out and disposed of. Observe any fire restrictions in place.
- If toilets, portable latrines or composting toilets are not available, dig latrines at least 50 m from water sources and camp sites. Cover the hole with natural materials and either burn or pack out your toilet paper.
- Wash clothing and cooking items well away from water sources and scatter grey water so that it filters through soil. If you must wash in streams, rivers or lakes, use biodegradable, phosphate-free soap.

Carbon offsetting

Carbon offsetting schemes aim to offset greenhouse gas emissions by donating to environmental projects such as tree planting or renewable energy schemes. For every tonne of CO_2 you generate through a fossil fuel-burning activity such as flying, you pay for an equivalent tonne to be removed elsewhere through a 'green' initiative. Although some conservation groups are concerned that carbon offsetting is being used as a smoke-screen to delay the urgent action needed to cut emissions and develop alternative energy solutions, it remains an important way of counterbalancing your carbon footprint. There are numerous online calculators (such as www.carbonfootprint.com). Alternatively, book with a travel operator that supports a carbon offset provider, such as TICOS (www.ticos.co.uk) or Reduce my Footprint (www.reducemyfootprint.travel).

Essentials A-Z

Accident and emergency

Police T10111; all emergencies from a landline T081-112; from a cell phone T112.

Children

Namibia is an ideal first introduction to Africa for children thanks to its excellent family-friendly facilities and low risk of holiday illnesses. The main supermarkets sell items like disposable nappies, formula milk powders and puréed foods; hygiene throughout the country is of a good standard; stomach upsets are rare and tap water everywhere is safe to drink. However, it is important to remember that children have an increased risk of gastroenteritis, malaria and sunburn and are more likely to develop complications, so care must be taken to minimize risks. Also be aware of the potential dangers of wild animals, snakes and insects in the bush.

Most accommodation welcomes families and many have either specific family rooms or adjoining rooms, and there are plenty of family self-catering chalets or bungalows, especially in the parks. Children get significant discounts; for example at the **Namibia Wildlife Resorts** (**NWR**) accommodation children under 6 go free, and those aged 6-12 are half price. There are also discounts for entry fees, especially in the main parks like Etosha, where children under 16 go free.

Seeing animals on safari is very exciting for children, especially when they catch their first glimpse of an elephant or lion. However, small children may get bored driving around a hot game park all day if there is no animal activity. Keep them interested by providing them with their own animal and bird checklists and perhaps their own binoculars and cameras. If you travel in a group, think about the long hours inside the vehicle sharing little room with other people. Noisy and bickering children can annoy your travel mates and scare the animals away. Most tour operators use minibuses for safaris so consider taking one for yourself or share it with another family.

Customs and duty free

There are no restrictions for residents from the Southern African Customs Union (Botswana, Lesotho, Namibia, South Africa, Swaziland). For all other visitors, the following items are allowed to be imported duty free: 400 cigarettes or 50 cigars or 250 g of tobacco, 50 ml of perfume and 250 ml of eau de toilette, 2 litres of wine and 1 litre of spirits. All hunting rifles must be declared on arrival; permits are issued by customs when entering the country; other firearms are not permitted. Once in Namibia, be careful about buying any wildlife-derived souvenirs. Any object made from an endangered species such as elephant ivory, sea turtle products and the skins of wild cats, is prohibited. If you were to buy such items, you should always consider the environmental and social impact of your purchase. Attempts to smuggle controlled products out of Namibia can result in confiscation, fines and imprisonment under the Convention on Trade in Endangered Species (CITES), www.cites.org.

Within the country, be aware that you are not permitted to transfer any animal products as you travel from the Far North, Caprivi or northwest regions across the Red Line (veterinary fence) to the south. This includes souvenir animal horns and skins and fresh meat, ostensibly to prevent the spread of foot-and-mouth disease, without prior clearance from a vet.

Disabled travellers

Namibia is fairly well developed for the needs of disabled travellers, although wheelchairs are not accommodated on public transport, so the options are to self-drive or go on an organized tour. Most of the modern hotels and lodges have rooms with disabled facilities, including most of the **Namibia Wildlife Resorts (NWR)** accommodation, and it is worth asking about this even in the smaller or more remote establishments. An organized safari isn't totally out of the question given that a fair amount of the time is spent in the vehicle. Wheelchair-bound travellers may want to consider a camping safari which provides easy access to a tent at ground level. Most tour operators are able to make special arrangements, so being disabled should not deter you from going to Namibia. **Sunbird Tours**, www.sunbirdtours-namibia.com, in Windhoek have safari vehicles adapted to wheelchairs.

Electricity

220/240 volts AC at 50 Hz, using 3-point, round-pin (1 x 10 mm and 2 x 8 mm prongs), 15-amp plugs. Check supermarkets and hardware stores for adaptors. Hotels usually have 2 round-pin sockets for razors and phones.

Embassies and consulates

For a list of Namibian embassies abroad, see http://embassy.goabroad.com/embassies-of/Namibia.

Gay and lesbian travellers

The climate is not particularly welcoming for gay and lesbian visitors. Ex-president Nujoma has made comments denouncing homosexuality on several occasions and homosexuality is still officially illegal in Namibia. Therefore it is wise for gay and lesbian visitors to be discrete. By doing so you should encounter no problems.

Health

Before you go
See your GP or travel clinic at least 6 weeks before your departure for general advice on travel risks, malaria and recommended vaccinations. Make sure you have comprehensive medical insurance, get a dental check (especially if you are going to be away for more than a month), know your own blood group and if you suffer from a long-term condition such as diabetes or epilepsy make sure someone knows or that you have a Medic Alert bracelet/necklace with this information on it.

Vaccinations and malaria precautions
First of all confirm that your primary courses and boosters are up to date (usually diphtheria, tuberculosis, typhoid, polio and tetanus). Vaccines commonly recommended for travel in Namibia are hepatitis A, meningitis and rabies. A yellow fever certificate is only required if entering from an infected area; check

requirements if travelling from other African countries to Namibia.

Malaria is present in the northern third of the country from Nov to Jun and along the Kavango and Kunene rivers throughout the year. Prophylactics should be taken, and the final decision on which anti-malarials to take should be based on a consultation with your GP or travel clinic. Make sure you finish the recommended course of tablets.

A-Z of health risks
Bites and stings

While venomous and non-venomous snakes are present in Namibia as well as biting spiders and scorpions, it's rare to be bitten by them. Nevertheless, if camping its always wise to shake boots and shoes out, check backpacks before putting them on, and check shower floors before stepping in.

Bites from scorpions are very painful but rarely dangerous to adults. Seek medical advice if a young child is bitten. Do not immerse the bite in cold water as this increases the pain. It should be cleaned with an antiseptic lotion, which also wipes away any remaining venom.

Most snake species are non-venomous and even venomous snakes often inflict a 'dry bite' where no venom is injected. But if you are unlucky (or careless) enough to be bitten by a venomous snake, try to identify the culprit, without putting yourself in further danger. Do not apply a tourniquet, suck or cut open the bite wound; victims should be taken to a hospital or a doctor without delay.

Ticks usually attach themselves to the lower parts of the body – often after you've been walking in areas of long damp grass or where cattle have grazed – then swell up as they suck blood. You should use a pair of tweezers to remove a tick, gently rocking it out and being careful not to leave the head embedded in your skin as this can cause a nasty infection. Do not use petrol, Vaseline, lighted cigarettes. If travelling with children, check them over for ticks.

Cholera

There are sporadic cholera outbreaks in Namibia, but given that cholera is spread through consumption of contaminated water and food, these have been in areas with very poor sanitation and lack of clean drinking water. The main symptoms are profuse watery diarrhoea and vomiting, which in severe cases may lead to dehydration and death. However, most travellers are at extremely low risk of infection and the disease rarely shows symptoms in healthy well-nourished people. The cholera vaccine, Dukoral, is only recommended for certain high-risk individuals such as health professionals and volunteers. All travellers should carefully observe food and water precautions.

Diarrhoea

Diarrhoea can refer to either loose stools or an increased frequency of bowel movement. Both can be a nuisance but symptoms should be relatively short lived. Adults can use an antidiarrhoeal medication to control the symptoms but only for up to 24 hrs. Keep well hydrated by drinking plenty of fluids and eat bland foods. Oral rehydration sachets taken after each loose stool are a useful way to keep well hydrated. They should always be used when treating children and the elderly. If there are no signs of improvement the diarrhoea is likely to be viral and not bacterial and antibiotics may be required. Also seek medical help if there is blood in the stools and/or fever.

The standard advice to prevent problems is to be careful with water and ice for drinking. If you have any doubts then boil the water or filter and treat it. Food can also transmit disease. Be wary of salads (what were they washed in, who handled them), re-heated foods or food that has been left out in the sun having been cooked earlier. There is a simple adage that says wash it, peel it, boil it or forget it. Also be wary of unpasteurized dairy products as these can transmit a range of diseases.

Hepatitis

Hepatitis means inflammation of the liver. Viral causes of the disease can be acquired anywhere in the world. The most obvious symptom is a yellowing of your skin or the whites of your eyes. However, prior to this all that you may notice is itching and tiredness. Pre-travel hepatitis A vaccine is the best bet. Hepatitis B (for which there is also a vaccine) is spread through blood and unprotected sexual intercourse; both of these can be avoided.

HIV/AIDS

Africa has the highest rates of HIV and AIDS in the world. Visitors should be aware of the dangers of infection from unprotected sex and always use a condom. If you have to have medical treatment, ensure any equipment used is taken from a sealed pack or is freshly sterilized. If you have to have a blood transfusion, ask for screened blood.

Malaria → See also Vaccinations and malaria precautions, above.

Malaria can start as something just resembling an attack of flu. You may feel tired, lethargic, headachy, feverish; or, more seriously, develop fits, followed by

coma and then death. Have a low index of suspicion because it is very easy to write off vague symptoms, which may actually be malaria. If you have a temperature, go to a doctor as soon as you can and ask for a malaria test. On your return home if you suffer any of these symptoms, get tested as soon as possible.

To prevent mosquito bites wear clothes that cover arms and legs, especially at dusk, and use effective insect repellents. Repellents containing 30-50% DEET (Di-ethyltoluamide) are recommended; lemon eucalyptus (Mosiguard) is a reasonable alternative. Rooms with a/c or fans also help ward off mosquitoes at night.

If you are a popular target for insect bites or develop lumps quite soon after being bitten, use antihistamine tablets and apply a cream such as hydrocortisone.

Rabies

Avoid dogs and monkeys that are behaving strangely. If you are bitten by a domestic or wild animal, do not leave things to chance: scrub the wound with soap and water and/or disinfectant, try to determine the animal's ownership, and seek medical assistance at once. The course of treatment depends on whether you have already been satisfactorily vaccinated against rabies.

Sun

Protect yourself adequately against the sun. In Namibia do not be fooled into thinking the sun cannot harm you even when it is foggy – the UV rays will still penetrate the mist. Apply a high-factor sunscreen (greater than SPF15) and also make sure it protects against UVB. Prevent heat exhaustion and heatstroke by drinking enough fluids throughout the day (your urine will be pale if you are drinking enough). Symptoms of heat exhaustion and heatstroke include dizziness, tiredness and headache. Use rehydration salts mixed with water to replenish fluids and salts and find somewhere cool and shady to recover. If you suspect heatstroke rather than heat exhaustion, you need to cool the body down quickly (cold showers are particularly effective).

If you get sick

It is essential to have travel insurance as hospital bills need to be paid at the time of admittance, so keep all paperwork to make a claim. Namibia has state hospitals in most of the larger towns. However, these can be poorly equipped and understaffed and should be avoided if at all possible. The much better alternative is the private hospitals, which have 24-hr emergency departments and pharmacies, and provide a high standard of healthcare. The best are in Windhoek, Swakopmund and Ongwediva. Owing to the large distances and remoteness of many areas, air evacuation is much more common than in other countries and the service is well developed. Unfortunately, the majority of accidents involving tourists are road accidents by drivers unaccustomed to driving on the gravel roads. See also Driving, page 18.

In the event of a medical emergency in Namibia **International SOS Namibia**, T061-289 0906, www.internationalsos.com, is likely to be the medical company that comes to your assistance. It offers 24-hr emergency medical rescue specifically for tourists, with permanent bases in Windhoek, Swakopmund, and Tsumeb, and air ambulances that can reach every corner of the country. When arranging medical insurance it is a good idea to ask if your insurer will cover you for the use of this service.

Useful websites

www.btha.org British Travel Health Association.
www.cdc.gov Centers for Disease Control and Prevention. US government site which gives excellent advice on travel health and details of disease outbreaks.
www.fco.gov.uk British Foreign and Commonwealth Office travel site with useful information on each country, people, climate and a list of UK embassies/consulates.
www.fitfortravel.nhs.uk A-Z of vaccine/health advice for each country.
www.travelhealth.co.uk Independent travel health site with advice on vaccinations, travel insurance and health risks.
www.who.int World Health Organization, updates of disease outbreaks.

Holidays

The dates of school holidays can have a significant bearing on your visit. Prices will be higher and popular destinations will be fully booked. In Swakopmund over Christmas there won't be anywhere to stay if you have not made an advance reservation. This also applies to national parks accommodation in late Aug, in particular at Etosha National Park. School holidays are: mid-Dec to mid-Jan; end of Apr to end of May; and end of Aug to early Sep. For exact dates of Namibian school holidays check www.natron.net, and for South African dates go to www.schoolterms.co.za. See the Festivals listings in each chapter for local events.

1 Jan New Year's Day.
21 Mar Independence Day.
Mar-Apr Good Fri and Easter Mon.
May-Jun Ascension Day.
1 May Worker's Day.

4 May Cassinga Day.
25 May Africa Day.
26 Aug Heroes' Day.
10 Dec International Human Rights Day.
25 Dec Christmas Day.
26 Dec Boxing Day/Family Day.

Internet

Internet cafés are widely available in Windhoek and Swakopmund and all the main towns. **Hosea Kutako International Airport** has Wi-Fi, as do many restaurants and coffee shops. Increasingly many hotels offer Wi-Fi for a fee. However, most lodges in the more remote places won't have internet, and if they do it is likely to be via an expensive satellite connection. There is the option of buying a USB/dongle connection and loading it with airtime once in Namibia; this can be organized at any of the mobile phone shops including the desks at the airport– try MTC or Telecom.

Language

→ *See Useful words and phrases, page 410.*
The official language is English and it is widely spoken by almost everyone, but Namibia has an ethnically diverse population that includes the Bantu-speaking Ovambo, Kavango and Herero, the Damara, the San (Bushmen) and whites of South African, German and British descent. There are more than 11 indigenous languages, with the most common being Oshiwambo, which about 50% of the population speak; the majority of which are in the north, while Afrikaans is still the lingua franca in the central and southern parts of the country. Visitors who speak German will find that many white-owned businesses in the tourist industry are owned and run by German-speaking people, and Namibia is very popular with German tourists.

Insurance

Before departure, it is vital to take out comprehensive travel insurance. There are a wide variety of policies to choose from, so shop around. At the very least, the policy should cover medical expenses, including repatriation to your home country in the event of a medical emergency. There is no substitute for suitable precautions against petty crime, but if you do have something stolen whilst in Namibia, report the incident to the nearest police station and make sure you get a police report and case number. You will need these to make any claim from your insurance company.

Media

Newspapers
The main English-language newspaper is *The Namibian* (www.namibian.com.na), an independent daily with some international news, which is also available online. If it's local scandal, crime and debate that you're after, head straight for the *Namibian Sun* (www.sun.com.na). Others are the *Republikain* (daily, Afrikaans); and *Mail & Guardian* (weekly South African and international news). International newspapers from the US, UK and Europe are regularly available in Windhoek and Swakopmund (although a day or so late).

Radio
As well as the **Namibian Broadcasting Corporation** (**NBC**), available almost everywhere throughout the country, and broadcast in English, there are several commercial radio stations. The best for up-to-date music are *Radio Kudu*

(103.5 FM) and *Radio Wave (96.7 FM)*. Don't expect much reception (other than NBC) away from urban centres.

Television

The state broadcaster, **NBC**, broadcasts one television channel in English. Most hotels will have **DSTV** (Digital Satellite Television), South African satellite TV, with over 100 channels of movies, music, sport and light entertainment. The most popular are the sports channels, especially *Supersport*, which provides extensive coverage of rugby and European football. A number of hotels and bars have widescreen TVs for watching big sporting events.

Money

➜ *US$1 = N$10.96, £1= N$17.69, €1 = N$14.14 (Sep 2014).*

The Namibian dollar is pegged 1:1 with the South African rand and both currencies can be used in Namibia interchangeably. However, outside Namibia the local currency is not convertible and you cannot use it in South Africa or anywhere else, so remember to spend any surplus Namibian dollars before your departure. Alternatively change it into rand which can be converted back into your own currency once back at home.

Currency

In 1993 Namibia issued its first set of bank notes, prior to which the South African rand had been legal tender (which it still is). Notes come in dominations of N$10, N$20, N$50, N$100 and N$200; coins come in 5c, 10c, 50c, N$1 and N$5. The N$10, N$20 notes feature a portrait of Sam Nujoma, while all the others have the face of famous Nama chief, Hendrik Witbooi.

As South African rand is still legal tender you will certainly come across notes and coins, particularly in national parks and in the south where you encounter a higher frequency of South African visitors. If your return flight is via Johannesburg, you might want to stash some rand away for a meal, drink, duty free or souvenirs on the way home. Additionally rand can be exchanged, and in more tourist-oriented places like lodges and shops, used, (though not interchangeably with the local currencies) in Botswana, Zimbabwe and Zambia. Ensure that you swap any leftover Namibian dollars into rand before crossing a border.

Changing money

Namibia's main banks are, **Bank of Windhoek, First National Bank, Nedbank** and **Standard Bank**, each of which have branches in all the towns.

US dollars, UK pounds and euros are the easiest currencies to exchange. If they have any, branches should also be able to sell you foreign currency (ie South African rand or US dollars) should you need the cash for continuing your travels in southern Africa or elsewhere after Namibia; you will need to produce your passport for all transactions.

For up-to-the-minute exchange rates, go to **www.xe.com**.

Credit and debit cards

Credit and debit cards are widely accepted all over the country; there are ATMs at every bank and some petrol stations and the larger hotels, shops and restaurants accept them, as do the airlines, car hire companies, tour operators and travel agents. However, most campsites, remote guest farms or smaller guesthouses may not have facilities. Visa is the most widely accepted card, followed by MasterCard, AMEX and Diners far less so. Remember your bank at home will charge a small fee for withdrawing from an ATM abroad with a debit and credit card, although withdrawing cash at an ATM usually attracts the most competitive exchange rate. Note that cards are not accepted at all petrol stations (yet) and in many places fuel can only be paid for in cash: ensure you have enough cash to fill up especially if your vehicle has a long-range fuel tank.

Currency cards

If you don't want to carry lots of cash, prepaid currency cards allow you to preload money from your bank account, fixed at the day's exchange rate. They look like a credit or debit card and are issued by specialist money changing companies, such as **Travelex** and **Caxton FX**, as well as the **Post Office**. You can top up and check your balance by phone or online.

Opening hours

Banks Mon-Fri 0800-1530, Sat 0800-1200.
Post offices Mon-Fri 0830-1600. Main branches also open Sat 0800-1200.
Shops Generally Mon-Fri 0800-1800. Larger branches of the supermarkets stay open until late in the evening and are open on Sun 0800-1300.

Post

NamPost (www.nampost.com.na) has post office branches across the country, even in the smallest of towns. Internal and international mail is generally reliable and letters to Europe and the USA should take no more than a week, although over the busy Christmas season can take longer. If you are sending home souvenirs, surface mail to Europe is the cheapest method but will take at least 6 weeks. It's probably best to use registered mail for more valuable items so that you can track their progress. The post office has its own domestic and international courier service, **NamPost Courier**, and the main international courier companies are also represented in Namibia: **DHL**, www.dhl.com, and **Fedex**, www.fedex.com. Check the websites for the nearest branch.

Safety

Generally speaking, Namibia is a safe country in which to travel, with far less petty crime than in neighbouring South Africa, although there are of course some exceptions. The most common crimes are pickpocketing and purse-snatching (usually in the busy shopping districts of towns) and thefts from parked vehicles. Overall, common sense precautions will be sufficient to ensure that your holiday is not spoiled by any unpleasant incidents. The general rules apply to prevent petty theft: don't exhibit anything valuable and keep wallets and purses out of sight; always keep car doors locked and windows wound up; lock room doors at night; avoid deserted areas and always take a taxi at night.

Car crime is particularly bad in the more populated northern part of the country, in towns such as Oshakati, Ondangwa and Grootfontein. Keep an eye over your shoulder when getting into your car or when unloading shopping and don't leave anything on the dashboard that could be grabbed through an open window.

It's not only crime that may affect your safety; you must also take safety precautions when visiting game parks and reserves. If camping, be cautious at night as wild animals wander around the camps freely, which is especially true of organized campsites where local animals have got so used to humans that they've lost much of their inherent fear. Exercise care during the day too; remember that wild animals can be dangerous.

Tax

VAT of 15% for accommodation and goods is included in the price. Visitors may reclaim the VAT back on purchases bought in Namibia exceeding the value of N$250 at the VAT reclaim desks at Hosea Kutako International Airport or at the main border posts when leaving the country.

Each item must be physically shown to the refund/customs officer as proof of purchase. At the airport, this needs to be done BEFORE checking in your luggage. Keep all receipts as they must accompany each item. Refunds only apply to new items taken out of the country and not on services rendered such as accommodation. If you are buying expensive items like diamonds, be sure to claim the tax back as the refund can be quite considerable. For more information pick up the *VAT Refund* leaflet at the airport or the tourist offices or contact the **Ministry of Finance**, T061-209 2931, www.mof.gov.na.

Telephone → *Country code +264.*

You can make international calls from public coin or card phones in boxes on the street or at post offices, which sell phone cards and are found in even the smallest towns. Most hotels and lodges offer international telephone services, though they will usually charge double the normal rate. In larger places like Windhoek and Swakopmund, private shops also offer international services, usually with additional internet. Calls between Namibia and Botswana and South Africa are charged at long-distance local rates rather than international. If you have a mobile phone with roaming, you can make use of Namibia's cellular networks, which cover all larger towns and main roads but not all the parks and reserves or the north of Namibia away from the towns. SIM and top-up cards are available for pay-as-you-go mobile providers – try MTC or Telecom. A better value alternative is to buy a Namibian SIM card which, along with pay-as-you-go top-up cards, are available from phone shops. Mobile phones are now such a part of everyday life in Namibia that many establishments have abandoned the local landline services and use the mobile network instead. You will see from listings such as hotels and restaurants in this book, mobile numbers are sometimes offered instead of landline numbers: they start T08.

Be Local, shop at Hosea Kutako International Airport, T061-305795, www.be-local.com, rents out mobile phones and SIM cards as well as satellite phones (very useful if you're going off the beaten track), which already have local emergency numbers programmed into them, and GPSs equipped with detailed coordinates for Namibia. You can collect these at the airport or they will deliver anywhere in Windhoek. Increasingly, car hire companies are also offering satellite phones and GPSs for hire; be sure to ask your company when booking your car. See Car hire, page 15.

Time

Winter: GMT + 1 hr (Apr-Sep); summer: GMT + 2 hrs (Sep-Apr). Daylight Saving Time (DST) begins at 0200 on the first Sun of Apr, and ends at 0200 on the first Sun in Sep. Bear this in mind for border crossings, as opening and closing times on the Namibian sides could be an hour earlier than the opposite countries (none of the neighbouring counties have DST).

Tipping

It is customary to tip waiters, hotel porters, chambermaids, taxi drivers and tour guides about 10-15% for good service. When leaving tips make sure they go where you intend, there is no guarantee that kitty money gets to everyone. Tip petrol pump attendants about N$5 for a fill-up and windscreen clean; N$10 for an oil and water check, and tyre pressure top-up – the latter being a frequent necessity because of Namibia's gravel roads. Photographing local people such as the Himba should be followed by a tip of some kind, which should always be negotiated first. If you are on a tour, your tour guide will arrange this (see box, page 196, for an explanation about visiting the Himba).

In the towns and cities, it is also customary to tip car guards N$2-5 if parking on the street. These are usually identified by a work vest or badge, and the system is well worth supporting as they provide many well-needed jobs as well as helping to reduce car crime.

Tour operators

Tour operators in Namibia are listed under Windhoek, page 77, and Swakopmund, page 262. See also Overland trucks, page 12, for companies offering overland trips.

Australia and New Zealand
African Wildlife Safaris, T+61 (0)3-9249 3777, www.africanwildlifesafaris.com.au.
The Africa Safari Co, T+61 1 800-659279, www.africasafarico.com.au.
Classic Safari Company, T+61 1 300-130218, www.classicsafaricompany.com.au.
Peregrine Travel, T+61 (0)3-8601 4444, www.peregrine.net.au.

North America
Adventure Centre, T1 800-228 8747, T+1 51-0654 1879, www.adventure-centre.com.
Africa Adventure Company, T+1 954-491 8877, www.africa-adventure.com.

Bushtracks, T+1 707-433 4492, www.bushtracks.com.

South Africa
Compass Odyssey, T+27 (0)21-783 0360, www.compassodyssey.net.
Go2Africa, T+27-(0)21-4814900, www.go2africa.com.
Pulse Africa, T+27 (0)11-325 2290, www.pulseafrica.com.
Wild Frontiers, T+27 (0)72-927 7529, www.wildfrontiers.com.
Wilderness Safaris, T+27 (0)11-807 1800, www.wilderness-safaris.com.

UK and Ireland
Abercrombie & Kent, T0845-070 0600, www.abercrombiekent.co.uk.
Acacia Africa, T020-7706 4700, www.acacia-africa.com.
Africa Travel Centre, T0845-450 1520, www.africatravel.co.uk.
Africa Travel Resource, T01306-880 770, www.africatravelresource.com.
Expert Africa, 10 & 11 Upper Sq, Old Isleworth, TW7 7BJ, T020-8232 9777, www.expertafrica.com. Also has an office in New Zealand.
Explore, T0870-333 4001, www.explore.co.uk.
Global Village, T0844-844 2541, www.globalvillage-travel.com.
Odyssey World, T0845-370 7733, www.odyssey-world.co.uk.
Okavango Tours and Safaris, T020-8347 4030, www.okavango.com.
Rainbow Tours, T020-7226 1004, www.rainbowtours.co.uk.
Safari Consultants Ltd, T01787-888590, www.safari-consultants.co.uk.
Somak, T020-8423 3000, www.somak.co.uk.
Steppes Africa, T01285-880980, www.steppestravel.co.uk.

Tribes Travel, T01473-890499, www.tribes.co.uk.
Wildlife Worldwide, T0845-130 6982, www.wildlifeworldwide.com.
Your Safari, Our Namibia, T01273-891275, www.yoursafari.co.uk.

Tourist information

The head office of the **Namibia Tourism Board** (**NTB**) is at 1st floor, Channel Life Towers, 39 Post Street Mall, Windhoek, T061-290 6000, www.namibiatourism. com.na. They can also be contacted at one of the worldwide offices, or through the website. The **NTB** produces an extensive array of publications each year listing tour operators and accommodation options and the information available is staggering. Among other publications the **NTB** produces are *Welcome to Namibia – Official Visitors' Guide*, which offers information about visiting the parks and contains extensive accommodation listings, and the very good *Namibia Map*, which shows all the minor road numbers and tourist highlights and is essential if you are on a self-drive holiday. Get in touch before you leave home and they will send them to you. The maps are published in English and German. Of the many free publications available to tourists to Namibia, firstly take the (complimentary) **Air Namibia** in-flight magazine from the plane, *Flamingo* (www.flamingo.com.na), which has good Namibia travel articles and facts for visitors. Also look out for the free bi-monthly magazine *Travel News* (www.travelnewsnamibia.com), which covers all aspects of travel in Namibia with some interesting ideas. Local tourist offices are listed under the relevant town.

Tourist offices overseas

France c/o LS Promotions, 31 Blvd Suchet, 75016 Paris, T140-508863, ntbfrance@orange.fr.

Germany 42-44 Schiller Strasse, 60313 Frankfurt, T69-1337360, info@namibia-tourism.com.

South Africa Ground floor, Pinnacle Building (beneath the Cape Town Tourist Office), Burg St, Cape Town, T+27(0)21-422 3298, namibia@saol.com. Also here is the desk for **Namibia Wildlife Resorts (NWR)**, T+27(0)21-422 3761, ct.bookings@nwr.com.na. If starting a trip to Namibia from Cape Town this is the perfect place to get ideas and make reservations for parks accommodation.

UK, c/o Hills Balfour Synergy, Colechurch House, 1 London Bridge Walk, London, SE1 2SX, T020-7367 0962, namibia@hbportfolio.co.uk.

Useful websites

www.economist.com.na Business news and economic outlook.

www.fco.gov.uk UK's Foreign Office site, for the 'official' advice on latest political situations.

www.met.gov.na Website of the Ministry of Environment and Tourism (MET), which manages the national parks and issues permits for fishing and access into protected areas.

www.mha.gov.na Namibia's Ministry of Home Affairs government site, for up-to-date visa requirements.

www.namibia-1on1.com A plethora of information on Namibia, from visa and customs requirements to general travel services.

www.namibian.com.na The country's independent newspaper online, with useful classifieds.

www.namibian.org Comprehensive tourism information from the **Cardboard Box Travel Shop** in Windhoek (see page 78).

www.namibianews.com Comprehensive news and sport.

www.namibiatourism.com.na Official site of the Namibia Tourist Board, indispensable.

www.namibiaweather.info Weather (obviously) but interestingly data is collected from private weather stations at lodges and guest farms, so provides a little information about these too.

www.namibweb.com The website for Elena Travel Services, a travel agent in Windhoek and a good source of online information.

www.nwr.com.na Website of Namibia Wildlife Resorts (NWR) which manages accommodation in the national parks; offers online bookings. See also page 24.

Visas and immigration

All visitors must be in possession of a passport which is valid for a minimum of 6 months from their date of entry. Most nationalities do not require visas including visitors from the UK, Ireland and European countries, the USA, and Australia and New Zealand, and can stay in the country for a period of 90 days with a permit issued on arrival at the point of entry. Extensions have to be applied for from the **Ministry of Home Affairs**, Cohen Building, corner of Independence Av and Casino St, Windhoek, T061-292 2111, www.mha.gov.na, Mon-Fri 0800-1600.

Weights and measures

The metric system is used in Namibia.

Women travellers

In Namibia normal caution is required. In particular, dress modestly, be wary of unsolicited male company, avoid quiet places, move around in a group where possible, and take taxis at night.

Working and volunteering

There are no opportunities for travellers to obtain casual paid employment in Namibia and it is illegal for a foreigner to work without an official work permit. Most foreign workers in Namibia are employed through embassies, development or volunteer agencies or through foreign companies. For the most part these people will have been recruited in their countries of origin. However, voluntary work can be combined with a sightseeing holiday and a number of NGOs and voluntary organizations can arrange placements for volunteers in Namibia for periods ranging from a few weeks to 3 months. Visit www.volunteerafrica. org, www.goabroad.com, or www. gooverseas.com. In Namibia there are projects specifically orientated around wildlife conservation such as tracking and collecting data on cheetahs or desert elephants, some of which are open to families; visit www.volunteersnamibia.com or www.desertelephant.org.

Contents

48 Windhoek
48 Arriving in Windhoek
51 Background
53 Places in Windhoek
66 Listings

86 Around Windhoek
86 Daan Viljoen
87 North to Okahandja
87 Düsternbrook
88 Okahandja
92 Listings

96 East to Botswana
96 Windhoek to the border
100 Listings

Footprint features

46 Don't miss …
60 War memorials

Border crossings

Namibia–Botswana
99 Buitepos–Mamuno

Windhoek & Central Namibia

At a glance

⊖ **Getting around** Windhoek city centre is compact enough to walk around. To explore outlying areas it's best to hire a car.

⟳ **Time required** One full day for Windhoek. Other places can be visited en route to Botswana, the north or the coast.

❀ **Weather** Days are mostly warm and sunny throughout the year. Rain occurs in summer and winter nights can be cool.

✘ **When not to go** Good all year round.

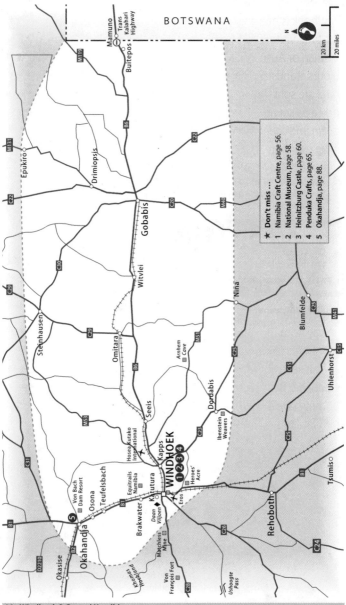

BOTSWANA

N

20 km
20 miles

Mamuno
Trans Kalahari Highway
Buitepos

★ Don't miss ...
1 Namibia Craft Centre, page 56.
2 National Museum, page 58.
3 Heinitzburg Castle, page 60.
4 Penduka Crafts, page 65.
5 Okahandja, page 88.

Epukiro

Drimiopsis

Gobabis

Witvlei

Nina

Blumfelde

Uhlenhorst

Steinhausen

Omitara

Arnhem Cave

Dordabis

Seeis

Kapps

Hosea Kutako International

WINDHOEK
1 2 3 4

Ibenstein Weavers

Katutura

Heroes' Acre

Tsumis

Equitrails Namibia

Von Bach Dam Resort

Osona

Teufelsbach

Brakwater

Daan Viljoen

Eros

Rehoboth

Okahandja

Okasise

Ithomas Rheinland

Matchless Mine

Von François Fort

Ushoogte Pass

With its neatly laid out grid of streets and orderly atmosphere, Windhoek is nothing like a bustling, chaotic African city and first-time visitors might think they have arrived in a medium-sized Bavarian or Austrian town. German colonial architecture in soft colours stands alongside gleaming high-rise office blocks; African crafts are sold from street stalls next to the trendy shopping malls and cafés serving up traditional African food as well as German *eisbein* and *sauerkraut*.

The city's interesting museums and historical buildings warrant at least a day of exploration, and there's good shopping and eating on offer too. The streets themselves are generally busy without being intolerably crowded, traffic pollution has yet to become a serious issue and gridlock is, for the time being, unheard of. Windhoek is home to the country's international airport and the smaller Eros airport, which is the central base for regional flights. The city is in a strategic central location for easy access to all parts of Namibia, so visitors may well find themselves passing through on more than one occasion.

Away from the city the countryside opens up in all directions over vast camelthorn savannahs, and within only an hour's journey you can visit several worthwhile guest farms. The regional towns such as Gobabis, Rehoboth and Okahandja don't warrant too much time, but they have a few worthy distractions if passing through and offer good facilities for those heading out to more remote regions.

Windhoek

Windhoek, Namibia's capital city, and its surrounding suburbs are spread out over a series of picturesque valleys in the central highlands, with the Auas Mountains to the southeast, the Eros Mountains to the northeast and the hills of the Khomas Hochland rolling away to the west. Located 650 km north of the Orange River and 360 km from the Atlantic, and thanks to a brilliant stroke of Germanic planning, it is in the geographical centre of the country and is the crossroads of all Namibia's major road and rail routes. With a population of 322,500, it is relatively small and sleepy for a capital city by international standards, but remains the political, judicial, economic and cultural centre of the country.

Arriving in Windhoek → *Phone code: 061. Colour map 1, C5. Pop: 322,500. Alt: 1646 m.*

Getting there

There are two airports serving Windhoek, which can confuse first-time visitors. However, all international flights arrive at **Hosea Kutako International Airport (HKIA)** ① *45 km east of the city centre on the B6 road towards Gobabis, T061-295 5600, www.airports.com.na.* It is named after Chief Hosea Komombumbi Kutako who was an early Namibian nationalist leader. Airport facilities include banks with ATMs, bureaux de change, post office, restaurant and bar, Wi-Fi, car hire desks, shops, a VAT tax refund desk for outgoing passengers, and there are taxis and shuttle buses to meet flights. The taxi fare into the city is roughly N$400-600 to the centre of town depending on destination and time of day. A slightly cheaper option is to catch one of the several minibus shuttles which cost around N$300 for one person, N$500 for two people, N$650 for three people, and N$800 for four people and so on. These drop off at any hotel or guesthouse in town and will also go to Eros Airport. You will find both the taxis and the shuttle company vehicles directly outside the Arrivals hall. Alternatively an airport pick-up or drop-off can be pre-arranged through any hotel, or pre-book directly with one of the shuttle companies, which include **Windhoek Airport Transfers and Tours** ① *T061-258792, www.namibiatours.com.na,* **Airport Shuttle Namibia** ① *T061-210532, www.airportshuttlenamibia.com,* or **Shuttle Namibia** ① *T061-302007, www.shuttlenamibia.com.*

Some car hire companies have desks at the airport; alternatively if you've hired a car from a company in Windhoek (see page 82) they will meet you at the airport with your car. Journey time to downtown Windhoek is about 30 minutes, and you will pass through a police checkpoint; no need for alarm, they are only on the lookout for shabby vehicles and drunk, unbelted or unlicensed drivers. Enjoy your first glimpse of the straight roads and the camelthorn trees, and keep an eye out for kudu, warthogs, meercats, baboons, foxes and squashed snakes on the road.

1 Greater Windhoek

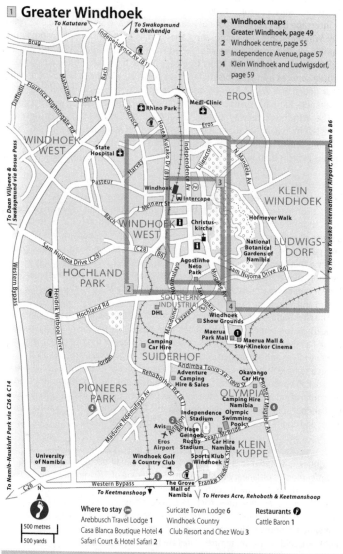

→ Windhoek maps
1 Greater Windhoek, page 49
2 Windhoek centre, page 55
3 Independence Avenue, page 57
4 Klein Windhoek and Ludwigsdorf, page 59

Where to stay
Arebbusch Travel Lodge 1
Casa Blanca Boutique Hotel 4
Safari Court & Hotel Safari 2

Suricate Town Lodge 6
Windhoek Country
Club Resort and Chez Wou 3

Restaurants
Cattle Baron 1

Many domestic and charter flights use the smaller **Eros Airport (ERS)** ⓘ *5 km south of the city centre off Rehobother Rd (B1), Aviation Rd, T061-295 5501, www. airports.com.na, next to the Safari Court Hotel (see page 67).* Taxis wait outside, and again you can pre-arrange a transfer with the shuttle companies above and car hire companies will meet you off your flight.

Intercape buses on the route between Windhoek and Swakopmund and Walvis Bay, Windhoek and Oshikango, and Cape Town in South Africa and Livingstone in Zambia via Windhoek, arrive and depart from the Intercape office opposite the railway station off Bahnhof Street (see page 16, for timetable). There are also daily shuttle services using micro/sprinter buses between Windhoek and Swakopmund (four hours) and Walvis Bay (4½ hours). On the way they pick up and drop off at Okahandja, Karibib, Usakos and the other towns on the B2 road.

The **Windhoek railway station** ⓘ *T061-298 1111, www.transnamib.com.na,* is accessed from Bahnhof Street at the northern end of Mandume Ndemufayo Street. All TransNamib Starline passenger services depart from here, so too does the luxury **Desert Express** train. ▶▶ *See Transport, page 80.*

Getting around

The most obvious feature of the city centre is its size – or lack of it. The central district consists of **Independence Avenue** running from south to north, where the main shops, banks, post office, tourism offices and larger hotels can be found, and a series of well-ordered streets laid out on a grid around it. **Zoo Park**, with its lawns and palm trees, lies on Independence Avenue right at the heart of the city, and offers a green and shady place used by Windhoekers to relax at lunchtimes. **Post Street Mall** is close by with its cafés and traditional arts and crafts street market; at the far end lies the main shopping mall, **Wernhil Park Mall**, on the corner of Fidel Castro and Mandume Ndemufajo streets.

The city centre is compact enough to walk around, although always get a taxi after dark. There are some City of Windhoek blue buses that ply the major main roads, as well as shared minibus taxis, which serve most areas of the city but on informal/ variable routes and are flagged down on the street. Regular taxis are not hailed on the street and have to be pre-booked by phone (any hotel or restaurant can call one for you) or can be found at several taxi ranks dotted around the city centre, including on the corner of Independence Avenue and Fidel Castro Street, outside the railway station off Bahnhof Street, in the car park opposite the Gustav Voigts Centre/Kalahari Sands Hotel, and on the northern side of the Wernhil Park Mall. ▶▶ *See also Transport, page 80.*

Best time to visit

Windhoek is situated in a semi-desert region. Rainfall occurs mostly during the summer months of January to March with an average of 370 mm annually. Days are mostly warm and sunny, though it gets quite hot during between December and February when temperatures reach 34°C. By contrast, even during this period and because of the surrounding hills, nights can be cool, so bring adequate clothing. The winter months of June to August are generally dry, mild and sunny, though nights are cold. Minimum temperatures are between 5°C and 18°C.

Tourist information

The Windhoek head office of the **Namibia Tourism Board (NTB)** ① *1st floor, Channel Life Towers, 39 Post Street Mall, T061-290 6000, www.namibiantourism.com.na, Mon-Fri 0800-1700*, has various brochures and publications, including a very good map that shows all the minor road numbers (essential if you're driving). There are two **Windhoek tourist information offices** ① *Post Street Mall, T061-290 2092, Mon-Fri 0730-1630; and corner of Fidel Castro St and Independence Av, T061-290 2596, www. windhoek.my.na, Mon-Fri 0700-1900, Sat and Sun 0900-1300*. Both offices are run by the council and provide information about the whole country and have plenty of leaflets to pick up including a decent city map. **Namibia Wildlife Resorts (NWR)** ① *Erkrathus building, Independence Av, T061-285 7200, www.nwr.com.na, Mon-Fri 0800-1700 (for information), 0800-1500 (for reservations)*, has a range of information about their park accommodation, and if you haven't already made reservations before your arrival (which you should have done) then head here to see if you can get last-minute bookings. Alternatively you can book online, or visit the offices in Swakopmund (see page 228) or Cape Town (see page 24).

Safety

Despite being a sleek and modern city with good infrastructure and services, don't be deluded. Windhoek is far from crime free, and obvious tourists are usually the ones to be targeted. Muggings and bag snatchings do occur, so be vigilant when walking around the city centre, especially at the weekend and when the shops start to close in the late afternoon and there are fewer people on the streets. Always take a taxi after dark and ask your hotel, guesthouse or tour operator to recommend a reputable taxi company. If you are driving, never put things on display and keep car doors locked and windows shut, especially in heavy traffic and at intersections and petrol stations and ensure that your accommodation has off-street parking.

Background

Windhoek's history reflects the movements of different peoples through the country, and in particular offers an insight into the past hundred years of colonial conquest, apartheid and struggle for independence. Originally Windhoek was known by the Khoi-khoi or Nama people as *Ai-gams,* correctly spelt /A //Gams to indicate the click sound (steam or fire-water), and by the Herero people as *Otjomuise* (place of smoke) due to the hot water springs found in what is now the Klein Windhoek district. These springs had been used for centuries as watering holes by the San (Bushmen) and Khoi-khoi (Nama), nomadic and semi-nomadic peoples who trekked through the area with their animals.

The roots of today's city, however, lie in the settlement established by the Oorlam leader Jonker Afrikaner in the 1840s and 1850s at *Ai-gams*, stretching along the ridge of the Klein Windhoek Valley. In 1836 Jonker urged the British explorer Sir James Alexander, who called the settlement Queen Adelaide's Bath, to organize a missionary for him. In 1842 the Rhenish missionary Hahn arrived to find a well-established settlement, which he called Elberfeld after a centre of the Rhenish mission in Germany. He was so impressed by the settlement that he was drawn to comment, "The location of Elberfeld is superbly beautiful ... seeing the extensive thorntree forest with its delicious green and curious forms, the lovely gardens, and the beautiful greensward ... " Jonker himself, in an 1844 letter to the Wesleyan Mission Station, referred to the settlement as *Wind Hoock*, and despite much speculation that he named the settlement after *Winterhoek*, his ancestral home in the Cape, there is no solid evidence to suggest this. However, it is certain that Windhoek was the original name given by Jonker and his followers when they settled here around 1840.

Under Jonker, the settlement flourished and served both as a trading station between the Oorlam/Namas and Herero, as well as a headquarters from which Jonker and his commandos launched cattle raids on the Herero living north of the Swakop River. Following Jonker's death at Okahandja in 1861, Windhoek was temporarily abandoned until the missionary Schröder installed himself in the remains of the original buildings in the 1870s.

In 1890 the Germans, under **Curt von François**, were still not well established in Namibia, and having been effectively driven out of Otjimbingwe and Tsaobis by the Nama leader Hendrik Witbooi, made a strategic retreat to Windhoek. This move neatly coincided with the death of Herero leader Maherero, and by the time his successor Samuel Herero sent envoys to Windhoek a few weeks later, the Germans were already halfway through the completion of the original fort. This served as the headquarters for the **Schutztruppe** (colonial troops) and is known as the **Alte Feste** (Old Fort). It now houses the historical section of the National Museum and is the oldest surviving building in Windhoek.

The German colonial settlement of Windhoek emerged around the Alte Feste and the springs surrounding it. The settler John Ludwig established substantial vineyards and fruit and vegetable gardens which fed the small settlement; the modern suburb, Ludwigsdorf, is named after him. The Klein Windhoek Valley continued to be agriculturally productive until the beginning of the 1960s with the hot springs below the Alte Feste 'smoking away'.

With the completion, in 1902, of the railway to Swakopmund on the coast, the settlement was able to expand and develop as the economic and cultural centre of the colony. In 1909 Windhoek became a municipality and this period saw the construction of a number of fine buildings, including the **Tintenpalast**, the present site of Namibia's parliament, and the **Christuskirche** with its stained-glass windows donated by Kaiser Wilhelm II.

During the 1960s the South African government pursued a policy designed to incorporate Namibia into South Africa as the fifth province, and this period saw a further era of rapid development and growth, not just in Windhoek but in the country as a whole. In Windhoek, the government started forcible movements of people from the 'Old Location' in 1959, and as the black population was gradually obliged to settle in Katutura, the white suburbs of Hochland Park and Pioneer's Park were developed on the western side of the city.

The period since independence has seen further growth characterized by some distinctly post-modern buildings in the city centre. The still very much low level skyline is dominated by the **Kalahari Sands Hotel** (built in 1974), the **Namdeb Centre** (built in 1989 and the home of Namdeb Diamond Corporation Ltd), the **Mutual Tower** (built in 2010 and home to Old Mutual Namibia, an insurance company, which is currently the city's tallest building with 21 floors), the **Hilton Windhoek** hotel (built in 2011) and the **Independence Memorial Museum**, brand new in 2014.

Places in Windhoek → *For listings, see pages 66-85.*

As virtually all the sites of interest are in the city centre, the most obvious way to see them is on foot. One full day will allow visitors with limited time the opportunity to appreciate the German colonial architecture and visit a couple of the museums. Note that the city centre virtually closes down at the weekends from around 1300 on Saturday and all day Sunday, when most of the shops, restaurants and attractions close; so weekends are not the best time to explore. For people with two or three days to spare, a fairly thorough exploration will be possible including one or two half- or full-day tours to the outlying areas.

Clock tower and Zoo Park

A good place to start a walk around the city is by the **clock tower** on the corner of Independence Avenue and Post Street. The tower itself is modelled on that of the old Deutsch-Afrika bank built in 1908, but long since gone. Cross the road, turn right and walk along Independence Avenue as far as **Zoo Park**. The park was established in the late 1800s to early 1900s and once featured marble water fountains, birdbaths and benches, and a little zoo and bird aviaries were here between 1916 and 1932. Kudu, gemsbok, red hartebeest, common duiker and even a leopard and wild dog were among the animals kept in the zoo. Today there is a children's playground, open-air theatre and a café.

Walk into the park about 20 m and you will see a 2-m-high **sculptured column** depicting scenes of a prehistoric elephant kill believed to have taken place some 5000 years ago on this site. The fossilized remains of two elephants and a variety of Stone Age weapons were found when the park was reconstructed in 1962, evidence that the hot springs were already attracting game to the area in pre-historic times. A message to that effect is carved into the side of the column. On top of the column is part of a fossilized elephant skull, however, the rest of the bones and tools were removed to the National Museum's research collection in 1990. Also in the park is the **Kriegerdenkmal** (Soldiers Memorial). This is an obelisk-shaped memorial unveiled in 1897 to honour the Schutztruppe who were killed in the 1893-1894 war against the renowned Nama Chief Hendrik Witbooi. It had been pre-built in Germany and is a smallish iron obelisk about 2 m tall, topped with a gilt eagle; on all four sides are panels bearing the names of the fallen men.

Adjacent to the park there is a small open-air crafts market specializing in excellent baskets from the north and woodcarvings from the Kavango – with the 2-m-tall giraffes the stars of the display. Before walking into the park itself, look back across the road and you will see three buildings designed by Willi Sander, a

German architect responsible for the design of a number of Windhoek's original colonial buildings.

The **Erkrathus Building**, the furthest right of the three, was constructed in 1910 on what was known as Kaiser Wilhelm Street and is typical of this period, incorporating business premises downstairs and living quarters upstairs. The second floor is now home to the central reservations office of Namibia Wildlife Resorts (NWR), see page 51. The building to the left is **Gathemann House**, commissioned in 1913 by the then Mayor of Klein Windhoek, Heinrich Gathemann, and now home to **Restaurant Gathemann** (see page 70). The stepped roof was of European design intended to prevent the roof from collapsing under the weight of a build-up of snow. Between 1927 and 1928 an extension was added to the earlier building, and Gathemann is credited with blending in the later design so perfectly with the original one, it has been assumed that the two buildings are in fact one. The fourth building on the left bears the inscription '*Kronprinz*', the name of the hotel which occupied the building until 1920 when it was converted into a shop, and the date of its completion in 1902 can also be seen carved in the stone.

If you're interested in African arts and crafts, the **Bushman Art Gallery** ⓘ *187 Independence Av, T061-228828, www.bushmanart-gallery.com, Mon-Fri 0830-1730, Sat and Sun 0900-1300*, is opposite Zoo Park and is worth a visit as it has one of the best selections of souvenirs in Windhoek. Local curios include carpets woven from the wool of the karakul sheep. In the back of the museum-like interior there's an interesting display of carvings, metalwork, jewellery, weapons, musical instruments and pottery that will give visitors a quick but insightful look into the many divergent traditional cultures of the Namibian people including the Himba, San (Bushmen), Caprivians, Kavangos and Owambos.

Post Street Mall

Right in the heart of Windhoek and off Independence Avenue, you can't miss the open-air **Post Street Mall** with its many shops and restaurants. In the middle of it are the **Gibeon Meteorites** or **Meteor Fountain**, claimed to be the largest collection of meteorites in the world. They were collected and first brought to Windhoek between 1911 and 1913 and have been fashioned into a series of sculptures sitting on top of steel columns set around a fountain. The meteorites get their name from the area in which they were found, southwest of Mariental, and are believed to have belonged to the world's largest ever meteor shower which took place some 600 million years ago. Although they look like fairly ordinary rocks, the meteorites are in fact made from solid metal: 90-95% iron, 8% nickel, and some smaller amounts of cobalt, phosphorus, carbon, sulphur, chrome, copper and other trace elements. In total 77 rocks were recovered, of which 31 are on display here and some have been cut in half to display their metallic interior. The average weight of the meteorites in Post Street Mall is an impressive 348.5 kg, but the largest of the Gibeon Meteorites, weighing 650 kg, was donated to the South African Museum in Cape Town. Others can be seen in the British, Budapest and Prague museums, as well as the Washington and New York natural history museums.

The **Crafts Market**, running most of the way down Post Street Mall, is an enjoyable place to wander around, whether you're planning on buying any souvenirs or not.

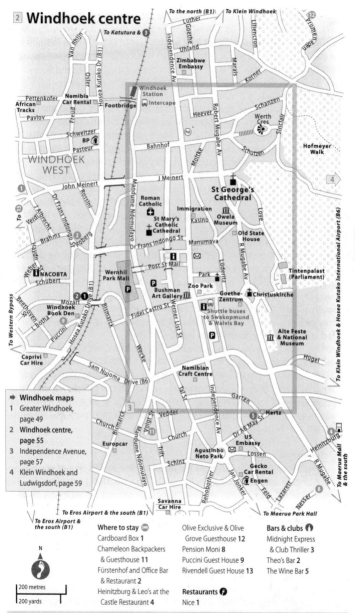

2 Windhoek centre

To the north (B1)
To Klein Windhoek
To Katutura & ❸

Luther
Goethe
Independence Av
Uhland
Lilliencron
Promenade
Marais
Korner
Schanzen
Sinclair
Werth Cres
Schutzen
Hofmeyer Walk

Zimbabwe Embassy

Pettenkofer
Namibia Car Rental
African Tracks
Pavlov
Van Rhijn
Ozter
Freud
Hosea Kutako Dr (B1)
Windhoek Station
Intercape
Footbridge
Heever
Robert Mugabe Av

Schweitzer
BP
Pasteur
WINDHOEK WEST
John Meinert
Dr Frans Indongo St
Rossini
Albrecht
Verdi
Haydn St
Weber St
Brahms
Roberg
Bahnhof
Mozart
Mandume Ndemufayo
J Meinert
Roman Catholic
St Mary's Catholic Cathedral
Dr Frans Indongo St
Manumava
St George's Cathedral
Immigration
Kasino
Owela Museum
Old State House
R Mugabe Av
Love

NACOBTA
Schubert
Mozart
Windhoek Book Den
Bismarck
Hosea Kutako Drive (B1)
Puccini
Botha
Beethoven
Caprivi Car Hire
Sam Nujoma Drive (B6)
Wecke
Fidel Castro St
Wernhil Park Mall
Post St Mall
Bushman Art Gallery
Park
Zoo Park
Goethe-Zentrum
Christuskirche
Shuttle buses to Swakopmund & Walvis Bay
Alte Feste & National Museum
Tintenpalast (Parliament)
Hugel

Werner List St
Namibian Craft Centre
Tal St
Independence Av
Garten

Windhoek maps
1 Greater Windhoek, page 49
2 Windhoek centre, page 55
3 Independence Avenue, page 57
4 Klein Windhoek and Ludwigsdorf, page 59

To Western Bypass
To Eros Airport & the south (B1)

Church
Bismarck
Mandume Ndomulayo
Vedder
Bülow
Church
Trift
Schinz
Rehoboth
Jan Jonker
Europcar
Agustinho Neto Park
US Embassy
Lossen
Gecko Car Rental
Engen
Hertz
Dr AB May St
Heinitzburg
Feld
Lazarett
R Mugabe
Nesser
Maerua Mall

To Klein Windhoek & Hosea Kutako International Airport (B6)
To Maerua Park & the south

Savanna Car Hire
To Eros Airport & the south (B1)
To Maerua Park Hall

N
200 metres
200 yards

Where to stay 🛏
Cardboard Box **1**
Chameleon Backpackers & Guesthouse **11**
Fürstenhof and Office Bar & Restaurant **2**
Heinitzburg & Leo's at the Castle Restaurant **4**

Olive Exclusive & Olive Grove Guesthouse **12**
Pension Moni **8**
Puccini Guest House **9**
Rivendell Guest House **13**

Restaurants 🍴
Nice **1**

Bars & clubs 🍸
Midnight Express & Club Thriller **3**
Theo's Bar **2**
The Wine Bar **5**

If you do decide to buy, be prepared to barter the price down. You should be able to pick up some objects at considerably lower prices than in the boutiques around town. At the end of the Post Street Mall is the entrance to the indoor **Wernhil Park Mall** (see Shopping, page 76), which has all the modern shops you may need, including supermarkets.

Fidel Castro Street

Back at Zoo Park, the road that crosses Independence Avenue to the south of the park is Fidel Castro Street. One block to the west and on the left of Fidel Castro is the **Windhoek Conservatoire**, built 1911-1912, which was formerly the Regierungsschule (Government School) and today is the home of the College of Arts. It has an impressive ornamental weather vane perched on top of its pyramidal tower.

Heading east, at the top of the steep hill, on the corner of Lüderitz Street, is the **Hauptkasse**, built in 1899 and the former home of the German colonial government's finance department. The building now serves the Ministry of Agriculture. Directly opposite is **Ludwig Van Estorff House**, named after the former Schutztruppe commander who lived here from 1902 to 1910. Over the last century it has housed senior officers, a hostel and a trade school and the National Reference Library (usually referred to as the Van Estorff library). It is now the **Goethe-Zentrum** (the German cultural centre, see page 84). On the far side of the library stands the **Supreme Court Building**, opened in October 1997, which looks down over the parking area and over to the **Hilton** and **Kalahari Sands** hotels.

South of Fidel Castro Street, the statue of **Curt von François** stands outside the Windhoek Municipality on Independence Avenue, and was unveiled in 1965 on the 75th anniversary of the 'founding' of the city.

Nearby next to the Warehouse Theatre, the **Namibia Craft Centre** ① *40 Tal St, T061-242222, www.namibiacraftcentre.com, Mon-Fri 0900-1730, Sat-Sun 0900-1330*, is located in the old breweries building, built in 1902 and originally called the Felsenkeller (cellar of rock). This is an indoor market on two floors with more than 30 outlets selling a variety of Namibian crafts (see Shopping, page 75). It also houses an internet café, an information desk where you can book local tours, and the earthy **Craft Café** (see Restaurants, page 72).

Christuskirche

At the top of the hill on an island in the middle of the road is one of Windhoek's striking landmarks, the **Christuskirche** ① *Wed and Sat 1100-1200, Mon, Tue, Thu and Fri 1400-1700, free*, often called the 'fairy cake' church. Designed by Gottlieb Reddecker, the church's foundation was laid in 1907 and the building was consecrated in 1910. The church was built by the Germans to commemorate the 'peace' between the Germans and the Nama, Herero and Owambo peoples and inside there are seven plaques bearing the names of German soldiers killed during the wars. Of the Nama, Herero and Owambo dead there is no record.

This Lutheran church was constructed from local sandstone and its design is an interesting mix of neo-Gothic and art nouveau styles. As the sun moves across the sky, the colours on the church walls change to reflect the colours on the hills of

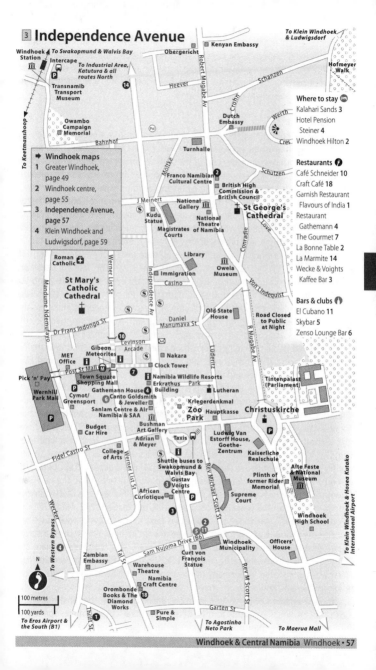

3 Independence Avenue

To Klein Windhoek & Ludwigsdorf

Windhoek Station

To Swakopmund & Walvis Bay

Intercape

Kenyan Embassy

Obergericht

Hofmeyer Walk

To Industrial Area, Katutura & all routes North

Transnamib Transport Museum

Heever

Robert Mugabe Av

Schanzen

Dutch Embassy

Werth

Crohn

Cres

Where to stay

Kalahari Sands 3
Hotel Pension
  Steiner 4
Windhoek Hilton 2

Owambo Campaign Memorial

Bahnhof

Montte

Psd

Turnhalle

Schützen

Restaurants

Café Schneider 10
Craft Café 18
Garnish Restaurant
  Flavours of India 1
Restaurant
  Gathemann 4
The Gourmet 7
La Bonne Table 2
La Marmite 14
Wecke & Voights
Kaffee Bar 3

Franco Namibian Cultural Centre

British High Commission & British Council

St George's Cathedral

J Meinert

National Gallery

Kudu Statue

National Theatre of Namibia

Magistrates Courts

➡ Windhoek maps
1 Greater Windhoek, page 49
2 Windhoek centre, page 55
3 Independence Avenue, page 57
4 Klein Windhoek and Ludwigsdorf, page 59

Bars & clubs

El Cubano 11
Skybar 5
Zenso Lounge Bar 6

Caprivi

Love

Library

Owela Museum

Jon Lindequist

Immigration

Casino

Old State House

Road Closed to Public at Night

R Mugabe Av

Lüderitz

Roman Catholic

St Mary's Catholic Cathedral

Werner List St

Independence Av

Daniel Manumwa St

Mandume Ndemufayo

Dr Frans Indongo St

Levinson Arcade

Gibeon Meteorites

MET Office

Post St Mall

Nakara

Clock Tower

Town Square Shopping Mall

Gathemann House

Canto Goldsmith & Jeweller

Namibia Wildlife Resorts

Erkrathus Building

Park

Lutheran

Tintenpalast (Parliament)

Pick 'n' Pay

Wernhill Park Mall

Cymot/ Greensport

Sanlam Centre & Air Namibia & SAA

Kriegerdenkmal

Zoo Park

Hauptkasse

Christuskirche

Budget Car Hire

Bushman Art Gallery

Adrian & Meyer

Taxis

Ludwig Van Estorff House, Goethe-Zentrum

Kaiserliche Realschule

Alte Feste & National Museum

Fidel Castro St

College of Arts

Werner List St

Shuttle buses to Swakopmund & Walvis Bay

Gustav Voigts Centre

African Curiotique

Rev Michael Scott St

Plinth of former Rider Memorial

Supreme Court

Windhoek High School

To Klein Windhoek & Hosea Kutako International Airport

Tal St

Zambian Embassy

Warehouse Theatre

Namibia Craft Centre

Orombonde Books & The Diamond Works

Pure & Simple

Sam Nujoma Drive (B6)

Curt von François Statue

Windhoek Municipality

Officers' House

Rev M Scott St

To Western Bypass

Mandume St

To Eros Airport & the South (B1)

N

100 metres
100 yards

Garten St

To Agostinho Neto Park

To Maerua Mall

the Khomas Hochland to the southwest. The church looks most striking at sunrise and sunset, which are also the best times to take photographs. The stained-glass windows were donated by Kaiser Wilhelm II and the altar bible by his wife Augusta; though not particularly impressive looking from outside, it is well worth climbing the steps to the balcony to get a better look.

Alte Feste area

The walk along Robert Mugabe Avenue, running south from the church, takes you towards the whitewashed walls of the **Alte Feste** (the Old Fort), which has looked over central Windhoek since the end of the 19th century. It was built in 1892 as the headquarters of the first Schutztruppe (protection troop) to arrive in Namibia (in 1889) and is Windhoek's oldest surviving building, an impressive sight shimmering in the sunlight on top of the hill. The plaque on the wall by the entrance states that the fort was built as a "stronghold to preserve peace and order between the rivalling Namas and Hereros". This statement was a convenient justification for the colonization and subjugation of Namibia, and typical of the European rhetoric of the time.

The Alte Feste currently houses the **National Museum** ⓘ *Robert Mugabe Av, T061-293 4362, Mon-Fri 0900-1800, Sat and Sun 1000-1300, 1500-1800, free but donations appreciated.* There is an exhibition depicting significant events in Namibia over the last 100 years and includes photographs, flags, uniforms and other memorabilia of the transition period from South African colonial rule to independence. There are also displays of the early household implements, tools and musical instruments of the first missionaries and European settlers. Alongside these are similar objects used by the different ethnic Namibian peoples, making for an unorthodox, but nevertheless interesting, display. Climb the turret before leaving and you'll be rewarded by a splendid view of Windhoek and the hills of the Khomas Hochland to the west.

At the time of writing most exhibits were being moved across to the new triangular-shaped **Independence Memorial Museum**, the latest addition to the Windhoek skyline, located between the Alte Feste and the Christuskirche on Robert Mugabe Avenue. Construction of the 40-m-high tower began in 2009 and it was built as both a museum and monument to commemorate Namibia's liberation struggle. It was finally inaugurated by Namibia's President Pohamba on the country's 24th Independence Day on 21 March 2014, and is expected to open in the near future. Also on Independence Day, President Pohamba unveiled the new **Sam Nujoma Statue**, which stands on a pedestal on the hill where the Reiterdenkmal stood for more than 102 years (see War memorials box, page 60).

Founded in 1917, Windhoek High School is next to the fort and across the road opposite the school is the old **Officers' House** built in 1906-1907 to house senior officers of the Schutztruppe, now serving as the Office of the Ombudsman. The highly decorative and rather attractive brickwork is a recreation of Putz architecture which was fashionable in Germany at the time. The architect, Gottlieb Redecker, designed the building after returning from a year's visit to Germany, and this was the first building of its style in Namibia. Walking back in the direction of the Christuskirche you'll pass the former **Kaiserliche Realschule**, which opened in 1909 as the first German primary school in Windhoek. After the Second World

4 Klein Windhoek & Ludwigsdorf

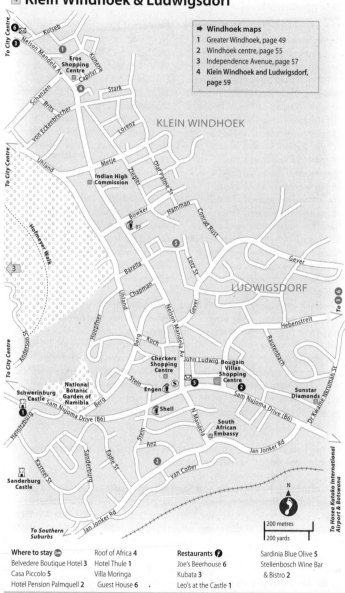

→ **Windhoek maps**
1. Greater Windhoek, page 49
2. Windhoek centre, page 55
3. Independence Avenue, page 57
4. Klein Windhoek and Ludwigsdorf, page 59

KLEIN WINDHOEK

LUDWIGSDORF

Indian High Commission

Hofmeyer Walk

National Botanic Garden of Namibia

Schwerinburg Castle

Sanderburg Castle

Checkers Shopping Centre

John Ludwig

Bougain Villas Shopping Centre

South African Embassy

Sunstar Diamonds

To City Centre

To Southern Suburbs

To Hosea Kutako International Airport & Botswana

Eros Shopping Centre

Sam Nujoma Drive (B6)

Jan Jonker Rd

200 metres
200 yards

Where to stay
Belvedere Boutique Hotel 3
Casa Piccolo 5
Hotel Pension Palmquell 2
Roof of Africa 4
Hotel Thule 1
Villa Moringa
Guest House 6

Restaurants
Joe's Beerhouse 6
Kubata 3
Leo's at the Castle 1
Sardinia Blue Olive 5
Stellenbosch Wine Bar & Bistro 2

War memorials

All over Windhoek are war memorials dating back to the German colonial occupation that commemorate German losses during wars with the different Namibian people. Among these are the Kriegerdenkmal in Zoo Park, the plaques on the walls of the Christuskirche, and the Owambo Campaign Memorial next to the railway station. As with all such memorials the victors have remembered their own dead and casualties in war without any acknowledgement of those conquered or defeated. Since Namibia's independence, there has been much debate about what should be done with these relics of the country's colonial past. Some argue that these are symbols of oppression and occupation and have no place in a free and independent Namibia and should be removed, while others argue that they are part of history and should remain.

A perfect example of this conflict can be demonstrated by the ongoing story of the Reiterdenkmal; translated as the Rider Memorial, and also commonly known as the Equestrian Monument. It was originally erected on a hill to the north of the Alte Feste on 27 January 1912; the 53rd birthday of German emperor Wilhelm II. The 5-m-tall plinth was made from 180 granite rocks from Okahandja and the imposing 4.5-m bronze statue depicts General Lothar von Trotha, the Scutztruppe commander during the Herero and Nama wars of 1904-1907, on his steed. The monument's plaque remembers the German soldiers and civilians that died:

"Remembering and honouring the brave German warriors that died for emperor and empire to save and protect this land during the Herero and Hottentot uprisings between 1903 and 1907, and during the Kalahari Expedition in 1908. Also remembering and honouring German citizens that died from the hands of the indigenous. Fallen, missing, died from accident, succumbed to their injuries or sickness: Of the Protection Force: 100 officers, 254 non-commissioned officers, 1180 soldiers, of the marine: 7 officers, 13 non-commissioned officers, 27 seamen. Killed during the uprising: 119 men, 4 women, 1 child."

War the building became an English-speaking school and now functions as the administrative part of the National Museum.

Schwerinburg, Heinitzburg and Sanderburg castles

A short distance from the city centre, sitting atop a series of hills to the southeast of the museum, between Robert Mugabe Avenue and Sam Nujoma Drive, are Windhoek's three elegant castles. All three were designed by the architect Willi Sander, the first for Graf Schwerin in 1914, and the second for his wife as her residence. The design of Schwerinsburg incorporates an original stone structure built by Curt von François and used as a lookout post in the early days of the Schutztruppe's presence in Windhoek. Sander designed the third castle for himself in 1917. Heinitzburg Castle, on Heinitz

The Reiterdenkmal has long been controversial not only because of its representation of German superiority, but because of its one-sided implication of loss of life. In reality Lothar von Trotha defeated the Herero and Nama by driving them into the desert where most of them died of thirst; an estimated 100,000 Herero and 10,000 Nama died between 1904 and 1907. In an investigation decades later, the United Nations' Whitaker Report of 1985 classified the war as an attempt by the Germans to exterminate the Herero and Nama peoples of Southwest Africa, and classified it as one of the earliest attempts of genocide in the 20th century. Later, in 2004, the German government acknowledged this and formally apologized for the events.

After Namibia gained independence in 1990, the monument became a symbol of injustice for modern Namibians and many wanted it destroyed. But for a while this was not a priority of the new SWAPO government, which preferred to build its own memorial sites to remember the independence struggle. But then

in 2008, demonstrators erected wooden crosses around the statue, and a Namibian flag was inserted into the rider's rifle barrel; actions to re-stimulate the discussion about the justification of a monument glorifying German colonialism. In 2009, when the government began the construction of the Independence Museum (see page 58), it was removed to make way for the new building. But then in 2010 it was inexplicably re-erected in front of the Alte Feste, 50 m from its original site. Again there was widespread objection, and by 2013 and during Heroes' Day celebrations in August, President Pohamba announced; "this monument is a symbol of victory on the side of the Germans...The horse rider must be removed". As a result, it was de-proclaimed as a national monument, and on Christmas Day 2013, the statue was lifted off its plinth by the police. Today it remains out of public display in the Alte Feste. Pohamba had added into his Heroes' Day speech; "If they want to take it back to Germany it is also fine, we will not have any objections."

Strasse, is today a luxury hotel (see page 66) and anyone can go to the terrace for coffee or a sundowner, which offers one of the best views of central Windhoek and the hills of the Khomas Hochland to the west. It is well worth the effort of walking up from the city centre to enjoy the views. Sanderburg Castle is privately owned and Schwerinburg Castle is used as the Italian embassy.

Robert Mugabe Avenue

Walk back in the direction of the Christuskirche and down Robert Mugabe Avenue until you see some public gardens on your right. These gardens were laid out in the 1930s and contain an olive grove consisting of three trees and a bowling green. More significantly, they surround Namibia's parliament, the **Tintenpalast**, an impressive yellow and white double-storied building with a veranda running around it. This building was also designed by Gottlieb Redecker, and first opened for business in 1914 as the German colonial government headquarters. It reputedly acquired its name, the 'Ink Palace', from the amount of paper work that went on here. Over the course of the 20th century the palace housed successive governments, before being renovated at independence in preparation for its role as the home of an independent Namibian parliament. At the top of the steps leading up to it are three modern statues depicting heroes of the Namibian liberation struggle: Hendrick Witbooi, Hosea Kutako and Theophilus Hingashikuka Hamutumbangela.

Further down Robert Mugabe Avenue you will find the **Old State House** on your left-hand side. This grandiose building in pretty gardens was built in 1958 and was formally the official residence of the South African Administrator-General, and then home to Namibia's post-independence presidents. However, the much larger New State House was built 2002-2008 on a 25-ha site in the suburb of Auasblick and was funded by a grant from North Korea. Namibia has large reserves of uranium (with its nuclear programme, perhaps this explains North Korea's interest in Namibia), and in 2008, the New State House was officially opened by President Pohamba in the presence of Kim Yong-nam, chairman of the Presidium of the Supreme People's Assembly of North Korea. Pohamba moved into the new official residence in 2010 and the Old State House is today the official prime minister's office and residence.

Next to Old State House, the **Owela Museum** ① *Robert Mugabe Av, T061-293 4358, Mon-Fri 0900-1700, Sat-Sun 1000-1230, 1500-1700, free but donations accepted*, a section of the National Museum, is located just below the Old State House and houses the ethnology hall. The exhibition consists of a series of dioramas intended to provide a picture of the lifestyles of the inhabitants of the country within their various environments. They include depictions of the cultivation of *omahangu* (millet), fishing in the Kavango, the Kalahari San (Bushmen) and the Owambo *oshanas* (water pans). The foyer of the museum has an ever-changing temporary display. There is also has a permanent cheetah exhibition which seeks to educate people about Africa's most endangered cat, the largest population of which is found in Namibia. Owela is a traditional African game played with pebbles.

In contrast to the plethora of German-inspired architecture, **St George's Cathedral** on Love Street offers a taste of rural England with its solid brown brickwork and exposed beams inside. It is the smallest functional cathedral in southern Africa and is the spiritual home of the Anglican community in Namibia. Designed by GHS Bradford and dedicated in 1925 the bell tower houses a bell cast in 1670, one of a set made for St Mary's Church in Northwall, Canterbury.

The **National Theatre of Namibia** (**NTN**) building lies at the bottom of Robert Mugabe Avenue on the corner of John Meinert Street (see page 73). Turn left onto John Meinert Street to the **National Gallery** ① *T061-231160, www.nagn.org.na, Mon-Fri 0900-1700, Sat 0900-1400, free*, where you'll find a permanent display reflecting a spectrum of both historical and contemporary Namibian art, as well as temporary exhibitions. There are crafts and CDs of Namibian music for sale in the gallery's shop.

Cross over Lüderitz Street where the **Magistrates Courts** are located until you find yourself back at Independence Avenue. Unveiled in the 1950s, the bronze statue of a kudu on the corner is a familiar Windhoek landmark (often referred to by Windhoekers when giving directions), commemorating the kudu which died during the 1896 rinderpest epidemic.

Bahnhof Street

A short walk north up Independence Avenue takes you to the intersection with Bahnhof Street, where to the west is the **Owambo Campaign Memorial**, a stone obelisk in the garden next to the railway station. It was erected in memory of German soldiers killed on 6 February 1917 in a battle against the uprising of King Mandume Ndemufayo of Kwanjama. He was killed in action and his head was cut off, which is reputed to be buried beneath the memorial.

Upstairs in the railway station is the **TransNamib Transport Museum** ① *T061-298 2624, Mon-Fri 0800-1300, 1400-1700, N$5, children (under 18) N$3*, a well-laid-out and extensive collection depicting the history of rail and other transport in Namibia dating back to German colonial times and the South African administration. Dozens of interesting photographs line the walls, including several of the Swakopmund Jetty built in 1904, and one small room has been fashioned as an interior of an early train compartment complete with original wash basin and linen. Railway buffs can buy original locomotive number plates and copies of historical timetables from the museum shop. The **railway station** itself is an interesting building that was built in 1912 by German Railways to replace the original prefabricated building, which could no longer handle the increased rail traffic once the Windhoek–Keetmanshoop railway line was completed. It was enlarged in 1929 by South African Railways and the addition was made in the same style and now you can see no difference between the two parts of the building. Outside sits a narrow-gauge German steam locomotive called *Poor Old Joe*, which was shipped to Swakopmund in 1899 and reassembled for the run to Windhoek. By 1906, another 100 steam locomotives had been shipped from Germany to the territory.

Further east on Bahnhof Street is the **Turnhalle**, which is a building currently not in use but it has an interesting history. It was built in 1909 for the Gymnastic Society and had a 22 m x 14 m gymnastic hall with high roof and decorative gables, plus changing rooms, a clubroom and accommodation for gymnasts; over the entrance, an ornate balcony with three arches supported by pillars. When it was built, the newspapers reported that the Turnhalle was the most beautiful building in town. During the First World War, the Schutztruppe stored their provisions there, and it served as accommodation for the South African Union Troops. In the 1920-1930s it was a gymnasium again and a stage was added which was used for theatre performances and bioscope shows. Later it played a historical role in the process of Namibian independence when representatives of the 11 ethnic groups in Southwest Africa started to meet there from 1975 to discuss independence and constitutional progress in the territory, in what was to become known as the Turnhalle Conference. One of Namibia's political parties today, the Democratic Turnhalle Alliance (DTA), still lends its name to the building from the events of this era. In 2007 it was refurbished after a fire and from then until 2012 hosted the well-publicized SADC Tribunal – the highest policy institution of the Southern African Development Community (SADC).

In one of its cases, the tribunal ruled that the government of Zimbabwe could not evict farmers from their land, and that farm seizures were deemed illegal under an amendment of the Zimbabwean constitution. Following this ruling, Zimbabwe left the SADC Tribunal and challenged its legitimacy. A sentiment that legal and human rights groups agreed with in that one member state did not have the legal or moral authority to take another member state to court. The necessity of the institution became doubtful and it was disbanded in 2012.

Windhoek suburbs and around

The **National Botanic Garden of Namibia** ① *Sam Nujoma Drive, Klein Windhoek, not far from Schwerinsburg Castle, T061-202 2014, www.nbri.org.na, Mon-Fri 0800-1700, first Sat of each month 0800-1100, free,* is Namibia's only botanic garden. It's a lovely 11-ha patch of greenery with neatly laid out paths with benches and birdbaths and there are examples of the country's flora from all its regions either in the gardens or display houses. The desert section is divided into winter rainfall and summer rainfall areas and is landscaped to represent the rocky outcrops, sandy plains and gravel plains of the Namib Desert. There's also a particularly dense stand of Aloe littoralis, the symbol of the city of Windhoek, and the bright orange-red flowers provide a vibrant display during April and May.

Heroes' Acre ① *10 km south of the city off the B1, not far after the police check on the road, daily 0800-1700, N$80, children (under 16) free, cars N$10,* a controversial monument covering 292 ha and surrounded by a 3-km fence, was built as a symbol of nationalism and patriotism. It was inaugurated in 2002 by the then president Sam Nujoma to mark Namibia's 10 years of independence. As well as being the resting place for 174 war graves (many still empty), there is a platform, a pavilion with a capacity for seating up to 5000 people, a 30-m-high white obelisk, an 8-m-high statue of the unknown soldier, and various bronze statues of soldiers and notable figures from the period leading up to independence. One of its main features is a frescoed wall that exhibits scenes of the various uprisings throughout Namibia's history including the forced removal of blacks to the Katutura township during the era of the Group Areas Act, and the SWAPO armed liberation struggle. The site is used for major political and celebratory functions including Heroes' Day (26 August). The controversy lies in the fact that it cost a staggering US$10 million, and was built not by Namibians but by North Korean architects and construction workers; the contract was awarded without any competitive tendering process, and eventually the construction cost doubled. The idea was in fact nurtured in the first place when Nujoma visited the similar National Heroes' Acre outside of Harare in Zimbabwe in 1997; that one was built by the North Koreans in 1981 soon after Zimbabwe's own independence. Additionally, the statue of the Unknown Soldier carrying an AK47 in one hand and an anti-tank grenade in the other, bears a strong resemblance to Nujoma himself. The criticism is that SWAPO has in fact erected a monument to itself. Nevertheless, it's worth a visit, perhaps because of its grandiose absurdity.

Some 6 km northwest of the city is the former black township of **Katutura**, which can be accessed from a variety of routes including the B1 and Independence

Avenue. Most people with a rudimentary knowledge of South Africa have heard about townships – locations for the (sometimes forced) removal of blacks and other non-white groups to separate designated living areas during apartheid ('living apart' in Afrikaans). What is perhaps less well known is that towns in the central and southern regions of Namibia (then Southwest Africa) also had townships while the country was under South African control, and thus under the same policies of apartheid. These were usually far from the town centre and well hidden from the white suburbs, and were home to the vast majority of black and coloured Namibians.

From the late 1950s Windhoek was separated into three major areas: the City of Windhoek, mainly for the whites; Khomasdal for the coloured community; and Katutura (variously translated as 'we have no dwelling place' or 'the place where we don't want to stay') for the black community. Katutura was than itself divided into suburbs (including Soweto, Havana, Babylon and Wanaheda) along ethnic lines with different sections for the Damara, Herero, Owambo and so on. While no expense was spared when it came to providing facilities for the white community, the opposite applied to the creation of Katutura. Thousands of uniform shoebox houses were built, lining the dirt and dust roads of the township and, until the late 1970s, black people were not even entitled to own property and businesses in their own communities.

In the 1980s, the Group Areas Act that restricted the freedom of movement of all people in the country was finally scrapped as apartheid policies began to breakdown. Although people were no longer legally required to live in a specific area, Katutura by then now represented a thriving community with real homes and people didn't necessarily want to move out or indeed have anywhere to move to. It also saw both an influx of newcomers from rural areas and an emergent class of business people that provided Katutura with its own infrastructure and services in now-legal black-owned businesses. The original Katutura was much smaller than the Katutura that exists today; of Windhoek's total population of around 320,000, about 60% of these people live in Katutura.

The word 'township' is rarely used these days, and it is now a fully functioning suburb of Windhoek (albeit with some poorer communities). However, as a lively, bustling place with a confusing network of roads, driving through the area unaccompanied is generally not recommended. You can visit on an informative organized tour and a walk or bike ride through Katutura is interesting and worthwhile, not least when one bears in mind that this former township is now larger than the main part of the city and is, additionally, a melting pot for Namibians from all parts of the country. Tours typically last around three hours and introduce the visitor to the history and development of the township, and take in the busy commercial centres such as the Soweto Market, where everything and anything is for sale, and the notorious Eveline Street, which is locally dubbed 'the street that never sleeps' thanks to its plethora of *shebeens* (bars), hairdressers, cell phone stalls, car washes and other informal traders. Tours also visit Penduka (below).

▶ *See What to do, page 77.*

Penduka ⓘ *follow Independence Av through Katutura, cross Otjimuise Rd and continue into Eveline St past the Queen Supermarket, turn left into Green Mountain*

Dam Rd and left again at the Penduka sign, T061-257210, www.penduka.com, Mon-Sat 0800-1700, is an initiative by women in Katutura that combines a number of small local enterprises. Penduka means 'to wake up' and a visit, with or without spending the night, is the perfect opportunity to get out of the city and see a local community project. The well-stocked shop has a range of locally produced craft items and you can watch the women at work. There is also a *boma* restaurant and you can spend the night in a simple but cheerful thatched rondavels, for around US$50 for a double or US$10 for a dorm bed. There's secure parking or they can pick up overnight guests from the city centre. **Katu Tours,** (see page 76) also operates a popular and fun bike tours of Katutura from here.

⊙ Windhoek listings

For hotel and restaurant price codes and other relevant information, see pages 21-28.

⊙ Where to stay

Windhoek *p48, maps p49, p55, p57 and p59*
Windhoek offers a good range of hotel and guesthouse accommodation, from 5-star luxury to backpacker dorms. There are also a number of guest farms within striking distance of Windhoek if you prefer a more rural type of accommodation. These are listed in the chapters where routes out of Windhoek are described. All accommodation can arrange airport transfers.
$$$$ The Olive Exclusive,
22 Promenaden St, T061-239199, www.theolive-namibia.com. A chic luxury boutique hotel under the same ownership and next door to the **Olive Grove Guesthouse** (see below). 7 large suites with stunning decor, themed and named after a different region of Namibia (for example Caprivi features reeds, rocks and splashes of green, while all-white Etosha has giant photographs of gemsbok and elephant). Each has a private deck with plunge pool, laptop with Wi-Fi,

iPod docking station, minibar and coffee machine. Swimming pool, spa, excellent restaurant, breakfast served on cake stands like an afternoon tea.
$$$$-$$$ Hilton Windhoek, Rev Michael Scott St, T061-296 2929, www3. hilton.com. One of the newest additions to the city's skyline (opened in 2011), in a commanding position in the heart of the centre on what used to be a massive car park. Good service and standards expected of a Hilton, 150 well-equipped rooms, gym, spa, 5 restaurants, bars and lounges including the rooftop **Skybar** (see page 72) with its 18-m heated swimming pool. There's an extra fee for parking.
$$$$-$$$ Hotel Heinitzburg,
22 Heinitzburg St, T061-249597, www.heinitzburg.com. A castle built in 1914 set high on a hill with magnificent views over the city, atmospheric and professionally run with 16 charming rooms, stylish decorated with 4-poster beds, brilliant white bedding, silver furnishings, and all mod cons including Wi-Fi and DSTV. Heated pool and elegant restaurant, **Leo's at the Castle**, run by a French chef and serving superb gourmet food (see Restaurants, page 70).
$$$$-$$$ Kalahari Sands Hotel,
129 Independence Av, above the Gustav

Voigts Centre, T061-280 0000, www.suninternational.com. A Windhoek landmark right in the centre of the city with good views, and with the Hilton now across the road as competition, it benefited from a multi-million refurbishment in 2011. 173 a/c rooms, rooftop swimming pool, gym and casino, the **Dunes Restaurant** with a terrace overlooking Independence Av, and the **Oasis Bar & Lounge** in the lobby.

$$$ Hotel Fürstenhof, 4 Frans Indongo St, T061-237380, www.proteahotels.com. A well-run **Protea** (South African chain) hotel within easy walking distance of the city centre, 33 modern, comfortable but small rooms with a/c, Wi-Fi and DSTV, in a block with balconies overlooking the swimming pool, secure parking, and the reasonable **Office Bar and Restaurant** serving continental food and game dishes.

$$$ Hotel Thule, 1 Gorges St, T061-371950, www.hotelthule.com. Set behind imposing gates and flanked by palms, this hotel is perched on the lip of a hill above Eros with fantastic views. 25 very stylish and modern a/c rooms, swimming pool. The restaurant is rather special (see Restaurants, page 70) and a drink in the **On the Edge** bar at the top of the complex is recommended, but not for those who have a fear of heights as the steep hill seems to fall away beneath you.

$$$ Windhoek Country Club Resort, on the B1 Western Bypass, south of the city centre just beyond Eros Airport, T061-205 5911, www.windhoekcountryclub.co.za. A modern glitzy hotel with 152 a/c spacious and comfortable rooms, and a good range of facilities; it is completely surrounded by an 18-hole golf course (see page 77), there's a swimming pool with a 'lazy river' for kids, tennis courts, 2 quality restaurants, poolside snack bar,

cigar lounge and casino. Transfers are available into the city.

$$$-$$ Olive Grove Guesthouse, corner of Promenaden Rd and Ngami St, T061-239199, www.olivegrove-namibia.com. Stylish upmarket guesthouse in a quiet residential location, 11 rooms with large verandas and lovely stone bathrooms, comfortable communal lounge with fireplace, wellness room for massages and facials, plunge pool in pretty gardens. Well regarded for its food, the restaurant serves lavish breakfast buffets and beautifully presented gourmet 3-course dinners.

$$$-$$ Safari Court & Hotel Safari, corner of Rehobother and Aviation Rds, (B1 South), T061-296 8000, www.safarihotelsnamibia.com. Slightly dated but well located for Eros Airport, this is 2 hotels in 1 on a 13-ha plot offering 415 rooms in total (those in **Safari Court** are nicer and in a high-rise block, while the **Hotel Safari** has simpler but cheaper drive-up motel-style rooms), all have DSTV, a/c, and made-for hotel furnishings. Several restaurants and bars, swimming pool, gym and spa, and free transport 0700-1900, every 30 mins into city centre and Maerua Mall (see page 76).

$$ Belvedere Boutique Hotel, 76-78 Gever St, Ludwigsdorf, T061-258867, www.belvedere-boutiquehotel.com. A little out of town but a popular choice with 18 a/c lavishly decorated rooms in a lovely group of bright white buildings surrounding a courtyard which has a heated swimming pool and jacuzzi with wooden decks. Floodlit tennis court, spa, lounge with fireplace and good breakfasts. Good value for the quality.

$$ Casa Blanca Boutique Hotel, corner of Gous and Fritsche Sts, T061-249623, www.casablancahotelnamibia.com. Built in the style of an old castle, the original house with its arches and terracotta tiles was built in 1970 by a game ranger in the style of Fort Namutoni, in Etosha. 15 spacious and smart individually decorated a/c rooms with DSTV and Wi-Fi, swimming pool, romantic dinners served on the patio, reasonable selection of South African wines, library, lovely tropical gardens.

$$ Casa Piccolo, 6 Barella St, T061-221994, www.natron.net/tour/casapiccolo. This family-run pension in a bright yellow sunny complex on a quiet street in Klein Windhoek, offers 16 comfortable and modern a/c tiled rooms with DSTV, Wi-Fi, verandas and tasteful curios hanging on the walls, some sleep 4, a swimming pool, comfortable lounge, generous breakfasts and secure parking.

$$ Hotel Pension Palmquell, 60 Jan Jonker Rd, T061-234374, www.palmquell.com. Austrian-run with 16 spacious and immaculate rooms in pleasant neutral colours with interesting Namibian artwork, some of which can sleep 3-4 so represent good value. Bar, lounge and superb restaurant (guests only) specializing in Austrian dishes, good-sized swimming pool in gardens full of tall palms, fruit trees and creepers.

$$ Hotel Pension Steiner, 11 Wecker, T061-222898, www.natron.net/tour/steiner/main.html. Standard and functional motel-style establishment with 16 small rooms with DSTV and Wi-Fi but benefits from its proximity to the city centre; it's just a short stroll to Independence Av and Wernhil Park Mall. Swimming pool, *braai* and bar area, lounge, breakfasts are very good with unusual sweet and savoury crêpes, light meals at lunchtime, friendly staff.

$$ Roof of Africa, 124-126 Nelson Mandela Av, corner with Gusinde St, T061-254708, www.roofofafrica.com. Neat set-up in the northern areas of Klein Windhoek close to **Joe's Beerhouse** (see page 71), with 27 rooms, though some are very small (price reflects the size), restaurant and bar under thatched roof with trees growing through the roof, secure off-street parking, Wi-Fi in public areas, swimming pool (heated in winter), sauna and lovely gardens.

$$ Villa Moringa Guest House, 111a Joseph Mukwayu Ithana St, (formerly Gloudina St), Ludwigsdorf, T061-422 4472, www.villa-moringa.com. An elegant guesthouse close to the **Belvedere Boutique Hotel**, with bright modern decor and 11 a/c rooms with DSTV, Wi-Fi, minibar with complimentary wine and soft drinks, pool with sun loungers, breakfast included, dinner of fish or game meat on request. Also runs **Dunas Safari** (see page 78).

$$-$ Arebbusch Travel Lodge, Rehobother Rd (B1), on the outskirts of town on the way to the **Windhoek Country Club Resort**, T061-252255, www.arebbusch.com. A large attractive and very secure complex set in lovely gardens with a wide choice of accommodation; Arebbusch Square is the hotel section with 37 smart B&B rooms and its own pool, plus there are budget en suite motel-style rooms, 2- and 6-bed self-catering bungalows, and **camping/caravan** sites in a bushveld setting with power, shade and spotless ablution and kitchen blocks with cooker; some have their own private bathrooms and storage lockers. Excellent restaurant and bar (0630-2200) open to non-guests and has a popular Sun lunch, shop selling basic food items, ice, firewood and beer, laundrette and pool.

$$-$ Hotel Pension Moni, 7 Rieks van der Walt St, T061-228350, www.monihotel.com. Friendly and good value, with 13 simple but spotless rooms in a modern block with DSTV, Wi-Fi and fans, bar, swimming pool, good cooked buffet-style breakfasts, dinner on request, and a short walk up the hill to the **Hotel Heinitzburg** for a sundowner.

$$-$ Suricate Town Lodge, 18 Daphne Hasenjager St, Olympia, T061-419100, www.suricatetownlodge.com. Small and personable with easy access from the B1 and Eros Airport, run by a friendly Swiss couple the lodge has a quirky desert theme of thatched roofs and burnt-red colours. 9 rooms (1 for families and 4 with kitchenettes), small heated pool and outdoor bar under an acacia tree in the landscaped garden with birdbaths, breakfast extra and other meals on request. 'Suricate' is the Latin name for meerkat.

$ Puccini Guest House, 4-6 Puccini St, T061-236355, www.puccini-namibia.com. Colourful budget guesthouse in a good location just a short walk to the city centre, 14 single, double or triple rooms, en suite or shared bathrooms, rates include continental breakfast. Kitchen, laundry, secure parking, lockers, swimming pool, nice thatched bar area with *braai* and pretty gardens.

$ Rivendell Guest House, 40 Beethoven St, T061-250006, www.rivendellnamibia. com. Deservedly popular budget guesthouse in the west of the city with 8 homely rooms, 4 with en suite bathrooms, swimming pool, B&B or there is a kitchen for guests to use, very helpful and can organize all travel arrangements.

$ Cardboard Box, 15 Johan Albrecht St, T064-228994, www.cardboardbox. com.na. A reasonable choice if **Chameleon** (below) is full but more of a party place and the accommodation is a little crowded. Double and triple rooms, dorms, and some space for tents, all rates (even camping) include a breakfast of coffee and pancakes, TV lounge, bar, restaurant, swimming pool, cooking facilities, Wi-Fi, laundry and helpful travel desk.

$ Chameleon Backpackers & Guesthouse, 5-7 Voigt St, T061-244347, www.chameleonbackpackers.com. Just 5 mins' walk from the city centre, very neat and professionally run in 2 adjoining houses with a traditional backpackers set-up with dorms, double and triple rooms with en suite or shared bathrooms, camping space, and a more upmarket guesthouse section with smart en suite rooms including a honeymoon suite with a 4-poster bed and private balcony, all rates are B&B. Facilities include self-catering kitchen, lounge with DSTV, Wi-Fi, heated swimming pool, thatched bar and *braai* area, secure parking, travel booking office. All round an excellent and friendly place to stay and popular with backpackers, older travellers and independent overlanders. Runs **Chameleon Safaris**, good value and comprehensive tours of Namibia (see Tour operators, page 78).

⑦ Restaurants

Windhoek *p48, maps p49, p55, p57 and p59*

There are a few individual restaurants in Windhoek worth seeking out that offer a more varied menu than those in the smaller towns of Namibia, and there are also many franchises of South African chain restaurants that offer the same meaty fare of steak, ribs, schnitzel and hamburgers. For snacks and takeaways, the numerous fast food outlets all over central Windhoek include **KFC**, **King Pie** and **Nando's Chicken**, and the large supermarkets such as **Pick 'n' Pay** and

Checkers have good deli counters selling takeaway hot and cold food. Be aware that Sun is very quiet in Windhoek and many restaurants may be closed; even **Wimpy** closes at 1300.

$$$ Hotel Thule (see Where to stay, page 67). Daily 0700-2200. Located in this stylish hotel which has dramatic views from its position on top of a steep hill, delicately presented food includes hung beef and game meat, and seafood such as oysters and crayfish shipped in from the coast. With its long wine and cocktail list, the bar is a perfect place to watch the sun go down over Windhoek. Reservations essential for dinner.

$$$ Leo's at the Castle, in the **Hotel Heinitzburg**, (see Where to stay, page 66). Daily 0700-1030, 1200-1400, 1830-2200. Expensive but beautifully presented haute cuisine dishes with crystal glassware, silver cutlery, fine linen, and a wonderful romantic atmosphere in this renovated castle. More than 10,000 (mostly South African) wines to choose from and its own French patisserie, so you can also go for tea or sundowners on the terrace for the superb views over the city.

$$$ Restaurant Gathemann, 139 Independence Av, T061-223853. Mon-Sat 1200-2200. Upstairs dining with terrace in the historic Gathemann building, with exceptional seasonal local and continental cuisine, impressive winelist, and good ambience and service. To whet the appetite, example dishes include steenbrass with caper and citrus sauce or kudu fillet with apple and grape chutney. Recommended for an elegant lunch, afternoon tea and cake, or special dinner.

$$$-$$ Chez Wou, upstairs above the casino in the **Windhoek Country Club Resort** (see Where to stay, page 67). Daily 1900-2300. With big Chinese dragon statues on either side of the doorway, an upmarket Asian restaurant with an excellent menu and also serves local specialities such as ostrich meat and Swakopmund asparagus cooked Chinesestyle. The resort also has the **Kokerboom Restaurant**, 0630-2300, for breakfasts, à la carte lunches and buffet dinners.

$$$-$$ Nice, 2 Mozart St, T061-300710, www.nice.com.na. Mon-Fri 1200-1400, daily 1800-2200. NICE stands for the Namibian Institute of Culinary Education, which is a training school for chefs that has this very stylish restaurant. Spread over several rooms and outside decks, it's worth going just to see the incredible interiors, contemporary furniture, chandeliers, and giant black and white photos of the chefs (with their pots and pans) posing in Namibia's deserts. And then there's the food: the ever-changing menu can be described as fusion cuisine but the chefs come up with traditional dishes from time to time, and it's quite delicious and beautifully presented. You can watch the chefs at work behind glass in the state of the art kitchen.

$$$-$ The Gourmet, Post St Mall, T061-232360, www.thegourmet-restaurant. com. Mon-Sat 0730-2200, Sat 0800-2200. Excellent and very popular restaurant with outside tables beneath giant palm trees in the shady courtyard or dining room of the historic Kaiserkrone building (1910), with a varied menu including fresh seafood; try the drunken prawns or Henties west coast sole, a good range of vegetarian dishes and cheaper light meals and healthy breakfasts. Good service and relaxed atmosphere.

$$ Cattle Baron, Maerua Mall, Centaurus Rd, opposite the cinema, T061-254154, www.cattlebaron.co.za. Mon-Thu 1130-1530, 1730-2330, Fri-Sun 1130-2330.

Despite being in a shopping mall, this has a cosy dark-wood interior with long bar, leather booth seating, TVs to watch sport, and a vast menu with every kind of meat dish imaginable including steaks, ribs, burgers and a variety of sauces.

$$ Garnish Restaurant Flavours of India, 2 Trift St, near the German school, T061-258119. Tue-Sun 1130-1400, 1730-2100. A simple place with plain decor and clinical lighting, but the most delicious Indian food in Windhoek served in copper pots, cooked from scratch by Indian chefs so there's a very authentic range of kebabs, mouth-watering curries, breads and desserts, and excellent choice for vegetarians.

$$ Joe's Beerhouse, 160 Nelson Mandela Av, T061-232457, www.joes beerhouse.com. Mon-Thu 1630-late, Fri-Sun 1100-late. A veritable Windhoek institution that first opened its doors in 1991 and is popular with residents and tourists alike. A great atmosphere in what is something of a rabbit warren or dining rooms, wooden decks and thatched bars with memorabilia from German beer labels to American flags filling all the nooks and crannies. The menu features lots of meat – the Bushman *sosatie* (kebab) of ostrich, crocodile, zebra, kudu and gemsbok is the best-seller – but also offers Swakopmund seafood, salads and baked veggie dishes, and plenty of icy draught beer on tap.

$$ Kubata, 151 Nelson Mandela Av, Eros, T061-272900 40 1944. Daily 1200-2300. Great Portuguese cuisine, good wine, popular with well-heeled Angolans for the traditional coastal dishes, choose fish from the display cabinet, tables inside with bare brick walls and large arched windows or on the small terrace, though it can get windy outside.

$$ La Marmite, 383 Independence Av, T061-240306. Daily 1200-1500, 1730-2330. A little out of the way on an industrial part of Independence Av, but delicious West African food and run by a Cameroonian chef. Try chicken, fish and meat cooked in spicy tomato sauces or peanut butter, *ndolé* (a spinach dish), okra stew or pepper soup accompanied by Senegalese rice or couscous. West African masks adorn the walls and there are tables under a mulberry tree in the garden. The name means 'cooking pot' in French.

$$ The Stellenbosch Wine Bar & Bistro, Bougain Villas shopping complex, Sam Nujoma Dr, T061-309141, www. thestellenboschwinebar.com. Mon-Sat 1200-2200. It's no surprise this is a celebration of South African wine given that all of Namibia imports it, and there's a great selection from the racks and fridges on every wall. Good menu from aged Namibian steaks to Norwegian salmon with a good selection of sauces and sides. Outside tables in the leafy mosaic courtyard.

$$-$ Sardinia Blue Olive, Schoemanns Building, Sam Nujoma Dr, T061-258183. Tue-Sat 0900-2230. Good-value, lively and always busy Italian family-run restaurant/ deli specializing in great pizzas, pasta and a small number of traditional Italian dishes, excellent espresso, cappuccino and ice creams and good choice of South African and Italian wines.

$ Restaurant La Bonne Table, 118 Robert Mugabe St, T061-253976, www.fncc.org.na. Mon-Fri 0800-2130, Sat 0800-1400. Located in one of the oldest houses in Windhoek (1908), and attached to the Franco-Namibian Cultural Centre (see page 84), offers a French-inspired bistro menu using lots of fresh Namibian produce and they make their own bread, pasta and pastries.

You can also come here just for coffee and don't miss the lemon meringue pie. Interesting art and photography on the walls and sculptures in the garden.

Cafés

Café Schneider, 8 Levinson Arcade, Independence Av, T061-226304. Mon-Sat 0700-1730. German café that's been around for decades with a delightful time warp feeling of 1970s Germany, popular at lunchtime with office workers for the daily specials like *leberkäse* (a sort of meatloaf), schnitzels, *bratwurst*, or pork knuckles, and the *brötchen* (bread rolls) are always good. Also offers breakfasts and cakes and service is fast and friendly.

Craft Café, at the **Namibia Craft Centre**, Tal St, T061-249974, www.craftcafe-namibia.com. Mon-Tue 0900-1800, Wed-Fri 0900-sunset, Sat-Sun 0900-1530. Light meals amongst all the crafts; quiches, omelettes, open sandwiches, salads, muffins, cheesecake, coffee, yoghurt shakes and unusual juices made from wild figs and plums. Fully licensed and organic wines and craft beers on offer and stays open later than most cafés to watch the sunset over the Windhoek skyline from the balcony. You can also buy preserves, chutneys and olives.

Wecke & Voigts Kaffee Bar, Gustav Voigts Centre, Independence Av, T061-377000, www.weckevoigts.com. Mon-Fri 0830-1700, Sat 0830-1400. Delightful café in the Wecke & Voigts department store with old-fashioned counters and stools as well as tables on the street, famous its filled brötchens, quiches, cakes and pastries, and the coffee is strong and flavoursome.

O Bars and clubs

Windhoek *p48, maps p49, p55, p57 and p59* There is not a huge choice of evening drinking places but many of the restaurants also serve as bars.

El Cubano, in the basement of **Hilton Windhoek**, T0812-385622. Fri-Sat 1700-0200. As the name suggests, with a Havana atmosphere and tastefully decorated, trendy bar and lounge popular with the media and for special launches and events, offers Cuban cigars and light snacks.

Midnight Express & Club Thriller, 212 Samuel Shikoma St, Katutura, T0814-135097. Mon-Thu and Sun 1700-0200, Fri-Sat 1700-0500. Authentic African bar and disco which plays a mixture of the latest club sounds and African dance music, with the occasional live band outside in the beer garden, a taxi is the best way to get there and it's best to go with a local or a guide. This place has been pumping tunes since before independence.

Skybar, at **Hilton Windhoek**, (see page 66). Daily 1000-2400. Located on the 9th floor next to the swimming pool with panoramic views over the city, this transforms from a restful pool bar by day to a chic and stylish lounge by night. Best enjoyed for sunset, there are birds' eye views of the Christuskirche, Alte Feste and Supreme Court with its hugging arms on the eastern side, a glorious view down Independence Av to the north and the sunset framed by the Khomas Hochlands to the west. Drinks are expensive for Windhoek but are accompanied by generous portions of snacks.

The Wine Bar, 3 Garten St, T061-226514 www.thewinebarshop.com. Mon-Thu 1600-2230, Fri 1600-2330, Sat 1700-2230. Situated in a historical house built in 1927, a vast range of South African

wines and wine-based cocktails, light Mediterranean-inspired meals and snacks, good cheese board with olives, often live jazz or classical music, has its own **Wine Club** with regular tastings and shop.
Theo's Bar, adjoining **Nice** (see page 70), 2 Mozart St, T061-300710. Mon-Sat 1600-0200. Operates independently to the restaurant with an upmarket stylish modern interior of moody lighting and plenty of comfy seating, South African wines by the glass, good snack menu or you can eat at **sushi@nice**, also part of the culinary school.
Zenso Lounge Bar, Gutenberg Platz, off Werner List St, T0816-894575. Mon-Sat 0900-0200. Lively late night city bar and restaurant with a weekly program of events ranging from cocktail parties, live acoustic music performances, karaoke or student nights, and there's a flea market outside in the palm-filled courtyard on the first Sat morning of the month. Varied menu of European and African dishes from pizza to goat stew.

⊕ Entertainment

Windhoek *p48, maps p49, p55, p57 and p59*
Casinos
The larger and smarter casinos are: the Desert Jewel Casino at the **Windhoek Country Club Resort** (see page 67), Western Bypass, T061-205529, slots daily 1000-0400, table games Mon-Fri 1500-0400, Sat-Sun 1200-0400; and at the **Kalahari Sands Hotel**, Gustav Voigts Centre, Independence Av, T061-280 0000, daily 1000-0400.
Ster-Kinekor, Maerua Mall, Centaurus St, T061-215912, www.sterkinekor.com. Mainstream 7-screen cinema with showings from 0930-2030. Tue is half price.

Theatre
National Theatre of Namibia, Robert Mugabe Av, T061-374400, www.ntn. org.na. Plays, musicals, opera, ballet and performances by the Namibian National Symphony Orchestra; check the website or local press to see what's on.
Warehouse Theatre, 48 Tal St, T061-225059, www.warehousetheatre.com.na. Sharing the old breweries building with the Namibia Craft Centre, and with 3 venues; the Warehouse Theatre, the Boiler Room and Cellar of Rock, hosts regular plays and live music including jazz and cabaret. Many of these above events are performed by students at the College of Arts, the Performing Arts Department of the University of Namibia, and the Nedbank of Namibia Theatre School. Always an excellent atmosphere and there's a late bar; check the website or local press to see what's on.

⊕ Festivals

Windhoek *p48, maps p49, p55, p57 and p59*
Apr Windhoek Carnival, www. windhoek-karneval.com. A week-long traditional German festival with various cabaret evenings and a costume ball and culminates with a parade of floats and dancing troupes down Independence Av. In the German carnival tradition, it features a royal couple, royal guards, a jester and *frühschoppen* (open-air pub).
26 Aug Maherero Day. Also commonly known as Herero Day, a gathering and parade of the Herero people to commemorate their deceased chieftains held in Okahandja (see page 88), 70 km north of Windhoek. It is the day and place Herero chief Samuel Maharero's body was reburied alongside his ancestors in 1923. The men wear military uniforms, and the women traditional dress of

the Herero; a voluminous skirt and hat twisted into 2. On 26 Aug Namibia also celebrates Heroes' Day as a national holiday commemorating the Namibian War of Independence which began on 26 Aug 1966. Events take place usually in the north of Namibia near important battle zones, but also at Heroes' Acre in Windhoek (see page 64).

Sep Bank Windhoek Arts Festival, www.bankwindhoekarts.com.na. Provides a platform for a number of artistic genres from theatre, dance and visual arts, to fashion design, poetry and creative writing. Unlike similar arts festivals where events are crammed into 2-4 dedicated weeks, the banks sponsor events throughout the year at venues around the city such as the National Art Gallery of Namibia and Warehouse Theatre.

Late Sep/early Oct Windhoek Industrial and Agricultural Show, Windhoek Show Grounds, off Jan Jonker St near the Maerua Mall, T061-224748. Local business fair but commonly known as the Windhoek Show, which first exhibited in 1899, and with side stalls, food and beer, and entertainment like a funfair, bucking broncos and live music.

Late Oct Windhoek Oktoberfest, Sport Klub Windhoek (SKW), Sean McBride St, Olympia, T061-235521, www.skw.com.na. Usually held on the last weekend of Oct with beer, very large sausage consumption, and 'oompah' bands from Germany. Attracts more than 5000 and those in traditional Bavarian costume get free beer.

Early Dec FNB Desert Dash, www. desertdashnamibia.com. Starting in Windhoek, this is a 369-km 24-hr mountain bike endurance race. The route climbs the Khomas Hochland up to a level of 2000 m before descending to cross the Namib Desert and finishing on the coast in Swakopmund.

O Shopping

Windhoek *p48, maps p49, p55, p57 and p59*
Bookshops
CNA, Wernhil Park Mall, T061-224090, www.cna.co.za. Mon-Fri 0900-1730, Sat-Sun 0830-1330. South African stationery/ magazine chain, limited choice on just-released books, but good for coffee table books, maps and foreign magazines. There's another branch in Maerua Mall.
Orombonde Books, at the main entrance of the Namibia Craft Centre, Tal St, T081-148 8462. Mon-Fri 0900-1700, Sat 1000-1400. Interesting collection of novels and classics in a variety of languages, also historical books on Namibia. Orumbonde is the Herero word for a camelthorn pod.
Windhoek Book Den, corner Hosea Kutako Dr and Puccini St, T061-239976, Mon-Fri 0900-1700, Sat 0900-1300. The largest and most comprehensive bookshop in the country, with an excellent range of African fiction and up-to-date international novels and autobiographies, plus coffee table, wildlife and history books on Namibia in both German and English.

Camping equipment
Just about all the car hire companies will hire 4WD vehicles fully equipped with camping equipment (see Car hire, page 82). When renting equipment, expect to pay around 50% of the total rental price as a deposit.
Adventure Camping Hire & Sales, 33 Tacoma St, Suiderhof St, T061-242478, www.adventure-camping-hire.com. Mon-Fri 0800-1300, 1400-1700. Everything needed for a camping trip for hire from tents, tables and jerry cans to shovels, chemical toilets, and frying pans. Prices are reasonable with tents costing about N$3560 per day and small items such as axes or pillows for as little as N$5-7.

Camping Hire Namibia, 78 Mosé Tjitendero St, Olympia, T061-252995, www.orusovo.com/camphire. Again anything for hire from a tent to a teaspoon and they can put everything together in a 'pack' for 2-4 people from N$110-200 per day.

Cape Union Mart, Maerua Mall, Jan Jonker St, T061-220424, www.capeunionmart.co.za. Mon-Fri 0900-1730, Sat 0900-1400, Sun 0900-1300. Branch of the excellent South African chain selling outdoorsy quality items including sleeping bags, backpacks, hiking boots, pen knifes, head torches, etc, and a good range of fashionable and well-made clothing.

Cymot/Greensport, 60 Mandume Ndemufayo Av, T061-2957000, www.cymot.com.na. Mon-Fri 0800-1700, Sat 0800-1230. Quality company selling a full range of camping, fishing and outdoor equipment, plus car and bicycle accessories. There are branches in Namibia's other major towns.

Curios and crafts

African Curiotique, 16 Gustav Voigts Centre, Independence Av, T061-236191, www.african-curiotique.com. Mon-Fri 0830-1730, Sat 0900-1400, Sun 1100-1430. Very stylish and carefully chosen crafts, jewellery, decorated ostrich eggs, textiles and clothes, glassware and ornaments.

Nakara, 165 Independence Av, T061-224209 www.nakara-namibia.com. Mon-Fri 0900-1730, Sat 0900-1400. Boutique for Namibia Karakul Leathers (NAKARA) considered the country's best tannery for Karakul sheep leather – bags, belts, wallets, etc. There's another outlet in Swakopmund.

Namibia Craft Centre, 40 Tal St, in the old breweries building next to the Warehouse Theatre, T061-242222, www.namibiacraftcentre.com. Mon-Fri 0900-1730, Sat-Sun 0900-1330. This is an indoor market on 2 floors and is the best place in the country to buy Namibian crafts including carvings, pottery, baskets, leatherwork, jewellery and paintings. Items are sourced directly from the producers to make sure rural people have an outlet for their crafts and receive an adequate income. The centre can arrange international shipping for larger or heavier items. What was the breweries cold room, now sells an excellent selection of local books, CDs and photographs of Namibia. Also see page 56.

Pure & Simple, 33 Garten St, T061-240165, www.pureandsimpleshop.net. Mon-Fri 0900-1700, Sat 0900-1300. A lovely little shop near the Craft Centre with well-displayed crafts and decor items with an emphasis on recycled products. The gallery exhibits local artists and displays are changed every 3 months, and on Thu is a farmers market and deli.

Diamonds and jewellery

See Shopping in Namibia, page 29, for information about buying diamonds, and box, page 347.

Adrian & Meyer, 250 Independence Av, Mon-Fri 0900-1700, Sat 0900-1300, T061-236100, and Maerua Mall, T061-223635, Mon-Fri 0830-1900, Sat 083-1600, Sun 0900-1300, www.adrian-meyer.com. Very modern designed jewellery made in a state-of-the-art workshop; they also sell single diamonds. It's named after Mr Meyer who began selling diamonds in Namibia in 1907 and Mr Adrian who joined the company in 1957.

Canto Goldsmith & Jeweller, Mutual Towers, 223 Independence Av, T061-222894. Mon-Fri 0900-1700, Sat 0900-1300. Very modern and unusual designs from a jeweller established in 1955, diamonds as well as amethyst and topaz. Staff speak many European languages.

The Diamond Works, in the Namibia Craft Centre, Tal St, T061-230156, www.thediamondworks.co.za. Mon-Fri 0900-1730, Sat-Sun 0900-1330. Stocks loose polished diamonds and other precious stones from Namibia, as well as tanzanite from Tanzania, and creates some contemporary jewellery.

Sunstar Diamonds, 4 Dr. Kwame Nkrumah St, T085-630 6054, www.sunstar.com.na. Open daily by appointment. This large showroom in Klein Windhoek is often visited by tour groups and sells loose diamonds and export quality jewellery and visitors can watch a film about Namibia's diamond history and see a diamond cutter at work.

Shopping malls

Grove Mall of Namibia, Frankie Fredricks St off the B1 opposite the Windhoek Country Club Resort. By the time you read this, Namibia's newest and largest shopping mall will have opened, which will have nearly 60, 000 sq m of retail space, a food court and various entertainment facilities.

Maerua Mall, Centaurus Rd, at the junction of Robert Mugabe Av and Jan Jonker St, Suiderhof, T061-239251. Mon-Sat 0800-1930, Sun 0900-1800 (restaurants and entertainment later). Hundreds of shops, plus restaurants and cafés, a post office, enormous branches of **Checkers** and **Spar** supermarkets, the 7-screen **Ster-Kinekor cinema** and a **Virgin Active** gym.

Wernhil Park Mall, corner Fidel Castro and Mandume Ndemufajo Sts, T061-226480, www.wernhilpark.com. Daily 0800-1900. The principal mall in the city centre that features mostly South African chain stores and large branches of **Pick 'n' Pay** and **Woolworths** supermarkets, and adjacent to the pedestrian zone Post Street Mall which is lined with stalls selling crafts and clothes.

Wecke & Voigts, Independence Av, T061-377000, www.weckevoigts.com. Mon-Fri 0830-1700, Sat 0830-1300. This traditional department store was established in 1892 and is still owned by the Voigts family today (4th-5th generations). It features old-fashioned departments from lingerie to luggage and items are gift-wrapped for free. It's now part of the modern **Gustav Voigts Centre** under the Kalahari Sands Hotel, which is also home to a number of other shops including a branch of **Checkers** supermarket.

⏺ What to do

Windhoek *p48, maps p49, p55, p57 and p59*

Cycling

Katu Tours, based at **Penduka** in Katutura (see page 65), T061-210097, www.katutours.com. This fun half-day guided bike tour of Katutura departs from Penduka at 0830 and is an excellent way to explore the township. The 7-km route is not physically demanding and stops include Eveline St and the lively Soweto Market. No under 14s. N$350.

Football

Football is a hugely popular spectator sport and there are 12 teams in the Namibia Premier League. The national team is nicknamed the Brave Warriors, and though they've never qualified for the World Cup, they have qualified for the Africa Cup of Nations. Matches are played at the Independence Stadium in Olympia, just off the B1 heading south, which has a 25,000 capacity, or the Sam Nujoma Stadium in Katutura, which holds 10,300. Matches can be lively and exciting to watch, but do not take anything of value with you as the stands get very crowded and theft is rife. For details of fixtures check local press or contact the **Namibia Football Association**, T061-265691, www.nfa.org.na.

Golf
Windhoek Golf and Country Club, adjacent to the **Windhoek Country Club Resort** (see page 67), south of the city on the B1, T061-205 5223, www.wccgolf.com.na. The club's 72-par 18-hole course surrounds the hotel. Visitors welcome.

Hiking
The scenic **Hofmeyer Walk** follows a ridge of the Klein Windhoek Valley. At an easy pace it takes about an hour and gives hikers elevated views of the city. In the winter months, Apr-May, aloes flower in a fiery orange and attract sunbirds and mousebirds. The walk starts from Sinclair or Uhland streets on the city centre side, about 5 mins' walk from Independence Av, and takes walkers through bushland until the path meets the junction of Orban and Anderson streets in Klein Windhoek. Even though it is generally safe, muggings have occurred, so don't walk alone or carry valuables. Also leading off Sinclair St is Werth Crescent, from where there are steps to a circular lookout point which offers splendid views across Windhoek to the north, west and south.

Horse riding
Equitrails Namibia, 15 km north of Windhoek, turn right at the Brakwater junction off the B1, clearly signposted, or transfers can be arranged from Windhoek, T061-264429, www.equitrails.org. Horse riding on a local farm with great views of the Eros Mountains. All abilities catered for, from 1 hr to overnight rides. The sundowner rides include snacks; breakfast rides include breakfast.

Rugby
Rugby has been played in Namibia since 1916 when it was introduced by South African soldiers who had invaded the German-run colony. Until independence, players for Namibia were also eligible to represent South Africa, with Namibian-born Springboks including Jan Ellis and, more recently, Percy Montgomery. Namibia's national team today is nicknamed the Welwitschias and does well internationally including participating in the Rugby World Cup. Matches are played at the Hage Geingob Rugby Stadium in Olympia, just off the B1 heading south and next to the Independence Stadium. For details of fixtures check local press or contact the **Namibian Rugby Union**, T061-251775, www.nru.com.na.

Swimming
Most accommodation has a swimming pool, though only for their guests. Windhoek's public pool, **Olympia Swimming Pool**, corner of Sean McBride and Frankie Fredericks Sts, Olympia, T061-290 2690, is located close to the Independence and Hage Geingob Rugby stadiums. It's newly built to replace the former Jan Jonker Swimming Pool which was demolished to make room for the extension of Maerua Mall. It has an Olympic-size pool, children's paddling pools, changing rooms, life guards, a kiosk and spacious lawns for sunbathing. Open daily 0700-1900 during the warmer months, Aug-May, but closed in Jun-Jul.

Tour operators
As long as you are up to walking around the city centre there isn't really any need to sign up for a guided tour, but if you're short of time, most tour operators can organize a half-day tour to see the major

historical and architectural sights for around N$350. An informative guided tour, however, is the best way to visit Katutura (see page 64) and there are lots of options to visit this vibrant and most interesting part of contemporary Windhoek, again from about N$350 for half a day. There is also the option of going on tours to outlying game/guest farms around Windhoek for a day in the bush to see some animals. The most popular are to Düsternbrook (see page 87) and Okapuka Ranch (see page 93) from around N$700 for a day trip with lunch.

Good tour operators in Namibia should be members of the **Tour and Safari Association (TASA)**, www.tasa.na; check that the TASA logo is displayed on their websites.
Acacia Namibia, T061-229142, www.acacianamibia.com. Tailor-made arrangements and tours, deals with upmarket lodges and camps.
Albatros Travel Africa, T061-221656, www.albatros-africa.com. Multilingual operator offering scheduled and tailor-made tours and self-drive itineraries.
ATI Holidays, based at **Rivendell Guest House**, 40 Beethoven St, T061-228717, www.infotour-africa.com. Organizes self-drive safaris and guided tours.
Cardboard Box Travel Shop, 15 Bismark St, T061-256580, www.namibian.org. Good friendly company for all travel arrangements and tours especially for budget travellers, book through the comprehensive website or visit them at the backpackers of the same name (see Where to stay, page 69).
Chameleon Safaris Namibia, based at **Chameleon Backpackers & Guesthouse**, 5-6 Voigt St North, T061-247668, www.chameleonsafaris.com. Great value and well-run small-group tours, staying in well-placed eco-friendly

accommodation. The 6-day 'Dunes and Wildlife Safari' covers the highlights of Sossusvlei and Etosha with a weekly departure. The new 11-day 'Namibian Adventurer' option includes Sossusvlei and Etosha, a mix of accommodation and camping, with free time in Swakopmund for adrenaline activities, perfect for solo travellers. Can also arrange self-drive and tailor-made safaris for all budgets. Recommended.
Cheetah Tours & Safaris, T061-230287, www.cheetahtours.com. Scheduled and tailor-made minibus tours, guided 4WD self-drive itineraries, hotel bookings, fly-in safaris.
Dunas Safari, based at the **Villa Moringa Guest House**, T061-231179, www.dunas-safari.com. Self-drive itineraries and tailor-made safaris, and a 17-day tour to Etosha, the coast and Sossusvlei ending at Maun in Botswana for the Okavango Delta.
Elena Travel Services, T061-244558, www.namibweb.com. Day trips including local game farms and agent for longer tours, airport shuttles and transfers between towns.
Focus Travel, T061-257825, www.focusnamibia.com. Fly/drive tailor-made itineraries, car hire and rents out camping equipment. Staff speak English, French and Dutch.
Hello Namibia Safaris, T061-238118, www.hello-namibia-safari.com. City and Katururu day tours, trips to Okapuka Ranch, and longer lodge and camping safaris.
The Kangaroo Traveller, T061-223255, www.thekangaroo-traveller.com. Mid-range operator with scheduled 7- to 9-day tours of southern and northern Namibia, plus tailor-made trips and Windhoek day tours.
Kidogo Safaris, T061-243827, www.kidogo-safaris.com. Exclusive lodge safaris with all the trimmings for 2-6 people, also

camping for 4-6 people, and can make arrangements for disabled travellers.

NatureFriend Safaris, T061-234793, www.naturefriendsafaris.com. Specialists in upmarket fly-in safaris in Namibia, Botswana and Zambia.

Namibia Travel Connection, 4 Lorentz St, T061-246427, www.namibiatravel.com. General travel agent for all tours, car hire and accommodation reservations.

Ondese Safaris, T061-220876, www.ondese.com. Tailor-made safaris in Namibia and beyond, self-drive or escorted tours, professional company dealing with the upper end of the market.

Orupuka Transfers & Tours, T061-302979, www.orupuka.iway.na. Katutura half-day tour plus 3- to 5-day camping itineraries to Etosha and Sossusvlei.

Pasjona Safaris, T061-223421, www.pasjona-safaris.com. Scheduled tours

including a 11-day comprehensive Namibia trip using mid-range guesthouses, and an 11-day self-drive itinerary. Can organize visits to Angola.

Sense of Africa, T061-275300, www.senseofafrica-namibia.com. Scheduled and tailor-made tours, fly-in safaris, self-drive, car hire, activities and day trips, a good all-round operator.

Skeleton Coast Safaris, T061-224248, www.skeletoncoastsafaris.com. As the name suggests, organizes fly-in safaris from 4-6 days along the coast and Sossusvlei using luxury, and quite often very remote, tented camps.

Southern Cross Safaris, T061-251553, www.southern-cross-safaris.com. Well-established camping operator with over 20 years' experience in Namibia, tailor-made trips that can go well off the beaten track, also covers Botswana.

Springbok Atlas, T061-215943, www.springbokatlas.com. Large coach company offering comprehensive tours of Namibia and South Africa, probably best suited to the older traveller who doesn't mind being in a big group. Their 14-day **Classic Namibia** tour covers all the major highlights.

Sunbird Tours, T061-272090, www.sunbirdtours-namibia.com. Fly-in safaris and small group tours to lodges in Namibia, Botswana and Zambia. Has a vehicle adapted for wheelchairs.

SWA Safaris, T061-221193, www.swa safaris.com. Another large coach tour company with a comprehensive brochure offering scheduled tours and over 50 years' experience in southern Africa.

Wild Dog Safaris, T061-257642, www.wilddog-safaris.com. Long-established tour operator that covers just about all of Namibia on regular scheduled camping tours using minibuses, affordable and fun and again aimed at the backpacker/adventure travel market. Regular departures for the 10-day **Namibian Explorer**, 7-day **Northern Adventure**, and 3-day **Etosha** and **Sossusvlei** safaris. Longer trips go to the Okavango Delta in Botswana and Victoria Falls in Zambia.

⊖ Transport

Windhoek *p48, maps p49, p55, p57 and p59*

Windhoek is in the centre of the country, all the surfaced highways and railways radiate out from here. The pattern of the road network makes it difficult to do a circuit of the country without having to return to Windhoek at some point – unless you want to spend a lot of time driving on gravel roads of variable condition. It is 1375 km to Johannesburg (South Africa); 1096 km to Gaborone (Botswana); 1218 km to Katima Mulilo; 482 km to Keetmanshoop; 850 km to Lüderitz; 533 km to Namutoni (Etosha NP); 786 km to Noordoewer (South Africa border); 435 km to Okakuejo (Etosha NP); 350 km to Swakopmund; 1435 km to Victoria Falls (Zimbabwe) via the Caprivi Strip.

Air

There are 2 airports serving Windhoek. International, regional and some domestic flights arrive and depart from **Hosea Kutako International Airport** (**HKIA**), 45 km east of the city centre on the B6 road towards Gobabis, T061-295 5600, www.airports.com.na. Many domestic and charter flights use the smaller **Eros Airport** (**ERS**), 5 km south of the city centre off Rehobother Rd (B1), T061-295 5501, www.airports.com.na. For details of getting to and from the airports, see page 48. For details of international airlines serving Namibia, see page 9.

    Air Namibia flies to and from Hosea Kutako and **Lüderitz**, **Oranjemund**, and **Walvis Bay**. From Eros they fly to and from **Katima Mulilo**, **Ondangwa**, and **Rundu**.
Airline offices Air Namibia, Sanlam Centre, corner of Independence Av and Fidel Castro St, T061-299 6333, Hosea Kutako International Airport, T061-299 6600, Eros Airport, T061-299 6508, www.airnamibia.com; **South African Airways** (**SAA**), Sanlam Centre, corner of Independence Av and Fidel Castro St, T061-273340, Hosea Kutoko International Airport, T061-540082, www.flysaa.com.

Bus

Local There is a fleet of around 80 'City of Windhoek' blue buses that ply the major main roads. Bus stops are clearly denoted and fares are N$6-8; enquiries T061-290 2528. In theory they run from 0530-1800 but generally the majority only run during commuter times to ferry people in and out of the city centre (most bus stops are along Robert Mugabe Av) and Katutura and its surrounding suburbs to the north. However, there are also some sporadic services between the city centre and Eros, Hochland, Klein Windhoek, Olympia, Pioneers Park, University of Namibia and Windhoek West.

There is also a system of shared minibus taxis, which serve most areas of the city but on informal/variable routes and with no timetables or formal stops; they are flagged down on the street and you can get out wherever you want. These are generally fine to use for a short journey along a main road, but there is no way of knowing what the final destination will be and many of the vehicles are overcrowded, in poor condition and are driven rather recklessly. Most trips cost around N$8-12, and they stop running at around 1900. The easiest place to catch them is in front of the Gustav Voigts Centre/Kalahari Sands Hotel on Independence Avenue south of the intersection with Fidel Castro St. Ask other passengers which one you should get on if you know your destination.

Long distance Intercape, T061-227847 or T+27 (0)21-380 4400 (South Africa), www.intercape.co.za, see timetable page 16. The long-distance buses between Windhoek and Swakopmund/Walvis Bay, Windhoek and Oshikango, Windhoek and Upington in South Africa, and on the route between Cape Town in South Africa and Livingstone in Zambia, all arrive and depart from the Intercape office opposite the railway station off Bahnhof St.

There are daily shuttle services using micro/sprinter buses between Windhoek and Swakopmund (4 hrs) and Walvis Bay (4½ hrs). Expect to pay in the region of N$250 one way to Swakopmund, and N$270 one way to Walvis Bay and there are discounts for children under 12. On the way they stop at Okahandja, Karibib, Usakos and the other towns on the B2 road. Check the websites for pick-up and drop-off places and most are in large car parks in the centre of the towns, and for a small extra fee they will pick up/drop off from your hotel. Confirm times with the company as they maybe 1 hr earlier in winter.

Tok Tokkie Shuttles, T061-300743, www.shuttlesnamibia.com, depart Windhoek daily from the car park opposite the Kalahari Sands Hotel at 0900, and arrive in Swakopmund at 1300 and Walvis Bay at 1330. They then depart from Walvis Bay at 1400, Swakopmund at 1430 and get back to Windhoek at around 1900.

Town Hoppers, T064-407223 (Swakopmund), www.namibiashuttle.com, depart daily from Walvis Bay at 0645, Swakopmund at 0730 and arrive in Windhoek at 1200. They then depart from Windhoek at 1430, and gets back to Swakopmund at 1900 and Walvis Bay around 1930.

Welwitschia Shuttle, T064-405105 (Walvis Bay), www.welwitschiashuttle. com, depart daily from Swakopmund at 0700, arrive in Windhoek at 1100, depart again at 1400, and arrive back in Swakopmund at 1800. They operate a separate shuttle service between Swakopmund and Walvis Bay; check the website for times.

Car

Car hire For further information on car hire and driving in Namibia, see page 15. All companies will meet you with the vehicle at either of Windhoek's airports or at accommodation in Windhoek. If you are hiring extra equipment with the car such as a fridge, GPS, rooftop tent and other camping gear, ensure you go through a checklist carefully to confirm everything is supplied before driving away. Additionally if you are taking a vehicle over the border (South Africa, Botswana, Zimbabwe and Zambia), ensure you have the relevant paperwork and the company has provided a NA sticker for the car.

Advanced 4x4 Car Hire, 74 Aschenborn St, Pioneers Park, T061-246832, www.advancedcarhire.com.
African Tracks, 10 Pettenkofer St, Windhoek West, T061-245072, www.africantracks.com.
Andes Car Rental, 25 Voigt St, Southern Industrial Area, T061-256334, www.andescarrental.com.
Avis, **Safari Court** & **Hotel Safari**, Aviation Rd, T061-233166, Hosea Kutako International Airport, T062-540271, Eros Airport, T061-233166, www.avis.com.na.
Budget, 72 Mandume Ndemufayo Av, T061-228720; Hosea Kutako International Airport, T062-540150; Eros Airport, T061-228720, www.budget.co.za.

Camping Car Hire, 36 Joule St, Southern Industrial Area, T061-237756, www.camping-carhire.com. Good-value fully equipped vehicles with excellent service and back-up, can organize self-drive itineraries which takes the hassle out of pre-booking campsites, etc. Also hires out satellite phones.

Caprivi Car Hire, 135 Sam Nujoma Dr, T061-256323, www.caprivicarhire.de.

Car Hire Namibia, Sean McBride St, T061-254253, www.carhirenamibia.info.

Europcar, 24 Bismarck St, T061-385100, Hosea Kutako International Airport, T061-385100; Eros Airport, T061-227103, www.europcar.co.za.

Gecko Car Rental, 174 Jan Jonker Rd, T061-309408, www.geckocarrental.com.

Hertz, corner of Garten and Dr AB May Sts, T061-256274; Hosea Kutako International Airport, T062-540118, www.hertz.co.za.

Maui Motorhome Rentals/Kea Campers, Hosea Kutako International Airport, T062-540660, www.maui.co.za.

Namibia Car Rental, corner Hosea Kutako Dr and Pettenkofer St, T061-249239, www.namibiacarrental.com.

Okavango Car Hire, 124 Andimba Toivo Ya Toivo St, T061-306553, www.windhoekcarhire.com.

Savanna Car Hire, 80 Trift St, T061-229272, www.savannacarhire.com.na.

Taxi

There are several taxi ranks dotted around the city centre including on the corner of Independence Av and Fidel Castro St, outside the railway station off Bahnhof St, in the car park opposite the Gustav Voigts Centre/Kalahari Sands Hotel, and on the northern side of the Wernhil Park Mall. It is not usual to hail taxis in the street but any hotel or restaurant can call one for you. Always use a reputable company, identified by name stickers on both sides of the vehicle, as these have transport passenger liability cover and vehicles are usually in good working condition. All regular taxis have meters.

The shuttle services including **Windhoek Airport Transfers and Tours**, T061-258792, www.namibiatours.com.na, **Airport Shuttle Namibia**, T061-210532, www.airportshuttlenamibia.com, and **Shuttle Namibia**, T061-302007, www.shuttlenamibia.com, will not only provide transport to and from the airport but can do transfers in minibuses to anywhere in and around Windhoek and the outlying guest/game farms.

Train

TransNamib Starline Passenger Service, central reservations T061-298 2032/2175, www.transnamib.com.na. The office at Windhoek railway station on Bahnhof St is open Mon-Fri 0700-1900. There is economy and business class (seat size varies), and children under 6 are free, and under 12s half price. There are presently services between Windhoek and **Swakopmund** (9½ hrs) and **Walvis Bay** (11½ hrs); and Windhoek and **Karasburg** (17 hrs, 40 mins), via **Rehoboth** (2 hrs 20 mins), **Mariental** (6 hrs 20 mins), and **Keetmanshoop** (11 hrs 20 mins). From Keetmanshoop it's possible to get buses to South Africa. There have in the past been services between Windhoek and Gobabis and Windhoek and Tsumeb, so check with TransNamib in the event that these services resume again. For now the Windhoek to Swakopmund and Walvis Bay train departs daily except Sat at 1955, arrives the next day in Swakopmund 0520 and Walvis Bay 0715. In the opposite direction it departs daily except Sat, from Walvis Bay at 1900, Swakopmund at 2045, and arrives in Windhoek at 0700 the next day. Fares start from N$85 one way. Windhoek to Keetmanshoop runs daily except Sat and departs at 1940 and arrives at 0700 the next day. In the opposite direction it runs daily except Sat and departs at 1850 and arrives at 0700 the next day. Fares start from N$95. In Keetmanshoop there's an additional service from there to Karasburg on Wed and Sat and in the opposite direction Sun and Thu; check with the stations for times and fares. These passenger trains also include freight wagons, so while they are reasonably comfortable, are very slow. There are vending machines but no restaurant or buffet car, so take your own food and drink. Also see Essentials, page 14 for details of train travel in Namibia.

TransNamib also runs the far more appealing overnight luxury service from Windhoek to Swakopmund once a week; the **Desert Express** reservations: Windhoek railway station, Bahnhof St, T061-298 2600, www.transnamib.com.na, Mon-Fri 0800-1700. It departs Windhoek Fri at 1130 (1230 in summer) and includes a stop at a game farm for a game drive, and dinner in the on-board **Welwitschia Restaurant** before spending the night on the train. After breakfast, there is a stop for a dune excursion before arriving in Swakopmund at 1000. The return journey leaves Swakopmund on Sat at 1430 and the itinerary runs in reverse. Facilities on board the train include accommodation in 24 a/c en suite sleeper compartments that are converted to lounges during the day, an elegant lounge carriage, and a dining car which serves 3-course dinners. The experience is pretty good value at around N$3250 per adult twin share, one way, N$4700 return; children under 3 are free and there are discounts for children

under 12. The train is also equipped to take cars; this costs N$90 and must be arranged in advance.

The 7-day **Swakopmund & Etosha Holiday** has several departures throughout the year. The itinerary includes off-train excursions to Okahandja, Walvis Bay, Swakopmund and Otjiwarongo, as well as a 2-night side-trip to Etosha National Park. The trip costs N$20,000 per person twin share, and includes all costs except drinks.

ⓘ Directory

Windhoek *p48, maps p49, p57, p55 and p59*
Courier companies
DHL, corner Kelvin and Dalton Sts, Southern Industrial, T061-378300, www.dhl.com. Mon-Fri 0700-1700, Sat 0745-1115.

Cultural centres
British Council, T061-274800, at the British High Commission, 116 Robert Mugabe Av, www.britishcouncil.org. Has a library and offers language and education courses.
Franco-Namibian Cultural Centre, 118 Robert Mugabe St, T061-387330, www.fncc.org.na. A wonderful and stylish modern venue cleverly incorporating an older house dating back to 1908, which hosts lectures, film screenings, concerts and exhibitions; check the website and press for details. The excellent **Restaurant La Bonne Table** is also here (see Restaurants, page 71).
Goethe-Zentrum, in the Ludwig Van Estorff House, 1-5 Fidel Castro St, T061-255700, www.goethe.de. The German cultural centre, which again has art exhibitions and shows movies and holds German language classes.

Embassies and consulates

For a full list of foreign representatives in Windhoek, visit the government's Ministry of Foreign Affairs website www.mfa.gov.na.

Emergencies

T10111.

Immigration

Ministry of Home Affairs, Cohen Building, corner of Independence Av and Casino St, T061-292 2111, www.mha.gov.na. Mon-Fri 0800-1600.

Medical services

The state hospital, Harvey Rd, T061-303 9111, is in poor shape and anyone with adequate medical insurance should head for the private hospitals. **Medi-Clinic Windhoek**, Heliodoor St, Eros, T061-433 1000, www.mediclinic.co.za. **Rhino Park Private Hospital**, Rhino Park, Hosea Kutako Drive, T061-375000, www.hospital-namibia.co. **Roman Catholic Hospital**, 92 Werner List St, T061-270 2911, www.rchwindhoek.org. Pharmacies are found at the hospitals and in the shopping malls.

Police

Central Police Station, corner of Jan Jonker and Lazarett Sts, T061-209 3111, www.nampol.gov.na. There's another station on Bahnof St.

Post office

Windhoek Central Post Office, corner of Independence Av and Daniel Manumava St, T061-201 3006, www.nampost.com.na, Mon-Fri 0800-1630, Sat 0800-1200.

Around Windhoek

To the north of Windhoek along the B1 is the small town of Okahandja which is worth a brief stop if passing through, especially for its craft markets. Nearby the Von Bach Dam Resort is a worthy distraction for birdwatchers and campers that can also be visited on a day trip from the city. To the east of Windhoek, the main B6 road heads through the fringes of the Kalahari Desert to Botswana, and a drive along the Trans-Kalahari Highway through the flat, dusty cattle-rich scrubland offers a glimpse of the scenery that lies across the border. Throughout this region are a number of guest farms which make a more peaceful and rural accommodation alternative to the city hotels.

Daan Viljoen → *For listings, see pages 92-95. Colour map 1, C5.*

ⓘ *24 km west of Windhoek on the C28, T061-232393, www.sunkarros.com.na. Sunrise-sunset. Entry N$40, children (under 16) free, vehicle N$10.*

The Daan Viljoen game park is in the Khomas Hochland Hills to the west of Windhoek and lies at an altitude of 1000 m. Proclaimed in 1962, it was named after Daan Viljoen, the former South African administrator to South-West Africa who took a major part in establishing the park. It covers just 40 sq km and is smaller than some of the country's farms, but features pretty hills and dams with plains' game and abundant birdlife and has long been a popular retreat for Windhoekers. The vegetation in the park is typical of that of the central highlands, with an abundance of thorn trees such as blue, mountain and red umbrella, and thorn bushes such as trumpet and honey thorn. After the summer rains the hills are covered with new grass, but as the months pass they turn from green to yellow and then become barren just before the next rains. The views over the highlands and Windhoek itself are spectacular all year round. Game includes various species of antelope such as springbok, gemsbok, kudu and red hartebeest and blue wildebeest; giraffe are also present. Birds include colourful rollers and bee-eaters, hornbills and weavers and by the two small dams there is a fantastic assortment of water birds. A bird checklist of more than 200 species is available in the park office.

The park closed to visitors in 2008 when Namibia Wildlife Resorts (NWR) tendered it out to private investment. The former NWR camp was then refurbished by new owners and the park reopened in 2010. It is now known as the **Sun Karros Daan Viljoen Resort**, although the old name of Daan Viljoen game park is often still used. The resort has chalets, a campsite, restaurant, swimming pool and other facilities, see Where to stay, page 92, and day visitors are welcome. It can be explored on a self-drive 6.5-km game route or two self-guided hiking trails: the shorter 1.5-km **Wag-'n-Bietjie Trail** that goes to the Stengel Dam and is popular with birdwatchers; and the more energetic 9-km **Rooibos Trail** that takes hikers past the Augeigas Dam and snakes up and down the rocky hills. Mountain biking is also allowed and the park is a popular spot for Windhoek's mountain biking fraternity. The resort has the **Kraal Restaurant** where day visitors can also have lunch (there are buffets on Saturday and Sunday) and there's also a kiosk for snacks and drinks.

North to Okahandja → *For listings, see pages 92-95. Colour map 1, C5. Phone code: 062.*

The B1 north out of Windhoek leads to Okahandja (72 km), where it branches into the B2 for Swakopmund (350 km) and the B1 north for the Waterberg Plateau, Otjiwarongo and the 'Triangle' towns of Otavi, Tsumeb and Grootfontein.

For the first 15 km the road is an impressive four-lane highway but then, just before the turn-offs for Döbra and Brakwater, it slims down to a more modest two lanes. As well as being the main route to Swakopmund and the north, this road is a commuter route between Windhoek and Okahandja. It therefore gets very busy during daily 'rush' hours and on Friday and Sunday afternoons with traffic leaving and returning to Windhoek. Care should be exercised when driving this stretch.

The light industry that surrounds Windhoek is soon left behind and the road then snakes its way through the attractive mountainous **Khomas Hochland**, with cattle ranches and guest farms situated on either side of the road. About 10 km before Okahandja the road passes the Osona Military Base and soon after on the right is the turn-off for **Von Bach Dam Resort** (see page 91). Just before the turn-off for Okahandja itself, the road passes over the Okahandja River, a dry, wide sandy riverbed with some market gardening practised along its banks.

Düsternbrook → *For listings, see pages 92-95.*

① *50 km northwest of Windhoek, follow the B1 north for 30 km towards Okahandja, then take the D1499 for 10 km and then follow signs, T061-232572, www.duesternbrook. net. Entry N$60 pp, 50-min leopard and cheetah drive/feeding, 1400 (Apr-Sep), 1530 (Oct-Mar), N$280 pp, 90-min game drive 1530 (Apr-Sep), 1700 (Oct-Mar), N$280 pp.*
Around 1850 the area of the present 14,000-ha Düsternbrook Guest Farm was called Otjihorongo ('the place of the kudu') and was on an ox-wagon route to transport supplies from the coast to the hinterland. During that time a spring at Otjihorongo called 'Dabi Poort' served as the first veterinary quarantine station in the country and was under the control of Jan Jonker Afrikaner. The spring was used to prevent the expansion of lung sickness that had been introduced from South Africa, and at this station the oxen from the north travelling to the south had to be exchanged with the 'clean' oxen owned by Jonker Afrikaner. In 1908 Captain Lieutenant Matthiesen bought the farm, built a fine house with a spectacular view onto a dry riverbed and the Khomas Hochland hills, and named it Düsternbrook after a suburb of the

German sea port Kiel. In 1942 he sold the farm to the Vaatz family, who renovated and enlarged the original farmhouse in 1949 to what it is today.

In the beginning the farm was used for beef production and dairy farming, but due to an outbreak of foot-and-mouth disease in 1962 and the resulting prohibition on selling cattle, the Vaatz family had to look for an alternative income and initiated the first guest farm in Namibia. This idea quickly gained support among drought-stricken farmers, and in 1967 legislation gave the farmers ownership of the game on their land; the first country in Africa to do so. The result was to have a cattle-dependent income but also to put a value on the resident game under a wildlife management scheme to attract visitors. Today there are hundreds of guest farms and lodges and many communal and private conservancies in Namibia.

Today game at Düsternbrook includes giraffe, zebra, blue wildebeest, eland, springbok, ostrich, red hartebeest and, in 2010, a family of hippo were introduced into the farm dam and are expanding well. Birdlife is also good and about 160 species have been recorded many of which can be spotted around the farmhouse and campsite. The highlight though is to see the leopard and cheetah, which are in spacious 50-ha natural drive-through enclosures. Excursions go every afternoon to watch them being fed. Pre-booked day visitors are welcome to go on the leopard and cheetah excursion and also go on a game drive; self-drivers with 4WDs can go on a 14-km mountain drive into the Khomas Hochlands and if lucky may spot kudu, gemsbok, or the rare Hartmann's mountain zebra. If you don't have your own transport, tour operators can organize a half-day trip here from Windhoek for around N$700. There's also comfortable accommodation and a campsite (see page 92).

Okahandja → *For listings, see pages 92-95. Colour map 1, C5. Phone code: 062.*

As a crossroads between the routes west to the coast and north to Etosha, Okahandja is a busy, bustling place with a railway station, shops, banks, 24-hour petrol stations and two large outdoor craft markets. The last few years have seen a growth in light industry in the town and an increasing number of people are choosing to live in Okahandja and work in Windhoek; the town currently has a population of around 25,000. The word Okahandja is derived from Otjiherero (a local language) and means 'the place where two rivers flow into each other to form one wide one'. This confluence is to the northeast of town and the rivers are the Okakango and the Okamita which join to form the Okahandja River; all of which flow only during the summer season and are dry throughout most of the year. Although the period of German rule saw the construction of a number of attractive early 20th-century buildings which can still be seen scattered around the town, unfortunately none of them has yet been turned into a museum and, apart from a casual glance, there is not much to see. But Okahandja is one of the oldest-established settlements in Namibia and is rich in history that revolves mostly around the Herero people. An annual procession through the town to the Herero graves commemorates Herero dead during various wars against the Nama and the Germans.

Background

During the 1840s, the Herero chiefs Tjamuaha and Katjihene both established themselves at Okahandja, having moved away from Oorlam leader Jonker Afrikaner's base in Windhoek, and in 1850 missionary Kolbe set up a mission station here. The establishment of this mission ran contrary to the wishes of Jonker Afrikaner, at the time the most powerful leader in central Namibia, as he felt that European influence over the Herero would interfere with his self-declared rights over Herero cattle. In August 1850 he raided the settlement, destroying the mission and killing men, women and children indiscriminately. The site where most of the atrocities took place was named **Moordkoppie** or **Blood Hill** in memory of those who fell there, and today the site is situated behind the town's school to the west of town. Jonker Afrikaner himself settled at Okahandja in 1854 – using the settlement as a base from which to launch his cattle raids in Hereroland – and lived here until his death in 1861. In 1894 the Germans established a military station and fort (which no longer exists) and this date was later regarded as the date on which Okahandja was officially founded (although curiously German businessmen Wecke & Voigt had established a shop here two years earlier in 1892). Soon after the first postal services were established, with camels being used to transport the mail from Windhoek; the post office at Okahandja, dating to 1896, still stands in the main street. In January 1904, the great Herero uprising under Chief Maherero began in Okahandja. The rebellion quickly spread through the whole of Hereroland and Damaraland and Maherero led the Herero into exile in Botswana in 1904 after a final pitched battle against the Germans at the Waterberg Plateau (see page 110).

Okahandja

To ④⑤⑥ & Otjiwarongo (B1)
Caltex
Curios
Water
Engen
Shoprite
Ossmann
FNB
Closwa Biltong
Standard
Football Ground
Dinter
Bahnhof
Herero Cemetery
Okahandja Hospital
Voigts
Library
Spar
B Templin
Bottle Shop
Rhenish Mission
Church of Peace
Kolbe
To Blood Hill
To ①, Shell Ultra, curio market, Intercape bus stop, Van Bach Dam Resort & Windhoek (72 km)
To ② & Windhoek (B1)
To Swakopmund (B2) & Otjiwarongo (B1)
Mose
Brand
Nzaraza
Kaiser
Walden
Hoof
Uitspan
Heroes
A Doeseb
M Nelb St
Voortrekker
M Nelb
Heroes

N

100 metres
100 yards

Where to stay 🛌
Auberge Omulonga **2**
Okahandja Country Hotel

5
King's Highway Rest Camp **1**
Ombo Rest Camp **6**
Sylvanette Guesthouse **3**

Restaurants 🍴
Garden Café **3**
Reit Club Okahandja **4**

Places in Okahandja

To the east of the main road in the south of town, the **Rhenish Mission Church** was built from the early 1870s and consecrated in 1876 and is not only the oldest building in Okahandja, but in Namibia. It is built in the shape of a cross and has narrow windows set in high walls, and a small bell tower is separate and sits a few metres from the entrance. The cemetery contains the graves of many missionaries and Herero people who converted to Christianity including that of Wilhelm Maherero, the eldest son of the late 19th-century Herero leader, who would have succeeded his father as leader of the Herero if he had not been killed in a skirmish with Jan Jonker's men on 11 December 1880. Another Herero leader, Nikodemus Kavekunua, is also buried here after being court-martialled and executed by a German firing squad on 13 June 1896. The church and cemetery were proclaimed a national monument in 1975.

Opposite is the **Church of Peace**, consecrated in 1952, which contains the graves of three influential Namibian leaders: the 19th-century Oorlam leader Jonker Afrikaner, who died in 1861; Herero leader Chief Hosea Kutako who died in 1970 and is widely credited as the leader of post-Second World War resistance to South African rule in Namibia; and Chief Clemens Kapuuo, Kutako's successor and former Democratic Turnhalle Alliance (DTA) President, who was assassinated in 1978.

Every year on the last Sunday of August and closest to the 26 August, is **Maherero Day** in Okahandja, which is formerly and still commonly known as Herero Day.

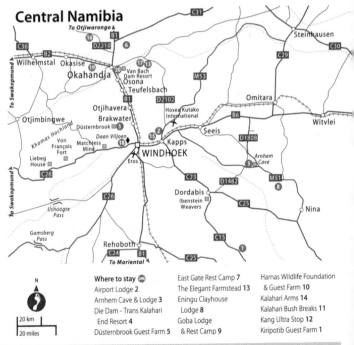

Central Namibia

Where to stay
Airport Lodge 2
Arnhem Cave & Lodge 3
Die Dam - Trans Kalahari
　End Resort 4
Düsternbrook Guest Farm 5

East Gate Rest Camp 7
The Elegant Farmstead 13
Eningu Clayhouse
　Lodge 8
Goba Lodge
　& Rest Camp 9

Harnas Wildlife Foundation
　& Guest Farm 10
Kalahari Arms 14
Kalahari Bush Breaks 11
Kang Ultra Stop 12
Kiripotib Guest Farm 1

26 August 1923 is the day the body of Chief Samuel Maharero (who led the Herero into exile in Botswana in 1904), was reburied in Okahandja alongside his ancestors. The Herero people gather to honour their forefathers and those fallen in battle and visit the various graves in the churches (above), and those in the **Herero Cemetery** to the east of town, which include Maherero and his son Samuel. It's a colourful procession (numbering perhaps a couple of hundred), and the women wear traditional Herero dress, voluminous Victorian-style dresses and horn-shaped headgear, while the men wear khaki military uniforms. Tourists are always made to feel most welcome at this important event.

Von Bach Dam Resort

ⓘ *Just under 70 km north of Windhoek and 3.5 km south of Okahandja signposted off the B1, T062-500162, www.tungeni.com. 0600-1900 for day visitors. MET (Ministry of Environment & Tourism) entry fee N$40 pp, N$10 vehicle, resort entry fee for day visitors N$40, children (12-15) N$15, under 12s free (overnight visitors to do not need to pay this).* What was the Von Bach Recreation Dam Resort is now officially called the Tungeni Von Bach Dam Resort, which again, like some of the other former NWR properties (like Daan Viljoen, above) was tendered out to private investment in 2008. The accommodation was refurbished and the resort reopened in 2011. The dam itself was built in 1970 and has since been the main water supply for Windhoek and belongs to the Swakop river drainage system. Fringed by the Auas Mountains, the small 43-sq-km game park around the dam was proclaimed in 1973 and covers an area that can be classified as thornbush savannah. Animals present include kudu, zebra, gemsbok, eland, springbok, red hartebeest, baboon and ostrich. The dam and surrounding reed beds attract large numbers of birds, in particular waterbirds such as moorhen, teal and coot. There are also large numbers of Monteiro's hornbill, lilac-breasted roller and crimson-breasted shrike with their distinct black and crimson markings. Benches on the edge of the dam are excellent places from which to twitch and there is a list of 187 species to tick off. However, despite the newly refurbished accommodation and campsites being pleasant enough, apart from swimming in the blue water and birdwatching, the dam offers little for overseas visitors and it's a destination

Okapuka Ranch **16**
Ombo Rest Camp **6**
Otjisazu Guest Farm **17**
The Rock Lodge **19**
Sun Karros Daan
 Viljoen Resort **18**

Trans-Kalahari Inn **15**
Tungeni Van Bach
 Dam Resort **20**

primarily for angling (for barbel, bass and carp) and watersports by people from Windhoek who bring their own boats and equipment. Tungeni, the new owners, have also taken over the former NWR campsites at Jakkalsputz, Mile 72 and Mile 108 in the Dorob National Park (formerly the West Coast Recreation Area), see page 277.

⊕ Around Windhoek listings

For hotel and restaurant price codes and other relevant information, see pages 21-28.

⊜ Where to stay

Daan Viljoen *p86*
$$$ Sun Karros Daan Viljoen Resort, 24 km west of Windhoek on the C28, T061-232393, www.sunkarros.com.na. 19 comfortable and modern a/c chalets sleeping up to 4 with veranda, *braai*, tea and coffee station, Wi-Fi and DSTV. The 12 **campsites ($)** are on a grassy terrace with views of the Augeigas Dam and have lights, power points, *braai*, sink and Wi-Fi. Facilities include the **Kraal Restaurant**, a kiosk selling snacks and curios, a swimming pool and the 2 hiking trails, which start from reception.

Düsternbrook *p87*
$$$-$$ Düsternbrook Guest Farm, (see page 87) follow the B1 north from Windhoek towards Okahandja, after 30 km take the D1499 and follow it for 10 km and then follow signs, T061-232572, www.duesternbrook.net. Accommodation is in 5 comfortable rooms in the German colonial farmhouse, 2 permanent en suite safari tents or a rustic double chalet next to the farm dam where the hippos live. Meals include game and beef dishes and home-made bread, swimming pool and thatched *lapa*. Rates include all meals and leopard and cheetah viewing, and there are

birdwatching and hiking trails. You can also **camp ($)** at sites along the dry riverbed and join in on the activities. Transfers available from Windhoek.

Okahandja and around *p88, map p89*
$$$-$$ Tungeni Von Bach Dam Resort, (see page 91) the turn-off is 3.5 km south of Okahandja on the B1, T062-500162, www.tungeni.com. 22 double or family thatch and stone a/c chalets set on a hill overlooking the dam (not self-catering), plus 11 campsites **($)** on the lakeshore, each with their own boat parking bay, *braai* area and small thatched shelter. Facilities include attractive semi-open restaurant with reasonable set meals, swimming pool, boat cruises, canoe hire and short walking trails which radiate from the resort.
$$ Okahandja Country Hotel, 2 km north of town on the B1, T062-504299, www.okahandjalodge.com. The smartest option in town with 22 thatched doubles and 2 family a/c rooms with DSTV and tea and coffee facilities, tastefully decorated in contemporary African style. There's a **campsite** (N$100 per person) on the banks of the dry Okahanja River with good reed hut shared ablutions and cooking facilities. With its beer garden and swimming pool in manicured grounds, good restaurant serving buffet and à la carte meals, this is a good place to stop for lunch if driving through.
$$-$ Ombo Rest Camp, 12 km north of Okahanjia, turn right off the B1 on

to the C31 for 2 km, T062-502003, www.ombo-rest-camp.com. On an ostrich farm with 2 family and 2 double self-catering a/c stone chalets, plus 3 cheap backpacker rooms which share facilities with the **campsite** that has warm showers, power points, *braai* pits and shade cloth. Swimming pool, bar, the restaurant specializes in ostrich steaks and eggs, and the farmstall here sells *braai*-packs, firewood, ice, soft drinks and some souvenirs.

$ Auberge Omulonga, 455 Dr Vedder St, T062-500341, www.omulonga.iway.na. Comfortable B&B in a family house run by a French couple, with pool, outdoor *lapa*, rustic wooden bar, good home-cooked French food (makes a nice change from Namibia's meaty fare), and pretty gardens.

$ King's Highway Rest Camp, opposite the Shell petrol station at the B1 turn-off for town (immediately north of the bridge over the Okahandja River), T062-504086, www.kingshighway.co.za. Well maintained and nicely laid out with plenty of trees for shade, the best-value option in town with 5 en suite chalets sleeping 2-3, equipped with fan, kettle, microwave and fridge, and 4 small double rondavels which share the good communal ablutions and camp kitchen with the **campsite** which has lights, power points and *braai* pits.

$ Sylvanette Guesthouse, 311 Hoogenhout St, T062-505550, www.sylvanette.com. Comfortable and pleasant, fairly central, with 9 a/c rooms with fridge and tea and coffee-making facilities, Wi-Fi, lovely shaded garden, swimming pool, secure off-street parking, B&B and other meals on request. The owners have a boat and can organize fishing excursions to Van Bach Dam Resort.

Guest farms

Most guest farms can organize transfers from the airports in Windhoek.

$$$ The Elegant Farmstead, from the B1, turn right on to the D2102 for 28 km past Von Bach Dam Resort, reservations Windhoek T061-301934, www.the-elegant-farmstead.com. An excellent professional set-up and more of a country hotel than a guest farm with (as the name suggests) elegant and contemporary interiors in old farmstead buildings. 9 double/twins, 2 triples and a family unit sleeping 5, restaurant, bar and cigar lounge, wine cellar, pool and wooden deck overlooking a waterhole, Wi-Fi. Activities include game drives and walks and sundowner trips in the surrounding hills. Rates include dinner and breakfast.

$$$ Okapuka Ranch, off the B1, 30 km north of Windhoek, T061-234607, www.okapuka-lodge-namibia.com. 18 thatched rooms decorated with locally made karakul rugs and paintings of Namibian landscapes, restaurant specializing in game dishes, attractive bar fashioned out of camelthorn trees, and well-stocked wine cellar. Activities include game drives and hikes on the ranch, there's a tennis court and sauna and some lions in an enclosure which you can watch being fed. The tour operators can organize a day tour here for lunch, game drive and to see the lions for about N$700.

$$ Otjisazu Guest Farm, next to **The Elegant Farmstead**, from the B1, turn right on to the D2102 for 27 km past Von Bach Dam Resort, T062-501259, www.otjisazu.com. The original farmhouse was built in the 19th century as a mission station, though the 12 rooms are purpose-built, swimming pool and thatched poolside *lapa*, mountain biking, hiking trails and game drives, and kudu, hartebeest, duiker, warthog, ostrich and jackal are present on the farm.

$$ The Rock Lodge, just off the B2, 12 km west of Okahandja, T062-503840, www.rocklodge.com.na. 18 simple thatched rooms and 4 houses each with 3 en suite bedrooms and open-plan lounge (not self-catering), many with fine views of the 'Rock', attractive wooden and stone walkways, swimming pool, restaurant and bar with outside deck, fireplaces and good country cuisine, game walks and drives on offer.

⦿ Restaurants

Okahandja and around p88, map p89
If you are just driving through there are coffee shops attached to both the 24-hr **Shell** and **Engen** petrol stations, both of which also have ATMs.

$$-$ Reit Club Okahandja, 500 m north of town on the B1, T0812-232720. Mon-Sat (closed Tue) 1000-2300, Sun 0900-1500. With its old-fashioned green corrugated-iron roof, this was originally the 1909 home of Dr Fock, the first Mayor of Okahandja. Today it's a lively restaurant and bar with large-screen TVs for sports and family-friendly outdoor areas. Good food in big portions, popular with local farmers so expect the likes of enormous T-bone steaks and chips, plus there's excellent freshly ground coffee. Wood carvings and other souvenirs from Okahandja's craft markets are for sale in the shop and there's free Wi-Fi. You can also camp here (**$**) and the sites in the spacious grassy grounds have taps and power points.

$ Garden Café, 261 Martin Neib St, T062-500887. Tue-Thu and Sat 0800-1700, Fri 0800-2000. Pleasant café and bakery run by an American couple who

operate a Christian NGO in Okahandja, profits go to teaching vocational skills in the community – as such the young people working in the café are very polite and friendly. There can be few places in Namibia to get a proper American fat burger with all the trimmings or a chocolate and peanut butter milkshake, also serves delicious cakes and coffee, and light dinners on Fri evening. Indoor and outdoor tables and has its own car park.

⦿ Shopping

Okahandja and around p88, map p89
Crafts and curios
There are 2 outdoor craft markets in town, which are run by woodcarvers from around Rundu in the north, who sell their carvings here on a co-operative basis – Okahandja gets a lot of tourist traffic passing through. The bigger one is on the corner of B1 as you turn into town from the south, opposite the Shell Ultra, while the smaller one is on Voortrekker St by the railway crossing. Good quality, and bargains to be had, but beware of crafts from Zimbabwe being sold; ask for locally made goods to get a feel for what is produced where in the country.

Food
There are both **Spar** and **Shoprite** supermarkets in town. The petrol stations are a good stop for cold drinks and ice for cool boxes. There is a bottle store on the main street (not open Sun) for beers, etc.
Closwa Biltong, Voortrekker St, T062-501123, www.closwa.com. Mon-Fri 0800-1715, Sat 0800-1300. There are a couple of kiosks on the main street that sell biltong (dried spicy, chewy but tasty meat snacks), which is produced in the region. Closwa is a factory that distributes throughout Namibia and South Africa,

and you can buy family packs of beef and game biltong and *droëwors* (great for long car journeys), and there's also a coffee and curio shop that doubles up as the town's local tourist info office.

⊖ Transport

Okahandja and around *p88, map p89*
Okahandja is 72 km to Windhoek, 179 km to Otjiwarongo, and 292 km to Swakopmund.

Bus
There are 3 routes for **Intercape** central reservations T061-227847, www.intercape.co.za, buses that stop in Okahandja; between Windhoek and **Swakopmund** and **Walvis Bay**; between Windhoek and **Oshikango**: and between Windhoek and Livingstone in Zambia. See timetable on page 16. The coaches arrive/depart about 1 hr before or after Windhoek and stop at the Shell Ultra on the B1. The daily shuttle services using micro/sprinter buses between Windhoek and Swakopmund and Walvis Bay also pick up and drop off at Okahandja; again 1 hr before/after Windhoek at the Shell Ultra, see Windhoek transport, page 80, for details and contacts.

Train
TransNamib Starline Passenger Services, central reservations T061-298 2032/2175, www.transnamib.com.na. The train service departs from **Windhoek** daily except Sat at 1955 and arrives in Okahandja at 2155, then arrives in **Swakopmund** at 0520, and **Walvis Bay** at 0715. In the other direction it leaves Walvis Bay at 1900, gets to Swakopmund at 2035, and arrives in Okahandja at 0500 and then Windhoek at 0700.

East to Botswana

The main road, B6, east out of Windhoek passes through the suburb of Klein Windhoek before it starts to weave its way through the Eros Mountains and out onto the plains past Hosea Kutako International Airport and on to Botswana. After passing the airport the road is a dull straight drive to Gobabis, the regional centre and the last settlement of any note before you reach the Botswana border. If you are planning on exploring the Kalahari in Botswana, this is the best place to stock up with supplies. Keep your eyes peeled along the road for warthogs, baboons, antelope (including kudu) and birds of prey. There are rest stops clearly signposted every few kilometres for a picnic. The terrain is relatively flat and, as you approach Witvlei, there are few trees. Most of the country is owned by large commercial cattle and sheep farmers. After good rains the countryside turns a beautiful green, but for most of the year it is a dull burnt brown covered with scrub vegetation.

East of Windhoek

Traffic is only 'heavy' on the B6 when there is an international flight arriving or departing from the airport, 45 km out of town. The airport was built here because of the need for level land and a clear approach for larger aircraft; closer to Windhoek there are too many mountains. On the way to the airport about 20 km from Windhoek, you will pass the **Trans-Kalahari Inn** (see Where to stay, page 100). It not only offers accommodation but if you have the luxury of owning your own vehicle in southern Africa, this is where you can park your car safely when not in Namibia.

Windhoek to the border → *For listings, see pages 100-101.*

About 11 km east of the airport, you'll go past **Seeis** in the blink of an eye, but 96 km on is **Witvlei**, which while it is a godforsaken, dusty place in the dry season, does have a petrol station, bottle store, small shops, police station and clinic. Witvlei Meat was established here in 2006 and is a major exporter of beef to Scandinavian countries, and now practically employs the whole town. From here it is another 52 km to Gobabis.

Dordabis → *Colour map 1, C6.*

The tiny settlement of Dordabis makes an interesting detour to see the karakul carpet weavers. From the B6 between Windhoek and Hosea Kutako International Airport turn onto the C23 and Dordabis is 64 km on a tar road. **Ibenstein Weavers** ① *4 km south of the village (left at the T-junction) on Klein Ibenstein Farm, T062-573524, www.ibenstein-weavers.com.na, Mon-Fri 0800-1200, 1430-1800,* offer tours of the farm and weavery. They produce a range of animal and African designs in varying sizes as carpets and wall hangings. The weavery has been going since 1952 and today it supports 20 weavers. The sheep's wool arrives in varying colours of grey, fawn, black and white, some of it is then dyed, before being spun and weaved by hand. If you don't make it this far, the carpets are for sale at the **Namibia Craft Centre** in Windhoek (see page 56).

Arnhem Cave

① *43 km northeast of Dordabis on the D1482, or 58 km south from the B6 on the D1808, 4 km (signposted) from the road, T062-581885, www.arnhemcave.com. Tours of the cave at 0800 and 1500, N$100, children (under 10) N$80.*

If you have plenty of time or are particularly interested in caves and bats then a detour to Arnhem Cave is recommended. The cave is situated on a private farm in the Arnhem hills south of the B6. There is a lodge and campsite here (see page 100) and tours of the cave last up to three hours; helmets, torches and refreshments are included in the tour. Wear old clothes as a visit may get messy.

The cave system is 4500 m long, making it the longest in Namibia. The entrance is divided in two by a thick column of rock; both sides lead down into an enormous cavern measuring 122 m long and 45 m wide. This leads down to smaller crevices and passages. It is a dry cave and thus there are few of the typical cave formations such as stalagmites. After it was discovered in 1931, it was exploited as a source of bat guano; today the cave remains a home to six different species of bat: the Egyptian slit-faced bat, leaf-nosed bat and giant leaf-nosed bat, horseshoe bat, and the long-fingered bat. The best time to visit is just after the first summer rains, when the insect-eating mammals are at their busiest; sitting by the cave entrance at night is a spectacular experience.

Gobabis → *Colour map 2, C1. Phone code: 062.*

Bordering the Kalahari Desert, Gobabis is 160 km east of Hosea Kutako International Airport on the B6 and is a typical Namibian rural town; it is the capital of the Omaheke Region, surrounded by important cattle country, which produces a third of all Namibia's red meat. The importance of cattle in this region is attested to by the large statue of a Brahman bull and a sign saying 'Cattle Country' on the roundabout on the B6 as you enter town. Although arid, the region has excellent grazing (and browsing for small game) especially after a few years of good rains. Visitors might find the Friday stock sales interesting (at the *kraal* on the left of the B6, 3 km before town as you approach from Windhoek), and there are both meat and dairy processing facilities in town.

The name 'Gobabis' is derived from a Nama word meaning 'the place where people had quarrelled', and referred to several conflicts which flared up between the Herero and the Nama people, as well as with settlers from the Cape colony that occupied the land. However, many locals believe it comes from *goabbes*, meaning 'the place of the elephants'; this is plausible, as the area along the Nossob River once had a population of elephants, and the settlement itself was a base for ivory hunters and a trading post for elephant tusks. The first Europeans to settle in the district were Rhenish missionaries and, in August 1856, Amraal Lambert decided to move to Gobabis and build a church and small school, and for many years the settlement was a popular stop-over for hunters and traders between what are now Namibia and Botswana. However, once all the profitable wild animals had been killed the trade and interest moved elsewhere and it was difficult to persuade people to come and settle in this dusty region on the edge of the Kalahari. The future of the town was only secured when the railway service was opened in November 1930, which greatly facilitated the export of cattle from the district to Windhoek and South Africa. In more recent years the prosperity of the town and region has been buoyed by the Trans-Kalahari Highway, which has greatly increased the number of people to the region and many hauliers use the road to transport goods from Walvis Bay to landlocked Botswana and onto Johannesburg.

The town itself has little to recommend it beyond its pretty churches (the greatest density in Namibia). For visitors driving across the Kalahari from Botswana this will be your first introduction to urban Namibia. Afrikaans is the very much the spoken tongue, and the white population is very conservative in its outlook. On your way through, a quick stop at the churches and a glimpse of Herero women and their 'traditional' costumes will probably suffice. It is a place for stocking up on supplies or a base for exploring the surrounding farms, which offer Bushmen art and 'experiences' (game viewing on foot and, for those interested, cattle ranching). In town there are petrol stations, banks, and a good range of shops including a large branch of **Shoprite** supermarket.

To the border
The 110 km road from Gobabis to the Buitepos–Mamuno Botswana border is straight and dull all the way, but it is in good condition, with a good number of guest farms and rest camps to tempt the weary; many will provide a decent breakfast or lunch. Traffic volume has increased considerably with the opening of the Trans-Kalahari Highway (tarred all the way), the best and quickest way to reach Namibia from Johannesburg. Just before you arrive at the border there are a couple of petrol stations and, on your left, the East Gate Service Station which has accommodation and a campsite (see Where to stay, page 101).

Border crossing

Buitepos (Namibia)–Mamuno (Botswana)

The border is open 0700-2400, but remember Namibia's daylight saving time is from the first Sunday of April to the first Sunday in September, meaning the times could be an hour earlier. Most visitors do not need visas for Botswana. As Botswana is part of the Southern Africa Development Community (SADC), you just have to sign a book to take a vehicle across the border and pay a road levy for Botswana in Namibian dollars, South African rand or Botswana pula..The Namibian dollar is not used in Botswana but the South African rand is, so ensure you've changed over any Namibian dollars over to rand before you reach the border. If in a hire car ensure you have documentation of permission to take a car into Botswana and have third-party insurance. It is not permitted to take meat into Botswana and you will be asked to step out onto the foot-and-mouth 'pad' to wipe your feet and your vehicle's tyres will be sprayed (like you do at the Red Line veterinary control fences elsewhere in Namibia).

The roads on the Botswana side are smooth tar, but they are long and straight with hardly any distractions; be careful of falling asleep at the wheel and do not be enticed into speeding – despite the remoteness, the Botswana traffic police (and their speed traps) are present. Do NOT drive at night along these roads. Unlike in Namibia, they are not fenced and stray animals on the side of the road, especially donkeys, and raptors actually on the road hunting for mice, can cause accidents. Plan your journey so you are driving in daylight hours.

After crossing the border there are two options; you can drive along the Trans-Kalahari Highway (A2 in Botswana), all the way to Johannesburg (1054 km) via Kang, Sekoma and the border at Lobatse/Zeerust, or alternatively branch off the Trans-Kalahari/A2, 210 km from the border and head north on the A3 to Maun (495 km); the springboard town for the Okavango Delta. At present there are only a few petrol stations along these routes, so make a point of filling your tank at the border. On the Trans-Kalahari Highway, fill up again at Kang, 391 km from Buitepos, and again at Jwaneng, 241 km from Kang, after which you are nearing Gaborone and petrol stations become more frequent. Towards Maun, the next fuel is at Ghanzi, 210 km from Buitepos, and again in Maun.

From the border the first suitable overnight accommodation for motorists is either in Kang or Ghanzi respectively. In Kang, the **$$-$ Kang Ultra Stop**, T+267-651 7294, www.kangultrastop.com, has guesthouse double/twin rooms with DSTV, plus cheaper family and budget rooms with showers, all rooms have a/c and tea and coffee stations, a well-equipped campsite, restaurant, bar and swimming pool, and there's an Engen petrol station next door with an ATM. In Ghanzi the **$ Kalahari Arms Hotel**, T+267-596298, www.kalahariarmshotel.com, has comfortable a/c chalets sleeping up to four people, with DSTV and tea and coffee facilities, a campsite, kids' playground, rather astonishingly a half-Olympic-size swimming pool to help you cool off after a long drive, and a menu that will warm the carnivore's heart. There is a Barclays Bank and a Spar supermarket in town.

⊛ East to Botswana listings

For hotel and restaurant price codes and other relevant information, see pages 21-28.

⊛ Where to stay

Windhoek to the border *p96, map p90*
$$$ Kiripotib Guest Farm, 160 km southwest of Windhoek; take the B6 east for 28 km, turn south on the C23 for 63 km to Dordabis, continue on the C23 towards Uhlenhorst for 55 km and follow signs for 10 km from the turning onto the D1488, T062-581419, www.kiripotib. com. A colourful jewellery workshop, spinning/weaving factory, working sheep farm and guest farm on the edge of the Kalahari with wide savannah views. 10 rooms, 2 chalets and 2 safari tents, with modern African decor, Wi-Fi, swimming pool, good home cooking, bar, hiking trails, a birdwatching hide, high-powered equipment for star-gazing, and informative, friendly hosts. Transfers from Windhoek and the airport. Items made here are also sold in the **Kirikara** shop in Swakopmund (see page 257).
$$ Arnhem Cave & Lodge, 43 km northeast of Dordabis on the D1482, or 58 km south from the B6 on the D1808, 4 km (signposted) from the road, T062-581885, www.arnhemcave.com. 4 self-catering chalets with 2 or 4 beds, though breakfast is included in the price, plus a **campsite ($)** with ablutions and field kitchen, bar and swimming pool, excellent meals on request. Guided nature walks and tours of the caves.
$$ Eningu Clayhouse Lodge, 1 km southwest of the D1471/D1482 junction, just off the M51, 65 km from Hosea Kutako Airport, T062-581880, www.eningulodge.com. Built of clay

bricks to blend into the dry Kalahari landscape, 9 rooms with attractive designs, central dining and lounge area, swimming pool, craft shop, good food and choice of wine, ideal for hiking and birding plus some game viewing (the waterhole is regularly visited by porcupines) and you can try archery. Transfers from Windhoek and the airport.
$$-$ Trans-Kalahari Inn, on the B6, midway between the airport and Windhoek, 23 km to each, T061-222877, www.transkalahari-inn.com. 9 neat rooms with African decor and bright white linen, **camping** on grass with electricity and *braais* and good views over the surrounding hills. Nice restaurant, homely bar with counter made from knarled tree trunks, pool, Wi-Fi, friendly German owners. They also operate a vehicle workshop and a facility to park up vehicles long term. Offers transfers from Windhoek and the airport.
$ Airport Lodge, on the B6 22 km from the airport and 23 km from Windhoek, T061-231491/2, www. airportlodgenamibia.com. 6 thatched self-catering chalets sleeping up to 4 with terraces and minibars, **campsite** with laundry and electric points, à la carte restaurant and bar, and swimming pool, and pleasant views. A good budget bet if you don't fancy staying downtown. Offers transfers.

Gobabis *p97, map p90*
$$-$ Goba Lodge & Rest Camp, Elim St (follow signs 1 km out of town), T062-564499, www.goba.iway.na. The best option in town, with 12 a/c rooms with DSTV, a big swimming pool, restaurant and plenty of Africanalia such as dugout canoes and carvings dotted

around. It's in the Nossob riverbed, and there is good birdwatching from its hide. There are also 10 budget rooms at the **campsite** 200 m from the main lodge which share ablutions and a fully equipped kitchen with campers.

$ Die Dam – Trans Kalahari End Resort, 1 km north of town, T062-565656, www.transkalahariendresort.com. Sitting on the pretty Tilda Viljoen Dam, 6 fully equipped self-catering thatched chalets, each with a loft with 2 extra beds, the restaurant here is in Gobabis's old jail – some of the windows still have bars, campsite with good hot showers and covered kitchen area, swimming pool.

To the border *p98, map p90*
$$$-$$ Kalahari Bush Breaks, on the B6, 26 km before the border, T062-568936, www.kalaharibushbreaks.com. A fabulous 3-storey thatched lodge with 8 rooms, plus 2 separate chalets and a **campsite** (**$**) overlooking a waterhole with open-air reed-wall ablutions and some sites have electricity and lights. Restaurant and bar with outdoor wooden deck, plunge pool, San (Bushmen) paintings nearby, hides for bird/game watching, horse riding, and there's a 20-km self-drive 4WD trail.
$$$-$ Harnas Wildlife Foundation & Guest farm, take the B6 for the border, turn north on the C22, it's a further 85 km, follow signs, T062-568828, www.harnas.org. Accommodation to suit all budgets from 7 smart a/c stone and wooden en suite chalets with kitchenettes, 3 self-catering tented igloos, or camping. Restaurant, lively bar, and swimming pool. The focus of the foundation is rehabilitating injured and orphaned game, and releasing animals back to the wild where possible. The

drives and walks around the centre are educational and you can see a large variety of animal and bird species in generous enclosures. There are some tame cheetahs that have been stars of a number of movies, leopard and a large lion enclosure, and the night-time walk offers the glimpse of the nocturnal creatures and includes a short drive out from the main farmhouse to see porcupine. Recommended especially for children.
$$-$ East Gate Rest Camp, on the B6 400 m before the Buitepos border, T062-560405, www.eastgate-namibia.com. Popular overnight stop at the border and a surprise in such a desolate region, with 13 bright blue self-catering bungalows sleeping 2-6, 13 cheaper cabins for 1-2 with shared bathrooms, and a campsite with good facilities on bright green lawns; great value from N$130 pp for a bed and N$70 pp camping. Restaurant and coffee shop that also offers takeaway packed lunches, swimming pool, shop selling *braai* packs (meat), ice and firewood and next door to a petrol station.

🍴 Restaurants

Gobabis *p97, map p90*
The restaurant in the **Goba Lodge & Rest Camp** is the best bet in town and is open to non-guests (see Where to stay, above). It has a long menu from salads and toasted sandwiches to grills and seafood. There is also a **Wimpy** attached to the Engen petrol station on Church St. Also on Church St near the FNB Bank is a large **Shoprite** supermarket, and the petrol stations in town are a good stop for snacks like hot pies, cold drinks and ice for cool boxes.

Contents

106 Otjiwarongo and around
107 Otjiwarongo
108 Around Otjiwarongo
110 Waterberg Plateau Park
113 Outjo
115 Listings

119 Etosha National Park
124 Listings

130 The Triangle
131 Road to the Triangle
131 Otavi
132 Tsumeb
134 Around Tsumeb
135 Grootfontein
138 Listings

142 Bushmanland and Kavango
143 Bushmanland
145 Khaudum National Park
147 Kavango
149 Listings

152 Caprivi
154 West Caprivi
159 East Caprivi
166 Listings

Footprint features

104 Don't miss …
111 The Battle of Waterberg
153 Berlin Conference – carving up the strip

Border crossings

Namibia–Botswana
144 Dobe
158 Mohembo
164 Ngoma Bridge
Namibia–Zimbabwe
164 Kazungula
Namibia–Zambia
165 Kazungula
165 Wenela–Sesheke

Etosha & the Northeast

At a glance

⊖ Getting around 2WD is sufficient in most places. Guided tours are on offer to Etosha from Windhoek.

⏱ Time required A minimum of 3 nights in the Etosha region. 1 week to head north and explore the Caprivi Strip.

☁ Weather Hot in summer, the cool, dry winter months are best for game-viewing in Etosha.

✕ When not to go Avoid Namibian and South African school holidays in Etosha (Dec-Jan) and the wet season in Caprivi (Feb-Mar).

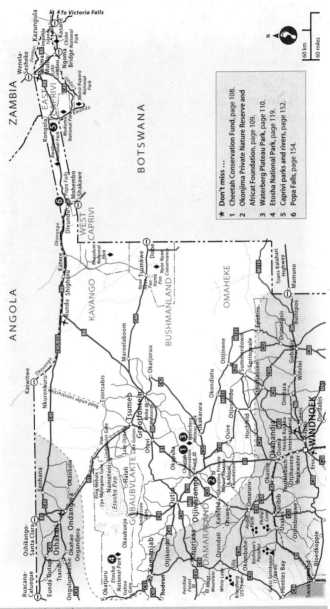

★ Don't miss ...
- 1 Cheetah Conservation Fund, page 108.
  Okonjima Private Nature Reserve and
  AfriCat Foundation, page 109.
- 3 Waterberg Plateau Park, page 110.
- 4 Etosha National Park, page 119.
- 5 Caprivi parks and rivers, page 152.
- 6 Popa Falls, page 154.

The north of Namibia is home to some of the country's principal attractions and is an almost inevitable part of any tour, due largely to the stunning landscapes and abundant wildlife in Etosha National Park. Visitors should allow at least a couple of days to view the game at this magnificent park, one of the highlights of any trip. As well as comfortable and accommodation within the park, a number of the country's most luxurious lodges are located on its perimeter, where game from Etosha wanders freely, providing an unforgettable and upmarket bush experience.

Lesser-known game reserves in the region include the well-stocked Waterberg Plateau Park, which offers some excellent hiking across an unusual limestone terrain. To the northeast, Khaudum National Park is in one of Namibia's more remote areas, deep in the flat and dry wilderness known as Bushmanland.

Also in the northeast, the Kavango and Caprivi regions provide a welcome change from the relentlessly dry landscapes for which the rest of the country is famous. The landscape here is dominated by rivers and green forests and, for overseas visitors, it offers something of 'real' Africa and presents a new range of vegetation and wildlife. Souvenir hunters will find some of Namibia's finest local crafts at the community-run markets and roadside stalls. The northeast is certainly a long drive from Windhoek but many hail it as their favourite corner of the country, and it provides easy access to attractions over the border in Botswana, Zambia and Zimbabwe.

Otjiwarongo and around

Meaning the 'place of the fat cattle' in Herero, the town of Otjiwarongo is a fast-growing commercial centre serving the farming communities in the surrounding area. It is strategically located in the central-north of Namibia on the B1 road linking Windhoek, with the triangle towns of Otavi, Tsumeb and Grootfontein, and is also a regular stopping-off place for people travelling to Etosha and the Waterberg Plateau. Nearby are the Cheetah Conservation Fund and Africat Foundation, which are both important organizations in the protection of Namibia's big cats and are well worth supporting. Namibia is home to 25% of the world's cheetah and 90% of these live on commercial farmland. Consequently they are under threat from farmers when they prey on their livestock. A day trip to the Cheetah Conservation Fund or an overnight visit to the Africat Foundation's guest farm, Okonjima, is highly recommended; not only is it the best place in Namibia to get close to cheetah and leopard, but also to learn about the plight of these creatures in Africa.

Arriving in Otjiwarongo

From Windhoek, the B1 heads north for 247 km and neatly dissects Otjiwarongo, as it runs through town as Hage Geingob Street. Along here you will find all the town's petrol stations, shops and banks. Intercape buses stop in Otjiwarongo at the Engen petrol station on Hugo Geingob Street on the route between Windhoek and Livingstone in Zambia. ▶ *See Intercape timetable, page 16, and Transport, page 118.*

Background

The town is officially deemed to have been founded in 1906 upon the arrival of the narrow-gauge railway linking the important mining centre of Tsumeb with the coast. However, as with many places of Namibia, there is evidence that San (Bushmen) were living in the area thousands of years ago. It is believed that groups of Damara settled here in the late 14th century where they lived as hunter-gatherers until the arrival of the Herero in the early part of the 19th century. The land was ideal for cattle grazing and the Herero gradually forced the Damara off the land and into the surrounding mountainous areas.

Where to stay 🛏

Acacia Park **6**
Bush Pillow Guest House **1**
C'est Si Bon **2**

Hadassa Guest House **3**
Out of Africa B&B **4**
Out of Africa Town Lodge **5**

Restaurants 🍴

Bäckerei Carstensen **3**
Kameldorn Garten & Restaurant **1**

In 1891 the Rhenish Mission Society secured the agreement of Herero Chief Kambazembi and a mission was established, opening the way for adventurers and traders to move further north. The Herero 'revolt' of 1904 and their eventual retreat from the German troops into the Omaheke *sandveld*, where thousands died of thirst and hunger, provided the colonial authorities with the opportunity to take control of the area. German (and later Afrikaner) cattle farmers were the principal benefactors.

Places in Otjiwarongo

The **Narrow Gauge Locomotive 'No 41'** sits outside the railway station. The locomotive is one of three manufactured by **Hensel & Son** in Germany in 1912 for Namibia's original narrow-gauge railway and remained in commission until 1960, when the Usakos–Otavi track was widened from 600 mm to 1067 mm (the Cape standard gauge).

To the east of town, the **Otjiwarongo Crocodile Ranch** ⓘ *T067-302121, Mon-Fri 0900-1600, Sat-Sun 1100-1400 N$20, children (under 16) N$10,* primarily rears the beasts for their skins and meat, and the skins are exported for use in making expensive leather shoes, wallets and briefcases, while the meat is sent to restaurants around the country. You can see plenty of breeding crocs and their young swimming around the pens, and guides are on hand to tell you anything you wanted to know about crocodiles, but the creatures appear a little lacklustre in the dank pools. There is also a small restaurant where you can grab a drink or snack; unsurprisingly the menu includes crocodile burgers and spare ribs.

Around Otjiwarongo → *For listings, see pages 115-118. Colour map 1, B5.*

Cheetah Conservation Fund

ⓘ *44 km east along the D2440 from Otjiwarongo, T067-306225, www.cheetah.org, daily 0800-1700, 2-hr tour to see the cheetah in the main facility, museum and education centre, N$180, children (under 12) N$90; 1-hr 'Cheetah Drive' N$480, children (under 12) N$240; 30-min 'Cheetah Run', daily 0800, N$480, no under 16s.*

The Cheetah Conservation Fund is a non-profit organization which was established in 1990 to research and conserve cheetahs and to provide information on their plight in Namibia. As well as providing a home and refuge for rescued cheetahs, the CCF monitors numbers in the wild and keeps an up-to-date health/gene pool database, it advises on predator management and relocation techniques, and works with all parties to promote awareness of their sleek protégés. You can visit to see the cheetahs in large spacious enclosures and see the very interesting museum dedicated to cheetah and the ecology of Namibia. As well as the standard tour, other activities include a drive inside the larger enclosures which is great for photography from the open-sided vehicles, and watching the cheetahs being exercised for about half an hour in the morning, when if lucky, you'll get to see an adult run at full pelt (cheetahs are capable or running up to 80 kph, but only over a short distance). If you are here Monday-Friday at 1400 or Saturday-Sunday at 1200, you'll also get to see the cheetahs being fed in addition to any of the activities. There's a gift shop selling everything and anything cheetah related and the

Cheetah Café serves breakfast, lunch and tea and cakes, as well as cheese platters and homemade ice cream from the farm's own goat's milk creamery. There's also a pleasant guesthouse here in a restored farm building (see Where to stay, page 116), and overnight rates include all activities.

Okonjima Private Nature Reserve and Africat Foundation

ⓘ *48 km south of Otjiwarongo on the B1 take a well-signposted private road west for 18 km, T067-687032, www.okonjima.com. 1½-hr tours depart Sep-Mar 1100 and 1330, Apr-Aug 1030 and 1230, N\$385, children (under 12) N\$240, no under 4s.*

Okonjima means 'the place of baboons', in Herero, and is a 20,000-ha private nature reserve on a former farm and is also home to the Africat Foundation; a non-profit organization dedicated to the conservation and protection of Namibia's

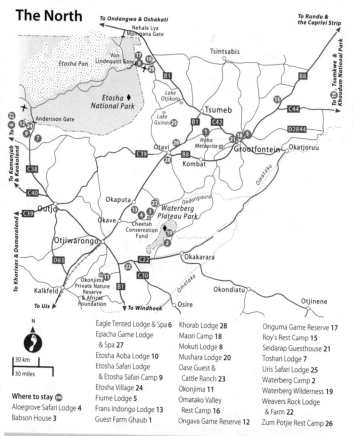

The North

Where to stay 🛏
Aloegrove Safari Lodge **4**
Babson House **3**
Eagle Tented Lodge & Spa **6**
Epacha Game Lodge & Spa **27**
Etosha Aoba Lodge **10**
Etosha Safari Lodge & Etosha Safari Camp **9**
Etosha Village **24**
Fiume Lodge **5**
Frans Indongo Lodge **13**
Guest Farm Ghaub **1**
Khorab Lodge **28**
Maori Camp **18**
Mokuti Lodge **8**
Mushara Lodge **20**
Oase Guest & Cattle Ranch **23**
Okonjima **11**
Omatako Valley Rest Camp **16**
Ongava Game Reserve **12**
Onguma Game Reserve **17**
Roy's Rest Camp **15**
Seidarap Guesthouse **21**
Toshari Lodge **7**
Uris Safari Lodge **25**
Waterberg Camp **2**
Waterberg Wilderness **19**
Weavers Rock Lodge & Farm **22**
Zum Potjie Rest Camp **26**

30 km
30 miles

wild carnivores. It was founded in the early 1990s and started out primarily as a welfare organization rescuing cats like cheetah and leopard from farmland where they have been traditionally regarded as pests. But over the years it has developed into an education and research facility to find other ways in which to preserve the wild cheetah and leopard population. For example, they advise farmers how to avoid conflict in the first place by corralling their livestock at night and employing herders to protect the animals. They also run outreach programmes to educate young people in Namibia about conservation; it is after all the youth that are the future farmers.

Day visitors can go on the tour to meet some of the resident leopard and cheetah that are housed in the rehabilitation enclosures and guides explain the work Africat do. Ensure you get there in time for lunch (1130-1400) either before or after the tours start in the pleasant restaurant and information centre decorated with stunning photographs of the cats. There are four lodges in the reserve and overnight guests have a full, informative agenda, including viewing the cats in the centre, as well as tracking the free-roaming leopard in the reserve by vehicle or on foot, and there are also guided San (Bushmen) trails, and after dinner guests can watch nocturnal creatures such as porcupine and honey badgers from a hide. Although Okonjima does not guarantee leopard sightings, there is certainly a good chance and one of the highlights is watching leopard in the early evening, a wonderful opportunity for photos. ▸▸ *See Where to stay, page 116.*

Waterberg Plateau Park → *For listings, see pages 115-118. Colour map 1, B5.*

ⓘ *T067-305001, www.nwr.com.na, gates open 0600-1800 (for day visitors), until 2100 (for overnight visitors), entry N$80, children (under 16) free, cars N$10, 4-hr game drives 0700 & 1500, N$300 pp, no under 6s. The rest camp has a shop, a restaurant (0700-0830, 1200-1330, 1900-2100) and bar (1200-1400, 1800-2200), petrol station and swimming pool with pool bar (0900-1800).*

The Waterberg Plateau is located 280 km north of Windhoek, and the mountain owes its name to the springs surfacing on its lower slopes. Known to the Herero-speaking people as *Oueverumue*, or 'narrow gate', it is Namibia's only mountain game park, and the plateau rises up to 200 m above the surrounding plain, extending some 50 km by 16 km. The sharp barrier of the plateau presents a stark contrast to the monotonous, scrubby, bushveld plain below, and has operated as a game sanctuary for endangered species since 1972. Today, it is of interest for its rare animal populations, atypical flora and striking sandstone topography, as well as being the scene of a historic encounter between German and Herero troops.

Arriving in Waterberg Plateau Park

Turn off the B1, 22 km south of Otjiwarongo, onto the C22. Follow this road for 42 km before turning left onto the D2512. Follow this for a further 17 km to the Waterberg Camp. No self-driving is allowed in the park but there are 10 gentle one- to three-hour demarcated walking trails around the camp and up onto the

The Battle of Waterberg

In January 1904, the Herero people, led by Chief Samuel Maharero, facing increasing pressure to take action over lost lands or for Maharero to stand down as Paramount Herero Chief, initiated a revolt against the Germans. Initial Herero attacks were successful, but following the appointment of General von Trotha as German commander in the middle of the year, with the expectation that Trotha was to end the revolt with decisive military victory, the tide started to turn against the Herero. As a growing number of Herero men, women and children retreated to the springs on the Waterberg Plateau with their cattle, the scene was set for the most decisive battle of the war.

The Waterberg lay 100 km east of the railhead source of German supplies, so Trotha spent nearly three months (June, July, and part of August) transporting troops and supplies by ox-drawn carts from the railhead to the site of the expected battle. In the meantime, the Herero, estimated around 60,000 men, women, and children, with an equal number of cattle, drew on meager grass and water supplies on the Waterberg while awaiting overtures from the Germans.

The Battle of Waterberg took place on 11 August 1904. The Germans had a total of about 1500 men, as well as 30 cannons and a dozen machine guns. Estimates of the strength of the Herero forces range from 35,000 to 80,000 with between 5000 and 6000 guns at their disposal. As the day progressed, the battle moved deeper into the bush, stretching over a 40-km front, with neither side able to establish a telling advantage. However, on the morning of 12 August, a German signal unit on the plateau noticed a huge cloud of dust heading southeast. The Herero were retreating into the Omaheke sandveld rather than surrendering to the enemy.

The Germans had won a tactical victory by driving the Herero from the Waterberg, but had failed in their intention to end the Herero revolt with a decisive battle. Trotha soon ordered the pursuit of the Herero eastward into the desert, with the intention of preventing Herero reorganization by depriving them of pastureland and watering holes. Over the next months, while Maherero and between 500 to 1500 men crossed the Kalahari into Bechuanaland, many thousands of Herero men, women and children, with their cattle, died of hunger and thirst on the trek into exile.

In the years immediately following the battle and the exodus of the Herero, the land around the Waterberg was sold off to European settlers. The small graveyard near the rest camp is testimony to some of the Germans who fell during the battle, but there is no record here of the many more Herero that were killed.

plateau, as well as longer four-day wilderness trails. Additionally three- to four-hour game drives set off early morning and mid-afternoon from the rest camp, and stop at game-viewing hides, often well frequented with game. Book these on arrival since this is a popular activity.

Vegetation and wildlife

Vegetation on the plateau is lush-green, subtropical dry woodland, with tall trees, grassy plains and a variety of ferns, which is in stark contrast to the acacia savannah at the base of the plateau. The mixture of very sandy soils and the Etjo sandstone cause the plateau to act like a sponge, absorbing any water that falls. The water is sucked into the soil until it reaches a layer of impermeable stone, from where it runs off underground to emerge on the southeast side of the plateau as springs. It is from the springs that the plateau gets its name.

The 40,549-ha area was proclaimed a park in 1972, originally as a sanctuary for rare and endangered species, including buffalo and roan and sable antelopes which were relocated from the Kavango and Caprivi regions. The aim was to breed these animals and then restock the areas from where they originated. Blue wildebeest were brought from Daan Viljoen game park, near Windhoek, and white rhino from then-Natal (South Africa), followed. Black rhino were reintroduced to the area from Damaraland in 1989. Today, among the game roaming on the plateau are buffalo, gemsbok, eland, giraffe, kudu, black-backed jackal, brown hyena, leopard and baboon, as well as those animals mentioned above. The environs of the rest camp are home to several delightful small mammal species including the diminutive Damara dik-dik, banded mongoose and bush babies might reveal themselves at dusk.

In addition to the game, the park has an estimated 200 species of birds. These include Namibia's only surviving colony of the Cape vulture, along with birds of prey such as the black eagle, the booted eagle and the pale chanting goshawk. There are also plenty of smaller birds such as the red-billed francolin (whose distinctive call can be heard at sunrise), five different hornbills, and the pretty rosy-faced lovebird.

Hiking in Waterberg Plateau Park

Camp trails There are 10 demarcated walking trails around the camp and up onto the plateau. Photocopied maps should be available from reception; if not, get your bearings using the three-dimensional display at reception and strike out along the well-marked trails. These gentle one- to three-hour walks are an excellent way of seeing the ruins of the **Old Mission**, as well as enjoying the flora and fauna, without undertaking a major expedition. There are two excellent four-day trails in the park and after days in the solitude and silence of the plateau it can feel strange going back down the mountain into civilization again.

Waterberg Wilderness Trail ⓘ *50 km, 4 days, N$250 per person, no children under 12.* This is a guided wilderness trail across the plateau, starting from the resort at 1400 on every second, third and fourth Thursday of the month, and arriving back on the Sunday afternoon (April to November only). The hike, which is led by an (armed) expert on the region's flora and fauna, overnights at the rustic base camps in the wilderness area. The distances covered in a day will depend on the fitness and requirements of the group but you should expect to walk 10-15 km each day. Only one group (six to eight people) is permitted per week and reservations should be made in advance with NWR in Windhoek or Swakopmund. Hikers must bring their own food and sleeping bag. Vehicles may be parked safely at the park gate at the beginning of the trail and transport is provided back at the end.

Waterberg Unguided Trail ⓘ *42 km, 4 days, N$100 per person, no children under 12.* This unaccompanied trail starts at the resort on Wednesday at 0900 and heads up onto the plateau before returning to the resort on Saturday (April to November only). Once up on the plateau itself, the trail winds around the sandstone *koppies* on the southeastern edge of the plateau, through glades of weeping wattle, silver bushwillow and laurel fig trees. It is aimed at reasonably fit, self-sufficient hikers and nature lovers who want to enjoy the scenery and wildlife and to have an adventure. Accommodation is in stone shelters with pit latrines; water is provided, but hikers must take everything else. Hikes are 7-14 km per day, only one group (three to 10 people) is permitted per week and since rhino and leopard inhabit the area, the trail is undertaken at the hiker's risk; you must stay on the tracks and not deviate at any time. Again, reservations are through NWR.

Outjo → *For listings, see pages 115–118. Colour map 1, B5. Phone code: 067.*

Just under 70 km northwest of Otjiwarongo on the B1, Outjo means 'little hills' in Herero and serves as a commercial centre for the large farms of the region and is considered the gateway to Etosha National Park from the southerly direction. It is located in an area of woodland savannah supporting both cattle and abundant game, and if you have been travelling in the south of the country, or have come

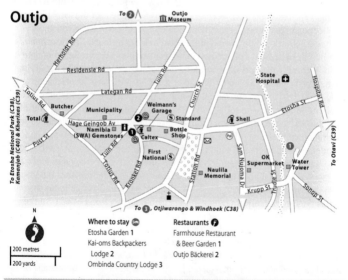

Outjo

Where to stay 🛏
Etosha Garden **1**
Kai-oms Backpackers
  Lodge **2**
Ombinda Country Lodge **3**

Restaurants 🍴
Farmhouse Restaurant
  & Beer Garden **1**
Outjo Bäckerei **2**

up from the coast, you will notice a far greater number and variety of trees in the landscape. As you continue north towards Etosha, keep an eye out for antelope sheltering in the shade of the trees and warthog crossing the road.

Arriving in Outjo

Most visitors to Outjo are en route to or from Etosha and travelling on the C38, and the town is 117 km south of Okaukuejo rest camp in the park. Outjo is also a good jump-off point for Damaraland and Kaokoland (see pages 176 and 192), with both Kamanjab and Khorixas within easy striking distance on good roads, the C40 and the C39, respectively. **Namibia (SWA) Gemstones** ① *8 Hage Geingob Av, T067-313072, www.namibiagemstones.com, Mon-Fri 0900-1700, Sat 0900-1200,* sells semiprecious minerals and gemstones, and also doubles as the tourist office and is very helpful on local information. You will also find a decent spread of Etosha information and souvenir books available in the park itself.

Places in Outjo

The first Europeans to settle here were big game hunters and traders in around 1880. By 1895, part of the German army was stationed here when they constructed several solid buildings, some of which still stand today. One of the more important roles for the army when they were not at war was to help to try and prevent the spread of rinderpest from the Kaokoland and Angola. They also acted as early anti-poaching units.

Overnighters won't miss much if they head off first thing in the morning, but anyone with an interest in local history might enjoy a visit to the museum as well as admiring the old Water Tower. The **Outjo Museum** ① *at the north end of Tuin Rd, Mon-Fri 1000-1200,1400-1600, N$5,* contains an account of the local history and a collection of gemstones, examples of which can still be found if you know where to look. The museum building is also known as **Franke House**. This was one of the first homes to be built in Outjo and dates from around 1899. Its first occupant was Major Victor Franke who was one of the last local commanders who made a name for himself in leading a punitive raid against the Portuguese in Angola in 1914.

In 1900, the settlement ran into water supply problems; the natural fountain could no longer provide for all the extra people and livestock. At the end of the year the German troops started to dig a well in the dry riverbed, while concurrently beginning construction of the **Water Tower**. The role of the tower was to house a wooden pump powered by wind sails. In March 1902 the first water started to flow, it was lifted into a concrete dam and was then carried over 600 m by pipes to the army barracks, a hospital and the stables. The 9.4-m-high tower remains, being made from local stone and clay, but the sail mechanism has not survived. Today the tower stands on a stone platform between the **Etosha Garden Hotel** (who own the land it stands on) and the dry riverbed; it is protected as a national monument and is an important local landmark, rather like the Franke Tower in Omaruru (see page 285). A lesser known monument from the past is the **Naulila Memorial** standing in the old German cemetery near the post office. In October 1914 a group of German officials and soldiers were massacred by the Portuguese near Fort Naulila on the

Angolan side of the Kunene River. More troops were killed a couple of months later, on 18 December 1914, when a force under the command of Major Victor Franke was sent to avenge the earlier loss of life. In 1933 the Naulila Memorial was built in memory of both expeditions.

◉ Otjiwarongo and around listings

For hotel and restaurant price codes and other relevant information, see pages 21-28.

◉ Where to stay

Otjiwarongo *p107, map p107*
$$ Bush Pillow Guest House, Son St, T067-303885, www.bushpillow.com.
A tidy set-up with friendly hosts knowledgeable about the local area, and 7 rooms with fans, DSTV, colourful well-designed decor, welcoming lounge and small library, Wi-Fi, restaurant and bar, dinner on request, small swimming pool, secure parking.
$$ C'est Si Bon Hotel, Swembad St, turn left between the BP petrol station and the church if entering town from Windhoek, T067-301240, www.cestsibon. com. The nicest accommodation in town, laid out like a resort with 56 large a/c rooms with DSTV in thatched bungalows, some with lofts for children, a central grassed courtyard with swimming pool, cosy bar and restaurant. Immaculately tended, friendly, tasty à la carte food, and not unreasonably priced.
$$-$ Hadassa Guest House, 36 Lang St, T067-307505, www.hadassaguesthouse. com. Smart newly built guesthouse run by a French couple with 9 nicely decorated a/c rooms with Wi-Fi and DSTV, motel-style parking, pool, restaurant with outside terrace and good pre-booked dinners, little luxuries like flowers and free car wash make it excellent value.

$ Out of Africa Town Lodge, on the B1 at southern edge of town, T067-302230, and **Out of Africa B&B**, 94 Tuin St, T067-303397, www.out-of-afrika.com.
2 venues in town, the lodge is more business traveller orientated with 20 rooms with a/c and DSTV, in a modern, bright white, Cape colonial-style building, swimming pool, bistro restaurant, lounge bar and coffee shop. The B&B has a more personable atmosphere with 10 comfortable a/c rooms with DSTV, sunny breakfast room, lounge, swimming pool, and friendly hands-on hosts focused on tourists' needs and willing to answer your questions. Both are excellent value and can also arrange car hire; www. namibia-rent-a-car.com.

Guest farms
$$$ Frans Indongo Lodge, 43 km on the B1 towards Otavi, T067-687012, www.indongolodge.com. 12 comfortable modern rooms in either the main house or chalets with DSTV and a/c, some with wheelchair access, swimming pool, lovely central *lapa* area under thatch with pretty gardens, all meals available and guests can go for walks in the area which is home to a number of antelope. Owner Frans Indongo is famous as being one of northern Namibia's biggest entrepreneurs, who owns a number of businesses.
$$$-$$ Aloegrove Safari Lodge, 18 km north of town on the B1 turn right for another 18 km, T067-306231/232, www. aloegrove.com. Perched on top of a

hill with good views of the open bush, 6 spacious rustic cabins built of stone and reed, 3 with self-catering facilities, built around a small swimming pool, restaurant and bar offering farm-style cuisine, game drives on offer as well as visits to the nearby Cheetah Conservation Fund.

$$-$ Weavers Rock Guest Farm, 27 km south of town on the B1, take the C22 for 5 km, T067-304885, www.weaversrock. com. In an elevated position with great views across this cattle farm, 4 smart bungalows sleeping up to 4, plus a clutch of cheaper stone double/twin chalets with open reed shower/toilet and *braai*, and a shady campsite. Good farm-style food, swimming pool, friendly hosts, and activities include a hiking trail or sundowner drives to the top of the Hohenfels Mountain on the farm, and the owners' dogs will guide you to a nearby waterhole.

Around Otjiwarongo *p108, map p109*
Cheetah Conservation Fund
$$$$ Babson House, 44 km east along the D2440 from Otjiwarongo, T067-237294, www.cheetah.org. The CCF's guesthouse with 3 stylish rooms in a restored 1940s farm building, the veranda has views of the Waterberg Plateau and the cheetahs live only a few meters away, lounge with deep leather couches and a private chef prepares meals. Rates include food and all activities at the CFF centre and on the farm including game drives.

Okonjima Private Nature Reserve & Africat Foundation
$$$$-$$$ Okonjima, 48 km south of Otjiwarongo on the B1, turn west for 18 km along a well-signposted private road, T067-687032, www.okonjima.com. **Plains Camp** has 14 rooms overlooking a waterhole with tasteful locally crafted furnishing, the separate **Bush Camp**, 3 km from Plains Camp, has 9 large, thatched rondavels where beds look straight through the open walls on to the savannah. The **Bush Suite** and **African Villa** are 2 exclusive luxury lodges and have their own chefs, guides and game-driving vehicle. All 4 camps offer gourmet food, indoor and outdoor dining areas and bar, lounge and library, swimming pool, and rates are all-inclusive of activities. The **campsite ($)** has 4 large pitches, each with their own kitchen, shelter and private bathroom, they cost N$550 per person which sounds expensive but includes one free activity such as the leopard or cheetah tracking. You really need 2 nights here to appreciate everything on offer.

Waterberg Plateau Park *p110*
Waterberg Camp, reservations through Namibia Wildlife Resorts (NWR), Windhoek, T061-285 7200, www.nwr. com.na. Fairly densely packed alongside each other but nicely refurbished in recent years and with great views of the plateau's sandstone cliffs above, accommodation is in 33 well-equipped self-catering chalets sleeping 2-5 and 34 double/twin rooms with tea and coffee stations; all rates include breakfast. Caravan and **campsite ($)** with ablution blocks, camp kitchens with gas burners and *braai* pits. Keep an eye on your possessions as thieving baboons can be a problem here. Facilities include a shop, restaurant (in the old German police station built in 1908), kiosk, petrol station and swimming pool, and game drives can be organized from reception.

Guest farms

\$\$\$ Waterberg Wilderness, well signposted 8 km northeast of the park entrance on the D2512, T067-687018, www.waterberg-wilderness.com. A private reserve with 10 rooms in the main lodge, which is set by a small river at the foot of the plateau in a shady, peaceful location, and 7 more expensive chalets with fireplaces and plunge pools a 15-min drive up in the valley beneath the sandstone cliffs. Very stylish decor, guided hikes, rates are full board and include afternoon tea. Also a shady **campsite (\$)** high up on the hill with hot showers, swimming pool and a bar/kiosk selling drinks and *braai* meat.

Outjo and around *p113, map p113*
Also see **Bambatsi Guest Farm** and **Vingerklip Lodge**, page 189, or the lodges on or around the C38 between Outjo and Etosha.
\$\$-\$ Ombinda Country Lodge, signposted 1 km south of Outjo on the C38, T067-313181, www.ombindalodge. com. Nothing special but adequate if you choose to overnight in Outjo, 20 simple chalets, most thatched with reed walls, some have bathrooms partially open to the sky, à la carte menu served in a large thatched *lapa* by the swimming pool, basic **campsite** with *braais* and electricity.
\$ Etosha Garden Hotel, Krupp St, T067-313130, www.etosha-garden-hotel. com. Old-style town hotel in an historic sandstone building, 20 rooms set around the tranquil and shady garden with jacaranda trees, small swimming pool, restaurant offering game specialities, home-baked bread and the likes of apple strudel, and a pretty beer garden.
\$ Kai-oms Backpackers Lodge, corner Harold and Meester Sts, T067-313597,

www.kai-oms.com. The name means 'big house' in Damara, and this building dating to the 1940s has been in the past a stables, a car repair shop and school hostel. Brightly decorated doubles/twins, dorm with 9 beds and sandy camping spaces around the back with *braai* pits, good shared ablutions and a self-catering kitchen. The owners are helpful with advice on Etosha.

🍴 Restaurants

Otjiwarongo *p107, map p107*
\$\$-\$ Kameldorn Garten & Restaurant, 17 Hindenburg St, opposite Shell, T0812-445967. Mon and Thu 0700-1700, Wed 1100-1700, Fri 0700-1500, 1800-2100, Sat 0800-1500, Sun 1200-2100. The best place to eat in town and a pleasant café/bistro with tables outside in the lush flowering garden with a parrot perched on a gnarled log at the entrance. Meals are prepared with fresh, local ingredients; Namibian oysters, dairy and meat supplied by local farmers, and home-grown vegetables and herbs. Breakfasts and light meals, and dinner Fri and Sun, free Wi-Fi.
\$ Bäckerei Carstensen, St George's St, near Shoprite, T067-302326. Mon-Sat 0800-1600. Bakery selling the freshest of breads and *brötchens* of all shapes and sizes, great apple strudel and cheesecake, strong filter coffee and light meals during the day.

Outjo *p113, map p113*
Outjo is definitely worth working into an itinerary to stop for lunch on the way to/from Etosha thanks to the 2 great restaurants opposite each other; both offer Wi-Fi.
\$\$-\$ The Farmhouse Restaurant & Beer Garden, 8 Kronkel Rd, T067-

313444, www.thefarmhouse-outjo.com.
Mon 0700-1700, Tue-Sun 0700-2100.
Swiss-owned (look for the Swiss flag),
lovely café serving home-made cakes,
excellent coffees, good light lunches and
suppers including pizza, kudu burgers
and generous salads, wine and beer.
Shady outdoor tables and also offers
4 B&B rooms (**$**).

$ Outjo Bäckerei, 9 Hage Geingob St,
T067-313055. Mon-Fri 0630-1600,
Sat 0700-1400. Friendly old-style
bakery established in 1950 with a nice
courtyard and an ideal stop on an early
start from Outjo to pick up a morning
hot roll or meat pie. Also delicious meals
like schnitzels, burgers, vegetarian
quiche, game meat steaks and sweet
and savoury filled pancakes. As well as
Wi-Fi also has computer terminals; worth
emailing home from here if only for an
excuse to tuck into the pastries.

O Shopping

Otjiwarongo *p107, map p107*
Shoprite, is on St George's St, while
Pick 'n' Pay and **Spar** are in the centre of
town on Hage Geingob St. All sell ice and
firewood and have takeaway counters.

Outjo *p113, map p113*
There are several very different routes
from Outjo; whichever you choose make
sure you have refuelled and have plenty
of water, all the routes lead into remote
regions, where supplies in small village
centres cannot be relied upon. Outjo
has small grocery stores and butchers,
but if you're coming from the south,
Otjiwarongo has a far better choice of
provisions in its large chain supermarkets.

⊖ Transport

Otjiwarongo *p107, map p107*
249 km to Windhoek; 70 km Outjo;
187 km Okaukuejo (Etosha); 379 km
to Swakopmund.

Road
For **Intercape** coaches to **Windhoek** via
Okahandja and north to **Katima Mulilo**,
see timetable on page 16. Buses stop at
the Engen petrol station on Hage Geingob
St. It is possible to use Intercape for the
3-hr journey to/from Windhoek, but the
buses arrive and depart at inconvenient
times during the night. Okaukuejo is
also well served by shared taxis on the
Windhoek–Oshakati route, though there
is a limited service towards Outjo.

Outjo *p113, map p113*
318 km to Windhoek; 117 km to
Okaukuejo; 155 km to Kamanjab; 132 km
to Khorixas; 70 km to Otjiwarongo.

ⓘ Directory

Otjiwarongo *p107, map p107*
Medical services State Hospital,
T067-300900, Hospital St, eastern edge
of town. The best private hospital in
the region is the 24-hr **Medi Clinic
Otjiwarongo**, Son St, T067-130 3734,
www.mediclinic.co.za.

Outjo *p113, map p113*
Mechanical repairs Weimanns
Garage, T067-313111, 10 Hage Geingob
Av. Stop here for final checks before
going north – it's been serving Outjo
since 1952. **Medical services** State
Hospital, T067-313 044, Hospital Rd.

Etosha National Park

Etosha is one of Africa's great national parks and the game viewing here is on a par with South Africa's Kruger, Zimbabwe's Hwange, Kenya's Masai Mara and Tanzania's Serengeti. Some 114 mammal species, 110 reptile species and more than 340 different bird species have been identified. The park sees hundreds of visitors daily, who are catered for in three well-appointed rest camps and the two newer exclusive camps. Each rest camp has a floodlit watering hole, which offers overnight visitors the chance to see good numbers of game in an unusual environment.

The central feature of the park is the Etosha Pan, a huge depression that becomes a lake during summers of exceptional rainfall, although even then the water is rarely more than a few centimetres deep. Most of the time it is a blinding expanse of flat, white, cracked and dried mud that shimmers with mirages and is dotted with spiralling dust devils. Seeing animals pace across this surreal landscape is one of the sights that make Etosha so special. Indeed, the name Etosha is usually translated as 'great white place' or 'place of emptiness'.

There are no roads across the pan, but along the southern fringe a network of gravel roads offers some exceptional views of this natural feature which can be seen clearly from space. Another unique aspect of Etosha is the fine white dust during the dry season – your car will certainly be covered with it but in some cases so are the animals, so to follow a white elephant as it ambles down a gravel road is a delightful experience. A visit to Etosha is deservedly one of the highlights of any visit to Namibia.

Arriving in Etosha National Park → *Colour map 1, A4. Phone code: 067.*

Getting there Each of the three **Namibia Wildlife Resorts** (NWR) main rest camps within the park (Okaukuejo, Halali and Namutoni) have their own **airstrips** which are used by tour operators and charter companies, from where guests are also transferred to the two NWR exclusive camps (Dolomite and Onkoshi). Some of the smarter lodges on the edge of the park also have airstrips and can arrange **fly-in safaris**.

By road there are three gates open to the public, so where you enter the park depends on what direction you've come from: **Andersson Gate** is to the north of Outjo and is 17 km south of Okaukuejo; **Von Lindequist Gate** is at the eastern end of the park and is 12 km from Namutoni; and **King Nehale Lya Mpingana Gate** is in the northeast off the B1 between Tsumeb and Ondangwa. A fourth gate, **Galton Gate** lies at the southwestern end of the park off the C35, but can currently only be used for self-drive visitors who book a night at the new Dolomite Camp, in the formerly restricted western region of the park. Access to this wilder area of the park is set to change as infrastructure improves and the general public may soon be allowed to use this gate. Additionally, on the route from Okaukuejo to Dolomite there are about 15 waterholes,

Etosha National Park

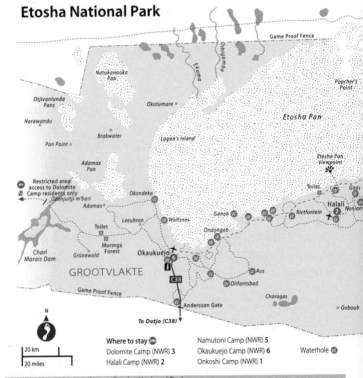

Where to stay 📍
Dolomite Camp (NWR) 3
Halali Camp (NWR) 2

Namutoni Camp (NWR) 5
Okaukuejo Camp (NWR) 6
Onkoshi Camp (NWR) 1

Waterhole 📍

which – though they have been there for several years now – are only beginning to attract animals, as it takes time for the wildlife to become aware of them.

The shortest route from Windhoek, 447 km, is to follow the B1 north as far as Otjiwarongo; from here, take the C38 for Outjo and continue north to Andersson Gate. For visitors approaching from the Caprivi, follow the B8 south as far as Grootfontein; from here take the C42 to Tsumeb where the road joins the B1 north, follow the signs for Etosha, Ondangwa and Oshakati. The turn-off for the Von Lindequist Gate is clearly signposted 74 km from Tsumeb. Namutoni camp is just inside the park. If coming from the far north, King Nehale Lya Mpingana is accessed off the B1, 101 km south of Ondangwa. Bear in mind that as there is no camp near this gate you need to arrive here about two hours before sunset so there's enough time to drive to Namutoni. If you plan to travel to Namibia's far north from Namutoni, this gate will save you a 100-km drive around Etosha's eastern border.

It is a good idea to plan an itinerary so you are entering the park either at Okaukuejo, or through the Namutoni or King Nehale Lya Mpingana gates, and exiting the park at the opposite end. This way you will not only be able to explore all the game-viewing roads linking the three main rest camps (Okaukuejo, Halali and Namutoni), but you will avoid doubling back on your route.

Best time to visit The park is open year round, but there are three distinct seasons that affect the nature-viewing experience. Many regard the best time to visit the park as the cooler, drier winter months (August and September) when a shortage of natural pools draws animals to the 50 or so artificial water points, many of which are visible from the rest camps or reachable by car. The other popular time of year for visitors is December and January (when it is very hot); this is more to do with local school holidays than any particular condition within the park. It may be difficult to book accommodation during the most popular periods, especially at weekends, and during school holidays. If visiting from overseas, consider booking your accommodation prior to your arrival in Namibia. For bird enthusiasts the best time to visit the park is during and after the rains, November to April.

Background

The central feature of Etosha is the large pan which covers 23% of the park and is 130 km long and 72 km wide; a fantastic and most unusual natural feature. The first Europeans to see the pan and write about it were Charles Andersson of Sweden and Francis Galton from Britain, who came here in 1851 en route to Owamboland. Having been told it was a large lake, they were very disappointed to find it was bone dry.

There is a San (Bushmen) legend that tells of a group who strayed into Heiqum lands only to be surrounded by brutal hunters who killed all the men and children. One of the young women rested under a tree with her dead child in her arms; she wept so much that her tears formed a giant lake. After the sun had dried her tears the ground was left covered in salt – and so the Etosha Pan was formed. The pan is indeed very alkaline, sediment samples have a pH of higher than 10, with a sodium content of more than 3%. This attracts the local wildlife, which requires salt in its diet.

The first European interference in the region came in the 1890s when the German administration was faced with the rinderpest outbreak. To try and control the spread, a livestock-free buffer zone was established along the southern margins of the pan. In order to enforce the restrictions on the movement of cattle, two small military units were posted in tiny forts at Namutoni and Okaukuejo. The park was created in 1907 by Governor Friedrich von Lindequist (it celebrated its centenary in 2007; the same year the three camps got extensive refits). Since its proclamation, the boundaries have been significantly changed on a number of occasions but the park has covered today's area of 22,912 sq km since 1970.

The German forts at Okaukuejo and Namutoni were converted into police posts to help establish control over the Owambo kingdoms to the north. The fort at Namutoni was made famous after it was attacked on 28 January 1904 by several hundred Ndonga warriors serving King Nehale, and was burnt to the ground. The present building at Namutoni dates from 1906 when a new and larger fort was completed. The last troops stationed here surrendered to the South African forces under the command of General Coen Britz on 6 July 1915. In 1957 the fort was restored as a tourist camp.

Visiting Etosha National Park → For listings, see pages 124-129.

① Entry N$80; children (under 16) free; N$10 per car; fees are for 24 hrs. Guided morning or afternoon game drives N$300, night drives US$400, children (6-16) half price, no children under 6.

Gates are open from sunrise to sunset; the times are posted daily at each rest camp and gate. By sunset, visitors must either have left the park through one of the gates, or have arrived at their overnight camp. Do not stay out in the park after sunset or you may find yourself in serious trouble. In any case, if staying overnight, each camp has a wonderful floodlit waterhole and three-hour guided night drives are on offer. The distance between **Halali** in the middle of the park to both **Namutoni** and **Okaukuejo** is 70 km. The speed limit throughout the park is 60 kph, but you will probably average 20-30 kph when you factor in plenty of stops to watch the game. The roads are gravel but in very good condition and perfectly negotiable in a saloon car. It is prohibited to get out of your car except at the toilet stops, and never go off road; tyre tracks leave scars and damage the environment. In the event of a breakdown or a puncture do not leave your car, you may be attacked; stay in the vehicle until help arrives.

There are countless drives and waterholes that you can visit for game-viewing, and they all have their different merits so it is difficult to offer recommendations. The rangers are the best source of advice as to where game is congregating and where the cats and large mammals have been spotted each day. Each camp reception also has a game-viewing book where visitors write up the location of the most recent sightings. Remember that it pays to be patient – once you have found a waterhole that appeals to you turn the engine off, keep quiet and wait. In addition to your own self-drive excursions, it's possible to sign up for a guided game drive in the early morning, late afternoon or at night. These can be booked at the reception of each rest camp and have the added attraction of being in open-topped safari vehicles with raised seating and with a guide who has a well-trained eye.

Vegetation and wildlife The most commonly occurring species are the animals that prefer open savannah country. You can expect to see large herds of blue wildebeest, gemsbok, Burchell's zebra, eland, giraffe, springbok and elephant, as well as hyena, warthog and the ubiquitous ground squirrel. Another good reason for visiting Etosha is to see the endangered black rhinoceros. While it is difficult to spot these animals in thick bush during the day, they frequently visit the floodlit waterhole at Okaukuejo. All of the large cats are found in Etosha and there are good numbers of lion, which are frequently seen, especially around Fischer Pan in the northeast, and late-night visitors to the Okaukuejo waterhole maybe be rewarded with lions coming down to drink. Cheetah are most easily seen in the short flat grasslands to the north of the main road along the edges of the pan where they prey on springbok. Although there are good numbers of both leopard and caracal, they are seldom seen.

The park is home to three uncommon antelope species: the black-faced impala, Damara dik-dik and roan antelope. The roan antelope was introduced to the park in 1970. In one of the earliest cases of moving animals by aircraft, a small herd was transported by Hercules from Khaudum National Park in Bushmanland. These are shy animals and tend to be only seen in the inaccessible western areas. The black-faced impala is easily recognized as an impala but with a distinctive black facial band. Originally from Kaokoland, a large herd was translocated and released within the park. The largest groups used to occur near Namutoni, but like all wild animals they will move to the water and pasture. The Damara dik-dik is the smallest antelope in Namibia, the adult weighs just 5 kg. They are shy animals favouring wooded areas; you may catch a glimpse of family groups, but such a small animal can hide quickly. Other small animals, such as jackal and banded mongoose, can often be spotted within the rest camps when they slip through the fence on night-time raids of the rubbish bins. Halali honey badgers can also be seen within the camp.

Of the 340 species of birds recorded in the park, about one-third are migratory including the European bee-eater and several species of waders and raptors. There are several species of owls and vultures and larger birds include ostrich, Kori bustard, and greater and lesser flamingo; the latter congregate on the pan during rainy seasons. About 80% of Etsoha's vegetation is mopane trees, plus dwarf savannah shrub and grasslands, and to the west of Okaukuejo is the well-known Sprokieswoud, or phantom or fairy forest; and area of unusual, lofty and slender African moringa trees (*Moringa ovalifolia*), which normally grow in more sub-tropical and hilly climates.

⊙ Etosha National Park listings

For hotel and restaurant price codes and other relevant information, see pages 21-28.

⊙ Where to stay

There are 5 camps within the park managed by **Namibia Wildlife Resorts** (**NWR**), www.nwr.com.na. The main camps are Okaukuejo, Namutoni and Halali; the exclusive camps are Dolomite and Onkoshi. Remember park entry fees are for 24 hrs, so make sure your entry and exit times allow for a night's accommodation. There is also the option of staying outside the park in one of the private lodges clustered around the roads leading to Andersson or Von Lindequist gates, which are also areas rich with game.

NWR camps

The 3 main rest camps have similar facilities and the accommodation was completely refurbished and remodelled several years ago. Apart from camping, the accommodation is no longer self-catering but each room has a fridge and a tea and coffee station while the larger chalets have *braais*, and some units have outside showers. The most luxurious units include dinner, bed and breakfast (dinner, B&B) in the rates, while in all the others rates are bed and breakfast (B&B). Children under 6 are free and children 6-12 are charged half the adult rate.

At each of the main camps there is a parks office/reception, a shop selling a few craft items and food and drink for campers, restaurants serving 3 meals per day (and a kiosk serving drinks and snacks open when the restaurant is shut), a bar, a petrol station (you can cover a surprising distance while game viewing), a swimming pool and a post box (Okaukuejo has a proper post office).

Booking

The **NWR** central booking office in Windhoek is in the Erkrathus building, 189 Independence Av, T061-285 7200, reservations@nwr.com.na. There is also a booking office in Swakopmund, T064-402172, Bismarck St, sw.bookings@nwr. com.na; and Cape Town in South Africa, ground floor, Pinnacle Building, (beneath the Cape Town Tourist Office), Burg St, T+27(0)21-422 3761, ct.bookings@nwr. com.na. The reservations office in each is open Mon-Fri 0800-1500. Alternatively you can book online at www.nwr.com.na.

Bookings are accepted 12 months in advance, and while this process is clearly designed for local residents and tour operators, there is no reason why overseas visitors should not apply from abroad several months prior to arriving in Namibia if you have decided on your itinerary.

Although you are encouraged to book accommodation in advance, it is possible to obtain a room on the day if there is space. Check on arrival in the park at the office at Namutoni or Okaukuejo for availability, either of these offices can advise you of the situation in all 3 camps. Also, if you want to change pre-booked accommodation from one camp to another, the offices can help with this too.

If **camping**, you will rarely by turned away even in peak season, and there seems to be little control over what constitutes 'full'. While at Okaukuejo campers are assigned a numbered site upon check-in, sites at Halali and Namutoni are not pre-assigned but it's best to arrive early to ensure a choice of sites. While there can be frustratingly long queues at the ablutions, and you may find yourself sharing cooking facilities with your neighbours, a full camp has its own distinctive, excited atmosphere, which all adds to the fun.

Okaukuejo map p120
Okaukuejo is 18 km from Andersson Gate, 70 km from Halali, 140 km from Namutoni, T067-229800. This is the largest of the 3 NWR camps and serves as the administrative hub and houses the Etosha Ecological Institute from where conservation management is conducted. It was formerly a German military outpost founded in 1901 and the central feature of the camp is a circular limestone water tower close to the administration block that was added in 1963. A few minutes at the top is worthwhile, both for the views of the plains and Etosha Pan in the distance, and to help orientate yourself within the camp. In addition to the accommodation, there is a camping and caravan site with communal facilities, a swimming pool, restaurant and an attractive thatched bar.

Away from the offices and shops is a floodlit waterhole which can get quite busy but is always rewarding for game viewing and is considered the best of the 3 camp waterholes. Bench seats are arranged behind a protective wall and there is a thatched miniature grandstand. Avoid talking loudly when in the vicinity of the waterhole, it is very easy to startle a shy animal, especially at night, and you will not make yourself popular with other guests. There is a good chance of seeing black rhino and elephant with young, and the 3 big cats also regularly drink here.

National parks accommodation
$$$$ Premier Waterhole Chalet, adjacent to the waterhole, there are 5 double-story chalets sleeping 4 people, with balconies overlooking the waterhole. At around N$2400 per person these are the most expensive in the park but are extremely comfortable and in an unbeatable location. Although they tend to offer less privacy, as the rest of the camp arrives at dawn and dusk, you may be rewarded with your own private views in the middle of the night. Dinner, B&B.
$$$$-$$$ Family Chalets, 2 chalets each with 2 rooms spacious enough for 4 adults, *braai*. B&B.
$$$ Waterhole Chalet, 30 chalets with 1 double/twin room still near the waterhole but without the direct views. B&B.
$$$ Bush Chalet, 25 chalets with 1 double/twin room, *braai*. Some of these have facilities for wheelchairs. B&B.
$$$ Double/Twin Rooms, 40 rooms, slightly cheaper than the bush chalets but with no *braai*. B&B.
$ Campsite, pricey at N$200 per site per day plus N$110 per person per day for up to 8 people (reasonable for groups but not for a couple). Shaded sites, electricity points, good communal

facilities with clean, hot showers and baths and camp kitchens with hotplates and sinks for washing up. However, queues can develop in busy periods, take your chance for a shower when you can; popular with overland trucks.

Private lodges/camps near Okaukuejo

On and around the C38 between Outjo and Andersson Gate are a number of lodges, which make a fine alternative to the accommodation in the park as there's still plenty of game around. See map, page 109.

$$$$ Epacha Game Lodge & Spa, from Etosha's Andersson Gate, drive south 44 km to the turning to the right along the D2695, then 27 km to the turning to the lodge which is 4 km from the road, lodge T067-697047, reservations Windhoek T061-375300, www.epacha-lodge.com. Located on the 21,000-ha Epacha Private Game Reserve, close to **Eagle Tented Lodge & Spa** (below). Animals on the reserve include 21 species of antelope including the rare sable and black rhino. 18 very stylish thatched a/c chalets decorated with specially commissioned antique Victorian furniture, each with luxury bathroom outside shower, and balcony. Comfortable lounges overlooking waterholes, library, billiards room, swimming pool with bar, spa with jacuzzi, steam room, sauna and splash pool, and activities include excursions into Etosha, game drives, bush walks and clay pigeon shooting.

$$$$ Ongava Game Reserve, entrance by Andersson Gate, then 9 km to the lodge, 18 km to the tented camp, T067-687187, www.ongava.com, part of the highly regarded **Wilderness Safaris**, www.wilderness-safaris.com. A super-luxury option set on a private

66,000 ha reserve, Ongava Lodge, has 13 beautifully crafted, thatched chalets with glass doors leading to a veranda, and views from the swimming pool that are hard to tear yourself away from. **Little Ongava**, is the most exclusive with just 3 suites with plunge pools, outdoor showers and private vehicles and guides. **Ongava Tented Camp**, has 8 spacious safari tents which are the least expensive option but still firmly in the luxury bracket with a pool and thatched dining area overlooking a waterhole. All offer excursions into Etosha, day and night game drives and walks including rhino tracking on foot.

$$$$-$$$ Eagle Tented Lodge & Spa, T067-687161, on Epacha Private Game Reserve (see **Epacha Game Lodge & Spa** for directions), T067-687161, www.eagle-tented-lodge.com. The lodge is built of natural rock and thatched roofs on a prominent hill in the reserve with broad views, accommodation is in 16 spacious luxury safari tents, the deluxe ones have outdoor baths on the balcony. 2 restaurants, main bar and pool bar, swimming pool and spa and activities on offer include game drives in the reserve as well as into Etosha, and clay pigeon shooting.

$$$ Etosha Safari Lodge & Etosha Safari Camp, 10 km from Andersson Gate on the C38, reservations Windhoek T061-230066, www.gondwana-collection.com. A well-priced mid-range option, good for families; the lodge boasts 65 bungalows perched on a small hill and sharing 3 swimming pools, while the camp offers 50 cheaper chalets dotted amongst *mopane* trees with a pool; both have a restaurant and bar serving buffet meals and South African wines. Activities include game drives in and out of Etosha, and their **Etosha Safari**

Shuttle package includes 3 nights' B&B accommodation, breakfast, game drives and transport from Windhoek. There's a **campsite ($)** with grassed, shady sites, power points and kitchen sinks is only a 2-min walk from the **Safari Camp**, where campers can eat and use the facilities.

$$ Etosha Village, 2 km before Andersson Gate on the left, T067-687190, www.etosha-village.com. A friendly and affordable option very close to the gate with a rustic African village theme, 40 simple safari tents with semi-open bathrooms in reed walls, some with extra beds for children, and the self-catering ones have outdoor kitchen with *braai*, stove and fridge. Swimming pool, buffet restaurant, bar, shop for curios and some fresh food. Etosha excursions and packed breakfasts and lunches can be arranged if self-driving.

$$ Toshari Lodge, 26 km south of Andersson Gate then signposted off the C38, T067-333440, www.etoshagateway-toshari.com. One of the least expensive options with 35 a/c rooms with patios and contemporary African decor, the family option is excellent value from N$1500 per room for 5, pleasant thatched restaurant, 4-course dinners N$230, swimming pool, terrace for sundowners, and Etosha game drives. **Campsite ($)** with good facilities and each site has a private wooden and stone bathroom with open roof, power point, *braai* and little herb garden.

Dolomite Camp *map p120*
The latest **NWR** exclusive offering is in the restricted western side of the park and guests can drive here via Okaukuejo or through the Galton Gate in the southwest of the park, which is for Dolomite guests only. Perched on the top of a little hill, the camp is unfenced

allowing animals to roam freely between the tents and communal area. There's a restaurant, rim flow swimming pool, curio shop, viewing deck overlooking a waterhole and the Etosha plains, game drives to areas not open to the public where you'll see no other vehicles.

National parks accommodation
$$$$-$$$ Safari Tents, 20 luxurious tents either west or east facing for sunset/sunrise views from the decks, some with plunge pools, contemporary African decor, golf carts take guests to the main facilities at the top of the hill.

Halali *map p120*
More or less midway, 70 km, between the other 2 **NWR** rest camps, T067-229400. This was the 3rd camp to be opened in the park, and has a refreshingly large (20 m) swimming pool, restaurant, shop, kiosk and bar. The floodlit waterhole is beautifully located at the base of a *koppie* and is popular with elephant. There are walks all around the camp, including up and over the small *koppie*; make sure you are quiet as you approach. One of the advantages of staying at this camp is that there are more waterholes within a short driving distance. It is also less popular with overland trucks and the campsite is quieter.

National parks accommodation
$$$$-$$$ Family Chalet, 2 chalets, each sleeping up to 4 adults in 2 rooms. B&B.
$$$ Bush Chalets, 40 chalets, sleeping 2-4 in 1 room, *braai*. B&B.
$$$ Double/twin rooms, 39 rooms, slightly cheaper than the bush chalets but with no *braai*. B&B.
$ Campsite, dusty but fairly well shaded, clean communal facilities with hot water, electricity; N$200 per site per

day plus N$100 per person per day for up to 8 people.

Namutoni *map p120*
Some 140 km from Okaukuejo, T067-229300. Allow at least 3 hrs to drive between the 2 camps, you are always likely to stop for something, even if it is to allow an elephant to cross the road. For many visitors, this is their favourite camp, with its striking, whitewashed, converted fort, palm-fringed swimming area and picturesque, floodlit waterhole surrounded by tall grasses and reeds. However, in saying that, some have reported that they have been disappointed that the majority of chalets have no view, just a tiny gravel courtyard surrounded by a tall fence.

As a reminder of its military past, a bugle accompanies the hoisting of the Namibian flag on top of the fort each day at sunrise and sunset. The fort is a hive of activity with a swimming pool, 2 restaurants, a bar, and shops selling crafts, jewellery and books.

National parks accommodation
$$$ Bush Chalets, 20 chalets, sleeping 2, outdoor showers and *braai*. B&B.
$$$ Double rooms, 24 rooms, sleeping 2, slightly cheaper than the bush chalets but with no *braai*. B&B.
$ Campsite, a greener site than at the other 2 camps but with less shade. Electricity available. N$200 per site per day plus N$110 per person per day for up to 8 people; communal kitchen and excellent ablution blocks, separate **Boma** bar, can get crowded, popular with overland trucks.

Onkoshi Camp *map p120*
The other exclusive **NWR** offering set on a secluded peninsula with stunning

views over Etosha pan. It is not a self-drive camp; guests arrive at Namutoni and are transferred by **NWR** vehicles. Facilities include a restaurant, lounge, bar, sunset deck and infinity pool overlooking the pan. Activities include game drives to exclusive areas of the park and moonlight walks on the Etosha pan.

National parks accommodation
$$$$ Chalets, 15 freestanding spacious units on stilts with thatched roofs, canvas walls, and elevated wooden decks for panoramic views. Spread out in a long line right on the edge of the pan and linked to the main facilities by boardwalks.

Outside the park *map p109*
From Von Lindequist Gate in the east of the park it is 35 km to the main Tsumeb–Ondangwa road, the B1, and there are a few excellent luxury lodges in the region.

Private lodges and camps near Von Lindequist Gate
$$$$-$$$ Mokuti Lodge, about 2 km from the main road just outside Von Lindequist Gate, lodge T067-229084, reservations Windhoek T061-207 5360, www.mokutietoshalodge.com. An enormous and impressive set-up and the main complex is in a huge, thatched barn; it won't appeal to those looking for a more intimate safari experience, but if you like to be anonymous in large, impersonal establishments, this could be for you. It's also ideal for families; children under 15 half price and under 6s free. 106 a/c, thatched rooms of varying size, set in a small woodland area with neat garden, restaurant, bar, pool bar, 2 swimming pools, playground, tennis courts, spa, gym, reptile park and large curio shop. Activities include game drives

in open-sided overland trucks and walks on the property.

$$$$-$$$ Mushara Lodge, 8 km before Von Lindequist Gate, and 1 km from the main road on the left, reservations Windhoek T061-240020, www.mushara-lodge.com. Unusually for this area, the lodge is privately owned by a young and energetic German couple. It is immaculately tended, with not a blade of grass out of place. Accommodation is in the main lodge with 10 comfortable chalets and 2 sumptuous villas with plunge pools, thatched restaurant, bar with wine cellar, lounge and library, large swimming pool. **Mushara Outpost** has 16 safari tents with the communal facilities in an old farmhouse; while **Mushara Bush Camp** has another 16 safari tents which are family orientated with kids' swimming pool, play area and child minders. Game drives in Etosha and walks around the property.

$$$$-$$$ Onguma Game Reserve, turn off to the right just before Von Lindequist Gate, then 8 km to the camps, reservations Windhoek T061-237055, www.onguma.com. Onguma means 'the place you don't want to leave' in Herero and covering 34,000 ha right on the edge of Etosha this is considered one of the finest private reserves in Namibia. There are 6 different types of accommodation here from luxury rooms for more than US$700 per couple to a simple inexpensive campsite. Some don't accept children under 12; check first. Overall, this is an excellent option in a game rich area close to the eastern edge of Fisher's Pan. **Onguma the Fort**, a super-luxury stone lodge designed like a fort with a tower overlooking Fisher's Pan, 13 a/c suites set 50 m apart with decks and plunge pools, stylish minimal decor mixed with antiques. Restaurant, bar and pool in one of the best vantage points for sunset views on the reserve.

Onguma Etosha Aoba Lodge, 11 thatched bungalows with veranda, comfortable, without being pristine, hidden among indigenous *tamboti* trees. Small swimming pool, large thatched bar/ restaurant area that overlooks a waterhole.

Onguma Tented Camp, 7 huge luxury tents overlooking a waterhole and a comfortable lounge and dining deck with earthy decor incorporating stone, wood and steel. Restaurant, bar, evening fire pit and rim flow pool.

Onguma Tree Top Camp, 4 suites with canvas walls and a main building with lounge and dining area entirely built on stilts among shady trees, overlooking a waterhole with wooden boardwalks lit by lanterns.

Onguma Bush Camp, the least expensive accommodation centered around a busy waterhole but still a very high standard in 19 thatched stone a/c rooms, some with lofts for families, swimming pool, a *lapa* for meals and a bar.

Onguma Tamboti & Leadwood Campsites ($), exceptionally well maintained, each site has its own private bathroom and power point, a bundle of firewood is provided, and they are fenced so a good option for small children. **Tamboti** has its own restaurant overlooking a waterhole, and campers at Leadwood can use the facilities at **Onguma Bush Camp**.

The Triangle

When you look at a map of northern Namibia, the roads that link the towns of Otavi, Tsumeb and Grootfontein quite clearly form a triangle. They are part of a prosperous region, which produces a significant proportion of the country's maize crop and is also an important mining centre. Because of their proximity to Etosha and the Waterberg Plateau, and being en route to and from the Caprivi, a significant number of visitors pass through these small, simple towns. The museum in Tsumeb and the Hoba Meteorite are worth a detour, and there are some beautifully located guest farms to accommodate you. This is the last outpost of German colonial influence – north of here the countryside and atmosphere is totally different to the rest of the country. All three towns are suitable (although Otavi only barely) for stocking up with supplies and cash, but none merit a stopover of any length. Of the three, Tsumeb is the most attractive and has the best facilities.

Road to the Triangle

Which of the triangle towns you arrive at, rather depends on which direction you have come from. Heading north from Otjiwarongo, it is 119 km on the B1 to Otavi. It is in this tiny town, on the southwestern point of the triangle, where the road splits. As the B1, it continues for 65 km to Tsumeb, the northern point of the triangle. From Tsumeb the B1 takes you past Otjikoto and Guinas lakes (see page 134), which are found in the bush close to the main road, and after 73 km there is the left turning to Etosha's Von Lindequist Gate. The B1 then heads northwest to Ondangwa and Oshakati. This region used to be known as Owamboland, but it has now been divided up into four new regions (see page 208 for details of the Far North). If coming from the north, it makes sense to use the King Nehale Lya Mpingana Gate to Etosha, which is on the B1 roughly 100 km south of Ondangwa.

Back in Otavi where the main road from Windhoek splits, you are also faced with the second option. If you need to stop and look at a map with a cup of coffee, stop at the large **Fourways Total** petrol service station here at the intersection of the B1 and B8 (see page 140). While the B1 heads northwest, the B8 is the main road to the Caprivi Region in the northeast; first via Grootfontein, 94 km from Otavi and the eastern point of the triangle, after which it begins the lonely 258-km drive though the bushveld to Rundu at the eastern end of the Caprivi (see page 148). The final road that makes up the three sides of the triangle is the C42, which links Tsumeb with Grootfontein, a distance of 62 km.

Otavi → *For listings, see pages 138-141. Colour map 1, B5. Phone code: 067.*

Otavi is the first of the three 'triangle' towns you reach when driving north from Windhoek on the B1. It is also the smallest and offers little of interest to the tourist, and is a base for local farming. It lies in a pleasant wooded and fertile plain, beneath the Otavi Mountains, and its name is derived from the Herero word 'ondavi' meaning 'branch of a tree'.

It was **copper** that brought the boom period to the town. Work on a narrow-gauge railway began in November 1903 and was completed in August 1906, after being interrupted by the Herero-German war. The railway was built to carry copper ore to Swakopmund. The German colonial company which ran the mine and built the railway was the **Otavi Minenund Eisenbahn-Gesellschaft (OMEG)**; there are some excellent photographs of the railway on show in the museum in Swakopmund (see page 231). The only mining operations that continue today are near Tsumeb.

The only local site of any note in Otavi is the **Khorib Memorial**, 2 km north of the town on a dirt road; there's a sign at the Otavi Municipal Office. Unlike some memorials in Namibia this one is particularly plain but nevertheless it represents a little piece of Namibian history. It was unveiled in 1920 to mark the end of German rule in South-West Africa in July 1915, when local officials surrendered to the Commander of the Union Forces, General Louis Botha. The German officials were the Commander of the German forces in South-West Africa, Colonel Victor Franke and the Governor of South-West Africa, Dr Seitz. There is a small stone plaque explaining this close to the railway.

Tsumeb → *For listings, see pages 138-141. Colour map 1, B6. Phone code: 067.*

Tsumeb is the largest of the three triangle towns in northern Namibia and was developed as a major mining centre in about 1905. The name Tsumeb is generally pronounced 'Suu-meb' and derives from the Hain/Ohmbushman word *Tsomsoub* meaning 'to dig a hole in loose ground', and the Herero word *Otjitsume* meaning 'place of frogs'. The reference to frogs derives from the green, red-brown and grey streaks of copper and lead ores found in the local rock. These are supposed to resemble frogspawn scooped out of a waterhole and sprinkled around on the surrounding rocks. The town's coat of arms acknowledges both Tsumeb's mining and frog connections by depicting a pair of frogs squatting alongside mining tools.

Thanks to the wealth generated by the mines, Tsumeb is an attractive town with some fine old colonial buildings and a palm-tree-lined central park with wide lawns. It is a practical stop en route to Etosha's Von Lindequist Gate and destinations in the far north, and has plenty of services such as cafés, shops and petrol stations. It is also the last stop before passing north of the so-called '**Red Line**', separating the enclosed commercial cattle farms to the south from the communally owned lands to the north. Once over the Red Line one moves away from 'European' Namibia and into the heart of Owamboland – today divided into four regions: Omusati, Ohangwena, Oshana and Oshikoto – where almost half of all Namibians live.

Arriving in Tsumeb

Tsumeb lies on the B1 431 km north of Windhoek. At the time of writing the new 267 km Tsumeb–Katwitwi road was under construction which goes 267 km to the newly opened Katwitwi border post with Angola (see page 149). By the time you read this it should be open and branches off the B1 just north of town near the sewage works (follow signs for Tsintsabis). Intercape buses stop in Tsumeb on the route between Windhoek and Livingstone in Zambia, but the buses arrive and depart at inconvenient times during the night.

Tourist information in Tsumeb can be found at the privately run **Travel North Namibia** ① *Sam Nujoma Dr, T067-220728, Mon-Fri 0800-1700, Sat 0800-1200*, which is the reception for the **Travel North Guesthouse** (see Where to stay, page 138) and has a small coffee shop with internet facilities. It is also the agent for **Europcar** car hire.

Background

There is evidence of the smelting and mining of copper in the Tsumeb area as long ago as the Stone Age, and certainly both Damara and Owambo communities were known to be skilled smelterers and workers of the metal. As the different groups came into increased contact with each other during the second half of the 19th century, so disputes arose over the ownership of the land around Tsumeb.

White traders, active in Namibia by this time, were also interested in the minerals in the area and a number succeeded in gaining land concessions around Tsumeb.

Serious European interest in the area was signalled in 1892 when the London-based **South-West Africa Company** obtained a mining concession, and early the following year the geologist Matthew Rogers visited Tsumeb to carry out further investigations. In 1900, a new company, the Otavi Minen-und Eisenbahn-Gesellschaft (OMEG), was formed in order to raise more money to develop mines in the area.

Following the construction of a road between the settlement and the mines and the sinking of two new shafts, the first nine tonnes of copper left Tsumeb for Swakopmund at the very end of 1900. Although this first copper was carried by ox-wagon, by August 1906 the narrow-gauge railway to Swakopmund had been constructed. This improved export channel proved a massive boost to the efficiency of the whole operation, and by 1908 the company was already generating significant profits.

Tsumeb

Where to stay	Restaurants
Makalani 1	Dros 3
Minen 2	Etosha Café
Kupferquelle Resort 3	& Beer Garden 1
Travel North Guesthouse 5	Wimpy 2

This was to signal the start of almost a century of mining at Tsumeb, interrupted only by the two World Wars. Ownership of the mines passed into the hands of the Tsumeb Corporation (TCL) following Germany's defeat in the Second World War, and it continued to develop mining capacity. However, by 1999 the costs of deep mining were exceeding output and that, coupled with a miners' strike in 1996, forced the mines to close. For the Tsumeb community it was a devastating blow, one that is still felt today as the town struggles to find jobs for the ex-miners. However, since then the Khusib Springs Mine has opened between Tsumeb and Grootfontein, which produces copper, lead and zinc, and some of the miners have found gainful employment again. Today the De Wet Shaft at the former mine can still be seen on President Street and serves as reminder of Tsumeb's mining past.

Places in Tsumeb

Located on President Street facing the park, and in the old German Private School building (look for the old steam engine out front), dating back to 1915, the **Tsumeb Museum** ① *T067-220447, Mon-Fri 0900-1200, 1400-1700, Sat 0900-1200, N$20*, has a fine display of the town's mining history including a display of minerals. There are also exhibits of traditional costumes, artefacts and photographs, and a fascinating collection of German First World War weapons and ordnance retrieved from Lake Otjikoto, where they were dumped prior to the German surrender to South Africa in 1915. This is one of the best museums in the country.

The **St Barbara Catholic Church**, on the corner of Main and Third streets, consecrated in 1914, was dedicated to the patron saint of mine workers, and for 13 years served as the town's only church. It dominates the centre of the town, and the unusual tower above the entrance is particularly eye-catching.

Around Tsumeb

Lake Otjikoto and Lake Guinas → *Colour map 1, B5.*
① *Lake Otjikoto is 24 km north of Tsumeb, well signposted off the B1, open daily sunrise-sunset, N$20, children (under 12) N$10, there is a car park and kiosk selling curios and cold drinks. Lake Guinas has no facilities or entry fee.*
Lake Otjikoto is set back 100 m from the main road amongst the trees, but it is well signposted and is a popular stop to or from Etosha via the Von Lindequist Gate. The name Otjikoto is said to come from the Herero and can be loosely translated as 'the place which is too deep for cattle to drink water'. The San (Bushmen) name for it is 'Gaisis', which means 'very ugly' and as it was probably the only lake they'd ever seen they were afraid of its deep water. When the sun shines the water looks very blue and clear. It is possible to climb down to the lake shore via a rock stairway; this is not encouraged and swimming is forbidden.

Just before you reach the lake there is another turning on the right, the D3043. If you follow this for 19 km and then take a turn onto the D3031 you will find yourself beside **Lake Guinas**. It is clearly signposted, but the site has not been developed. There is no easy access to the lake shore as the sides are precipitous.

Each of the lakes was formed by the collapse of a ceiling in a huge dolomite underground cavern. They are technically known as sink holes. The caverns were formed after water leaked into the dolomite rocks, following a minor earthquake which fractured the rocks. Once in contact with the limestone, the water slowly dissolved the rock. The cross-sectional view of the lake can be described as an upside-down mushroom. A popular myth is that Lake Otjikoto is bottomless; this is not so, but the flooded cave system extends for much further than was originally believed. Lake Guinas is considerably deeper; it has been measured to over 200 m. The levels in both lakes fluctuate as water is pumped for irrigation.

Lake Otjikoto is home to an interesting range of fish, most of which are 'alien' species. A sub-species of the common tilapia was introduced to the lake in the 1930s, and the lake is home to a very unusual type of bream. The bream has a protective habit of carrying its eggs and, when they are first born, the young fish, in its mouth. The dwarf bream, *Pseudocrenoolabrus philander disperses*, live in the dark depths of the lake too. Scientists have postulated that these fish moved to the depths after the shallower waters became overpopulated due to the absence of predators.

The first Europeans to come across these lakes, Francis Galton and Charles Andersson, camped beside Lake Otjikoto in May 1851. In 1915 the retreating German army took the decision to dump their weapons in Lake Otjikoto so the South Africans could not make use of them. There are mixed accounts about what was actually thrown in, but there is no doubt about the pieces which are on show in Tsumeb Museum. A large ammunition wagon is also on display in the Alte Feste Museum in Windhoek. In 1916, a team of divers under Sergeant G Crofton and J de Villiers of the Special Intelligence Unit of the Union forces was sent to try and recover some of the armaments. They managed to find a mix of small arms and ammunition, five cannons, 10 cannon chassis and three machine guns. In 1970, an ammunition wagon was found at a depth of 41 m, in surprisingly good condition. In the early 1980s, divers recovered some more pieces, including a Sandfontein cannon. All of the most recently discovered items have been carefully restored and are now on show in the excellent Tsumeb Museum. Legend has it that one of the German soldiers got his leg caught in the riggings of one of the cannons as it was thrown in the lake and was dragged down and drowned. Reputedly his ghost still haunts the lake.

Grootfontein → *For listings, see pages 138-141. Colour map 1, B6. Phone code: 067.*

Blessed in Namibian terms by a high annual rainfall (450-650 mm), the Grootfontein area supports a wide range of agriculture on its predominantly white-owned farms. Apart from the usual livestock farming of cattle, sheep and goats, the farms here produce most of Namibia's commercially grown maize, sorghum, cotton, peanuts and sunflower.

The third triangle town of Grootfontein is a pleasant enough place with limestone buildings and tree-lined streets, and is particularly attractive in September and October when the purple jacaranda blossom and red flamboyants appear. It's another good place to stop for petrol and provisions and the nearby Hoba Meteorite is worth visiting. However, accommodation is limited, and there have been problems of theft from vehicles in Grootfontein, especially cars belonging to tourists; do not leave your car unattended and be vigilant.

Background

With an abundant supply of water and good grazing, the area has been home to both game and humans for many thousands of years. In pre-colonial times the town was known to the Herero as *Otjiwandatjongue*, meaning 'hill of the leopard'. The earlier Nama and Berg Damara inhabitants called the area *Gei-ous*, meaning 'big fountain', from which the Afrikaans name Grootfontein is derived. The fountain and the Tree Park, planted by the **South-West African Company**, can both be seen today on the northern edge of town.

In the 1860s, two elephant hunters, Green and Eriksson, used the fountain as a base from which to launch their hunting expeditions. However, the first Europeans to settle in the area arrived around 1880, followed soon after by the so-called 'Dorsland Trekkers' who in the mid-1880s established their own republic on land purchased from Owambo chief, Kambone. The Republic of Upingtonia, as it was called, survived for a mere two years before collapsing.

In 1893 the **South-West Africa Company** established its headquarters at Grootfontein and in 1896 the settlement was enlarged by a group of settlers from the Transvaal. In the same year the Schutztruppe constructed a fort and administrative centre, and in 1904 a tower was constructed, providing the garrison with an excellent vantage point from which to survey the surrounding area. In 1922 the limestone extension was added.

Between 1923 and 1958 the fort served as a school hostel, after which it was abandoned. A public appeal in 1974 saved the building from demolition, and in 1975 it was declared a national monument, and also served as an assembly point for Angolan refugees. In 1977 it was renovated and in 1983 Das Alte Feste (The Old

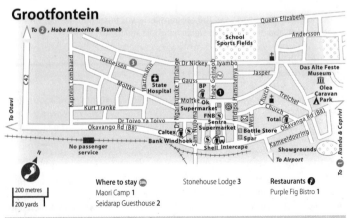

Grootfontein

Where to stay
Maori Camp 1
Seidarap Guesthouse 2
Stonehouse Lodge 3

Restaurants
Purple Fig Bistro 1

Fort) Museum was opened, with a local history exhibition inside and a display of industrial and agricultural items outside.

Grootfontein itself officially became a town in 1907, and the following year the narrow-gauge railway linked the town with Otavi and Tsumeb. The town has subsequently grown to become the centre of Namibia's maize industry, evidenced by large silos at the end of the railway line. It also has a significant cattle industry and holds a large agricultural show every September.

Places in Grootfontein

Das Alte Feste Museum ① *off Eriksson St, T067-242456, www.altefortmuseum.de, Mon-Fri 0900-1230, 1400-1630, closes at 1600 in winter, free,* is worth visiting for its history of the town and the local area. Exhibits include local minerals, restored carpenter's and blacksmith's shops with working machinery, and traditional crafts. One room is dedicated to the Himba people with items on display such as jewellery and clothing and some good photographs of everyday Himba life.

Around Grootfontein

The **Hoba Meteorite** ① *follow the C42 towards Tsumeb for 3 km, then take the D2859 for about 15 km, following the sign to the meteorite, open sunrise-sunset, N$20, children (under 12) N$10,* is an impressive lump of metal: it is the largest known single meteorite in the world, weighing in at around 60 tonnes and measuring 2.95 m by 2.84 m. It was discovered by Johannes Brits in 1920 whilst he was hunting in the area. It is believed to be between 190 and 410 million years old and fell to earth some 80,000 years ago. After various people tried to get a souvenir piece of it, the meteorite was declared a national monument in 1955. Made of 82% iron (which really shows when you see it up close), the meteorite also contains 16% nickel, which South-West Africa Company manager, T Tonnessen, proposed mining in 1922 – fortunately he never got round to it. There are suggestions that the Hoba Meteorite is merely the largest fragment of an even larger meteorite which broke up during entry into the earth's atmosphere, in which case there may be other fragments lying around in the area waiting to be discovered. Next to the meteorite, there are some panels with information, a basic nature trail (birders should look out for Kalahari robins and waxbills), good *braai*/picnic facilities, toilets and a small kiosk selling information leaflets, souvenirs and drinks. It really is an unusual lump, worth the short detour to see this mysterious visitor from space.

For hotel and restaurant price codes and other relevant information, see pages 21-28.

Where to stay

Otavi *p131, map p109*
$$$ Khorab Lodge, 3 km south of Otavi on the B1, T067-234352, www. khorablodge.com. 10 thatched bungalows with 2 bedrooms, swimming pool with *lapa*, good restaurant, bar in large thatched barn popular with tourists and local farmers. Also a well-maintained **campsite ($)** with private hot showers and thatched shelters, and the lodge sells *braai* packs. There are some antelope in the grounds and chickens, ducks and geese wander around. Also the agent for **Avis** car hire (see page 141).
$ Palmenecke Guesthouse, 96 Hertzog Av, T067-234199, www.palmenecke.co.za. Friendly and comfortable and the only decent choice in town with 5 large and bright a/c B&B rooms, other meals available on request and can organize a *braai* in the cosy thatched *lapa* surrounding the tiny swimming pool.

Guest farms
$$$-$$ Guest Farm Ghaub, 25 km from the B1 between Otavi and Tsumeb on the D3022, T067-240188, www.ghaub.com. Located in the middle of the triangle, this is your best bet in the region. The main house is an old Rhenish Mission Station (established 1895), and the impressive trees date from that time, giving the feel of an English country estate, but with African touches everywhere. 10 large rooms with veranda and great views over a huge lawn, the swimming pool and across the valley, plus a shady **campsite ($)**. Good farm-

style meals and lots of activities including farm drives, guided walks in the hills to see San (Bushmen) engravings, an excursion to the nearby bat caves (the 3rd largest in Namibia) or large underground reservoir/ cave for those who are interested and free mountain bikes are available.
$ Zum Potjie Rest Camp, 8 km north of Otavi, 2 km off the B1, T067-234300, www.zumpotjie.com. 5 neat en suite bungalows and a **campsite** with simple ablutions and camp kitchen, swimming pool, and small farm museum. The attraction is the home-cooking; the resourceful Afrikaner hosts source most of their ingredients from the farm, including fruit from the orchards to make juice and jams. The *potjies* (stews cooked in iron 3-legged pots) are very good.

Tsumeb *p132, maps p109 and p133*
$$ Minen Hotel, Omeg Allee St, T067-221071, www.minen-hotel.com. Set in pleasant mature gardens, 49 faded but comfortable a/c rooms, pub lunches served in the garden, restaurant with extensive menu, swimming pool. An atmospheric old-style German-owned hotel, full of character but quality and size of the rooms can be a hit or miss; ask to see a few.
$$ Travel North Guesthouse, Sam Nujoma Dr, T067-220728, www.travelnorthguesthouse.com. 6 comfortable B&B rooms with a/c, mini-fridge, tea and coffee making facilities, breakfast taken in the dining room or garden, internet access, laundry, and secure off street parking. Also agent for **Europcar** car hire, and friendly owners are helpful with local tourist information.
$$-$ Kupferquelle Resort, B1 southern edge of town, T067-221139, www.

kupferquelle.com. This new resort is on what used to be the municipal campsite and is set on lovely brilliantly green lawns. 35 chalets with 1 or 2 bedrooms DSTV, neat kitchenettes, smart modern decor and balconies with *braais*. The campsite is vast and the 25 shaded sites are well spaced apart and have power points. Facilities include an Olympic-size swimming pool (the only one outside Windhoek), shop, large bar and the **Dros** restaurant (see Restaurants, page 140).
$$-$ Makalani Hotel, Ndilimani Cultural Troupe St, T067-221051, www.makalanihotel.com. Central location, 28 a/c rooms with DSTV and tea- and coffee-making facilities, some with 4 beds, swimming pool surrounded by palms, restaurant and attractive bar/beer garden. Friendly, good value and a nice lunch stop if driving through.

Guest farms
$$$ Uris Safari Lodge, 10 km northwest of Tsumeb towards Etosha on the B1, turn left at the sign for 14 km, T067-687060, www.uris-safari-lodge-namibia.com. A lovely lodge fashioned from old 1900s miner's cottages, 14 stone and thatch chalets, 2 with loft accommodation for children, and separate **campsite ($)** with *braai* and washing up facilities and hot showers. Large thatched bar and dining area with wooden decks, wine cellar, small library with some mining history of the region, swimming pool with island feature, wheelchair access. Activities include walks or drives around the farm to visit old mine sites and spot the several species of antelope including eland.

Grootfontein *p135*, maps *p109* and *p136*
$ Maori Camp, off the B8, 3 km from Grootfontein towards Rundu, 2 km off the main road, T0608-038689. If

camping, there's the grim municipal **Olea Caravan Park** near the museum in town, but security is an issue so it's not recommended. Far better to head out of town to this pleasant site on a German-run citrus farm. 10 camping spots and 10 simple thatched rondavels, each with shade and a *braai* pit, firewood, hot showers. You can climb a mock castle-like tower for sunset views and the shop at the bottom sells *braai* meat, drinks and Bushman crafts.
$ Seidarap Guesthouse, 5 km from town on the C42 towards Tsumeb, T067-242817, www.seidarap.com. A B&B with friendly owners set in an historical farmhouse on the C42 in lovely gardens with flowering plants and lemon and avocado trees. 6 neat rooms, generous breakfasts, dinner on request, swimming pool. The name is the backward spelling of 'Paradies' – German for paradise and was so named by the owner's grandparents.
$ Stonehouse Lodge, 10 Toenessen St, T067-242842, www.stonehouse.iway.na. A neat B&B in town in a modern stone house with secure parking, 6 a/c spacious rooms with DSTV and tea and coffee stations, set around an inner courtyard with a swimming pool, and the front covered terrace has views over town.

Guest farms
There are a couple of good options north of Grootfontein off the B8 if you're heading north towards the Caprivi.
$$$ Fiume Lodge, on the B8 30 km north of Grootfontein, 3 km from the main road, T067-240486, www.fiume-lodge.com. Set on a 1400-ha game farm, this lovely lodge has 6 large stone and thatch a/c chalets in beautifully tended gardens, restaurant, bar, fire pit for evening drinks, swimming pool. The

highlight is the sensitive excursion to meet the u/'Hoansi San (Bushmen) as the owner Jörn speaks their language fluently and knows much about their way of life. There are also game drives to see the resident antelope or you can join in the cattle farming activities for the day.

$$ Roy's Rest Camp, on the B8 at the Tsumkwe junction (C44), 57 km north of Grootfontein, 1 km from the main road, T067-240302, www.roysrestcamp. com. Tranquil spot hidden in the bush with friendly hosts, 5 double/twin and 2 family rustic thatched chalets built of local materials, green, shaded **campsite** (**$**) with **braai** sites. Nice bar by swimming pool set into rock, restaurant (book meals in advance), short hiking trail, it is sometimes possible to see zebra and small antelope in and around the camp. With notice, can organize day trips to a San (Bushmen) village located 86 km from Roy's on the C44.

🍴 Restaurants

Otavi *p131, map p109*

$$-$ Camel Inn Restaurant & Bar, at the **Fourways Total** service station at the intersection of the B1 and B8, T067-302121. Daily 0800-2200. Lovely thatched building surrounded by palms with a wooden bar and cosy tables, expect the likes of rump steaks and all things meaty, and the Hungry Camel is a full-on English cooked breakfast with additional steak, Russian sausage and chicken wings. Fourways is in fact Total's top-rated service station in southern Africa (it wins awards!) and also has an ATM, a biltong shop and butcher, chicken and chips and pizza takeaway, coffee shop, and even a fresh vegetable market. This is probably all you'll need in Otavi. Don't forget to fill up the car.

Tsumeb *p132, maps p109 and p133*

$$ Makalani Hotel (see Where to stay). Daily 1100-1400, 1730-2200. Standard small town hotel restaurant offering the likes of fairly predictable steaks, schnitzels and salads, plus Irish coffees and don pedros (ice cream and whisky). Tables outside among the palms.

$$ Minen Hotel (see Where to stay). Daily 0800-2130. Similar set-up to **Mekalani** serving breakfast, lunch and dinner, popular with local business people and German tour groups. German dishes include sauerkraut and sausage.

$$-$ Dros, at **Kupferquelle Resort** (see Where to stay) on the B1 at the southern edge of town, T067-221040, www.dros. co.za. Mon-Sat 0700-2200, Sun 0700-2100. The only Namibian franchise of this popular South African steakhouse chain, with a pleasant veranda and a supervised kids' playroom with jungle gym and a Playstation. Grills, burgers, ribs and steak and seafood combos, and decent giant cooked breakfasts.

$ Etosha Café & Beer Garden, 21 President St, T067-121207. Mon-Fri 0700-1700, Sat 0800-1300. Pinafored waitresses, excellent cakes and coffee, light meals plus tourist shop selling books, cards and gifts, flower-filled garden, and a few simple B&B rooms at the back (**$**).

$ Wimpy at the Engen petrol station on the approach to town on the B1. The usual burgers, recommended for breakfast and Wimpy mega-coffee in a whoosh of a/c.

Grootfontein *p135, maps p109 and p136*

Like accommodation, there is little choice of restaurants in Grootfontein, but you can get takeaways at the petrol stations and supermarkets.

$ Purple Fig Bistro, 19 Hage Geingob St, T0811-242802. Mon-Fri 0700-1700, Sat 0800-1300. Not a bistro as such but a pleasant daytime café serving cakes, light meals and excellent coffees – try the ice-cream and chocolate flake in a mug with a separate espresso to pour on top. Pleasant surroundings with outdoor tables under the shade of enormous trees.

O Shopping

Tsumeb *p132, maps p109 and p133*
Tsumeb is the self-caterers' final chance to stock up en route to Etosha and there are large branches of **Shoprite**, **Spar** and **Pick 'n' Pay** in town. Note in this region meat is always good and plentiful, but the quality of fruit and vegetables can be a bit hit or miss depending on if you've arrived before or after a delivery from Windhoek.
Tsumeb Arts & Crafts Centre,
18 President St, a couple of doors from the **Etosha Café & Beer Garden**, T067-220447. Mon-Fri 0830-1730, Sat 0830-1300. Supports and displays crafts made by people in the local community, and has some nice items for sale including baskets and karakul rugs, as well as wood carvings from the north and Tsumeb minerals.

Grootfontein *p135, maps p109 and p136*
Spar, with a coffee shop and bottle store next door is on the main drag, Okavango Rd, while the **OK** supermarket is off this on Hage Geingob St.

O Transport

Otavi *p131, map p109*
368 km to Windhoek, 62 km to Tsumeb, 94 km to Grootfontein.

Bus
Intercape, reservations Windhoek, T061-227847, www.intercape.co.za, buses stop at the **Fourways Total** petrol station on the B1. See timetable, page 16.

Tsumeb *p132, maps p109 and p133*
431 km to Windhoek, 64 km to Grootfontein, 112 km to Etosha (Namutoni), 250 km to Ondangwa.

Bus
Intercape buses, central reservations, Windhoek, T061-227847, www.intercape.co.za, stop at the **Engen** petrol station and **Wimpy**, on Sam Nujoma Dr. See timetable on page 16.

Car
The possibility here to keep car hire costs down, is to get the **Intercape** bus to Tsumeb and hire a car from here to explore the Etosha region. However, both these companies use agents in Tsumeb, so check what vehicles maybe available and book well in advance.
Avis, the agent is Khorab Lodge near Otavi (see page 138) will also arrange cars in Tsumeb, T067-234111, www.avis.co.na.
Europcar, at **Travel North Guesthouse**, (see page 138), Sam Nujoma Dr, T067-220728, www.europcar.co.za.

Grootfontein *p135, maps p109 and p136*
460 km to Windhoek, 278 km to Tsumkwe, 258 km to Rundu.

Bus
Intercape, see timetable on page 16.

O Directory

Tsumeb *p132, maps p109 and p133*
Medical services Private Hospital, Hospital St, T067-224 3000.

Grootfontein *p135, maps p109 and p136*
Medical services State Hospital, Hartmann St, T067-248150.

Bushmanland and Kavango

When you look at a road map of Namibia there is a large blank area in the northeast, on the border with Botswana, with very few roads or settlements. This is the area known as 'Bushmanland'. The San (Bushmen) are the oldest ethnic group in Namibia having inhabited southern Africa for an estimated 20,000 years. The South African 'homeland' policy forced them to settle in this remote semi-desert area, which forms part of the Kalahari. In a wilderness of over 22,000 sq km Tsumkwe is the only settlement of any note. The countryside is flat and dry, the few roads that are marked are no more than tracks in places and there aren't many signposts. Every now and then, narrow sandy paths lead into the bush and the San (Bushmen) settlements. These friendly people still live a traditional life as hunters and gatherers, and they have a deep understanding of nature and ecology. They are able to identify hundreds of plant species and are known to be excellent animal trackers. An estimated 30,000 San (Bushmen) live in Namibia, but only about 2500 of them still follow a traditional way of life in this region. There are a few options to visit a settlement but, like the Himba in the northwest, this must always be done with the utmost respect and sensitivity.

Further north, the arid lands are left behind as you enter Kavango, between Grootfontein and Rundu; also part of today's Otjozondjupa Region. This is the wettest part of Namibia where the average annual rainfall is more than twice that of the south, although most of the rain falls between November and March. There is a marked shift in both vegetation and human influence. Even more striking is the contrast in the style of farming, from the commercial low-intensity farming south of the Red Line to the subsistence living of the small farmers and communities of the north. Almost all the tourist lodges and camps are located in strategic positions along the lush riverbanks, where the scenery is at its most beautiful and game and birdlife is at its most plentiful.

Arriving in Bushmanland

On the B8, 58 km north of Grootfontein, is the turning east on the C44 for Tsumkwe (220 km) and Khaudum National Park. Like Kaokoland in Namibia's northwest, this is a tough part of the country to travel in – you should not even consider exploring here unless you are familiar with 4WD in soft sand and off-road. There are no facilities for tourists and visitors must be completely self-sufficient: food, water, tents and so on must all be brought with you. There are no petrol stations after Grootfontein and Tsumkwe (not to be relied on) so you need to carry extra jerry cans of fuel. On Namibia's border with Botswana is the remote and little-visited Khaudum National Park. Visitors to Khaudum must be in a convoy of at least two vehicles, and elsewhere in the region it would also make sense to travel with another vehicle.

Tsumkwe → *Colour map 2, B2. See also map, page 109.*

Tsumkwe is the former district capital of Bushmanland, and today it administratively falls within the Otjozondjupa Region. But it is no more than a crossroads with a police station and a ramshackle collection of shops, trading stores and bottle shops. There is a petrol pump but don't rely on it. Also here is the Nyae Nyae Conservancy Office (see below). Dotted about this level landscape are the occasional baobab tree and patches of savannah forest, as well as paths leading off to the remote San (Bushmen) communities. You may find San (Bushmen) art for sale on the side of the road: ostrich egg bracelets and necklaces and colourful beaded bags are the most common items. The options from here are to go east for 53 km on a sandy road to the remote border post with Botswana at Dobe (see Border crossing box, page 144), or head north for just over 60 km to Sikereti Camp in the Khaudum National Park (see page 145).

Nyae Nyae Conservancy → *Colour map 2, B3.*

The Nyae Nyae Conservancy is the ancestral home of the Ju/'hoansi San (Bushmen). Through ash taken from fires below the calcrete layer, archaeologists claim the Ju/'hoansi have lived in the region for at least 40,000 years. Historically the inhospitable surrounding desert protected them from Bantu tribes and European settlers making inroads into the region. This relative isolation makes the Ju/'hoansi the most untouched and traditional of all the San (Bushmen) groups, and up until the early 1950s they practised a lifestyle of hunters and gatherers in the greater Kalahari ecosystem almost undisturbed. However, with the building of a fence along the Namibia/Botswana border in 1965, the Ju/'hoansi were squeezed into an ever-diminishing landscape by the South African government. Bushmanland was created as a 'homeland' in attempt to segregate ethnic groups under apartheid, leaving the Ju/'hoansi with 10% of their former territory. This dramatic reduction in land forced the Ju/'hoansi to adapt to new lifestyles, which has resulted in their dispersement across the region and its various communities today.

In 1998 the Nyae Nyae Conservancy became the first communal area in Namibia to be declared a conservancy by the Ministry of Environment and Tourism (MET).

Border crossing

Dobe (Botswana)

This remote border 53 km east of Tsumkwe along a sandy track has little more than a farm gate with a couple of tin sheds on either side, but all formalities are conducted here. Its open 0730-1630 but remember Namibia's daylight saving time is from the first Sunday of April to first Sunday in September, so times could be an hour earlier. Most visitors do not need visas for Botswana. As Botswana is part of the Southern Africa Development Community (SADC), you just have to sign a book to take a vehicle across the border and pay a road levy for Botswana in Namibian dollars, South African rand or Botswana pula. The Namibian dollar is not used in Botswana but the South African rand is, so ensure you've changed over any Namibian dollars over to rand before you reach the border. If in a hire car ensure you have documentation of permission to take a car into Botswana and have third-party insurance. It is not permitted to take meat into Botswana and you will be asked to step out onto the foot-and-mouth 'pad' to wipe your feet and your vehicle's tyres will be sprayed (like you do at the Red Line veterinary control fences elsewhere in Namibia). On the Botswana side It's 135 km to the village of Nokaneng on the A35 (the road that runs down the eastern side of the Okavango Delta). **Note** The road from the border to Nokaneng is very sandy and maybe impassable after heavy rains. A 4WD is essential and even in good conditions, do not expect to travel more than 50 kph; ensure you have everything needed to get yourself out if stuck, and to camp, and travel in convoy if possible. The nearest fuel is 37 km north of Nokaneng at Gumare or at Maun.

This gave the Ju/'hoansi the rights to hunt traditionally, manage natural resources including wildlife and promote tourism. It covers 9003 sq km and stretches from about 30 km west of Tsumkwe and 35 km east to the Botswana border. From north to south it extends for about 100 km.

Tsumkwe lies in the centre of the conservancy, but is not part of it; this means that people from any language group can live in Tsumkwe, but not inside the conservancy borders. Nyae Nyae surrounds a couple of pans, Nyae Nyae and Nama, which tend to flood after rain and then attract wildlife from all over the Kalahari region, including eland, springbok, blue wildebeest and gemsbok. But the real attraction is that the Ju/'hoansi let visitors take part in some of their traditional activities. You can go hunting with the men for spring hare, watch the women gathering and preparing seeds and plants or make local crafts such as ostrich egg jewellery, or see them perform healing rituals or traditional games.

The Nyae Nyae Conservancy Office in Tsumkwe can arrange a guide who will take you out to an outlying village in your own vehicle. Always arrange payment before going on an outing; the office will give you an idea of fees. Expect to pay from N$100 per person for a short walk or N$80 per person for a demonstration of traditional dancing. Crafts are also usually for sale. When you do come into contact with the San (Bushmen) be courteous and respectful at all times.

For overnight stays, several simple campsites have been developed close to their villages in the conservancy, and you can camp for a small fee which goes back into the local community. Again ask at the office or ask your guide where you should camp – under no circumstances set up camp anyway as while the land may look empty and not utilized, it may be in a place that the Ju/'hoansi use for hunting and gathering.

Khaudum National Park

ⓘ *Entry N$40 per person, N$10 per car, per 24 hrs, paid at the ranger's post at Sirkereti Camp, 60 km north of Tsumkwe.*

Khaudum covers an area of 384,200 sq km along the Botswana border on the edge of the Kalahari. It was established to conserve one of the few true wilderness areas in Namibia, and was proclaimed as a game reserve in 1989 and then upgraded to a national park in 2007. Although it has a fairly wide variety of animals and birds, it is a desperately remote park with no facilities, and visitors have to be totally self-sufficient. Many of the tracks are very sandy and it is easy to get stuck, and it should not be explored by inexperienced off-road drivers even if you have the right vehicle.

Arriving in Khaudum National Park

From Tsumkwe follow the road north behind the village school and look out for the signs to the park. It is 60 km to Sikereti Camp. If approaching from the north from the B8, take the D4800 south off the B8 at a village called Shighuru, 90 km east of Rundu. Once you are on the road driving south, check with people at regular intervals that you are on the right route; there are plenty of tracks, masses of sand and no signposts. Note that a minimum of two vehicles per group is allowed to travel in the park.

There are two designated free campsites in the park, Sikereti and Khaudum camps, but there are no facilities whatsoever and it is essential that you carry water (100 litres per vehicle is recommended) and all the food and firewood you may need. The distance between Sikereti and Khaudum camps is about 100 km and the distance takes a full day to drive. You'll need to deflate your tyres and be prepared for your vehicle to be scratched by bushes and trees along the track.

The climate of the area has two distinct seasons: the rainy season extends from late November until March, which is also the hottest time of the year when temperatures can reach 45°C. The rest of the year, April to November, is a long dry season. It's best to avoid late summer, December to March, when rain renders the vegetation very dense and the roads impassable. This is, however, the best time for birds. During the winter, June to October, game numbers seem to improve in the park, particularly close to the artificial waterholes along the *omuramba* (fossil rivers), see below.

Vegetation and wildlife

The vegetation is a dense mix of short and tall dry woodland; in winter, most trees shed their leaves and game viewing is much easier. The dominant trees are wild teak, wild seringa and copalwood. The shorter trees, those less than 5 m in height, include the Kalahari apple-leaf, silver cluster leaf and the shepherd's tree. All of these trees are able to grow on the thin sandy soils of the Kalahari. Running through the park are several fossil rivers known as *omuramba*. The soil along the margins of these have a high clay content and therefore support a different range of trees, a mix of thorns – camel, umbrella and candle as well as leadwood. After the first summer rains look out for the flowering knob thorn.

The *omuramba* no longer flow as rivers, but they fill up and store water which is gradually released during the dry season. They are made up of peat beds and are often identifiable by the abundant reed beds. The lush vegetation within them and along their margins make them a natural east–west migration route for game.

If you wish to see animals around each corner, then this is not the game park for you. Here, game viewing is a real skill; you have to be patient and know something about the animals – what they eat, when they eat, where they prefer to be at different times of the day, and so on. Since very few people visit the park the animals are not used to the sound of engines and they are more likely to bolt than ignore you. But if you look carefully and use some bush skills, there is every chance of a rewarding safari experience.

Animals present include kudu, eland, steenbok, gemsbok, blue wildebeest, giraffe, hartebeest, reedbuck, tsessebe, jackal, spotted hyena, lion, leopard and perhaps cheetah. Notably its home to the rare roan antelope and wild dog, and a highlight is seeing exceptionally large herds of elephant – some 300-strong – that migrate over the border from Botswana. The mix of vegetation habitats provides a wide variety of birds: over 320 species have been recorded, with more than 70 migrant species after good rains.

1 Kavango & Caprivi

Where to stay
Caprivi River Lodge 9
Drotsky's Cabins 6
Hakusembe River Lodge 3

Ichingo Chobe River Lodge 10
Impalila Island Lodge 11
Kaisosi River Lodge 2

Kalizo Lodge 12
Nhoma Safari Camp 4
N'Kwazi Lodge 1
Ntwala Island Lodge 13

North from Grootfontein

After the Tsumkwe turning, there are no other junctions of note before the B8 reaches Rundu. You will encounter a checkpoint at the **Red Line**, the fence dividing the north and south of the country, built to prevent foot-and-mouth disease and rinderpest from migrating south into the large commercial ranches. Its name derives because the German administration used red ink to draw it on maps. Later it was also used by the police to control north–south travel of the indigenous population in South-West Africa during the apartheid era. At the checkpoint, 131 km south of Rundu, there is a small shop, takeaway and petrol station. You will also be asked to step out onto the foot-and-mouth 'pad' to wipe your feet and your vehicle's tyres will be sprayed. The change in landscape and roadside activity north of this divide is striking, you are entering a very different Africa.

Depending on the season, between the Red Line and Rundu you will probably see by the roadside heaped piles of watermelons, contorted gourds or bowls of monkey oranges, as well as some local handicrafts. Avoid driving this stretch after dark as goats and cattle regularly stray into the road; in daylight, enjoy the homesteads, perhaps purchase crafts or fresh produce from roadside stalls. While the road is tarred all the way, beware of potholes and roadworks. Malaria is a risk in the northeast, especially during the wet season.

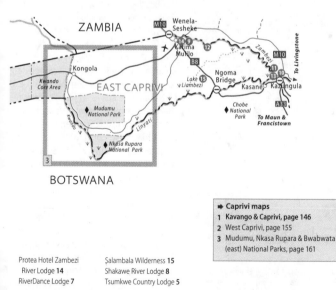

ZAMBIA

Wenela-Sesheke M10

Katima Mulilo B8

12

Kongola

Kwando Core Area

EAST CAPRIVI

Zambezi M10

To Livingstone

Ngoma Bridge

Lake Liambezi

Kasane Kazungula

A33

Mudumu National Park

Kwando

Linyati

Chobe National Park

To Maun & Francistown

Nkasa Rupara National Park

3

BOTSWANA

➡ **Caprivi maps**
1 Kavango & Caprivi, page 146
2 West Caprivi, page 155
3 Mudumu, Nkasa Rupara & Bwabwata (east) National Parks, page 161

Protea Hotel Zambezi River Lodge **14**
RiverDance Lodge **7**
Şalambala Wilderness **15**
Shakawe River Lodge **8**
Tsumkwe Country Lodge **5**

Rundu and onwards → *Colour map 2, A2. Phone code: 066.*

After the long straight drive of 258 km northeast from Grootfontein the sprawl of Rundu is a welcome sight. It was originally built as a bus stop in the 1940s to transport local labour to German-owned farms in the region, and is now a thriving commercial town of about 80,000 people spreading inland along the banks of the Okavango River, the opposite bank is Angola where the river is called the Cubango; in Botswana it becomes known as the Okavango. Since 1993, Rundu has been the provincial capital of the Kavango Region and consequently is home to an impressive number of municipal offices, schools, hospitals and banks, as well as supermarkets and petrol stations. The character of the town is quite different from other Namibian towns; the Portuguese influence from across the border is strong, and there is no legacy of the German past. You will see far fewer white faces than in the south, and outside the formal suburbs shanty towns symbolize the rapid urbanization of the town and high unemployment rate.

While there are lovely views over the Okavango River, particularly from the **Kavango River Lodge**, most tourists use Rundu as a staging post to the quieter and longer established destinations further east, where the abundant rivers and plentiful game offer a compelling package. Remember to refuel in Rundu before continuing; supplies east of here are limited and there's some distance between petrol stations.

There are several options for continuing your journey. It is possible to drive straight through to **Katima Mulilo** (513 km) on the B8. If you have already driven from Grootfontein, this would make for a tough day's driving, and you should ensure there is sufficient time to arrive in daylight. At the small village of **Katere**, 117 km east of Rundu on the B8, is the well-signposted turning south to Khaudum National Park (4WD only, see above). Once at Khaudum, the intrepid might want to exit via the south and complete a circuit back to the main road just north of Grootfontein. Another popular option is to drive along the B8 for roughly 200 km as far as **Popa Falls** and spend the night at the Namibia Wildlife Resorts (NWR) camp, **Ngepi Camp**, or one of the private lodges along the banks of the Okavango River. The next day you have the option of exploring the **Bwabwata National Park**, entering Botswana, or continuing east through Caprivi towards Katima Mulilo.

The other option is to head west along the C45; the first 135-km section

Where to stay 🛏
Hakusembe River Lodge 2
Kaisosi River Lodge 5
Kavango River Lodge 1
N'Kwazi Lodge 6
Omashare 3
Tambuti Lodge 4

to Nkurenkuru has recently been renamed the B10 and has been tarred. This is because it leads another 35 km northwest to the newly opened **Katwitwi border post** with Angola (0700-1800). It is at the end of the new 267-km Tsumeb–Katwitwi road (under construction) which will carry traffic from the interior of Namibia via Tsumeb to the border. By the time you read this it should be open. The road on the other side goes roughly 360 km to Menongue in Angola and is also presently being upgraded; check locally for up-to-date news of these developments and for more information about crossing into Angola. ▸ *See Border crossing box, page 216.*

Nkurenkuru itself lies on the Okavango River opposite the town of Cuangar in Angola. It started life as a Finnish mission base in 1929 and like most of the other towns along the river, was a base for the South African Defence Force during the Angolan Bush War. Today it has a modest population of around 7000, a few small shops, a branch of Bank Windhoek and petrol stations. The town and the Katwitwi border are expected to develop considerably once the road is in use. The C45 continues west for another 364 km to Oshakati (see page 214).

◉ Bushmanland and Kavango listings

For hotel and restaurant price codes and other relevant information, see pages 21-28.

◉ Where to stay

Tsumkwe *p143, maps p109 and 146*
$$$$ Nhoma Safari Camp, turn off the B8 onto the C44 towards Tsumkwe, the turn-off north to Nhoma is 185 km from the B8 and the sign reads Nhoma/ Aasvoelnes, Nhoma is 40 km further on. The road is normally suitable for 2WD vehicles but check ahead, T0812-734606, www.tsumkwel.iway.na. This lodge exclusively offers a 2-day/2-night package of accommodation, meals and interaction with the Ju/'hoansi San (Bushmen) in the Nyae Nyae Conservancy including walks, hunting and evening performances. This is an authentic San (Bushmen) experience and profits support the local village. Only pre-booked visitors are permitted. 10 furnished tents on wooden decks under the shade of Zambezi teak trees, with bathrooms in reed compounds, a restaurant and bar under thatch. You can also **camp ($)**, hot showers, and pay extra for the activities. They can arrange guides to go with you to the Khaudum campsites.
$$$ Tsumkwe Country Lodge, reservations Windhoek T061-374750 or book through **Temba Safaris**, South Africa, T+027 (0)21-855 0395, www.temba. co.za. This is the only place to stay in Tsumkwe, with 25 canvas-sided, en suite bungalows, restaurant with set menu, bar, swimming pool, half- and full-day guided excursions to Nyae Nyae Conservancy and San (Bushmen) villages. There's also a small **campsite ($)** with hot showers.
$ Omatako Valley Rest Camp, turn off the B8 onto the C44 towards Tsumkwe for 111 km, www.omatakovalley.com. Sandy campsites under shady trees, with a thatched hut and table, *braai* pits and taps, no electricity but flush toilets and solar-powered warm showers in an open-roofed reed ablution block. You can buy firewood and San (Bushmen) crafts and village visits and guided walks can be arranged here for around N$50-80 per person.

Nyae Nyae Conservancy *p143*
$ Nyae Nyae Conservancy Campsites,
These campsites are basically simple
clearings beneath the arms of baobab
trees with no facilities. There are several
in the region and to get directions and
GPS coordinates go first to the Nyae Nyae
Conservancy Office. Camping fees of
about N$50 per person should be paid
at the nearest village, where you can
also get water and firewood. All rubbish,
including toilet paper, should be burnt
or removed.

Rundu and onwards *p148, maps p146
and p148*
The lodges are all fairly well signposted.
Most offer boat trips on the Okavango
River, but these may not be possible
May-Nov when water levels are low.
However, if you're energetic you may
enjoy a paddle in a canoe.
$$$ Hakusembe River Lodge, 16 km
west of Rundu, reservations Windhoek,
T061-230066, www.gondwana-collection.
com. Take the B8 towards Grootfontein,
after 2 km turn northwest on the C45/
B10 towards Nkurenkuru, turn right after
10 km and follow signs for a further 4 km.
Stunning riverside location and recently
refurbished to a high standard by the
Gondwana Collection, 22 thatched a/c
chalets with patios and river views set
under shady trees, excellent restaurant,
stylish wooden bar, swimming pool, and
small **campsite ($)** with 8 grassy pitches.
Activities include pontoon champagne
trips and fishing for tiger fish.
$$$ Kavango River Lodge, 14 Fish Eagle
St, Rundu, T066-255244, www.natron.
net/kavango-river-lodge. Set high above
the river looking west, with fabulous river
views in the evening, with 18 a/c chalets,
8 are B&B and 10 self-catering, restaurant
and bar, activities include fishing and

boat cruises. Lovely position and friendly
but dated so hence slightly overpriced.
$$ Kaisosi River Lodge, 7 km east of
Rundu, 2 km north of the B8, T066-267125,
www.kaisosiriverlodge.com. A green,
shaded area by the river, 16 thatched a/c
chalets, square and simply decorated,
restaurant and bar with wooden deck,
swimming pool, boat for breakfast and
sundowner cruises. **Campsite ($)** with
16 sites which are a little close together
but each has its own bathroom, power
point and thatched *braai* area.
$$ N'Kwazi Lodge, 21 km east of Rundu
off the B8, then 3 km towards the river
on the D3402, well signposted, T0812-
424897, www.nkwazilodge.com.
A simple place with 12 spacious,
thatched bungalows dotted along the
riverbank, can put extra beds in to sleep
4, campsite set in neat, well-kept grounds
with plenty of shade. Restaurant and bar
with outdoor deck, can prepare packed
lunches for onward journeys, swimming
pool, good birdwatching, and can
organize village visits.
$$ Omashare Hotel, Maria Mwengere
St, opposite FNB bank, Rundu, T066-
266600, www.omasherehotel.com.
A town hotel and nothing fancy but
worth mentioning if you arrive in Rundu
late, 20 rooms with DSTV, restaurant, long
wooden veranda, 'ladies' bar, swimming
pool set in large lawn where peacocks
roam, views of river in the distance.
$$ Tambuti Lodge, 1.2 km north of the
centre of Rundu, T066-255711, www.
tambuti.com.na. On the river with good
views of village life on the other side in
Angola, with 8 pretty, large whitewashed
bungalows with DSTV and Wi-Fi, set in
beautiful lush gardens, swimming pool,
good, small restaurant/bar, and a sandy
area on the river with tables and *braai* pits
and a launching ramp for canoes.

🍴 Restaurants

Rundu and onwards *p148, maps p146 and p148*

Eating out is limited, but there are a few takeaways around town, **Wimpy** at the Engen petrol station on the B8, and all the lodges have restaurants. If driving through the **Omashare Hotel** has a decent à la carte restaurant with some Portuguese-inspired dishes like peri-peri chicken and chips. For the more adventurous, there is street food behind the main market.

🛍 Shopping

Rundu and onwards *p148, maps p146 and p148*

A large number of Angolans cross the border by boat to do their food shopping in Rundu, although it's not an official border crossing. There are several supermarkets; the **Shoprite** is located north of the **Total** petrol station on Eugene Kakakuru St, while **Pick 'n' Pay** is in the Mangetti Mall on Markus Siwarongo St. Rundu's bottle stores have some of the most extensive ranges in the country, there are numerous clothes and 'From China' shops, and enough furniture shops to supply half of Namibia. Also in town opposite the Mangetti Mall is a useful branch of **Cymot** to stock up on camping/fishing supplies and car accessories (Mon-Fri 0800-1700, Sat 0800-1300). The region is also known for its woodcarvings and these can be purchased for not unreasonable prices at the **Rundu Open Market**, Maria Mwengere St, which, is in fact, one of the largest markets in Namibia with more than 350 stalls selling everything from fruit and veg to bed sheets (Mon-Fri 0600-2100, Sat 0600-1800).

🚌 Transport

Rundu and onwards *p148, maps p146 and p148*

258 km to Grootfontein, 205 km to Popa Falls, 201 km to Divundu, 233 km to Mohembo border (Botswana), 513 km to Katima Mulilo.

Air

Air Namibia, reservations Windhoek T061-299 6333, www.airnamibia.com.na. Has flights between Rundu and **Windhoek's Eros Airport** in each direction on Mon, Wed, Fri and Sun. They depart Windhoek at 1015, arrive in Rundu at 1130, depart Rundu at 1150 and arrive in Katima Mulilo at 1250. They depart again at 1335, and get back to Eros at 1515. Those returning from Rundu to Eros will need to go via Katima Mulilo.

Bus

Intercape buses between Windhoek and **Livingstone**, stop at the Engen petrol station on the B8 2 km south of town. See timetable, page 16.

Taxi

There are plenty of long-distance shared taxis arriving and leaving from the large rank opposite the Engen petrol station on the B8, 2 km south of town.

🏢 Directory

Rundu and onwards *p148, maps p146 and p148*

Mechanical repairs FDS Auto Electric & Repairs, Eugene Kakuru St, T066-255760. **Medical services** State hospital, off Markus Siwarongo St, T066-265500. The largest hospital in Kavango Region but particularly poor: avoid if possible and head to the private **Medi Clinic Otjiwarongo** (see page 118).

Caprivi

The pan-handle shaped Caprivi Region is a land of fertile, flat flood plains surrounded by perennial rivers, a far cry from the arid lands of the Kalahari or the Namib-Naukluft. The area is crossed by three major rivers; the Zambezi, the Okavango and the Kwando/Linyati/Chobe (names confusingly change depending on what country you're in), which form the boundaries between Namibia, Zambia, Botswana, Angola and Zimbabwe. The regional centre is Katima Mulilo, a busy commercial town on the banks of the Zambezi. Don't dwell in town: the attractions of the region are the tranquil lodges, plentiful game and birdlife and beautiful river scenery, centred in the rarely visited national parks. All three parks – Mudumu, Nkasa Rupara (formerly Mamili) and Bwabwata – offer a similar experience, with few tourist facilities, made up for by pristine woodland and riverine flood plain with abundant local and migrant wildlife. The lodges in this region make the most of their riverside settings and are well worth settling in for a few days to enjoy the scenery and the activities. These include sunset river cruises on pontoons, canoeing, fishing and game viewing, before continuing into Botswana to visit the magnificent Chobe National Park and Zimbabwe or Zambia for the famous Victoria Falls. It is only a two-hour drive from Katima to Livingstone in Zambia and a three-hour drive from Katima to Victoria Falls. At the extreme eastern end of the strip and usually accessed from Botswana, are the isolated lodges surrounded by rippling beds of water lilies and tall baobabs on Impalila Island where the Zambezi and Chobe rivers converge. In the Zambezi at the eastern end of the island is the exact point where Namibia, Botswana, Zambia and Zimbabwe all meet.

Berlin Conference – carving up the strip

The Caprivi Strip owes its origins to the Berlin Conference when the European colonial powers decided how to carve up Africa between themselves. On 1 July 1890, Britain traded Heliogoland and the Caprivi Region for Zanzibar and parts of Bechuanaland, present-day Botswana. Germany planned to use the strip as a trade route into central Africa, but even before the outbreak of the First World War this plan was thwarted by the activities of Cecil Rhodes in modern-day Zimbabwe.

The strip was named after the German Chancellor, General Count Georg Leo von Caprivi di Caprara di Montecuccoli. Unlike the rest of Namibia the region has little to show from the German period of rule. The strip returned to British control at the outbreak of the First World War, less than 25 years after the Germans had assumed control of the region. The return to British control came about in a most unusual fashion. The story goes that the German governor was having afternoon tea with a senior British official from Rhodesia, when a message arrived saying that war had just been declared between the two countries. The governor was placed under arrest and the territory under his control annexed.

In 1918 the land was incorporated into Bechuanaland and thus ruled by the British. In 1929 it was handed over to the South African ruled South-West Africa, and at independence it remained part of Namibia.

Arriving in Caprivi

All the attractions in the region are on or off the B8, also known in the Caprivi as the Trans-Caprivi Highway, which runs for 513 km from Rundu to Katima Mulilo. The Katima Mulilo Bridge spans the Zambezi to the Zambian town of Sesheke from where a recently upgraded paved road runs to Livingstone joining the main southern highway to Lusaka, which connects onwards to Zambia's Copperbelt. This route is a section of the Walvis Bay Corridor, a trade route linking land-locked Zambia (and neighbouring countries such as the Democratic Republic of Congo, Malawi and Zimbabwe) to the port at Walvis Bay. The highway is in great condition, but beware when driving off the main tarred road: in this waterlogged part of Namibia, sand, mud or water can slow progress and fray nerves.

Background

The Caprivi Strip is a classic example of how the former colonial powers shaped the boundaries of modern Africa (see box, above). The strip is 500 km long, at its narrowest only 32 km wide, while at the eastern end it bulges to almost 100 km wide before narrowing to a point at the confluence of the Zambezi and Chobe rivers where the boundaries of Zimbabwe, Namibia, Zambia and Botswana convene.

From the early 1960s until 1990 the region was in a constant state of turmoil, notably the Angolan Bush War (see box, page 212), and the Caprivi Region was home to the South African Army and police and, as a consequence, no one really knows what went on up here. There were secret army camps, the airfield at Mpacha (now Katima Mulilo) was used for air strikes into Angola and Zambia, and the region was closed to anyone who didn't live here or have a legitimate reason for visiting. There was a brief resurgence of 'trouble' in 1999 between the Namibian government and the Caprivi Liberation Army (CLA), a rebel group aiming for the secession of the Caprivi Strip led by Mishake Muyongo. The main eruption occurred on 2 August 1999 when the CLA launched an attack in Katima Mulilo, occupying the state-run radio station and attacking a police station, the Wenela border post, and an army base. Namibian armed forces quashed the attempt at secession within a few days.

Added to this, West Caprivians, in particular, had to live for 27 years with the Angolan Civil War on their border, until peace was restored in Angola in 2002. Today the local communities remain poorly off, economically, as a result of many years of conflict and also because of their relative isolation from the rest of Namibia. The population is mostly made up of subsistence farmers who make their living on the banks of the various rivers. But now-accessible and new borders with Angola, (and the inevitable trade associated with borders), means that the region is enjoying a burgeoning prosperity.

The Caprivi Region became one of Namibia's 13 regions when the country gained independence in 1990. In 2013 it was officially renamed the Zambezi Region in a step to eliminate names of colonial administrators from Namibia's maps. However, it will be some time before this is reflected to its full extent and people become used to the new name.

West Caprivi → *For listings, see pages 166-172.*

Divundu → *Colour map 2, A4.*

Divundu is the village at the bridge where the Trans-Caprivi Highway (B8) crosses the Okavango River 201 km east of Rundu. The river marks the border of Namibia's Okavango Region and Caprivi Region (recently renamed the Zambezi Region). When you arrive all you will see is a Engen petrol station (0600-2100) just before the bridge, where there is a fairly well-stocked supermarket that also sells engine oil and tyres, as well as a small takeaway. Note that this is the last place to fill up with fuel until Kongola (202 km). From Divundu, just a few kilometres south on the C48, is Popa Falls, where the river runs through the rapids with amazing force. Below the rapids lies the former Mahango Game Reserve (now incorporated into the Bwabwata National Park). Also along this stretch of river are many lodges and campsites to accommodate visitors to this section of the park, and for those en route to and from Botswana's Okavango Delta, crossing the Namibia–Botswana border at Mohembo, 35 km south of Divundu (see box, page 158).

Popa Falls → *Colour map 2, A4.*

ⓘ *Namibia Wildlife Resorts (NWR), www.nwr.com.na. Just before the B8 crosses the Okavango River, turn south on the C48 for 5 km, the entrance is clearly signposted. Day visitors are permitted sunrise-sunset, N$10, children (under 16) free.*

The NWR camp at Popa Falls has long been a popular overnight destination, dating from the days when the road between Rundu and Katima Mulilo was all gravel and an overnight limb-restoring rest was a necessity. Be warned, Popa Falls are not falls at all, rather a series of rapids, waterways and islands on the Okavango River. When the river is low the highest visible drop is about 3 m. There is a walkway into the middle of the river, after this you are free to scramble over the rocks from where birds, a few hippo and some crocodile may be seen. At this point it's about 1 km wide with the river split into a series of channels making their way through the rocks. It's dangerous to swim in the river because of crocodiles and there is also biharzia in the water. The comfortable NWR accommodation at the camp (see page 167) has recently been extensively refurbished, and in parts rebuilt including the addition of a thatched riverside pub with good views. The campsite suffers from the inflated NWR charges, but is set among lovely grassed lawns, by the water's edge. This is a popular spot for travellers on the way to Botswana and a convenient stopping place when travelling between Kavango and East Caprivi.

Bwabwata National Park → *Colour map 2, A4.*
ⓘ *If you are just passing through on the B8, or the C48 between Divundu and the Mohembo border with Botswana, you do not have to pay. Entry fees only apply if you venture off the B8 or C48 on to the park tracks, N$80 per person, children (under 16) free, N$10 per car.*

② West Caprivi

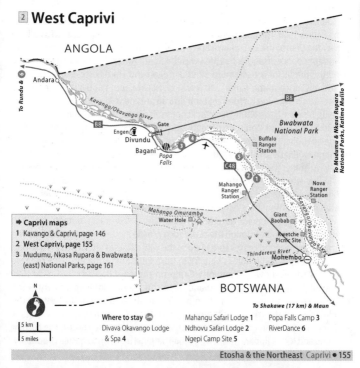

➔ Caprivi maps
1 Kavango & Caprivi, page 146
2 West Caprivi, page 155
3 Mudumu, Nkasa Rupara & Bwabwata (east) National Parks, page 161

Where to stay 🛏
Divava Okavango Lodge & Spa 4

Mahangu Safari Lodge 1
Ndhovu Safari Lodge 2
Ngepi Camp Site 5

Popa Falls Camp 3
RiverDance 6

On either side of the Trans-Caprivi Highway (B8), the Bwabwata National Park was proclaimed in 2007 from the former Mahango Game Reserve and the Caprivi Game Park. The park is sandwiched between the Kavango/Okavango and Kwando rivers, with the northern boundary formed by Angola and to the south, Botswana. The park is 40 km wide and 190 km long covering a vast area of 7600 sq km, and now includes what has become known as the Kwando, Buffalo and Mahango core areas. It is a region of swamps, flood plains and riverine woodland, and is generally flat with a few sporadic sand dunes rising on the horizon. At present visitors can see the park on the 190-km section of drive through the park along the B8 between Divundu and Kongola, and on the C48 between Divundu and the Mohembo border with Botswana. The mixed forest and bush country is beautifully scenic and full of life; keep an eye out for game, particularly elephant, in the morning and evening, and more than 450 species of bird have been recorded in the park, so these are rewarding drives for birdwatchers. However, the best way to explore Bwabwata, and to spend time to really appreciate this environment that is so different to other parts of Namibia, is to stay for a day or two at the riverside lodges at either the Divundu or Kavango ends of the park (see Where to stay, page 166), from where activities include boat trips, game drives and walks.

Background

The Caprivi Game Reserve was first proclaimed in 1966 and upgraded to the Caprivi Game Park in 1968. The park has had a chequered history as it was declared a military area by the South African Defence Force during Namibia's war of liberation. During the independence struggle, this area was the South African Army Buffalo Base, the training grounds for the infamous 32nd Battalion and Third Force. Sadly, the army hunted out much of the game, and it is said that Western Caprivi was kept as the private hunting ground for former South African president John Vorster who used to come up here and go hunting from helicopters. It was not until after Independence in 1990 that the park could be properly run as a conservation area. From 1999, it was decided that the former rather disjointed reserves of Caprivi and neighbouring Mahango would be amalgamated and be renamed as the Bwabwata National Park, to become under the one management of the Ministry of Environment and Tourism (MET). This was to benefit the environment for the wildlife and also the people in the area, and certain areas were de-proclaimed and the land given over to the isolated rural communities living along the B8, centred on the old military posts.

Bwabwata was formerly gazetted in 2007, and a few tracks suitable for 4WD vehicles have been cut through the bush. Today cattle movement around the park is controlled to prevent diseases spreading to the wild game. In return there is a strong focus on the local communities benefiting from tourist infrastructure. One of these projects is the **Nambwa Community Camp** on the Kwando River (see page 169). Additionally, the lodges, campsites, and safari concessions on the periphery of the park run by private operators, in turn provide much needed employment for the people living on the fringes of the newly declared park boundaries. Bwabwata is definitely a work in progress and is expected to expand to also contain the current Mudumu and Nkasa Rupara (formerly Mamili) national parks on its eastern boundary.

Arriving in Bwabwata National Park The Trans-Caprivi Highway (B8) runs through the entire length of Bwabwata and does not require a permit. Upon entering the park just beyond Divundu, you will pass through a police and MET checkpoint, where you may be asked to produce your driver's licence and be asked to step out onto the foot-and-mouth 'pad' to wipe your feet and your vehicle's tyres will be sprayed (like you do at the Red Line veterinary control further south on the B8 towards Grootfontein). The same happens at the checkpoint at the other end of the park on the west side of the Kwando River and 2 km east of Kongola if coming from the other direction.

Entry permits are, however, applicable if you are venturing off the road at the Kongola end to go to **Susuwe Lodge** or **Nambwa Campsite** (see Where to stay, pages 168 and 169); both of which are in the park on the western side of the Kwando River down a sandy road (4WD only). Fees are paid at the Susuwe Ranger Station on the B8 at the park boundary. There is no fuel along the B8 as it runs through the park; Divundu is a fairly safe bet, but be sure to fill up in Rundu and Kongola.

On the C48 between Divundu and the Mohembo border with Botswana in the Mahango Core Area of Bwabwata, again there is no entry permit if just driving through. But in addition to the main road running through the park, there are two side tracks, one for ordinary cars and the other only suitable for 4WD vehicles, for which entry fees are applicable. The ordinary track to the east follows the river. When in full flood it can be impassable, but the staff at the Mahango Ranger Post on the C48 (where you also pay entry fees) will let you know. This track is about 15 km; there is a large baobab and a picnic spot overlooking the river at Kwetche. The western trail is 31 km and follows the course of the two *omurambas* in the park. These roads are very sandy in the dry season, and slippery after the rains. Nevertheless, this is a special drive through unspoilt bush country, though if you have limited 4WD experience it is best to stick to the ordinary road which offers game (and driving challenge) enough.

Best time to visit There are two distinct seasons. Between 500 mm and 600 mm of rain is expected in the rainy season (December to March) when it gets hot, with the average daily maximum over 30°C. The dry season extends from April to November with no rain expected and evening temperatures falling to around 7°C. The best time to visit during the winter months is from June to October, when game will be found close to the river and waterholes. Birdlife is prolific from November to March, after the rains, when insects are abundant and many of the trees flower and carry fruit. The same climatic conditions also apply to Mudumu and Nkasa Rupara (formerly Mamili).

Vegetation and wildlife The reed-lined rivers of Bwabwata National Park are a Namibian rarity – they are perennial. The Kavango/Okavango, which is the source of the Okavango Delta in neighbouring Botswana, acts as a 400-km-long border between Namibia and Angola. During high waters, normally in April, river levels rise between 3-4 m above the low watermark. This overflow feeds the floodplains and is essential to the wetlands in both Namibia and Botswana. The Kwando forms the

Border crossing

Mohembo (Botswana)

The Mohembo border post is 35 km south of Divundu on the C48. If you are just transiting through the Mahango section of the Bwabwata National Park on the main road and don't deviate on the game-driving tracks, you don't have to pay entry fees. Note that no motorbikes are permitted in the park, and therefore on this section of the C48. The border is open 0600-1800, but Namibia's daylight saving time is from the first Sunday of April to the first Sunday in September, meaning the times could be an hour earlier.

Most nationalities do not need visas for Botswana. As Botswana is part of the Southern Africa Development Community (SADC), you just have to sign a book to take a vehicle across the border and pay a road levy for Botswana. If in a hire car ensure you have documentation of permission to take a car into Botswana and have third-party insurance. Fees are paid for in US dollars, rand or Botswana pula. Note that Namibia dollars are not used in Botswana but the South Africa rand is, so ensure you've changed over any Namibia dollars to rand while still in Namibia.

The road on the Botswana side is the A35, and the first settlement is Shakawe, 17 km from the border. There are a couple of good options to stay here, both of which overlook the papyrus-dotted channels of the Okavango River:
$$$ **Shakawe River Lodge**, 12 km south of Shakawe, T+267-684 0403, www.shakawelodge.com. 10 lovely canvas-walled and thatched a/c rooms decorated with African artefacts, dining room and bar in a thatched boma, swimming pool. The grassy and popular campsite ($) has its own restaurant and bar, and sites have electricity and lights, there are four pre-erected dome tents for those without their own camping gear.
$$-$ **Drotsky's Cabins**, 11 km south of Shakawe, then 2 km off the road, accessible by 2WD but drive carefully, T+267-687 5035, www.drotskycabins.com. Six A-frame thatched chalets sleeping up to four and a campsite, restaurant and bar in a lovely location on stilts and can organize fishing.

From Shakawe, the road then continues south for 377 km to Maun with the 'panhandle' of the Okavango Delta to the east. Maun is the principal town for excursions into the delta as well as scenic flights. If you are driving, there are numerous campsites where you can park up your vehicle while spending three or four days exploring the tranquil delta on foot and by *mokoro*. For further information visit Botswana Tourism's website; www.botswanatourism.co.bw.

border between East and West Caprivi, and seasonal rains (November to March), often accompanied by dramatic displays of thunder and lightning, create temporary pans known as *omurambas*. These environments are ideal for numerous species of flora and fauna to thrive

The dominant tree species are Kalahari apple-leaf, water pear and jackal-berry; along the flood plain margins you will see the wild date palm. If you visit one of the private lodges or **Popa Falls Camp** you will find many of these riverine trees have been helpfully labelled. A tree that every visitor quickly learns to recognize is the baobab. There are several groups within the park, including a distinctive clump just before the Kwetche Picnic Site in the Mahango Core Area.

If you are fortunate you will encounter a wide variety of animals, and the park is home to some rare (certainly in Namibia) antelope: sable and roan (both shy but readily indentified by their magnificent curved horns), reedbuck, tsessebe and sitatunga. The sitatunga is very difficult to spot since it is small and lives in thick swamp areas; if you manage to see one, consider yourself very lucky. They are only found in large numbers in the Okavango Delta. Reedbuck and red lechwe are also quite difficult to spot and they tend to inhabit the flood plains. Along the riverbank are good numbers of kudu and Chobe bushbuck, and in addition to antelope, you can expect to see hippo and crocodile in the rivers, and buffalo, warthog, baboon and vervet monkey in the wooded areas and from the roads. Main predators such as lion, leopard, cheetah and hyena are present, and the park is one of the last refuges for wild dog in Namibia, but these are rarely seen. Easily seen, however, and one of the highlights of the park, are the large herds of elephant that migrate across from Botswana.

There are more than 450 species of birds – the most of any national park or reserve in Namibia – and twitchers can expect to spot more than 50 different species in a couple of hours sitting by the rivers at one of the lodges or from the Kwetche Picnic Site in the Mahango Core Area. The different habitats in the park appeal to wide variety of species, and birds include wattled crane, African skimmer, western banded snake eagle, wood owl, Pel's fishing owl, narina trogon, Cape parrot, both red billed and yellow billed oxpeckers, and various herons and egrets.

East Caprivi → *For listings, see pages 166-172.*

At the eastern end of **Bwabwata National Park**, and 202 km from Divundu, the Trans-Caprivi Highway (B8) crosses the Kwando River, which effectively divides West and East Caprivi. Here the narrow Caprivi Strip opens up into a triangle of land that constitutes the pan section of the pan-handle. A closer look at a map of East Caprivi reveals the unusual feature that except for a 90-km strip of land along the northern border, between the Kwando River and the Zambezi River, the region is completely surrounded by rivers. The Kwando-Linyanti-Chobe forms the border to the west, south and southeast, with the Zambezi, the border with Zambia, to the northeast. Enclosed by these rivers is a landscape which is largely flat, with numerous flood plains, oxbow lakes, swamps and seasonal channels.

The hydrography of the area is particularly interesting because in years of good rain the flow of water in stretches of the rivers can be reversed and water can actually spill into the Okavango Delta system, a completely different (internally draining) watershed. With a map in hand, consider the complexities of the river system, starting in Angola, where the **Kwando River** rises in the Luchazes Mountains. As this river flows southeast it forms the border between Angola and Zambia before it cuts across the eastern end of the narrowest part of the Caprivi Strip (the eastern border of the Bwabwata National Park). Where the river cuts through Namibia (past Kongola) it is known as the **Kwando**. Having cut across the Caprivi Strip, the river once again becomes an international boundary, this time between Botswana and Namibia. At Nkasa Island, the southwest corner of Nkasa Rupara (formerly Mamili) National Park, the river channel turns sharply for 90 degrees from the southeast to the northeast and becomes known as the **Linyati River** Inside the corner of this bend is a swamp that lies in Nkasa Rupara and is similar in appearance to the Okavango Delta. The **Linyati** reaches the Ngoma border post, and from here it becomes the **Chobe**, which flows into the **Zambezi** at Impalila Island. Confused? It's even worse 'on the ground'!

Kongola and around → *Colour map 2, A5.*
Kongola is the village straddling the B8 about 3 km east of the boundary of Bwabwata National Park. It is little more than a petrol station, a few buildings and a series of signs advertising camps and lodges along the road south, the C49, to two of Namibia's least developed national parks: **Mudumu** and **Nkasa Rupara** (formerly Mamili). Both of these are set in beautiful countryside, and as with Bwabwata, both are just starting to see the return of substantial amounts of wildlife.

At the B8/C491 junction in Kongola, by the Engen petrol station, is the **Mashi Craft Market** ⓘ *daily 0900-1600.* Opened in 1997 as a community project, it sells a range of traditional handicrafts from all over the Caprivi region. As well as baskets and mats made from the *makalani* palm, there are interesting bracelets, earrings and other pieces of traditional jewellery made from seeds, and some woodcarvings that are distinctive to the Caprivi region.

Mudumu National Park → *Colour map 2, A5.*
ⓘ *N$80 per person, children (under 16) free, N$10 per car, which are paid at the Ngenda Ranger Post on the C49.*
Mudumu National Park was proclaimed in 1990, just before independence, and covers 785 sq km. The main attraction is the riverine habitat of the Kwando River, while inland the Mudumu Mulapo fossilized river course and the dense mopane woodland shelter numerous species of game and birds. Its charm lies in its simplicity, with no residents (though there are some lodges and simple bush camps in the area), few visitors and increasing numbers of game. The best place to stay is the upmarket **Lianshulu Lodge** (see page 168) in the south of the park by the Kwando River, which is a special place that offers plenty of activities to enjoy the environment. Today the lodge is very much associated with the park, although not for day-to-day management, and at present the park remains a backwater as far as the Ministry of Environment and Tourism (MET) is concerned. There are no gates at the entrance to the park, and you are unlikely to meet anyone as you drive along the few tracks in the park.

Arriving in Mudumu National Park Just east of the Kwando River, turn south off the B8 by the Engen garage at Kongola, onto the C49, which is a well-maintained gravel road – its only when you go into the parks or along the access roads to some of the lodges and camps that you may need to engage 4WD depending on the time of year. You will pass the turning to **Camp Kwando** and after another 30 km you'll see a sign indicating the park entrance at the Ngenda Ranger Station. There are plans by MET to develop Ngenda into a proper gate and visitors centre, and for now this is where you may or may not be asked for park entry fees. The park boundary is marked also by the sudden lack of subsistence farmers and land cleared for millet fields. It is 40 km from the B8 to the turning for **Lianshulu Lodge**.

Vegetation and wildlife A large part of Mudumu is dominated by *mopane* woodland, interspersed with camelthorn, Natal mahogany, mangosteen and mixed acacia. Within the woods are depressions that become flooded after the rains. The western boundary of the park is marked by plentiful reeds along the

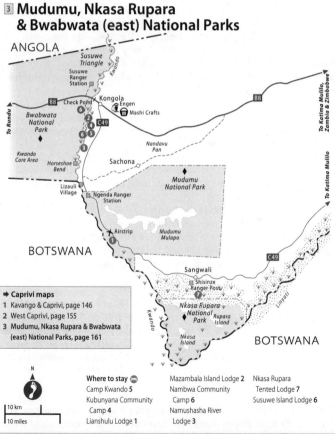

③ Mudumu, Nkasa Rupara & Bwabwata (east) National Parks

Where to stay 🛏
Camp Kwando **5**
Kubunyana Community
  Camp **4**
Lianshulu Lodge **1**

Mazambala Island Lodge **2**
Nambwa Community
  Camp **6**
Namushasha River
  Lodge **3**

Nkasa Rupara
  Tented Lodge **7**
Susuwe Island Lodge **6**

➡ Caprivi maps
1 Kavango & Caprivi, page 146
2 West Caprivi, page 155
3 Mudumu, Nkasa Rupara & Bwabwata (east) National Parks, page 161

10 km
10 miles

Kwando River, and remnants of riverine forest (with woodland waterberry trees) and grassed flood plains. Soil is primarily Kalahari sandveld with belts of clay and alluvium where the forest occurs.

The best game viewing is in winter, from June to October, before the heat and, more importantly, before the rain comes. After the rains, numerous ponds of water form away from the perennial Kwando and sightings become more rare. Between 1974 and the early 1980s the region was managed as a private hunting concession and much of the game was shot, and there remain occasional poachers (for food), but game numbers are on the increase, regardless. Animals present include hippo, crocodile, elephant, buffalo, kudu, impala, steenbok, warthog, Burchell's zebra, southern reedbuck, red lechwe, oribi and baboon. Although once hunted out, giraffe, eland and sable have been reintroduced in recent years. If you are lucky you may catch a glimpse of tsessebe, sitatunga, spotted hyena and lion, and leopard, cheetah and even wild dog have been seen in the area, but sightings are extremely rare. Birdwatchers should be on the lookout by the water for slaty egret, rufous-bellied heron, wattled crane, wattled and long-toed plovers, red-winged pratincole, coppery-tailed coucal and the occasional coppery and purple-banded sunbird. Woodland areas are home to Bradfield's hornbill, mosque swallow, Anrot's chat, long-tailed and lesser blue-eared starlings, broad-billed roller and yellow-billed and red-billed oxpeckers.

Nkasa Rupara (formerly Mamili) National Park → Colour map 2, A5.

ⓘ N$80 per person, children (under 16) free, N$10 per car, which are paid at the Shisinze Ranger Post near the village of Sangwali on the C49.

Created at the same time as Mudumu, this is a seldom visited park tucked in the southwestern corner of East Caprivi, across the Kwando River from Botswana. It is centered around the Nkasa and Rupara islands in the river (hence the new name) and the entire area is flat, consisting of channels of reed beds, lagoons and islands. It is Namibia's largest formally protected wetland area, of which 8% of the 318-sq-km park is underwater after significant rains (usually between May and August). The landscape resembles the Okavango Delta in Botswana, but with hardly any development and there is only one new lodge here. The principal attraction is the birdlife (an amazing 430 recorded species), but there is plenty for the game viewer too.

Arriving in Nkasa Rupara National Park From the B8, travel south along the C49 through Mudumu until you see signposts for Nkasa Rupara (formerly Mamili) National Park. Two new steel bridges were built in 2010 on the road to the park, which also provide access to the only lodge in the park, **Nkasa Rupara Tented Lodge**, but a 4WD is still essential (thick sand or mud, year round). Alternatively safe parking is available in Sangwali village (75 km from Kongola) at the park's Shisinze Ranger Post (where you also pay park entry fees) and pick up can be arranged from the lodge.

Wildlife The variety of animals you can expect to see is more or less the same as for Mudumu. The large area of swampland means that you are more likely to see the antelope that favour this environment – red lechwe, sitatunga and waterbuck. If you are lucky you may also see puku, another swamp antelope, which is only found along the Chobe River and is quite rare. Overall, the game viewing in this park is unpredictable as a large proportion of the animals still migrate between Angola and Botswana. Poaching and hunting have also left their mark. During the dry season the park has a reputation for large herds of buffalo and migrant elephant. Lion and leopard also live in the park, but you are likely, at best, to see only their spoor.

Katima Mulilo and around → *Colour map 2, A6. Phone code: 066.*

Katima Mulilo (sometimes shortened to 'Katima') is 513 km east of Rundu and is the capital of the Zambezi Region with a population of around 30,000. Visitors to the area can be excused for thinking that it feels more like Zambia than Namibia, as it is the country's most remote outpost: 1225 km from Windhoek, but only 500 m from Zambia looking over the Zambezi River. Also being near the point where five countries meet (Namibia, Zambia, Zimbabwe, Botswana and Angola), several languages and a myriad of dialects are spoken. But it is an ugly town whose position on the banks of the Zambezi is easy to forget once you're there. Use it to replenish and refuel, and then enjoy the picturesque accommodation and plentiful water and land activities in East Caprivi, before moving on to the fabulous Chobe National Park in Botswana and the Victoria Falls from either Zimbabwe or Zambia.

Arriving in Katima Mulilo Katima Mulilo Airport, is on the B8 18 km southwest of town and is served by **Air Namibia** flights. The B8 splits at Katima Mulilo; the Zambezi River is straight ahead; a left turn takes you to Zambia (4 km), right goes through town, then on 70 km to the border with Botswana at Ngoma Bridge (see box, page 164). >> See Transport, page 171.

Your first stop should be **Tutwa Tourism and Travel** ① *just before the T-junction at the Zambezi where the B8 splits, T066-252739, www.tutwatourism.com, Mon-Fri 0800-1700*, which has numerous maps and is well informed about excursions and lodges. It can also arrange car hire, day trips over the borders and airport transfers. There's a coffee shop selling curios and with internet access.

Background

The name Katima Mulilo is loosely derived from a Lozi expression meaning 'quenches the fire', and is probably a reference to burning embers carried by travellers being extinguished by rapids as they crossed the Zambezi. The town was founded by the British in 1935 to replace the previous German colonial regional capital of the Caprivi Strip at Schuckmannsburg (now the village of Luhonono, 65 km east of Katima Mulilo on the Zambian border). The British built the first brick-and-mortar regional office under a giant baobab; the hollow tree became known as the **Toilet Tree** (for obvious reasons). Given its proximity to important transport routes, particularly the railway bridge at Victoria Falls, the location of Katima Mulilo became strategically important during the Second World War, when military supplies, people, and goods had to be flown in. The town's first car arrived in 1940 and belonged to the airstrip operator.

Border crossings

For all these borders, remember Namibia's daylight saving is from the first Sunday of April to the first Sunday in September so times could be an hour earlier. Also note that the Namibian dollar is not used in Botswana, Zimbabwe or Zambia but the South African rand is, so ensure you've changed over any Namibian dollars to rand before you reach the borders. Border fees are paid in US dollars, rand, or the local currency.

Ngoma Bridge (Botswana)

This border (0700-1800) crosses a bridge over the Chobe River and is 70 km southeast of Katima Mulilo at the end of the B8. Most visitors do not need visas for Botswana. As Botswana is part of the Southern Africa Development Community (SADC), you just have to sign a book to take a vehicle across the border and pay a road levy for Botswana. If in a hire car ensure you have documentation of permission to take a car into Botswana and have third-party insurance. It is not permitted to take meat into Botswana and you will be asked to step out onto the foot-and-mouth 'pad' to wipe your feet and your vehicle's tyres will be sprayed (like you do at the Red Line veterinary control fences elsewhere in Namibia). Once in Botswana you are now in Chobe National Park and its 55 km to Kasane, which has petrol stations, banks with ATMs, shops and accommodation. If you are only transiting, you do not have to pay park fees, but keep your speed down as there are often elephant on this road. Note that motorbikes are not permitted to drive through Chobe so motorcyclists will have to use a different border.

Kazungula (Zimbabwe)

Kazungula is 13 km east of Kasane on the south banks of the Chobe and Zambezi rivers and is from where the A33 road heads south to Maun and Francistown. It's also the location of both the road border crossing between Botswana and Zimbabwe and a ferry crossing between Botswana and Zambia (see below). Beyond the Kazangula road border (0600-2000), the road heads 72 km to the town of Victoria Falls in Zimbabwe. Again look out for elephant on this road and keep your speed down. The drive from Katima Mulilo to Victoria Falls (210 km) should take not much more than three hours including the two border crossings. Most nationalities need visas for Zimbabwe which are available at the border and can be paid for in US dollars or South African rand. Single-entry visas are valid for 90 days, but if you are going into Zambia and back to Zimbabwe (to see the Victoria Falls from both sides for example) it's better to get a multi-entry

In 1971 the area around Katima Mulilo was part of the Angolan Bush War, and it was a military base during the occupation by the South African army. As in the Second World War, it was a strategically important, this time for troop transports into and out of Zambia and Angola. The settlement also was at the centre of the Caprivi conflict

visa – also available at the border. Contact Zimbabwe diplomatic missions for up-to-date costs. Not all car hire companies in Namibia and South Africa permit you to take cars into Zimbabwe, so if that's the case, taking your car into Zambia is the alternative option to visit the Victoria Falls from Livingstone. If you are in your own vehicle and travelling on a carnet de passages, then it is here on the Zimbabwe (or Zambia – see below) border that you will need to stamp out your car from the joint customs organization of the Southern Africa Development Community (SADC) as these countries are not members. You will also need to take out a short-term policy for third-party insurance which can be bought on the Zimbabwe side of the border.

Kazungula (Zambia)

A motorized pontoon vehicle ferry operates between the Botswana side and the Zambia side of Kazungula and crosses 400 m of the Zambezi River. It has a capacity of 70 tons so can fit several cars or a couple of trucks at a time and goes when full (0600-1800). The fees for a car are US$30, plus road fees and third-party insurance for Zambia, and the paperwork needed to take a vehicle into Zambia is the same as crossing into Zimbabwe (above). Most nationalities need visas for Zambia which are available at the border and can be paid for in US dollars or South African rand, and again if you are going to and from Zambia and Zimbabwe a multi-entry visa is the best option – also available at the border. Contact Zambian diplomatic missions for up-to-date costs. Once off the ferry its 3 km through the village to the tarred M10 (the Sesheke–Livingstone road; see below), and then it's 60 km to Livingstone, which shouldn't take longer than an hour.

Wenela (Namibia)–Sesheke (Zambia)

This border (0600-1800) is 4 km north of Katima Mulilo and therefore is often also referred to as the **Katima border**. On the Zambian side it's called Sesheke. The crossing is over the impressive 900-m-long Katima Mulilo Bridge over the Zambezi. Again formalities to take a car into Zambia are the same as Zimbabwe, and visa requirements are the same as the Kazungula ferry. Although the Sesheke–Livingstone road (the M10) is tarred, drive slowly as there are potholes, and the 193 km from the bridge to Livingstone can easily take three to four hours. It's not advisable to drive after dark, and ensure you've filled up with fuel and bought some snacks/drinks in Katima Mulilo. However, in the last 30-40 km on the approach to Livingstone, there are some very nice lodges next to the Zambezi; visit the Livingstone Tourism Association's website, www.livingstonetourism.com.

in the 1990s, an armed conflict between the Caprivi Liberation Army (CLA), a rebel group working for the secession of the Caprivi Strip, and the Namibian government.

Since then Katima Mulilo's economy has boomed thanks to it becoming a service town to the traffic passing through since the opening of the Katima Mulilo Bridge in 2004 that spans the Zambezi. The bridge completed the 2200-km Trans-Caprivi Corridor – a trade/truck route – that links the port of Walvis Bay with Zambia's capital Lusaka and the Zambian Copperbelt.

Impalila Island → *Colour map 2, A6.*

At the eastern tip of Caprivi, by the confluence of the Chobe and Zambezi rivers, is the easternmost outpost of Namibia: Impalila Island (sometimes spelt Mpalila). The island sits in the Kasai channel between the Zambezi and Chobe. At its eastern end is another small island, Kakumba, which lies opposite the Botswana town of Kazungula where Zimbabwe, Zambia, Botswana and Namibia all meet (officially in the middle of the Zambezi).

Impalila Island and the banks of Botswana at Kasane are home to a number of upmarket lodges, which offer excellent boat excursions, and all have game drives into the remote riverbank area of Chobe National Park to see the abundant game. It's strange to think of these lodges as part of Namibia, but that's what their tax bill (if not their phone number) says. They are accessed by boat from Kasane in Botswana, which is 55 km from the Ngoma border post (see page 164) via the tarred road through Chobe National Park, or by plane to the small airstrips at Kasane and on the island. There are customs and immigration facilities on the island. The aquatic attractions include superb fishing and rapids (Mombova and Chobe), as well as excursions up the Indibi River (western end) for game viewing in the papyrus fringed flood plain. The stunning location of this island, with its abundant wildlife, tranquil rivers and beautiful lodges makes getting here well worth the effort. En route, if you have come by 4WD, it is certainly worth spending some time along the river in **Chobe National Park**, www.botswanatourism.co.bw.

◉ Caprivi listings

For hotel and restaurant price codes and other relevant information, see pages 21-28.

◉ Where to stay

Divundu and around *p154, map p155*
Charter flights for any of the upmarket lodges in the region use Bagani airstrip, close to the entrance to Popa Falls. There is also the option of flying to the Shakawe airstrip in Botswana and arranging a transfer with the lodges from there.
$$$$ Divava Okavango Lodge & Spa, on the C48, 6 km from the B8 and just after Popa Falls, T066-259005,

www.divava.com. 20 luxurious thatched, a/c bungalows with contemporary earthy decor, freestanding baths, outdoor showers, wooden decks or verandas and views over the Okavango River. Swimming pool in pleasant shaded lawns, attractive restaurant and bar, sundowner deck 10 m above the water for safe views of the hippos and crocs, spa, and activities include fishing, boat cruises, *mokoro* (dugout canoe) rides, and visits to Popa Falls and Bwabwata.
$$$$ River Dance Lodge, on the B8 24 km before Divundu turn left at the Shadikongoro turn off, follow signs for 6 km to the river, T0811-243255,

www.riverdance.com.na. A beautifully designed new luxury lodge on the Okavango River northwest of Divundu on the Angolan border, with 7 large wood and glass rooms with decks at the water's edge, each having its own unique character and decor. Restaurant and bar, swimming pool and activities include romantic dinners on an island, sundowner and game-watching cruises, tiger fishing and cultural visits to a local village and school. The **campsite ($)** is very special and right on the river's edge with its own wooden deck, each site has its own bathroom and you can order pizzas from the lodge.

$$$ Ndhovu Safari Lodge, on the C48, 17 km from the B8, about 2 km down a track towards the river, T066-259901, www.ndhovu.com. Tented camp at a beautiful spot by the Okavango River with 7 fairly basic but comfortable tents under thatch with veranda, one is rather uniquely on a floating pontoon in the river. Restaurant and bar on a lovely wooden deck built out on the river, pool, shaded lawn and curio shop. Guided game drives into Bwabwata and boat excursions include a day trip to Popa Falls or an overnight safari on a houseboat. There are also a few grassed and shady **campsites ($)** on the river's edge.

$$$ Popa Falls Camp, on the C48, 5 km south of the B8 (see page 154), reservations Namibia Wildlife Resorts (NWR), Windhoek, T061-285 7200, or their other offices in Swakopmund and Cape Town, www.nwr.com.na. Recently rebuilt, this NWR camp will possibly be renamed a 'lodge' by the time your read this. 14 river-facing thatched a/c chalets with kitchenettes, and *braais* on the balconies, and 3 family units facing the woodland side of the resort, plus a **campsite ($)**, green and picturesque, with

smart ablution blocks and a bush kitchen. There's a new restaurant and bar with wooden decks next to the river, and a boat jetty with its own pub for numerous excursions including sunset cruises and fishing (from N$200-700 per person). A lovely spot with the sound of the rapids to soothe you to sleep, but mosquitoes can be a problem – cover up in the evening and use plenty of insect repellent.

$$$-$$ Mahangu Safari Lodge, next door to **Ndhovu Safari Lodge**, T066-259037, www.mahangu.com.na. German-run with 10 a/c thatched bungalows and 6 slightly cheaper safari tents in a shaded, green spot by the river, swimming pool with a view of the river, bar and restaurant, and game drives and fishing trips can be arranged. **Campsites ($)** also available on the river's edge with *braais* and wooden shades.

$$-$ Ngepi Campsite, T066-259003 or T081-2028200, www.ngepicamp.com. 5 km off the C48, 12 km from the B8, 5 km from the D3430. A stunning spot next to the Okavango River with a rustic collection of delightful partially open double en suite treehouses plus family thatched chalets sleeping 4, as well as **campsites**, beautifully set by the Kavango River, grassed and well shaded, with hot showers, a central dining *braai* area and lively bar. Activities include fishing, boating or trips in a *mokoro* (dugout canoe), birdwatching and with a good and interesting guide, and there's a cage sunk in the river so you can effectively swim with crocodiles.

Kongola and around *p160, map p161*
Only **Lianshulu Lodge** has an airstrip in this region; some of the other upmarket places can organize transfers from Katima Mulilo Airport, on the B8, 95 km to the east of Kongola.

$$$$ Lianshulu Lodge, Mudumu National Park, well signposted off the C49, 40 km south of the B8, then a further 4 km to main lodge, reservations, Windhoek T061-224420, www.caprivicollection.com. The only lodge inside the park with 11 enormous luxurious thatched tastefully decorated suites with decks right on the Kwando River, some with outdoor showers, strategically placed among the trees so each is very private. Large, beautiful, central dining area, lounge and bar, swimming pool, attractive gardens often visited by elephants. Excursions include walks, boat trips and game drives, including a night drive with liqueurs.

$$$$ Nkasa Lupala Tented Lodge, Nkasa Rupara (formerly Mamili) National Park, vehicles park at Sangwali village, 75 km from Kongola, from where it's an 11-km transfer to the lodge, T0811-477798, www.nkasalupalalodge.com. This new luxury option offers the only accommodation at Nkasa Rupara and its on Lupala Island just 300 m from the park boundary; hence guests are likely to have this wonderful watery wilderness to themselves. Well designed and constructed from steel, canvas and wood, 10 tents with decks and outside freestanding baths (from where elephant are likely to be spotted below), bar, dining room and lounge. Activities include day and night game drives, bush walks, boat cruises and village visits.

$$$$ Susuwe Island Lodge, Bwabwata National Park near Kongola, if you don't have a 4WD park at the police check point next to the Kongola Bridge and transfers are arranged, reservations Windhoek, T061-224420, www.caprivicollection.com. On an island in the Kwando River in Bwabwata, with 6 beautiful, spacious suites with plunge pool and balcony overlooking the river, central lounge and dining area, library, and curio shop. Game drives go to Horseshoe Bend in Bwabwata, a scenic bend in the Kwando which is a favourite spot for elephant, plus there are boat and fishing excursions.

$$$ Camp Kwando, well signposted off the C49, 5 km south of the B8, T066-686021, www.campkwando.com. 13 reed and thatch chalets on an island in the Kwando facing Bwabwata built on poles so close to the water you can fish from the balconies, with bathrooms with open roofs lit by paraffin lamps, plus 5 canvas and thatch tree houses, and a grassy **campsite ($)** with hot showers. Attractive restaurant and bar with good views of hippo and crocs in the river. Activities include day game drives in Muduma National Park, overnight trips to Nkasa Rupara (formerly Mamili) National Park, village visits and boating and fishing.

$$$ Namushasha River Lodge, well signposted 20 km south of the B8 on the C49, 4 km from turning, past its airstrip and a few large baobabs, reservations: Windhoek T061-230066, www.gondwana-collection.com. 47 thatch-and-reed chalets set in shaded gardens by river, swimming pool, bar, buffet restaurant, and lovely deck with views over groups of hippo in the river. Boat and 4WD excursions on offer, generally caters for German tour groups. The **campsite ($)** has shaded, grassy sites.

$$ Mazambala Island Lodge, signposted off the B8, 4 km east of Kongola, 2 km to the car park and campsite, T066-686041, www.mazambala.com. A rustic bush camp on an island with 16 comfortable thatch-and-reed bungalows, some triple or family units. The bar, lounge and restaurant area is built on 3-m-high stilts with excellent views of the flood plain below, and there's a swimming pool. Activities include canoe trips, walking trails, fishing or visits to local villages. The **campsite ($)** is on the 'mainland' and lodge guests can park here and be transferred to the lodge by a 15-min boat ride (campers can also go to eat and use the facilities).

$ Kubunyana Community Camp, turn off the C49, 7 km south of the B8, then it's 4 km to the camp and river, reservations by email through **Spitzkoppe Reservations**, www.spitzkoppereservations.com. On the banks of a tributary of the Kwando River, the final few hundred metres may be underwater; there's a place above high water to park. 3 pre-erected tents set on thatched shaded structures, bedding not provided, plus 4 campsites, decent communal ablutions with hot showers and simple field kitchen. Note there is no electricity and you need to bring your own drinking water.

$ Nambwa Community Camp, inside the Bwabwata National Park, the turn off the B8 is the same as **Susuwe Island Lodge**, at the police checkpoint next to the Kongola Bridge, the 14-km road to the camp is very soft sand and a 4WD is essential, reservations by email through **Spitzkoppe Reservations**, www.spitzkoppereservations.com. A beautiful remote spot on a tributary of the Kwando River with 6 sandy sites, simple ablutions in reed huts with warm showers but bring all drinking water, and wooden viewing deck overlooking the floodplains. The camp is frequently visited by elephant, and it's a short drive to the Horseshoe Bend in Bwabwata; the piece of cut-off river that is a haven for wildlife. Don't forget to pay park entry fees first at the Susuwe Ranger Station on the other side of the turn-off on the B8.

Katima Mulilo and around *p163, map p146*

There is a good selection of lodges in the Katima Mulilo area. Note that while the fishing is excellent, boat trips for game viewing are better in Kasane or Victoria Falls, assuming you are travelling in this direction, or the lodges on the Kwando River accessed from Kongola (above) – there is little wildlife on this wide stretch of the Zambezi.

$$ Protea Hotel Zambezi River Lodge, 4 km northeast of town on the banks of the Zambezi to the north of the golf course, T066-251500, www.proteahotels.com. Excellent riverside location and the best option if you need/want to stay in town, first opened in the 1970s but now pleasantly refurbished by **Protea** (a quality South African hotel chain). 42 neat a/c rooms in cottages with decor that gives a nod at Caprivi baskets (lightshades and headboards, etc), pool, restaurant and a floating moored pontoon bar.

$$-$ Caprivi River Lodge, signposted off the B8 towards the Ngoma Bridge border, 5 km from town, T066-252288, www.capririverlodge.com. 8 cosy and pretty thatched chalets, on request can set up tents outside the chalets for children, plus 3 budget cabins sharing good ablutions with the **campsite**, shaded lawns, small pool, bar and dining area overlooking the river, lounge with TV and library. Activities include kayaking, boat trips and fishing.

$$-$ Kalizo Lodge, 37 km from Katima Mulilo, take the B8 for Ngoma Bridge for 18 km, then the D3508 signposted for Kalimbeza, next signpost after 11 km, 5 km to the lodge (4WD needed after rain), offers transfers from Katima Mulilo, Kasane and Victoria Falls, T066-686802, www.kalizolodge.com. A simple no-frills place on a broad sweep of the Zambezi. 7 rooms in A-frame wood, reed and thatch chalets, plus 4 family self-catering cottages with 2-3 bedrooms and kitchenette, restaurant, bar, pool, plenty of river activities including fishing for tiger fish and bream and sunset cruises to see hippo and crocs. **Campsite** with *braai* spots on the water's edge.

$ Salambala Wilderness, at the Salambala Pan, 48 km south of Katima Mulilo, off the B8, a signpost points to Salambala on the right on the way to the Ngoma Bridge border, 15 km further on. The track is sandy in patches but is suitable for 2WD vehicles, except during the rainy season (Oct-May) when it may only be accessible by 4WD, T066-252108, www.salambala.com. 4 separate sites with room for 4 tents, each with its own wash block with hot water and flush toilet, *braai* area and simple camp kitchen. A short walk takes you to and a hide for viewing the regular elephant and small game that come to drink and bathe.

Impalila Island *p166, map p146*
Accommodation here is only at the very top end of the market. Access is usually by charter flights or the lodges will collect guests from Kasane, Victoria Falls, or Livingstone.

$$$$ Ichingo Chobe River Lodge, reservations South Africa T+27-(0)798-717603, www.ichobezi.co.za. 8 beautifully decorated luxury tents with open-air bathrooms and balcony overlooking the Chobe River. Attractive dining room serving gourmet food, lounge and bar, boat or *mokoro* trips into the Caprivi flood plain, walks around the island, fly fishing for tiger fish and bream, excellent game viewing and birdwatching. Alternative accommodation is offered on 2 luxury fully catered houseboats, each with 4 double cabins, a plunge pool and tender boats for excursions.

$$$$ Impalila Island Lodge, reservations South Africa T+27 (0)861-010200, www.africananthology.co.za. 8 suites overlooking the Mombova Rapids, swimming pool, craft shop, lounge, small library, elevated bar above the river with the roar of the rapids in the background, the centerpiece is the dining area which is built around 2 large baobab trees. Activities include trips in *mokoros*, sunset game cruises and tiger fishing.

$$$$ Ntwala Island Lodge, reservations South Africa T+27 (0)861-010200, www.africananthology.co.za. Ntwala Island is in the Mombova Rapids at the confluence of the Zambezi and Chobe rivers just to the south of Impalila and is a lovely isolated spot with little white-sand beaches. Ultra-luxurious with only 4 suites with private plunge pools and outdoor showers. Each has its own boat and guide for game cruises. The main building has a walk-in wine cellar and sort of sunken kitchen where guests can interact with the chef.

🍴 Restaurants

Katima Mulilo and around *p163, map p146*
There is very little choice in town but the petrol stations and supermarkets offer takeaways such as pies, grilled chicken, Vienna sausage and chips and the like. The best bet is the restaurant in the **Protea Hotel Zambezi River Lodge** (see Where to stay, page 169). Reasonable restaurant with a good choice, the highlight is eating on the deck with views of the Zambezi gliding by or an early evening drink on the pontoon bar that juts out into the river.

O Shopping

Katima Mulilo and around *p163,
map p146*
The town has reasonable facilities
including 24-hr petrol stations, a
post office, banks, bottle stores and
supermarkets, most of which are situated
around a central square which is the
centre of all activity. There's a branch of
Shoprite supermarket on Hage Geingob
St near the main intersection in town,
and a **Pick'n'Pay** at the entrance to town
from the B8.
Caprivi Arts Centre, between the market
and the hospital, T066-252670. Daily
0800-1730. Also known as the **Katima
Craft Centre**, this offers an excellent
selection of crafts brought to the shop
by villagers from the surrounding area.
They include a variety of woven baskets
made from *makalani* palm fronds; many
have geometric patterns created with
natural dyes in mauves, pinks, greens
and blacks. They make very attractive
souvenirs and many lodges in Namibia
and Botswana use them as decorations
on walls. Also sells wooden carvings and
lovely clay pots with slender necks, and
some regional crafts from neighbouring
Zambia and Zimbabwe.
   You'll smell the **market** next door,
open daily sunrise to sunset, which has
stalls erected under shade netting, where
women sell fresh vegetables, and in a
separate area a meat market where cows
and goats are slaughtered and where
fish – a staple in the diet of people living
along the rivers – is dried and sold. In the
clothing section, lookout for a colourful
shitenge (a piece of cloth used as a
wraparound skirt).

Transport

Katima Mulilo and around *p163,
map p146*
1170 km to Windhoek, 513 km to Rundu,
125 km to Kasane (Botswana), 208 km
to Livingstone (Zambia), 210 km to
Victoria Falls (Zimbabwe). From Katima
Mulilo there is the option of crossing
into Zambia at the border at Wenela or
Botswana (and ultimately Zimbabwe) at
Ngoma Bridge (see box, page 164). If you
don't have a vehicle, many of the lodges
in the region offer transfers or tours to
Livingstone, Kasane and Victoria Falls.

Air
Katima Mulilo Airport is 18 km southwest
of town off the B8, T066-254404. As
it used to be a military airport there is
nothing to do except to sit on incredibly
uncomfortable wood and brick seats.
Make sure you have arranged in advance
to be collected by your lodge as there
are no taxis or buses. **Air Namibia**,
reservations Windhoek T061-299 6333,
www.airnamibia.com.na. Has flights
between Katima Mulilo and **Windhoek's
Eros Airport** in each direction on Mon,
Wed, Fri and Sun. They depart Windhoek
at 1015, arrive in **Rundu** at 1130, depart
Rundu at 1150 and arrive in Katima Mulilo
at 1250. They depart again at 1335, and
get back to Eros at 1515. Those returning
from Rundu to Eros will need to go via
Katima Mulilo.

Bus
Intercape buses bound for **Windhoek**
or **Livingstone** stop at the Shell petrol
station on Hage Geingob St; see
timetable on page 16. Local minibus
long-distance taxis converge near
the market.

⚐ Directory

Katima Mulilo and around *p163, map p146*
Mechanical repairs Katima Engineering Works, 24-hr breakdown service, T066-252986. **Medical services** State Hospital, on Hospital St north of the market and Caprivi Arts Centre, T066-251400.

Contents

176 Damaraland
- 178 Spitzkoppe
- 179 Brandberg –
  the White Lady
- 180 Uis
- 181 Khorixas
- 181 West of Khorixas
- 184 East of Khorixas
- 186 Northern Damaraland
- 187 Listings

192 Kaokoland
- 203 Listings

208 Far North
- 210 Ondangwa
- 217 Listings

Footprint features

- 174 Don't miss …
- 179 The White Lady
- 182 Desert elephants
- 185 Desert rhino
- 196 The Himba
- 200 Kunene River
- 211 The oshana environment
- 212 A brief history of Angola's wars

Border crossings

Namibia–Angola
- 202 Ruacana–Calueque
- 216 Oshikango–Santa Clara

The Northwest & the Far North

At a glance

⊖ **Getting around** 2WD hire car in Damaraland, 4WD essential for Kaokoland. Guided tours from Windhoek.

↻ **Time required** 3 days for Damaraland. 1-2 weeks to explore the Far North.

⬢ **Weather** Generally warm and dry.

⊗ **When not to go** The heat in the middle of summer may be too stifling for some visitors.

ANGOLA

KAOKOLAND

NORTHERN
DAMARALAND

DAMARALAND

SOUTHERN
DAMARALAND

GOBAUBVLAKTE

Atlantic Ocean

Skeleton Coast National Park

Dorob National Park

Namib-Naukluft Park

Etosha National Park

Etosha Pan

Enyandi
Epupa Falls
Baynes Mountains
Otjinungwa
Otjihipa Mountains
Omuhonga
Okongwati
Ehomba
Ruacana
Ruacana Falls
Ruacana-Calueque
Oshikango-Santa Clará
Oshikango
Outapi
Eenhana
Oshikuku
Eunda
Tsandi
Ongulumbashe
Okahao
Oshakati
Ongwediva
Ondangwa
Okankolo
Ongandjera
Otjitanda
Van Zyl's Pass
Red Drum
Otjiveze
Steilrand Mountains
Tonnesen Mountains
Opuwo
Marienfluss Valley
Hartmann's Valley
Nadas
Orupembe
Sanitatas
Etendeka Mountains
Giraffen Mountains
Otjiu
Joubert Mountains
Okatjuru
Puros
Tomakas
Sesfontein
Owen Gorge
Warmquelle
Khowarib
Galton Gate
Okaukuejo
Halali
Andersson Gate
Hoarusib
Hoanib
Mowe Bay
Seal Beach
Terrace Bay
Palmwag
Grootberg
Otjikonde
Kamanjab
Outjo
Uniab
Bergsig
Fransfontein
Springbokwasser Gate
Petrified Forest
Wondergat
Koichab
Torra Bay
Twyfelfontein
Organ Pipes
Burnt Mountain
Khorixas
Vingerklip
Ugab
Doros Crater
White Lady
Ozondati
Kalkfeld
Ambrose Bay
Brandberg West
Brandberg (2573 m)
Uis
Otuwe
Durissa Bay
Ugabmund Gate
Okombahe
Anjbib Farm
Erongo Mountains
Omaruru
Bacack's Bay
Cape Cross Seal Reserve
Omaruru
Spitzkoppe (1784 m)
Phillip's Cave
Usakos
Wilhelmstal
Henties Bay
Cape Farilhaa
Karibib
Otjimbingwe
Bosua Pass
Rock Bay
Rössing Uranium Mine
Swakopmund
Moon Landscape & Welwitschia Drive
Bloedkoppie
Groot Tinkas
Pelican Point
Walvis Bay
Vogelfederberg
Ganab

30 km
30 miles
N

★ Don't miss ...
1 Damaraland, page 176.
2 Rock art at Spitzkoppe, page 179.
3 Twyfelfontein, page 183.
4 Visiting the Himba, page 196.
5 Marienfluss and Hartmann's valleys, page 199.
6 Kunene River, page 200.
7 Epupa Falls, page 201.

With its stunning landscapes, Kaokoland, in the extreme northwest of Namibia, is one of the last true wilderness areas in southern Africa. From the Kunene River in the north, down the Skeleton Coast National Park to Damaraland in the south, the area is rugged and mountainous. Both the Damara, with their clicking tongue, and the photogenic Himba, with their ochre-skinned beauty, live in simple villages, mostly subsisting as goat and cattle herders. Namibia's best-known rock art is located in the hills of Damaraland, while desert elephant and black rhino roam the harsh environment.

In the very north, the Kunene River flows sedately to the sea from the Ruacana Falls Hydroelectric Power Station and for 300 km this forms the now peaceful border with Angola. The 32-m Epupa Falls are roughly halfway to the Atlantic; a beautiful rift in the rock, dotted with precariously perched baobab trees and bathed in glorious palm-fringed sunsets with plenty to entice birders and fishermen. The area is often inaccessible to saloon cars, preserving Kaokoland as a world unto itself.

The Far North, or what was once known as Owamboland, is a dusty, overgrazed, overpopulated area with few attractions for most tourists. However, for those with the time and energy, there is plenty to discover. The towns are an interesting mix of urban and traditional tempered with a vibrant Portuguese/Angolan influence. Out of town, the landscape is dominated by the fascinating geography and agronomy of the *oshanas*, on which so many rely.

Damaraland

This sparsely populated region is a highland desert wilderness, home to uniquely adapted animal species such as the desert elephant and the last free-roaming black rhinos in the world, as well as rare raptors such as the peregrine falcon and booted eagle. A huge area stretching almost 600 km north to south and 200 km east to west, Damaraland is bordered by the Hoanib River to the north, the tar road to Swakopmund to the south, and Etosha and the Skeleton Coast to the east and west. It encompasses some of Namibia's most dramatic natural features such as the Spitzkoppe and Brandberg mountain ranges, which dominate southern Damaraland and are particularly impressive because they rise out of the flat gravel plains. Heading north, the plains give way to rolling hills, dissected by numerous seasonal rivers. Also well suited for exploration on foot with local guides are the Petrified Forest, west of Khorixas, and the Burnt Mountain, and Organ Pipes near Twyfelfontein, which is the site of Namibia's largest collection of San (Bushmen) rock art. The majority of Damaras are engaged in subsistence livestock farming. There are no sizeable towns in the region; however, a network of lodges and campsites, some community-run, provide comfortable and scenic accommodation for visitors to this beautiful region.

Arriving in Damaraland

Most of the tour operators include Damaraland in longer tours of the country. See tour operators in Windhoek (see page 77) and Swakopmund (see page 262). If you are in your own vehicle, Damaraland can be approached from a number

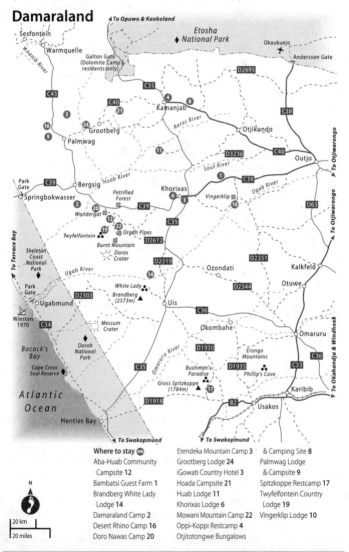

Damaraland

To Opuwo & Kaokoland

Sesfontein

Warmquelle

Woanib River

Etosha National Park

Okaukuejo

Andersson Gate

Galton Gate (Dolomite Camp residents only)

D2695

C43

C35

C40

Kamanjab

Aeros River

Otjikondo

C38

Grootberg

C40

Outjo

To Otjiwarongo

Palmwag

Sout River

D3236

Huab River

Bergsig

C39

Ugab River

C39

Park Gate

Springbokwasser

Petrified Forest

Khorixas

Vingerklip

D63

C35

To Otjiwarongo

Wondergat

Twyfelfontein

Organ Pipes

Burnt Mountain

Doros Crater

D2612

Skeleton Coast National Park

Ugab River

D2319

Ozondati

D2351

Kalkfeld

Park Gate

Ugabmund

White Lady

Brandberg (2573m)

D2344

Otuwe

Winston 1970

C34

Messum Crater

Uis

C36

Okombahe

Omaruru

To Okahandja & Windhoek

Dorob National Park

D2303

D1930

Erongo Mountains

Phillip's Cave

C33

C36

Bocock's Bay

Cape Cross Seal Reserve

C35

Onamuru River

D1935

Bushman's Paradise

Gross Spitzkoppe (1784m)

Karibib

Atlantic Ocean

D1918

B2

Usakos

Henties Bay

To Swakopmund

To Swakopmund

Where to stay
Aba-Huab Community Campsite **12**
Bambatsi Guest Farm **1**
Brandberg White Lady Lodge **14**
Damaraland Camp **2**
Desert Rhino Camp **16**
Doro Nawas Camp **20**

Etendeka Mountain Camp **3**
Grootberg Lodge **24**
iGowati Country Hotel **3**
Hoada Campsite **21**
Huab Lodge **11**
Khorixas Lodge **6**
Mowani Mountain Camp **22**
Oppi-Koppi Restcamp **4**
Otjitotongwe Bungalows

& Camping Site **8**
Palmwag Lodge
& Campsite **9**
Spitzkoppe Restcamp **17**
Twyfelfontein Country Lodge **19**
Vingerklip Lodge **10**

N

20 km
20 miles

of directions. If you travelled north from Windhoek and made Etosha National Park your first stop you would be likely to arrive via Kamanjab. Another option is to visit a guest farm in the Omaruru Region and then head west into the heart of Damaraland. The following text follows one of the more popular routes, which is to head north out of Swakopmund to Henties Bay and then head inland to either Spitzkoppe (D1918), or via the C35 to Uis.

In Damaraland most places of interest can be visited in a saloon car during dry weather. After rain, a 4WD, or at least a vehicle with high clearance is necessary to get across normally dry riverbeds that may hold some water. Because of the remoteness and lack of traffic, travellers should keep fuel tanks topped up, and carry sufficient water and food.

Background

Inhabited for centuries by the Damara people, the area around Okombahe (between Omaruru and Uis) was first proclaimed a 'reserve' for the Damara by the German colonial administration in 1906. Following the Odendaal Commission report in 1964, which led to the creation of Bantustans in Namibia, a separate Damara tribal 'homeland' was proclaimed in this region. Further acts in 1968 and 1969 cemented this arrangement and, in 1971, a Damara Advisory Council was formed. This was part of an overall strategy on the part of the South African government to incorporate Namibia as the country's fifth province and mirrored similar apartheid policies in South Africa itself. At independence in 1990, Damaraland was incorporated into the newly proclaimed administrative regions: the southern section now lies in the Erongo Region while the north forms part of the Kunene Region. The name Damaraland is still commonly used in tourism circles to refer to this exceptionally scenic part of Namibia.

Spitzkoppe → *For listings, see pages 187-191. Colour map 1, C4.*

ⓘ *Turn off the B2 onto the D1918, 24 km west of Usakos. Turn right almost immediately onto the D1930 for 19 km, and left onto the D3716 for 13 km; it's well signposted and the gravel roads are suitable for saloon cars. T064-464144, www.spitzkoppe.com, open sunrise to sunset, N\$30 per person, car N\$50, 1- to 3-hr guided tours N\$50 per person per hour. Accommodation and camping available (see Where to stay, page 187) and there's a café and curio shop.*

One of Namibia's most recognizable landmarks, the Spitzkoppe, or 'pointed hill', rises some 700 m above the surrounding plain and is 1784 m above sea level. The mountain's distinctive shape has given rise to its nickname as the Matterhorn of Namibia. The main peak, or **Gross Spitzkoppe**, is one of three peaks in the area, the others being the **Klein Spitzkoppe** at 1572 m and the dome-shaped **Pondok Mountains**, whose highest point sits at 1530 m.

Geologically, these three mountains are grouped with the Brandberg range to the north; all are ancient volcanoes. The violent break up of Gondwanaland 500-750 million years ago caused explosive activity through these volcanoes; their granite cores have been exposed by millions of years of erosion, creating the inselbergs or 'island

The White Lady

The White Lady is the best known of a number of San (Bushmen) paintings situated in a 1.5-km radius of each other in the Tsisab Ravine. The first paintings in the area were 'discovered' in 1909 by a German soldier, Hugo Jochmann, however, the White Lady itself was only found in 1917 following a successful ascent of the Königstein peak by three friends, Reinard Maack, A Griess and George Schultz.

Initially the paintings were believed to have been influenced by early Mediterranean art, mainly due to their superficial resemblance to early Cretan art, but also as a result of contemporary European belief that nothing original could possibly have originated from southern Africa. The main authority on rock art at the time, Abb, Henri Breuil, was shown a watercolour of the White Lady at a science congress in Johannesburg in 1929, and concluded that the principal figure in the painting was a woman of European origin. This theory came to be widely accepted. More recently, however, after detailed further research, it has been concluded that the painting is indeed of local origin, most likely the work of San (Bushmen). In fact, the White Lady is no longer believed to be a woman at all, rather it is thought that the figure is actually a man, probably a shaman or medicine man daubed with white body paint.

mountains' that we see today. The northwest face of Spitzkoppe was first climbed in 1946, the west face in 1960, and today the mountain still attracts climbers. The area is a great place to hike, camp, enjoy the clear desert air and fine views, and visit a number of San (Bushmen) paintings – the best known are found at **Bushman's Paradise**.

Rock art

After checking in at the gate and obtaining a map (and possibly a guide), make the short but steep hike from Pondok to Bushman's Paradise; the smooth, precipitous slopes are rendered easily accessible with the help of a well-positioned chain. At the top is a richly vegetated natural amphitheatre and large overhang that protects the paintings from the elements, but unfortunately not from vandals. Nevertheless, there are still interesting paintings of humans and animals and the views of the surrounding countryside make the climb worthwhile. Local guides will also be able to take visitors to the sites of other San (Bushmen) paintings, in particular the **Golden Snake** and **Small Bushman's Paradise**.

Brandberg – the White Lady → *For listings, see pages 187-191. Colour map 1, B3.*

ⓘ *From Uis take the C35 north for 14 km then turn west onto D2359 for a further 28 km; the car park and guides' office is at the foot of the mountain. The gravel roads are suitable for saloon cars, open sunrise to sunset, White Lady Tour 1½ hrs, N\$50, children (6-17) N\$30, car N\$20.*

The immense Brandberg Massif lies south of the Ugab River about 40 km northwest of Uis. It has Namibia's highest peak, **Königstein**, at 2574 m and is the site of one of Namibia's most intriguing pieces of San (Bushmen) art – the so-called White Lady (see box, page 179). Like the Burnt Mountain further north, the Brandberg owes its name to its striking colouring, particularly vivid at sunset. In Khoekhoegowab, the language of the Damara and Nama people, it's known as Dâureb, meaning 'burning mountain'. The Germans translated it as Brandberg.

Getting to the White Lady involves an energetic hike up a well-marked track from the car park up the Tsisab Ravine. You must be accompanied by a guide and, depending on your level of fitness, the walk will take 45 to 90 minutes. Wear a hat and decent walking shoes and take water with you. The relative cool of early morning and late afternoon are the best times to make this walk. The last tour is at 1600.

The Damara guides are well informed about local fauna and flora, and will happily answer questions and show off their clicking prowess should you be interested in learning a few simple greetings in their language. There is plenty of birdlife, but the chance of seeing klipspringer, mountain zebra and the other indigenous mammals is small due to the number of visitors.

The site of the White Lady is in an overhang called Maack's Shelter, named after the surveyor who discovered it in 1917. There's a wooden boardwalk and viewing platform, as well as a toilet. A maximum of eight visitors, accompanied by a guide, are allowed to view the White Lady at any one time; there is a shaded seating area for those waiting their turn. This viewing 'protocol' is a welcome necessity – in years gone by, visitors were known to throw water on the paintings to make them stand out more clearly for photography – at the same time eroding them. The guides are well briefed on what is known about the paintings, although you should not expect a masterful thesis on rock art. While most people are content to turn back at this point, the guides will lead the adventurous over boulders to the other more remote and less famous paintings. There are another five to six sites about 20-30 minutes' walk beyond Maack's Shelter but ensure you choose a guide that's familiar with them and be prepared to pay a little extra.

Uis → *For listings, see pages 187-191. Colour map 1, C4. Phone code: 064.*

Uis was built on the mining of tin and the first thing you see when approaching the town, is a huge white mountain, which is in fact the old mine dump for processed tin ore. Although small-scale tin mining has taken place in the area since the first half of the 20th century, it was not until 1951 that a full-scale mining operation started. In 1958 the South African mining giant ISCOR took over the mining rights and built the town, which flourished until the mine's closure shortly after Namibian independence in 1990.

Today the population has dwindled to perhaps just 4000 and Uis is generally referred to as a village. It manages to eke out an existence based almost entirely on the traffic passing through the area. In recent years, modern technology has made it worthwhile reprocessing the excavated ore that was originally discarded and there is a tiny re-processing plant located near the old mine dumps. The old mine recreation club, with its 25-m swimming pool, and some of the miners' houses, now form the **Brandberg Rest Camp** (see Where to stay, page 187).

Arriving in Uis

Uis is 123 km northeast of Henties Bay and 120 km south of Khorixas on the C35. From Swakopmund, either head up the coast via Henties Bay or take the B2 towards Usakos and branch north on the D1918 and D1930. These gravel roads are windy but usually in good condition. From the east, Uis is 124 km from Omaruru on the C36.

At the T-junction of the C36 and Main Street is **Vicky's Coffee Shop** (see Restaurants, page 190). In the centre of town is a crossroads where most other amenities are to be found, including a petrol station (it is advisable to fill up here given the scarcity of petrol stations in the region), a small shop, butcher and bottle store. If any of these are closed during the day, ask around and someone will fetch the owner. This is how they do things in Uis.

Khorixas → *For listings, see pages 187-191. Colour map 1, B4. Phone code: 067.*

This bedraggled town lies just west of the junction between the C39 from Outjo and the C35 between Kamanjab and Uis. Khorixas is a derivation of the Damara word 'Gorigas' – a type of water bush that flourishes in the area. The 'Kh' is pronounced as a 'c', while the 'x' is pronounced as a hard guttural 'g' (those familiar with Afrikaans should be able to grasp it). But once you have got your tongue around the town's name there is not much more to say about the place. Before independence it was the administrative centre of Damaraland, but when this became part of the Kunene Region, the town's administrative functions were moved to Opuwo. Today it's another sprawling oversized village of perhaps 6000 and most of the inhabitants are impoverished Damara. There are, however, a couple of reasonable places to stay, a Standard bank with ATM, petrol station, bakery, butcher and supermarket. Curio hawkers approach tourists as they fill up with fuel.

West of Khorixas → *For listings, see pages 187-191.*

The C39 winds its way through the mountains, following the Aba-Huab Valley into the picturesque heart of Damaraland. If you are lucky, you might catch a glimpse of the desert elephants along the dry river course (and there is usually spoor to be seen on the road). During the heat of the day they tend to stand in the shade of the large trees, but given that these are rather spindly and leafless, the elephants may still be spotted.

Most tourists are heading for the stunning rock formation and plentiful rock engravings at Twyfelfontein. There are also unusual geological formations of the Petrified Forest, the Organ Pipes and Burnt Mountain. The Wondergat is a little more difficult to find and most organized tours will not bother to stop here. While Twyfelfontein, Organ Pipes, Burnt Mountain and Wondergat are often grouped together (they lie within a few kilometres of each other), it is the paintings,

Desert elephants

Namibia's desert elephants are one of only two populations of desert-adapted dwelling elephants in the world; the other is in Mali. In Namibia they have a range that covers 3000 sq km in the northwest of the country with the elephants trekking up to 200 km in search of water. They have larger feet and longer long legs than regular elephants, which can carry them 70 km in one a day. On average normal elephants drink about 100-200 litres of water a day, but desert elephants drink about this amount only every three to four days. During severe drought they use their trunks, feet and tusks to dig narrow holes in the dry riverbeds in search of water. They obviously are aware of the scarcity of food in the arid region as they hardly ever fell trees, break fewer branches and strip the bark off trees far less than other elephants. By the 1980s most of the 3000 elephants that lived in the region had been killed by hunters and poachers, but thanks to increased protection, the population has increased from 350 in 1975 to almost 700 today. If you come across elephants while driving around Damaraland or Kaokoland remember that these animals have poor eyesight but excellent hearing and smell and they can run very fast if agitated. Stay quietly in your vehicle at least 100 m away, never chase them if they move away, and leave if the animal appears nervous.

the walk and the geology of Twyfelfontein that are by far the most interesting attractions in the area. If pushed for time, ignore the other sites and focus your attention on Twyfelfontein.

From Khorixas, take the C39. The Petrified Forest is well signposted after 42 km, and has a large thatched information hut where plenty of locals offer their services as a guide. Beware the many 'false' forests set up by entrepreneurial locals, especially the 'All New Petrified Forest' further up the road. The real one has a large, brown Namibian Tourism signpost pointing off the road. Continue for a further 15 km and turn left on to the D2612 for 25 km to Twyfelfontein, clearly signposted. If coming from Uis, head north on the C35 for 58 km, turn left on the D2612; again, Twyfelfontein is clearly marked. The D2612 is not very suitable for ordinary vehicles as it may have sandy patches which are difficult to negotiate, especially after rainfall. From either direction you will turn off the D2612 southwest onto the D3254 towards Twyfelfontein and the other attractions, and on the way pass the community campsite by the Aba-Huab River (see Where to stay, page 188). If you are not planning to spend the night at Twyfelfontein, or in Damaraland at least, make sure you start early, as the road needs careful, slow driving, and the distance is considerable.

For 'inner' Damaraland, return to the C39 and continue west. You will pass a sign for the exclusive and highly regarded **Damaraland Camp**, before either heading north towards Palmwag or continuing west on the C39 for 92 km to Torra Bay, via the Spingbokwasser checkpoint. At Palmwag you have the choice of heading north to Sesfontein and Kaokoland, or joining the C40 as it loops east to Kamanjab.

Petrified Forest → *Colour map 1, B3.*

ⓘ *42 km west of Khorixas on the C39. Open sunrise to sunset. N$40, children (6-17) N$30, car N$20. Tours take 30-45 mins and guides may expect a tip.*

Declared a national monument in 1950 after farmers discovered it in the 1940s, the Petrified Forest lies on a sandstone rise in the Aba-Huab Valley, affording a fine view of the surrounding countryside. Around 50 fossilized trees reckoned to be 260 million years old lie scattered over an area roughly 800 m by 300 m, some of them so perfectly preserved that it is hard to believe that they aren't still alive. The absence of roots and branches suggests that the trees in the Petrified Forest do not originate from this area, rather that they were carried here by floodwaters resulting from retreating glaciers. After being deposited here the logs were saturated with silica-rich water which penetrated the cells of the trees, gradually causing petrification.

The largest trees here measure more than 30 m in length with a circumference of 6 m and belong to a type of cone-bearing plant that flourished between 300 and 200 million years ago. Still alive, scattered among the fallen trees, are some fine examples of *Welwitschia mirabilis*, ancient desert-dwelling plants, some of which are more than 1000 years old.

At the entrance are a pile of rocks that might interest the geologist or souvenir hunter, a few locally made low-quality crafts, a kiosk for cold drinks, toilets and a thatched *braai*/picnic area. Better light and cooler temperatures mean early morning or late afternoon are the best times to visit if possible.

Twyfelfontein → *Colour map 1, B3.*

ⓘ *25 km south of the junction with the D3254, 25 km south of the C49, open sunrise to sunset, N$50, children (6-17) N$30, including guided tour, car N$20. The Twyfelfontein Visitor Centre was built entirely out of recycled materials and houses a display on the rock engravings and their history. There are also shaded parking places, toilets (fed by water from the original spring), curios and a kiosk.*

Early inhabitants of the area must have been attracted to the valley by the small freshwater spring on the hillside and by the game grazing in the valley below. There is evidence of habitation more than 5000 years ago. The Damara who lived here named the valley **Ui-Ais** or 'jumping fountain' after this source of freshwater. However, it was renamed Twyfelfontein or 'doubtful fountain' in 1947 by the first white farmer to acquire the land; he considered the fountain too weak to support much life.

The site was declared a national monument in 1952, but sadly this did not prevent many of the engravings being defaced or stolen, and local Damaras are now employed as guides to protect the rocks and take visitors on tours. It was granted further protection in 2007, becoming Namibia's first UNESCO World Heritage Site.

More than 2500 engravings cut into the rockface of the huge boulders strewn around have been identified. These engravings have been categorized into six phases ranging in age from 300 BC to as recent as the 19th century. The majority of the engravings depict a wide range of game species, including elephant, rhino, lion and various antelopes. There are, interestingly, far fewer depictions of human figures. Although experts believe that rock paintings and engravings featured in ceremonies intended to imbue the hunters with the power to catch game, the picture of a seal on one of the rocks is particularly interesting considering that this site is more than 100 km from the sea. This suggests that some engravings may literally have been items in a gallery of game the San (Bushmen) and/or Damara artists were familiar with.

There are two guided trails to choose from depending on your level of fitness as the longer one involves a scramble over rocks; the **Dancing Kudu Route** takes half an hour, while the **Lion Man Route** takes about an hour. You must be accompanied by a local guide, who seem to show more enthusiasm about the engravings in the cooler parts of the day. It is advisable to wear a hat, stout shoes and to carry water with you. Even if you are not especially interested in rock art, Twyfelfontein is still a fantastic place to come and watch the sunset whilst imagining what life must have been like for the area's earliest inhabitants.

Organ Pipes → *Colour map 1, B3.*

For many visitors the Organ Pipes and Burnt Mountain are of only passing interest, however, for anyone interested in the early history of the earth and its geology, they are fascinating glimpses into the past. The Organ Pipes are a series of perpendicular dolerite columns set at the bottom of a shallow gorge 3 km after the turn-off onto the D3254. These elegant rocks, some up to 5 m long, were formed 120 million years ago when the cooling dolerite split into distinct columns which form the pipes we see today. The easiest way to approach the site is to drive past the small car park (no signpost) and turn left up a sandy riverbed a little further on. From here you can walk along the riverbed to the pipes without having to scramble down from above.

Burnt Mountain → *Colour map 1, B3.*

The Burnt Mountain or 'Verbrandeberge' is at the end of the D3214, a 12-km section of mountain rising 100 m above the plain. During the day the mountain is bleak and uninviting, however, the distinctive colouring of the rocks appears at sunrise and sunset when the imaginative might contest that the mountain is 'on fire'. The rocks are dolerite and are believed to have been formed more than 130 million years ago as a result of volcanic activity.

Wondergat → *Colour map 1, B3.*

The Wondergat, set down a short track off the D3254, 3 km before reaching Aba-Huab Campsite, offers an interesting view into the depths of the earth. There are no signposts or safety barriers so be careful near the edge. The hole is believed to have been created when a subterranean river washed away a chunk of earth. Its depth is still unknown – divers have turned back due to lack of oxygen at 100 m, without reaching the bottom.

East of Khorixas → *For listings, see pages 187-191.*

From Khorixas take the C49 towards Outjo, and after 54 km turn south on the D2743. After a few kilometres the Ugab River is reached where the view opens up

Desert rhino

Like desert elephant, Namibia's desert black rhino survive only in the country's northwest Kunene Region (Damaraland and Kaokoland); a region covering roughly 25,000 sq km. They are the only free-ranging black rhino in the world that inhabit communal land with no formal conservation status. Like the elephants, they have evolved with remarkable adaptations to allow them to survive in this tough arid landscape.

Compared to Africa's other black rhino, the desert rhino appears to be slightly larger and with slightly longer and thinner horns – believed to help them forage in barren environments. They are able to withstand sweltering heat in excess of 40°C during the day and below freezing temperatures at night. The dryness of the climate gives their skin a smooth glossy appearance and they have no lesions or visible parasites. Again like elephants, due to the scarcity of food, their range is much greater, measuring 500-600 sq km; and while regular rhino drink every night, the desert rhino may drink only every third or even fourth night. They are remarkably agile creatures and can climb up to mountain ledges to escape the heat of a valley and catch the cool wind from the Atlantic, or forage for succulents. The rhinos of the Kunene are also unlike other black rhinos in that they are usually found on their own and not in small groups, although a mother will stay with her calf for up to 2½ years, which is long enough for her to teach it how to survive in the tough conditions.

In the 1970s aggressive poaching took Namibia's black rhino to the brink of extinction and thousands were slaughtered. Little information was known about this animal's habitat, anti-poaching efforts did not exist and the black rhino population in the Kunene was reduced to dangerously low numbers; by the early 1980s the population had plummeted to an estimated 60 individuals. In 1982, the **Save the Rhino Trust** (SRT), www.savetherhinotrust.org, was formed to reduce poaching and save these animals from extinction. Their approach was simple but highly effective; offer poachers a more secure livelihood as wildlife guards. Today the SRT, in collaboration with the Namibian government, focuses on rhino management programmes, scientific research and raising public awareness and the population of desert rhino is now believed to be several hundred. Rhino-based tourism in the region is also growing steadily. The introduction of private sanctuaries and local conservancies has given communities the right to benefit from wildlife living on their land; local people are recruited as rhino monitors, guides and trackers and can also earn an income from other associated tourism such as working in the lodges.

to the amazing Ugab Valley with its table mountains and plateaus. This fascinating landscape looks a bit like the valleys seen in the US state of Arizona and is called the Ugab Terraces. Dominating the valley, and reached after 22 km from the turn-off on the C49, is the Vingerklip, (finger rock), a 35-m-high limestone rock sitting on a

44-m circumference base. Also known as the **Kalk Kegel** or 'limestone skittle', this unusual landmark was formed by erosion of the Ugab River flood plain over a period of 30 million years. There is no fee to explore the site, and there are numerous walks that offer different angles to view the unusual skittle. Perhaps the best is from the **Vingerklip Lodge** itself (see Where to stay, page 189), which will provide the heat-sapped day visitor with a meal or snack and even a swim in one of its pools. Back on the C49, it's a short drive to Outjo (see page 113) where there are numerous options including taking the C48 to the Andersson Gate of Etosha.

Northern Damaraland → *For listings, see pages 187-191.*

Loosely defined as the lands to the north of the Huab River, the landscape of northern Damaraland rolls beautifully, with small settlements dotted throughout the flat-topped mountains and boulder-strewn valleys. There are plentiful, freely roaming springbok and isolated herds of goats and their goatherds. The only settlement of any size is **Kamanjab**, 108 km north of Khorixas on the C35, which has a petrol station, basic supermarket, several bottle stores and police station; if heading north, fill up with fuel and provisions as this is the last source before reaching Opuwo or Ruacana. Recently the Kamanjab region has become a more popular overnight destination due to the opening of Galton's Gate, the most western entrance to Etosha National Park (see page 119). Only visitors with pre-booked accommodation for **Dolomite Camp** can use this new gate into the park; Kamanjab is the nearest town.

From Kamanjab there are a number of choices. In the easterly direction, the C40 goes to Outjo from where the C38 goes to **Etosha**, while the C35 continues north from Kamanjab towards Opuwo and Kaokoland. To the west the C40 heads to Palmwag, and another route into Kaokoland. Ask ahead about road conditions before heading north into Kaokoland in a saloon car: some roads require a 4WD and preferably a minimum of two vehicles.

Palmwag is nothing more than the junction (and a veterinary control gate) of the C40 and C43 lying 115 km west of Kamanjab. It has a petrol station, a small shop and bottle store and that's about it. It's important, however, because it's centred in what is loosely referred to as the Palmwag Concession (or sometimes Palmwag Reserve); an area covering roughly 5000 sq km between the western boundary of Etosha and the Skeleton Coast. The 'concession' is actually made up of a few private conservancies and the authorities have tried to embrace eco-tourism and get maximum return for minimum damage by granting these to a few private lodges. The area around Palmwag is a semi-desert wilderness, and is a habitat for a variety of species of plants and animals that are adapted to the arid conditions, some of which are quite rare. Most notable are desert elephant (see box, page 182), but gemsbok, springbok, kudu, Hartmann's mountain zebra, giraffe, cheetah, brown and spotted hyena and lion are also present, albeit in small and scattered numbers. In addition, this is the part of Damaraland that supports the world's largest population of black rhinoceros outside a national park (see box, page 185), and the loosely defined

Palmwag Concession is probably home to about 70% of these. For an opportunity to see the rhino, elephant and other species, and fully appreciate the expertise and knowledge of the local guides, aim to spend at least two nights at one of the lodges in this area. It's pricey and sightings are far from guaranteed but the experience of seeing these rare animals is very special.

◉ Damaraland listings

For hotel and restaurant price codes and other relevant information, see pages 21-28.

◉ Where to stay

Spitzkoppe *p178, map p177*
$ Spitzkoppe Restcamp, at the foot of the mountain, T064-464144, www.spitzkoppe.com. A well-run community initiative and a stunning spot to sleep under a starry sky. 31 secluded campsites around the mountain amongst the rocks, *braai* facilities and pit latrines, communal hot showers, also 3 basic thatched huts sleeping 3-4 (bedding included). Simple bar and restaurant, dinner must be booked by 1600, bring drinking water and firewood, though these can be bought at reception. No electricity.

Brandberg – the White Lady *p179, map p177*
$$$-$$ Brandberg White Lady Lodge, from the C35 follow the D2359 towards Brandberg, after 15 km is the signposted turn-off, then it's 12 km to the lodge, 36 km from Uis; drive to Brandberg on the D2359 and you will see the sign to the right, T064-684004, www.brandbergwllodge.com. Set on the banks of the dry Ugab River, the main thatched lodge houses a restaurant, bar, and grassed pool area. Accommodation some distance from the lodge; 8 stone and thatch chalets, simply furnished with veranda, a block of 15 cheaper compact

rooms, and a shady **campsite** (**$**) with sandy sites and a line of twin dome tents, reasonable ablution facilities, *braai* pits, firewood and ice available to buy. Excellent views of Brandberg, the area is regularly visited by desert elephant, daily game drives on offer in an open truck.

Uis *p180*
$ Brandberg Rest Camp, Main St, T064-504038, www.brandbergrestcamp.com. Formerly the mine's recreation club with double/twin a/c rooms or 4-bed self-catering flats, comfortable, facilities including Wi-Fi, restaurant, bar, large swimming pool, sandy **campsite** with electricity and *braais*. With notice, the enthusiastic owner can arrange tours in a Land Cruiser to nearby attractions.
$ White Lady B&B & Camping, 3rd Av, T064-504102, whitelady@iway.na. A long, thatched bungalow with 13 spacious but simple rooms (B&B and self-catering), large *braai* area, *lapa* where breakfasts are served, and swimming pool. Shady **campsite** with adequate ablutions, power points, a separate splash pool and *braais*. The small waterhole at the campsite attracts a number of birds.

Khorixas *p181, map p177*
$$ iGowati Country Hotel, King Justus Garoëb Av, T067-331592, www.igowatilodge.com. Lovely, smart low thatched building, 29 modern rooms decorated with African touches such

as fake leopard-skin throws. Pool, good friendly bar and à la carte restaurant and evening entertainment including talks about Damara culture. Day trips can be organized to the sites, or a donkey cart ride around Khorixas to meet the Damara people and sample local food. Grassy **campsite ($)** with electricity and *braais*.

$$-$ Khorixas Lodge, 1 km north of town, reservations Windhoek T061-285 7200, www.nwr.com.na. Run by **Namibia Wildlife Resorts (NWR)**, a very plain rest camp (not a lodge) with square concrete bungalows fenced in like a compound, but with adequate and cheap accommodation, 2 family units and 36 chalets, all with a/c, some with kitchens. Large swimming pool, restaurant, bar with TV, small food/curio shop, plus a dusty **campsite** with 20 sites.

West of Khorixas *p181, map p177*
$$$$ Damaraland Camp, signposted at the C39/C43 junction, 110 km west of Khorixas, guests leave their vehicles in a car park and are transferred 12 km to the camp by 4WD, reservations **Wilderness Safaris**, South Africa, T+27(0)11-807 1800, www.wilderness-safaris.com. An upmarket option with 10 luxury tents with shady verandas overlooking the valley, central bar and dining area, rock swimming pool and curio shop. Price is full board and includes activities: stargazing, 4WD excursions to find desert elephant, visits to Twyfelfontein and guided walks with guides.
$$$$ Doro Nawas Camp, off the C39, the turning is 800 m west of the turning (D2612) to Twyfelfontein, the lodge is 5 km down this track, suitable for 2WD, reservations **Wilderness Safaris**, South Africa, T+27(0)11-807 1800, www.wilderness-safaris.com. Luxury camp on the edge of the dry Aba-Haub riverbed

with 16 natural walled units with outdoor showers and verandas. The stylish main building is perched on top of a hill with panoramic views, and has a bar, indoor and outdoor dining areas, swimming pool and small art gallery.
$$$$ Mowani Mountain Camp, signposted off the D2612, just southeast of the turning (D3254) for Twyfelfontein, reservations Windhoek T061-232009, www.mowani.com. Exclusive, intimate camp with 15 thatched suites with canvas walls, on stilts among huge boulders, each with balcony and lovely views, some with outdoor baths and showers, swimming pool, trips to local sights and in search of desert elephants. Pricey but elegant and in a wonderful setting.
$$$ Twyfelfontein Country Lodge, well signposted off the D3214 just before the entrance to Twyfelfontein, T067-697021, www.twyfelfonteinlodge.com. This 3-star lodge has been built with natural materials to blend in with the landscape. 56 rooms decorated in earthy colours, restaurant and bar with excellent views, swimming pool, curio shop. Not intimate (it's popular with tour groups) but smart and in a fabulous location.
$ Aba-Huab Community Campsite, 5 km before Twyfelfontein, on the D3254, no phone. A simply stunning location next to the (normally dry) Aba-Haub River, but has become sadly neglected and ablutions are badly maintained. Nevertheless, it's cheap (N$50-80 pp) and only a 15-min drive from Twyfelfontein so you can be there early or late in the day for the best light and photography. The highlight is the regular visits by desert elephant (they have been known to knock down the reed shower enclosures looking for water). You can't pre-book, but there's plenty of camping space and small, thatched, open A-frame shelters

where you can lay out your sleeping bag, and the dry sandy riverbank is dotted with stone fireplaces, tables and benches. The rustic thatched bar usually has cold drinks where traditional dishes of the Damara people can be prepared with notice. **Note** Watch for scorpions here, especially in the A-frames and never leave shoes outside your tent. Caution may be required during the rainy season, as the river floods on rare occasions.

East of Khorixas *p184, map p177*
$$$ Bambatsi Guest Farm, signposted on the C39, 70 km west from Outjo, T067-313897, www.bambatsi.com. A well-run family guest farm located on a ridge with magnificent views, 7 simple but pleasant bungalows sleeping up to 4, swimming pool, dining room and bar, rates are full board including afternoon tea. There are also 2 isolated **campsites (\$)** on the farm with simple outdoor showers and toilets, ideal for a family or couple of vehicles and giraffe and antelope have been known to wander by.
$$$ Vingerklip Lodge, off the C39 next to the entrance to the Vingerklip (a 35-m-high limestone rock), T067-290319, www.vingerklip.com.na. 22 thatched bungalows, tastefully decorated, with veranda and views, 8 have loft space for children, 2 swimming pools, walking trails to the striking Vingerklip (2 km away) and for the adventurous on the nearby Ugab Terrace. Bar, restaurant and separate sundowner hut all have lovely views.

Northern Damaraland *p186, map p177*
$$$$ Desert Rhino Camp, Palmwag, off the C43, a short distance north of the veterinary control gate, reservations **Wilderness Safaris**, South Africa, T+27 (0)11-807 1800, www.wilderness-safaris. com. Close to **Palmwag Lodge** (below), the camp is run by Wilderness Safaris in conjunction with the Save the Rhino Trust, and although very expensive (US$800+ per night for a couple) some of the fee goes towards the rhino charity and a stay here includes rhino tracking on foot, game drives and all meals. Raised from the ground on wooden decking, 8 comfortable safari-style tents with private verandas and the tented restaurant and lounge and swimming pool have sweeping views of the plains below and the Etendeka Mountains.
$$$$ Etendeka Mountain Camp, off the C43, just north of Palmwag, follow the signs to the pick-up point where you leave your car and it's another 1½ hrs to the camp by 4WD transfer; or there's an airstrip. Reservations T061-226979 (Windhoek), www.etendeka-namibia. com. In the foothills of the Grootberg Mountains, 10 comfortable and spacious tents with outside showers, connected by wooden walkways to the communal area which has been cleverly constructed from giant boulders. Its isolation provides a genuine bush experience, and there is a fair amount of game in the area including black rhino and desert elephant. Rates include all food and drinks, game drives and guided hikes.
$$$$ Huab Lodge, 46 km north of Khorixas on the C35 towards Kamanjab, turn west on the D2670, then it's a further 35 km (this final access road may require 4WD in the wet), T067-687058, www.huablodge.com. Set along the normally dry Huab riverbed – a favourite haunt for desert elephant – are 8 large thatched bungalows with tasteful decor and balcony, delicious farm cooking and good wine list, swimming pool plus a hot spring to enjoy in the cool evenings, massages on offer, game drives and guided hiking.

$$$ Grootberg Lodge, on the C40, 22 km east of Palmwag and 95 km west of Kamanjab, T061-333212, www.grootberg.com. 16 very comfortable rooms in stone and thatched chalets with wooden decks, 2 for families, marvellous views down the Klip River Valley and Grootberg Mountain, swimming pool and good food. Guided elephant and black rhino tracking by vehicle and foot, and also day trips to Palmfontein in the north to visit a Himba settlement (see box, page 196, for details). A good spot for an all-round experience of the area.

$$$-$$ Palmwag Lodge & Campsite, Palmwag, off the C43, a short distance north of the veterinary control gate, reservations Windhoek T06-234342, www.palmwaglodge.com. Can sleep 40 people in simple bungalows or more expensive safari tents among *makalani* palm trees, exposed **campsite ($)**, so peg carefully against the wind, with power points and *braais*. Restaurant, pleasant swimming pool with poolside bar that serves snack meals to campers and passing drivers (a welcome stop as there's nothing else in the region). Game drives into the Palmwag Concession offer excellent opportunities to see elephant and rhino, and there are 3- to 5-hr hiking trails. A good base to explore the area, but popular so book well ahead.

$$-$ Oppi-Koppi Restcamp, at the junction of the C40 and C35 in Kamanjab, T067-330040, www.oppi-koppi-kamanjab.com. A new set-up in Kamanjab, the name means 'on a small hill' in Afrikaans. 13 neat doubles rooms or chalets, **campsite** with electricity, lighting, *braai* area and hot showers, friendly bar that's a focal point for local farmers, Wi-Fi, good restaurant that also offers packed lunches, swimming pool.

Organizes fun donkey-cart rides around town to meet the Damara people.

$$-$ Otjitotongwe Bungalows & Camping Site, 24 km east of Kamanjab on the C40, 8 km off the main road, T067-687056, www.cheetahparknamibia.com. Simple family guest farm with 6 en suite thatched bungalows lit by gas lamps, buffet meals are served at the main farmhouse where there's a small swimming pool, basic bush-style **campsite ($)** with ablutions and *braais*. The attraction here is the cheetah-viewing; the farm cares for a number that were bought from local farmers to prevent them from being killed. Organized feeding sessions afford good photo opportunities and you can pat the 3 tame ones.

$ Hoada Campsite, on the C40 40 km east of Palmwag and 95 km west of Kamanjab, 8 km south of the main road, T0812-890982, www.grootberg.com/hoada-campsite. A stunning spot and fantastically designed to incorporate giant boulders, and a joint initiative by the local community and **Grootberg Lodge** (see above). There's a clever system in that your fire in the *braai* heats the water for the open hot showers. Great swimming pool sunk in among the rocks with wooden deck and bar. Campers can participate in activities at the lodge including elephant and rhino tracking, but they must drive themselves to the lodge (25 km via the C40) and book by 1800 the day before.

🍴 Restaurants

Uis *p180*
$ Vicky's Coffee Shop, at the C36 entrance to town, T064-504212. Daily 0800-1700. Small café that can seat about a dozen people at any one time

on the pretty veranda (from where you can watch the donkey carts go up and down Uis's main street). Light meals such as toasted sandwiches and omelettes, muffins and cakes, coffee and tea. Also sells some local crafts and doubles up as the town's information office.

Khorixas *p181, map p177*
$$-$ iGowati Country Hotel, see Where to stay, page 187. The à la carte restaurant here is open to passers-by all day and offers steaks, schnitzels, pasta, salads, burgers and the like and there's also a pleasant partially open bar under thatch and a small curio shop.

Kaokoland

Kaokoland covers roughly 40,000 sq km of sparsely populated land and is often described as one of the last truly wild areas in southern Africa. Outside Opuwo, the regional capital, the area is devoid of amenities, with no fuel, very few shops, no telephones or cell phone reception and only a network of tough gravel and dirt roads. Its isolation is a large part of the appeal: a vast wilderness with small communities living a subsistence existence off the land. The attractions are the simple beauty of the mountain landscape, the ruggedness of the access routes and the tranquillity enjoyed by those reaching the northern and western corners. En route, as well as 4WD challenges, is the opportunity to see the unique and photogenic Himba villages and people, while the Kunene River on the border with Angola rewards weary travellers with the beautiful Epupa Falls and numerous riverside lodges and camps.

Like Damaraland, Kaokoland was established as a homeland for the Himba and other local people during the apartheid era under the South African government. It was abolished in 1990 with Namibia's independence, and these days the region is administrated as part of the Kunene Region but it is still referred to as Kaokoland, especially in tourist literature. It is bounded by the Skeleton Coast National Park on the west, the perennial Kunene River to the north, the C35 gravel road to the east and Damaraland to the south. The only sizeable settlement is the dusty town of Opuwo, which has the only banks in the region as well as supermarkets and petrol stations. Elsewhere in the region visitors need to have a degree of self-sufficiency, but allowing time in your schedule to visit Kaokoland will be amply rewarding.

Arriving in Kaokoland

Self-driving is the best way to explore, but with it comes the risk that the under-prepared may venture into the region and expose themselves unwittingly to danger. Maps of the area give the misleading impression that there is a well-established system of roads allowing free access to many parts of Kaokoland. Nothing could

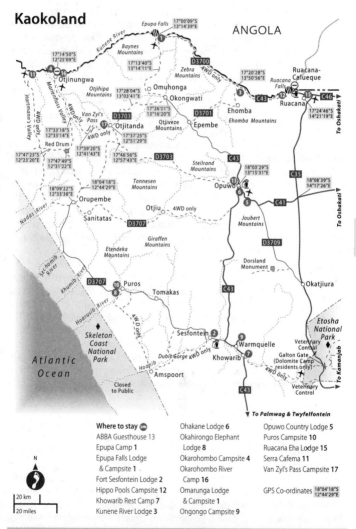

Kaokoland

Where to stay
ABBA Guesthouse **13**
Epupa Camp **1**
Epupa Falls Lodge
& Campsite **1**
Fort Sesfontein Lodge **2**
Hippo Pools Campsite **12**
Khowarib Rest Camp **7**
Kunene River Lodge **3**

Ohakane Lodge **6**
Okahirongo Elephant
Lodge **8**
Okarohombo Campsite **4**
Okarohombo River
Camp **16**
Omarunga Lodge
& Campsite **1**
Ongongo Campsite **9**

Opuwo Country Lodge **5**
Puros Campsite **10**
Ruacana Eha Lodge **15**
Serra Cafema **11**
Van Zyl's Pass Campsite **17**

GPS Co-ordinates 18°04'18"S
12°44'29"E

be further from the truth. Roads are often little more than dirt tracks, which can be hard to follow and become impassable bogs during the rainy season. The rocky, mountainous terrain of much of the region makes all travel extremely slow and hazardous. For example, it could take two hours to cover the 73 km between Okongwati and Epupa Falls, while you'll need to allow at least three hours just to cross Van Zyl's Pass.

One of the most important considerations when visiting Kaokoland is to carefully plan your route in advance and calculate distances and fuel consumption. Very few roads are passable by 2WD car, and it is advisable to travel in a high-clearance vehicle with 4WD, ideally with another vehicle in case of an emergency or breakdown. You should carry two spare tyres and puncture repair kits, basic spares such as oil and fuel filters, at least 160 litres of fuel, water and food, a decent medical kit, a good map and a GPS is a good idea (see pages 15-18 for details of hiring equipment). There are few lodges and campsites in the area and careful planning is needed to reach these before dark. Remember, bush or free camping is prohibited in Namibia, but nevertheless tolerated in very remote locations and is the only option on some of the back roads described below. If you find yourself exploring the area during the rainy season be prepared to wait several hours, even days, before being able to cross certain riverbeds (there are no bridges in the region). Do not be put off from visiting this region but do come prepared and take heed of all local advice. Finally, whatever the condition of the road, stick to existing tracks as off-road driving scars the landscape – there are still pre-Second World War tyre tracks visible in some coastal valleys. Most importantly, stock up well, allow plenty of time and get advice from lodge owners and fellow travellers as to the conditions ahead before embarking on each stretch of your journey.

You can also consider an organized tour of Damaraland and Kaokoland. These are not cheap, but may not be much more costly, given the expense of hiring two 4WD vehicles. There are a number of tour operators offering guided trips in the region and you'll get the added advantage of their knowledge of the difficult terrain (see Tour operators in Windhoek, page 77, and Swakopmund, page 262). The routes outlined below assume visitors arrive via Damaraland. However, self-drive visitors who entered Namibia via the Caprivi Strip are likely to follow all the routes in reverse – entering Kaokoland in the north from Oshakati and Ruacana, and then working their way south into Damaraland. ➤➤ *See Essentials, pages 18-20, for tips on driving in Namibia, and page 82 for car hire in Windhoek.*

Khowarib and Warmquelle → *Colour map 1, B3.*

Driving north from Palmwag and Damaraland, the C23 is suitable for a 2WD as far as Opuwo and it's a very scenic drive. However, going anywhere west of the C43 requires a 4WD. The first village you will reach is Khowarib, about 80 km from Palmwag, which no more than a collection of Damara houses spread out along the banks of the perennial Hoanib River, which irrigates a few small fields growing maize and vegetables. The Hoanib is generally referred to the boundary between Damaraland and Kaokoland and is one of Namibia's few flowing rivers. Here it flows through the low-lying Khowarib Gorge which creates a narrow floodplain that attracts many bird species as well as the region's desert elephants; hence a new enterprise, **Khowarib Lodge**, now occupies a lovely spot within the gorge where there's also a community-run campsite (see Where to stay, page 203).

Like Khowarib, the tiny settlement of Warmquelle, 11 km further on, has little to offer the visitor beyond refreshing patches of green in this dusty environment. Another good place to stay is the **Ongongo Community Campsite** (see Where to stay, page 203), in an impossibly pretty spot, with an enticing water feature: a year-round natural pool which is large enough to swim in. You could stop for a swim if just passing on the C43, but note that the 6-km track to the campsite is rocky and tough going and you'll need a 4WD and a bit of time to get there and back. From Warmquelle, its 11 km to the junction where the C43 heads north to Opuwo and the D3707 heads west for another 12 km to Sesfontein.

Sesfontein → *Colour map 1, B2/3.*

The name originates from six springs that surface in the area. In 1896, following the devastating rinderpest epidemic, which killed off huge numbers of both livestock and game, the German colonial authorities established a number of control checkpoints across the country; these now form the so-called **Red Line** which demarcates the boundary between commercial and subsistence livestock farming in the country. Sesfontein formed the most westerly in a string of such checkpoints.

Following the construction of a road between Outjo and Sesfontein in 1901, the German authorities transported materials to build a military outpost. This was designed to assist in the prevention of poaching and gun-running in the area and although a fort (complete with vegetable garden) was built, by 1909 Sesfontein had been relegated to the status of police outpost before being finally abandoned in 1914. The fort fell into disrepair but was given a reprieve in 1987 when the former Damara administration renovated it. Today it is home to the **Fort Sesfontein Lodge** (see Where to stay, page 203). Amenities in Sesfontein include an Engen garage with shop just before the lodge gate and puncture repair places.

North from Sesfontein

The choice from here is to go back 12 km east to the junction with the C43 and go north to Opuwo. In parts, this road runs through a valley that is so narrow elephants use the road but it's negotiable by a 2WD as far as Opuwo and it's a very scenic drive. About 13 km from the junction is the short but very steep **Joubert Pass**, but this section is tarred. Another option is to continue north on the D3707 towards Puros and Orupembe. If you are going to take this route, ensure you have sufficient supplies and fuel before leaving Sesfontein.

Sesfontein to Puros → *Colour map 1, A2.*

The tiny settlement of **Puros** (also spelt Purros) is 105 km northwest of Sesfontein and this stretch of the D3707 is relatively good and should take about two to three hours in a 4WD. If lucky you may spot some wildlife and the Puros area supports populations of desert elephant, black rhino, giraffe, gemsbok and ostrich making their way to and from the Hoarusib River. Although usually dry, it does flood

The Himba

The Himba people are a semi-nomadic, pastoral people who follow their cattle and goats in search of good grazing. They are descendants of the earliest Hereros, who migrated into this region early in the 16th century from Botswana. Around the middle of the 18th century the pressure of too many people and not enough cattle in this dry, fragile environment led to the migration of the main body of the Herero to the rich pasturelands further south, leaving behind the Himba in the inhospitable north. Some went across the Kunene River where they lived with the Ngambwe people in Angola. Here, they were named Himba, which in the Ngambwe language means beggar, simply because they begged for a place to live.

Today it is believed the Himba in Namibia number around 16,000. They live off mostly the meat and milk of their livestock and, like the Maasai in East Africa cattle are the central most important feature of their lives, which represent status and wealth. Their beehive huts are made from tree saplings covered with a mixture of mud and dung, surrounded by a *kraal*

where their animals are protected overnight against predators. Many settlements are often deserted when they move their herds in search of water and grazing, and visitors may often meet a family on the move carrying all their worldly goods wrapped in only animal skins.

Many Himba maintain traditional dress, language and behavioural codes. It is perhaps because the land they occupy is so harsh and unyielding that it has rarely been coveted by the colonialists and commercial farmers who have affected so much of the continent, that they have managed to keep their traditional lifestyles intact for so long. They plaster their skin and hair with butter, ash and red-hued ochre, a primitive protection against the sun, and also wear elaborate, heavy, metal-studded jewellery and weave their hair in complicated and intricate tresses. To signify their status, married women wear soft-skinned headpieces and a conch shell around the neck. They are without doubt strikingly beautiful and an evocative image of Namibia.

Today the Himba's traditional way of life is threatened by the intrusion of

between January and April. The name Puros stems from the Otjiherero word 'omburo' meaning underground water that seeps up to the surface. It could also refer to the holes that the elephants dig in the dry riverbed to reach the fresh water. The community-run **Puros Campsite** (see Where to stay, page 204) is in a beautiful spot on the Hoarusib River and desert elephant are so frequent in the camp you'd be unlucky not to see them. Local guides can be hired from here for visits to the outlying Himba villages around Puros.

North of Puros

North of Puros is the part of Kaokoland where all the advice and warnings about travel come into play and you must be very careful about carrying sufficient fuel.

traders, tourists and modern ways of living. More are starting to live in permanent settlements, such as the regional 'capital' Opuwo, and many are adapting their lifestyles to meet the demands of living in the 21st century. Just as the Nama and Herero peoples were exploited by European traders who introduced strong, mass-produced alcohol during the 19th century, today Himba communities are vulnerable too, as liquor is often bartered by Angolan and Owambo traders for goats or cattle. Tourists, too, pose a threat as they come into contact with a culture they know little or nothing about and whilst there is undoubtedly a place for tourism in Kaokoland and for contact with the Himba, caution and sensitivity should be exercised at all times. If possible, a local guide should liaise between tourists and the Himba to ensure that local customs and people are respected.

Meeting the Himba

→ Never take photographs without first having obtained permission and negotiate a fee beforehand. Rather than cash, this is usually in the form of provisions that are a daily part of the Himba's life – maize meal, cooking oil, sugar and the like (available from Opuwo's supermarkets). Never give cigarettes, alcohol or sweets.

→ If you are driving through the region and see the Himba walking along the roads, by all means stop and offer them a lift if it will help them get to their destination. As a thank you, it may possible that you will be granted permission to take a photograph.

→ Never enter a seemingly deserted settlement. As a semi-nomadic people, the Himba move around with their animals to return later to villages that may appear abandoned but in reality are not.

→ Finally, don't just stop and stare but interact and share; in many ways they are just as interested in learning about the people who have come to visit them. Children are delighted to see pictures of themselves on the back of a digital camera, and the women may want to see what other women's hair feels like or admire and compare items of jewellery. Earrings, tattoos, velcro sandals, even the contents of your wash kit may well be a source of fascination and amusement!

Driving sensibly you can expect to get from Puros to just beyond Red Drum before having to pitch camp in the wild. Marked by a windmill, **Orupembe** is 106 km from Puros, which should take roughly about two hours, and about midway the D3707 skirts the boundary of the Skeleton Coast National Park and you are only about 40 km from the Atlantic Ocean. However, this is part of the Skeleton Coast that is closed to the public. Once at Orupembe, the D3707 heads 185 km east to Opuwo. Alternatively, from Orupembe turn northeast for 15 km on the D3703 to another intersection. The right fork is still the D3703 and continues to Opuwo, roughly 200 km away, while the left fork goes another 50 km to **Red Drum**, literally a painted drum full of stones and bullet holes which was first put in place by the South Africa Defence Force in the 1970s as a navigation aid. Take a left here for Hartmann's Valley and a right for Marienfluss Valley. Remember it is not possible to get to Opuwo from Marienfluss Valley via Van Zyl's Pass as it can only be tackled from east to west. Instead you'll have to backtrack to the intersection with the D3703. For details of the east–west route from Opuwo to the two valleys via Van Zyl's Pass, see page 199.

Opuwo → *Colour map 1, A3. Phone code: 065.*

Surrounded by low-lying hills, Opuwo, which means 'the end' in Herero, is an uninspiring town in the middle of the bush. It is the administrative capital of the Kunene Region and has a rapidly growing population of around 12,000. Long occupied by the Himba and Herero, whose settlements of beehive huts still surround the town, Opuwo only grew into a permanent settlement during the Angolan Bush War prior to independence, when the South Africa Defence Force built the airport and used it as a base from which to launch expeditions into the surrounding area. After independence during the 1990s, FM radio, television and an automatic telephone system were introduced, and Opuwo finally got town status in 2000. More recently the route from Kamanjab via the C35 and C41 has all been tarred making access (and the supply of provisions) from the south much easier.

Opuwo's name is indeed appropriate as it is both the first and last place offering supplies, fuel and banks in the region. The main intersection in town is where the C41 from the east joins the C43 from the north and south. The C43 forms the main street (Mbumbiazo Muharukua Avenue) and near this intersection is a small shopping centre with a branch of First National Bank with an ATM, a 24-hour **Puma** petrol station and large **OK** supermarket. The residential areas are a few streets of bungalows built during the bush war for army and government personnel; these now house government officials and the few business people in the area. In every direction from town, are sandy tracks leading to the Himba and Herero settlements. You will see many of the striking Himba people on the streets of Opuwo, indeed you may find yourself in a queue with them in one of the shops, but do not take photos. If visiting one of the settlements, always be accompanied by a guide/translator who will negotiate a donation for taking photographs. ►► *See What to do, page 207, and box, page 196, about visiting the Himba.*

Arriving in Opuwo

Opuwo is 262 km north of Kamanjab via the C35 and C41 and this route is tarred all the way. If coming directly from Windhoek, this is the quickest option for the 710-km drive. The junction of the C45 and C41 is 58 km east of Opuwo, and from here the remaining 82 km of the C35 to north to Ruacana is good gravel. Alternatively from Kamanjab, it's 353 km via the C40 and C43 via Palmwag and Sesfontein. To the west it's 227 km from Opuwo to Oshakati on the C41, which is tarred for 58 km as far as the C45 junction, after which it is again good gravel. The routes from Opuwo to the far northwest are the C43 to Okongwati, 106 km, and the shortest route to Hartmann's Valley is via the D3703 through the Steilrand Mountains, but this involves negotiating Van Zyl's Pass, strictly 4WD only (see page 199). Whichever way you go, ensure you top up with fuel in Opuwo.

Okongwati → *Colour map 1, A2.*
This small settlement marks the end of the reasonable C43 from Opuwo. There is a police station, basic store, bottle shop and a few houses. There is a small sign for **Epupa Camp** (for Epupa Falls), which takes you across a wide sandy riverbed shortly after leaving the village. This road needs to be driven with care; allow three hours.

By the time you reach Okongwati you need to have already decided which route you are going to follow. The reason for this is simply the availability of fuel and the distances you plan to cover. There are a few possible routes you can follow and each will take you through beautiful country.

The adventurous and well-equipped can take the D3703 west from Okangwati towards Otjitanda, Van Zyl's Pass and Hartmann's Valley.

Van Zyl's Pass, Marienfluss and Hartmann's valleys → *Colour map 1, A1/A2.*
From Okongwati a rough track leads 36 km to **Van Zyl's Pass**, which is regarded as the most difficult mountain pass in Namibia. It gets its name from a Dutch explorer who found the way across in the 1920s with the help of a few hundred Himba and a Model T Ford, and is a tremendous feat of engineering. The narrow track, leading through the rugged Otjihipa Mountains, and consisting of coarse scree and jagged rocks, is not to be treated lightly and can only be crossed from east to west (downhill). It is strewn with large rocks, which you may have to remove, and you will need to engage low ratio and, at times, diff-lock. From the top of the pass there is a scary view of the final 3-km drop.

If you started your day's journey in Opuwo you will not manage to cross the pass before nightfall. Do not attempt the pass without plenty of daylight remaining – the descent from the top of the pass covers a distance of 10 km, which will take you three to six hours to negotiate. Stay the night at the small community-run Van Zyl's **Pass Campsite** (see page 205) near the village of Otjitanda, 20 km before the pass, and cross the pass in the morning.

From the bottom of the pass the track splits and goes north roughly 65 km to the **Okarohombo Campsite** and the **Okahirongo River Camp** (see Where to stay, page 204) on the Kunene River at the other end of the Marienfluss Valley, and south to Red Drum (see page 197) and the Hartmann's Valley. Having got this far, both valleys are worth visiting but you will need to be completely self-sufficient. Keep to existing tracks, which in places are soft sand. The only other lodge in the region is **Serra Cafema**, in the upper reaches of the Skeleton Coast National Park which can only be reached by air (see Where to stay, page 205).

The **Marienfluss Valley** is very scenic and relatively greener than Hartmann's Valley. It is known for its 'fairy circles' – round patches without any sign of vegetation thought to be the sites of ancient termite mounds. If you are interested in seeing the circles but can't get here, then a couple of days spent at the NamibRand Nature Reserve (see page 304) near Sossusvlei will teach you all that is currently known about their origins.

Hartmann's Valley is closer to the Atlantic and yet much more arid. It has a strange atmosphere when the sea mists drift inland, rather like at Swakopmund. The drive is a tiring one and you should allow three hours to complete the 91 km from Red

Kunene River

If you look at a map, the Kunene River heads south from its source in the central highlands of Angola (where it's spelt 'Cunene River'), and makes a sharp bend to the west at the Ruacana Falls to form the border between Namibia and Angola. The name Kunene was given to the river by the Herero, and in their language it means, 'right-hand side'; the name refers to the land north of the river. The name 'kaoko' derived from 'okaoko' in Herero, means 'small left arm' and was given to the area 'to the left' of the Kunene River; Kaokoland. From its source in Angola, the river travels for just over 1000 km and enters the Atlantic Ocean along the northern extremity of the Skeleton Coast National Park. Here it also marks the northern limits of the giant sand dunes which first appeared 1700 km south, along the banks of the Orange River. Along its course, the geometry of the Kunene riparian zone is distinctly narrow, with rugged arid landscapes on both sides of the river for long distances, and a virtual lack of any major floodplains. It is Namibia's most rapidly flowing river, descending through gorges and forming rapids and waterfalls along the border. These include the Epupa Falls and the Ruacana Falls (see page 201). Surrounded by waving makalani palms, wild fig trees and precariously placed baobabs, both these waterfalls are a pleasant and welcome sight after long drives through the thirst lands of Kaokoland.

Drum. Here the road meets a bank of sand dunes, which are part of the Skeleton Coast National Park proper, and you are not permitted to continue. You will have to turn back on the same road. For other options from Red Drum (see page 197).

As you drive up each of these valleys the sandy tracks lead through undulating grass savannahs where herds of springbok and gemsbok gallop across the white-yellow grass. It is difficult not to feel a certain sense of achievement and good fortune to be able to visit such a beautiful and fragile environment. Somehow nothing else in Namibia has quite the same impact as a week or more discovering the beauty of Kaokoland.

Okongwati to Epupa Falls → *Colour map 1, A2.*

From Okongwati, the road continues 76 km north to the beautiful **Epupa Falls** (allow three hours). The falls are a series of cascades where the Kunene River drops a total of 60 m over a distance of about 1.5 km. The main drop is roughly 32 m. As the river drops, it divides into a multitude of channels creating hundreds of small vegetated islands. While most people content themselves with a quick peek at the falls from the road, there is a path along the rocks high above the river, downstream of the falls, affording fine views back towards the falls. From here you can appreciate their extent and beauty, and see the range of vegetation including makalani palms and wild fig trees which attract a varied birdlife – look out for bee-eaters, fish eagles, the Malachite kingfisher and paradise flycatchers. Beware of snakes on land and crocodiles in the water. Just before sunset, drive a short way back towards the airfield and take the only track to the right. This leads up to the top of the hill where you are presented with a magnificent view of the falls and all the islands. An ideal spot for your sundowner.

Given that it is the end of the road for many adventurous road trips through Namibia, Epupa has a considerable amount of tourist activity. You will encounter other (mostly South African) self-drive visitors and the occasional tour group being ferried between the airstrip, Himba village, Epupa Falls and lodges in the area, but this is a truly beautiful spot and one can only hope that too much tourism doesn't spoil it. Part of its charm lies in the effort required to get here; it's worth spending a couple of days to enjoy the feeling of remoteness. It is essential to take sufficient fuel as there is none at Epupa. There are, however, a couple of small shops selling fresh bread (the clay oven is outside), and cold drinks and beer are available to refresh those without an onboard fridge. There are also thatched structures by the approach to the falls where the Himba sell local crafts.

Epupa Falls to Ruacana → *Colour map 1, A2.*
The most straightforward route is to head south to Okangwati and Opuwa and loop round to Ruacana via the C41 and C35. However, if you have sufficient fuel and a high-clearance 4WD (as well as off-road driving experience) you can follow the very rough D3700 next to the Kunene River. The narrow rocky track, whose course is vague in places, runs 135 km upstream from Epupa Falls to Ruacana via the **Kunene River Lodge**, which is about a three-hour drive from the falls. Note this road does not follow the river as closely as some people expect and is very hard going in places. If you are not experienced but still want to follow the river to Ruacana, we recommend that you drive back to Okangwati and then south to Otjiveze on the D3700 and then take the D3701/3702 signposted **Kunene River Lodge**. While this road is not smooth or easy, it is not as tricky as the first part of the D3700 between the Epupa Falls and **Kunene River Lodge**. The road onwards to Ruacana Falls is, however, rough again and the river often floods making it inaccessible. Ask at the lodge for the most up-to-date information.

Ruacana Falls → *Colour map 1, A3.*
These falls in the Kunene are located on the river's bend where it joins Namibia from Angola, 15 km west of the town of Ruacana, and well signposted from the C46. However, the Ruacana Falls are not the destination they once were. Built in 1975, the Calueque Dam 20 km upstream in Angola has stopped any flooding and the steady stream that does come through is deviated through the hidden turbines of Nampower's Ruacana Hydroelectric Power Station. But this now provides both an important source of power for Namibia and water for irrigation in Owamboland, the water being carried by the Ogongo Canal alongside the C46 to lands beyond Oshakati.

The falls can still be spectacular, and the water gushes in many single streams down into a 700-m-wide and 120-m-deep ravine, but this requires consistent heavy rains (ie summer). For views of water crashing over rocks, March and April are the best bet. Year-round, the flow of the river is increased and decreased with demand for electricity; it runs faster on weekdays in the morning and evening for example.

Border crossing

Ruacana (Namibia)–Calueque (Angola)

The border is 15 km from Ruacana at the junction of the C46 and D3400 and 2 km up the track to the main viewpoint of the Ruacana Falls – it's well signposted. There's little more than a police/army checkpoint here and it's open 0800-1800, but remember Namibia's daylight saving time is from the first Sunday of April to the first Sunday in September, meaning the times could be an hour earlier. Over the border the road is rough and overgrown (4WD only) and it's about 20 km to Calueque, the small village at the Calueque Dam on the Kunene River (Cunene in Angola). From here it's another 100 km to Xangongo on Angola's main north–south interior highway which is tarred all the way to Luanda (1150 km) and in the southern direction back towards Namibia, 130 km to Santa Clara and the border at Oshikango. For details of visa and vehicle requirements for Angola, see the Oshikango–Santa Clara border box, page 216.

Below the falls the gorge ends at **Hippo Pools** where there are a couple of small islands in the middle of the channel. There is a campsite here, where local guides will take people for walks along the river and to the falls and to see the Himba and their villages. The border with Angola runs down the middle of the river below the main falls and the Ruacana border post with Angola is on the track to the main viewpoint (see box, above).

Ruacana → Colour map 1, A3. Phone code: 065.

Although Ruacana is where the Kunene River enters Namibia from Angola, the town actually lies in the country's administrative Omusati Region on the border with the Kunene Region. The town itself only came into existence as a camp for workers involved with the construction of the Ruacana Hydroelectric Power Station in the late 1970s, although it was also an important South African military base in the 1980s during the Angolan Bush War (the dam and pumping station were bombed in a Cuban airstrike in 1988). In 2010 it was granted the status of a town and the population is little more than 3000.

It is a useful supply stop for those heading to or returning from northern Kaokoland. There is a **Puma** petrol station, the only fuel in the area, with a well-stocked shop, a small supermarket 200 m further along the same road, hospital, post office and one good place to stay (see Where to stay, page 206).

From Ruacana there are a few options. If you have approached through Oshakati you can avoid backtracking by returning south via the C35 past the western end of Etosha National Park to **Kamanjab**, a 286-km drive. This road is good gravel for the first 82 km and navigable with a saloon car. It then becomes tar at the junction of the C45 and C41, 58 km east of Opuwo. For **Epupa**, 4WDs can take the D3700 westward along the banks of the Kunene via the **Kunene River Lodge** (see Epupa Falls to Ruacana, above).

For hotel and restaurant price codes and other relevant information, see pages 21-28.

◉ Where to stay

Khowarib *p194, map p193*
The following places are both signposted off the D3706 in the village and are close to each other in the Khowarib Gorge with its lovely floodplain on the Hoanib River. Campers have a choice; the campsite at the lodge or the community-run camp. Both are similar in price so it's just a case of looking to see which individual camping spot you like best. You can eat dinner at the lodge if you order before 1600.
$$$-$$ Khowarib Lodge 1 km from the D3706, reservations Swakopmund T064-402779, lodge T814-965450, www.khowarib.com. A sister operation to the excellent **Kunene Tours & Safaris** which runs tours in Kaokoland and Damaraland (see Swakopmund tour operators, page 262). 14 tented chalets with open-air bathrooms in rocky walls, verandas with river views, a *lapa* built around boulders with lounge, dining area and curio shop. Excursions include elephant and rhino tracking and Himba visits. **Campsite ($)** 8 sites, electricity, showers with warm water and sells *braai* packs and cold drinks.
$ Khowarib Community Campsite 2 km off the D3706, no phone. Perched on a cliff overlooking the Khowarib Gorge and river, 4 attractive sites, each has its own *lapa* with kitchen counter, *braai* pit, sink, toilet and hot shower heated by a donkey boiler. There's always a small flow of water in the Hoanib River

and you can carefully climb down and enjoy a splash in one of the small pools. The staff can take you on lovely walks through the gorge.

Warmquelle *p194, map p193*
$ Ongongo Community Campsite, 6 km north from Warmquelle up a narrow track, if you fail to see the signs just keep following the water pipe. This track is very stony and while you may not need to engage 4WD, a high-clearance vehicle is essential. Set in picturesque limestone valley, there are several reasonably flat sites cleared of rocks and shaded by reed shelters with *braai* pit, basic communal toilets and showers, firewood and sometimes cool drinks for sale. The highlight is swimming in the natural pool here formed by Hoanib River filtering through the huge boulders and at one end is a waterfall which flows during the rainy season (Nov-Apr). Look out for the terrapins that live in the pool; they have been known to attach themselves to men's nipples! This is a wonderful stop, and if you climb to the top of the hills behind the camp the views at sunset over the gravel plains are tremendous.

Sesfontein *p195, map p193*
$$$ Fort Sesfontein Lodge, T065-685034, www.fort-sesfontein.com. 13 rooms in the 1896 historical fort, which in the past has been a police station and veterinary checkpoint, cool spacious restaurant in what was the police officers' mess, bar, large swimming pool, pleasant shaded courtyard with palms and bougainvillea. The lodge can pick up from the airstrip at Sesfontein and arrange local 4WD trips in the region.

Puros *p195, map p193*

$$$$ Okahirongo Elephant Lodge,
just outside the village, T065-685018,
www.okahirongolodge.com. Set on
the dry Hoarusib River, a luxury camp
with 7 terracotta cottages with outdoor
showers and separate day beds in their
own gazebos, ethnic earthy furnishings,
stunning rim-flow pool, African and
Italian cuisine for dinner served by
candlelight, and activities include game
drives in search of desert elephant and
black rhino, and visits to Himba villages.
It's possible to drive here but most guests
are ferried in by charter flights. Costing
more than N$8600 for a double, this is
the place to enjoy real luxury in such a
remote area.

$ Puros Campsite, 2 km northeast
of the village on a single sandy track,
only accessible by 4WD, no phone
but reservations are not necessary.
Shaded by large camelthorn trees and
community-run, 6 sites with space for
4 tents each, with flush toilet, shower,
braai, sink, tap and donkey boiler for hot
water. Bar, walking trails, firewood for
sale, visits to the Himba with local guides
can be arranged, lots of game in the area
and desert elephant are frequent visitors
to the camp. A fabulous spot and well
worth spending a couple of nights in
order to fully appreciate the beauty and
appeal of the region.

Opuwo *p198, map p193*

There are few options, and campers
should head for the **Opuwo Country
Lodge** and spoil themselves with the
facilities after a long drive.

$$$ Opuwo Country Lodge, T065-
273461, www.opuwolodge.com.
On a hill to the northwest of town
with breathtaking views of the valley
and sunset from the patio and pool,

this is the best of Opuwo's limited
accommodation with 50 a/c rooms, the
vast main thatched building houses a
restaurant, bar and craft shop. Visits to
Himba villages and day trips to Epupa
Falls can be arranged. Also 12 **camping
sites ($)** on terraces on the hillside with
braai pits and electrical points, washing
up area and hot showers.

$$ Ohakane Lodge, north of OK
supermarket on Mbumbiazo Muharukua
Av, T065-273031. Not well located
and noisy, and the 13 a/c rooms are a
little shabby, but worth mentioning if
the **Opuwo Country Lodge** is full or
beyond your budget. The thatched main
building has a bar and restaurant with set
3-course dinners next to the swimming
pool and curios are for sale. A good place
to pick up a guide to visit the Himba in
your own or their vehicle.

$ ABBA Guesthouse, near the police
station on Mbumbiazo Muharukua Av,
T065-273155, www.abbaguesthouse.
com. No reference to the Swedish super
group – ABBA stands for Affordable,
Beautiful, Budget Accommodation...
15 neat rooms with a/c or fans and DSTV,
you can also camp in the compound,
again a little noisy on the main road,
breakfast included and there's a self-
catering kitchen and the OK supermarket
is close by. Prices start at N$130 pp.

**Marienfluss and Hartmann's
valleys** *p199, map p193*

$$$$ Okahirongo River Camp,
reservations Windhoek, T065-685018,
www.okahirongolodge.com. Also
operates **Okahirongo Elephant Lodge** at
Puros (see above), this is another luxury
offering in a beautiful wilderness at
the top of the Marienfluss Valley on the
banks of the Kunene River. 6 wood and
canvas suites, 4-poster beds and outdoor

showers, swimming pool, walks, drives, Himba visits, fishing and boat cruises. You can drive here through the valley or there's an airstrip.

$$$$ Serra Cafema, reservations **Wilderness Safaris**, South Africa, T+27. (0)11-807 1800, www.wilderness-safaris. com. In the extreme northwest on the Kunene River, used only for fly-in safaris and probably one of the most remote camps in Africa. 8 beautifully furnished tents with 4-poster beds and wooden decks, swimming pool and thatched dining area in shaded, grassed riverside site. Walking, quad bike and 4WD trails into the valleys, plus boating and fishing on the river and visits to Himba villages.

$ Okarohombo Campsite, by the Kunene River at the northern end of the Marienfluss Valley, no phone. Managed by the local Himba, very little English spoken, although you might find someone who understands Afrikaans. 5 simple campsites with communal flush toilets, showers, taps and shade provided by a few camelthorn trees, a scenic camp that helps make the long and tiring journey worthwhile. Bring all supplies including firewood and drinking water. Be sure to ask the safest spot for swimming in the river – there are crocodiles.

$ Van Zyl's Pass Campsite, roughly 20 km before the pass coming from the east, near the Himba village of Otjihende, no phone. A community camp with 3 shady sites are alongside a sandy dry riverbed, each with its own flush toilet and hot shower heated by a donkey boiler in little reed and stone structures, kitchen area with sink and *braai* areas. You will need to camp here if there are not enough daylight hours to tackle the pass.

Epupa Falls *p200, map p193*
The lodges here are set in the lush vegetation along the Kunene River and can organize sundowner drives to 'Sundowner Hill' (a prominent point overlooking the falls), rafting some of the gentler rapids on inflatable boats, guided birdwatching boat trips, and visits to Himba villages. A minimum of 2 nights is essential, given all the activities and that it's a long way to come.

$$$$-$$$ Epupa Camp, about 1 km from the falls, follow the track upstream past the village, T065-685053, www. epupa.com.na. An attractive camp nestled amongst baobab trees and palms and just a short walk from the falls with 9 safari-style tents, a *lapa* with eating area and bar. The 5 **camping sites ($)** have a river view and private ablutions, *braai* and kitchen sink. As dinner in the restaurant is a set menu at a 7-m-long dining table, campers must pre-book.

$$$ Epupa Falls Lodge & Campsite, next to the falls, T065-695106, www. epupafallslodge.com. The closest lodge to the falls (fall asleep to the sound of the rapids) on what was the first development at Epupa (it became a campsite in the early 1990s). Now offers 5 attractive chalets set on stone stilts under the Makalani palms, a **campsite ($)** with good ablutions, electricity and firewood, and meat and ice is available, and bar and restaurant on a fantastic wooden deck over the falls from where crocodiles and African fish eagles may be spotted.

$$$ Omarunga Lodge & Campsite, next to **Epupa Falls Lodge**, reservations Swakopmund, T064-403096, www. omarungalodge.com. 14 comfortable canvas-sided, thatch-roofed chalets, all with views and some with river frontage, open dining area, afternoon tea and generous buffets for dinner, swimming pool and pool/sports bar where there are sometimes BBQs. **Campsite ($)** with hot showers, lights, taps, plenty of shade, and close enough to hear the roar of the falls.

Ruacana Falls *p201, map p193*
$$$-$ Kunene River Lodge, 56 km west of the C46 junction for Ruacana, on the D3700; this route is normally navigable with a high-clearance car; however, if the river levels rise, you must instead use the route from Opuwo via the C43 and then turn off on to the D3201 at Epembe to get to the lodge, T065-274300, www.kuneneriverlodge.com. Accommodation is in 8 smart a/c rooms sleeping 2-4, 4 double simple, stone and thatch A-frame chalets, and a **campsite** with 12 shady sites with *braais* and good ablution facilities, most next to the river. Swimming pool, bar and restaurant with a lovely wooden deck that goes right over the river, activities include rafting and canoeing, fishing, birdwatching, and the sundowner cruises are a highlight. There's an airstrip at Swartbooisdrift, 12 km from the lodge for charter flights.
$ Hippo Pools Community Campsite, close to the falls, 17 km west of the C46 junction for Ruacana, 4 km after the Ruacana border post, just 200 m behind the Nampower Hydroelectric Power Station, where the D3700 forks off from the C46, no phone. Lovely spot under *mopane* trees and acacias right on the riverbank (there's a lot of hippo here), each site has a *braai* area, communal ablution block with solar hot showers and eco-toilets. At the reception you can usually buy firewood and borrow paraffin lamps, and there are some local crafts for sale. Guided walks to Himba settlements and to the falls.

Ruacana *p202, map p193*
$$-$ Ruacana Eha Lodge, Springbok Av, T065-271500, www.ruacanaehalodge. com.na. Nothing special but the only option in town and comfortable enough with 21 modern a/c motel-style rooms and a campsite that also has 6 simple 2-bed huts with spotless shared hot showers, washing up facilities and *braai* pits. Restaurant, bar, swimming pool with sun loungers in pretty gardens, can arrange day trips with notice to the Ruacana Falls and Himba villages.

O Shopping

Opuwo *p198, map p193*
Opuwo has a number of very basic takeaways and shops selling goat meat and chips, a few tinned goods, crisps and not much else. There's a decent shop at the **Puma** petrol station selling meat pies and cold drinks. The best bet is the **OK** supermarket in the small shopping centre at the intersection in with the C41 and C43, which also usefully has a bakery and sells charcoal, ice, wine and tyres. There's also a butcher and bottle store in the centre. However, deliveries of provisions in this remote region are infrequent so it's best to stock up on fresh food further south if possible.

Local crafts can be bought from the **Kaoko Information Centre**, on the main street, which sells locally made and used baskets, jewellery, Himba dolls, carvings, clothing and ornaments. These, thankfully, are no longer the family heirlooms of the vendors, but are now produced for sale, with designs sometimes adapted to be more appealing to tourists.

Ruacana *p202, map p193*
In the centre of this small town is a 24-hr **Puma** petrol station with a mini-market that sells charcoal and ice, and a bottle shop across the road. The next, fuel, shops and banks are in Outapi, 69 km east along the C46.

What to do

Kaokoland *p192, map p193*
Most of the lodges and campsites in Kaokoland can organize an excursion to meet the Himba in their traditional villages with a Himba guide. But if you want to visit one of the outlying Himba villages around Opuwo with a guide in your own vehicle, then go to the **Kaoko Information Office** opposite the offices of the Regional Council (daily 0800-1800). The guides speak English and will be able to translate for you. A half-day visit will cost in the region of N\$100-150 per person/N\$150 per car for the guide,

plus the cost of taking provisions to the Himba. It is a way of putting a little money into the local economy as crafts and other souvenirs can be bought directly from the people themselves. See box, page 196, about visiting the Himba.

Directory

Opuwo *p198, map p193*
Medical services The State Hospital, is in the middle of town, T065-272800, but avoid if at all possible; it suffers from a shortage of doctors and even running water. For minor ailments go to the **Kunene Pharmacy**, in the same shopping centre as the OK supermarket, T065-273221, which rather uniquely/usefully doubles up as the town's print and photocopying shop. **Mechanical services** Kunene Fitment Centre, again in the same centre as OK, T065-273 519, sells tyres, batteries, oil, and does puncture and other small repairs.

Far North

Formerly known as Owamboland, the far north of Namibia is a dusty, overgrazed, over-populated area with few attractions for tourists. This area is home to about one million people, almost half the country's population, on land that constitutes less than 10% of Namibia's total area. The reason for this is that Owamboland was declared as the 'homeland' for the Owambo people under South Africa's apartheid policies in the 1960s. Unsurprisingly, support for SWAPO and armed resistance to South African rule was at its most intense here and the result was that the region became a war zone under martial law for most of the 1970s and 1980s. The region is now divided into four political regions (Oshikoto, Ohangwena, Omusati and Oshana) and is often referred to as the Four-Os region.

This part of Namibia is typified by a different relationship between man, animal and land: you will notice a significant increase in traffic; herds of goats and cattle criss-crossing the roads; rows of wooden, fenced homesteads; strings of children making their way to and from school; and the tireless collectors of water going about their daily grind. Most of the landscape comprises subsistence farming and while the *makalani* palm trees have survived in the harsh landscape – perhaps because of their inefficiency as firewood – and offer attractive silhouettes at sunset, the *mopane* trees have long since been cut down for firewood or used to build homesteads.

A great deal of money is flowing into the region from government and overseas aid, which is being spent on education, health care, the civil service, police and military, and there are significant visible infrastructure investments. With the ending of the civil war in Angola, the Four-Os region has also become a feeder for supplies and services into once war-ravaged southern Angola. The area is evidently booming, but visitors will quickly appreciate that tourism is not the engine for this growth.

Namibian Wildlife

A large proportion of people who visit Namibia do so to see its spectacular wildlife. This colour section is a quick photographic guide to some of the more fascinating mammals you may encounter, including pictures and information about habitat, habits and characteristic appearance to help you when you are on safari. It is by no means a comprehensive survey and some of the animals listed may not be found throughout the whole country. For further information about Namibia's mammals, birds, reptiles and other wildlife, see the Wildlife section of the Background chapter.

The Big Nine

It is fortunate that many of the large and spectacular animals of Africa are also, on the whole, fairly common. They are often known as the 'Big Five'. This term was originally coined by hunters who wanted to take home trophies of their safari. Thus it was, that, in hunting parlance, the Big Five were elephant, black rhino, buffalo, lion and leopard. Nowadays the hippopotamus is usually considered one of the Big Five for those who shoot with their camera, whereas the buffalo is far less of a 'trophy'. Equally photogenic and worthy of being included are the zebra, giraffe and cheetah. But whether they are the Big Five or the Big Nine, these are the animals that most people come to Africa to see and, with the possible exception of the leopard, you have an excellent chance of seeing them all.

Below: Hippopotamus

Above: Black rhinoceros
Right: White rhinoceros

■ **Hippopotamus** *Hippopotamus amphibius*. Prefers shallow water, grazes on land over a wide area at night, so can be found quite a distance from water, and has a strong sense of territory, which it protects aggressively. Lives in large family groups known as 'schools'. They are not common in the dry interior of Namibia, but flourish in the rivers along the Caprivi Strip.

■ **Black rhinoceros** *Diceros bicornis*. Long, hooked upper lip distinguishes it from white rhino rather than colour. Prefers dry bush and thorn scrub habitat and in the past was found in mountain uplands. Males usually solitary. Females seen in small groups with their calves (very rarely more than four), sometimes with two generations. Mother always walks in front of offspring, unlike the white rhino, where the mother walks behind, guiding calf with her horn. You might be lucky to see

free-roaming black rhino in Damaraland and Kaokoland. Like the desert elephant, it has adapted its behavior to the harsh environment.

■ **White rhinoceros** *Diceros simus*. Square muzzle and bulkier than the black rhino, they are grazers rather than browsers, hence the different lip. Found in open grassland, they are more sociable and can be seen in groups of five or more. The distribution of both black and white rhino has been massively reduced by poaching, but visitors to Etosha National Park have a good chance of seeing them at the waterholes.

■ **Giraffe** *Giraffa camelopardis*. Yellowish-buff with patchwork of brownish marks and jagged edges, usually two different horns, sometimes three. Found throughout Africa in several differing subspecies.

■ **Common/Burchell's zebra** *Equus burchelli*. Generally has broad stripes (some with lighter shadow stripes next to the dark ones) which cross the top of the hind leg in unbroken lines. The true species is probably extinct but there are many varying subspecies found in different locations across Africa. **Hartmann's mountain zebra** *Equus zebra hartmannae* is also present in

Namibia and occurs in mountainous areas in the Namib Desert.

■ **Leopard** *Panthera pardus*. Found in varied habitats ranging from forest to open savannah. They are generally nocturnal,

Right Giraffe
Below: Common zebra
Opposite page: Leopard

Above: Cheetah
Left: Lion
Bottom: Buffalo
Opposite: Elephants

hunting at night or before the sun comes up to avoid the heat. You may see them resting during the day in the lower branches of trees.

■ **Cheetah** *Acinonyx jubatus*. Often seen in family groups walking across plains or resting in the shade. The black 'tear' mark is usually obvious through binoculars. Can reach speeds of 90 kph over short distances. Found in open semi-arid savannah, never in forested country. Endangered in some parts of Africa, Namibia is believed to have the largest free-roaming population on the continent. More commonly seen than the leopard, they are not as widespread as the lion.

■ **Lion** *Panthera leo*. The largest of the big cats in Africa (adult males can weigh up to 200 kg) and also the most common, lions are found on open savannah all over all over eastern and southern Africa. They are often not at all disturbed by the presence of humans and so it is possible to get quite close to them. They are sociable animals living in prides or permanent family groups of up to around 30 animals and are the only felid to do so. The females do most of the hunting (usually ungulates such as zebra and antelope).

■ **Buffalo** *Syncerus caffer*. Were considered by hunters to be the most dangerous of the big game and the most difficult to track and, therefore, the biggest trophy. Generally found on open plains but also at home in dense forest, they are fairly common in most African national parks but, like the elephant, they need a large area to roam in, so they are not usually found in the smaller parks.

■ **Elephant** *Loxodonta africana*. Commonly seen, even on short safaris, the largest land mammal weighing up to six tonnes with an average shoulder height of 3-4 m. They form large family groups led by a female matriarch. Namibia also has a sizeable population of desert-adapted elephant in Damaraland and Kaokoland.

Larger antelopes

■ **Gemsbok** *Oryx gazella*, 122 cm. Unmistakable, with black line down spine and black stripe between coloured body and white underparts. Horns (both sexes) straight, long and look v-shaped (seen face-on). As they favour semi-desert country, the handsome gemsbok is commonly seen throughout Namibia.

■ **Nyala** *Tragelaphus angasi*, 110 cm. Slender frame, shaggy, dark brown coat with mauve tinge (males). Horns (male only) single open curve. The female is a different chestnut colour. They like dense bush and are usually found close to water. Gather in herds of up to 30 but smaller groups are likely.

■ **Common waterbuck** *Kobus ellipsiprymnus* and **Defassa waterbuck** *Kobus defassa*, 122-137 cm. Very similar with shaggy coats and white marking on buttocks. On the common variety, this is a clear half ring on the rump and around the tail; on the Defassa, the ring is a filled-in solid white area. Both species occur in small herds in grassy areas, often near water.

Top: Waterbuck
Above: Nyala
Below: Gemsbok

Above: Sable antelope
Left: Greater kudu
Below: Topi

■ **Sable antelope** *Hippotragus niger* 140–145 cm (below), and **roan antelope** *Hippotragus equinus*, 127–137 cm. Both similar shape, with ringed horns curving backwards (both sexes), longer in the sable. Female sables are reddish brown and can be mistaken for the roan. Males are very dark with a white underbelly. The roan has distinct tufts of hair at the tips of its long ears. Sable prefers wooded areas and the roan is generally only seen near water. Both species live in herds.

■ **Greater kudu** *Tragelaphus strepsiceros*, 140–153 cm. Colour varies from greyish to fawn with several vertical white stripes down the sides of the body. Horns long

and spreading, with two or three twists (male only). Distinctive thick fringe of hair running from the chin down the neck. Found in fairly thick bush, sometimes in quite dry areas. Usually live in family groups of up to six, but occasionally larger herds of up to about 30.

■ **Topi** *Damaliscus korrigum*, 122–127 cm. Very rich dark rufous, with dark patches on the tops of the legs and more ordinary looking lyre-shaped horns.

■ **Hartebeest** In the hartebeest the horns arise from a bony protuberance on the top of the head and curve outwards and backwards. **Coke's hartebeest** *Alcephalus buselaphus*, 122 cm, is a drab pale brown with a paler rump; **Lichtenstein's harte-beest** *Alcephalus lichtensteinii*, 127-32 cm, is also fawn in colour, with a rufous wash over the back and dark marks on the front of the legs and often a dark patch near the shoulder; the **red hartebeest** *Alcephalus caama*, 127-132 cm, the most colourful hartbeest, has black markings contrasting against its white abdomen. All are found in herds, sometimes they mix with other plain dwellers such as zebra.

■ **Blue wildebeest** or **gnu** *Connochaetes taurinus*, 132 cm, only found in southern Africa, is often seen grazing in herds with zebra. Blue-grey coat with a few darker stripes down the side, black muzzle and buffalo-like horns.

■ **Eland** *Taurotragus oryx*, 175-183 cm. The largest of the antelope, it has a noticeable dewlap and shortish spiral horns (both sexes). Greyish to fawn, sometimes with rufous tinge and narrow white stripes down side of body. Occurs in groups of up to 30 in grassy habitats.

Top: Hartebeest
Above left: Blue wildebeest
Above right: Eland

Smaller antelope

■ **Bushbuck** *Tragelaphus scriptus*, 76-92 cm. Shaggy coat with white spots and stripes on the side and back and two white, crescent-shaped marks on front of neck. Short horns (male only) slightly spiral. High rump gives characteristic crouch. White underside of tail noticeable when running. Occurs in thick bush, near water. Either seen in pairs or on its own.

■ **Klipspringer** *Oreotragus oreotragus*, 56 cm. Brownish-yellow with grey speckles and white chin and underparts with a short tail. Has distinctive, blunt hoof tips and short horns (male only). Likes dry, stony hills and mountains.

■ **Bohor reedbuck** *Redunca redunca*, 71-76 cm. Horns (male only) sharply hooked forwards at the tip, distinguishing them from the oribi. Reddish fawn with white underparts and a short bushy tail.

Above right: Bushbuck
Right: Bohor reedbuck
Bottom: Klipspringer

They usually live in pairs or in small family groups. Often seen with oribi, in bushed grassland and always near water.

■ **Steenbok** *Raphicerus campestris*, 58 cm. An even, rufous brown colour with clean white underside and white ring around eye. Small dark patch at the tip of the nose and long broad ears. The horns (male only) are slightly longer than the ears: they are sharp, have a smooth surface and curve slightly forward. Generally seen alone, prefers open plains, often found in arid regions. Usually runs off very quickly on being spotted.

■ **Springbok** *Antidorcas marsupialis* or springbuck, 76-84 cm. The upper part of the body is fawn, and this is separated from the white underparts by a dark brown lateral stripe. It is distinguished by a dark stripe which runs between the base of the horns and the mouth, passing through the eye. This is the only type of gazelle found south of the Zambezi River. You no longer see the giant herds the animal was famous for, but you will see them along the roadside as you drive around Namibia. They get their name from their habit of leaping stiff-legged and high into the air.

■ **Common (Grimm's) duiker** *Sylvicapra grimmia*, 58 cm. Grey-fawn colour with darker rump and pale colour on the underside. Its dark muzzle and prominent ears are divided by straight, upright, narrow pointed horns. This particular species is the only duiker found in open grasslands Usually the duiker is associated with a forested environment. It's difficult to see because it is shy and will quickly disappear into the bush.

■ **Oribi** *Ourebia ourebi*, 61 cm. Slender and delicate looking with a longish neck and a sandy to brownish-fawn coat. It has oval-

Above: Steenbock
Above right: Oribi
Below right: Duiker
Opposite page: Springbok

Above: Suni
Right: Impala

shaped ears and short, straight horns with a few rings at their base (male only). Like the reedbuck it has a patch of bare skin just below each ear. Found in small groups or as a pair and never far from water.

■ **Suni** *Nesotragus moschatus*, 37 cm. Dark chestnut to grey-fawn in colour with slight speckles along the back, its head and neck are slightly paler and the throat is white. It has a distinct bushy tail with a white tip. Its longish horns (male only) are thick, ribbed and slope backwards. One of the smallest antelope, it lives alone and prefers dense bush cover and reed beds.

■ **Impala** *Aepyceros melampus*, 92-107 cm. One of the largest of the smaller antelope, the impala has a bright rufous-coloured back and a white abdomen, a white 'eyebrow' and chin and white hair inside its ears. From behind, the white rump with black stripes on each side is characteristic and makes it easy to identify. It has long lyre-shaped horns (male only). Above the heels of the hind legs is a tuft of thick black bristles (unique to impala) which are easy to see when the animal runs. There's also a black mark on the side of the abdomen, just in front of the back leg. Found in herds of 15 to 20, it likes open grassland or sometimes the cover of partially wooded areas and is usually close to water.

Other mammals

There are many other fascinating mammals worth keeping an eye out for. This is a selection of some of the more interesting or particularly common ones.

■ **African wild dog** or hunting dog *Lycacon pictus*. Easy to identify since they have all the features of a large mongrel dog: a large head and slender body. Their coat is a mixed pattern of dark shapes and white and yellow patches and no two dogs are quite alike. They are very rarely seen and are seriously threatened with extinction (there may be as few as 4000 left). They are particularly vicious when hunting. The only place where they survive in Namibia is in Khaudum National Park.

■ **Brown hyena** *Hyaena brunnea*. High shoulders and a low back give the hyena its characteristic appearance. The spotted variety, larger and brownish with dark spots, has a large head and rounded ears. The brown hyena, slightly smaller, has pointed ears and a shaggy coat, and is more noctural. Although sometimes shy animals, they have been know to wander around campsites stealing food from humans.

■ **Rock hyrax** *procavia capensis*. The rock hyrax lives in colonies amongst boulders and on rocky hillsides, protecting itself from predators like eagle, caracal and leopard by darting into the rock crevices.

■ **Caracal** *felis caracal*. Also known as the African lynx, it is twice the weight of a domestic cat, with reddish sandy-coloured fur and paler underparts. Distinctive black stripe from eye to nose and tufts on ears. Generally nocturnal and with similar habits to the leopard. It is not commonly seen, but is found in hilly country.

■ **Vervet monkey** *Chlorocebus pygerythrus*, 39-43 cm. A smallish primate and one of the most recognized monkeys in Africa and often seen at campsites and lodges. Brown bodies with a white underbelly and black face ringed by white fur, and males have blue abdominal regions. Spends the day foraging on the ground and sleeps at night in trees.

Left: African wild dog
Below: Vervet monkey
Bottom left: Spotted hyena
Bottom right: Rock hyrax
Next page: Caracal

Arriving in the Far North

There are two main arteries through Owamboland: the B1/C46, and the smaller C45. The unnatural division in the structure of life in the country is the **Red Line**, 120 km south of Ondangwa on the B1, the fence that separates the animals of Etosha and the large commercial farms of the south from those of the communal small farmers of the north. The movement of livestock, meat and animal products from north to south is forbidden, ostensibly to prevent foot-and-mouth disease and rinderpest from infecting the commercial herds of the south. For the tourist, this means any meat, skins, horns, trophies or other animal products should either not be brought north in the first place, or require a veterinary note specifying the health of your souvenir before being allowed to re-enter the south. There's another checkpoint on the Red Line on the B8, 131 km south of Rundu.

Given that the towns of the Four-Os region are so populated, there is plenty of public transport in the way of shared minibus taxis. However, they are generally driven rather recklessly as they race north along the B1 from Windhoek. A better option is the daily **Intercape** bus that goes from Windhoek via Okahandja, Otjiwarongo, Otavi, Tsumeb, Omuthiya, Ondangwa, Ongwediva and Oshakati, from where it goes on to the Angolan border at Oshikango (see box, page 216).

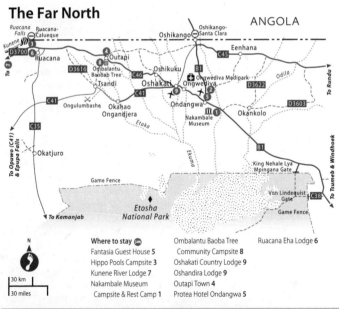

The Far North

Where to stay 🛏️
Fantasia Guest House **5**
Hippo Pools Campsite **3**
Kunene River Lodge **7**
Nakambale Museum
 Campsite & Rest Camp **1**

Ombalantu Baoba Tree
 Community Campsite **8**
Oshakati Country Lodge **9**
Oshandira Lodge **9**
Outapi Town **4**
Protea Hotel Ondangwa **5**

Ruacana Eha Lodge **6**

This is the second largest town in the region (after Oshakati), and is a lively busy place that caters to many people in the Oshana and Oshikoto regions in terms of shopping and other vital services. There are numerous roadside stalls, open markets and wholesale cash-and-carry warehouses around town that cater for the *cuca* owners. A feature of the north are the thousands of distinct square, tin-roofed informal trading shops/bars, known as *cucas*. The name is derived from the tin shacks (often attached to people's homes) on the Angolan border that sold the Portuguese Cuca Beer during the Angolan Bush War. The beer was illegal at the time but was widely drunk by soldiers of the South African Defence Force thus creating a lucrative business for the local people. Today the little shops still serve beer, plus other provisions and provide a sociable hub for the communities. The town has a population of about 30,000 residents, but this figure increases by more than double during the day as many people come in from the nearby villages to shop.

If you're passing though there are modern shopping centres with banks, supermarkets and bottle shops, but there is no need to dally as it's a scruffy place with a particularly bad litter problem and abandoned gutted cars seem to be a prominent feature along the dusty streets. The only tourist attraction is the informative Nakambale Museum at Olokonda, signposted off the B1 before you reach town.

Arriving in Ondangwa

You can get to Ondangwa either from Tsumeb (252 km) and the triangle towns along the B1, which crosses the Red Line (where there is a 24-hour Engen garage, bottle shop and takeaway), or from the far north on the C46 from Ruacana (192 km) via Oshakati (35 km) and Ongwediva (28 km), or from Opuwo on the C41 (262 km), both of which are fairly good gravel roads. From Ondangwa, the border with Angola at Oshikango is 61 km at the end of the B1 (see box, page 216). Air Namibia serves Ondangwa Airport, which effectively serves all the towns in the Four-O's region. Intercape also has a service from Windhoek to these towns.➤➤ *See Transport, page 219.*

Background

Ondangwa was first established as a missionary station in 1893 by the Finnish Missionary Society. In 1914 it became a government station when the British bought the mission and surrounding land off the Finns. In the late 1950s and 1960s during the apartheid era the town swelled as it became the assembly point for those living in the north that were travelling south for employment in the large towns and the South African mines. During the Angolan Bush War, Ondangwa, along with the other towns in the Four-Os region, was an important staging area for the South African Defence Force during its campaigns in neighbouring Angola. Airstrips were built in Ondangwa, as well as at Oshakati, and local road links were also improved by authorities to facilitate the rapid movement of military vehicles. Prior to 1970, Namibia's main north-south road (now the B1) was unpaved beyond Otjiwarongo; by the end of the decade the tarmac had been extended through

The oshana environment

The local agronomy in the far north relies on the *oshanas*, a system of shallow watercourses and *vleis* which only flow for a few weeks a year after heavy rains. They appear in the landscape from south-central Angola and reach as far south as the Etosha Pan. Aerial photography reveals a pattern of watercourses akin to a river delta emptying into the ocean, but in this case they drain internally into pans, the largest of which is Etosha. Most of these 'rivers' are several hundred kilometres long, and when they fill with water, pale pink and white lilies miraculously appear, and they attract a host of water birds such as herons, storks, ducks and waders.

When the rains come it is locally called *efundja*, an Oshiwambo name which means 'flood'. An optimal season sees the rains start in November and fall regularly from December to March, and there is water in the *oshanas* from January until July. Farmers prepare their fields, cattle are herded back from distant grazing to benefit from the new pasture near home, and crops are reaped before the water evaporates in July and August. This is the time to witness the local spectacle of groups of women with handmade fishing baskets wading in shrinking muddy pools, doing their best to catch some extra protein for the supper pot.

Then, after the *oshanas* have turned into dry, sandy riverbeds, the groundwater level drops and boreholes run dry, pastures return to barren fields and cattle have nothing to eat. Quickly, a land of plenty becomes a desolate, desperate place with dust, heat and breath-sapping hot winds, and the signs of overgrazing, erosion and deforestation become all too apparent. For the region's inhabitants, it's back to eating *mealie pap* for the remainder of the year as they wait for the rains and the *oshanas* to fill up again.

Ondangwa to Oshakati (today it's tarred to the border at Oshikango). Ondangwa was officially granted town status in 1998.

Nakambale Museum and Campsite → *Colour map 1, A4.*
ⓘ *At the village of Olukonda, 13 km southeast of Ondangwa, off the B1. A signpost, 8 km southeast of Ondangwa, points west onto the gravel D3629 to Olukonda, the road is suitable for all vehicles. Mon-Fri 0800-1300, 1400-1700, Sat 0800-1300, Sun 1200-1700. N$10, plus a tip for a guided tour.*

Housed in the original (1893) mission house, much of the collection here is devoted to the lives and impressive work of the Finnish missionaries in northern Namibia since the 1870s; in particular, to Martti Rautunen, who translated many (particularly religious) works into local languages and was given the Owambo name 'Nakambale'. There are some excellent displays of traditional musical instruments, household utensils, clothing, tools, snares and clothing. Surrounding the house are a large church and a cemetery with beautifully maintained marble graves for the Rautunen family, which is now a national monument, and a traditional Ndonga homestead,

A brief history of Angola's wars

To label Angola's wars as complex would be the understatement of the century. They variously involved Portugal, South Africa, Namibia, Cuba, Russia, the USA and, of course, the Angolans themselves.

The issues started in the 1950s, when the Portuguese colonial 'masters' who'd had a presence in Angola for 400 years were asked by the indigenous population to leave. They refused and, in 1961, an armed conflict began between Portuguese authorities and various independence groups. These included the People's Movement for the Liberation of Angola (MPLA), and the National Front for the Liberation of Angola (FNLA); in 1966, these were joined by the National Union for the Total Independence of Angola (UNITA). This armed conflict was the **Angolan War of Independence** (1961-1974).

The war ended when a leftist military coup in Lisbon in April 1974 overthrew Portugal's Estado Novo regime, and the new regime immediately stopped all military action in the African colonies, declaring its intention to grant them independence without delay.

Angola gained its independence from Portugal in 1975, to a coalition of the three liberation groups. But they were undecided on who would best fill the power vacuum that had been left behind, which eventually led to armed conflict, with FNLA and UNITA forces, encouraged by their respective international supporters, attempting to wrest control of Luanda from the MPLA. So began the **Angolan Civil War** (1975-2002). Global cold war superpowers became involved, with US-backed South Africa siding with FNLA and UNITA while the

where the guides explain about the everyday life of the Ndonga. There's a restcamp here (see Where to stay, page 217).

Oshikango → *Colour map 1, A4.*

Oshikango is 61 km directly north of Ondangwa at the end of the B1 and is the principal and busiest Namibian border post with Angola, as it joins Angola's main north–south highway (see box, page 216). Oshikango is a strange place indeed. Initially after the Angolan Civil War ended in 2002, it grew almost overnight from a ramshackle dusty, and war-torn village, into a thriving town and one of the most important business hubs of northern Namibia. As there was little available in their own country outside the capital, Luanda, Angolan village traders headed south for much needed supplies. Wealthier Angolans come to spend their newly acquired US dollars in this land of relative plenty, while some Namibians ventured north, mainly for cheaper petrol, cattle and goats. Many foreign (particularly Chinese) and local investors chose it as their stepping-stone for exports into Angola, and the road leading to the border was lined with traders, warehouses and car yards that supplied Angolans with whatever they wanted.

communists, namely Soviet-backed Cuba, got into bed with the MPLA.

Meanwhile, the South African Border War, commonly referred to as the **Angolan Bush War** (1966-1989), was a conflict that took place in Southwest Africa (now Namibia) and Angola about South-West Africa being administered as a fifth province of South Africa during its period of apartheid policy, and was fought between South Africa and its allied forces (mainly UNITA) on the one side, and the **South-West Africa People's Organisation** (SWAPO) and their allies (mainly Cuba), on the other. It was very closely intertwined with both the Angolan Civil War, and the **Namibian War of Independence** (1966-1989), which was the internal guerrilla warfare campaign by SWAPO against South Africa.

Both the Angolan Bush War and the Namibian War of Independence ended when the New York Accords were signed at the United Nations headquarters in New York in 1988 by representatives of the governments of Angola, South Africa and Cuba. The agreement also ended direct involvement of foreign troops (including Cuban) in the Angolan Civil War. This lead to Namibia's independence in 1990 but the Angolan Civil War went on until 22 March 2002, when Jonas Savimbi, the leader of UNITA, was killed. After Savimbi's death, the Angolan MPLA government came to a crossroads over how to proceed and agreed to a ceasefire, while UNITA's new leadership declared the rebel group a political party and officially demobilized its armed forces. After 27 years, the Angolan Civil War was over, ushering in a new era of stability and peace which has endured ever since.

In 2004, Oshikango, along with several other villages and settlements that were booming with this sudden trade along the B1 on its approach to the border, were amalgamated under the new town name of Helao Nafidi. However, this name has failed to be reflected on signs or maps much and most people still commonly use the old names.

Today, Oshikango's fortunes have made a dramatic downturn. The Angolan economy is now in full recovery, entry to the country is much easier, and the main roads in southern Angola are now sleek highways that have been demined. As such many of the businesses that made Helao Nafidi a boomtown have migrated into Angola, and abandoned buildings (which were only hastily put up just a few years ago) testify to the decline of business at Oshikango. While there are still hundreds of trucks queuing up along the B1 to cross the border, these are in fact in transit with goods not from Oshikango but from the port in Walvis Bay and from South Africa. Even the Chinese are now abandoning Oshikango to establish shops in Angola.

You'll pass through if crossing the border, but be warned it's an unappealing and untidy place and as with any crowded transient frontier town, opportunist crime is a problem so carefully guard vehicles and belongings. Nevertheless, there are shops, banks, takeaways, petrol stations and a couple of places to stay.

Ongwediva → *Colour map 1, A4.*

At Ongwediva, 28 km after Ondangwa and 10 km before Oshakati on the C46, there is a small concentration of a shops, a **Standard Bank** with ATM, **Spar** supermarket and **Engen** garage. Again, this sprawling town was developed in the 1960s by the occupying South African military forces during the Angolan Bush War. Today an annual trade fair takes place in the huge, conference facility, the Sam Nujoma Multi-Purpose Centre, built in 2003, and there's a modern private hospital, the **Ongwediva Medipark**, which services the whole region. Drivers may want to stop at **Bennie's Entertainment Park and Lodge** ① *Auguste Taanyanda St, T065-231100, www.benniespark.net, daily 0700-2200, N$20 per person day fee,* for a swim and a meal. It's an odd set-up aimed at the local conference/wedding market with more than 100 rooms (see Where to stay, page 217) but the two swimming pools with a curly waterslide, picnic and *braai* areas are set in lush relaxing gardens where peacocks roam (although it seems an excessive use of water), and the restaurant serves good salads, pizzas and Portuguese-style peri-peri chicken.

Oshakati → *Colour map 1, A4. Phone code: 065.*

Surrounded by *oshanas*, palm trees, farmland and settlements, the much-developed Oshakati is the capital of the Oshana Region, and along with Ongwediva and Ondangwa which sprawl along the C46 to the east, this is where the largest population concentration in Namibia after Windhoek lives. The University of Namibia has its northern campus in town, and you will notice a major influence of municipal buildings including the town council complex, which rather oddly perhaps, was opened in 2006 by then-president of Botswana Festus Mogae. In the local Oshiwambo language the town's name means 'that which is between' and again it was officially founded in 1966 as a base of operations by the South African Defence Force during the Angolan Bush War.

Oshakati has many faces, and town planning seems to have been a fairly haphazard affair. There is the 'town', the former South African military base, where government employees, expatriates and the 'successful' live in detached houses set in leafy gardens close to the private schools and public library. While around town are the various townships where shanty-type dwellings of corrugated iron and scrap metal are dotted with NGO and municipally built public lavatories and stand pipes. Unfortunately, a fair chunk of these were devastated by floods in 2008, and the town's council relocated some to higher (and no doubt drier) places, but there have been no visible signs of improvement in infrastructure.

The main road is lined with a collection of *cuca* shops and *shebeens* (bars), as run-down taxis, donkey carts and luxury vehicles jostle for position along the streets. Services here include banks, several petrol stations, vehicle repair places, a large open market, supermarkets (notably the large **Shoprite** is worth stopping at), and a branch of **Cymot** for camping equipment and vehicle parts. While there is certainly money in the area, the impression remains that life for the majority in Oshakati is hard.

Northwest of Oshakati

Continuing north from Oshakati, the sense of being somewhere becomes elusive as the ribbon development peters out. Only the scattered homesteads and schools are a reminder that this is still one of the most densely populated parts of Namibia.

The direct route from Oshakati to Ruacana follows 157 km of good tar road, the C46, along the Ogongo Canal. This route will take you through **Oshikuku**, 32 km, and Outapi, 90 km. The most striking feature of the landscape is its flatness, and depending upon the time of year you will either pass through the flood plains (usually January to July), or the dry sandy pans (the rest of the year) of the *oshanas*, dotted with homesteads and *mahangu* fields, clusters of *makalani* palms and wonderful baobabs.

Outapi → *Colour map 1, A4.*

Outapi, also known as Uutapi and Ombalantu, along the C46 between Oshakati and Ruacana, is the capital of the Omusati Region and another former South African army base and rapidly developing town in the Four-Os region. As you approach from the south you will notice the large number of government buildings and shops, including some small roadside restaurants and a supermarket. Opposite the town council buildings there is an exceptionally large baobab tree with a wide girth that in the past its huge hollow trunk has been used in the past as a prison, post office and a chapel. Known as the **Ombalantu Baobab Tree**, it is almost 30 m tall, 25 m in diameter and is reputedly to be about 800 years old. It is something of a national monument and has a door and they say about 35 people can stand in it. There's a community campsite here (see Where to stay, page 218) and a craft shop, which offers a wide range of wire products, from replicas of the baobab tree to wire giraffes, but also traditional Owambo baskets and clay pots.

Ongulumbashe → *Colour map 1, A4.*

To the south of Outapi, about 36 km along the gravel D3612 and signposted from the village of Tsandi, is the historic site where the first shots of the liberation struggle were fired on 26 August 1966. Deep in the bush, a group of PLAN (Peoples Liberation Army of Namibia) combatants at their training camp were ambushed by eight helicopters and a team of South African Defence Force soldiers. When visiting the site it is hard to believe that the PLAN combatants were not totally taken aback by the South Africans' precise knowledge of their whereabouts. It really is the middle of nowhere; far from any main routes or settlements and not a hint of landscape, the countryside is flat, scrubby *mopane* woodland. Before setting their ambush, the South Africans apparently harassed the civilian population in their search for the 'terrorists'. There were in fact only 17 PLAN members in the camp at the time of the attack, many other members were in secret exile, and those that weren't killed were captured and sent to Robben Island, the notorious prison outside of Cape Town, to begin long life sentences.

PLAN, the active military wing of the South-West Africa People's Organization (SWAPO), was not deterred by this set back, and went on to engage in guerrilla attacks on South African military bases in South-West Africa until the end of the 1980s. Ogulumbashe is regarded as the event and site where the struggle for

Border crossing

Oshikango (Namibia)–Santa Clara (Angola)

The border is open 0700-1900 but remember Namibia's daylight saving time is from the first Sunday of April to the first Sunday in September, meaning the times could be an hour earlier. Oshikango is currently the busiest Namibian border post with Angola, and as a busy truck route, expect lengthy queues for customs, immigration and vehicle formalities. The Ruacana–Calueque border, see page 202, is a much quieter entry point (take the C46 from Ondangwa) but the condition of the roads on the other side can be a little challenging.

Obviously Portuguese is the language on the Angolan side, but there are entrepreneurial 'fixers'; young boys hanging around the border that for a tip can help you negotiate the formalities and change money. The currency in Angola is the kwanza, and border fees can be paid in US dollars, Namibian dollars/rand or kwanza. There are petrol stations on both sides of the border. From Santa Clara its 139 km to Xangongo and the turn off to the Ruacana–Calueque border, and after Xangongo its 1151 km to Luanda on Angola's main north–south interior highway which is newly tarred all the way.

All foreigners need visas for Angola which must be obtained in advance. Tourist visas are valid for 30 days but are notoriously difficult to obtain so it's best to try the Angolan diplomatic missions in your home country. Alternatively given that you must enter Angola within 60 days of being issued with a visa, you may need to try the diplomatic missions in southern Africa: the **Angolan Embassy** in Windhoek (3 Ausspann Street, T061-227535, Monday-Friday 0800-1600), or the **Angolan Consulate General** in South Africa (1030 Francis Baard Street, Hatfield, Pretoria, T+27 (0)12-342 0049, www.angolanembassy.org, Monday-Friday 0800-1300; there are also consulates in Cape Town, Johannesburg and Durban, check the website for details). It is also compulsory to have a yellow fever vaccination certificate for entry into Angola; if you haven't already got one, get the vaccination in Namibia or South Africa.

Drivers will need the vehicle registration certificate, a letter of authority from the registered owner, if the vehicle is not owned by the driver, ideally an international driver's licence but one with a photo on should do, and make sure you know where the engine/chassis numbers are on the vehicle as these will be checked. By law you must have red warning triangles and a fire extinguisher in the vehicle. You will need to buy a **Temporary Import Permit (TIP)**, and have third-party insurance; you can get this at the Oshikango–Santa Clara border, otherwise make sure you insurance covers Angola. Driving is on the right in Angola.

Namibian independence was born, and in commemoration of the day of the attack, August 26, it is a public holiday in Namibia; Heroes' Day. There is little to see or do here, but the site is marked with an obelisk-like monument, and you may want to visit on Heroes' Day when there is a low-key ceremony when speeches are made by local politicians and the Namibian flag is raised.

For hotel and restaurant price codes and other relevant information, see pages 21-28.

🍽 Where to stay

Ondangwa *p210, map p209*

Staying overnight in the dreary and unattractive towns of the Four-Os region has little appeal, but nevertheless there is adequate accommodation; most is aimed at government officials, business people, conferences and, given the population density in the region, weddings.

$$ Protea Hotel Ondangwa, on the B1 at the northern end of town, just as the road turns towards Oshikango, T065-241900, www.proteahotels.com. Fairly square and impersonal but well run by the South African chain and the best option in town with 90 modern and functional a/c rooms with DSTV and Wi-Fi, restaurant, bar, coffee shop with good cakes and snacks, swimming pool.

$ Fantasia Guest House, Brian Simata St, signposted north of the FNB bank on the B1 in the middle of town, T065-240528. Simple brick guesthouse, but with friendly owners and 8 neat a/c B&B rooms, each with fridge, toaster, microwave, cutlery, coffee and tea facilities and a shaded parking spot, and there's a bar and *braai* area.

Nakambale Museum and Restcamp *p211, map p209*

$ Nakambale Restcamp, at the museum. Spacious but not very attractive campsite in the village, with dusty sites and 5 traditional Ndonga mud huts with mattresses on reed mats on the floor and thatched roof. Very basic

showers and toilets, tap and sink for washing up, *braai* pit, with a little notice traditional meals like chicken/meat and *pap* can be arranged.

Ongwediva *p214*

$ Bennie's Entertainment Park & Lodge, Auguste Taanyanda St, T065-231100, www.benniespark.net. Built for the local conference/wedding market, this large thatched and brick complex has a rather surprising 100 rooms, some sleeping 3-4, with a/c and DSTV, swimming pool with sun loungers and a water slide, decent restaurant serving Portuguese fare, a couple of tacky bars and neat spacious gardens which are a green oasis in these parts.

Oshakati *p214, map p209*

$$ Oshakati Country Lodge, Robert Mugabe Av, T065-222380. Hardly in the country; turn off the C46 in the middle of town at the KFC. The large thatched structure with reception and bar looks impressive from the outside, but the 45 rooms arranged in blocks at the back are pretty mediocre, though they have a/c, DSTV, desk and kettle. Restaurant serving varied food and swimming pool in pleasant lawned garden.

$$-$ Oshandira Lodge, Airport Rd, T065-220443. Near the airstrip, go south from the **Oshakati Country Lodge** for 1.5 km. The best option in town with 16 rooms, decorated with African touches and DSTV and a/c, the open-sided restaurant and bar surrounds the small pool, and there's a decent choice including seafood, pizza, vegetarian dishes and South African wine.

Outapi p215, map p209
$$-$ Outapi Town Hotel, to the west of town off the main road behind the town council buildings, T065-251029, www.outapith.iway.na. Simple concrete motel style complex with 27 rooms with TV, fridge and kettle, secure shaded parking, pool with thatched *lapa*, pleasant gardens with palms, restaurant and bar for basic but cheap meals.
$ Ombalantu Baobab Tree Community Campsite, opposite the town council building, T065-251005. Campsite next to the huge baobab tree with 4 sites under bamboo shades with tap, fire place and good shared ablutions, the office rents out *braai* grills and sells firewood and there's also a craft shop.

🍴 Restaurants

Far North p208, map p209
Eating in the far north is restricted to the few lodges where the à la carte restaurants are open to passing trade even if you're not staying there, as well as the many takeaways/*cuca* shops and market stalls in the regional towns where you can get a taste of what the locals eat, and perhaps enjoy a beer while listening to a blast of *kazomba*; infectious dance music from Angola. Most of the petrol stations have small shops selling snacks and drinks. Self-caterers can stock up in the town's supermarkets and bottle shops.

🛍 Shopping

Far North p208, map p209
The towns feature all the shops you may need. There are branches of the **Shoprite**, **Spar** and **Pick 'n' Pay** supermarkets, as well as bottle shops aplenty – the range of spirits and special

liqueurs is final evidence, if necessary, of Namibians' love of drinking. There cannot be many places in Africa where 5 different brands of tequila are on offer in one bottle shop. A word of warning: theft from vehicles may be a problem so if stopping to shop in the towns, guard your car carefully even if it's within a shopping centre/supermarket car park.

You should see roadside stalls selling traditional baskets woven from the *makalani* palm leaves, bowls and calabashes. The revenue derived from these items is important to the individual craftsmen and women who produce them. The stalls may look unattended, but stop your car and someone will be there in a flash. The markets in Ondangwa and Oshakati, also worth browsing, may have carved cups, bowls, snuff containers, knives and colourful material. None of these crafts is produced for tourists; they are the preferred implements and materials of the homesteads.

Oshakati p214
As well as the usual shops and petrol stations, there is a branch of **Cymot** on the main street (C46), T065-220916, www.cymot.com, Mon-Fri 0800-1700, Sat 0800-1200, for camping and fishing gear and vehicle accessories and spares.

Outapi p215
The craft shop at the **Ombalantu Baobab Tree** (see page 215) is worth stopping at for wire souvenirs, clay pots and baskets.

🚌 Transport

There are hoards of shared minibus taxis in the Four-O's towns, often called 'Ovambo-Taxis' in the north, and they not only ply the streets (drivers will honk at anyone standing on the pavements) but link the towns – the 35 km between Ondangwa and Oshakati for example will take little more than half an hour and cost in the region of N\$10. They also frequently run down the B1 south to **Windhoek** and destinations en route. Again all warnings about travelling on these must be heeded, as the vehicles are in a poor state, overcrowded and driven recklessly.

Ondangwa *p210*
686 km to Windhoek, 252 km to Tsumeb, 35 km to Oshakati, 192 km to Ruacana, 262 km to Opuwo.

Air
Ondangwa Airport, (and Air Namibia office) is 5 km northwest of Ondangwa on the C46, T065-240476. **Air Namibia**, reservations Windhoek, T061-299 6111, www.airnamibia.com.na. Has 2 flights a day between Ondangwa and **Windhoek Eros Airport**, 1 hr 5 mins, with the exception of Sat, which has one daily flight. Taxis meet the flights, or arrange for a transfer with a hotel.

Bus
Intercape buses, central reservations, Windhoek, T061-227847, www.intercape. co.za, buses arrive and depart at the Engen petrol station at the Olunkono Centre on the main road (C46). See timetable on page 16.

Car hire
Avis, Olunkono Centre, where the Spar supermarket is, T065-241281, www.avis. com. **Europcar**, Ondangwa Airport, T065-240261, www.europcar.com. Both can organize cars at the airport and hotels, but they use local car hire companies so

reserve cars in advance. The option here is to fly from Windhoek to Ondangwa, pick up a vehicle and drop it back in Windhoek (or vice versa). Also discuss these arrangements with the car hire companies in Windhoek (page 82).

Ongwediva *p214*
Bus
Intercape buses, central reservations, Windhoek, T061-227847, www.intercape. co.za, arrive and depart at the Engen petrol station on the main road (C46). See timetable on page 16.

Oshakati *p214*
Bus
Intercape buses, central reservations, Windhoek, T061-227847, www.intercape. co.za, arrive and depart at the Engen petrol station at the Yetu Centre on the main road (C46). From here the bus goes on to the Oshikango border (see box, page 216). See timetable on page 16.

① Directory

Ongwediva *p214*
Medical services Ongwediva **Medipark**, Auguste Tanyaanda St, 600 m from the main turn-off into Ongwediva, T065-232911, www.ongwedivamedipark. com. This is the largest private hospital in the north of Namibia, opened in 2006, and anyone with medical ailments and decent insurance should head here. There are several pharmacies in town.

Oshakati *p214*
Mechanical services Approaching Oshakati on the C46 from Ondangwa, you'll pass many roadside vehicle repair workshops on entering town. **Northern Auto Repairs**, is on the main road near the post office, T065-221802,

for breakdown service and general repairs. **Medical services** Oshakati Pharmacy, 249 Main Rd, T065-220964, www.oshpharm.com. This is part of a private medical centre that also has doctors, a dentist, and a laboratory for malaria tests.

Contents

224 Swakopmund and around
  225 Arriving in Swakopmund
  228 Background
  230 Places in Swakopmund
  238 Around Swakopmund
  241 Walvis Bay
  247 Listings

267 Skeleton Coast
  268 Dorob National Park
      (formerly the West Coast
      Recreation Area)
  272 Skeleton Coast
      National Park
  277 Listings

280 The Hinterland
  280 Three Passes
  282 Usakos
  283 Erongo Mountains
  283 Karibib
  284 Omaruru
  285 Kalkfeld
  286 Listings

291 Namib-Naukluft Park
  292 Arriving in Namib-
      Naukluft Park
  292 Background
  293 Namib Section
  296 Naukluft Park
  301 Sossusvlei
  304 NamibRand Nature
      Reserve
  307 Listings

Footprint features

222 Don't miss …
230 Roads, railways and the desert
232 Lappiesdorp – tent city
    on the beach
238 Martin Luther – the steam ox
243 The amazing Benguela Current
269 Hentie's Bay
270 Twitching for a tern
293 Desert conservation
294 Nara melons
297 War in the Naukluft Mountains
305 The Dune Sea

The Coast & Namib-Naukluft

At a glance

⊜ **Getting around** 2WD hire car for major routes. Guided tours from Windhoek and Swakopmund.
⏱ **Time required** Minimum 3 days along the coast, at least 2 days in the Namib-Naukluft region.
☁ **Weather** Warm and dry most of the year.
✖ **When not to go** Avoid Swakopmund during Namibian and South African school holidays.

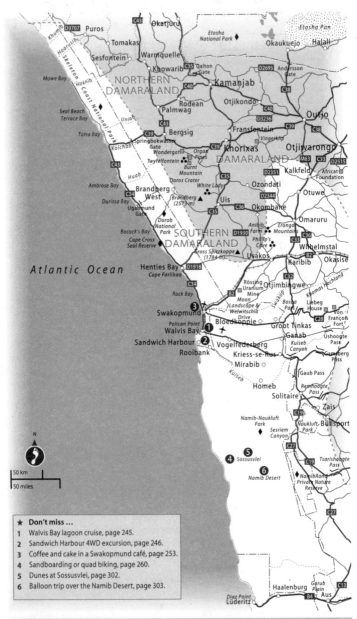

★ Don't miss ...

1 Walvis Bay lagoon cruise, page 245.
2 Sandwich Harbour 4WD excursion, page 246.
3 Coffee and cake in a Swakopmund café, page 253.
4 Sandboarding or quad biking, page 260.
5 Dunes at Sossusvlei, page 302.
6 Balloon trip over the Namib Desert, page 303.

The coast provides a series of striking contrasts between the dunes of the desert and the wild southern Atlantic Ocean, epitomized by the rusting hulks of sunken ships lying along the Skeleton Coast. However, for many visitors the coast provides a relaxing and cool contrast to the heat and dust of the interior. Each year thousands of Namibian and South Africans descend on the cheerful seaside town of Swakopmund and the other coastal resorts for a few weeks' fishing and boating. Increasingly, foreign visitors are attracted to Swakopmund for its variety of adventure activities, as well as the opportunity to see marine wildlife like seals and pelicans, and welcome distractions like comfy guesthouses and seafood restaurants.

Further inland is the Namib Desert, which has the oldest and most evocative desert scenery in the world. Here giant sand dunes march determinedly towards the sea in a dune field 300 km wide. The ever-changing landscape supports gravel plains, rugged canyons, towering walls of volcanic rock and vast dune seas. The dunes are best appreciated in the Namib-Naukluft Park around Sossusvlei or, if you have the extra cash, from the air on a scenic flight from Swakopmund or a balloon ride from Sesriem. Witnessing the changing colours of the shifting sands at sunset or sunrise is easily one of the highlights of a trip to Namibia.

Swakopmund and around

Surrounded on three sides by the arid Namib Desert and on the west by the cold waters of the Atlantic, Swakopmund is surely one of the most unusual and fascinating colonial towns in the whole of Africa. In a period of a little more than 25 years the German Imperial Government built a succession of extravagant buildings, which today represent one of the best-preserved collections of German colonial architecture still standing. When approached from the desert, especially during the morning fog, the turrets, towers and pastel-coloured buildings on the skyline appear as a hazy mirage, and the quirky town comes as quite as surprise on the barren coastline.

Swakopmund is Namibia's premier holiday resort. With its olde-worlde charm and relaxed atmosphere, it receives a steady flow of local visitors all year round, culminating in December and January when thousands descend from the hot interior to enjoy the temperate climate of the coast. Few foreign visitors pass through Namibia without visiting this popular coastal town, and a couple of days here is recommended to shake the desert dust out of your shoes and enjoy the bracing fresh sea air. There are lots of things to do, a wide choice of hotels, guesthouses and pensions, and several good restaurants and coffee shops selling traditional German pastries. You will not have a problem finding an apple strudel or a flagon of beer in this town.

Getting there

Swakopmund is easily reached from Windhoek along the tarred B2 via Okahandja. This route is 363 km and can be covered in half a day and is well served by the regional towns of the Hinterland with plenty of shops and petrol stations along the way. **Intercape** runs a daily bus service between Windhoek to Swakopmund along the B2, and there are also several shuttle bus companies using smaller vehicles. However, if you have your own transport, there are more scenic approaches from

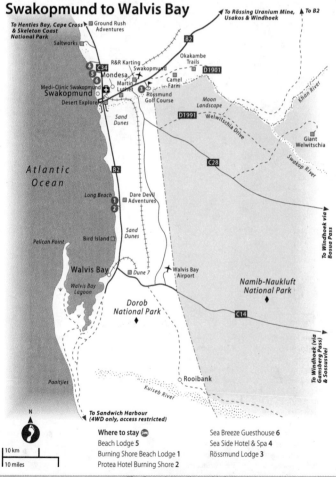

Swakopmund to Walvis Bay

To Henties Bay, Cape Cross & Skeleton Coast National Park

To Rössing Uranium Mine, Usakos & Windhoek

To B2

Ground Rush Adventures

Saltworks

C34

R&R Karting

Okakambe Trails

B2

Swakopmund

D1901

Mondesa

Camel Farm

Medi-Clinic Swakopmund

Martin Luther

Swakopmund

Rössmund Golf Course

Moon Landscape

Khan River

Desert Explorers

D1991

Welwitschia Drive

Sand Dunes

Giant Welwitschia

Atlantic Ocean

B2

C28

Swakop River

Long Beach

Dare Devil Adventures

Bird Island

Sand Dunes

To Windhoek via Bosua Pass

Pelican Point

Walvis Bay

Dune 7

Walvis Bay Airport

Namib-Naukluft National Park

Walvis Bay Lagoon

Dorob National Park

C14

To Windhoek (via Gamsberg Pass) & Sossusvlei

Paaltjies

Rooibank

Kuiseb River

N

10 km

10 miles

To Sandwich Harbour (4WD only, access restricted)

Where to stay
Beach Lodge **5**
Burning Shore Beach Lodge **1**
Protea Hotel Burning Shore **2**

Sea Breeze Guesthouse **6**
Sea Side Hotel & Spa **4**
Rössmund Lodge **3**

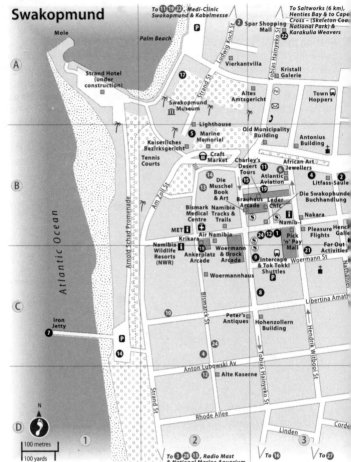

Swakopmund

Where to stay 🛌
Alte Brücke Resort **3** *D2*
Amanpuri Traveller's
  Lodge **1** *C5*
Beach Lodge **22** *A2*
Brigadoon **2** *A2*
Dunes Backpackers **7** *C2*
Deutsches Haus **8** *B4*
Eberwein **17** *B4*
Europa Hof **4** *C2*
Gruner Kranz **26** *C3*
Hansa & The Equestrian
  Room Restaurant **6** *B3*

Pension a la Mer **10** *C2*
Pension Rapmund **13** *B2*
Prinzessin Rupprecht
  Heim **12** *D2*
Sam's Giardino **23** *B5*
Schweizerhaus &
  Café Anton **14** *B2*
Sea Breeze
  Guesthouse **19** *A2*
Sea Side Hotel & Spa **11** *A2*
Secret Garden
  Guesthouse **24** *C2*
The Stiltz **28** *D2*

Swakopmund Hotel &
  Entertainment Centre &
  Platform One Restaurant
  16 *A4*
Swakopmund Municipal
  Restcamp **27** *D3*
Villa Margherita
  & Villa Tulipano **15** *B4*
Villa Wiese Backpackers
  Lodge **29** *A5*

Restaurants 🍴
3 N'amigos Mexican Bar
  & Grill **2** *C3*
22 Degrees South **5** *B2*
Bits'N' Pizzas **6** *B3*
Bojos Café **11** *B3*
Café Tref **1** *B3*
Café Treff Punkt
  & Hansa Bäckerei **12** *B3*
Cosmopolitan Restaurant
  & Lounge Bar **3**
Erich's **4** *B3*
Jetty 1905 **7** *C1*

the interior to the coast on the gravel roads. From Windhoek the C28 goes to Swakopmund through part of the Namib-Naukluft Park, and this is a very scenic 325-km drive though you will require a permit for part of it. Another route that goes through the park is the C26 and then the C14 from Windhoek to Walvis Bay, 30 km to the south of Swakopmund; this 386 km route goes over the Gamsberg and Kuiseb passes and again offers a wonderfully scenic drive. For more information on these routes, see the Hinterland section, page 280. Air Namibia has flights between Windhoek and nearby Walvis Bay, and there is also the option of taking the luxury (expensive) Desert Express train from the capital to the coast.
» See Transport, page 264.

Getting around

Swakopmund is entirely negotiable by foot, although at night it is advisable to catch a taxi back to your hotel even over short distances (see Safety, page 228). The town is dissected neatly in a grid pattern and signposts are clear. The main road that runs from east to the coast on the west and is the extension of the B2 is Sam Nujoma Avenue. To reach the outlying regions of Swakopmund, you need to be on a tour or have a car. All the operators provide pick-ups in town (eg to the Swakopmund Airport for skydiving), which are almost always included in the price.

Tourist information

The Ministry of Environment and Tourism (MET) ① corner of Bismarck St and Sam Nujoma Av, T064-404576, www.met.gov.na, Mon-Fri 0800-1700, Sat-Sun 0800-1300, is the place to get permits for the Welwitschia Drive

KFC **21** C3
Kücki's Pub **8** C3
Lighthouse Pub
  & Restaurant **17** A2
Napolitana Grill
  & Pizzeria **10** B3
Pandora's Box & Café **18** B2
Stadtmitte Café **9** C3
Swakopmund
  Brauhaus **19** B3
Tug **14** C1
Village Café **24** B3
Western Saloon **15** B2

Wimpy & Debonairs
Pizza **22** A3

Bars & clubs 🌢
Desert Tavern **16** D3
Gruniz Pub **25** C3
Tiger Reef Beach
  Bar **13** D2

(page 240) if you are driving independently and not on a tour. You also need to come here to get fishing permits if you are not booked with a fishing operator.

Namibia Wildlife Resorts (NWR) ① *Bismarck St, T064-402172, www.nwr.com.na, Mon-Fri 0900-1630*, is a helpful office where you can make bookings for any NWR accommodation, including the Skeleton Coast National Park (Torra and Terrace Bay), and the Namib-Naukluft Park. The office can provide a little local information too.

Far Out Activities ① *44 Nathaniel Maxulili St, T064-405989, farout@africaonline. com, daily 0800-1900* is a one-stop shop for booking all adventure activities in town. **Namib-i** ① *Sam Nujoma Av, T064-404827, namibi@iway.na, Mon-Fri 0830-1300, 1400-1700, Sat-Sun 0900-1300,* is centrally located and the best place for tourist information; the helpful staff can reserve accommodation, and book local tours and transport.

Best time to visit

Although the town lies in a true arid desert, the cold Benguela Current that flows from south to north along the coast acts as a moderating influence. The climate on the coast is temperate, with temperatures of 15-25°C. The sea temperature is 14-18°C, too cold for swimming for any period without a wet suit. Swakopmund receives less than 15 mm of rain per year; as you walk about town note how most buildings have no gutters or drain pipes and on the rare occasion the town gets a lot of rain it floods. The only moisture comes in the form of a sea mist that can reach up to 50 km inland (see box, page 243). Swakopmund is fairly quiet at the weekends. Except for the large supermarkets and tourist shops, other businesses close from 1300 on Saturday until Monday morning and most restaurants are closed on Sunday nights.

Safety

On the whole Swakopmund is fairly safe, though, like Windhoek, there are occasional instances of pickpocketing and theft from vehicles and it's usually tourists that are targeted. As in all urban areas it pays to be vigilant; something you may have forgotten if you've been out in the wilds for a while. Ensure that room windows are locked, make use of hotel safes and avoid carrying valuables around. At night always take a taxi or walk home in a large group. Always lock your car and do not leave valuables on show, and make use of the car guards in the street who usually wear yellow work vests and an ID badge. They'll watch your car in exchange for a N$2 tip (more at night or if you leave your car for a lengthy period of time). Try and ensure that your accommodation has secure off-street parking.

Background

"The municipality since 1909 has made every effort to create an up-to-date township. The water supply is the best in the whole Protectorate and shortage is never felt in the town. There is an Electric Power Station, Ice and Mineral Waters Factories, a first-class Hospital and Nursing Home, Public Library, German, Dutch and English Churches, High-class Schools and Hostels and a lot of Corporations and Clubs" (Swakopmund Publicity Association, 1924-1925). This is how Swakopmund (meaning 'mouth of the Swakop' in German') proudly promoted itself during the inter-war years, yet 30 years earlier no more than 30 Europeans lived in the newly established town. As a visitor, it is always worth pausing and questioning why and how the town came to be here. If ever there was a town in Africa that owed its origins to colonialism it was Swakopmund.

The first Europeans to encounter the barren Namibian coastline did not stop; the Portuguese sailors left monuments to mark the points where they had ventured ashore, but there was no attempt made to settle anywhere along this section of the Atlantic coast. But when the German protectorate was proclaimed in 1884 the British had already claimed possession of Walvis Bay, forcing the Germans to look elsewhere for a suitable coastal port. While there were other more suitable sites along the coast, the Germans selected Swakopmund as the point to develop a future harbour and settlement because, first, the immediate hinterland was not a mass of sand dunes that inhibited the inland development of transport routes, and second, a short distance up the Swakop River valley there was a fresh water supply.

In August 1892 the German gunboat, *Hyena*, landed just north of the Swakop River and two beacons were raised by the crew to mark their position. At the time this was one of many possible locations for a port along the coast that the Germans were looking for. Today history recounts that the landing in 1892 marked the origins of Swakopmund, however, it was a combination of chance and a tough spirit that saw the establishment and growth of a town at this point on the coast. The first 40 settlers were landed in 1893 by four boats, but thereafter they had to fend for themselves. They started with nothing; many of these early settlers ended up living in what have been described as 'caves' on the beaches. Today the town can be a grim place on a misty day, so imagine how it was for the first settlers at the turn of the last century. Gradually a town developed and people were able to move inland and establish trading posts and mission stations, but it was the resilience of the earliest settlers that set the pattern. After the First World War the town fell into decline as the nearby port of Walvis Bay assumed the role as the main town on the coast. Many businesses and government offices also moved. Until the 1970s Swakopmund may have been a forgotten town, but many of the citizens made their mark.

Today it is one of the most unusual and vibrant communities along the western coast of Africa; what's more, it has a special place in German history. Tourism is now an integral part of the local economy, and many people in the area depend upon the thousands of visitors each year. During the month of December the permanent population of roughly 50,000 on the coast is said to double; hotels are full, restaurants require a booking and to the frustration of local residents there are no parking places in the town centre. In recent years, Swakopmund has witnessed development on a large scale, and the modern town is experiencing a building boom that is taking many people by surprise. Already a number of resorts and holiday homes have been built at Long Beach between Swakopmund and Walvis Bay. To the north of Swakopmund the former bleak campsite at Mile 4 is long gone and the region is now part of the built-up area of the town.

Roads, railways and the desert

Much of Swakopmund's early history was a battle to establish a port that could supply the settlements inland. Like all colonial regimes of the period, the colonies were regarded as an important source of raw materials and new territories for trade. If they were to exploit the interior effectively, the Germans had to overcome the inhospitable Namib Desert, which in the age before railways and motorcars represented a tremendous natural barrier.

The first road to be constructed between the coast and the interior was known as the 'Baaiweg'. It was built by the local leader Jan Jonker in 1844. Most of the early traffic consisted of ox wagons carrying copper from Matchless Mine to Walvis Bay, but the 350-km journey proved to be uneconomic and the route was seldom used. All this changed when a harbour was built at Swakopmund, and records show that in 1896, the road was used by 880 ox wagons. But this heavy traffic quickly exposed the local weaknesses: each year more than 12,000 oxen had to be fed and watered across the Namib Desert; there were no waterholes and no suitable pastures; losses were very high. In 1897 the government was forced to turn to the railways to overcome the problems posed by the desert.

Work on the first railway started in September 1897, and like the Mole construction project the work greatly contributed to the growth of the town as workshops, supplies and storage sheds were provided. This first railway was a narrow gauge (60 cm), a great achievement for the times considering the obstacles and the remoteness of the colony. The first stage went as far as Jakalsswater, 100 km inland; by July 1900 the railway had reached Karibib, and on 19 June 1902 the first train from Swakopmund arrived in Windhoek, a journey of 382 km. This part of the state railway remained open until March 1910.

In 1903 work had begun on a second narrow-gauge railway, known as the Otavi railway line. In 1900 the Otavi Mine and Railway Company (OMEG: Otavi Minen-und Eisenbahngesell-schaft) had started to mine copper ore in Tsumeb, but because of the unreliable state service they opted to build their own railway line. Their chosen route into the interior proved to be a more sensible one than that followed by the state railway, and the

---

Places in Swakopmund → *For listings, see pages 247-266.*

For Namibian residents, Swakopmund is popular as a beach resort which provides a comfortable contrast to the hot interior. International visitors come here for the sea, the desert and the fine collection of German colonial buildings. Although most of these old buildings are closed to the public, much of their elegance lies in their exteriors and can be enjoyed while strolling around town. The buildings are listed in a sequence that could be followed on a walk starting from the Swakopmund Museum. If you choose to follow the route allow a couple of hours and there are plenty of

quality of engineering was much higher. When the full line opened on 12 November 1906 it was the longest narrow-gauge line in the world at 567 km. The running of the line was taken over by the government when the state railway was closed in 1910. The stretch between Tsumeb and Usakos was only widened in 1960.

Up until 1914 all the German efforts had been concentrated on connecting the port of Swakopmund with the rest of the country. But once the colony had been taken over by the British, the site of Walvis Bay was favoured and Swakopmund went into decline. During the First World War the troops from the Union of South Africa built a railway line between Walvis Bay and the Swakop River in just over two months, but unlike the German-built railways this was a broad-gauge track, measuring 106.7 cm. The problem proved to be crossing the Swakop River; the first railway bridge was washed away in 1917. As the German army retreated inland they destroyed the existing narrow-gauge railway, but this merely paved the way for the South African engineers to replace the tracks with a broad-gauge railway. Following the Treaty of Versailles the railway network was taken over by the South African Railways and Harbour Administration. While the network was improved and extended in the interior, the problem of crossing the Swakop River remained unaddressed. A railway bridge was built between 1925 and 1926, but in January 1931 the structure was washed away by the river in flood. It was not until 1935 that a secure bridge was built, a short distance inland from the current road bridge. If you visit Swakopmund today, you may well wonder what all the fuss was about, but during the town's early years, the river caused great damage as well as loss of life. The dry riverbed may well look innocuous today, but with sufficient rainfall inland the flood waters can drastically alter the current landscape.

As you drive along the surfaced road between Swakopmund and Walvis Bay it is worth remembering that this stretch of road was first opened in August 1959, and was only surfaced in 1970. The railway that ran between the two towns had to be re-routed in 1980 when the sand dunes finally reclaimed it. You will feel very safe driving between the two towns today, but 100 years ago the Namib was a real threat.

cafés and bars to call in on along the route. Alternatively, guided walking tours of Swakopmund are worthwhile if you are interested in the town's history and related anecdotes, though not necessary if you just want to see the colonial architecture as most of the interesting buildings are centrally located and easy to find.

Beach area

The **Swakopmund Museum** ⓘ *T064-402046, www.swakopmund-museum.de, daily 1000-1700, N$25, children (6-16) N$10,* was founded in 1951 by Dr Alfons Weber and transferred to its present site in 1960. The collection is very strong on local German

Lappiesdorp – tent city on the beach

In 1947 the municipality set aside an area, close to the present-day Municipal Restcamp, as a temporary campsite with 10 tents to cope with the large number of holidaymakers. This proved to be a great success and the following year 50 tents were erected; the site became known as 'Lappiesdorp'. In 1949 the site had swollen to 400 tents occupied by an estimated 2000 people. Each year the council was faced with the same problem of providing enough accommodation for the Christmas influx of holidaymakers. In 1952 the council built the first small bungalows (which are still in use today); by 1972 more than 200 bungalows had been built, ranging from luxury self-catering units to the most basic of shelters. The camp continues to be very popular, particularly since most hotels in Swakopmund are too expensive for the average Namibian. Just below the camp is the sandy bed of the Swakop River, where the original concrete pillars from the first railway bridge can still be seen leaning in all directions after being washed away by the great flood in 1932.

history and the geography of the Namib Desert. A small museum shop stocks a wide selection of historical leaflets (mostly in German) plus the usual choice of postcards and books on Namibia. Visitors interested in rocks and minerals will find an impressive collection to the right of the entrance. Next to the uranium mine exhibits are a series of shops and rooms recreating the days of German occupation, and this is one of the most interesting displays in the museum. There is also an impressive room dedicated to the peoples of Namibia, and a section devoted to transport and photography in and around Swakopmund during the German occupation. Note the diving helmets that were used during the construction of the jetty, each weighing 15 kg. The museum also houses the largest collection of birds' eggs in the country. Overall this is a worthwhile museum and, given that there are not that many museums worth visiting in Namibia, an hour spent here should be of interest to most visitors young and old.

In front of the museum is the **old harbour** with the Mole jutting out to the left. Swakopmund was never the ideal place for a harbour or port, as there was no natural bay or sheltered spot, so, in 1898 the government decided that a mole (sea wall) should be built in order to create an artificial harbour basin. The whole project acted as a great stimulus for the fledgling settlement. Such a giant engineering project required a lot of preparation and additional facilities; these took more than 10 months to put in place and included a piped water supply for making cement, a small railway line, the opening of a quarry and the provision of housing for the labour force. The foundation stone was laid on 2 September 1899, and the Mole officially opened on 12 February 1903. It had proved to be a far greater job than imagined; the 375-m construction had cost 2.5 million marks. Along the Mole were three steam-powered cranes that could transfer the freight from ships to barges. Unfortunately the planners were totally ignorant of the ocean currents and within two years of completion large amounts of silt started to build up on the south side of the Mole. By July 1904 the tugs could only enter the artificial basin at high tide. By 1906 the whole basin had silted up and in the process created **Palm Beach** that is so enjoyed by today's tourist. After the Herero War the government looked for an alternative solution and plans were drawn up for the construction of a jetty. A wooden jetty was quickly built, which in turn was replaced by the iron jetty which can still be seen today. These days the Mole is used as a launch point for pleasure boats and the original harbour basin is a pleasant sheltered swimming area, though while the ocean is calm, the water is very, very cold. If you are lucky you may see a dolphin or two swimming around in the bay as you walk out to the end of the Mole.

Tucked away in the gardens behind the museum is the port **lighthouse**. The first version, built in 1903, stood at only 11 m; in 1910 a further 10 m was added. The lighthouse marked the harbour as well as warning ships off the treacherous Skeleton Coast – the light can be seen more than 30 km out to sea. The old administration buildings and the gardens at the base are today home to the **22 Degrees South**, (see Restaurants, page 253), which is a fine place for lunch or coffee and so named as Swakopmund lies on the 22nd parallel south of the equator. Next to the lighthouse is the **Kaiserliches Bezirksgericht**, which serves as the presidential holiday home. The presence of heavily armed soldiers will alert you to his presence and it is advisable to keep well clear during such visits. The building was originally the first magistrates court in Swakopmund.

Close to the lighthouse is the **Marine Memorial**, a monument to members of the First Marine Expedition Corps who died during the Herero War, 1904-1905. The statue was designed and cast in Berlin, and presented to the town by the crew of the German gunboat, *Panther*, in July 1908. The figure represents a marine standing by his wounded colleague, ready for action.

As you walk north from the lighthouse, Strand Street turns into Ludwig Koch Street, where there are a couple of contrasting colonial buildings along the seafront. At No 5 is **Vierkantvilla**, the last house assembled by the 'Hafenbauamt' for the construction of the harbour mole. The interesting thing about this building is that it was prefabricated by Fa Zadek in Germany for the Kaiser government. It was shipped out to Africa and erected on a stone foundation in 1899. Further along the street is a solid double-storey building built in 1901 for the **Eastern and South Africa Telegraph** company. **Kabelmesse** was the principal office for the employees who installed the undersea cable from Europe to Cape Town. It is now the offices of the Ministry of Education.

Alte Gefängnis

Away from the centre of the town, in Garoeb Street, is the Alte Gefängnis (Old Prison). When the prison was completed in 1909 it stood right out of the town. The building has such a fine façade that it has frequently been mistaken for a hotel or private mansion. There is a tale that recounts the first visit of an official in the South West-Africa administration who on seeing the solitary building for the first time exclaimed: "I wouldn't mind staying there." Local dignitaries politely replied, "That, your honour, is the prison." The building is still used as a prison today so be very discreet if taking a photograph.

Theo-Ben Gurirab Avenue (formerly Bahnhof Street)

Close to the police station on the corner of Theo-Ben Gurirab Avenue and Tobias Hainyeko Street is a lemon yellow building in a well-kept garden full of succulents and palm trees. This is the **Altes Amtsgericht**, built in 1906 as a school but then used as the magistrates office after the state had to complete the building when the private source of funds ran out. After falling into disrepair the building was restored in 1976. It's now used by the municipal council and during office hours you may be able to get a glimpse of the interior. The building was designed by Otto Ertl who was also responsible for designing the prison and the Lutheran church; notice the similarities of features, such as the gables and turrets, of these buildings.

A short walk along Theo-Ben Guriab Avenue will bring you to the **Swakopmund Hotel and Entertainment Centre**, one of the most comfortable hotels in town (see Where to stay, page 247). Until the early 1990s this was the **railway station**, and passengers from Windhoek would alight here into this fine colonial building. While all the building work has destroyed any trace of the railway line, there are plenty of old photographs on display in the hotel restaurant and reception area which capture the scene perfectly. Before the conversion took place there was only one structure here, which is now the hotel reception and evening bar. The original platform is the terrace which overlooks the swimming pool. The building was designed by the architect C Schmidt, and constructed in 1901, while the central tower was added at a later date by W Sander. In 1910 the main railway line was closed, but the station continued to act as a terminus for the narrow-gauge railway, of the **Otavi Railway Company**. After the First World War the broad-gauge railway was once again opened and continued to terminate here until a new station was built a short distance inland on the other side of Garoeb Street.

Daniel Tjongarero Avenue (formerly Post Street)

Daniel Tjongarero Avenue is a pleasant wide road with some palm trees on the centre island, and a variety of old buildings to admire along its length.

The **Old Municipality Building** dates from 1907 when it started life as a post office, telephone exchange and living quarters for the personnel. Perhaps the fact that this and many other buildings are still standing is due to the high standard of craftsmanship and attention to detail that was typical of the period. The architect, Redecker, included the following clause in the contract with the builders: "the building must be built as stipulated in the contract and associated plans; all wood must be seasoned and dry; qualified artisans must be engaged for each task; the roof nails must be 4 cm apart and countersunk." The Swakopmund Council has recently moved to a new office block on Rakotoka Street, so the future of the building is unclear, but as it's a listed building new owners must restore and maintain it.

A short distance along Daniel Tjongarero Avenue is the **Antonius Building**. Over the years there have been many additions to this building, but between March 1908 and 1987 it was Swakopmund's only hospital. In the early days it was staffed by sisters of the Franciscan order; later on it was run by the Roman Catholic church.

It may not be the most interesting sight but the **Litfass-Saule** on the corner of Daniel Tjongarero Avenue and Nathanael Maxilili Street has an unusual background.

This rather tatty looking pillar is an original advertising post dating from the days before radio and television. There were similar posts all over the town to which people used to stick their promotional posters. This is the only post still standing. Litfass was a printer in Berlin who first thought of the pillars in 1855.

The neo-baroque **German Evangelical Lutheran Church** was designed by the government builder, Otto Ertl, in 1909, and built by FH Schmidt. The parsonage was completed in 1911 and, as with several other important buildings and homes of the wealthy, the church roof was covered with copper. On 7 January 1912 the inaugural dedication service was held in this grand building. At the time the white population of Swakopmund was about 1400. Today it holds regular services and organ recitals.

Across the road from the Lutheran Church is the **Old German School** building. Still in use as a private school, its new extension to the right has none of the baroque style of the original building which was opened in 1913 and was designed to fit in with the church.

Central Swakopmund

Villa Wille, Otavi Street, now enjoying a renaissance as a Victorian period-piece hotel (see **Hotel Eberwein**, Where to stay, page 248), is a fine example of a comfortable private residence of the colonial period. This was built in 1910 and was the home of Hermann Wille who was responsible for building some of the most elegant buildings in Swakopmund. By contrast to the more 'rustic' colonial style of the earlier buildings of Swakopmund, he integrated design elements of the neo-baroque and art deco styles. Originally he designed his own home as a bungalow but then decided to add a second floor and today it is one of the most noteworthy buildings in Swakopmund with a fine balcony and a turret (a popular feature of the time) with a copper roof. Unfortunately, Wille only enjoyed a short life in Swakopmund; he was killed in action in 1915.

If you walk along Sam Nujoma Avenue for a couple of blocks you will reach the **Otavi-Bahn Building** and **Living Desert Snake Park** ① *59 Sam Nujoma Av, T064-405100, Mon-Fri 0900-1700, Sat 0900-1300, N$30, snake feeding Sat at 1000*. The Otavi-Bahn Building was built as a station in 1906 by OMEG (the Otavi Mining and Railway Company), which ran a railway from here to the copper mines in Tsumeb. OMEG Haus, which was the goods shed, now serves as the reception for the snake park in the garden. This is home to over 25 species of Namibian snakes including black mamba, boom-slang and four types of cobra, as well as small lizards, chameleons and scorpions. It doesn't take long to walk around and children especially will be curious about these creatures. You can also get wrapped up in a non-venomous snake for a photo.

Around the corner in Windhoek Street is the excellent **Sam Cohen Library** ① *T064-402695, Mon-Fri 0900-1300, 1500-1700, Sat 1000-1300, free*, which will fascinate anyone with an interest in Namibian history. Here you will find most of the material that has ever been published on Swakopmund. Of particular interest is the collection of historical photographs and old newspapers. Those able to read German will find plenty of reading material here.

One of the finest colonial buildings in Swakopmund is the **Hohenzollern Building**, on the corner of Libertina Amathila Avenue and Tobias Hainyeko Street. The most obvious feature, on the roof above the front door, is the statue of a kneeling Atlas holding up a globe of the world. In 1988 the original cement figure had to be replaced with the present plaster-of-paris version. The building dates from 1909 when it started life as a hotel but in 1912 it was taken over by the municipality after the hotel licence had been revoked by the local magistrate. The hotel had become a well-known gambling den. When the municipality moved out, the building was converted into private flats.

The **Alte Kaserne (Old Schützenhaus)** was built in 1906 as a fort for the Second Railway Company who were involved with the construction of a wooden jetty. The style of the fort was considerably different from other forts of the period, notably Fort Namutoni. The front of the building measured 55 m with a tower in the centre facing out to sea, the other sides measured 45.5 m. A turret was built at each corner; the turret loopholes were included more for decoration than practical purposes. Crests of the then German federal states and a plaque commemorating those killed in action during German-Herero wars adorn the walls of the entrance hall. It was used as a school from 1927 to 1975 and today is owned by the Ministry of Education.

On the opposite corner of Bismarck and Anton Lubowski Avenue is another original colonial building, the **Prinzessin Rupprecht Heim** a fine single-storey building dating from 1902. It was first used as a military hospital, but in 1914 it was taken over by the Bavarian Women's Red Cross who renamed the building after their patron, Princess Rupprecht, the wife of the crown prince of Bavaria. For many years the building served as a peaceful nursing home until it was converted, and some out-buildings added, into a small hotel (see Where to stay, page 249).

Bismarck Street

Heading back along Bismarck Street, the **Woermannhaus** ① *Mon-Fri 1000-1200, 1500-1700, Sat 1000-1200*, is easily recognized as the building on the high ground with a decorated tower. Visitors can climb the tower and visit the **Swakopmund Arts Association** on the first floor, which has exhibits of traditional Namibian art alongside some contemporary European art and the local library. The Woermannhaus dates from 1905 and was designed by Friedrich Höft as an office for the **Damara and Namaqua Trading Company**. In 1909 the building was bought by another trading company, **Woermann, Brock & Co**. In the early days the Damara Tower was used as a lookout position to see when ships arrived at sea, and when ox wagons arrived from the desert. Between 1924 and 1972 the building served as a school hostel. When it was closed in 1972 it was in such a poor state of repair that the municipality planned to demolish the building. Fortunately a successful campaign saved the building; restoration was completed in 1975 and the public library moved into part of the building.

At the lower end of Libertina Amathila Avenue you can view the town from a different angle by walking to the end of the jetty. In 1910 the German government decided that it was time to build a permanent **iron jetty**. A contract was entered with the bridge builders, Flender, Grund and Bilfinger to complete the jetty in 3½ years at a cost of 3½ million marks. Before work on the jetty could start, workshops and storage rooms had to be built on the shore; these were only finished in November

1911. The original plans were to build a bridge reaching 640 m out to sea, carrying two parallel railway lines of 490 m. These lines would carry a loading platform with two cranes; a third crane was planned for the shipping of marble from the Karibib Region. Each of the iron posts supporting the jetty were filled with cement. Progress was slower than planned and by September 1912 only 100 m had been completed.

At this stage the contractors ran into the first problems with shifting sandbanks. When work stopped at the outbreak of the First World War a third of the jetty had been completed for a cost of 2½ million marks. In 1919 one side of the jetty was covered with planks so that it could be used by visitors and fishermen. In 1931 and 1934 the Swakop River flowed for more than four months after exceptionally good rains in the interior. In 1934 parts of the town were destroyed by the floodwaters and silt from the Swakop River pushed the sea 3 km back from the present coastline. The jetty stood high and dry with a set of steps added at the end to help people get to the ocean. Slowly the sea washed away the silt and the present coastline was restored.

A rather delightful story surrounding the jetty is about what happened to the first women settlers who arrived from Germany in the early days. The men had already been on the coast for a number of years, when German women aged between 18 and 20 (an age that was considered past the prime for marriage at home), were shipped out to the new colony as nurses. The young male settlers would line the jetty in wait for the boat carrying the women and when they landed on shore, the women were grabbed and whisked away immediately, some marrying within a few days. Many Swakop residents tell how their ancestors were married to complete strangers in this way. The story also goes that those women who did not quite live up to the young men's expectations of a wife, ended up in the town's first brothel.

The jetty was declared unsafe in the mid-1980s and it briefly closed as 17 pillars of the first section were encased in concrete. It was then closed to the public in 1998 because it was again no longer deemed safe to walk on. But a 'Save the Jetty Fund' was established to raise funds for renovation, and it finally reopened in 2010. The 'new' 300-m jetty has been built with the southern side dedicated for walking and the northern side for angling (entrance is free and there are toilets). Well worth the bracing walk is **Jetty 1905**, at the end; a fine seafood restaurant and oyster bar which has an upper deck offering uninterrupted views over the Atlantic Ocean (see Restaurants, page 252). If you have been following the recommended walk the jetty marks the end of the tour, and **The Tug** by the jetty is also another pleasant place for a good fish meal (see Restaurants, page 252). To get back to the **Swakopmund Museum** you can head north along the Arnold Schad Promenade.

Alternatively head south for 500 m to the **National Marine Aquarium** ① *Strand St, T064-410 1000, Tue-Sun 1000-1600, feeding by divers in the main tank is on Wed, Sat and Sun at 1500, N$10 per person.* Opened in 1995, this is Namibia's only aquarium and is owned and run by the Namibian Ministry of Fisheries and Marine Resources. It recently reopened after undergoing major refurbishment. Although small (you'll need no more than 45 minutes to walk around), it is well worth a visit and is especially recommended for children. Sea water, drawn from the jetty, is pumped through a series of filter systems before reaching the exhibition tanks. They feature

Martin Luther – the steam ox

Just out of town, in a brand new brick and glass shed, beside a clump of palm trees on the Windhoek road, stands one of Swakopmund's most famous historical monuments, an old steam engine known as 'Martin Luther'. In 1896 a First Lieutenant Edmund Troost of the Imperial Schutztruppe on a trip back to Germany came across a mobile steam engine at the engineering works in Halberstadt. Aware of the heavy losses suffered by the ox wagons he saw this new machine as the answer to Swakopmund's problems. He was so sure of the idea that he paid for the steam engine out of his own pocket and arranged for its transportation from Hamburg to Swakopmund. But when the ship arrived in Swakopmund the offloading equipment could not cope with the 280 cwt iron machine, so the boat proceeded to Walvis Bay

where the engine was successfully landed. Troost was forced to leave the machine at the harbour for four months because of his military obligations elsewhere. When he finally returned to Walvis Bay he found that the engineer he had retained to drive the steam engine had left and returned home when his initial five-month contract had expired.

The first attempt to drive the steam engine to Swakopmund was undertaken by an American who, it quickly became apparent, knew little about such machines. The going was very tough, the machine continually got stuck in the sand, and by the time a Boer had completed the journey for Troost a further three months had elapsed. The whole venture was never that successful – apart from the problems of weight, the machine consumed vast amounts of water and

the aquatic life found in the coastal waters of Namibia that are specific to the cold Benguela Current (see box, page 243). Species include swordfish, yellowfin tuna, West Coast steenbras, mako and ragged-tooth shark, octopus, green and hawksbill turtle, hermit crab, and little creatures like the horseshoe sea cucumber and the delightfully named crumb-of-bread sponge. Diners may also be interested to see what their rock lobsters, anchovies, pilchards and mackerels look like in the water. The highlights are the 320,000 litre tank, 12 m long and 8 m wide with a glass tunnel beneath it that you can walk through, and the 'petting' tidal pool which gives visitors a chance to touch and even feed certain species of marine creatures such as sting rays. Another feature is the digital rock pool on the floor close to the entrance; if you step into it, a ripple effect is created and the digital fish swim away.

Around Swakopmund → *For listings, see pages 247-266.*

Swakopmund Saltworks → *Colour map 1, C3.*
Located 6 km to the north of town off the C34 towards Henties Bay, the saltworks should be on the itinerary of any keen birder. Follow the dirt track around the salt

there was no-one able to carry out regular maintenance and repairs. In all, about 13 tonnes of freight were transported inland; two trips were made to Heigamchab and several journeys to Nonidas, the first source of water inland. In 1897 the engine broke down where it stands today and Troost was forced to give up his venture. Fortunately by now the government in Germany had released funds for the construction of a railway.

One of the most frequent stories you will come across in Swakopmund is how the steam engine got its name. The tale goes that shortly after it had ground to a halt a Dr Max Rhode said during a meeting at the Bismarck Hotel: "Did you know that the steam ox is called 'Martin Luther' now because it can also say – 'Here I stand; I cannot do otherwise'?" The original statement was made by the German reformer, Martin Luther, in 1521 in front of the German parliament in Worms.

In 2005, the steam engine got its new home in a glass and brick shed to protect it from the elements and vandalism. It was completely renovated by students of the Namibia Institute of Mining and Technology as a class project. The students – young black Namibians, not older white people with a penchant for German history – spent a lot of time researching and got original sketches of steam engines from all over the world. They discovered, somewhere in Russia, the only other engine type similar to the *Martin Luther* in the world today. They matched the steel and repaired the rust and followed the original design to the letter. Visitors can stop at any time to peer through the glass to look at the engine.

lakes; on the coastal side is the **Seabird Guano House**, and drivers in a saloon car will have to stop by the fence. The terrain is a mix of ponds and canals surrounded by a gravel plain; off the sandy beach is a guano platform. It is advisable to arrive here in the early morning before human activity at the works and on the beach disturbs the birds. In addition to the resident population of waders, many migrants can be seen between September and April. Species recorded at the saltworks include: (resident) avocets, chestnut-banded plovers, oyster catchers, Cape teals, Cape shovellers, grey heron and black-winged stilts, pelicans and cormorants, the latter two breed on the guano platform; (migrants) whimbrel, turnstones, little stint, knot, ringed plover, sanderling and bar-tailed godwit. Salt no longer naturally occurs in the area, but water is pumped from the ocean into the shallow pans and during the following 15 months evaporation results in the formation of salt crystals which are then collected.

Other birdwatching sites include the **Swakop Estuary**, accessed from the bridge that crosses the river just south of town on the B2. It easily be visited by foot from the centre of town. Here there is a mix of reed beds and sandy beach; find a sheltered spot and you should be rewarded with a variety of waders and land birds.

Welwitschia Drive
ⓘ *Permits must be purchased in advance from the Ministry of Environment and Tourism (MET) office on Bismarck St (page 227), N$80, children (under 16) free, valid for 24 hrs. With the permit you get a map and information sheet that corresponds with the markers next to the road.*

A popular self-drive excursion is to follow the Welwitschia Drive in the Namib section of the Namib-Naukluft Park. The full round-trip from Swakopmund is about 135 km and can be covered in four or five hours. However, if you take a picnic this can be turned into a pleasant, leisurely day trip. It is well signposted and drivers must keep to existing roads at all times; the desert is well patrolled by MET staff and you will be fined if you don't have a permit. Follow the B2 out of town for the airport and Windhoek, take a right turn on to the C28 just beyond the Martin Luther steam engine signposted for Windhoek via the Bosua Pass. Continue along this road, crossing the Swakop River, until you reach the entrance to the Namib-Naukluft Park. After a short distance you will see the signpost at the start of the trail. Turn left here and you will come across the first of the 13 numbered stone beacons that indicate places of particular interest. These include viewpoints over the Swakop River Valley, spectacular rock formations and moonscapes, as well as areas of lichens, lithops, hoodias and other desert-adapted plants that survive on the fog that rolls in from the Atlantic. Number 10 is a picnic site where you can relax under the shade of a clutch of camelthorn trees, while at Number 11 you will find the 1500-year-old giant welwitschias. The return route backtracks to Number 8 and rejoins the C28 back to town. This an enjoyable trip and if you don't want to drive, you can join a guided tour. ▸ *See Tour operators, page 262.*

Rössing Uranium Mine
ⓘ *68 km from Swakopmund on the B2 near Arandis, T064-402046, www.rossing.com, every 1st Fri of the month, 1000-1330, except during mine holidays, N$50, bookings must be made in advance at the Swakopmund Museum where the tours depart, see page 231.*

Uranium was discovered in the Namib Desert in 1928, and Rössing Uranium Mine started operations in 1976. It is now one of the largest open-pit uranium mines in the world and Namibia produces some 8% of the global output of uranium. Once a month, a tour to the mine departs from the Swakopmund Museum. While this is undoubtedly a fascinating glimpse into a major mining operation and one that provides much-needed employment in this part of the country, like everything associated with the nuclear industry there is a sense of 'look how good and safe we are'. Even if this is the case, the giant scar on the landscape could never be passed off as environmentally sound but it is impressive to look at.

Mondesa
ⓘ *Hata Angu Cultural Tours, T064-461118, www.hata-angu.com, or Mondesa Township Tours, T0812-734361, or book through the Namib-i office (page 228); tours 2- to 3-hr tours start from N$400 and depart mid-morning or mid-afternoon.*

Just outside central Swakopmund to the northeast, Mondesa is the town's former black township that was created in the 1950s during the Apartheid era. It is the more

African part of town that has been home to many generations of black families for decades and is currently home to some 17,000. You will be picked up from hotels by minibus taxi and this well-organized and enjoyable excursion is recommended for tourists wishing to see all aspects of Namibia through the eyes of the different ethnic groups. Tours visit Mondesa's thriving market and areas where the Damara and Herero live, and a *shebeen* (pub) where you will be invited to sample a local meal such as *mahangu* porridge, wild spinach and barbecued chicken, and learn a few words of the local languages, such as Nama with its distinctive 'clicks'. You may also visit the new low-cost housing developments on the edge of Swakopmund known as the Democratic Resettlement Community and nicknamed the DRC. Some of the fees go towards community projects

---

Walvis Bay → *For listings, see pages 247-266. Colour map 1, C3. Phone code: 064.*

Had it not been for two colonial powers seeking to gain a foothold on this remote coastline, it is unlikely that both Swakopmund and Walvis Bay would have thrived. Nevertheless, today, Walvis (as it is affectionately known) represents a pleasant alternative if the Disney-esque charms of Swakopmund leave you cold, particularly if you enjoy birdwatching or just want a convenient base from which to explore the Namib-Naukluft Park. However, the town is not as pretty as Swakopmund and there is less choice of accommodation and fewer eating options. In truth, much of the town is a grid of characterless modern buildings, although it is currently enjoying a renaissance after the quiet years following its return to Namibia. The highlight is the Walvis Bay Lagoon, which is home to hundreds of thousands of birds throughout the year, most notably flamingos. It has been declared a Ramsar site for its importance as a wetlands area and a feeding ground for many of species of bird on migratory routes from Africa to the Arctic Circle.

Arriving in Walvis Bay
Getting there The town is well serviced by public transport. Walvis Bay Airport has regular flights from Windhoek, and the train and Intercape bus services that pass through Swakopmund terminate in Walvis Bay. The 34-km (40-minute) drive down the coast from Swakopmund snakes between the rolling sand dunes inland to the east and the Atlantic Ocean to the west. Occasionally, after strong winds, JCBs are employed to push the sand back off the road. On your way, you will pass the holiday resorts of Long Beach or Langstrand (in Afrikaans) and Dolphin Beach. Opposite the beach are the dunes where adrenaline seekers can try out quad biking or parasailing. Finally, the two townships of Narraville and Kuisebmond appear on either side of the road just before a roundabout that signals the start of Walvis Bay proper. ► *See Transport, page 265.*

Getting around The town is laid out in a large grid pattern, and apart from the few shops in the centre that you can walk around, you really need a car, especially to reach the Waterfront at the western end, from where boats depart to explore the lagoon. If you don't have your own wheels, there are plenty of taxis in Walvis Bay.

Tourist information The **Walvis Bay Tourism Centre** is privately run by **Levo Dolphin Tours** ① *corner of Union St and 5th Rd, located where the road curves at the entrance to the Golf Club on the way to the lagoon and jetty for boat cruises, T064-200606, www.levotours.com, Mon-Fri 0800-1700, Sat-Sun 0900-1300.* Levo Dolphin Tours is an operator for the popular dolphin and seal cruises (see page 263) but this is also a one-stop shop for local information, and the friendly staff can book all activities around Walvis Bay. Also here is the **Lemon Tree Café** (see Restaurants, see page 255), a curio shop, the office for **Hertz** car hire (see page 265), and **Photo Ventures** for trips to Sandwich Harbour (see page 264). It also operates three comfortable self-catering chalets (**$**) behind the complex, sleeping up to four.

Background

The first known European to visit Walvis Bay was Bartholomeu Diaz who entered the bay on 8 December 1487 in his flagship, the *São Christovão*, while searching for the tip of Africa and a possible sea route to Asia. He named the sheltered lagoon the Golfo de Santa Maria de Conceição. The bay was one of the finest natural harbours

Walvis Bay

Where to stay 🛏
Free Air Guest House 1
Lagoon Lodge 11
Langholm 5
Loubser's B&B 2
Oyster Bay Guesthouse 4
Protea Hotel Pelican Bay 7

Protea Hotel Walvis Bay 9

Restaurants 🍴
Anchors @ the Jetty 6
Crazy Mama's 2
KFC 9
Lemon Tree Café 3

Lothar's Steak House 7
Lyon de Sables
  & Cuppa Musselcracker 10
Raft 5
Vlooi's Nest Coffee Shop 8
Willi Probst Bakery 1

The amazing Benguela Current

The Benguela Current flows from Antarctica to the southernmost tip of Africa where the Atlantic steers it up the western coast as far as Mossamedes in Angola. As the current flows so close to the coast, sea temperatures are colder by the land than further out to sea. On most days a dense belt of sea fog hangs over the ocean on the Namibian coast that is generated by the cool air of the Benguela Current meeting the warmer air inland. During the night when the desert surface cools, the humid sea air of the day is transformed into visible clouds of mist because of condensation and each morning the coast wakes up in a fog. On most days the fog penetrates inland for about 50 km, some days reaching 100 km. As the sun rises and the land surface warms up, heat is radiated into the fog and it gradually disperses into a hazy belt along the coast. As the day progresses, the sea breezes blow away any remaining moisture over the desert. It is because of this mist that the coastal strip of the Namib Desert has a unique living environment. There is sufficient moisture to support more than 50 different lichen species and many other larger plants. These plants in turn provide food and water for hardy animals such as the gemsbok and springbok that live in the desert. Without the fog the desert would be almost completely devoid of life. The Benguela Current also plays an important role in Namibia's economy by providing ideal conditions for fish to breed in. The current is rich in nitrogen which supports an excess of plankton, the favourite diet of whales and pelagic fish such as pilchards and anchovies, which live in giant shoals. The fishing sector provides about 22% of all exports and remains a large source of employment.

along a barren coast, having been formed by the floodwaters of the Kuiseb River, before the natural silt load blocked the delta.

The modern town of Walvis Bay is located on the edge of this deep-water bay and tidal lagoon. An 18-km-long sandspit forms a natural breakwater against the Atlantic Ocean, and the tip of the spit is marked by an automatic lighthouse, Pelican Point, which doubles as a small seal colony. The spit joins the mainland to the south of Walvis Bay forming a shallow lagoon famous for its superb variety of birdlife, an important wetland providing many species with feeding and breeding grounds. In all, a total of 45,000 ha are now protected as a nature reserve.

Back in 1487 it was not the birdlife that was of interest to the Portuguese sailors, it was the shelter from the ocean, but when they landed they found no surface fresh water. Accordingly Diaz named the area the Sands of Hell. For the sailors this was not the wealthy country they were seeking to trade with and so they quickly pushed on further towards the cape.

The name Walvis Bay, or bay of whales, originates from the 16th-century Portuguese maps which showed the bay as Bahia das Bahleas, due to the large numbers of migratory whales passing this way. In 1487 Diaz and his crew had taken note of the abundance of fish in the coastal waters and when the first chart of the area was drawn up he had called the area around the bay Praia dos Sardinha, the 'coast of sardines'. During the 17th century, British and American ships frequented the area in search of whale meat and seals, from time to time using the natural harbours at Walvis Bay and Sandwich Harbour, but no attempts were made to explore the interior. Eventually the Dutch in Cape Town decided to investigate the hinterland, prompted by the rumours of great cattle and copper wealth. On 26 February 1793 Captain F Duminy, in the ship *Meermin*, landed and annexed the Bahia das Bahleas, renaming it Walvis Bay. But the land remained in Dutch hands for only a few years; in 1795 the British occupied the cape and Captain Alexander travelled up the coast to Walvis Bay, where he hoisted the British flag.

The growth of the settlement was very slow; a few traders made the epic journey from Cape Town and some missionaries passed through for the Rhenish Missionary Society. Up until the time that the Germans started to develop Swakopmund, the small community at Walvis Bay prospered on the cattle trade, and copper from the Matchless Mine in the Khomas Hochland close to Windhoek. The coast at this time was linked with the interior by a road known as the Baaiweg, built by Jan Jonker in 1844. Most of the early traffic consisted of ox wagons.

During the 1870s, unrest in the interior led to the British government in the cape being asked to intervene to protect missionaries and traders. However, the British concluded that the lands were too poor and not worth adding to the territory of the British Empire. Instead they decided to consolidate their position at Walvis Bay: by controlling the movement of goods and people to the interior they hoped to be able to influence or even control the events inland. On 12 March 1878 Commander RC Dyer formally annexed the area, the boundaries being described as follows: "on the south by a line from a point on the coast 15 miles south of Pelican Point to Scheppmansdorf; on the east by a line from Scheppmansdorf to the Rooibank, including the Plateau, and thence to 10 miles inland from the mouth of the Swakop River; on the north by the last 10 miles of the course of the said Swakop River". Rooibank had been included since it was the closest place with fresh water and greenery. The rest of the 750-sq-km enclave was desert.

For the next 50 years the fortunes of Walvis Bay were influenced by the development of the German colony of South-West Africa; as Swakopmund grew and prospered so the amount of traffic using Walvis Bay declined. The outbreak of the First World War was to change everything for good. Once the South African troops had built the broad-gauge railway the port was quick to develop, and in 1927 a newly dredged harbour was opened by the Earl of Athlone, governor-general of South Africa. At the same time a new source of fresh water was discovered in the bed of the Kuiseb River, which helped guarantee the future of the town.

At the end of the First World War, Walvis Bay was given to South Africa to govern as part of the mandated territory of South-West Africa. This remained the case until 1977 when South Africa declared Walvis Bay to be part of the Cape Province. Despite pressure from the United Nations, South Africa refused to give up the small enclave as it served both as an important commercial port and as location of a South African military base. In 1992 South Africa relented and agreed to a joint administration without any border controls; on 28 February 1994 South Africa returned Walvis Bay to Namibia.

The port is a great asset for Namibia and competes with ports such as Durban in South Africa and Maputo in Mozambique for trade. In 1996, two years after the town rejoined Namibia, the private **Walvis Bay Export Processing Zone Management Company**, was established to attract more businesses to Walvis Bay and to take advantage of the port and its improved access to the hinterland. Both the Trans-Kalahari and Trans-Caprivi highways were completed in 1998, thus reducing the transport time of commodities to and from Zambia, Zimbabwe, Botswana and South Africa by up to 14 days. Today the port also accommodates oil rigs from Angola for servicing. The town has benefited much from the improved economic climate and today has a population of around 90,000.

Places in Walvis Bay

Despite its long history the town has surprisingly few old buildings. For most visitors the attractions here are in the sea, not on the land. The earliest building in Walvis Bay is the **Rhenish Mission Church ① *5th Rd***, a small structure surrounded by modern private homes. It was made in Hamburg as a prefabricated kit in 1879 and in 1880 the wooden building was erected on the waterfront. As the harbour grew in importance it was decided to move the church to its present site. Once reassembled, the wooden walls were plastered to help prevent wood rot.

About 7 km north of Walvis Bay on the way to Swakopmund look out for a large wooden platform in the sea. This is known as **Bird Island** and was built during the 1930s depression by Adolf Winter, a carpenter from Swakopmund on a rock that is only exposed at low tide to provide a nesting site for seabirds from which guano could be collected. Mr Winter actually noticed the rock as he was travelling between Swakopmund and Walvis Bay on the train, and on the return trip he noticed the guano had been washed away by the sea. Still in use today, the platform can yield close to 650 tonnes in a single year. Although about 90% of the birds are cormorants, there are always plenty of seabirds to watch in the vicinity including about 15-20 breeding pairs of great white pelicans. Beyond the platform you may occasionally see one of the drilling platforms which are being used to look for off-shore oil and gas fields, and you will certainly see the ships lining up out to sea waiting to get into Walvis Bay port.

The **Walvis Bay Lagoon** to the southwest of town is regarded as one of the most important wetlands for birds along the southern African coast and since 1995 it has been a proclaimed Ramsar site (an important wetland area for birds). This site covers the shallow lagoon, the beach and the inter-tidal areas of Pelican Point and the saltworks. The lagoon is tidal – low tide is best for birdwatching. The region is a feeding site for around 80% of all the lesser flamingos found in southern Africa and about 50% of greater flamingos. It also attracts large numbers of chestnut plovers, pelicans, damara, Caspian and swift terns, white-fronted plovers and Hartlaub's gulls. There are an estimated 170,000 resident birds around the lagoon, with some 200,000 more stopping off on migratory routes. The lagoon can also be explored by boat or kayak; most of the tour operators can organize trips around the lagoon, to

Bird Island and to Pelican Point which forms the most westerly lip of the lagoon, and it is also a popular spot for windsurfing. ⟫ *See What to do, page 263.*

The town's newest attract is the **Walvis Bay Waterfront** development that lies around the Walvis Bay Yacht Club and the jetty where the boat cruises depart from. It was partly developed for the benefit of cruise liner passengers; it's one of the few places along the southwest African coast with a deep-water habour where cruise ships can dock. To get to the waterfront from town, drive along Union Street until it passes the **Walvis Bay Tourism Centre** (see page 242) and becomes 5th Road. Continue and turn left into Atlantic Street to avoid the harbour gates and proceed to Walvis Bay Yacht Club. It's a lovely paved area with a clutch of gift shops, restaurants, booking offices for the water-based activities, and it's a fine place for a bracing stroll to enjoy the ocean and the view of the moored boats bobbing about – you may well be joined by the odd waddling pelican. It also very conveniently faces west; perfect for sunsets and if you're lucky you might get flamingoes wading in the shallows as you take a photograph.

Other minor attractions include **Dune 7**, 10 km from town, on the C14, the highest dune in the area. A small picnic site has been set up amongst some palm trees. The best time of the day to visit the dune is close to sunset, when the views are spectacular but the sand is not so hot for walking on.

Sandwich Harbour → *Colour map 3, A1.*

Sandwich Harbour is 52 km south of Walvis Bay and is now part of the newly established Dorob National Park (see page 268). The Dorob extends along the coast from the Ugab River in the north to the southern end of the Sandwich Harbour floodplains. The name may well be derived from an English whaling ship, *The Sandwich*, which operated in this region in the mid-1780s. Today it's an area of wilderness and part of the Namib-Naukluft Park. It was never actually a harbour; the area was surveyed in the 1880s by the Royal Navy but it was considered inferior to Walvis Bay and no development took place. Occasional sealing vessels used it as an anchorage, possibly to avoid the authorities at Walvis Bay, and there were some temporary settlements used by seasonal fishermen catching snoek. The lagoon here was once an open bay that became silted up over the years by sand. Do not attempt this road without a 4WD as much of it goes through soft sand; the last bit can only be tackled on foot and permits are required from the Ministry of Environment and Tourism (MET). Most people visit with the tour operators which offer fun guided half- or full-day trips that start from around N$1000 (see What to do, page 264).

The drive down is long and tough and the journey is as dramatic as the landscape, and it soon becomes clear why Sandwich Harbour is often described as inaccessible. Spring tides and shifting sands ensure an unpredictable route, but as you approach the towering, wind-sculptured dunes at the edge of Sandwich Harbour, there is a sense of entering a different world. All that is left of the old whaling station is a solitary deserted building and the strange greenery around the lagoon. Some 40,000 birds (34 different species) have been recorded in this area during recent surveys. There is time to take a leisurely walk around the lagoon and you may also see seals, dolphins and even whales in the water, and possibly brown hyena and jackals in the surrounding dunes.

For hotel and restaurant price codes and other relevant information, see pages 21-28.

⊙ Where to stay

Swakopmund *p224, maps p225 and p226*
Swakopmund has a vast range of hotels, pension (or *garni*) hotels, guesthouses, rest camps and self-catering apartments – indeed far too many to list. As a result of Namibia Tourism Board's confusing grading system, we have listed recommended establishments by type; it is personal preference whether you want the anonymity of a large hotel, the intimacy of a pension or hosted guesthouse, or the independence of a fully equipped self-catering apartment (many of which are on or close to the beach).

Note that all accommodation in Swakopmund is likely to be fully booked around the peak Christmas period. Even at other times of the year occupancy rates may be very high. You are therefore strongly advised to book in advance or at the very least to check on availability before arriving.

The cool fog that collects over the coast each night means camping can be cold and you may well want to consider treating yourself to a bed whilst on the coast. However, if you have your own tent or campervan it's possible to camp at the **Alte Brücke Resort**. In hotels on the coast, a/c is not required – in fact, heaters in winter are of more importance.

Hotels

The **Strand Hotel**, www.strandhotel swakopmund.com, has historically and enviably occupied a prime position on the Mole, but the old one was demolished

a few years ago. A new one is presently being constructed and will have 85 rooms, restaurants, spa and swimming pool and is due to open in 2015-2016. Check the website for progress.

$$$$ Swakopmund Hotel and Entertainment Centre, Theo-Ben Gurirab Av, T064-410 5200, www. swakopmundhotel.co.za. An excellent hotel with high standards that caters primarily for international visitors with 90 a/c, light and airy rooms with DSTV and Wi-Fi, the **Platform One**, restaurant for à la carte and buffet meals, casino, heated swimming pool, gym, spa, shops and car hire. The front building is the original railway station built in 1901; look at the old photographs to see where the trains used to pull up.

$$$$-$$$ Sea Side Hotel and Spa, 5 km north of Swakopmund off the C34 towards Henties Bay, T064-415900, www.seasidehotelandspa.com. Right on the beach with sea and sunset views with 36 a/c rooms with DSTV, Wi-Fi, large picture windows, some with balconies, decor is stylish and fresh, restaurant, wine cellar, room service, bar, indoor pool which is part of the spa. Good modern set-up but mixed reviews about the level of service.

$$$ Beach Lodge, 1 Stint St, Vogelstrand, 4 km north of town, T064-414500, www.beachlodge.com.na. On the seafront with sweeping ocean views, 19 spacious rooms with DSTV, patios or balconies, some have fireplaces, a quirky building constructed to look like ships with enormous circular porthole-style windows, the restaurant is called **The Wreck**, but there's nothing 'wreck-ish' about it; the choice of food and wine is excellent and beautifully presented.

$$$ Hansa Hotel, 3 Hendrik Witbooi St, T064-414200, www.hansahotel.com.na. Historic hotel built in 1905 with 58 rooms with DSTV arranged around a garden courtyard with palm trees, bar with fireplace, and 2 restaurants. **The Terrace** offers light meals and overlooks the inner gardens, and the **Equestrian Room** has a good selection of Namibian fare (see Restaurants, page 252). A smoothly run hotel in the centre of town which many still regard as the best in Swakopmund.

$$ Hotel Deutsches Haus, 13 Lüderitz St, T064-404896, www.hotel.na. Family-run mid-range place that is deservedly popular for its friendly service and sensible rates with 20 rooms, a little plain but comfortable, pub, restaurant and beer garden with good atmosphere and meaty Namibian style-meals. Despite the name, the hotel does cater for non-German speakers.

$$ Hotel Eberwein, Villa Wille (see page 235), Sam Nujoma Av, T064-414450, www.eberwein.com.na. A splendid colonial-era home tastefully converted into a Victorian-style hotel with 17 comfortably furnished rooms equipped with all mod cons including under-floor heating. Breakfast included, nice bar and lounge with a good range of South African wines, recommended for those who want the colonial experience.

$$ Hotel Europa Hof, 39 Bismarck St, T064-405061, www.europahof.com. Looks a little out of place in Swakopmund (the black-and-white timber frame and flower boxes seem more suited to the Alps) but a comfortable and homely old-style hotel popular with tour groups. 35 rooms with DSTV and Wi-Fi, restaurant with pleasant terrace and a menu that will make anyone from Germany feel at home – try the pork knuckle with sauerkraut.

$$ Hotel Schweizerhaus, 1 Bismarck St, T064-400331, www.schweizerhaus.net. Under family management since 1965 this place is rather old-fashioned but has a couple of redeeming features; its location at the top of the steps down to the Mole and the Swakopmund Museum, and the fact that the 24 B&B rooms are on the 1st floor above **Café Anton** (see page 254), which is under the same ownership. Some rooms have ocean views, and there's a private residents' bar in the back garden.

Pensions and guesthouses

$$$ Villa Margherita & Villa Tulipano, 37 Daniel Tjongarero St, T064-400122, www.villamargherita.com.na. An upmarket guesthouse with 10 individually decorated stylish rooms in 2 converted colonial villas (1908-1913), with DSTV and Wi-Fi, luxurious decor, wall colours in bright reds or lime greens, interesting modern paintings, lounge with fireplace, pretty garden, and in-house bistro for meals with an Italian twist.

$$$-$$ Brigadoon, 16 Ludwig Koch St, T064-406064, www.brigadoon swakopmund.com. Classy small place with a nod at boutique style, with 7 rooms decorated in muted browns and greys with minimalist decor and bright white linen, Wi-Fi and DSTV, small garden overlooking Palm Beach, breakfast included and is delivered to your wooden veranda. Secure parking and a short walk from the museum and **Café Anton**.

$$$-$$ Sea Breeze Guesthouse, 48 Turmalin St, 3 km north of town, T064-463348, www.seabreeze.com.na. Stylish Italian-run establishment offering 10 individually decorated rooms, each with vibrant splashes of colour, DSTV, Wi-Fi, some with garden patios and kitchenettes and can sleep up to 5, from the breakfast room there is a terrific view down the beach to the town centre. If you don't want to go into town, you can eat dinner at **The Wreck** restaurant at the nearby **Sea Side Hotel and Spa** (see page 247).

\$\$ Hotel Pension à la Mer, 4 Libertina Amathila Av, T064-404130, www. pension-a-la-mer.com. Funky B&B with unusual quirky furniture and brightly coloured decor, in a good location just seconds away from the jetty and **Tug** restaurant, 23 rooms from singles to quads, works out good value per person, off-street parking, Wi-Fi, bar and generous breakfasts.

\$\$ Hotel Pension Rapmund, 6-8 Bismarck St, T064-402035, www. hotelpensionrapmund.com. A good solid family-run option in a central location near **Café Anton**, with 24 homely rooms including triples and family flats, some with balconies and views of the lighthouse, breakfast is taken overlooking the garden and ocean. One of the most welcoming and popular pensions in town so book well ahead.

\$\$ Sam's Giardino, 89 Anton Lubowski Av, Krammersdorf, T064-403210, www. giardinonamibia.com. Located on the edge of town, this friendly, relaxed and service-minded guesthouse has been built in the style of a Swiss mountain chalet. 10 stylish rooms facing the garden, breakfast included and a 5-course gourmet dinner offered. There's a bar and well-stocked wine cellar, mini-library/reading room with plenty of information on Namibia and Wi-Fi.

\$\$ The Secret Garden Guesthouse, 36 Bismarck St, T064-404037, www. secretgarden.com.na. Attractive orange building surrounding a courtyard with flowers, giant palms and *braai* area, 11 neat rooms, 2 have additional

kitchenettes and pull out beds for families/groups. Attached and sharing the garden courtyard is a small bistro restaurant and bar (Mon-Sat 1700-2130) serving pizzas and a 'meal of the day'.

\$\$ The Stiltz, T064-400771, www. thestiltz.com. A quirkily designed place with 9 smart wooden and thatched chalets, some for families/groups, with balcony, minibar and Wi-Fi. The chalets are over 3 m high, up on stilts and interlinked by walkways overlooking the Swakop riverbed, sand dunes and ocean. Generous breakfasts are taken in a dining area with wonderful views and birdwatchers will love it here.

\$\$-\$ Hotel Prinzessin Rupprecht Heim, 15 Anton Lubowski Av, T064-412540, www.hotel-prinzessin-rupprecht. com. In a historic building (see page 236) that used to be a hospital, this is a simple but peaceful option with 24 rooms, 5 of which are singles with shared bathroom, and 2 are for families, good value for anyone on a medium budget, off-street parking and a lovely sheltered garden at the back, breakfast included.

Self-catering and rest camps

Apartments can be booked through a number of agents acting on behalf of the owners. Try **Namibia Holiday Services**, T064-405442, www.namibiaholiday services.com, or **Nel's Estates**, T064-405226, www.nels-estates.com.na.

\$\$-\$ Alte Brücke Resort, 200 m from the beach at the southern end of Strand St near the aquarium, T064-404918, www.altebrucke.com. A great value and well-run resort with 23 self-catering chalets sleeping up to 6 with TV and *braai* spots, cleaners make beds and wash up each day, rates include a good and filling buffet breakfast. Also very nice **camping** spots on green lawns, each with its own bathroom, *braai* spot and power point. Wi-Fi available throughout.

$$-$ Swakopmund Municipal Restcamp, Hendrik Witbooi St, to the left of the main road after crossing the bridge coming into town from Walvis Bay, T064-4104333, www.swakopmund-restcamp.com. A bit of a Swakop institution and the bright pink A-frames lying on the dry Swakop riverbed are unmissable, but primarily geared at local visitors (it gets fully booked during school holidays). Nevertheless, it's cheap with a range of self-catering bungalows: the most basic are known as 'Fisherman' and have bunk beds, shower, fridge and hot plate; at the other end of the scale are the A-frames with 6 beds and full bathrooms and kitchens. However only bedding is provided and there's no crockery, cutlery, or towels. It's suitable for those with their own fully equipped vehicles who want a warm bed for the night; rates are from N$200 pp. Breakfast is available in the dining room or can be delivered to your chalet.

Backpackers

$$-$ Gruner Kranz, also known as **Swakop Lodge**, 14 Nathaniel Maxuilili St, T064-402030, www.grunerkranz.com. A large corner block decorated with brightly painted African art with 30 rooms in total, arranged into en suite singles/doubles/twins/triples/quads with satellite DSTV and coffee/tea station, plus dorm rooms with shared bathrooms. Laundry, self-catering kitchen, buffet breakfast, secure parking and Wi-Fi. The upstairs pub/disco is deservedly one of Swakop's most popular nightspots, but some may find it a little noisy.

$ Amanpuri Traveller's Lodge, corner of Moses Garoeb St and Anton Lubowski St, T064-405587 www.amanpurinamibia.

com. Good, lively set-up with single, double, triple and quad en suite rooms, dorms sleeping 4-10, a large and social courtyard entertainment area with bar, DSTV and outdoor *braai*, good English cooked breakfasts, free Wi-Fi, and plenty of off-street parking. Helpful in booking local activities and the **Ground Rush Adventures** office is here for skydiving (see page 262).

$ Villa Wiese Backpackers Lodge, corner of Theo Gurirab St and Windhoeker St, T064-407105, www.villa wiese.com. Well-run and established backpackers in a lovely house originally built in 1905, cosy kitchen and dining area with vaulted ceiling and fireplace, some parking space behind a gate, doubles, twins, triples and dorms, all rates include cooked breakfast, upstairs pub with TV and courtyard where an old tree has been cleverly incorporated into the decor. Very friendly owners and recommended for all budget travellers including families.

Around Swakopmund *p238, map p225*
Long Beach

The area known as Long Beach, or *Langestrand* in Afrikaans, is midway between Swakopmund and Walvis Bay (about 15 km from each). It has a sheltered beach which is safe for swimming but it's gritty and not especially clean. The settlement grew as a cluster of holiday homes and there is also a couple of sprawling basic campsites aimed for the domestic market. It was made famous when Brad Pitt and Angelina Jolie holed up here for their Namibian soirée in 2006, and one can only imagine they chose the location for the solitude rather than for its beauty; it's unattractive and has the atmosphere of a building site, and won't hold too much interest for international visitors and you'll need a car to get here. In the event that you do want to stay, there are a couple of modern and well-run but very average hotels in the mid-range bracket (**$$**) with 25 rooms between them, run by the South African Protea Hotel chain, www.proteahotels.com; **Protea Hotel Burning Shore**, 152 4th St, Long Beach, T064-213700, and **Protea Hotel Long Beach Lodge**, Long Beach Circle, T064-218820.

Walvis Bay *p241, map p242*

There are a number of comfortable options in Walvis Bay for tourists and business travellers, but it will always be the poor cousin of Swakopmund, which is a far more attractive place to stay with a much better choice of places to eat out in the evening. In contrast to Long Beach (above) **Protea Hotels** run a couple of the best options in Walvis Bay.

$$$-$$ Lagoon Lodge, 2 Kovambo Nujoma Drive, T064-200850, www.lagoonlodge.com.na. Run by a French couple, 8 comfortable individually styled rooms with DSTV, Wi-Fi and excellent views of the lagoon, in a bright yellow building, lovely decor, swimming pool, the warm hospitality make this one of the most pleasant places to stay in town. Rates are B&B or full board. Also runs the **Lyon des Sables** restaurant at the Walvis Bay Waterfront (see Restaurants, page 254).

$$$-$$ Protea Hotel Pelican Bay, The Esplanade, T064-214000, www.proteahotels.com. Lovely location at the edge of Walvis Bay Lagoon, a modern option with white walls and lots of slate and marble, 48 a/c rooms with balconies and lagoon views, DSTV, Wi-Fi and minibar. Facilities include a smart restaurant and bar and 24-hr coffee shop.

A highlight is the pelican-feeding from the jetty at the front of the hotel.

$$ Langholm Hotel, 24 2nd St West, T064-209230, www.langholmhotel.com. A sensibly priced small hotel suitable for business travellers or tourists alike, 15 rooms and 1 self-catering suite that can sleep 5 arranged around a pretty garden patio, DSTV and smart furnishings, lounge and bar, generous 3-course dinners and the **NightCap** bar is uniquely decorated with caps from around the world.

$$ Oysterbox Guesthouse, The Esplanade, T064-249597, www.oysterboxguesthouse.com. Modern B&B with a beach-house feel thanks to the large windows that let lots of light in, 10 rooms, DSTV, Wi-Fi, it's worth paying a little more for lagoon views and balconies, breakfast is included and there's a pleasant bar which offers light meals until 2100, or walk to restaurants at the waterfront.

$$ Protea Hotel Walvis Bay, corner of Sam Nujoma Av and 10th Rd, T064-213700, www.proteahotels.com. Striking modern building painted in a variety of pastel colours, 58 a/c rooms, DSTV, Wi-Fi, breakfast available and dinner can be ordered in from local restaurants. A functional, smart hotel located in the centre of town, business orientated but with equally good standards as the **Pelican Bay**.

$$-$ Free Air Guest House, The Esplanade, T064-202247, www.namibia-walvisbay-guesthouse.com. Another good location on the Esplanade opposite **The Raft** (see Restaurants, page 254) and overlooking the lagoon in a bright yellow building, striking architecture with floor-to-ceiling windows, 10 rooms and 1 family room sleeping 4, bar with large-screen TV and Wi-Fi, B&B and again you can walk to the waterfront.

$ Loubser's B&B, 11 3rd St West, T064-203034, www.loubseraccommodation.com. In a bright white modern house 350 m from the lagoon, one of the cheapest options and popular with backpackers and kitesurfers, 3 double en suites, 1 self-catering unit sleeping 4, and a couple of 4-bed dorms, each with their own kitchenette and bathroom. Friendly laidback vibe, cosy lounge with TV and can organize all local activities.

⊙ Restaurants

Swakopmund *p224, maps p225 and p226*
Swakopmund has the best choice of restaurants in Namibia outside Windhoek, and most offer the usual high-quality Namibian meaty fare as well as excellent and affordable seafood. Another lesser known Swakopmund speciality is asparagus, which is grown out of town in the dry Swakop riverbed. Check opening times as quite a few restaurants close on Sun or Mon evenings. During the day there are plenty of cafés offering cakes, pastries and German-style sandwiches, some of which also serve beer; a Swakop must-do is to have coffee and cake at the famous **Café Anton**. Fast food can be found at **KFC** on Hendrik Witbooi St, **Wimpy** and **Debonairs Pizza** in the Spar Shopping Mall.

$$$ Cosmopolitan Restaurant & Lounge Bar, 37 Daniel Tjongarero St, T064-400133. Mon-Sat 1600-late. A fairly new Italian-run place in a bright red house, the dining and lounge areas are in different rooms, classy modern decor, fine art on the walls and a slick cocktail bar. Food varies from excellent and innovative sushi, to seafood spaghetti and game steaks in red wine jus.

$$$ The Equestrian Room, at the Hansa Hotel, 3 Hendrik Witbooi St, T064-414200, www.hansahotel.com.na. Daily 1900-2200. Elegant formal dining room in this historic hotel with old world charm, a tinkling piano and uniformed waiters. Specialities include lobster bisque, prawns with Swakop asparagus and chateaubriand. The chef's complimentary gazpacho and sorbet between courses is a tasty touch.

$$$ Erich's, 21 Daniel Tjongarero Av, T064-405141. Mon-Sat 1800-2200; the adjoining takeaway and coffee shop is open Mon-Sat 0830-1630. A dull tiled interior, but a vibrant seafood restaurant during the season, which also serves game meat such as kudu, springbok, eland and crocodile steaks and a fair choice of vegetarian dishes. Professional bow tie-clad waiters and a well-chosen wine list.

$$$ Jetty 1905, at the end of the jetty, T064-405664. Tue-Thu 1200-1400, 1700-2200, Fri-Sat 1100-2200, Sun 1100-2100. A magical spot especially at sunset at the end of the jetty and 300 m out to sea in a double-storey wooden and glass structure (some of the floors are glass so you can see the crashing waves below), which also incorporates some of iron girders of the original jetty. A good and varied menu of seafood, sushi and steaks – standouts are the baked garlic oysters and seafood skewers.

$$$ The Tug, Strand St, by the jetty, T064-402356, www.the-tug.com. Opens at 1700 for sundowners and dinner is 1800-2200, lunch Sat-Sun 1200-1500. A great sunset with an ocean view, and a good place to relax and enjoy fantastic seafood including the delicious seafood soup with calamari, prawns, mussels and linefish or the 600-g crayfish platter. The bar is in part of an old ship complete with portholes, whilst the dining area is built around the ship with chunky brick walls and heavy wooden furniture. There are over 70 South African wines on offer plus French champagne. Good atmosphere and service and bookings essential.

$$$-$$ Kücki's Pub, 22 Tobias Hainyeko St, T064-402407 www.kuckispub.com. Mon-Sat 1800-late. A long-time favourite with all visitors to Swakopmund and has been going strong since 1981, with a traditional restaurant downstairs and lively pub upstairs. A great place for seafood, though there's a long menu of meat, pizza, pasta and vegetarian dishes. Make a reservation in high season.

$$$-$$ Lighthouse Pub & Restaurant, the Mole, next to the Swakopmund Museum, T064-400894. Mon-Thu 1600-2400, Fri-Sun 1200-2400. Outdoor terrace overlooking the sea or inside bar and dining. Offers a wide range of dishes from excellent fresh seafood to steaks, burgers and pizzas. Good social atmosphere, suitable for families and large groups, sensible prices and great views.

$$ 22 Degrees South, in the lighthouse at the Mole (see page 233), T064-400380. Tue-Sun 1200-2200. With tables set in the old administration buildings of the lighthouse and scattered around the grassy gardens, this has a menu of home-made pastas and pizzas and be sure to check the specials board for fresh local produce like cob, steenbras, mussels or game steaks.

$$ Napolitana Grill & Pizzeria, 33 Nathanael Maxilili St, T064-402773. Tue-Sun 1200-1400, 1800-2200. Huge pizzas prepared in a wood oven and a range of pastas and meat dishes including 750 g steaks and foot-long ribs. Popular with locals and tourists, prices are very reasonable and the atmosphere friendly and relaxed.

$$ Swakopmund Brauhaus, Brauhaus Arcade, Sam Nujoma Av, T064-402214, www.swakopmundbrauhaus.com. Mon-Sat 1000-1430, 1800-2130. Bistro pub offering traditional German dishes, Namibian game and fish and a great cooked breakfast. Tables under umbrellas outside, plenty of German beer on tap, and children's portions available. A good place to stop and relax during a walk about town.

$$-$ Western Saloon, 8 Tobias Hainyeko St, T064-405395. Daily from 1700. The name sums up the Wild West theme. The seafood is good and so are the steaks, specials include game meat and oysters, easy-going medium priced restaurant.

$ 3 N'amigos Mexican Bar & Grill, 19 Nathanael Maxilili St, T064-406711. Mon-Thu 1700-0200, Fri-Sat 1200-0200. Mexican decor and a courtyard with fairy light covered palm trees, this has a reasonable menu of fajitas, nachos, enchiladas, chili-poppers, plus pizzas, steak and fish. Service is very slow though and it's a better venue for a late night beer or cocktail with perhaps some tapas.

$ Bits 'N Pizzas, 30 Daniel Tjongarero Av, T0817-263126. Tue-Sat 1200-1400, 1600-2100, Sun 1700-2100. Informal family-run place in a 1924 historical building with swift service. An eat-in or takeaway menu of great gourmet (square) pizzas, delicious steaks, salads, pastas or traditional fish and calamari and chips.

Cafés

Swakopmund is well known for its many European-style street-side daytime cafés serving light snacks and excellent coffees and cakes – they make a pleasant stop on a walk around town.

Bojos Café, 13 Daniel Tjongarero Av, in the **Hansa Hotel** building, T064-400774.

Mon-Fri 0700-1700, Sat 0800-1500, Sun 0900-1400. Buzzy café with Wi-Fi that spills out onto the palm-shaded street. Excellent coffee and cappuccino, breakfasts, pastries, and lunches are chalked up on the specials board. Ideal for catching up on emails while sitting in the sunshine.

Café Anton, in the lobby of the **Hotel Schweizerhaus** (see page 248), 1 Bismarck St, T064-400331. Daily 0700-1900. Established in 1966, the dated furniture and decor give it a time-warped charm and it's a Swakop must-do for the delicious German confectionary, lovingly presented in old-fashioned glass display cabinets. Try the apple strudel, black forest gateaux, florentines or bee-sting cakes, also does decent breakfasts and light meals like brötchens filled with German cold meats and cheeses.

Café Tref Punkt & Hansa Bäckerei, Sam Nujoma Av, T064-402034. Mon-Sat 0800-1700. Coffee, cakes, some hot meals like pumpernickel (German rye bread that is tastier than it sounds) and German-style bratwurst and bockwurst sausages. The bakery has a good range of items to buy to take on road trips.

Pandora's Box & Café, Ankerplatz, Bismarck St, T064-403545. Mon-Fri 0900-1800, Sat 0900-1300. A well-stocked curio shop that doubles up as a café and sells home-made chocolates. Breakfasts, schnitzel and goulash for lunch, lemon meringue pie and excellent cakes, beer and wine. From 1200 on Fri, they serve *kartoffelpuffer*; delicious potato pancakes. Outside tables next to a babbling water feature.

Stadtmitte Café, 2 Woermann St, T064-400893. Mon-Sat 0700-1900. Popular with locals for the huge and cheap breakfasts, a canteen-style place where you order at a counter, lunchtime specials

like lamb curry or chicken and avocado burger, plus coffees, shakes, smoothies, sandwiches and cakes. The signs/menus are a blatant copy of the Starbucks logo. Free Wi-Fi.

Village Café, 21 Sam Nujoma Av, T064-404723, www.villagecafenamibia.com. Mon-Fri 0700-1600, Sat 0700-1400. A travellers' favourite with bright and colourful decor with some interesting local art on the walls and nooks and crannies to explore, serving breakfasts, pancakes, scones and waffles, unusual salads, and an excellent range of coffees to go with the free Wi-Fi.

Walvis Bay *p241, map p242*

Thanks to the opening of the new Walvis Bay Waterfront (see page 246), dining in Walvis Bay has improved considerably of late; even if you don't eat there, it's a fine place for a drink and to watch the sunset. For fast food, again there is a **KFC** in town and plenty of bakeries and supermarkets with takeaway counters; especially useful if you need a picnic before heading to the Namib-Naukluft Park.

$$$ Lyon des Sables, at the Walvis Bay Waterfront, T064-221220. Tue-Fri 1200-1430, daily 1830-2130. Run by a French chef, this attractive spot in the new waterfront development offers beautifully presented seafood including crayfish in season, meat and game, vegetarian dishes, specials like Kalahari truffles, and save room for the decadent desserts. A recommended fine dining experience.

$$$ The Raft, Esplanade, T064-204877, www.theraftrestaurant.com. Mon-Sat 1200-1500, 1800-2200, the bar is open 1200-late. A fantastic structure built on stilts in the lagoon with a long boardwalk to reach it. A wide selection of dishes, seafood, pasta, fresh salads and the usual choice of steaks and a snack menu is available throughout the day. Always worth a visit to watch the sunset from the bar and the pelicans flying into the lagoon.

$$ Lothar's Steak House, 112 6th St, T064-220884. Daily 1200-1400, 1800-2300. Informal steakhouse, plainly decorated but good value and large portions of meaty fare, including game meat, hearty homemade soups, some grilled fish and seafood, and some German dishes. The separate bar opens at 1700 and stays open late if there is the demand.

$$-$ Anchors @ The Jetty, at the Walvis Bay Waterfront, T064-205762. Mon and Sun 0730-1500, Tue-Sat 0730-2200. Attractive setting on the new waterfront with a nautical theme of fishing nets and buoys and the like, popular with people going on or coming off lagoon cruises serving breakfasts, brötchen, toasted sandwiches, seafood dishes (try the *cocochas* – fish cheeks in garlic butter, or succulent calamari), burgers, steaks and home-made desserts.

$$-$ Crazy Mama's, Sam Nujoma Av, T064-207364. Mon-Fri 1200-1500, 1800-2300, Sat 1800-2300. An unmistakable thatched building with stone cladding, good-value steaks, seafood, pizzas and pasta dishes, and popular amongst locals and budget travellers alike. The unusual bar is fashioned out of a split tree and there's a beer garden and large TV to watch sports.

$ Cuppa Musselcracker, at the Walvis Bay Waterfront below **Lyon des Sables**, T0816-178537. Mon-Thu 0700-1900, Fri-Sun 0700-1900. Predominantly a daytime café but stays open in the early evening for drinks and tapas and it's another lovely spot to watch the sunset from the waterfront. The bar and deck are furnished with cane hanging chairs and upturned *makoros* (dug-out canoes). The

interesting tapas have names like 'à la seaside' (seafood), 'à la oink-oink' (pork), 'à la crunch-crunch' (vegetarian), and 'à la kids' (aka fish fingers)!

Cafés

Lemon Tree Café, at the Walvis Bay Tourism Centre (see page 242), corner of Union St and 5th Rd, T064-206959. Mon, Tue and Thu 1000-1900, Wed and Fri, 1000-2200. An ideal stop while deciding what you want to do at the adjoining information office. There's sushi and Asian dishes, wraps and burgers and the decor is colourful with art on the walls for sale.

Vlooi's Nest Coffee Shop, in a small shopping centre called **The Place** on Hage Geingob St, T064-220157. Mon-Fri 0700-1800, Sat 0800-1400. Simple coffee shop serving cakes and light meals with chunky wooden furniture and some outside seating, and complemented by the **Amazing Things** gift shop and **Crazy Daisy** nursery next door.

Willi Probst Bakery and Restaurant, corner of Theo Ben Gurirab St and 12th Rd, T064-202744. Mon-Fri 0630-1730, Sat 0630-1400. A popular German bakery and restaurant, unmissable thanks to the 2 giant palm trees outside, recommended for breakfasts, cakes, bread and rolls, and especially for the lunchtime hot 'teller-essen' (buffet, from 1215-1400). Also a good place to start the day for early fishermen (it opens at 0630), and it makes up picnic baskets. Rather astonishingly, it's been here since 1957.

⬤ Bars and clubs

Swakopmund *p224, maps p225 and p226*
Most restaurants have a bar area where you can go just for a drink. Recommended for sundowners as they have great ocean

views are **Jetty 1905**, the **Lighthouse Pub & Restaurant** or the **Tug**. Other late-night drinking venues that cater for a mix of overlanders (overland trucks are in town most weekends) and the young Swakop crowd are the upstairs bar at **Kücki's Pub**, **The Naps Bar**, at the Napolitana Grill & Pizzeria, and **3 N'amigos Mexican Bar & Grill**.

Desert Tavern, Swakop St, opposite the very end of Tobias Hainyeko St, T064-404204. Mon-Fri 1600-0200, Sat 1600-2400. Traditional-style pub with friendly bar and fireplaces, pub food like steak and chips or giant burgers with all the trimmings. The only venue in town for live music and often hosts local bands or guitarists.

Gruniz Pub, upstairs at **Gruner Kranz** (see Where to stay, page 250). Daily 1800-late. Centrally located on Nathaniel Maxuilili St, an always lively place with a long wooden bar, enormous TV screen, dance floor, pool tables, and a long list of cocktails, so if you are in the mood for a party, try your luck here. Particularly busy at the weekends when the overland trucks are in town.

Tiger Reef Beach Bar, Strand St, just south of the aquarium, T064-400935. Tue-Fri 1200-2400, Sat-Sun 1100-2400. Informal reed and tented beach bar situated right where the Swakop River meets the ocean (it does get flooded from time to time). Lie in the sand or lounge on chairs on the wooden deck during the day, and it becomes a lively bar from sunset onwards. Some light meals available on a self-service basis.

☺ Entertainment

Swakopmund *p224, maps p225 and p226*
Mermaid Casino, at the Swakopmund Hotel and Entertainment Centre (see Where to stay, page 247). T064-402743. Daily 1000-0400. The comfortable and glitzy bar here is the latest place to close in town and has a decent snack menu, and you can have a flutter at the 200+ slot machines (from 1000) and 12 gaming tables (blackjack, roulette, poker; from 1900). Also at the hotel is the tiny 2-screen **Atlanta Cinema**, which shows new releases and the first movie starts around 1200 and the last around 2000.

○ Shopping

Swakopmund *p224, maps p225 and p226*
Bookshops
Die Muschel Book & Art, Brahaus Arcade, T064-402874, www.muschel.iway.na. Mon-Sat 0830-1800, Sun 1000-1800. Professional bookshop with a charming art gallery upstairs and soft music playing, full range of intelligent books in English and German and a good selection of souvenir books on Africa. The café serves coffee and cakes and has outside tables.
Die Swakopmunder Buchhandlung, 22 Sam Nujoma Av, T064-402613. Mon-Fri 0800-1730, Sat 0800-1300, Sun 0930-1230. A full range of coffee-table books, calendars, local guides and maps, also sells postcards and stamps. This is Namibia's first and oldest bookshop and during the First World War it was the issuer of emergency banknotes in Swakopmund.

Camping equipment
Cymot, Sam Nujoma Av, T064-400318, www.cymot.com. Mon-Fri 0800-1700, Sat 0800-1300. A very large branch selling a full range of camping equipment and car accessories.

Curios
Swakopmund has a particularly good selection of crafts and curios for sale;

not all of these are as tacky as you might imagine, and there are some quality shops and some interesting art studios. Also well worth a browse is the informal craft market on the pavement at the bottom of the steps below **Café Anton**.

Henckert Gallery, 39 Sam Nujoma Av, T064-400140, www.swakopmund. henckert.com. Daily 0830-1900. A showroom with its sister branch in Karibib, selling hand-woven carpets, wall hangings, minerals and semi-precious stones, wood carvings and drums, can buy polished stones by weight.

Karakulia Weavers, 2 Rakotoka St, in the industrial area to the northeast of town at the end of Tobias Hainyeko St, T064-461415, www.karakulia.com.na. Mon-Fri 0900-1700, Sat 0900-1300. Good selection of karakul rugs and wall hangings, some of the finest Namibian products to take back home, all of a high standard. You can take a tour around the factory here to see how the carpets are made.

Kirikara, Ankerplatz Arcade, T064-663146, www.kirikara.com. Mon-Fri 0900-1300, 1430-1730, Sat 0900-1300, 1600-1800, Sun 1000-1200. A brightly painted orange shop with an excellent variety of quality crafts, textiles, ceramics, baskets, tribal art and jewellery. Many items are made in the studios and workshops of **Kiripotib Guest Farm** on the edge of the Kalahari (see page 100).

Leder Chic, Brauhaus Arcade, T064-404778, www.lederchic.net. Mon-Fri 0900-1800, Sat-Sun 0900-1300. Luggage and leather shop selling quality ostrich and kudu wallets, belts, handbags, briefcases and laptop bags.

Nakara, Brauhaus Arcade, T064-405907, www.nakara-namibia.com. Mon-Fri 0900-1730, Sat 0900-1400. Boutique for Namibia Karakul Leathers (NAKARA), considered the country's best tannery for Karakul sheep leather – bags, belts, wallets, etc. Also sells items in game leather. There's another outlet in Windhoek.

Peter's Antiques, 24 Tobias Hainyeko St, T064-405624, www.peters-antiques.com. Mon-Fri 0900-1300, 1500-1800, Sat 0900-1300. This is a must for anyone interested in German colonial history, excellent collection of Africana books, as well as some genuine tribal antiques. Not cheap but the quality is excellent and the shop now covers 400 sq m and Peter is happy for people to visit it as a museum even if not buying anything.

Jewellery

African Art Jewellers, 1 Hendrik Witbooi St, T064-405566. Mon-Fri 0830-1800, Sat 0830-1300. One of Swakopmund's top outlets for modern contemporary handcrafted jewellery including diamonds and other precious stones.

Kristall Galerie, corner of Tobias Hainyeko St and Theo-Ben Gurirab Av, T064-406080, www.namibiangemstones. com. Mon-Fri 0800-1700, Sat 0800-1300. A large modern gallery with a display of crystals and other semi-precious stones and replica of the original Otjua Tourmaline Mine as the hook to get you to come into the jewellery boutique. Worth it if this sort of thing appeals to you as the giant quartz cluster on display is impressive; it measures 3 m by 3.5 m and weighs 14 tons, and was found on a farm near Karibib district in 1985, 45 m underground. It took 5 years to unearth the crystal in one piece.

Shopping malls

There are several shopping malls in Swakopmund. For specialist tourist shops try the **Brauhaus Arcade** between Hendrik Witbooi and Tobias Hainyeko Sts; the **Ankerplatz** off Sam Nujoma Av which backs on to the Woermann House; and the **Woermann & Brock Arcade** on the corner of Sam Nujoma Av of Tobias Hainyeko St. For food and clothes, standard South African chain stores and supermarkets can be found at the **Pick 'n' Pay Mall** on Hendrik Witbooi St close to the Namib-i office, which also has a branch of **Woolworths** (quality South African chain for clothes; there's another branch on on Libertina Amathila Av), or at the **Spar Shopping Mall** to the north of the centre on Thobias Hainyeko St with several shops and takeaways. Going out of town the **Shoprite Centre** on Sam Nujoma Av, is probably the easiest place to pick up provisions for self-catering where there's also a bottle shop, pharmacy and ATMs. Opposite here, the Engen petrol station has a shop which is open 24 hrs.

Walvis Bay *p241, map p242*
There's a cluster of gift and curio shops at the new Walvis Bay Waterfront, while in the centre of town are the usual supermarkets; the **Pick 'n' Pay Shopping Centre** is on Theo-Ben Gurirab St, the **Spar** supermarket is on Sam Nujoma Av, and **Shoprite** is on 10th St.

○ What to do

The many adventure and adrenaline activities available on land and at sea are the highlight of this region – so much so that Swakopmund is giving Victoria Falls a run for its money as Adventure Capital of Africa. Regional tourists on their annual holiday tend to stick to angling, *braaing* and relaxing in their self-catering accommodation, while international tourists arrive throughout the week on tour buses and overland trucks to throw themselves into a couple of days of action-packed frenzy such as quad biking, sandboarding or skydiving. There are also numerous half-day, full-day and longer sightseeing tours that can be taken with one of the many tour operators listed below. To book, you can contact the companies directly or, in most cases, your accommodation will be able to make reservations. In Swakopmund, simply go along to the **Namib-i**, or the **Far Out** booking offices (see Tourist Information, see page 228), and in Walvis Bay, the **Walvis Bay Tourism Centre** (see page 242), and they will organize an action-packed itinerary for you.

Swakopmund *p224, maps p225 and p226*
Ballooning
Africa Adventure Balloons, T064-403455, www.africanballoons.com. Passengers are picked up from hotels in Swakopmund and generally early morning 40-min sunrise flights are conducted in the vicinity of the Rössing Mountain beyond the belt of coastal fog. Expect magnificent views of the surrounding moon-like landscape, as well as Spitzkoppe to the northeast and the Naukluft Mountains in the south. A champagne breakfast is served after the flight. N$3000, children (under 40 kg) half price.

Camel riding
Camel Farm, 12 km from the town centre, off the B2, T064-400363, www.swakopmundcamelfarm.com. One of the more interesting ways of enjoying the desert landscape is to ride on a camel. The farm is also home to a traditional farmyard with cows, chickens, geese and donkeys, as well as an indigenous desert garden with a collection of unique Namibian flora. Fun rides can be organized every afternoon 1400-1700; N$100 for 20 mins or N$300 for an hour.

Fishing

The coastline either side of Swakopmund is famous for its superb fishing, and you will notice that many of the local cars seem to have a set of rods permanently attached to the roof. Tour operators offer day trips which include fishing gear, tackle and bait as well as lunch and refreshments. If you've never tried fishing before, this is a superb introduction. If you are successful, the operators will clean and gut the fish for you, and if you are staying in self-catering accommodation you can cook it for dinner over the *braai*. Always remember to protect yourself from the sun while fishing. Trips cost N$850-1400 per person, and there are 3 options;

Ski-boat fishing trips depart from The Mole in Swakopmund, and fishing takes place from 100 m to 1 km offshore. Depending where the best fishing is, it could be anywhere within a 20-km radius of Swakopmund. The most commonly caught fish are kabeljou, black tail, west coast steenbras and catfish.

The deep-sea fishing season is Nov-Mar and again trips depart from The Mole. Fishing is done at a distance of up to 25 km offshore and at depths of around 200 m. Fish include snoek, yellow tail, mackerel and blue shark.

Angling from the beach takes place between Swakopmund and Mile 108 and trips use 4WDs to access some of the more remote spots; the distance travelled could be anything from 8 km to 120 km depending on where the fish are biting. Kob, West Coast steenbras, and various shark species can be caught; copper sharks can weigh up to 180 kg.
Aquanaut Tours, T064-405969, www.aquanauttours.com.
Levo Tours, T064-200606, www.levotours.com.

Go-Karting

R&R Karting, at Swakopmund Airport off the B2, T0813-502723, www.karting namibia.com. Tue-Fri 1500-sunset, Sat-Sun 1000-sunset. A 520-m track has been laid out in the desert and karters can reach speeds of 70 kph. Children above 1 m 45 cm are permitted and there are 'play' mini pedal go-karts for smaller kids. No need to book and there's a small bar and *braai* area. Costs are from N$70 for 5 laps to N$230 for 20 laps.

Golf

Rössmund Golf Course, 6 km east of Swakopmund on the B2, T064-405644. A par 72, 18-hole course with grass greens, palm trees and shrubs, which lies next to the (dry) Swakop River and is reputedly one of only 5 desert grass courses in the world. It opened in 1979 a couple of years after the Rössing Uranium Mine (Rössmund is an acronym of Rössing and Swakopmund). As the course is located beyond the coastal fog-belt you can play with good visibility at any time of day. Expect to pay in the region of N$250 for a round and golf clubs and golf carts can be hired from the shop. There's a restaurant in the club house that offers a good Sun buffet lunch. You can also stay here at the (**$$ Rössmund Lodge**), T064-414600, which has 20 modern rooms in stone chalets and meals are at the club house. There's a shuttle service to town.

Horse riding

Okakambe Trails, 11 km from town, follow the B2 towards the airport, take a right turn on the D1901, the stables are close to the camel farm, T064-402799, www.okakambe.iway.na. A variety of 1-hr rides or pony rides for kids to half-day, full-day or overnight rides which include camping out in the desert. If you are an experienced rider this is one of the most pleasant ways to explore the amazing desert landscape – good fun, recommended. If you are not a rider, it can also organize hikes in the region. Prices start from N$450 for a 1-hr ride.

Living Desert tours

This is a half-day 4WD tour into the dune-belt between Swakopmund and Walvis Bay, usually leaving Swakopmund at 0800 and returning at 1330. It's an excellent way to discover the creatures in the sand such as geckos, snakes, insects, dancing lizards, the white lady spider and desert chameleons. Whilst many people initially think they don't want to go and see insects and reptiles, they come back from the dunes fully rewarded and children simply love it. The guides also take out a magnet and draw the iron ore out of the sand in such a way you can write on a dune! You are also taught how to extract moisture from the desert plants and thus drink in the dunes. Rates are around N$650, children (under 12) half price.
Living Desert Adventures, T064-405070, www.livingdesertnamibia.com.
Tommy's Living Desert Tours, T0811-281038, www.livingdeserttours.com.na.

Quad biking

An excellent way to explore the dune field south of Swakopmund is by quad bike. This is one of the best ways to access parts of the Swakopmund sand dunes that even 4WDs can't reach. There are 2 types of bike: 160 cc semi-automatic bikes ideal for beginners; or, those who wish to go hell for leather and have some idea of what they are doing can ride the 200 cc manual quad bikes. Helmets, goggles and gloves are provided. Tours are multi-guiding with slow and fast

groups in the same tour, catering for both the adrenaline seeker and the complete novice. They start on the edge of the Swakop riverbed and cross flat gravel plains before going into the dune belt where the fun starts. Trails follow the crests of the dunes and there are some very steep ascents and descents where your bikes plough through the sand. Although there are variations between the companies, the standard full ride takes about 2½ hrs, covers 35-50 km and costs about N$500. Take something warm to wear later in the day as the ride back to Swakopmund can be cold.
Dare Devil Adventures, Long Beach, T0817-553589, www.daredeviladventures. com. This company offers quad biking trips from Long Beach and has a children's quad bike circuit.
Desert Explorers, on the main road to Walvis Bay just before the bridge over the Swakop River, T064-406096, www. namibiadesertexplorers.com. Daily 0800-1800. Book through any agent in town or just rock up, it runs 1- to 2-hr trips with a minimum of 2 people. There's a bar and lounge area at the office, and DVDs of your trip can be arranged with prior notice. Can also organize overnight or multi-day safaris using tented camp accommodation in the desert.

Sandboarding

There is no better way to conquer the towering dunes than to zoom down them head first on a traditional Swakop sandboard, or carve up the dune with style and skill on a snowboard adapted for sand. The dunes are constantly shifting and can move 10 m in a week; sandboard tracks soon disappear. The beauty about sandboarding is the sand is not abrasive, and as it's obviously not cold, you can board in shorts and

T-shirts. The worst that can happen is that you walk away covered in sand. For the lie-down option you're supplied with a large flat piece of waxed hardboard, safety hat, elbow guards and gloves before heading off to climb a dune. The idea is to lie on the board, push off from the top and speed headfirst down the sandy surface. Speeds easily reach 80 kph and some of the dunes are very steep though first you'll do a few training rides on the lower dunes. No experience is necessary; it's exhilarating and lots of fun. Stand-up boarding requires more skill. It is a very similar technique to boarding on snow and uses standard snowboarding equipment. If you've got snowboarding experience then this is an opportunity to try out those turns, free-style jumps and big spray curves. Prices are about N$300 for the lie-down option and N$400 for the stand-up, and stand-up boarders have the option to try lie-down boarding at no extra cost. Prices include transfers from town, a light lunch and a few drinks. **Alter Action**, at the **Far Out** office in town (see page 228), T064-402737, www. alter-action.info. Beth Sarro invented sandboarding at Swakopmund in 1996 and has taken many thousands of people through the dunes over the years. A fun half-day excursion with a lot of laughs. Suitable for 10 years and up, though younger kids can ride with the guides.

Scenic flights

For those visitors short on time but long on cash a number of companies offer flying safaris. Flights vary from 1½-hr trips along the coast to all-day safaris to northern Namibia that include landings and 4WD adventures. From the air you can clearly see Namibia's desert landscapes, dried up riverbeds, moonscapes, rock formations,

mountains and gravel plains. Strongly recommended if you wish to appreciate the Namibian landscape from the air, the views are tremendous.

Most flights are high-winged single-engine 6-seater Cessnas, which have the wings above the windows for better sightseeing.

The most popular trip is a 2¼-hr flight from Swakopmund to Sossusvlei, which goes over the massive dune field and returns along the coast over the flamingos, seals and shipwrecks. Other sample flights include a 1½-hr trip along the coast; a full-day trip over Sossusvlei and the Fish River Canyon which includes a stop in Lüderitz to visit Kolmanskop; a day trip over Sossusvlei, the coast and a stop in the Kalahari for lunch and a visit to the San (Bushmen); or a day trip over the Skeleton Coast in the north and a stop to visit the Himba in the far north. Costs vary enormously depending on the length of the trip and the number of people in the plane, but the cheapest and shortest flights of about 1 hr start from around N$1100 if there are 5 people in the plane. Obviously the prices increase significantly if there are fewer people though the companies will endeavour to find other people to fill the plane. The companies listed below also can arrange fly-in safaris to the remote lodges.

Atlantic Aviation, 5 Hendrik Witbooi St, next to **Hansa Hotel**, T064-404749, www.flyinnamibia.com.

Pleasure Flights and Safaris, corner of Sam Nujoma Av and Hendrik Witbooi St, T064-404500, www. pleasureflights.com.na.

Wings Over Africa, office at the **Swakopmund Hotel and Entertainment Centre**, T064-403720, www.flyinafrica.com.

Skydiving

Ground Rush Adventures, office at **Amanpuri Traveller's Lodge** (see Where to stay, page 250), corner Moses Garoeb St and Anton Lubowski Av, the 'drop zone' and airstrip is 10 km north of town on the C34 past the Saltworks, T064-402841, www.skydiveswakop. com.na. Extremely popular tandem free-fall jumps for novices. Jumps take place daily, normally after the fog has lifted in the morning. After a brief safety chat, you board a small plane for a short scenic flight over Swakopmund and the surrounding coast and desert as you prepare yourself for your jump. This involves being strapped between the thighs of your tandem jump master and shuffling to the door of the plane. At 3500 m you both tumble into the sky for a mind-blowing 35-second free-fall at around 200 kph – a totally exhilarating experience. Then the parachute opens and you float to the ground for a 5-min canopy-ride enjoying the breathtaking desert scenery. A cameraman jumps with you with either a hand-held camera or a camera strapped to his helmet. The jump costs N$2250 and includes pick-ups from hotels in town; optional DVD N$500, DVD and photos N$950. Also runs static line courses, which involve 6 hrs of ground school before the initial jump at 1000 m.

Tour operators

All of the companies offer a selection of similar tours and the **Namib-I** and **Far Out** offices (see page 228) can make recommendations and reservations. Day tours on offer include **Cape Cross Seal Reserve** (see page 270), the **Welwitschia Drive tour** (see page 240), **Sandwich Harbour** (see page 246) and **Spitzkoppe** (see page 178). You can do 'town' tours of Swakopmund and Walvis Bay, but it's just as easy (and cheaper) to visit the sights yourself; however they will appeal to those who would like to hear a little about the history. Day tours cost approximately N$500-900 per half day, and US$900-1300 per full day depending on the distance travelled, how many people are in the vehicle and if lunch is included. There are usually significant discounts for children under 12. Some companies also offer multi-day trips further afield, so if you haven't yet decided what you want to see in Namibia before arriving, then you can discuss longer trips with these companies.

Africa Leisure Travel, T064-463812, www.africaleisure.net. Day tours and can organize dinner *braais*, in the desert under marquees for large groups.

Batis Birding Safaris, T064-404908, www.batisbirdingsafaris.com. Day trips with an emphasis on birding including dune and wetland walks around Swakopmund to look for specific species like the rare Gray's lark and Damara tern.

Charly's Desert Tours, Brauhaus Arcade, T064-404341, www.charlysdeserttours. com. Well-established company with a large fleet of vehicles and their own booking office, the usual day tours and they also run their own Living Desert Tour (see page 260).

Kallisto Tours, T064-402473, www. kallisto.com.na. Day tours including a specialized mineral tour into the desert and can organize longer trips to Etosha and Sossusvlei in a/c minibuses.

Kunene Conservancy Safaris, T064-406136, www.kcs-namibia.com.na. Offers 4WD camping safaris from 3-9 days from Swakopmund into Kaokoland and the far north including specialized trips to join desert elephant and desert lion conservation projects.

Kunene Tours & Safaris, T064-402779, www.kunenetours.com. Based in

Swakopmund but runs guided 4WD tailor-made camping tours to the more remote corners of Kaokoland and Damaraland with renowned experienced guide Caesar Zandberg (who's a favourite with film crews); recommended to really get off the beaten track.

Namibia Tours and Safaris, T064-406038, www.namibia-tours-safaris.com. 4WD tours to regions around Swakopmund, camping and lodge safaris for small groups, fly-in safaris.

Namibia Tracks & Trails, 14a Sam Nujoma Av, T064-416820, www.namibia-tracks-and-trails.com. Tailor-made camping safaris from 6-14 days to most places in Namibia, can also organize self-drive and fly-in itineraries. Has a walk-in office in town and can also book local day trips.

Sunrise Tours and Safaris, T064-404561, www.sunrisetours.com.na. Guided lodge/camping safaris using minibuses or 4WDs from 3-11 days including Etosha and fishing trips to the Caprivi Strip.

Turnstone Tours, T064-403123, www.turnstone-tours.com. A Sandwich Harbour specialist, and camping trips into the Namib Desert, Damaraland and the Erongo Mountains.

Walvis Bay *p241, map p242*
See also under Swakopmund tour operators, above.

Dolphin and seal cruises

Cruises by ski-boat or catamaran from Walvis Bay go through the harbour to **Bird Island** and **Pelican Point** and back via the lagoon, and you can expect excellent sightings of seals (some may jump aboard for a fishy snack), dolphins, flamingos and pelicans. For those contemplating a trip up to **Cape Cross** to see the Cape fur seal colony, these

tours offer an excellent alternative that avoids both the long drive and the pungent smell. A further possibility – if you are lucky – is the chance of spotting southern right and humpback whales as they make their way up and down their migratory routes to and from the Antarctic. Boats usually depart from the **Walvis Bay Waterfront** or the **Walvis Bay Yacht Club** each morning at 0800-0900 and arrive back around 1200-1300, and in season there are also departures at 1400. The trips are good value at N$500, children (under 12) N$350 and under 6s free, and are recommended. Most include oysters, snacks, beers, wine and soft drinks. For an extra cost, transport from Swakopmund can be arranged, and can be combined with the Sandwich Harbour trip (below).

Catamaran Charters, at the Willi Probst Bakery in town (see Restaurants, above), T064-200798, www.namibiancharters.com.

Laramon Tours & Catamaran Cruises, at the Walvis Bay Waterfront, T0811-240635, www.laramontours.com.

Levo Dolphin Tours, at the Walvis Bay Tourism Centre (see page 242), corner of Union St and 5th Rd, boats leave from the tanker jetty in the harbour, T064-200606, www.levotours.com.

Mola Mola, Atlantic St, opposite the entrance to Walvis Bay Yacht Club, T064-205511, www.mola-namibia.com.

Pelican Tours, Walvis Bay Yacht Club, T064-207664, www.pelican-tours.com.

Kayaking

Eco Marine Kayak Tours, at the **Mola Mola** office (see above), T064-203144, www.emkayak.iway.na. Kayak tours for both the experienced and the beginner in single or double kayaks. 4WD transfers to Pelican Point depart the office at 0745, before boarding the kayaks and paddling out to the Cape fur seal colony off the coast, and return about 1200. You'll literally float with the seals and they have been known to playfully jump over the paddles. Rates are N$600, children (under 12) N$400, and include tea, coffee and a light breakfast and waterproof jackets are provided. Again it can be combined with the Sandwich Harbour trip (below).

Sandwich Harbour

For the excursion to Sandwich Harbour (page 246), expect to pay in the region of N$1200, children (under 16) N$1000, for a day trip (1000-1630), which includes lunch and perhaps oysters and drinks in the dunes; N$1000/800 for the morning excursion (0830-1230), or afternoon excursion (1300-1730). Most of the boat companies (above) work in conjunction with the 4WD companies (below), so the option from Walvis Bay for a full day out (approximately 0800-1630) is to take a morning dolphin and seal cruise or a morning kayak, combined with an afternoon half-day 4WD trip to Sandwich Harbour. The cruise/4WD combo is around N$1600, children (under 12) N$1200, while the kayak/4WD combo is N$1700, children (under 12) N$1300.
Photo Ventures, office at the Walvis Bay Tourism Centre (see page 242), T0814-261200, www.photoventures-namibia.com.
Sandwich Harbour 4x4, office at the Walvis Bay Waterfront, T064-207663, www.sandwich-harbour.com.

Windsurfing and kite-boarding
Walvis Bay Kite and Wind Surf Centre, The Esplanade, near **The Raft**, restaurant, T0813-739402, www.namibiakite.com. Offers lessons and short courses and rents out equipment. With light morning winds and stronger winds in the afternoon, the secluded Walvis Bay Lagoon offers a range of conditions, allowing the beginner to take on more wind as skill and confidence increases. Once you know what you're doing, you can progress to the beaches between Walvis Bay and Swakopmund. The water is cold so wetsuits are provided.

The **Walvis Bay Speed Week**, www.walvisbayspeedweek.co.za, is a windsurfing and kite-boarding challenge usually held in Sep, which attracts international participants in a bid to break world-speed records.

⊖ Transport

Swakopmund *p224, maps p225 and p226*
34 km to Walvis Bay, 363 km to Windhoek, 70 km Henties Bay, 119 km to Cape Cross, 192 km to Uis.

Air
Although there is a small airfield at Swakopmund, flights go to and from Walvis Bay Airport (see page 241). However there is an office for **Air Namibia**, 11 Sam Nujoma Av, T064-405123, central reservations, Windhoek, T061-299 6333, www.airnamibia.com.

Bus
Intercape buses, central reservations, Windhoek, T061-227847, www.intercape.co.za, between **Windhoek** and **Walvis Bay** stop in Swakopmund. Buses arrive and depart from the car park behind Pick 'n' Pay supermarket on Hendrik Witbooi St. See timetable on page 16.

For details of the daily shuttle services using micro/sprinter buses between Windhoek and Swakopmund (4 hrs) and Walvis Bay (4½ hrs), see Windhoek transport, page 80. In Swakopmund,

Tok Tokkie Shuttles, arrive and depart from the car park behind Pick 'n' Pay supermarket on Hendrik Witbooi St; Town Hoppers, on the corner of Theo-Ben Gurirab and Nathanael Maxuilili Sts opposite the Swakopmund Hotel and Entertainment Centre; and Welwitschia Shuttle, at the Woolworths car park on Libertina Amathila Av.

Car
Some of the major car hire companies have an office in Swakopmund. Note, however, that if you want a fully equipped car with camping gear there is a much better choice in Windhoek. Avis, Theo-Ben Guirab Av, in the Swakopmund Hotel and Entertainment Centre, T064-402527, www.avis.com.na. Budget, 3 Moses Garoeb St, T064-463380, www.budget.co.za. Crossroads 4x4 Hire, 3 Moses Garoeb St, T064-403777, www.crossroads4x4hire.com. In the same building as Budget (above), the best option for a 4WD fully equipped with camping equipment, and for anglers they also rent out fishing equipment such as rod holders for the vehicle's front bumpers. Hertz, GIPF Building, Sam Nujoma Av, near the Living Desert Snake Park, T064-461826, www.hertz.co.za.

Taxi
There are taxis all over Swakopmund; if you find a driver you like, get his mobile number. Bay-Route Shuttle Services runs a door-to-door shuttle service on demand between the airport in Walvis Bay, Long Beach and Swakopmund, T0812-077651.

Train
The railway station is on the desert side of Moses Garoeb St; reservations, T064-463538. If time is not an issue then the

TransNamib Starline Passenger Service, central reservations T061-298 2032, www.transnamib.com.na, between Windhoek and Swakopmund/Walvis Bay is a comfortable alternative to the bus, but it's very slow (see details of the service in Windhoek transport, page 83).

TransNamib also runs the far more appealing overnight luxury service between Windhoek and Swakopmund once a week: the Desert Express, reservations Windhoek T061-298 2600, www.transnamib.com.na, arrives in Swakopmund at 1000 on Sat and departs on the same afternoon at 1430 (for details, see Windhoek, page 83).

Walvis Bay p241, map p242
34 km to Swakopmund, 397 km to Windhoek (via the B2), 338 km (via the C28).

Air
Walvis Bay Airport is 16 km east of town off the C14, T064-271102, www. airports.com.na. There is a restaurant, gift shop, car rental desks and, as you can imagine, great desert views when taking off and landing. Air Namibia office, at the airport, T064-202867, in town in the Old Mutual Building, Nangola Mbuma Dr, T064-203102, central reservations Windhoek T061-299 6333, www.airnamibia.com. There are direct daily flights between Walvis Bay and Windhoek's Hosea Kutako International Airport, 40 mins.

Bus
Intercape buses, reservations Windhoek, T061-227847, www.intercape.co.za, to Windhoek (5 hrs) via Swakopmund, and the towns on the B2 (see timetable, page 16). Buses arrive and depart from the car park at the Pick 'n' Pay shopping centre on Theo Ben Gurirab St.

For details of the daily shuttle services using micro/sprinter buses between Windhoek and Swakopmund (4 hrs) and Walvis Bay (4½ hrs), see Windhoek, transport, page 80. In Walvis Bay, **Tok Tokkie Shuttles**, **Town Hoppers** and **Welwitschia Shuttle**, arrive and depart from the car park at the Pick 'n' Pay shopping centre on Theo-Ben Gurirab St, and will pick up/drop off at the airport on request.

Car

Avis, corner 11th Rd and Hage Geingob St, T064-209633, Walvis Bay Airport, T064-207527, www.avis.com.na. **Budget**, at the Protea Hotel Walvis Bay, corner of Sam Nujoma Av and 10th Rd, T064-204128, Walvis Bay Airport, T064-204624, www.budget.co.za. **Europcar** at the Protea Hotel Pelican Bay, T064-207391, www.europcar.co.za. **Hertz**, at the Walvis Bay Tourism Centre (see page 242), corner of Union St and 5th Rd, T064-209085, www.hertz.co.za.

Train

The railway station is at the end of Station St near the harbour. www.transnamib.com.na. See under Swakopmund for contact details. Walvis Bay is at the end of the line from Windhoek and the train arrives at 0715 and departs again the same afternoon at 1900. To illustrate just how slow the trains are in Namibia, the train between Swakopmund and Walvis Bay takes almost 2 hrs – a distance of 34 km!

❶ Directory

Swakopmund *p224, maps p225 and p226*
Medical services Bismark Medical Centre, 17 Sam Nujoma Av, T064-40500. With good medical insurance, this is the best bet for doctor's consultations (including malaria tests) and dentistry emergencies, and it has a well-stocked pharmacy. **Medi-Clinic Swakopmund**, corner of Mosley and Fransica Van Neel Sts, 3 km north of town off the Henties Bay road (C34), T064-412200, www.mediclinic.co.za. Private hospital with 24-hr emergency.

Walvis Bay *p241, map p242*
Medical services Welwitschia Hospital (formerly Walvis Bay Medipark), Rikumbi Kandanga Rd, T064-218911, www.erongomedical.com. Private hospital with 24-hr emergency.

Skeleton Coast

To the north of Swakopmund, Namibia's bleak coastline follows its course to the Angolan border. Firstly it passes through the Dorob National Park (formerly the National West Coast Recreation Area, renamed in 2010) and then through the evocatively named Skeleton Coast National Park. Inland are the inhospitable mountains and gravel plains of Damaraland and Kaokoland.

The Skeleton Coast got its name from the ships and unlucky sailors who perished after being shipwrecked on the barren shores over the centuries. The first stretch of coast through the Dorob National Park is open to all and, although flat, is foggy and featureless; the beach here is hugely popular with anglers in search of the Benguela Current's big-game fish. The only settlement of note is Henties Bay, primarily a regional centre that supports the fisherman. Further north is the Cape Cross Seal Reserve, one of the largest breeding grounds of seals in the southern hemisphere, where thousands of Cape fur seals unfathomably decide to sit on the same overcrowded rock.

In the Skeleton Coast National Park proper, permits are needed for any stay longer than a transfer through to the interior. Staying overnight in the park offers the chance to experience complete isolation in this eerie and desolate environment.

Arriving on the Skeleton Coast

Driving from Swakopmund north on the C34 through the Dorob National Park, takes you through flat monotonous stony plains to Henties Bay. This road is a 'salt' road (a combination of brine and sand), not too dissimilar to a regular tarred road. It's generally in excellent condition though can get a little slippery in heavy mist. Motorists must have their headlights on even during daylight hours as visibility can be poor and mirage affects are common. From Henties Bay there are three different routes to explore. The easiest route is the D1918 inland, which passes close to the Klein Spitzkoppe (1572 m) and Gross Spitzkoppe (1784 m) before joining the B2 near Usakos. The other two routes will take you into some of Namibia's finest wilderness areas. Just north of the town, the C35 turns east into the heart of Damaraland; this is the road to Uis and the Brandberg (2573 m). Finally, you can follow the C34 along the coast. It is possible to drive as far north as Terrace Bay; once you have crossed the Ugab River you are in the Skeleton Coast National Park (southern section). To travel through the park on the C34 and then the C39, you need to pay entrance and vehicle fees at the gate. Both roads that lead inland from the coast go through a sparsely populated region; care should be taken when driving on these gravel and sand roads. If you have an accident or a breakdown you may have a long wait before the next vehicle comes along.

Dorob National Park (formerly the National West Coast Recreation Area) → *For listings, see pages 277-279. Colour map 1, C3.*

The Dorob National Park stretches from the northern boundary of the Namib-Naukluft Park to the Ugab River. It extends for around 200 km along the coast and covers an area of 16,400 sq km. The Ugab forms the southern boundary of the Skeleton Coast National Park. It was renamed in 2010 and the name simply means 'dry land'. Its proclamation is a key piece of the puzzle along Namibia's coast which now allows for the entire 1570-km coastline of the country to be protected under national park status. However this area is not subject to quite the same stringent controls as those that apply to areas of the Skeleton Coast National Park. The park is open all year round and there are no restrictions on when you can travel. For most visitors the only sight of interest is the seal colony at Cape Cross; the rest of the coastline is flat and monotonous, and most visitors come here for the fishing. If you are not heading to the Skeleton Coast National Park there is no point travelling beyond Cape Cross – shipwrecks such as the *Winston* are very disappointing and the Messum Crater can only be visited with a guide and a 4WD.

Henties Bay and the coast road → *Colour map 1, C3. Phone code: 064.*

Named after Major Hentie van der Merwe who started fishing here in 1929 (see box, opposite), this is the most northerly settlement of any note on the Namibian Atlantic seaboard and is 70 km (about an hour's drive) from Swakopmund. For much of the year it is just a quiet collection of bungalows on a windswept sand-blasted coast, with a resident community of about 5000. During the summer season it comes

Hentie's Bay

In 1929 Major Hentie van der Merwe, a motor dealer in Kalkveld, discovered a freshwater spring in an old delta of the Omaruru River while on a rhino hunt/expedition in the desert. He immediately fell in love with the place and returned there on his next December holiday and built himself a wooden shack from crates used for the importation of motor cars in those early years. For years it was his own private spot that he escaped to every December. Later, he started inviting his friends along who referred to it as Hentie's Bay, which eventually became Henties Bay as more people claimed their own little place amongst the dunes. In 1966 it was decided that the people must move out of the riverbed and 27 people were given land to the north and south of the dunes, either side of the riverbed. In 1967 the **De Duine Hotel** was built and after that the town started to develop.

to life and the population is doubled by visiting holiday-makers. Traditionally, the area has attracted Afrikaans speakers, either from the interior or from the Jo'burg/Pretoria areas, intent on some serious fishing. Apart from the splendid coastline and fine sandy beach, there is little to do, and the majority of international visitors are unlikely to find much of interest, unless it's solitude you want.

The very helpful **Henties Bay Tourism** ① *Nickey Iyambo Av, T064-501143, www.hentiesbaytourism.com, Mon-Fri 0900-1630, Sat 0900-1200*, is in a purpose-built building just after the right turn to Usakos. It has a coffee shop and arts and crafts for sale. If you are driving further north, make sure you fill up with petrol at Henties Bay, as well as drinking water and food. Beyond the petrol station is the post office on the corner of Pelican Street. A left here will take you to the seafront. The first main road to the left and north of the tourist office, Duineweg, leads to the best and oldest hotel in town, the De Duine Hotel (see box, above, and Where to stay, page 277). As you turn left, look out for Benguela Street on the left, where all the shops are. Opposite the hotel is a dramatic nine-hole **golf course** set in a valley leading down to the beach. It extends over a distance of 2.7 km and has very well-tended grass greens and tees while the fairways are virgin desert sand. Visitors can play for a minimal fee, but have to provide their own golf clubs. A round here will test your ability to cope with windy conditions.

There are two walking trails that start from town. The **Jakkalsputz Trail** (18 km) heads south either along the beach or the dune road, past some tidal pools which are visible at low tide, past Cape Farilhao where the ruins of an old lighthouse can be seen, to the Jakkalsputz camping site. The way back to Henties Bay further inland is through a wetlands area, where jackal may be spotted, and through the dunes. The **Omaruru River Trail** (20 km) goes north along the beach up to the mouth of the Omaruru River, then follows the river before turning back to town on an existing track through the desert where various species of lichen can be seen. Maps of these trails are available from the tourist office. If you are in a 4WD there are several routes in the region. Information and GPS coordinates are available at the tourist office.

Twitching for a tern

It has been estimated that more than 300,000 wading birds seasonally visit the Namib coast and most of the birds live along the coast since there are few areas of wetlands with fresh water inland. Some of the most popular birds are also those that are the easiest to identify: plovers, sandpipers, cormorants, flamingos and white pelicans. Further inland along the riverbeds you will come across birds that favour gravel plains and cliff faces: the augur buzzard, peregrine falcon, black eagle and rock kestrel have all been seen, and after a little rain the reed beds are home to a few weavers and warblers. The coast is also home to one of the rarest and smallest terns found in the world, the Damara tern (*Sterna balaenarum*), which favours the open coastline and sandy bays. In Namibia its range extends from Lüderitz to Walvis Bay and Swakopmund, and then further north along the Skeleton Coast to the Kunene River mouth. It has been estimated that the entire population consists of about 15,000 individuals, and 98% of these are found between the Orange and Kunene rivers; the remaining are found close by along the coast in South Africa and Angola. The Damara tern is only 23 cm long, with a white breast and a black head. In flight it is similar to a swallow. Such a small bird is not able to carry much food for the young so to limit the amount of flying they have to do they tend to nest close to the food supply. Their size also influences the more precise location of their nests. They are unable to defend their nests against jackals and hyenas, so to try and avoid predators they nest on the salt pans and the gravel plains up to 5 km inland. This is another reason for observing Namibia's off-road regulations, for once disturbed a breeding pair will abandon the chick.

The **Henties Bay Fish Festival** is held over a weekend either at the end of August or the beginning of September. It includes an angling competition, street fair, fish *braais*, live entertainment and the unfortunately named **Miss Fish Festival** beauty pageant. Contact the tourist office for more information and for recommended operators for fishing trips. ➸ *See What to do, page 279.*

Driving between Swakopmund and Henties Bay will quickly make you realize how repetitive and dull much of this coastline is, but once you get out of the vehicle and start to explore the dry rivers and the occasional salt pans on foot, the park can be enjoyed at a different level. The peace and solitude is amazing, the air is clean and fresh and at night the stars are like you've never seen them before. If this does not sound like fun then go no further north than Henties Bay, where you can take the C35 and head inland.

Cape Cross Seal Reserve → *Colour map 1, C3.*
ⓘ *55 km north of Henties Bay just off the C34, T064-501143, daily Dec-Jun 0800-1700, Jul-Nov 1000-1700, N$80, children (under 16) free, N$10 car. The entrance gate is 3 km from the junction where there is an office at which you pay entry fees and can pick*

up some leaflets. The colony is located just beyond the crosses, a short drive from the entrance. Facilities include a car park and picnic site with toilets, information boards. A 200-m walkway suitable for wheelchairs has been constructed out of recycled plastic.

Pick up any tour brochure in Swakopmund and you will see advertisements for trips to Cape Cross. There are 23 breeding colonies of Cape fur seals along the coast of southwestern Africa, of which 16 are in Namibia and Cape Cross is the largest and best known. It is also the most easily visited. The second largest colony covers Wolf Bay, Atlas Bay and Long Island, south of Lüderitz (see page 343). Most of the other colonies are offshore on small islands.

In addition to its seal colony, the reserve has had an interesting history. In 1485 the Portuguese navigator Diego Cão landed at Cape Cross. This was the furthest any European had travelled down the coast of Africa, and to mark the event he erected a stone cross on the isolated stony headland, inscribing it thus: "Since the creation of the world 6684 years have passed and since the birth of Christ, 1484 years and so the Illustrious Don John has ordered this pillar to be erected here by Diego Cão, his knight." Diego Cão died at Cape Cross and was buried in some high ground close by. His original cross was later removed and taken to Berlin by the Oceanographical Museum. In 1974 the whole area was landscaped and a couple of replica crosses now stand amongst the rocks.

As you walk to the shoreline from the office you pass a small graveyard, which dates from the turn of the 19th century. Between 1899 and 1903 there was a small thriving community at Cape Cross, which was involved in the collection of guano from salt pans on nearby islands. The records show that 124 people died and were buried here. Around 1900 this was a busy little port that was even served by a railway. The guano industry was so prosperous that a 16-km railway track was laid across the salt pan to facilitate its collection. In its heyday there were steam locomotives working here.

The Cape fur seal (*Arctocephalus pusillus pusillus*) is the largest of the world's nine species of fur seals and is only found on the coast of Africa from southern Angola, down Namibia's coastline and as far south as Algoa Bay in South Africa. Estimates of the number of seals at Cape Cross vary between 80,000 and as many as 250,000 during the breeding season (November/December). The bulls, which can weigh up to 360 kg, start to arrive here in October to claim the land for their cows. Some 90% of seal pups are born over a 34-day period in November and December. The female produces a single pup that begins suckling immediately after birth. Approximately a week later when a bond has been established between mother and pup, the mother will go into the sea to feed. When she returns she will bark for her pup who responds by bleating until they find each other again, usually by detecting scents. The whole scene during the birth of the young pups in November and December can be quite distressing as many of the newly born seals get crushed by adults, others drown, and then there is always the threat posed by the predators, jackals and hyenas that come to the colony to nab lone pups. It also has to be one of the smelliest places on earth – think pungent rotting fish/flesh – and it really is a relief to get away again after having taken in the sight of tens of thousands of seals basking on the rocks or surfing amongst the waves.

Before or after visiting the seals, be sure to stop in at the **Cape Cross Lodge**, 4 km north of the seal reserve (see Where to stay, page 277), which has a fascinating museum all about Cape Cross and a good restaurant for lunch or coffee. About 33 km north of Cape Cross the salt road divides in two. The salt road (C34) follows the coastline towards the campsite at Mile 108, while the side road (D2303) turns inland and then joins the D2342, the back road to Uis. These roads are heavily corrugated and best driven in a 4WD.

Skeleton Coast National Park → *For listings, see pages 277-279. Colour map 1, B2.*

ⓘ *Day visitors are only allowed in the park between sunrise and sunset. Permits are available at the 2 entry gates: the Ugab River in the south and Springbokwasser in the east, N$80, children (under 16) free, N$10 car.*

The Skeleton Coast is one of the finest and most unusual coastal wildernesses in the world and it protects about one-third of Namibia's coastline. It stretches for approximately 500 km between the Ugab River in the south and the mouth of the Kunene River in the north, marking the border with Angola. The strong currents and swirling fogs of this Atlantic coastline have long been a hazard to shipping and when the term Skeleton Coast was first applied in 1933 by newspaperman Sam Davis, the name stuck. Davis had been reporting on the search for a Swiss airman, Carl Nauer, whose plane had disappeared along the coast while trying to break the Cape Town to London solo air record. No trace was ever found. Today it is the elements previously responsible for so much loss of life – the desert, wide-open space, isolation and solitude – that attract the majority of visitors.

Arriving in Skeleton Coast National Park

The park can be entered in the south, from the Dorob National Park, or in the east from Damaraland. Driving through the park is one-way. You cannot leave and depart through the same gate unless you are staying overnight. Wherever you enter, you must make sure there are sufficient hours of daylight to either cross the park between the two gates or reach your camp at **Terrace Bay** or **Torra Bay**. The southern gate, by the Ugab River, is known as **Ugabmund** and is 207 km north of Swakopmund; it is a further 109 km to the camp at Torra Bay and 156 km to Terrace Bay, while it is 138 km from Ugabmund to the eastern gate, **Springbokwasser**. To get to either the camps or Springbokwasser, you need to be at Ugabmund by 1500. The same applies if coming in the opposite direction. From Springbokwasser it is 50 km to Torra Bay, 95 km to Terrace Bay, and again 138 km to Ugabmund. Day visitors are not permitted to Terrace Bay or Torra Bay and if you are staying overnight you will need to show proof of your reservation at the gate. From Springbokwasser it is 169 km to Khorixas on the C39, or you can veer off north before then on to the C43 to Palmwag, 98 km from Springbokwasser.

The quality of the road heading inland from the gate is not as good as the coast road. It features sharp gravel so ensure you have a spare tyre. Fill up with fuel at Henties Bay, Khorixas or Palmwag. There is a petrol station at Terrace Bay but only for the use of overnight guests.

The Skeleton Coast

Möwe Bay
Lighthouse
To ② (fly-in only)
◆ Skeleton Coast
Wilderness
Hoanib

(Limited access)
Dunes
Hunkab
Control Gate
Seal Beach
Terrace Bay 6

D2302
Uniab River
Delta
Uniab
Atlantic
1977
Torra Bay
Torra Bay
(Open Dec
& Jan only)
Henrietta
1968
Springbokwasser
Gate
C39
C39
Koichab
C34
Bergsig
Montrose II
1973
Salt
Pans
Luanda
1969
Huab
Atlantic
Pride
Toscanini Diamond Mine
Oil Rig
Sand
Dunes
Ambrose
Bay
Gravel Plains
South West
Sea - 1976
Skeleton Coast
National Park
Park Boundary
Durissa Bay
Ugab
Hike
Ugabmund Gate
Brandberg West
Winston
1970
Salt Pans
Mile 108
D2303
D2342
Messum
Crater
Bocock's Bay
Horing Bay
Dorob
National
Park
Cape Cross
Cape Cross
Seal reserve
Mile 72
C35
Omaruru
Henties Bay
D1918
Cape
Farilhao
Jakkalspütz
Lichen
Fields
Rock
Bay
C34
20 km
20 miles
Saltworks
Pelican
Point
Walvis
Bay
Swakopmund
Rössing
Uranium Mine
Khan

To Palmwag & Sesfontein
To Twyfelfontein & Khorixas
To Uis & Khorixas
To Spitzkoppe
To Windhoek

Where to stay 🛏
Cape Cross Lodge
& Camping 1
De Duine 3
Eagle Holiday Flats

Fisherman's Guest House 5
Hoanib Skeleton Coast
Camp 2
Terrace Bay 6

There are only three places to stay within the national park: Terrace Bay, Torra Bay and the upmarket camp run by **Wilderness Safaris** in the far north that can only be reached by plane (see page 278). Accommodation at Terrace Bay is in simple chalets. Torra Bay is a basic campsite only open December to January and you will need to bring everything with you (even the water for the showers has to be trucked in). Nevertheless, during the Christmas period these get booked up quickly, mostly by local fishermen. In order to get the most out of the park it is worth making the arduous journey as far north as Terrace Bay.

As in Swakopmund, it never gets too hot thanks to the cooling influence of the ocean, but during the winter months it can get cold at night.

Background

For many people the Skeleton Coast is synonymous with shipwrecks – just about every photograph promoting the wild coastline will include a rusting, beached hull. The Portuguese used to call the area the 'Sands of Hell' and before the days of modern communications and transport this 1600-km coastline represented a real threat to shipping. Sailors knew that if they did survive a wrecked ship then their problems had only just begun. The land behind them was a dry desert, and there were very few known natural sources of drinking water. The few places that did occasionally have drinking water (the riverbeds) were home to wild animals such as lion, leopard and elephant, which in turn represented another threat to the sailors' lives. A third factor that added to the dangers for survivors was the remoteness. Before 1893, when the first settlers arrived at Swakopmund, there was nothing for more than 1000 km of coastline. Unfortunately the most spectacular wrecks are all found in the areas which are closed to the public in the far north. A little background to some of the wrecks that can be seen has been included in the route description below.

Wildlife and vegetation

Between Ugabmund and Terrace Bay the coastal road crosses four westward flowing rivers: the Ugab, Huab, Koichab and Uniab. These rivers only flow when sufficient rain has fallen in the interior, and even then they only flow for a short period. For the rest of the year they represent long narrow oases that are home to migratory birds, animals and the few plants that can flourish in drought conditions.

The animals that may be seen in the park have all adapted in different ways to overcome some of the problems the desert creates. The smaller species such as genet, caracal, baboon, springbok, jackal and brown hyena live in the desert all year round; the larger animals, such as black rhino, elephant and lion, tend to migrate along the channels in search of food and water. The lion may well no longer occur along the coast, but when they were roaming the beaches they were known to have fed upon Cape cormorants, seals and the odd stranded whale. Gemsbok, kudu and zebra are occasionally seen inland in the mountainous regions; at the coast, the Uniab Delta is a good location for viewing gemsbok. During low tide, black-backed jackals can be seen on the beach scavenging on dead birds, fish and seals. There is stiff competition for scraps among the hyena, ghost crabs, crows and gulls.

Like much of the wildlife, most of the plants growing in the park occur in the four major riverbeds that dissect the park. Two of the most common shrubs are the dollar bush (*Zygophyllum stapfii*) and brakspekbos (*Zygophyllum simplex*), both of which can be found in the riverbeds. The former is a semi-deciduous shrub with small leaves shaped like a 'dollar' coin. It will only grow where there is some groundwater as it has not adapted to make use of the sea mist. Brakspekbos, a food source for the black rhino, can be recognized by looking for an off-green carpet in a shallow depression where rainwater would drain.

The only other vegetation you are likely to come across is lichen – of which there is an amazing variety. The bright orange lichens, which cling to rock outcrops facing the ocean, add a welcome splash of colour to the grey landscape. More than 100 different species have been recorded in the Skeleton Coast National Park, all dependent upon the coastal fog for moisture; in the moist air the plants become soft and many change colour.

Durissa Bay North → *Colour map 1, C2.*

As you approach the southern entrance to the Skeleton Coast National Park there is a signpost for the wrecked fishing boat, *Winston*. Do not drive on the salt pans; despite their dry appearance, it is easy to get stuck here. The boundary between the Dorob National Park and the Skeleton Coast National Park is marked by the Ugab River, which flows into Durissa Bay. The Ugab is one of Namibia's major rivers, rising over 500 km inland, east of Outjo; after good rains it is an important source of water in Damaraland. A skull and crossbones adorns the gate by the Ugabmund park office and this is a good spot to have your photo taken.

As you cross the wide river, notice the variety of trees and shrubs growing in the sandy bed. Some of the well-established plants are stunted since they have had to survive in windswept conditions with long periods of moisture stress. Whenever you approach these riverbeds try to be as quiet as possible as there is always a chance of seeing a small herd of springbok resting in the shade or a shy family of kudu browsing the acacia trees.

Once across the river the salt road stays close to shore. One of the first shipwrecks you see is the *South West Sea*, wrecked in 1976. Just after you have crossed the Huab River there is a signpost indicating an old oil rig. While you will see the remains of various mining ventures along the coast, this is the only case of oil exploration. In the 1960s, Ben du Preez went ahead and erected the rig despite numerous warnings that the scheme was unlikely to succeed. Today the rusty rig lies on its side providing the perfect nesting area for a breeding colony of Cape cormorants. During the September to March breeding season visitors are asked to stay in the car park so as not to disturb the birds. On the beach you can visit the wreck of the fishing schooner, *Atlantic Pride*.

About 50 km from the park entrance you reach the point marked **Toscanini** on most maps. This is the site of a derelict diamond mine – only a few small diamonds were ever found. Today the legacy of the operations are a few cement slabs which acted as foundations for the buildings and the ruins of the sorting plant. There are a couple more wrecks in the ocean here, but there is little to see.

Soon after crossing the Koichab River, which has more sand than vegetation, there is a junction in the road. This is the only other access road for the Skeleton Coast National Park, the C39. A right here leads to Springbokwasser Gate, 40 km inland. There are some fine sand dunes along this stretch of road as well as some welwitschia plants growing in the dry riverbeds.

Torra Bay → *Colour map 1, B2.*

Continuing north on the salt road you reach the seasonal fishing resort, Torra Bay. In the 16th century, Portuguese sailors named it 'Dark Hill' after the dark-capped hills that they could see while they were looking for fresh water. Anyone staying here must be totally self-sufficient, though during the holiday season petrol and basic groceries are available. Aside from the solitude, the great attraction of this site is the excellent fishing. Despite restrictions, there has been extensive damage caused by vehicles on the beaches. During the few months the camp is open it is necessary to book in advance (see Where to stay, page 278).

Uniab River Delta → *Colour map 1, B2.*

Between the temporary camp at Torra Bay and the permanent camp at Terrace Bay is one of the most interesting attractions in the southern part of the Skeleton Coast National Park, the Uniab River Delta. The river has split into five main channels plus a number of reed-ringed pools that are formed by seepage from the riverbed. After good rains this is the perfect spot for birders. There are a number of walks in the delta, including a trail to a waterfall and a small canyon, which lie between the road and the beach. Check with the park authorities on the current situation as the amount of rainfall and the size of the flood can change the lie of the land between seasons. If you hear that there is water here, then it is well worth the drive. Within the delta are several hides and parking spaces, each with a different view of the system. Look out for the shipwreck, *Atlantic*, at the rivermouth.

Terrace Bay → *Colour map 1, B2.*

Having enjoyed the delta it is a short drive to the final destination, Terrace Bay. The camp and all the outbuildings were once part of the mining operation owned by Ben du Preez. When the company was declared bankrupt, the state inherited all the facilities at the camp. There is a grocery shop with basic supplies and petrol is also available. The camp is built next to an old mine dump. There is an airstrip to the north of the complex. Visitors to the park are allowed to drive a further 14 km along the coast to **Seal Beach**, the absolute northern limit for private visitors. At this point you are more than 380 km from Swakopmund, in the heart of the Skeleton Coast National Park.

Skeleton Coast wilderness

When reading about Namibia's desert from Oranjemund to the Angolan border, a recurrent theme is fragility of the desert environment and the need to control access to the most sensitive areas. When the Skeleton Coast National Park was proclaimed in 1967 the park was divided into two zones, each covering about 800,000 ha. The southern zone is the 210-km-long coastal strip between the Ugab River in the south and the Hoanib River in the north. The boundary of the park extends no more than 40 km inland. Access to the northern zone is tightly controlled and, for the tourist, limited to those who join the exclusive fly-in safaris organized by the sole concessionaire in Windhoek (see page 79).

The northern section of the park extends from the Hoanib River to the Kunene River, which forms the border with Angola – a distance of 290 km. This section of the national park is managed as a wilderness area and is sometimes referred to as the Skeleton Coast Wilderness. While the government has chosen to allow one private operator, **Wilderness Safaris** (see page 42) access to this area, there are still tight controls in place on how the operation must be run in order to guarantee minimal environmental impact. Access to the northern section is limited to the area between the Hoarusib and Nadas rivers, a strip of coastline measuring about 90 km long by 30 km wide.

For hotel and restaurant price codes and other relevant information, see pages 21-28.

● Where to stay

Dorob National Park (formerly the National West Coast Recreation Area) *p268, map p273*

Between Swakopmund and the Skeleton Coast National Park there are 3 very basic campsites: **Jakkalspütz**, 12 km south of Henties Bay; **Mile 72**, 30 km north of Henties Bay; and **Mile 108**, 90 km north of Henties Bay. Designed to serve the needs of the angler more than the holidaymaker, each is in a grim and barren location with very few facilities (they are also not fenced, so security may be an issue). Each has communal toilets and showers and sheltered eating (and fish cleaning) areas. No booking is required though you may want to contact the management, **Tungeni Africa Investments**, in Windhoek, T061-400205. Rates are N$100 per person, children (under 7) free, N$5 per shower and N$30 per car.

Henties Bay *p268, map p273*

Most of the accommodation consists of holiday flats and houses; the tourist office (see page 269) is the best place to contact for information. They get booked months in advance over the peak Christmas period, but for the remainder of the year there should be no difficulty in finding somewhere to stay unless you happen to coincide with a fishing tournament. Nevertheless, the limited accommodation in Henties Bay is unlikely to appeal to overseas visitors and there are far superior choices in Swakopmund.

$$ Fisherman's Guest House, AuasSt, T0814-536324, www.huntandfishnamibia.com/wordpress. Tidy and neat lodge 200 m from the beach, 9 modern rooms with DSTV in a bright yellow building, pleasant restaurant and bar, delicious dinners (the Belgian owner is a chef), book in advance before 1600, can also provide packed breakfasts and lunches for early departures and fishermen.

$ De Duine Hotel, 34 Duine Rd, T064-500001, www.deduinehotel.com. The first hotel in town (see box, page 269) with clear views across the Atlantic from its high perch, 20 motel-style rooms with DSTV and room service, the restaurant is known for its reasonable seafood, attached bar with slot machines and oddly shaped pool tables, and there's a swimming pool and squash court. Quality has waned in recent years but new owners are in the throes of planning a refurbishment.

$ Eagle Holiday Flats & Backpackers, 175 Jakkalspütz Rd, T064-500032, www.eagleholiday.com. Whitewashed self-catering flats and chalets well-equipped for 4 with a fridge/freezer (for fish) and TV, plus twin and triple backpacker rooms with showers and there's a communal kitchen and *braai*. A bit stark but fine for an overnight stop, and part of the **Eagle Shopping Centre** complex where there is a supermarket, bakery, bottle store and Total petrol station.

Cape Cross Seal Reserve *p270, map p273*

$$$ Cape Cross Lodge & Camping, 4 km north of the seal reserve, T064-694012, www.capecross.org. Hotel in Cape Dutch style situated on the beach just north of the seal colony (but out of the 'smell zone'), with 20 rooms, all with balconies and sea views, stylish and modern throughout, great restaurant specializing in seafood (of course), plus a bar with veranda. The rate includes breakfast and dinner.

The **campsite ($)** has 21 sites with lights, power points and a sink, good ablutions, small shop selling basic groceries, fresh bread, ice and *braai* packs, and it has its own bar with pool table. If not staying you can stop here for lunch or coffee and cake before or after visiting the seals; well worth it as the lodge also has its own excellent little museum all about Cape Cross.

Skeleton Coast National Park *p272, map p273*

There are only 3 places to stay within the park and all accommodation, even camping at Torra Bay, must be booked in advance.

$$$$ Hoanib Skeleton Coast Camp, **Wilderness Safaris**, reservations Johannesburg T+27 (0)11-807 1800, www.wilderness-safaris.com. The only concessionaire permitted to run accommodation in the restricted northern area of the park, the camp is located on the Hoanib River, about 20 km inland from the coast, only accessible by plane. 8 super-luxury tents on raised wooden platforms, lovely decor using items found locally, dining room, lounge and bar. With luck you will see a wide range of desert-dwelling wildlife such as springbok, gemsbok, desert elephant and rhino, brown hyena, jackal, ostrich and, if you are extremely lucky, lion. The day starts with breakfast in camp and then a day out exploring on foot, by vehicle, in hides, and by air before returning to camp for sundowner and dinner. All-inclusive rates start from N$6000 per person.

$$ Terrace Bay, 316 km north of Henties Bay, **Namibia Wildlife Resorts (NWR)**, **Windhoek**, T061-285 7200, www.nwr. com.na. Clearly aimed at anglers and the chances of catching a variety of species of fish is excellent, though you need to bring all equipment and fishing permits are required. Walking along the beach and exploring the Uniab River Delta are the only other activities. 20 comfortable en suite twin rooms, plus 2 self-catering **beach chalets ($$$)** sleeping 3-10, restaurant, bar, freezer space for anglers, a small shop selling basic groceries, booze and *braai* meat and electricity is supplied by a generator.

$ Torra Bay, 265 km north of Henties Bay, **Namibia Wildlife Resorts (NWR)**, Windhoek, T061-285 7200, www.nwr. com.na. Only open Dec and Jan. Torra Bay is a very basic campsite again primarily aimed at anglers – you will need to bring everything with you, even the water for the showers has to be trucked in. The small shop sells firewood and a few basic goods and petrol is available.

❷ Restaurants

Henties Bay *p268*

As well as the restaurants in town, there are also a number of early morning/late-night takeaways and petrol station shops that sell snacks like sandwiches and pies, and drinks including beer.

$$ De Duine Hotel (see Where to stay, above). Daily 0800-2130. Reasonably priced food, steaks and grills, well known for its seafood and a good place to try oysters and crayfish in season. There's also a bar with pool tables.

$$-$ Fishy Corner, 19 Benguela St, next to the Spar complex, T064-501059. Tue-Sun 1100-2130. Small seafood restaurant (as the name suggests), with

marine decor and photos of local anglers on the walls, pine tables and chairs, serving local catches like kabeljou and steenbras, plus generous seafood platters and a good Greek salad and mussel soup. Also does takeaway fish and chips.
$ Skubbebar, Karas St, T0813-67818. Mon-Sat 1000-2200, Sun 1100-2100. Informal fisherman's bar and restaurant attached to a tackle shop where you can hire fishing rods and reels and buy bait, and usefully also has a car wash (to get the salt off) and a fish cleaning area. Food includes fish and chips and they are well known for their slow-cooked *eisbein*, plus beers and coffees, they can put together packed lunches.

O Shopping

Henties Bay *p268*
Henties Bay Spar Complex, Benguela St. Mon-Fri 0800-1800, Sat 0800-1300. Has a supermarket with bakery, butcher and bottle shop, sells ice, firewood and bait and there's also an ATM, pharmacy and a coin-operated laundry.

O What to do

Henties Bay *p268*
Fishing
Edible fish species most frequently caught include cob (kabeljou), West Coast steenbras, galjoen and blacktail.

The Skeleton Coast is also famous for excellent shark fishing, which include the copper shark and the spotted gully-shark. Sharks are fished on a tag-and-release system. Both these operators offer guided beach and surf angling and boat fishing. A day's fishing costs from around N$800 per person and includes permits, tackle, bait, and if desired, cleaning, freezing and packing of fish.
Henties Bay Angling Tours, T064-500903, www.hentiesbayanglingtours.com.
Sea Ace Adventure Angling, T064-500545, www.seaace.com.na.

O Directory

Henties Bay *p268*
Banks There are branches of **Bank Windhoek** and **Standard Bank**, on Jakkalsputz Rd, both with ATMs. This is the last stop for a bank for some distance if you are travelling away from Swakopmund. The next banks are located in Omaruru or Khorixas. **Fishing permits** The Ministry of Fisheries and Marine Resources has an office to the north of town off Nickey Iyambo Rd, T064-500320. Mon-Fri 0800-1300, 1400-1700, Sat-Sun 0800-1300. This is where fishing permits can be bought (you will also need these for fishing at Terrace and Torra Bay) **Mechanical services** Grobler Motors, Jakkelsputz Rd, T064-501211, repairs and breakdown service.

The Hinterland

There are several routes from Windhoek to the coast. The most straightforward is to take the main B2 via Okahandja, Karibib and Usakos to Swakopmund, which is 366 km and will take four to five hours. The turn-off north to Spitzkoppe is on the B2 approximately 120 km before Swakopmund. More interesting is to explore the hinterland and to travel via one of the three passes – the Bosua, Ushoogte or Gamsberg – and stop along the way to enjoy the spectacular views. Of the three, the Bosua is the quickest and provides the opportunity to stop and see the ruins of Liebig Haus and Von François Fort, while the Gamsberg is certainly the most dramatic.

Three Passes → *For listings, see pages 286-290.*

All three routes – via the Bosua, Ushoogte or Gamsberg Pass – are gravel roads without any petrol stations or shops along the way. Furthermore, they each include some extremely steep sections. If there has been heavy rain you may have difficulty negotiating certain sections in a heavily loaded, low-slung saloon car.

The **Khomas Hochland** is the rugged, upland area, lying between 1750 m and 2000 m, which joins the central highland plateau with the escarpment, where the land falls dramatically away to the gravel plains of the central Namib. The surface of the Hochland was laid down in Karoo times some 180-300 million years ago; subsequent erosion has carved out the sharp ridges and rolling hills characteristic of the area.

Bosua Pass → *Colour map 1, C5.*
The distance from Windhoek to Swakopmund via the C28 and the Bosua Pass is 325 km; shorter than the B2 but it will take longer; about five to six hours. Following the C28 out of Windhoek, just past the **Sun Karros Daan Viljoen Resort** (see page 92), the tar road turns to gravel about 25 km west of Windhoek. A further 16 km down the road is the abandoned **Liebig House**, built in 1912 for Dr R Hartig, director of a farming consortium, Liebig's Fleischextrakt Kompanie. This double-storey house must once have been a splendid place to live, with its fountain in the main downstairs room and fine views over the surrounding rolling highlands. On a hill to the right about 10 km further on lie the ruins of **Von François Fort** named after the 'founder' of Windhoek. The fort was one of a number of military outposts built after Von François established his headquarters in Windhoek, and was designed to protect the route between Windhoek and Swakopmund. It was, however, later turned into a **Trockenposten**, or 'drying-out post', for alcoholic German soldiers.

Some 180 km west of Windhoek, you eventually get to the pass itself, which has a 1:5 descent down to the gravel plains of the Namib and is not suitable for trailers or caravans. Because the pass is so steep, it is probably better to drive it from east to west, although the steepest part has been tarred. Some 25 km past the pass, you have the option of either driving a further 150 km on the C28 to Swakopmund, or turning south on a small farm road to the D1982 and returning to Windhoek via the Ushoogte Pass (below). West of here, the C28 heads straight as an arrow through the bleak plains of the Namib to Swakopmund.

The Hinterland

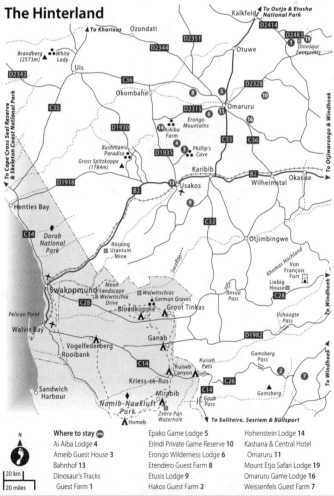

N

20 km
20 miles

| Where to stay |
| Ai Aiba Lodge **4** |
| Ameib Guest House **3** |
| Bahnhof **13** |
| Dinosaur's Tracks |
| Guest Farm **1** |

Epako Game Lodge **5**
Erindi Private Game Reserve **10**
Erongo Wilderness Lodge **6**
Etendero Guest Farm **8**
Etusis Lodge **9**
Hakos Guest Farm **2**

Hohenstein Lodge **14**
Kashana & Central Hotel
  Omaruru **11**
Mount Etjo Safari Lodge **19**
Omaruru Game Lodge **16**
Weissenfels Guest Farm **7**

Ushoogte Pass → *Colour map 1, C5.*

This route via the Ushoogte Pass (also known as the Us Pass) from Windhoek to Walvis Bay is the shortest; 309 km/five hours, but it is the least scenic. In Windhoek, take the main road towards the University of Namibia (UNAM) and ignore the turn-off south towards Rehoboth. Continue past the university out of town on the C26 for 32 km until the road branches right onto the D1982. This road continues to the 1:10 Ushoogte Pass before eventually joining the main C14 highway to Walvis Bay.

Gamsberg Pass → *Colour map 3, A2.*

At some 2330 m high, the Gamsberg Pass is Namibia's highest and longest mountain pass – here the C26 tumbles off the central plateau and is probably the most popular of the three passes and certainly offers spectacular scenery. It is 354 km from Windhoek to Walvis Bay along this route, which again should take five to six hours. The name is a combination of the Nama word *gan* meaning 'flat' and the German *berg* meaning 'mountain', and refers to the flat-topped Gamsberg Mountain (2350 m) which dominates the view and is often referred to as Namibia's 'Table Mountain'. This 1000-million-year-old granite mountain rises 500 m above the surrounding highlands and has survived further erosion thanks to a sandstone cap formed about 200 million years ago when most of this area was covered by an inland sea. It is worth stopping at the top of the pass to enjoy the views of the surrounding hills and to contemplate the snaking descent towards the desert floor. Before reaching the Namib, however, the road must still make its way through the Kuiseb Pass (see Kuiseb Canyon, page 294) after which it joins the C14 for the final 110-km stretch to Walvis Bay.

Usakos → *For listings, see pages 286-290. Colour map 1, C4. Phone code: 064.*

The first town east of the Namib Desert on the main B2 road, 146 km from Swakopmund, Usakos lies on the southern bank of the Khan River nestled in the last hills before the Namib at the edge of a vast expanse of nothingness. In Damara, the name in fact means 'grab the heel' in reference to this geological location. The town originally developed around the railway workshops which were built to service the narrow-gauge Otavi line, completed in 1906. Until 1960, the town prospered but when the old steam locomotives were replaced by diesel engines it lapsed into its present sleepy state.

Nowadays the town's main role is one of service centre for vehicles between Swakopmund/Walvis Bay and Windhoek. It's worth stopping for refreshment here at either the Shell petrol station or the **Namib Wüste Farmstall**, although while there is a decent small hotel in town, there doesn't seem any reason to stay here. As a reminder of the town's heyday, *Locomotive No 40* stands in front of the railway station, one of three Henschel steam trains built in Germany for the colony's narrow-gauge railway.

Erongo Mountains → *Colour map 1, C4.*

The Erongo Massif of towering granite mountains is easily visible about 40 km north of Usakos and Karibib. They lie in the 200,000-ha **Erongo Mountain Nature Conservancy**, established to protect a number of endemic or near-endemic species. These include the Angolan dwarf python, white-tailed shrike and Hartlaub's francolin. Like the Brandberg and Spitzkoppe inselberg, the Erongo Mountain is the remnant of an ancient volcano. A further attraction is the Phillip's Cave national monument (see below), containing a number of San (Bushmen) paintings, first made famous by the pre-historian Abbé Breuil. Although most of the range is only accessible by 4WD, it is possible to visit the **Ameib Guest Farm** (see Where to stay, page 287), and take tours to the following sights and rock formations from there.

Phillip's Cave → *Colour map 1, C4.*
The cave is a short drive from **Ameib Guest Farm**, followed by a 25-minute walk over a series of low hills. It is in fact an overhang, rather than a cave, on one of the highest hills in the area and offers excellent views over surrounding countryside, making it easy to see why the San (Bushmen) used this place. There are numerous paintings of the San (Bushmen) themselves, as well as buffalo and the famous white elephant. It is named after Emil Phillip who owned the farm when the cave was discovered.

Bull's Party and **Stone Elephant Head** are two sites with interesting rock formations, in particular the 'balancing' rocks at the Bull's Head.

Karibib → *For listings, see pages 286-290. Colour map 1, C5. Phone code: 064.*

Just over 30 km east of Usakos, this tiny bustling town lies almost exactly halfway between Windhoek and Swakopmund on the B2. Although most people zip through on their way to and from the coast, there is more to the town than first meets the eye. There are a number of fine old colonial buildings on the main street, the Navachab Gold Mine just southwest of town and the internationally reputed Marmorwerke, or marble works, lying to the north of the town, though the latter two are not open to the public.

In the early years of the 20th century, the train between Windhoek and Swakopmund only travelled during the daytime, so passengers needed hotels for the overnight stop in Karibib. The present-day **bakery**, on the left-hand side coming from Okahandja, was one of these hotels; it survived until 1950 when it was converted into a bakery. The **Rösemann Building**, further down the road, was built in 1900 and the façade has remained virtually unchanged since. Originally the headquarters of the trading firm Rösemann and Kronewitter, it was later converted into a hotel. The granite building that resembles a church, was in fact used by a local merchant, George Woll, as both his shop and living quarters. The **Christuskirche**, made partially of marble from the nearby marble works, dates back to 1910.

Out of town, the **Marmorwerke** was started in 1904 and produces high-quality marble, considered to be the hardest in the world. About 100 tonnes of marble is quarried each month. This is first cut up into blocks and then processed into floor and bathroom tiles, ornaments and tombstones. It is hard to believe, but marble from Karibib is exported to Italy. The **Navachab Gold Mine**, lying southwest of town, was started in 1987, two years after gold was discovered on Navachab Farm. The gold is actually of quite low quality, but it is Namibia's only gold mine and today is operated by AngloGold Ashanti who employ about 600 people in Karibib. North of the town is the location of the (inactive) Karibib Airport with its 2600-m asphalt runway, parallel paved taxiways and apron, but oddly not a single airport building. It was built and used during the South African Air Force days, but was never used again after Namibia's Independence in 1990.

Omaruru → *For listings, see pages 286-290. Colour map 1, C5. Phone code: 064.*

The C33 tar road heads due north from just outside Karibib and 66 km later arrives at the small, sleepy, historical town of Omaruru. Set in the heart of game- and dairy-farm country, the town is surrounded by an impressive array of mountains, the most prominent being the Oruwe or Omaruru *koppie* southeast of town. Omaruru is renowned in Namibia these days for having one of the country's few vineyards, the Kristall Kellerei, and is a centre of mineral production and trading. It's location on the C36 makes it a logical stopover when heading to Uis and the Brandberg and to Khorixas.

Background

The area around the town has been home both to humans and game for thousands of years, evident from the numerous sites of San (Bushmen) art found here. The first Europeans reached the area in 1851, but it was only after the missionary, Gottlieb Viehe, arrived in 1870 that the town was 'officially' founded. The name is derived from the Herero 'omaere omaruru', meaning 'bitter curd', which is apparently how milk tasted after cattle had grazed on one particular local bush. In 1858, Charles Andersson, attracted by the area's plentiful game, established a hunting camp on the banks of the Omaruru River. In 1870, the hunter Axel Eriksson and brewer Anders Ohissen formed a partnership to exploit the game and by 1880 they had succeeded in wiping out all the elephant, rhino, lion and giraffe that had once lived in the area. Throughout the 1880s, Omaruru was a focal point for Herero-Nama battles and, as part of the consolidation of German rule in Namibia, a garrison was stationed here at the end of 1894. The town started to grow and by the end of 1896 Omaruru had the largest population of European settlers in Namibia. However, the great rinderpest epidemic of 1897 wiped out the last remaining game in the area as well as taking a heavy toll on the settlers' cattle; many were forced to leave the area. But the military garrison continued to grow and a new barracks and sick bay were completed by 1901. In 1904 the Herero rose up against the German occupiers and the town was besieged. At the time the military commander, Captain Franke, was away in the south helping to put down the Bondelswart uprising. Nevertheless, he marched 900 km in 20 days and broke the siege by leading a cavalry charge, thereby defeating the Herero.

Places in Omaruru

Franke Tower, on the southern bank of the Omaruru River, was built in 1907 to commemorate Franke's victory over the Herero. It was officially opened in 1908 and declared a national monument in 1963, and although it offers a good view over the town from the top, it's kept locked.

The **Mission House**, the oldest building in Omaruru, now serves as the town **museum** ① *collect the key from the Municipality building, Wilhelm Zeraua St, T064-570277*, focusing on the early history of the area. Made from clay bricks and featuring a cow-dung roof and low (1.75-m) doors, the house was built by missionary Gottleib Viehe and completed in 1872, and was where he completed the first translation of the gospel into Oshiherero. Later the house served as a temporary military post and a meeting place between Herero and German leaders. Until recently, it was neglected with graffiti on the walls and broken windows, but in 2010 the Municipality partially restored it, and it now holds additional temporary art exhibitions.

The **Kristall Kellerei** ① *4 km from town on the D2328, T064-570083, www.kristallkellerei.com, Mon-Fri 0800-1500, Sat 0900-1300, book ahead*, the only vineyard operating in Namibia, is certainly worth a visit before you leave town. Helmut Kluge planted 4 ha of Colombard and Ruby Cabernet vines in 1990 and since 1996 perfected his Colombard white (to which oak chips are added) and Ruby Cabernet red wine. In 2008, Micheal and Katrin Weder acquired the winery and they now also distil grapes to make brandy. Some 4000-6000 litres of wine are produced each year, split equally between white and red. A few select lodges and guesthouses sell the wine. Bottling (into 500 ml bottles) takes place every August. Wine tours are conducted personally throughout the year, each one ending with a tasting accompanied by a cheese platter. Also worth a taste are the various schnapps (lemon, prickly pear and wine yeast).

Ai Aiba Farm rock art

Ai Aiba Farm, 52 km west of Omaruru on the D2315 (follow signs), is said to have one of the largest collections of rock paintings in Namibia. Spread over an area of 2000 ha are a host of rock paintings depicting both humans and animals, as well as a range of Stone Age tools and jewellery which have been left in their original spots. There are daily guided walks and 4WD trips intended to give visitors a real insight into the paintings and tools and to ensure the preservation of the sites. Bookings should be made in advance through the **Ai Aiba Lodge** (see Where to stay, page 288).

Kalkfeld → *For listings, see pages 286-290. Colour map 1, B5. Phone code: 067.*

Kalkfeld is simply a staging post on the C33 between Omaruru and Otjiwarongo for those looking for the **dinosaur footprints**. The village has fuel station (not 24-hour), a small general and bottle store, a post office and police station.

About 150 to 200 million years ago, the 25-m tracks of a two-legged, three-toed dinosaur were embedded in the (at the time) soft, red Etjo sandstone. There are some 30 imprints with a distance between them of about 70 cm to 90 cm, so it is clear the creatures had a large stride. The dinosaur was probably one of the forerunners of modern birds and, much like an ostrich, had powerful hind legs.

Declared a national monument in 1951, the site at **Otjihaenamaperero Farm** is 29 km east of Kalkfeld on the D2414. Access to them is from the **Dinosaur's Tracks Guest Farm** which has a guesthouse and a campsite (see Where to stay, page 289), but you don't have to stay there and there's a pleasant picnic site and day visitors can visit the footprints for a small fee. Be careful not to turn north to **Mount Etjo Safari Lodge** by mistake; however, if you are staying at the lodge, it is a 20-minute walk to the footprints from there.

● The Hinterland listings

For hotel and restaurant price codes and other relevant information, see pages 21-28.

⊖ Where to stay

Gamsberg Pass *p282, map p281*
$$$-$$ Hakos Guest Farm, signposted 7 km north off the C26, 135 km from Windhoek, T062-572111, www.hakos-astrofarm.com. A stargazer's paradise, Hakos is Nama for 'the place where no-one will disturb you'. The owner was manager of the neighbouring Max Planck Institute for Astronomy observatory for 25 years, and it can still be visited. Hakos offers 'star tours' for beginners, and the skies can be relied on to be clear (and cold – it is 1830 m above sea level). 14 rooms and a **campsite ($)** with shade and hot showers, heated indoor swimming pool, guided mountain walks and challenging 4WD trails available. Recommended for an introduction to the southern hemisphere's night sky.
$$-$ Weissenfels Guest Farm, C26 towards Gamsberg Pass, 110 km from Windhoek, follow signs to follow. T062-572112, www.weissenfelsnamibia.com. Set on an Arabian horse stud with 10 simple rooms, the cheaper ones share bathrooms, and a **campsite**. Farm-style meals available including packed lunches,

swimming pool, horse riding, 2 farm dams that are good for birdwatching, and hiking trails. The climb up the granite hills behind the farm is well worth the effort; the view of the Gamsberg and surrounding mountains is breathtaking.

Usakos *p282, map p281*
$ Bahnhof Hotel, 22 Theo Ben Gurirab St, T064-530444, www.usakos.biz. This is an old hotel that has recently been extensively rebuilt and refurbished, with 10 large rooms with DSTV, a/c and Wi-Fi, bar, beer garden, swimming pool, restaurant, secure parking. Friendly, informative hosts, the best and only bet in town.

Game lodges and guest farms
$$$ Hohenstein Lodge, from Usakos turn on to the D1935 towards Okombahe, after 25 km turn right for 1 km, T064-530900, www.hohensteinlodge.com. 14 smart and spacious rooms with verandas leading on to rock gardens, superb views over the Erongo Mountains and Spitzkoppe, dinners are taken on a patio overlooking a waterhole frequented by wildebeest, springbok and warthog, and leopard have been spotted on the property, sundowner game drives, guided hikes and pool. The Damara staff will take guests on a tour of their nearby village.

$$-$ Ameib Guest Farm, from Usakos turn on to the D1935 towards Okombahe, after 12 km turn right on to the D1937, T0818-574639, www.ameib.com. Simple farmhouse with 9 rooms, 3 thatched chalets, pleasant garden, small plunge pool, restaurant and bar, plus a **campsite** with its own swimming pool and *braai* pits and a further 2 budget cabins. The owners can organize scenic walks and trips to the rock art in Phillip's Cave (see page 283), which is also on their farm.

Karibib *p283, map p281*
$$$ Etusis Lodge, 36 km south of Karibib off the C32, follow the signs from town, T064-550826, www.etusis.com. Set on the private Etusis Game Reserve, with 7 thatched bungalows and 6 slightly cheaper bush tents, along with the main thatch and stone construction all built entirely of natural resources found on the reserve. Restaurant, bar, swimming pool, waterhole which is lit up at night, game drives, 4 well-mapped hiking trails, mountain biking and horse riding, and for those who don't want to get on a horse there are also horse-carriage rides. On the expensive side, but rates are half board and include game walks.

Omaruru *p284, map p281*
$$ Kashana, Dr Ian Scheeper Dr, T064-571434, www.kashana-namibia.com. At the **Nawa Nawa Arts Centre** shop and restaurant (see Restaurants, below), the accommodation is in 8 comfortable a/c chalets with DSTV and veranda, 2 of which have lofts for children, plus 2 rooms in the main house which dates to 1907 and was once a casino for miners, delicious meals in the restaurant, swimming pool, a perfect base for exploring Omaruru.
$ Central Hotel Omaruru, Wilhelm Zeraua St, T064-570030, g.redler@iway.na.

A typical town hotel but behind the old façade is a very pleasant set up with 12 a/c rooms in tasteful, modern whitewashed and thatched bungalows, welcoming restaurant and bar with TV, beer garden, swimming pool in neat garden with palm trees. The original main colonial building has a classic shaded veranda where you can stop for a coffee.

Guest lodges and game farms
$$$$ Epako Game Lodge, 22 km northeast of Omaruru on the C33, T064-570551/2, www.epako.com. Booking Epako is on an exclusive basis, with only one group accommodated at any one time (whether 2 or 20 guests) and includes services of the entire lodge. It has 11,000 well-stocked ha, 10 luxury rooms, excellent cuisine and dinner is served over a floodlit waterhole, bar, swimming pool, guided walks, game drives to Bushman paintings, chance to see rhino, tame cheetah and a wide range of antelope. Lacking in 'African' feel as everything is very modern, but some may enjoy the stylish decor.
$$$$-$$$ Erindi Private Game Reserve, from Omaruru it's 60 km along the D2328 to the reserve gates, it's a further 9 km to Camp Elephant and 24 km to the Old Trading Lodge. The reserve can also be reached on the D2414 from Kalkfeld (90 km) and there are a couple of access roads from the B1 about 100 km south of Otjiwarongo, T064-570800, www.erindi.com. A 71,000-ha private reserve home to more than 15,000 game animals including lion, leopard, cheetah and black rhino – Erindi means 'The Place of Water,' in Herero. Accommodation is in 45 comfortable a/c rooms at the **Old Trading Lodge** which has a central thatched area with restaurant, bar, swimming pool, and a viewing deck over

a floodlit waterhole that is home to hippo and crocodile. Self-caterers can head to **Camp Elephant**, which has 14 chalets sleeping 2-6 set in a horseshoe around a floodlit waterhole and a **campsite ($)**, a shop for basic groceries and swimming pool. Various game activities on offer from day and night drives to hiking trails and some are specifically designed for children. A number of leopard on the property have been radio-collared as part of a research project, so there's a good chance of seeing them.

$$$$-$$$ Erongo Wilderness Lodge, 11 km southwest of Omaruru on D2315, reservations Windhoek T061-239199, www.erongowilderness.com. Part of the Erongo Mountain Nature Conservancy (200,000 ha), the lodge has 10 very comfortable stilted cabins with thatched covers, straddling enormous granite rocks. There's a central *lapa* with restaurant, bar and lounge, lovely evening views of the enormous ruddy granite blocks and a waterhole, small swimming pool built among the rocks, scenic drives to rock art, guided walks and plentiful game. Plenty of character and good range of activities including visits to (San) Bushmen paintings.

$$$ Ai Aiba Lodge, from Omaruru take the D2315 for 45 km, the lodge is 1.5 km from the gate at the road, T064-570330, www.aiaiba.com. Set in the Erongo Mountains, this lodge also calls itself the **Rock Painting Lodge** thanks to a number of ancient rock art sites on the farm. 20 comfortable rooms in neat thatched chalets nestled between giant balancing boulders, nice views from the restaurant and bar, very good food including game, swimming pool, 4WD trips to the rock art, sundowner drives and hiking trails.

$$$ Omaruru Game Lodge, 15 km southeast of Omaruru on the D2329,

T064-570044, www.omaruru-game-lodge.com. Set on a 3400-ha reserve with 13 pretty thatched bungalows, 5 of which are self-catering and work out a bit cheaper, set in shaded gardens with cactus-lined lit paths, restaurant and bar overlooking dam, swimming pool and *braai* area. Game drives to view all major antelopes, zebra, giraffe and, if you're lucky, black rhino, cheetah and leopard.

$$ Etendero Guest Farm, 36 km from Omaruru in the direction of Uis on the C36, T064-570927, www.etendero.de. Unusual farmhouse that was built in 1934 and modelled on a Prussian manor house with a grand pillared entrance, plain but comfortable rooms in the main building or in garden cottages, wholesome farm food and outdoor *braais*, pool, activities include donkey cart rides and drives around the farm, which has a good selection of game including gemsbok, kudu and springbok. Fairly German orientated.

Kalkfeld *p285, map p281*
$$$$ Mount Etjo Safari Lodge, 37 km from Kalkfeld, take the D2414, then D2483 (well signed after 22 km), T067-290173, www.mount-etjo.com. Named after the 2000-m-high, 18-km-long flat mountain that dominates the view and covering 30,000 ha, this game farm has been in the tourist business since the 1970s and was the site of the historic Mount Etjo Declaration (supervised by the UN) which effectively ended the Angolan Bush War. Today it's a little old-fashioned, the mock-castle structures slightly tacky and it's popular with tour groups, but the 27 stone rooms are cool and spacious and there are plenty of game activities on offer including walks and drives, though unfortunately the lion and cheetah are in enclosures, and it's about a 40-min walk to the dinosaur footprints (see

page 285). Gardens and comfortable lounges, plentiful buffet dinners served in a sheltered outdoor *boma*, and good curio shop. **Dinosaur Campsite ($)**, 6 shady sites overlooking a dam, 3 km from the main lodge and 20 mins' walk to the footprints, each with their own toilets and showers.

$ Dinosaur's Tracks Guest Farm, 29 km from Kalkfield on the D2414 turn left on to the D467 for 2 km, T067-290153, www.dinosaurstracks-guestfarm.com. Part of **Otjihaenamaperero Farm** where the dinosaur footprints are located, 3 comfortable rooms with patios, and a campsite well shaded by acacia trees, hot water is provided by donkey boilers. Filling farm breakfasts, dinner on request or self-cater in the farm kitchen, lounge with fireplace. You can visit the footprints and there are pleasant walks along the Omaruru River.

❼ Restaurants

Usakos *p282, map p281*
Eating is restricted to the **Bahnhof Hotel** (see Where to stay, above), or the takeaway at the **Shell Ultra** at the eastern edge, or the **Engen** at the western edge of town. Both are open 24 hrs. There is a supermarket, bottle store and butcher.

$ Namib Wüste Farm Stall, B2 on the western outskirts of town, T064-530283. Daily 0700-2000. Welcoming small restaurant and shop with a wooden deck and a fine place for a breakfast/ lunch/coffee stop, has excellent *biltong* and rusks for sale, and whatever local produce is in season.

Karibib *p283, map p281*
The 24-hr **Engen** on the B2 in town is the best bet for takeaways, and the **Karibib Bakery & Café**, entrance through the OK Supermarket a block to the east of

the Engen and the coffee shop at the **Henckert Tourist Centre** (see Shopping, below), serve pies, cakes, coffee and tea and cold drinks to passing motorists during the day.

Omaruru *p284, map p281*
$$-$ Kashana & Nawa Nawa Arts Centre, Dr Ian Scheeper Dr, T064-571434, www.kashana-namibia.com. Daily 1000-2100. A smart white colonial building with several galleries of crafts, fine gold and silver jewellery, linens, wooden carvings, baskets, etc, all produced locally and some made from recycled materials. The restaurant offers English breakfasts, lunches, afternoon teas and dinner, a small wine list, sunny garden tables and Wi-Fi. For accommodation, see page 287.

$ Main Street Café, 116 Wilhelm Zeraua St, T064-570544. Tue-Sun 0800-1500. Stylish café/gallery selling crafts and good photography of Namibia, menu includes breakfasts, toasted sandwiches, home-made cakes and ice cream, very good coffee and there's free Wi-Fi.

$ Wronsky Haus, 122 Wilhelm Zeraua St, T064-570230 www.wronskyhaus.com. Mon-Sat 0730-1730, Sun 0830-1730. Located in a historical house built in 1907 for a German trader, Wilhelm Wronsky. Excellent breakfasts, light lunches, afternoon tea with home-made cakes, and takeaways. It has a good curio shop, plant nursery and a beer garden at the back with a swimming pool which you can use for a small fee.

❍ Shopping

Karibib *p283, map p281*
For stocking up on provisions Karibib has a small **OK** supermarket, as well as a butcher, baker and biltong shop. **Henckert Tourist Centre**, Main St, T064-550700, www.karibib.henckert.com. Daily

0800-1700. This is the sister outlet to the one in Swakopmund (see page 257), and the branch here has a small tourist office, a token but functional weavery where you can watch the women at work, a few curios and an enormous range of gemstones, both local and imported. The restaurant sells coffee and filled rolls, there's internet access and a kids' playground.

Omaruru *p284, map p281*
There's a large branch of **Spar** supermarket at 66 Wilhelm Zeraua St, Mon-Sat 0800-1900, Sun 0900-1900, which is open late and has everything you may need including a bottle shop. Also check out the crafts for sale in the restaurants around town (see Restaurants, above).
Tikoloshe, to the east of town at the C33 turn off to Karibib, T064-570582, www.tikoloshe.iway.na. Daily 0900-1630. This gallery and workshop is well worth a stop and it sells carvings from 10 cm to 10 m high ingeniously made from weathered old tree trunks and roots. There are some unique abstract pieces, though the animal carvings are the most popular with visitors to Namibia. You can meet the talented Kavango carvers and watch them at work.

⊗ Transport

Usakos *p282, map p281*
218 km to Windhoek, 146 km to Otjiwarongo, 146 km to Swakopmund.

Bus
For **Intercape** buses, central reservations, Windhoek, T061-227847, www.intercape. co.za, to **Swakopmund**, **Walvis Bay** and **Windhoek**, see timetable, page 16. Buses arrive and depart from the **Shell Ultra City** on the B2. For details of the daily shuttle services using micro/ sprinter buses between Windhoek and

Swakopmund (4 hrs) and Walvis Bay (4½ hrs) which stop in the towns along the B2, see Windhoek transport, page 80.

Train
For trains to **Swakopmund**, **Walvis Bay**, and **Windhoek** via Okahandja, see details of the service in Windhoek transport (page 83), or contact the **TransNamib Starline Passenger Service**, central reservations, Windhoek T061-298 2032, www.transnamib.com.na.

Karibib *p283, map p281*
187 km to Windhoek, 203 km to Otjiwarongo, 177 km to Swakopmund.

Bus
For **Intercape** buses, central reservations, Windhoek T061-227847, www.intercape. co.za, to **Swakopmund**, **Walvis Bay** and **Windhoek**, see timetable, page 16. Buses arrive and depart from the Engen petrol station on the B2. For details of the daily shuttle services using micro/ sprinter buses between Windhoek and Swakopmund (4 hrs) and Walvis Bay (4½ hrs) which stop in the towns along the B2, see Windhoek transport page 80.

Train
For trains to **Swakopmund** and **Windhoek** via Okahandja, see details of the service in Windhoek transport (page 83), or contact the **TransNamib Starline Passenger Service**, central reservations Windhoek T061-298 2032, www.transnamib.com.na.

⊕ Directory

Omaruru *p284, map p281*
Medical services State Hospital, T064-572900, follow Hospital St south over the river.

Namib-Naukluft Park

First proclaimed in 1907 and progressively enlarged over the years until it reached its present size in 1986, the Namib-Naukluft Park is the largest nature reserve in Africa, covering an area more than twice the size of Wales. Geographically, the park is divided into four distinct areas of which three are covered here: the gravel plains of the central Namib between the Swakop and Kuiseb rivers, known as the Namib Section; the mountainous knuckle of land stretching inland south of Solitaire to just west of Büllsport, known as the Naukluft Park; and the towering sand dunes south of the Kuiseb River, which we label here simply as Sossusvlei. The fourth area, the seemingly endless sand sea south towards Lüderitz known as the Sperrgebiet ('Forbidden Zone'), has for many decades been declared out of bounds to tourists due to the presence of diamonds and the fragility of the ecosystem. These days, however, it is the Sperrgebiet National Park and while access is still very limited, excursions do go from Lüderitz. For more details on this region, see page 348.

This truly remarkable area attracts geographers, ecologists, hikers and tourists. On the larger scale, flights and balloon trips over the mountains and dunes in light aircraft provide breathtaking views of the magnificent natural formations. At the opposite extreme, researchers analyse and hikers enjoy a glimpse of the fascinating variety of life that survives in the inhospitable sand and heat.

Getting there

There are several approaches to the Namib-Naukluft Park, and where you enter it rather depends on where you have come from. From Windhoek, Swakopmund or Walvis Bay, the options are to drive between the capital and the coast through the top of the park on either the C28 or C26/C14. These routes are described on page 225. The most popular access to the park is at Sesriem, the entry to spectacular sand dunes at Sossusvlei further south, which can be reached from Windhoek in a day or alternatively from anywhere along the C14 as it heads south through Maltahöhe and Helmeringhausen.

Getting around

Most roads in the park are gravel, though normally navigable in a 2WD. The exceptions are the roads around **Groot Tinkas** and **Gemsbokwater** campsites, which require a 4WD. Permits are not necessary for visitors travelling on the public roads through the park (the C14, C26, D1982 and D1998). However, those planning to travel on any of the signposted tourist roads, or stay at any of the campsites here, must obtain permits which are available at all the gates, or from the **MET** offices in Swakopmund (see page 227) and Windhoek (see page 51). You can also make reservations for all the campsites through **Namibia Wildlife Resorts (NWR)** in Windhoek (see page 51), Swakopmund (see page 228), at the NWR office at the **Sesriem Rest Camp** (see page 310), or through the website www.nwr.com.na.

Background

The Namib Desert is a narrow strip of land stretching for 2000 km north to south and never extending more than 200 km from west to east. Bounded by the cold waters of the South Atlantic Ocean on its west and an escarpment to the east, the Namib passes through three countries: South Africa, Namibia and Angola. In this chapter, our coverage is limited to the central Namibian areas that are accessible to tourists, namely the portion between the Swakop River in the north and the dune fields of Sossusvlei to the south. The majority of the desert further south is out of bounds to visitors. For the other accessible portion within Namibia, encompassing the Dorob National Park (formerly the National West Coast Tourist Recreation Area) and Skeleton Coast National Park (see pages 268 and 272).

The Namib Desert is generally believed to be the 'oldest' desert in the world, having enjoyed or endured arid and semi-arid conditions for around 80 million years. This does not mean that the climate has remained static during that period, nor that the dunes are that old. On the contrary, the desert itself has been changing as a result of climatic shifts, one of the most significant being the development of the cold Benguela Current (see box, page 243) about five million years ago, which plays an important part in maintaining the Namib's extremely arid conditions.

Desert conservation

The desert is a fragile environment and both plant and animal species struggle to survive here. It is important that visitors leave the area in the same condition as they entered it, and consider carefully their impact on the environment: take only photographs and leave only footprints. Visitors to the desert should be extra-sensitive and abide by the following rules:

→ When driving, stick to existing roads and tracks, as tyre marks can scar the desert floor for decades. Similarly, lichens and other fragile plants which play an important role in the ecology of the desert can be easily destroyed.

→ Whatever their condition, always use public toilets when they are available. If it is absolutely essential to go to the loo in the desert, bury everything well away from roads, paths (including those made by animals) and ground water, and burn or take with you any toilet paper used.

→ Do not disturb or collect any samples of plant or vegetable life from the desert. Many of these, such as desert melons, are a life-giving source of food and water for many species of animals. Take photos or make sketches to keep as souvenirs.

→ When camping in the desert take firewood with you, never collect wood. Many dead-looking trees or bushes come alive again after rain.

→ Never drop litter or cigarette butts. Carry all rubbish with you until you reach the next bin, though remember that because of the remoteness of campsites in the desert, it is a difficult process to transport rubbish out of the desert so if possible carry it all with you until you next reach a town.

The great sand dune fields visible at Sossusvlei are also 'recent' occurrences, probably having developed after the Benguela Current was formed; they are migrating north and west in a constant cycle thanks to the prevailing wind.

The desert is also an archaeological storehouse, rich in a whole range of stone tools, pieces of pottery or paintings left by the earliest inhabitants of this region. The findings play an important role in informing us how early humans made use of the natural resources of the desert in order to survive. They also pose the question as to why humans spent periods of time in the desert when there was an abundance of better-watered land further inland?

Namib Section → *For listings, see pages 307-312. Colour map 3, B2.*

ⓘ *N$80, children (under 16) free, cars N$10, camping N$120 (maximum 8 people per site), per 24 hrs. Only payable if you are going off the public roads or are camping (see above).*

Although the common perception of a desert is a hot, dry barren wilderness, the Namib actually has distinct climatic zones. At an altitude of 300-600 m the desert is moistened each morning by a rolling fog caused by the cool offshore air meeting

Nara melons

The nara melon is endemic to the Namib desert, in particular the Kuiseb River area. A member of the cucumber family, the nara grows in sandy places where its roots are able to burrow deep down into the earth as far as the water table. In order to reduce water loss, the stems of the plant are almost leafless, thereby also preventing animals from eating it. The nara is dioecious, meaning it has separate male and female plants. The male plant, which flowers for most of the year, provides a ready source of food for one particular species of dune beetle. One crop of the melons, which grow to about 15 cm in diameter, is produced each year in late summer providing food for desert dwellers such as jackals, gerbils, crickets and beetles.

Traditionally the nara has also been a source of food for the Topnaar Namas, who have lived around the lower reaches of the Kuiseb River for several centuries. At harvest time the fruit is collected on donkey carts and carried back to camp, where the flesh and seeds are separated from the rind and roasted over a fire. The seeds are then separated from the pulp which can be eaten as it is or dried and eaten at a later date. Archaeological sites in the Namib provide evidence in the form of seeds that the nara melon was an important source of desert food to prehistoric humans.

the hot dry air from inland. This fog allows a host of life forms, such as lichens, succulents and small bushes and the insects and animals that feed off them, to exist in an otherwise inhospitable environment.

Closer to the escarpment, beyond the reach of the daily fog, the desert is hot and dry, sustaining only the hardiest forms of life. The gemsbok, for example, is specially adapted to these conditions and has an in-built cooling system to keep the blood flowing to its brain cool enough to survive in these otherwise intolerable temperatures. Ground squirrels position themselves so that their upturned tails serve as sunshades, and a number of species of beetle have extra-long legs which afford them 'stilts'. Raising their bodies above the surface of the desert allows them to benefit from cooler air just above ground level. Other animals have developed strategies such as retreating below the surface of the desert, either into the dunes themselves or by burrowing into the desert floor.

Kuiseb Canyon → *Colour map 3, A2.*

"We stared down in fascination. It was an impressive and intimidating sight, landscape inconceivable under a more temperate sky and in milder latitudes. Barren cliffs fell away steeply into deep ravines all around the main canyon like a wild and gigantic maze. They had a name, the *gramadoelas*, and as someone had aptly said, they looked as though the Devil had created them in an idle hour." So wrote Henno Martin, a German geologist, who during the Second World War spent 2½ years with his friend Hermann Korn living in the desert in order to avoid internment. His book *The Sheltering Desert* describes their experiences as they struggled to survive in the unforgiving Namib environment and is well worth reading before visiting the region.

The Kuiseb Canyon campsite is located on the C14 at the base of Kuiseb Pass by the Kuiseb River bridge in the river course. The river may flood during the rainy season and visitors should check when booking the site.

Kriess-se-Rus → *Colour map 3, A2.*

Named after an early European resident of Swakopmund who was interested in the game in the Namib area, the **Kriess-se-Rus Campsite**, 107 km east of Walvis Bay on the C14, is located in a dry watercourse surrounded by camelthorn trees. Short walks around the area give visitors access to three typical central Namib habitats: the watercourse, calcrete plain and the schist or crystalline rock.

Mirabib → *Colour map 3, A2.*

Off the C14 in the direction of Gobabeb, this is a granite inselberg rising above the desert floor accommodating two groups at a time. Rocky overhangs offer protection from the sun and carbon dating has revealed that early humans took advantage of this site some 8500 years ago. There is also evidence of more recent visits by pastoralists about 1600 years ago. A small waterhole, **Zebra Pan**, located 35 km southeast of here, is visited by mountain zebra, ostrich and gemsbok.

Homeb → *Colour map 3, A2.*

Turn off C14 towards Zebra Pan and continue on the track to the Kuiseb River. Located on the banks of the Kuiseb River, the **Homeb Campsite** – capable of accommodating several parties – offers excellent views of the nearby sand dunes. Although the river only flows when good rains are received in the highland areas west of Windhoek, this site demonstrates the role of the Kuiseb River in preventing the huge dune field south of here from encroaching onto the gravel plains to the north. Seasonal water from the river and occasional rain means that there is a sufficient supply of underground water to support substantial riverine vegetation and to provide water for animals and humans.

There is a good chance at Homeb of seeing game such as steenbok, gemsbok and baboons, as well as a fairly large number of birds. In particular look out for birds of prey such as the lappet-faced vulture, black eagle and booted eagles, as well as the noisy red-billed francolin, the well-camouflaged Namaqualand sandgrouse and the attractive swallow-tailed bee-eater. ›› *For information on the Gamsberg area, see page 282.*

Ganab → *Colour map 3, A1.*

This site, near a dry watercourse, is named after the Nama word for the camelthorn trees, which are found here. Although rather dusty, it gives a good idea of the expanse of the Namib Desert, and the nearby borehole and windmill are an attraction for game. A host of mammals have been spotted here, including gemsbok, springbok and zebra, as well as predators such as spotted hyena, aardwolf, bat-eared fox and caracal. To get here, turn off the C14 onto the D1982 in the direction of Windhoek.

Groot Tinkas → *Colour map 3, A2.*

Only accessible by 4WD, this is an ideal place to camp in the Namib. The surrounding area has some interesting hikes, although the heat means that early morning and late afternoon are the best times to do this. After good summer rains the nearby dam, an unusual site in the middle of the desert, is full of water and attracts game and birdlife. To get here, turn north off the C28 from Swakopmund to Windhoek, or north on the small track leading from Ganab.

Bloedkoppie → *Colour map 3, A2.*

Close to Groot Tinkas (55 km northeast of the C28 from Swakopmund) stands the 'blood hill' granite inselberg, a popular campsite in this part of the Namib. The sites on the western side of the hill are very sandy, requiring 4WD to get there. It is well worth exploring the immediate area, not least for the fascinating rock formations. About 5 km east of the campsite are the ruins of a German colonial police station and the graves of two policemen dating back to 1895.

Vogelfedeberg → *Colour map 3, A1.*

A smaller inselberg than Bloedkoppie, Vogelfedeberg is nevertheless an interesting place to visit, especially after summer rains. Water collects in the rock pools which, for a short while, become home to a host of small invertebrates, such as the crab-like *triops*. The development of these creatures has to be rapid as the water only remains in the pools for a few weeks. During this brief period the eggs, which have been waiting for the rain, must hatch, the creatures must mature, mate and lay eggs for the next generation to emerge when the rain returns. To get here from Walvis Bay, take the C14 east for 51 km and then turn off at the sign.

South of Vogelfedeberg lie the **Hamilton Mountains**, not officially on the tourist route, but nevertheless an interesting place for those with the energy for a hike. This limestone range climbs between 300 m and 600 m above the Namib plain and benefits from enough fog-water to allow a fascinating range of plants to grow here. In particular look out for blooming succulents following summer rains and the occasional lily.

Naukluft Park → *For listings, see pages 307-312. Colour map 3, A2.*

ⓘ *N\$80, children (under 16) free, cars N\$10, camping N\$120 (maximum 8 people per site) per 24 hrs. The latter is only payable if camping or going off public roads (see page 309).*
The Naukluft Park was proclaimed in 1964 as a sanctuary for the Hartmann's mountain zebra before being joined with the former Namib Desert Park in 1979 to form the Namib-Naukluft Park. The name Naukluft derives from the narrow *kloof* or gorge on the eastern side of the mountain range. This rugged, mountainous area hides deep ravines, plunging gorges, crystal-clear rock pools and a variety of game totally at odds with the desolate surrounding desert. Accessible only on foot or on horseback the Naukluft Park is an ideal place for hiking and has a number of superb trails, ranging from the 10-km **Olive Trail** to the 120-km eight-day **Naukluft Hiking Trail**.

War in the Naukluft Mountains

In 1894 the Naukluft Mountains were the setting for a series of skirmishes and battles between the Nama leader Hendrik Witbooi and the German forces led by Theodor Leutwein. The outcome played an important role in the consolidation of German control over Namibia.

In April 1893 the Germans, led by Captain Curt von François, had attacked Witbooi's stronghold at Hoornkrans west of Rehoboth, forcing Witbooi and his followers to flee. Signed affidavits by survivors of the attack (Hendrik Witbooi Papers, Appendix 3) give a vivid picture of this bloody raid. "A little before sunrise the German soldiers opened fire on us and stormed the place... When we heard the firing we ran out of our houses; we had no opportunity of making resistance but fled ... Houses were set on fire and burned over the bodies of dead women and children."

Following this attack Witbooi pursued a guerrilla war against the Germans, using his superior knowledge of the countryside to harass and outwit the German forces. Finally, however, Witbooi was forced to retreat and chose the inaccessible Naukluft Mountains as the last refuge for his followers, including women, children and livestock. The decisive battles of the war took place in the Naukluft between 27 August and 5 September 1894.

An account of the fighting by German commander Major Leutwein gives an idea of how tough it must have been for both sides to have waged a war in these mountains: "The troops followed the tracks left by the Hottentots' livestock; more often than not, however, it was extremely difficult to discern these tracks on the rocky ground. For this reason, the enemy could be pursued only during the day...the sun burned down from a cloudless sky, while the temperature dropped to several degrees below zero during the night... no fires could be lit... The troops were exhausted, clothing and shoes in tatters; casualties had reduced their already thin ranks..."

Despite superiority in arms and ammunition these deprivations prevented the German forces from defeating Witbooi; on the other hand Witbooi was not able to successfully break out of the siege. Eventually, the two sides came to a standstill and on 15 September Witbooi signed a conditional surrender which required him and his supporters to return to Gibeon, to accept the paramountcy of the German Empire and the presence of a German garrison at Gibeon. In return Witbooi retained jurisdiction over his land and people, and the right to keep guns and ammunition.

Concluding his account of the battle in the Naukluft, Leutwein wrote, "The enemy had suffered only minor losses... It proved that the Hottentot was far superior to us when it came to marching, enduring deprivation and knowledge of and ability to use the terrain...it was only in weaponry, courage, perseverance and discipline that the troops surpassed the enemy."

Arriving in Naukluft Park

The entrance to the park is 10 km south of Büllsport on the D854. From Windhoek take the B1 south to Rehoboth and then immediately south of the town turn west onto the gravel C24. This passes the small settlements of **Klein Aub** and **Rietoog** (petrol during daylight hours) before gradually descending from the central highlands into the semi-desert around **Büllsport**. From the coast, the C14 passes through the central Namib climbing steeply and tortuously through the Kuiseb and Gaub passes past Solitaire to Büllsport. From the south the most direct route is on the C14 from Maltahöhe.

Geology

The geological history of the area starts between 1000 and 2000 million years ago when the base of the mountains was formed by volcanic rocks, granites and gneisses. Between 650 and 750 million years ago the whole of this part of Namibia was flooded by a shallow tropical sea which formed the next layer of rock – mainly black limestone. The mountains themselves were formed between 500 and 550 million years ago during a period of crustal movement when large sheets of sedimentary rock formed and were set in place. These rock sheets give the tops of the Naukluft Mountains their characteristic nappes or folds. Porous limestone deposits caused by evaporating limestone-rich water are also common all over the range and suggest a much wetter past.

Vegetation and wildlife

For such a harsh environment the mountains are home to a surprisingly large number of plants and trees. These range from common gravel plain species such as corkwood trees and wild raisin bushes to mountain species such as shepherd's tree, quiver tree and mountain thorn bushes. The deep gorges with their perennial streams are home to a wide range of different species such as sweet thorn and cluster figs, which attract large numbers of birds.

The park is home to a host of small mammals, many of them nocturnal and therefore easily missed. These include Cape hare, ground squirrel, badger and yellow mongoose, as well as the common and easily spotted rock dassies, which make up the bulk of the black eagle's diet. Of the larger mammals, the Naukluft Park is home to the unique Hartmann's mountain zebra which live only in southern Angola and Namibia. A zebra sub-species, the Hartmann's differ from plains zebras by being about 14 cm taller and also by virtue of a slightly different pattern of stripes on the lower back. Antelopes such as klipspringers are common and easily spotted as they bounce from rock to rock, as are duiker and steenbok. The mountains with their rocky overhangs, gorges and caves are an ideal home to leopards, shy animals not easily spotted, but nevertheless the most significant predators in the area. Smaller predators like black-backed jackal, bat-eared fox, African wild cats and aardwolfs are also common in the park although, like many of the smaller animals, most of these are nocturnal and therefore difficult to spot.

Due to its position between the desert to the west and the highlands to the east, the park lies at the limits of the distribution of a large number of endemic Namibian species. Furthermore the perennial streams in the deep kloofs attracts birds that otherwise would not be found in this environment. Late summer (February–March) is an excellent time for bird-spotting in the park when species such as the Herero chat, Rüppell's korhan, Monteiro's hornbill, cinnamon-breasted warblers and African black ducks can be seen.

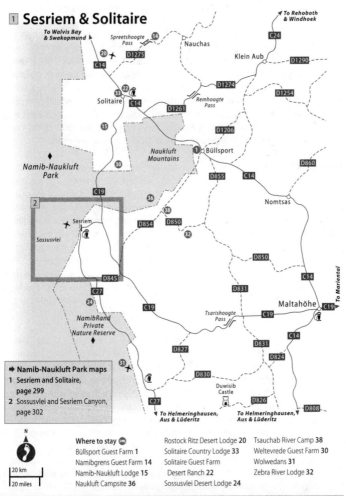

1 Sesriem & Solitaire

To Walvis Bay & Swakopmund ►
To Rehoboth & Windhoek

Where to stay
Büllsport Guest Farm **1**
Namibgrens Guest Farm **14**
Namib-Naukluft Lodge **15**
Naukluft Campsite **36**

Rostock Ritz Desert Lodge **20**
Solitaire Country Lodge **33**
Solitaire Guest Farm
Desert Ranch **22**
Sossusvlei Desert Lodge **24**

Tsauchab River Camp **38**
Weltevrede Guest Farm **30**
Wolwedans **31**
Zebra River Lodge **32**

➡ Namib-Naukluft Park maps
1 Sesriem and Solitaire, page 299
2 Sossusvlei and Sesriem Canyon, page 302

N
20 km
20 miles

Hiking

Without a doubt some of the most exciting hiking country in Namibia is found here in the Naukluft Mountains, both within the national park and on the neighbouring guest farms. There are hikes to suit just about anyone, but conditions can be hard and all hikers should make sure they come properly equipped with decent boots and a hat as well as ensuring they have enough water (minimum 2 litres per person per day). For those planning longer hikes involving overnight stops in the mountains it is absolutely essential to take warm clothing as the temperature at night, even in summer, can drop close to freezing. Windproof clothing is also recommended.

Olive Trail ① *10 km, 4-5 hrs*. Ideal as a starter for those unaccustomed to the conditions. The walk gets its name from the preponderance of wild olive trees along the route. The trail starts from the car park close to the **Naukluft Campsite** (see page 309) with a steep climb to the top of a plateau giving great views of the main Naukluft gorge. From here the path continues northwest as far as a huge social weaver nest, and then turns east into a river valley. This valley gradually deepens until a narrow gorge has to be crossed with the assistance of chains anchored into the rocks. Don't be alarmed, this is easily achieved by even the most timid. From here, the trail more or less follows a jeep track back to the starting point.

Waterkloof Trail ① *17 km, 6-7 hrs*. Considerably more demanding than the Olive Trail, but well worth it. This hike starts from the Naukluft Park office 10 km south of Büllsport on the D854; try not to leave later than 0800. It is an anti-clockwise circular route which leads past a weir up to a series of beautifully clear rock pools which, although cold, make for wonderful swimming. From here the trail climbs steadily up to a high point of 1910 m just over halfway round from where there are stunning views over the mountain range. As the path descends it follows part of an old German cannon road used in the campaign against Hendrik Witbooi in 1894. The last 6 km follow the Naukluft River back to the office. An alternative is to do a shorter hike on just part of the trail, which is a good introduction to the Naukluft Mountains. From the office you can hike as far as the 'last water', which takes about 1½ hours; you can have a swim then return the same way.

Naukluft Hiking Trail ① *120 km, 8 days, but possible to shorten to 58 km, 4 days*. Reputed to be one of the toughest hiking trails in southern Africa. Accommodation on the trail consists of a farmhouse on the first, third and last nights and simple stone shelters on the other nights. Water is provided at the overnight stops but fires are not permitted, making a camping stove essential. It goes without saying that this trail is only for fit and experienced hikers and you'll be asked for a recent medical report attesting to your fitness when booking. Due to extreme summer temperatures the trail is only open from 1 March to the third Friday in October to groups of between three and 12 people. The trek starts on Tuesday, Thursday and Saturday on the first three weeks of each month. Visitors must provide their own food and equipment. Demand is high so reservations should be made well in advance through the **Namibia Wildlife Resorts (NWR)** offices.

Solitaire → *Colour map 3, A2. Phone code: 063.*

The subject (in fact, title) of a Dutch novel by author Ton van der Lee about his stay in this place, Solitaire is actually just a dusty, desolate farm on the gravel plains among the dunes of the southern Namib. Standing on the junction of the C19 and C14 and 83 km from Sesriem, the name Solitaire is derived from the lone dead tree standing next to the service station, a motif frequently seen on publicity posters for tourism in Namibia, though of course it could also mean solitude or loneliness, which would describe its incredulous location. The mountains to the east are an extension of the Naukluft Mountains, to the north is the flat-topped Gamsberg Mountain and to the west lie the massive red dunes of the heart of the Namib.

Solitaire was founded in 1948 by Willem Christoffel van Coller, who bought 33,000 ha of land from the South West Administration to farm karakul sheep. He built a farmhouse and later the shop, which still stands today. There is more traffic than would be expected for such an isolated outpost, as most people stop at the shop for fuel, toilets, soft drinks, beer, ice, home-made bread and cake, meat and basic supplies en route to Sesriem; the shop is renowned for its delicious apple pie. The **Solitaire Country Lodge** is next to the shop, and its campsite is useful if the one at Sesriem is booked out. There are also a number of other places to stay in the area.

Note the next petrol south of Solitaire is at Sesriem (see page 304), followed by a BP petrol station on the C27, 5 km north of the D827 junction. This is particularly useful as it allows you to continue along this beautiful route, perhaps to Duwisib Castle (see page 324), rather than heading away from the dunes towards Maltahöhe.

Sossusvlei → *For listings, see pages 307-312. Colour map 3, A1/A2. Phone code: 063.*

For most visitors, one of the highlights of Namibia is a trip to the massive sand dunes surrounding Sossusvlei (actually the pan or valley floor that you will park on). This is one of the world's most striking, well-preserved and easily accessible desert landscapes, and is well worth the effort of getting there.

The huge pan, or *vlei*, is surrounded by towering sand dunes, reputed to be the highest in the world. While you will quickly realize this is an exaggeration when you arrive (there are towering dunes as far as the eye can see), it is a spectacular region of the Namib Desert. In years of extraordinary rains, such as 1997, 2001 and 2006 (when the **Sesriem Campsite** and **Sossusvlei Lodge** were flooded), the Tsauchab River breaks through the sand and flows all the way to Sossusvlei, filling the pan with water and presenting the surreal site of ducks and even flamingos wading amid the dunes. The water gradually seeps into the ground, where it is tapped by the long roots of the trees and plants living here, and subsequently there is the extraordinary sight of the red dunes covered with green swathes of grass.

Arriving in Sossusvlei

The C19 gravel road winds south out of Solitaire into the Namib Desert, through a 20-km section of the Namib-Naukluft Park where there is a good chance of seeing wild ostriches, springbok and gemsbok. It continues south through the red earth before turning east to the **Tsarishoogte Pass** in the **Tsaris Mountains** with stunning mountainscapes either side, and reaching the small town of Maltahöhe (see page 324). The C27 is the turn-off for Sesriem, approximately 80 km of fairly tricky, undulating, loose gravel from Solitaire, and is well indicated.

The tarred road to Sossusvlei lies beyond a gate inside the rest camp where a permit must be obtained before driving into the park. The gate is open from sunrise to sunset; times are indicated on the gate. It is 65 km to the pan itself, and it's worth stopping at the photogenic **Dune 45** (coincidentally, 45 km from the gate) and, if you've got the energy, climbing to the top for the view of the surrounding dune sea. It takes from 20 to 45 minutes to reach the main ridge depending on fitness. This is a lovely spot to watch the sun rise to the east in the early morning or setting over the dunes to the west in the evening before scurrying back to the gate before it closes (and you get fined).

Seeing the dunes
ⓘ *N$80, children (under 16) free, cars N$10, per 24 hrs.*

Sossusvlei is 65 km from the gates; access is either by 4WD or on foot. There is a car park for 2WD vehicles 5 km short of the *vlei*, while 4WD vehicles can park on the Sossusvlei pan itself. The gates are open from before sunrise to after sunset (and campers within Sesriem get a 15-minute headstart on 'outsiders') to allow visitors to

2 Sossusvlei & Sesriem Canyon

To Solitaire & Büllsport ▲

Naukluft Mountain Park ◆

Oorwinning

Namib-Naukluft Park

Elim Dune

Daytime access to Sossusvlei

C27

Sesriem

➡ **Namib-Naukluft Park maps**
1 Sesriem and Solitaire, page 299
2 Sossusvlei and Sesriem Canyon, page 302

Sesriem Canyon

Namib Sky Balloon Safaris

C19

D854

S a n d   D u n e

Tsauchab

Naravlei

Sossusvlei (4WD)

P

P (2WD)

C27

Dead Vlei

Dune 45

S a n d   D u n e

To Maltahöhe ▲

To NamibRand Nature Reserve ▼ & Helmeringhausen

N

5 km
5 miles

Where to stay 🛏
Betesda Lodge & Camping **10**
Desert Camp **6**
Desert Homestead & Horse Trails **7**

Kulala **1**
Le Mirage Desert Lodge & Spa **5**
Little Sossus Lodge & Campsite **3**
Sesriem Campsite **4**

Sossus Dune Lodge **8**
Sossus Oasis Campsite **9**
Sossusvlei Lodge **2**

enjoy the more photogenic and comfortable early morning and late afternoon. There is a sporadic shuttle from the 2WD car park between 0800 and 1600 (N$100 per person), which will transport you the final 5 km.

Our recommendation, especially if you are staying in the campsite, is to drive into the park first thing in the morning as soon as the gate opens (remember to drive slowly if it is still semi-dark as there may be game on the road) and stop at Dune 45 to watch the sunrise, before continuing to Sossusvlei. Once there, instead of following the herd straight up the nearest dune, we suggest that you walk a few hundred metres beyond the final car park to the **Dead** or **Hidden Vlei** to enjoy the tranquillity and scenery of the area, before climbing one of the less-crowded surrounding dunes. Being even one ridge away from the crowds transports you into your own silent and awesome desert wilderness; on clear days your view over the dune sea extends to around 100 km in all directions. There are no restrictions to walkers: orientate yourself from the top of a dune and explore at will. Remember, it very quickly gets warm, but if you set off before the sun gets too high you can easily cut straight across the dunes for the 3 km (as the crow flies) to the ordinary car park.

It is extremely important to respect that, while in the park, vehicles must remain on the road in order not to damage the fragile desert environment. Walking is permitted anywhere and good walking shoes with thick socks (going barefoot in summer will blister your soles and even sandals will expose your feet to the hot sand), snacks and plenty of water are strongly recommended.

Desert flights This is a fantastic way to appreciate the majesty and enormity of the dunes, marvel at their abrupt stop at the coast, see the geological shift at the mountains to the east and be back on the ground in time for breakfast. Any of the more expensive lodges with airstrips will be happy to arrange a flying excursion for you, and there are several pleasure flight companies in Swakopmund (see page 261) that offer a two- to 2½-hour sightseeing flight from Swakopmund over Sossusvlei and back, which costs about N$3700 per person if there are four people in the plane; they fly with a minimum of two and a maximum of five so obviously the price increases/decreases depending on numbers. Flights are rarely cancelled due to inclement weather or wind (unlike balloon trips) and can be arranged at the last minute (even the night before). Obviously, it's best to book in advance to ensure availability.

Ballooning This is another fantastic way to view the region from the air. However, the technological limitations of balloons means and they can be cancelled on days of inclement weather or wind direction. The trip is a very memorable way to start the day and is elegantly concluded with a champagne breakfast while the silk is stowed away. Contact **Namib Sky Balloon Safaris** (the office is 18 km south of Sesriem on the C27, T063-683188, www.namibsky.com) or book at any of the lodges or through the website (quite remarkably they have a mobile credit card machine at the balloon takeoff/landing sites). Rates are N$4250 per person; children over 1 m 30 cm can go up and smaller kids can follow the balloon in a vehicle with the ground crew. Half an hour before sunrise, clients are collected from **Le Mirage, Sossusvlei**

Desert Lodge, Kulala Desert Lodge, Sossusvlei Lodge and Sesriem Campsite. If you are staying elsewhere, speak to them the night before about the closest pick-up point. Passengers will be returned to the lodges approximately three to four hours later so ensure you factor this into your itinerary. You'll need to wear something warm as it's chilly before the sun rises.

Sesriem Canyon → *Colour map 3, A2.*

Located near the campsite and entrance to Sossusvlei is another interesting geological feature, the sharp schism in the earth known as Sesriem Canyon. The name Sesriem is derived from the *ses riems*, or six lengths of rope that were needed to haul water out of the gorge from the top. This narrow gorge is a deep slash in the earth 1 km long and up to 30 m deep running west before eventually flattening out as it approaches Sossusvlei. Needless to say, it is not recommended after heavy rain, however, it very infrequently acts as a channel these days.

The Tsauchab River, which today only runs after good rains fall in the Naukluft Mountains, cut the gorge some 15 to 18 million years ago during a significantly wetter period in the Namib's history. The canyon itself was created by continental upheaval somewhere between two and four million years ago, which resulted in the creation of most of the westward flowing rivers in the Namib Desert Region.

The canyon is located 4 km from the campsite; ask at the office and follow signs, it is a poor gravel road and the cars parked in the dust indicate your destination. It is an interesting place to walk and appreciate the multiple rock layers exposed there. After good rains pools of water form at the bottom of the gorge; take your swimming gear and enjoy a quick dip.

NamibRand Nature Reserve → *For listings, see pages 307-312. Colour map 3, B2.*

A short distance south of the dunes at Sossusvlei lies the largest private nature reserve in the country. The NamibRand extends over 172,000 sq km and incorporates some of the most beautiful and spectacular scenery of the Namib Desert. It shares a 100-km border with the Namib-Naukluft Park to the west and the Nubib Mountains border the eastern boundary. The special attraction of the reserve is the diversity of the desert landscapes: mountains plunging down on to endless grassy plains which are intercepted by red vegetated dunes. Game species in the reserve include gemsbok, mountain and plains zebra, bat-eared fox, spotted hyena and African wildcats. In the more rocky areas are baboon, kudu and leopard. The birdlife is particularly varied for this region, with more than 120 species recorded.

The development of the reserve has been carefully controlled and guests can enjoy exclusive insight into the ecology of this fascinating region with expert and enthusiastic guides. For anyone fearing the crowds of Sossusvlei, or the limited offering of some of the other lodges in the region, a stay at NamibRand is recommended. In order to fully appreciate the area it is best to spend up to three nights in the reserve.

The Dune Sea

The sand dunes of the Namibia south of the Kuiseb River are sometimes referred to as a dune sea. This is because the dunes are not stationary – on the contrary they are ever-moving and ever-changing as the wind blows the sand in different directions. All the dunes in the Namib are composed of grains of quartz with a few heavy minerals, such as ilmenite, also present. The dunes rest on a base of sand where the so-called 'mega-ripples' are found; these can be as large as 50 cm high and are shaped by the wind. Above this base is the 'dune slope' and then the 'slipface', the area at the top of the dune where the sand is constantly cascading.

Sand dunes come in many shapes. South of Walvis Bay and close to the coast are the transverse dunes, so called because the axis of the dune lies perpendicular to the strong winds blowing mainly from the south. Around Sossusvlei are found parabolic or multi-cycle dunes, formed by winds of more or less equal strength blowing from every direction. The third kind, the parallel linear dunes, are most commonly found in the Homeb area. It is believed that this series of 100-m-high north–south dunes, which generally lie about 1 km apart, are caused by strong south and east winds which blow at different times of the year. The most mobile dunes, the barchans, are visible in the Lüderitz area, especially in the deserted mining town of Kolmanskop, where they have invaded the abandoned houses.

Standing on top of a dune at Sossusvlei you can see the rippling dune sea extending far into the distance. It is a place of outstanding natural beauty where atmospheric conditions provide exceptional visibility of the landscape by day and the dazzling southern hemisphere sky at night. In 2013, the newly named Namib Sand Sea of the Namib-Naukluft Park was proclaimed a World Heritage Site by UNESCO – it is Namibia's second World Heritage Site after Twyfelfontein. The distinct, different types of sand found in the Sossusvlei area are the result of wind and water acting together. The yellow sand originates in the Namib itself, but the deep red sand usually found in the Kalahari Desert has reached the Namib by being washed down into the Orange River far to the south before being blown northwards again into the Namib. The main criterion for declaring the region as a World Heritage Site is that the massive dune field has been created by the natural phenomenon of material transported over thousands of kilometres from the interior of the African continent by river erosion, ocean currents and wind. Most dune fields elsewhere in the world are derived from bedrock eroded in situ.

The second criterion for its inclusion as a World Heritage Site is that the Namib Sand Sea is the only coastal desert in the world that includes extensive dune fields influenced by fog. This life-giving fog supports a large number of endemic plants and animals that are considered globally important examples of evolution and the resilience of life in extreme environments.

Arriving in NamibRand Nature Reserve

There are currently six camps/lodges in the area and the policy is to limit the number of beds to keep tourism to a minimum and the wilderness area intact – hence the high prices. Some of the fees paid by guests go towards conservation initiatives and have already been used to introduce black rhino into the reserve. Each lodge offers hiking or late-afternoon drives and will happily arrange a breathtaking light aircraft or balloon ride over the dunes, if this is not already included in your agenda. It is possible to organize fly-in safaris, each including a low-level flight over the dunes at Sossusvlei. Independent travellers wanting to splash out should make their own arrangements with private charter flight companies (see page 13). The lodges in the reserve are serviced by the **Dune Hopper** (see page 312).

Background

In the 1950s, the NamibRand area was allocated to individual farmers (ex-First World War soldiers) who introduced sheep to the area, cut roads and put up fences and water points. After 30 years of marginal farming it was obvious that the local environment was just not suited to commercial farming. A series of drought years in the early 1980s forced several farmers to sell their land. It was at this point that the idea of NamibRand started to emerge.

In 1984, Albi Brückner bought Farm Gorrasis, and later he bought two neighbouring farms, Die Duine and Stellarine. It quickly became apparent that throughout the drought years the game had survived and flourished. The reserve today is made up of a series of farms that removed their fences in order to allow the wildlife to roam freely; more than 200 km of fencing and 120 km of roads were removed, and pipelines serving water points installed. In order to support and develop the project, a series of different operators have taken out 'concessions' on the farms and now offer a range of activities designed to introduce and educate visitors about the wonders of the Namib Desert. All of these concessionaires make every effort to co-operate with one another so as not to interfere with each other's activities, such as drives, hikes, utilization of tracks and care of the environment. Additionally in 2012, the NamibRand was proclaimed as Africa's first **International Dark Sky Reserve** (www.darksky.org) meaning that the concessionaires take every effort to minimize artificial light and it is one of the best places in Namibia to star-gaze. As such **Sossusvlei Desert Lodge** now has its own observatory and state-of-the-art telescope, and there are guides trained in astronomy at the **Wolwedans** lodges and **Tok-Tokkie Trails**. The concessionaires collect a daily park fee from guests on behalf of the reserve which is included in accommodation rates. For information on the reserve, visit www.namibrand.com.

⦿ Namib-Naukluft Park listings

For hotel and restaurant price codes and other relevant information, see pages 21-28.

⦿ Where to stay

Namib Section *p293, map p299*
Accommodation within the park is at the 8 basic campsites at Kuiseb Bridge, Mirabib, Homeb, Kriess-se-Rus, Vogelfederberg, Bloedkoppie, Tinkas and Ganab, which are detailed on page 295. Visitors to these campsites need to be entirely self-sufficient, taking water and firewood with them. The only amenities are drop toilets, *braai* areas and picnic sites. Visitors to the region unwilling to camp should stay either at the coast (Walvis Bay or Swakopmund) or consider the lodges on the inland fringe of the desert and neighbouring mountains; for suggested routes and places to stay, see Hinterland, pages 280-289.

Naukluft Park *p296, map p299*
There are numerous places to stay in the area north and east of the Naukluft Park, centred around Solitaire and Büllsport. Take a good look at the road map before choosing your accommodation; make sure your overnight stops correspond to your daytime activities to minimize unnecessary gravel road driving. This guide assumes that you will be coming from or travelling to Sossusvlei, and so provides distances to the entry point to the dunes at Sesriem.
$$$ Büllsport Guest Farm, C14/ D854 junction, 124 km from Sesriem, T063-693371, www.buellsport.com. 14 comfortable rooms, swimming pool, petrol station, small store, hiking trails in the surrounding Naukluft Mountains.

Full board with communal farmhouse meals. Not as charming or pretty as others nearby, but there are a number of horses available for rides, overnight trips and lessons, and there's a full dressage and jumping arena. There's a **campsite** (**$**) 3 km from the farmhouse with toilets, and showers heated by a wood burning stove.
$$$ Rostock Ritz Desert Lodge, signposted off the C14, just south of the Gaub Pass, 120 km northeast of Sesriem, reservations Windhoek T061-694000, www.rostock-ritz-desert-lodge.com. A tasteful, peaceful lodge with 20 rooms with an unusual 'traditional' adobe design, restaurant overlooks the plains below, good food, swimming pool with shaded terrace and fairly tame meerkats can be spotted around the lodge. There are also several **campsites** (**$**) with ablutions and *braais* on the property. Good, long hikes to the nearby canyon, water and day packs provided, and drives to San (Bushmen) paintings.
$$$ Zebra River Lodge, from Solitaire, take the C14 to Büllsport, turn onto D854, after 42 km turn onto D850, farm is signposted 19 km down this road, T063-693265, www.zebra-river-lodge. com. A windy 91 km from Sesriem, deep in a canyon in the Tsaris Mountains, this is a superb lodge with 8 rooms leading out to a sheltered veranda that surrounds an imaginatively designed plunge pool. Rates are full board and the food is excellent. The oldest known shell fossil, 550 million years old, was discovered on the farm in 2000. Hiking to perennial springs, 4WD drives, and a waterhole attracts a number of game species.
$$$-$$ Namibgrens Guest Farm, 130 km from Sesriem, on the D1275,

a challenging 47 km from the C14 over the Spreetshoogte Pass, follow the signs, T061-304051, www.namibgrens. com. A typical farmstay with 11 rooms around the old farmhouse, 3 self-catering mountain villas and **camping** (**$**) in a pretty area with old farming memorabilia, large communal *braai* area and huge trees that provide shade in summer, a swimming pool, restaurant, bar, and a lovely conservatory. Located at 1760 m on the Spreetshoogte Pass, with superb views of the desert below (it gets cold at night) and there are 45 km of beautiful hiking trails in the mountains; maps are provided.

$$$-$ Namib-Naukluft Lodge, 18 km south of Solitaire off the C36, 70 km from Sesriem, reservations Windhoek T061-372100, www.namib-naukluft-lodge. com. 16 rooms each with veranda and superb views, some have 3 or 4 beds, restaurant, swimming pool with adjacent thatched bar overlooking the desert. There are also cheaper 15 canvas sided en suite chalets and a **campsite** not far from the lodge and hidden by one of the granite hills with communal kitchen and dining facilities, though guests can also eat at the lodge. Good-value early morning excursions to Sossusvlei including breakfast, and there are easy walks within the vicinity. Serviced by a daily shuttle from Windhoek.

$$$-$ Solitaire Guest Farm Desert Ranch, follow signs from Solitaire, 6 km north along a farm track, off the C14, 90 km from Sesriem, T062-682033, www.solitaireguestfarm.com. 5 neat rooms in a 1950s farmhouse, 1 self-catering house, comfortable lounge, peaceful garden, campsite and swimming pool. Good value in this pricey region, cheaper if you self-cater or camp but the farm cuisine is very good. Game

drives on offer and plenty of hikes and children will enjoy the 'pets corner' with rabbits, chickens, ducks and guinea pigs.

$$$-$ Weltevrede Guest Farm, 35 km south of Solitaire on the C36, 49 km from Sesriem, T063-683073, www. weltevredeguestfarm.com. 12 rooms, some with self-catering facilities, swimming in a large farm water holder, bar, rates are dinner and B&B with wholesome farm cuisine. Sunset drives and trips to Sossusvlei on offer. A simple but relaxing operation on a working farm. **Campsite** with 4 shady pitches and communal cooking and ablutions.

$$ Tsauchab River Camp, follow signs 1 km from the D854/D850 junction, 72 km from Sesriem, T064-464144, www.tsauchab.com. Set in imaginative locations along a 3-km stretch of the Tsauchab River, accommodation is in 7 individually designed thatched chalets with *braais* and 10 separate campsites, most with their own ablutions and some with bush showers set among wild fig trees, farm shop selling fresh bread and *braai* packs, bar, restaurant but book meals in advance. There are lovely hikes including the 5- to 6-hr (21-km) Mountain Zebra Hike into the Tsaris Mountains.

$$-$ Solitaire Country Lodge, next to the shop and petrol station in Solitaire, 83 km from Sesriem, reservations Windhoek T061-305173 www.solitairecountrylodge.com. A lodge popular with tour groups with 25 rooms with stone floors in low blocks surrounding a courtyard with a swimming pool, plus 15 sandy camping sites with good ablutions, restaurant and bar, good food buffet-style, curio shop, desert walks from 2-8 km and they'll drive you to sundowner spots with drinks and snacks. Not as much character as some of the guest farms but well managed and in a good location at Solitaire.

$ Naukluft Campsite, 12 km within the park from the gate, which is 10 km southwest of Büllsport on the D854, 84 km from Sesriem, book in advance through **Namibia Wildlife Resorts (NWR)** in Windhoek (page 51), Swakopmund (page 228), at the NWR office at the **Sesriem Rest Camp** (see page 310), or through the website www. nwr.com.na. 15 fairly simple sites with *braais* and stone picnic tables, shared ablution block, hot showers, kiosk for cold drinks and beers, drinking water and firewood available, there may be water in the river in rock pools to swim in. Information on the park's flora and fauna is available at the office and the Olive Trail and Naukluft Hiking Trail (see page 300) start from here.

Sossusvlei and Sesriem Canyon *p301 and p304, map p302*

These are the closest lodges to the dunes at Sossusvlei. Check times of sunrise at the entrance gate at Sesriem if you want to make an early morning excursion into the park in your own vehicle, or alternatively take a guided excursion from any of the lodges. It is recommended to spend at least 2 nights in this region to visit Sossusvlei in the morning and Sesriem Canyon in the afternoon, and to simply enjoy sleeping in the desert. There are an additional 5 upmarket lodges in the NamibRand Nature Reserve (see page 304).

$$$$ Kulala, 17 km south of Sesriem, access is off the C27, **Wilderness Safaris**, reservations Johannesburg T+27 (0)11-807 1800, www.wilderness-safaris.com. The Wilderness Safaris luxury accommodation here is on the 37,000-ha private Kulala Wilderness Reserve with a private entrance to Sossusvlei, and each camp is in a tremendous location with sweeping views. **Kulala Desert Lodge**, is family-friendly with 23 thatched and canvas *kulalas* (bungalows, with a roof you can sleep on or stargaze from), the main area includes a lounge, bar, dining area, plunge pool, and wrap-around veranda overlooking a dry riverbed. **Little Kulala**, is slightly more expensive as the 11 spacious *kulalas* each have their own plunge pool and outdoor shower, and the main area has a bar, lounge, dining room, wine cellar, library, curio shop and swimming pool.

$$$$ Le Mirage Desert Lodge & Spa, 21 km from Sesriem, reservations Windhoek T061-224712, www.mirage-lodge.com. Stunning and remote stone castle-style structure in the middle of a wide expanse of gravel desert, with very much the atmosphere of a North African desert medieval castle, 25 super luxury a/c rooms with balconies and fantastic desert views, gourmet food and wine, swimming pool and spa.

$$$$ Sossus Dune Lodge, 4 km west of the Sesriem campsite, reservations through **Namibia Wildlife Resorts (NWR)** in Windhoek (see page 51), Swakopmund (see page 228), www. nwr.com.na. Similar to the upgraded accommodation in Etosha, this is another of the NWR's efforts to compete with the luxury lodge market. Like the **Sesriem Campsite** it's located inside the Namib-Naukluft Park boundary, so you'll get a head start to Sossusvlei. 25 chalets built from wood, canvas and thatch with spacious rooms, floor-to-ceiling windows and stunning desert views, interlinked by elevated boardwalks in a long line with the 2 honeymoon suites at each end. The raised central building has a restaurant, bar, curio shop and swimming pool.

$$$$-$$$ Sossusvlei Lodge, adjacent to **Sesriem Campsite**, T063-693636, www.sossusvleilodge.com. 45 comfortable rooms in tent/bungalow structures designed to blend into the desert with lovely views, restaurant, bar, lounge where nature films are shown in the evening, swimming pool, curio shop. Well located and the closest non-campers can stay to the Sesriem gate to Sossusvlei, and apart from the 4WD excursion to the dunes, there are guided walks, star gazing through telescopes, and it has its own 6-seater Cessna plane for scenic flights.

$$$ Betesda Lodge & Camping, 40 km from Sesriem on the D854, T063-693253, www.betesdalodge.com. One of the less expensive options with 21 simple stone rooms built in a long line, swimming pool, horse riding, hiking, farm trips, rates include dinner. There's a small craft shop, lovely mountain views, daily trips to Sossusvlei and quad bikes can be hired. Stony **campsite ($)** by riverbed with *braai* pits and hot showers, dinner is available for campers.

$$$ Desert Homestead and Horse Trails, C19/D854 junction, 3 km from the road, 30 km from Sesriem, T063-683103, www.deserthomestead-namibia.com. Good value for the region with 20 large and tastefully decorated bungalows with fabulous views, small swimming pool, curio shop, bar and restaurant (drive-by visitors can stop for lunch), and given that it has its own stables, there are a number of horse rides on offer from sunrise and sunset trips, to overnight horseback safaris where mobile camps are set up in the desert.

$$$ Little Sossus Lodge & Campsite, 35 km from Sesriem at the junction of the C19 and D854, T064-464144, www.littlesossus.com. A sensibly priced option with 16 well-furnished stone chalets, some sleep 4, plus **campsite ($)** with 10 sites, each with their own bathroom and donkey boiler for hot water, and you can order *braai* packs and fresh bread. The main area of the lodge is an old farmhouse set in a lovely garden with succulents and a few palm trees, meals are taken on the veranda, cosy lounge and bar with ethnic African decor and comfortable leather sofas, and there's a pool.

$$ Desert Camp, beyond Sossusvlei Lodge, 8 km east of Sesriem, T063-683205, www.desertcamp.com. An impressive row of 20 self-catering wood and canvas units laid out in a long line with parking outside. Each has an extra sleeper couch for 2 children under 12, and a kitchenette on the veranda with sink, fridge, hot plate and *braai*. Eating and cooking utensils can be hired from reception if you don't have your own. There's a lovely outside bar fashioned out of tree trunks, a communal *boma* for use by large groups, and fabulous dune and mountain views from the swimming pool. If you don't want to self-cater, you can eat at **Sossusvlei Lodge**.

$ Sesriem Campsite, inside the gates to Sossusvlei, which is 63 km away, reservations through **Namibia Wildlife Resorts (NWR)**, in Windhoek (page 51) or Swakopmund (page 228), www.nwr.com.na. Already inside the park so campers have a 15-min headstart on 'outsiders' in the morning for those uninterrupted dawn views and photos. Large campsite with room for 24 groups of up to 8 people, each site has a *braai*, tap and a large camelthorn tree for some shade, communal ablution blocks, bar but no restaurant, but there is the option to eat at **Sossusvlei Lodge**, miniscule swimming pool that gets crowded, petrol stations and fairly well-stocked shop that sells firewood, cold drinks and beer, ice and occasionally meat – but don't rely on this. Book in advance; this site is, unsurprisingly, popular, otherwise you may find yourself in the much less attractive 'overflow' campsite next to the petrol station. Gates open sunrise to sunset only; no entry after sunset.

$ Sossus Oasis Campsite, on the C27, 300 m before the Sesriem gate, T063-293632, www.sossus-oasis.com. This fairly new set-up is a lot nicer than the **Sesriem Campsite** (which may in turn encourage NWR to improve facilities there). 12 shaded individual sites with thatched shelters, private bathroom, *braai* and kitchen area, as well as power points. There's also a pool and it's part of the **Sossus Oasis Service Station**; an Engen petrol station with a puncture repair workshop, and a shop (much better stocked than the one at the Sesriem Campsite) for ice, beer, meat, groceries and there's a bakery and café for snacks, drinks and ice cream.

NamibRand Nature Reserve *p304, map p299*

The reserve is by no means a cheap destination but each camp is in a perfect location and facilities and service are of the highest standard. Roughly 60% of the NamibRand Nature Reserve's income comes from park fees from guests at these camps.

$$$$ Sossusvlei Desert Lodge, C27, 9 km south of the D845 junction, 26 km from Sesriem, reservations through **And Beyond**, T+27 (0)11-809 4314 (South Africa), www.andbeyond.com. Looking out onto a broad rocky plain that rises towards the distant dunes, 10 stone and glass super-luxurious villas with all mod cons and a star-gazing skylight over beds, excellent food and extensive wine list, activities include game drives, balloon rides and quad biking. Whilst not part of **Wolwedans** (below), **Sossusvlei Desert Lodge** can be booked through them, as a stay is often combined with any of the Wolwedans properties. Rates are from N$5000 per person all inclusive.

$$$$ Wolwedans. The luxury lodges here are grouped close together 70 km south of Sesriem on the C27, reservations through **NamibRand Safaris**, Windhoek T061-230616, www.wolwedans.com. **Wolwedans Dunes Lodge** is a stunning set-up, located on the edge of the 250-m-high dunes, with 9 beautifully decorated chalets on stilts with canvas walls you can roll up to sleep under the stars. Central dining area, bar, comfortable lounge with fireplace, library, wine cellar, swimming pool and sundowner decks. **Wolwedans Dune Camp** consists of 6 luxury tents on raised wooden platforms linked by walkways, central dining and lounge where guests gather for their sundowner and chat to the chef in the open kitchen before enjoying an alfresco dinner. **Wolwedans Private Camp** is another wood and canvas property that is completely stuck out in its own private patch of wilderness. Again sumptuously decorated but with a kitchen and has 2 bedrooms that sleep 4, though it is located with honeymooners in mind to provide absolute seclusion in a magnificent desert setting. A chef and guide are provided. **Wolwedans Boulders Camp** (as the name suggests) is at the foot of a massif of boulders and has 4 spacious tents, a dining and lounge tent with a breakfast deck and open fireplace. You can drive or fly in, and all the camps offer exquisite food and service, game drives and walks in the reserve and rides in their hot-air balloon. Rates start at N$3300 per person all inclusive.

◉ Transport

Namib-Naukluft Park *p296, map p299*
The **Dune Hopper**, www.dunehopper. com, is a daily air taxi that runs a service between **Windhoek** and **Swakopmund** and **Wolwedans**, **Sossusvlei Desert Lodge**, **Sossusvlei Lodge** and **Kulala Desert Lodge**. There are several packages to choose from, from 2-5 days. Reservations through the website, or alternatively book through **Nature Friend Safaris**, in Windhoek, T061-234793, www.naturefriendsafaris.com.

Contents

316 Windhoek to Keetmanshoop
317 Rehoboth
319 Mariental
319 East of Mariental –
Stampriet and Gochas
321 Mariental to
Keetmanshoop
322 Keetmanshoop
via Maltahöhe
326 Listings

331 Keetmanshoop and around
331 Arriving in
Keetmanshoop
332 Background
333 Places in Keetmanshoop
335 West from
Keetmanshoop
339 Listings

343 Lüderitz and around
344 Arriving in Lüderitz
344 Background
346 Places in Lüderitz
350 Around Lüderitz
354 Listings

**358 The Far South and Fish
River Canyon**
359 Keetmanshoop to
South Africa
363 Fish River Canyon
366 Fish River Canyon
Hiking Trail
369 Listings

Footprint features

314 Don't miss …
320 The Kgalagadi
Transfrontier Park
334 Karakul sheep
337 Wild horses of the Namib
347 Namibia's diamonds
348 The Sperrgebiet
360 The |Ai-|Ais/Richtersveld
Transfrontier Park

Border crossings

Namibia–South Africa

320 Mata Mata
360 Sendelingsdrift
362 Ariamsvlei–Nakop
362 Noordoewer–Vioolsdrif

At a glance

Getting around 2WD hire car to most major sights. Guided tours from Windhoek.

Time required 1 week, longer if hiking the Fish River Canyon.

Weather Generally warm and dry inland, windy during summer on the coast.

When not to go The Fish River Canyon Hiking Trail is closed in summer.

★ **Don't miss ...**
1 Klein-Aus Vista, page 338.
2 A 4WD tour to Saddle Hill, page 349.
3 Kolmanskop Ghost Town, page 350.
4 Seafood in Lüderitz, page 355.
5 Canoeing on the Orange River, page 361.
6 Fish River Canyon, page 363.

SOUTH AFRICA

30 km
30 miles

The south of Namibia is an arid, sparsely populated region with isolated farmhouses and communities scratching a living from the rocky ground. While seemingly inhospitable, there is widespread cattle and karakul sheep farming and plentiful game, two perennial rivers (the Fish and Orange), the awesome Fish River Canyon and, on the coast, the unusual isolated existence that is Lüderitz. The distances are vast, but there is plenty to catch the eye, with mountain ranges, red Kalahari sand and quiver trees, herds of kudu and circling birds of prey, pleasant dams for watersports and the sand-enveloped diamond boom town of Kolmanskop. On the edge of the Namib Desert is the delicate Duwisib Castle, an outpost of European elegance in the middle of the veld; further south lie the brooding Brukkaros Mountain and the quirky Quiver Tree Forest.

Geographically, the south encompasses all the land from Rehoboth to the South African border and from the borders with Botswana and South Africa in the Kalahari Desert to the ancient Namib and cold waters of the South Atlantic Ocean. The central highland plateau runs like a spine down the middle of the region and it is along this narrow strip of land that the majority of the population lives.

The only towns of significant size are Rehoboth, Keetmanshoop and the old German coastal town of Lüderitz; the rest of the south is scattered with smaller towns and settlements. As such it's difficult to explore properly without your own vehicle. The Intercape bus sticks to the B1 on its way from South Africa to Windhoek, and the (painfully slow) rail service runs from Windhoek through Mariental and Keetmanshoop as far as Karasburg. To get to the sites of interest – in particular the Fish River Canyon – the only alternative is to drive yourself or to join an organized tour.

Windhoek to Keetmanshoop

Politically, the region immediately south of Windhoek is divided into the Hardap and Karas regions, with their administrative centres at Mariental and Keetmanshoop respectively. It is a semi-arid region of vast plains stretching as far as the Kalahari to the east, and to the west lie a series of mountain ranges demarcating the edge of Namibia's central plateau and the Namib Desert.

The economy of the south has always been based around livestock farming. In pre-colonial times the Nama people grazed their animals on the vast plains, watering them at the springs of Rehoboth, Hoachanas, Gibeon, Berseba and Bethanie, now all small settlements. Following the arrival of European missionaries, traders and settlers, the majority of the land was turned into vast white-owned ranches, many of over 10,000 ha, and for much of the 20th century the wealth of these farmers was built on the back of the trade in the wool of the karakul sheep (see box, page 334).

The drive south on the B1 is fairly uneventful although the towns such as Rehoboth and Mariental have sufficient services if you want a break from the monotonous landscape. From Mariental you can either head south to Keetmanshoop, or southwest to the quaint, rural villages of Maltahöhe and Helmeringhausen on the edge of the Namib Desert. Also in this region is the German-built Duwisib Castle, worth a stop to see what is a rather incredulous location for a sandstone fortress. If you have no pressing need to go to Keetmanshoop, this western route is a pleasant alternative to both Lüderitz and the Fish River Canyon.

South to Rehoboth

The B1 leaves Windhoek past Eros Airport and the Windhoek Country Club Resort and is a good, tarred road leading all the way to the two southern border crossings at Noordoewer and Ariamsvlei, 799 km and 819 km from Windhoek, respectively. Crossing both of these borders is uncomplicated (see box, page 362). Although there is little traffic on the B1, great care should be exercised when overtaking the large trucks which ply their way up and down the highway between South Africa and Windhoek. The busiest stretch of this road (by Namibian standards) is the first 87 km between Windhoek and Rehoboth, especially during morning and afternoon rush hours, as large numbers of Rehobothers commute to and from their jobs in the capital. Nevertheless it's a beautiful route, winding through the picturesque ranchland of the Auas Mountains. Baboons rooting around in the bush for food are a common sight; also keep an eye open for warthogs, mongoose, guinea fowl and yellow-billed hornbills. There is a clutch of places to stay along this stretch of road which make an alternative to staying in Windhoek and they are within easy reach of the airports.

Rehoboth → *For listings, see pages 326-330. Colour map 3, A3. Phone code: 062.*

Situated at the foot of the Auas Mountains, Rehoboth is home to the Basters (literally, 'Bastards'), a fiercely proud and independent people who are the descendants of a group of farmers of mixed European and Khoisan blood. The town has very little to recommend it; some say this is part of a deliberate policy to marginalize the Basters' hometown. The only real attraction in the area is the nearby Lake Oanob, which supplies Rehoboth with water and where the pleasant **Lake Oanob Resort** offers lakeside thatched chalets, well-tended camping and picnic sites and a range of watersports and entertainment for families.

Rehoboth's main street, which turns off the B1 east at the BP petrol station, is well equipped with ATMs, petrol stations (24-hour), supermarkets, butchers and biltong shops and bottle stores.

Background

The town was founded around some hot springs, which for centuries were known by the Swartbooi Namas as the place *Anhes*, meaning 'smoke', which referred to the steam rising from the hot water. A more permanent settlement was established in 1844 by Rhenish Missionary, Heinrich Kleinschmidt. This original mission station lasted for 20 years before being abandoned in 1864 following an attack by the Oorlam Afrikaners under Jonker Afrikaner.

The Basters migrated to the area from the Cape in 1870 and under the leadership of Hemanus van Wyk established a settlement at the site of the mission. The Basters are the descendants of Cape Colony Dutch and indigenous African women, and are similar to coloured people in South Africa. The name Baster is derived from the Dutch word for 'crossbreed' or 'bastard', but while some people consider this term demeaning, the Basters proudly use the term as an indication of their history. The name of the town comes from the Bible: "He moved on from there and dug another well, and no one quarrelled over it. He named it Rehoboth, saying, 'Now the Lord has given us room and we will flourish in the land.'" (Genesis Chapter 26, verse 22).

In the years following the arrival of van Wyk and his people, the mission station was rebuilt. One of the earliest buildings to be completed was the Lutheran church in Church Street; with its distinctive brickwork it is reminiscent of the Putz architectural style of the Ombudsman's Office in Windhoek.

The Baster community has traditionally been a farming community, living a more or less self-sufficient farming existence, similar to that of the white Afrikaner settlers. Fiercely independent, Christian and Western-oriented in their culture, the Basters have managed to hold on to their land despite attempts by the German and South African colonial governments to take it away from them.

Places in Rehoboth
Located in the former residence of the town's first postmaster, the **Rehoboth Museum** ⓘ *T062-522954, www.rehobothmuseum.com, Mon-Fri 0900-1200, 1400-1600, Sat 0900-1200, N$25*, was built in 1903. It houses an interesting record of the community's history and culture revealing the fascinating twists and turns in the history of this unusual 'Lost White Tribe'. There is also information on local flora and fauna, and in the garden a display of traditional huts of the different ethnic groups.

Lake Oanob Resort
ⓘ *7 km west, signposted off the B1, T062-522370, www.oanob.com.na, day visitors N$30, children (under 13) free.*
The blue water of this lake is a welcome sight amidst the arid thorn veld of the surrounding countryside. The pleasant resort here is justifiably a popular summer weekend and holiday spot for locals and it's a useful stopover for tourists on the way to or from the airports in Windhoek. There are shaded, grassy *braai* sites for day visitors as well as two picturesque and reasonable thatched bar/restaurants, one overlooking the heated pool.

The property is home to ostriches, springbok, baboons and other smaller mammals, and the birdwatching is excellent at the lake where there are colonies of cormorants, pelicans, darters and other waterbirds. There are one-hour game drives, or self-drivers can take themselves, a few marked trails laid out around the lake for easy walks and you can rent mountain bikes. Boat rides and waterskiing are on offer, or you can take a canoe out for a paddle.

South from Rehoboth
Just south of Rehoboth the C24 branches west off the main B1 and leads to the Remhoogte Pass, one of several spectacular routes which descend to the Namib Desert floor. From here you can head west into the Naukluft Mountains or southwest towards Sossusvlei. The B1 south from Rehoboth passes through the ranching land of the Baster community, and about 10 km south of town, it crosses the Tropic of Capricorn; there are signs and gravel patches on both sides of the road where you can pull over and take a photograph. After 103 km it reaches the tiny village of **Kalkrand** with its **Shell** petrol station (24 hour), bottle store and mini-supermarket. From here the B1 continues south for another 78 km to Mariental.

After Rehoboth the next major (and we use this term loosely) settlement on the B1 is Mariental, a small, quiet market town in the heart of southern Namibia and the administrative centre of the Hardap Region. It is not the most exciting place in Namibia and is windswept and dusty in spring and autumn, ferociously hot in summer and bitterly cold in winter. However, it's a useful stop for provisions, petrol and maybe a coffee at the Wimpy for weary drivers.

The nearby Hardap Dam, 15 km north of Mariental, crosses the upper reaches of the Fish River, and with a surface area of 25 sq km is the largest reservoir in Namibia. It provides water for irrigation for wheat, maize, lucerne, cotton, grapes and vegetables, all cultivated on large-scale farms in the area. A dam was first proposed in 1897 by German geologist Dr Theodor Rehbock but it took a number of surveys and a further 63 years before construction began in 1960. A game reserve surrounding the dam was later proclaimed in 1968. The name Hardap derives from the Nama word meaning 'nipple' or 'wart', which is how the surrounding area of low conical-shaped hills appeared to the early inhabitants. There was a resort here run by **Namibia Wildlife Resorts (NWR)**, but it has been closed for a few years now with no sign of reopening.

Background
Mariental was officially founded in 1920 following the construction of Namibia's first Dutch Reform Church; however, it was well known to the early Nama inhabitants who referred to the place as *Zaragaeiba* meaning 'dusty'. The present name is derived from 'Marie's Valley', bestowed upon the settlement by the first white settler, Herman Brandt, in honour of his wife. Following some rather turbulent early years during the anti-German war of 1904 to 1907 and the arrival of the railway in 1912, Mariental settled down to life as a quiet *dorp* in the middle of the veld. However, its peaceful existence was rudely shattered by a devastating flood in 2006. After several days of heavy rain, the Hardap Dam, which is fed by eight rivers, filled up, and its sluice gates had to be opened and the town was flooded. Houses were submerged, and people had to be rescued by boat and helicopter from farms in the region. A national disaster was declared, and it took many months for the town to recover to some sort of normality.

Some 10 km north of Mariental, the C20 heads east into the Kalahari Desert towards the cattle town of **Aranos**. En route it passes **Stampriet**, a small settlement where, thanks to artesian water flowing in from the Kalahari, fruit and vegetables are cultivated and its clutch of palms trees come as quite a surprise. It has a petrol station with a takeaway and punctures can be repaired. At Stampriet, the C15 heads south along the Auob River towards Gochas. Along this route lie a number of battle sites and memorials dating back to the 1904-1907 war of resistance against the Germans.

The Kgalagadi Transfrontier Park

Transfrontier parks were established across borders in Africa with the aim of both conservation and to stimulate good relationships between countries – by taking fences down, original migration routes for game are re-established and park authorities from neighbouring countries are encouraged to work as a team. The obvious benefit for the tourist is that, thanks to border facilities, they can move around within a single park regardless of which country they are in. The only transfrontier park in Namibia is the |Ai-|Ais/Richtersveld Transfrontier Park (see box, page 360) which straddles the border between Namibia and South Africa. However, while the Kgalagadi Transfrontier Park doesn't actually lie on any ground within Namibia and instead straddles the northwestern corner of South Africa and southern Botswana, it does have a boundary with Namibia. As such it can be accessed directly from Namibia through the Mata-Mata Gate.

The magnificent Kgalagadi is an amalgamation of the former Kalahari Gemsbok National Park in South Africa and the Gemsbok National Park in Botswana, and today covers a staggering 3.6 million ha – one of the largest conservation areas in the world. It offers some of the continent's finest game viewing and is characterized by Kalahari red sand dunes, sparse vegetation, and the dry riverbeds of the Nossob and Auob show antelope and predator species and birds of prey off to spectacular advantage. It is also remote with uncomfortably high summer temperatures, but few begrudge the long dusty roads when they glimpse their first black-maned lion surveying its territory from the crest of a dune.

The **Mata-Mata Gate** (0800-1630) is 188 km southeast of Gochas on the C15, and 268 km northeast of Keetmanshoop via the C17 and C15. It lies in the South African section of the Kgalagadi, managed by South African National Parks (SANParks), and entry fees are R248, children (under 12) R124, per 24 hours. Only visitors to the park are allowed to use this road (it is not a through road for commercial traffic) and you must stay at least two nights and have accommodation bookings when entering. The nearest rest camp to the gate is Mata-Mata which sits on the dry Auob River and is surrounded by thorny Kalahari dune bushveld. It has a swimming pool, shop and fuel facilities, and accommodation is in self-catering chalets and a campsite. There are also some wonderful Wilderness Camps that are unfenced and only accommodate a few people at a time.

If you are entering from Namibia and are returning to Namibia via Mata-Mata you can explore the park without even showing your passport. However, if you've arrived from Namibia and then leave the park into South Africa or Botswana, you go through customs and immigration at **Twee Rivieren Restcamp** on the southern boundary. For more information contact **SANParks**, Twee Rivieren park office, T+27(0)54-561 2000, head office and central reservations, T+27(0)12-428 9111, www.sanparks.co.za, or consult the *Footprint South Africa Handbook*.

South of Stampriet, 20 km along the C15, is the farm **Gross Nabas**, the site of one of the bloodiest battles of the war. A small monument on the main road commemorates the battle of 2-4 January 1905, during which the Witbooi Nama inflicted heavy losses on the German forces. Another monument, 24 km further on, indicates where a German patrol was ambushed and killed in March of that year. Although **Gochas** is a fairly desolate place, it is on the way (183 km) to the Mata-Mata border gate into the South African side of the Kgalagadi Transfrontier Park which spans the Botswana/South Africa border (see box, opposite). There is one simple hotel, the **Stoney's Country Hotel**, (page 327) an Engen petrol station, fairly well-stocked OK supermarket with an ATM, and cemetery with numerous German graves from the early 1900s.

Mariental to Keetmanshoop → *For listings, see pages 326-330.*

The B1 south from Mariental and Windhoek is a fairly dull straight drive. You will see Brukkaros Mountain to the west (see below) and a long, low ridge to the east, atop which is the **Commonwealth War Graves** (on the C18, quite a detour). Just over 100 km south of Mariental, you pass through the village of **Asab**, which has a shop but no fuel. Unfathomably the train between Windhoek and Keetmanshoop stops here in the middle of the night.

Although there's nothing to see now, a few kilometres to the east of Asab are the remains of the Mukurob, which was a rock pinnacle or 'finger rock' similar to the Vingerklip near Khorixas (see page 181). It was a popular and impressive attraction some 12 m tall standing on a pyramidal base about 20 m high. The narrow neck was only 1 m wide, and it resembled a chubby giant finger, and was hence dubbed the 'Finger of God'. It fell down in 1988, and although it wasn't recorded on film, the collapse must have been an incredible sight. The name Mukurob is derived from the Nama language; '*Mû kho ro*' means 'There, do you see that?' Nama oral tradition also related that the power of the 'white man' would end when this geological structure collapsed. Coincidentally (or not?) shortly after the rock collapsed on 7 December 1988, South Africa finally relinquished control of South-West Africa when the New York Accords were signed at the United Nations headquarters in New York on 22 December. This event ended the Namibian War of Independence and the Angolan Bush War, and paved the way to Namibia's independence in 1990.

From Asab the B1 continues for 52 km to the village of **Tses** (Caltex garage 0700-2000); turn here for Brukkaros, and then it's another 82 km to Keetmanshoop, passing the turning for the Quiver Tree Forest (see page 334) just 2 km before reaching the town.

Brukkaros Mountain → *Colour map 3, B4.*
① *Turn off the B1 at Tses and follow the C98 for 40 km towards the village of Berseba, then 1 km before the village take the D3904 north for 8 km to the foot of the mountain.*
This mountain dominates the skyline to the west of the B1 between Mariental and Keetmanshoop. A climb to the top is well rewarded with superb views of the

surrounding plains. The name 'Brukkaros' is the German equivalent of the Nama name *Geitsigubeb*, referring to the mountain's supposed resemblance to the large leather apron traditionally worn by Nama women around their waist.

Brukkaros is not an extinct volcano, as its shape would suggest, but the eroded remnants of a pile of fragmented rock produced by a gigantic gaseous explosion some 84 million years ago. Over the course of several hundred thousand years, sedimentation and erosion created the crater floor; simply put, rain washed the finely shattered rock fragments into the crater, which is roughly 2 km across. At its highest point the mountain is about 1580 m.

The Germans established a heliograph on the eastern rim around 1900, and from 1926-1931, the American Smithsonian Institute declared the mountain the perfect site to establish a research station to study the surface of the sun, thanks to the incredibly clear desert air. It consisted of a solar telescope at the mouth of a 10-m-deep tunnel in the flank of the mountain, and a variety of measuring instruments further in. The ruins of the station can still be seen today on the northwestern rim of the crater which is an ideal spot to take in the view over the surrounding gravel plains.

There used to be a community campsite here but sadly it is now abandoned and the facilities have been vandalized. However, the level campsites are still here; some are situated at the foot of the mountain around the car park at the end of the fairly good gravel road, while the others are about 1 km higher up on the slope and can only be reached with a 4WD (with high clearance). But as there are no restrictions where you can camp, pitching a tent in or around the crater rim is much more exciting and sleeping out under Namibian night skies which are astoundingly clear here is a magical experience. Alternatively it's possible to do the hike to the top of Brukkaros on a long day from Keetmanshoop, but set off early in the morning and avoid hiking in the heat of the middle of the day in summer.

Hiking Hikers have a moderate 4-km walk from the parking area on the path, such as it is, to the crater lip. From here you can either head into the crater and across a dried riverbed, past a number of ancient quiver trees, or follow the route which turns sharply left and climbs to the abandoned research station on the rim. This walk takes 2½ hours each way from the car park. There are still signs of the scientists' stay at the volcano – ancient rusting tins, a few old bottles and some graffiti etched into the trunks of the quiver trees. It's all fairly awesome and eerie. At any moment one expects a hungry creature from a Hollywood B-movie to come crawling over the lip of the volcano and gobble you up. The walk itself is not very tough, but does involve a lot of rock hopping and the rocks can be slippery in the wet, and there is no water and no shade on the mountain, so it is absolutely essential to take at least 2 litres of water per person.

Keetmanshoop via Maltahöhe → *For listings, see pages 326-330.*

Just south of Mariental on the B1, the tarred C19 crosses the Fish River, and heads west towards the small town of Maltahöhe, on the edge of the Namib Desert, 110 km away. From Maltahöhe there is a choice of roads: west through the spectacular

The South

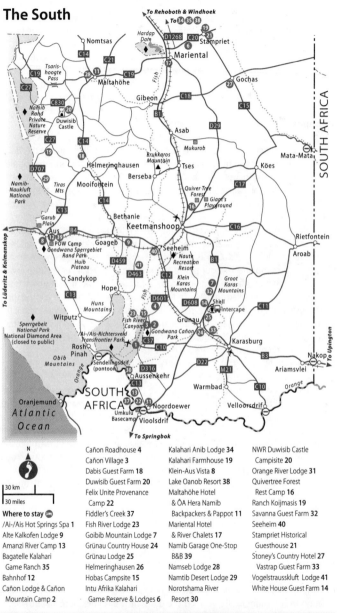

Where to stay 🛏

/Ai-/Ais Hot Springs Spa **1**
Alte Kalkofen Lodge **9**
Amanzi River Camp **13**
Bagatelle Kalahari Game Ranch **35**
Bahnhof **12**
Cañon Lodge & Cañon Mountain Camp **2**
Cañon Roadhouse **4**
Cañon Village **3**
Dabis Guest Farm **18**
Duwisib Guest Farm **20**
Felix Unite Provenance Camp **22**
Fiddler's Creek **37**
Fish River Lodge **23**
Goibib Mountain Lodge **7**
Grünau Country House **24**
Grünau Lodge **25**
Helmeringhausen **26**
Hobas Campsite **15**
Intu Afrika Kalahari Game Reserve & Lodges **6**
Kalahari Anib Lodge **34**
Kalahari Farmhouse **19**
Klein-Aus Vista **8**
Lake Oanob Resort **38**
Maltahöhe Hotel & ÔA Hera Namib Backpackers & Pappot **11**
Mariental Hotel & River Chalets **17**
Namib Garage One-Stop B&B **39**
Namseb Lodge **28**
Namtib Desert Lodge **29**
Norotshama River Resort **30**
NWR Duwisib Castle Campsite **20**
Orange River Lodge **31**
Quivertree Forest Rest Camp **16**
Ranch Koijmasis **19**
Savanna Guest Farm **32**
Seeheim **40**
Stampriet Historical Guesthouse **21**
Stoney's Country Hotel **27**
Vastrap Guest Farm **33**
Vogelstrausskluft Lodge **41**
White House Guest Farm **14**

Tsarishoogte Pass before descending into the Namib Desert and on to Sesriem and Sossusvlei; or south past Duwisib Castle and the Schwartzberge, through the hamlet of Helmeringhausen to Bethanie, Keetmanshoop and Lüderitz. The clear desert air and the absolute emptiness of the landscape make this part of southern Namibia well worth the effort of driving through for those with the time and inclination to prolong their journey. Once you have spotted a nice view, stop and turn off the car engine and drink it all in; this is surely one of the reasons you came.

Maltahöhe → *Colour map 3, A3. Phone code: 063.*

Although the pronunciation of Maltahöhe varies, the majority of locals draw out the end, pronouncing it 'Mataheeah'. It is a small village on the edge of the Namib Desert, and was founded in 1900 and owes its name to Malta von Burgdorff, wife of the German commander of the Gibeon garrison. Maltahöhe was once an important agricultural town; the nearby farm Nomtsas was established as a sheep farm of some 100,000 ha by the turn of the century. Later, it became the centre of the karakul trade, but years of drought and the collapse of karakul prices brought hard times to the town. Many of the white commercial farmers were forced to sell up and leave, and the resulting loss of revenue killed off many of the businesses in town. While Maltahöhe offers a few basic services such as a Standard Bank (with ATM), hotel, general store, bakery, bottle shop and 24-hour petrol station with tyre repair service, the town is now a run-down and faded reminder of its former self. It was in fact downgraded from town status to a village in 2000 and now has a tiny population of no more than a few thousand, many of whom live in the **Blikkiesdorp**, an informal settlement which means 'tin town' in Afrikaans. The area around the town, however, is spectacular, encompassing the Tsaris, Namgorab and Nubub mountain ranges that border the central highland plateau and there are many game farms in the region.

The only sight as such is the **cemetery** with its Schutztruppe graves from the battles fought against Hendrik Witbooi in 1894 and the Nama rebellion of 1903-1907. Serenaded by birdsong, the graves lie peacefully between palm trees and greenery. Additionally, the iron-clad **Maltahöhe Hotel** survives and as it dates to 1907 it's considered the oldest country hotel in Namibia (see Where to stay, page 328). When it was built it also served as a post office and farmers from miles around arrived by ox wagon to collect their mail. In the foyer are some interesting historical photographs of the village and rusty farm implements are dotted around outside. You can stop in for a cup of coffee or a cold drink if driving through; which you may well want to do as the tarmac stops in Maltahöhe and the C19 and C14 become gravel, dusty roads beyond here.

Duwisib Castle → *Colour map 3, B2. Phone code: 063.*

ⓘ *To get here from either Maltahöhe (82 km) or Helmeringhausen (104 km), take the C14, then the D831 before turning onto the D826; once in the grounds, take the turning away from the campsite. Daily 0800-1700. Entry and guided tour N$60, children (6-16) N$30, under 6s free, cafeteria and small curio shop.*

Duwisib Castle, a reminder of Namibia's colonial past, is situated in an improbable location in the rugged, dry veld on the edge of the Namib Desert southwest of

Maltahöhe. Designed by the architect Willi Sander who was also responsible for Windhoek's three hilltop castles, Duwisib was commissioned in 1907 by Hansheinrich von Wolf and his wife Jayta, an American heiress. Von Wolf had arrived in Namibia in 1904 to serve in the Schutztruppe as a captain in command of a regiment. It was during this time that he became interested in the area around Maltahöhe. In 1906 he resigned his commission and returned to Germany where he met Jayta. The two were married in April 1907 after which they arrived to settle in Namibia, buying Farm Duwisib from the Treasury.

The castle took two years to build, a remarkably short time considering that many of the building materials were imported from Europe via Lüderitz, from where they were hauled by ox wagon across the Namib Desert. Herero workers were employed to quarry stone from a nearby site; Italian stonemasons were brought from Italy to finish off the stone and actually build the castle; and carpenters from Germany, Sweden and Belgium were responsible for the woodwork.

Von Wolf and his wife soon became known as the Baron and Baroness by the local German and Afrikaner farmers in recognition of the lavish lifestyle they enjoyed. The von Wolfs employed seven Europeans to assist in managing the castle and the business. 'Baron' von Wolf bred horses from imported Australian and British stock and some people believe that the wild horses of the Namib seen today in the Aus area are survivors of his original stud. He also imported Hereford bulls from England and wool sheep from the Cape.

In 1914, just before the outbreak of the First World War, the von Wolfs left for England to buy further stock for their stud. During the voyage, war broke out and the boat they were travelling on was forced to seek shelter in Argentina where they were interned. Released a few months later, von Wolf was determined to join the German forces, which he succeeded in doing, only to fall at the Battle of the Somme in September 1916. Jayta never returned to Namibia to reclaim her property or to sell the farm, and died in New Jersey in 1946 at the age of 64. The farm itself was bought and sold twice before eventually, in 1979, the then colonial administration of South-West Africa bought the castle with the intention of preserving it as a heritage site.

The castle has elements of both Gothic and Renaissance architecture. In addition there is a collection of antique European furniture on display, as well as old armour, paintings, photographs and copperplate engravings. The courtyard at the rear has an ornamental fountain and a pair of large jacaranda trees, which provide shade during the heat of the day and, when in flower (September and October), fill the courtyard with their scent.

Helmeringhausen → *Colour map 3, B3. Phone code: 063.*

This small settlement was founded during the German colonial era as a farm by a member of the Schutztruppe, and lies 141 km south of Maltahöhe on the gravel C14. There is a petrol station (Monday-Saturday 0800-1800), a general store, bottle shop and small hotel. It is worth visiting the **Agricultural Museum** to look at the old farming implements, an old fire engine used at Lüderitz and one of the ox wagons used to transfer building materials and furniture from the coast to Duwisib Castle. Entry is free and the key is available from the **Helmeringhausen Hotel** next door (see

Where to stay, page 329). While you're there, the hotel is a good place to stop for a drink or meal in the lovely lush garden, especially if their famous apple crumble has just come out of the oven, and it also has a curio shop. From Helmeringhausen, the options are to loop back to Keetmanshoop and the B1 via the C14 and Bethanie and Goageb, or head towards Aus and Lüderitz on the C13.

◉ Windhoek to Keetmanshoop listings

For hotel and restaurant price codes and other relevant information, see pages 21-28.

◉ Where to stay

South to Rehoboth *p317, map p323*
$$$$ Goche Ganas, 20 km south of Windhoek on the B1, turn onto D1463 for 14 km, T061-224909, www.gocheganas. com. All-inclusive luxury lodge on a private 6000-ha reserve which is home to several species of game including rhino and giraffe. 16 superb suites under thatch with all mod cons and lovely stone bathrooms, a stunning indoor heated swimming pool in a Moorish stone-arched building plus outdoor pool, gym, extensive spa called the **Wellness Village**, hilltop restaurant and sundowner decks. Airport transfers available.
$$$-$$ Auas Safari Lodge, 23 km south of Windhoek on the B1, turn onto D1463 for 22 km, T064-406236, www. auas-safarilodge.com. German-run game ranch with 16 large rooms with patios, swimming pool, bar and restaurant offering farm-style meals. Activities include game drives and hiking trails from 20 mins to all day on the well-stocked 12,000-ha game farm which is home to giraffe, wildebeest, eland and blesbok. There's also a dam that is good for birdwatching. Airport transfers available.
$$$-$$ Lake Oanob Resort (see page 318), 7 km west of Rehoboth, well

signposted off the B1, T062-522370, www. oanob.com.na. The best option near Rehoboth are these large self-catering lakeside thatched chalets, some sleeping 6-8, and the terrace of neat double/twin B&B rooms with patios. The only possible complaint might be of over-exuberance from day visitors during the summer. 20 immaculate grassed, mostly shaded **campsites ($)**, adequate ablutions. Restaurant and bar, and numerous activities including walks and boat rides.

Mariental *p319, map p323*
There is little reason to stay in Mariental, but there are a couple of options for weary drivers. In the event you are arriving on the Intercape bus, it stops at the Engen petrol station between 2100-2200 in both directions.
$ Mariental Hotel, Marie Brandt St, T063-242466/7, www.marientalhotel.com. Typical simple town hotel which dates back to 1912, but was severely damaged during the town's devastating floods in 2006, after which a new wing was built. 18 plain but reasonably comfortable a/c rooms with DSTV, small swimming pool with thatched *lapa*, restaurant and bar with pool table and poker machines.
$ River Chalets, next to the Engen petrol station and Wimpy on the B1, T063-240515, www.riverchalets.com. 7 smart pastel-coloured self-catering a/c chalets with 2-7 beds, a/c and DSTV, patio with *braai* facilities, shaded parking, a

campsite with good ablutions, swimming pool, breakfast on request, and walking distance from town (though there's not much there to warrant the effort).

East of Mariental *p319, map p323*
$$$$-$$$ Intu Afrika Kalahari Game Reserve & Lodges, 72 km northeast of Mariental, from the B1 turn right on the C20 11 km north of Mariental, then left after 12 km on the D1268 and follow the signs, reservations Windhoek T061-375300, reserve T063-240855, www.intu-afrika. com. Set on a private 10,000-ha reserve, 2 lodges and a tented camp are set amidst the red sand dunes of the Kalahari with a total of 30 rooms. Price depends on the season and degree of elegance of your room. All guests share the swimming pool, restaurant and bar, and activities include dinners in the dunes, game drives by 4WD or quad bike, but the particular attraction is the opportunity to go on nature hikes with the !Kung San (Bushmen).
$$$ Bagatelle Kalahari Game Ranch, 50 km northeast of Mariental on the D1268, same directions as above, T063-240982, www.bagatelle-kalahari-gameranch.com. A Kalahari farmstead with accommodation in 4 chalets perched on stilts on bright red dunes, 6 bungalows in the valley below (rather unusually made from hay bales) or 4 garden rooms next to the main converted farmhouse, all nicely decorated, and 5 **camping sites** (**$**) between the dunes, each with their own ablution block. Swimming pool, bar, dining room and library, you can watch 3 cheetah in a spacious enclosure being fed, and horse riding, game drives and sundowners in the dunes are available.
$$$ Kalahari Farmhouse, Stampriet, reservations Windhoek, T061-230066, www.gondwana-collection.com.
A **Gondwana Collection** property on the fringes of the village in the fertile valley of the seasonal Auob River, the main building is a former farmhouse built some 50 years ago in the heyday of the Karakul sheep industry. 11 tastefully decorated rooms in Cape Dutch-style set in a row in front of the farmhouse, and a **campsite** with 8 sites under palm trees with hot showers and *braais*. Swimming pool, bar and restaurant, all cheese, milk, meat and vegetables come from the farm. A lovely, small and peaceful stopover but to experience the Kalahari, **Anib** (see below) is the better option.
$$$-$$ Kalahari Anib Lodge, 30 km northeast of Mariental, turn off the B1 11 km north of Mariental onto the C20 for 24 km, reservations Windhoek, T061-230066, www.gondwana-collection. com. A neat brick and thatched mid-range lodge also from the **Gondwana Collection** with 19 nicely decorated a/c rooms next to the farmhouse with their own swimming pool, plus another 35 rooms around a courtyard with another pool used for tour groups, and **campsite** (**$**) with 5 sites each with own ablution block and *braai*. Lush gardens full of palms, spacious restaurant, friendly service for a large lodge, curio shop, hiking trails and sunrise and sunset drives to see the Kalahari dunes.
$$ Stampriet Historical Guesthouse, Stampriet, T063-260013, www.stampriet guesthouse.com. Lovely little oasis with hospitable owners and 11 tastefully decorated rooms with patios and Wi-Fi, set in stone chalets in flowering gardens with swimming pool, the restaurant, bar and interesting gift shop is in an old farmhouse, drivers can stop in for coffee and freshly baked cakes.
$ Stoney's Country Hotel, on the main street in Gochas, T063-250237, www. gochashotel.com. Small town hotel

with 14 a/c rooms with modern decor, bar that is a focal point for local farmers, restaurant, swimming pool, and shady **campsite** with hot showers, a *lapa*, and lighted *braais*. Nothing special but a useful overnight stop on the way to the Mata-Mata border post to the Kgalagadi, 183 km from Gochas.

Maltahöhe *p324, map p323*
$$ Namseb Lodge, follow signs west from the C19/C14 junction in Maltahöhe for 17 km along the farm track, T063-683578, www.namseb.com. Set on a working ostrich farm with 5 self-catering bungalows, and 16 rooms in a long stone-built block, swimming pool, à la carte restaurant, bar with billiards table, curio shop and farm drives. A little old fashioned but popular with German families, and peaceful with good bush views from its elevated position.
$ Maltahöhe Hotel, if coming from Mariental on the C19, turn left at the first stop sign and the hotel is on the right, T063-293013, www.maltahoehe-hotel. com. Established in 1907, with 24 simple rooms and 3 family rooms each sleeping up to 6, and a swimming pool in shaded garden. The restaurant serves good-value home-cooked food including game steaks, and the quirky bar is the only place in town to sit and relax in the evening and is covered in flags and stickers. Nice enough and characterful, but you are better off in one of the guest farms/country lodges in the region.
$ ÔA Hera Namib Backpackers, Main St, near the intersection with the C19 and C14, T063-293028, www.oaheraart.com. Accommodation consists of 5 simple, brightly painted 2-bed mini dorms and the **campsite** has *braais*, tables, showers, toilets and washing-up facilities. There's also internet access and a café on site,

donkey cart rides can be arranged, the owner runs an excellent curio shop here selling locally produced wooden, metal and stone sculptures, plus batiks and baskets.
$ Pappot, on the main street next door to the backpackers (above), T063-293397, pappot@mweb.com.na. This is in fact the village shop and bakery, and doubles up as the local tourist information office and round the back there are 3 simple en suite brick bungalows and a **campsite** with *braai* pits and electricity. The shop (Mon-Fri 0700-1900), sells firewood, ice, meat, beers and wine and the helpful owners can organize meals with advance notice.

Duwisib Castle *p324, map p323*
$$-$ Duwisib Guest Farm, beside the castle, T063-293344, www.farmduwisib. com. Simple but peaceful when the tour groups have left, with 7 rooms in the main building with verandas, and 2 self-catering bungalows sleeping 4-8, plus 4 shady camping sites located close to the castle and kiosk, with modern, clean shared ablutions: note that this is not part of the NWR campsite below. Good home-cooked dinners such as venison stews or *braais*; day visitors to the castle and campers can also get hot and cold drinks and treats such as apple pie at the kiosk here, which also sells locally made curios, and is open until 1700.
$ NWR Duwisib Castle Campsite, by entrance to the grounds of the castle, reservations **Namibia Wildlife Resorts (NWR)**, T061-285 7200, www.nwr.com.na. 10 large pitches under huge camelthorn trees with *braai* pit, water, but no electricity and dingy ablution facilities with haphazard hot water. Campers can go to the guest farm's kiosk, above (it's far nicer to camp there anyway).

Helmeringhausen *p325, map p323*
$$-$ Helmeringhausen Hotel, at the crossroads, T063-283307, www.helmering hausennamibia.com. Part of the historic 11,000-ha Farm Helmeringhausen, this small, friendly country hotel has 22 small but comfortable rooms and a well-maintained **campsite** with grassy places for tents, *braais*, tables, and hot showers. Restaurant/coffee shop, bar, beer garden, swimming pool, good and cheap 3-course dinners are on offer using home-grown produce, activities include farm drives and the hotel has laid out a short walking trail and seats on the top of a nearby hill for sundowners.

Guest farms
$$$-$$ Namtib Desert Lodge, 99 km southwest of Helmeringhausen, signposted off the D707, northwest of the C13 junction, T063-683055, www. namtib.net. A peaceful spot located on the 16,400-ha private reserve at the foot of the red sandstone Tiras Mountains that border the Namib-Naukluft Park, about halfway between Lüderitz and Sesriem. Comfortable accommodation in 5 chalets and 4 rooms, good food, very welcoming owners, game drives, hiking trails, and star gazing. **Little Hunters Rest (\$)** is a beautifully remote campsite on the edge of the Namib Desert with 5 sites under shady camelthorn trees with simple ablution and cooking facilities. Well worth the out-of-the-way drive to get here.
$$$-$$ Ranch Koijmasis, off the D707, after 56 km south of the junction of the C27 turn on to the farm road for 22 km, if coming from the south turn on to the D707 from the C13 and its 75 km to the turn-off to the ranch past **Namtib Desert Lodge**, T063-683052, www. namibia-farm-lodge.com. Another guest farm in the beautiful Tiras Mountains on

the edge of the Namib-Naukluft Park and surrounded by red shining granite rocks. The name means 'meeting point' in the San (Bushmen) language. 4 chalets cleverly designed to blend into the rocks, restaurant, pool, and bar with terrace for mountain views, plus 2 cheaper self-catering chalets and lovely **campsites (\$)** scattered among the giant boulders. Activities include 4WD dune and mountain drives, horse riding (including cattle round-ups) and ostrich farm tours.
$$ Dabis Guest Farm, 10 km north of Helmeringhausen on the C14, then 7 km along the farm's road, T0813-108902, www.farmdabis.com. Fairly plain no-frills accommodation in 11 rooms, fresh farm food using home-grown produce, swimming pool and tennis court. Won't appeal to some but the trips around the working sheep farm (est 1926) with the friendly owners to learn about farming and living in this hostile environment are very interesting and great for children. A tour with lunch can be arranged for day visitors (minimum 4 people).

Restaurants

Rehoboth *p317*
There are no restaurants to recommend in town, but takeaways include the **Dolphin** fish and chip shop at the corner of the B1 and the turn-off to the southern part of town, and the **BP** on the B1 sells hot drinks and snacks such as fried chicken and pies. There's a **Spar** and **Shoprite** to pick up provisions if self-catering and they both also have takeaway counters.

Mariental *p319, map p323*
Mariental Hotel (see Where to stay, above), has a decent restaurant though expect plenty of meat on the menu. For provisions pop into the surprisingly

large **Spar** supermarket which also has a bottle shop, just off the B1 north of town. Next door at the **BP** petrol station is an ice-cream parlour and takeaway, while the large **Engen** petrol station on the B1 just south of town has a **Wimpy**, which is open daily until mid-evening, so you can still do steak, egg and chips or a burger as an early evening meal. Wimpy restaurants in southern Africa are not too bad, and have spotlessly clean toilets, a shop and ATM and many local people eat at them; cooked breakfasts and Wimpy mega-coffee are perfect 'fuel' for a long road journey.

Maltahöhe *p324, map p323*
Those wanting a break from the road have a great choice here; a drink in the characterful bar or lunch in the beer garden at the **Maltahöhe Hotel**, a coffee and snack, or eat your own picnic in the grounds of the **ÔA Hera Namib Backpackers**, and then browse the excellent locally produced arts and crafts on sale, or you can stop at **Pappot**, the all singing-all-dancing village shop/bakery that sells anything and everything from freshly baked bread and hot chips to children's toys and engagement rings. See Where to stay for details.

⊖ Transport

Rehoboth *p317*
Bus and taxi Intercape buses between **Windhoek** and **Cape Town**, and **Upington**, via **Keetmanshoop**, stop at the BP petrol station on the B1 (see timetable on page 16), as do local shared minibus taxis (frequent service to **Windhoek**, and south down the B1).
Train TransNamib Starline Passenger Service, central reservations T061-298 2032/2175, www.transnamib.com.na. The station is 10 km east of town off the C25, but this is a desolate spot, there's no public transport and trains arrive and depart at night. The train departs **Windhoek** daily except Sat at 1940, arrives in Rehoboth at 2210, and **Keetmanshoop** at 0700. In the other direction it leaves Keetmanshoop at 1850, gets to Rehoboth at 0425, then Windhoek at 0700.

Mariental *p319, map p323*
264 km to Windhoek, 228 km to Keetmanshoop.
Bus Intercape buses between **Windhoek** and **Cape Town**, and **Upington**, via **Keetmanshoop**, stop at the Engen petrol station on the B1, see timetable on page 16, as do local shared minibus taxis (frequent service to **Windhoek**, and south down the B1).
Train TransNamib Starline Passenger Service, central reservations T061-298 2032/2175, www.transnamib.com.na. The station dominates the middle of town. The train departs **Windhoek** daily except Sat at 1940, arrives in Mariental at 0200, and **Keetmanshoop** at 0700. In the other direction it leaves Keetmanshoop at 1850, gets to Mariental at 2335, then Windhoek at 0700.

❶ Directory

Mariental *p319, map p323*
Mechanical breakdown There are plenty of mechanics in town and **Supa Quick**, Koichas St, T063-242417, repairs and sells tyres. **Medical services**, State Hospital, Hospital Rd, to the east of the railway station, T063-245250.

Maltahöhe *p324, map p323*
Mechanical breakdown There are 2 petrol stations and **Marauns Garage**, Johan Albrecht St, T063-293110, offers breakdown recovery services in the Maltahöhe, Sesriem and Sossusvlei areas.

Keetmanshoop and around

Almost 500 km south of Windhoek, Keetmanshoop lies at the crossroads of southern Namibia and is principally a transit stop to and from South Africa. As with many Namibian towns, it developed around a German mission that was founded in the 1860s to spread their faith to the local Namas. Today it has a population of around 22,000 and is the administrative centre of Namibia's largest region, Karas. Its southern central location makes it a natural traffic junction, as well as the economic centre for the entire south of Namibia. The Karas region covers some 161,000 sq km (20% of Namibia) and is named after the mountains of the same name which lie to the southeast of town. As would be expected of a regional hub, Keetmanshoop offers travellers several accommodation choices as well as banks, shops and petrol stations. It is also a convenient stop-off on the way to explore the 'deep' south, in particular the Fish River Canyon and Lüderitz.

Arriving in Keetmanshoop → *Colour map 3, B4. Phone code: 063.*

Getting there

Keetmanshoop (pronounced 'keet-man-swoop', and referred to in Namibia as 'Keetmans') is the principal town in the south and a logical stop-off on the B1 between Windhoek and South Africa. It's 496 km south of the capital and the B1 reaches the South African border at **Noordoewer** after 299 km. On the way it reaches Grünau after 163 km, where the turn-off is on to the B3 heading east through Karasburg to the South African border at **Ariamsvlei**. Going west from Keetmanshoop, the B4 heads towards the Aus Mountains before descending to the desert, eventually arriving at the old German seaside town of Lüderitz 337 km away. Both the **Intercape** bus and the **TransNamib Starline Passenger Service** train stop in Keetmanshoop. ▸▸ *See Transport, page 342.*

Tourist information

The municipal **Tourist Information Office** ⓘ *corner of Hampie Plichta Av and 5th Av, T063-221266, Mon-Fri 0730-1230, 1330-1600,* in the old post office building is fairly helpful and can book accommodation in the region and there are plenty of leaflets to pick up.

Background

Keetmanshoop is one of the oldest towns in Namibia dating back to the late 18th century, and was originally known as Modderfontein due to the presence of a strong freshwater spring. Nama herders trekking north from the Cape settled here, calling the place Swartmodder, after the muddy river that ran through the settlement after good rains.

During the middle part of the 19th century, the Barmen Society gradually established a series of mission stations in the south of Namibia at places such as Bethanie, Warmbad and Berseba. In 1866, following a request by converted Namas living at Swartmodder, Johan Schröder was sent by Reverend Krönlein, the pastor at Berseba, to establish a mission station at Swartmodder. After struggling to build a church and home for himself and his family, Schröder appealed to the Barmen Society for funds to develop the station. Johan Keetman, a rich industrialist and chairman of the Barmen Society, personally donated 2000 marks to pay for the building of a church, and in appreciation Schröder renamed the settlement Keetmanshoop, which translates from the Afrikaans for 'the hope of Keetman'. He never actually visited the settlement himself.

Like many other settlements in Namibia at the time, Keetmanshoop functioned both as a mission station and as a trading post. A successor to Schröder, Reverend Thomas Fenchel, came into conflict with the European traders who bartered liquor, usually brandy, with the Nama herders in exchange for livestock which was then sold in the Cape.

In 1890, a freak flooding of the Swartmodder River washed away the original church, but Fenchel and his congregation had rebuilt it by 1895 from when it served a multiracial congregation until 1930. Abandoned for many years, the church was restored and declared a national monument in 1978 and today houses the Keetmanshoop Museum.

The year 1890 also saw a wave of German immigrants to the new colony, particularly to this area, and in 1894 a fort was established in the town. In the following years, as soldiers were discharged from the army, many bought farms or settled in the town that grew to support the surrounding farms. The growth of the town convinced the authorities of the necessity of improving communications, and the railway to Lüderitz was completed in 1908. In the following year the military handed over the town to a civil authority and Keetmanshoop became the administrative centre for the south of the country.

Economically, the town's prosperity was built upon the karakul sheep industry, which reached its peak in the early 1970s. Since the decline of the industry (see box, page 334) Keetmanshoop has earned its keep more mundanely as a transit point for goods and people travelling between Namibia and South Africa.

The old Rhenish Mission Church on Kaiser Street now houses **Keetmanshoop Museum** ⓘ *T063-221256, Mon-Fri 0730-1230, 1330-1630, no entry fee but donations are welcome.* It was built in 1890 on the site of the previous mission that was washed away during floods. For many years it was left neglected because of the Group Areas Act that forced most of the congregation to live in other regions away from Keetmanshoop. But it was reopened as a museum and declared a national monument in 1978. The displays focus on the history of the town, information on the surrounding area and a small art exhibition. Outside, by the rock garden of aloes, succulents and cacti, a traditional Nama hut stands cheek by jowl with early trekkers' wagons. The stone church itself is a fine example of early colonial architecture, with its original corrugated-iron roof and bell tower with weather vane, and inside there is an elegant pulpit and wooden balcony. The church looks particularly attractive at night when it is floodlit.

The former post and telegraph office, the **Kaiserliches Poststamp**, designed by government architect, Gottlieb Redecker, and built in 1910, is another of Keetmanshoop's fine early buildings. It was constructed of granite, a hard rock that at the time was used considerably because it needed little maintenance. The

Keetmanshoop

Where to stay ⬤
Bird's Mansions 1
Bird's Nest B&B 2

Canyon 3
Central Lodge 4
Pension Gessert 6

Karakul sheep

The use of karakul sheep pelts to make high-quality leather and fur clothes, formed the backbone of the farming industry in southern Namibia from the early 1920s to the mid-1970s. Often called Namibia's 'black gold' the karakul sheep originated in Bokhara in central Asia, from where they were imported to Germany in the early 1900s.

Experimental breeding started in Germany in 1903 and Paul Thorer, a prominent fur trader, started promoting the idea of exporting the sheep to German colonies. The then governor of German South-West Africa, Von Lindequist, supported the idea, and the first dozen sheep were brought into the country in 1907. In 1909 a further consignment of 22 rams and 252 ewes arrived, followed by smaller numbers of the animals in the years leading up to the First World War. After the end of the war an experimental government karakul farm was set up at Neudam near Windhoek, in order to develop and improve the quality of the pelts. Breeders succeeded in developing pure white pelts in addition to the more normal black and grey ones, and although the former Soviet Union and Afghanistan produced larger numbers of the pelts, Namibian karakul fur was internationally recognized as being of the finest quality.

In 1919 the Karakul Breeders Association was founded to consolidate this new industry, and by 1923 thousands of the pelts were being exported to Germany. Over the next 50 years the numbers of pelts exported each year mushroomed to a peak of 3.2 million in 1973, earning millions of dollars for the farmers of the south. However, a combination of severe drought and changing views in Europe during the 1970s about the ethics of slaughtering millions of lambs only 24 hours old for their pelts, sent the karakul fur industry into decline. In response to this, most farmers in the south switched to breeding dorbber sheep for their meat, which guarantees a more reliable source of income, not affected by swings in the fashion industry.

wood and corrugated iron for the roof were brought up from Cape Town and the windows and doors were imported from Germany. The building now houses the tourist office (see page 331). Adjacent is the Garden of Remembrance where the **Eagle Monument** was built sometime between 1897 and 1907 in remembrance of the German soldiers who were killed in the Herero and Nama wars. It is shaped in the form of an obelisk and topped with a bronze German imperial eagle.

Quiver Tree Forest and Giant's Playground → *Colour map 3, B4.*

ⓘ *13 km northeast of Keetmanshoop, from the B1 north of town, turn onto the D29 after 2 km and follow signs, T063-222835, www.quivertreeforest.com. Daily sunrise-sunset, N\$55 per person.*

The Quiver Tree Forest with its curious and picturesque trees, can be viewed on the Farm Gariganus, which also runs the **Quivertree Forest Rest Camp**, close to the entrance. ➤ *See Where to stay, page 339.*

The 'trees' are in fact aloe plants (*Aloe dichotoma*) which usually only grow singly, but which in a few places grow in large groups, and are ambitiously called forests. The plant's name derives from the former practice of some of the San (Bushmen) and Nama peoples of hollowing out the light, tough-skinned branches of the plant to use as quivers for their arrows. The forest was declared a national monument in 1959 and the quiver trees themselves are a protected species in Namibia. It is forbidden to carry off any parts of the trees. A good time to visit the forest is either early in the morning for sunrise or late afternoon for sunset, when the clear light offers good photo opportunities. The view south over the Karas Mountains is especially beautiful at these times.

Also on the farm, the **Giant's Playground** is 5 km further northeast on the D29. Let yourself in via the farm gate and drive up to a car park. From here there is a short trail through the most striking formations. This is an area covered in huge, black, basalt rocks balanced precariously on top of each other. Do not climb on them: they may be well balanced but they are not necessarily secure. These strange formations were caused by the erosion of sedimentary overlying rocks 170 million years ago. The playground is a pleasantly eerie place to go for a gentle late-afternoon walk, and look out for the rock hyraxes (dassies) scurrying around, before catching sunset at the Quiver Tree Forest.

West from Keetmanshoop → *For listings, see pages 339-342.*

Naute Recreation Resort → *Colour map 3, B4.*
ⓘ *The turn-off is signposted on the B4 32 km west of Keetmanshoop, from where it is 18 km to the dam, T063-250519. Daily 0700-1700, N\$7 per person.*
Located on the Lowen River, surrounded by flat-topped ridges and large rust-coloured boulders, the focal point of the recreation resort is the **Naute Dam**, which with a 470-m-long wall is Namibia's third largest dam, with a capacity of 83 million cu m of water. It's a lovely spot to escape the heat of the surrounding sandy hills. The dam provides Keetmanshoop with all its water, in addition to providing water for some large-scale irrigation of date palms and grapes. Visitors are few and far between though it does attract a handful of freshwater anglers. The months of inflow into the reservoir are usually February to April, when the sluice gates are often opened. It's quite a sight to see the flumes of water spouting into the usually dry desert at the bottom of the dam.

Birdwatchers will find colonies of pelicans, cormorants, darters, Egyptian geese and other water birds on the reservoir. There is a variety of game in the vicinity, as the animal spoor on the sand dunes testify, and kudu, springbok, ostrich and other small animals may be spotted. There are no facilities here except for rudimentary picnic sites, though you are permitted to camp here but there are no facilities except toilets and *braai* pits.

The B4 heads west for 47 km from Keetmanshoop over the high veld to **Seeheim**. There's nothing to see here, just the historical **Seeheim Hotel** that began life in 1896 as a base for the Schutztruppe, where you can stop for lunch or overnight (see Where to stay, page 340), and it is the junction with the C12 that heads south along the railway line which is an alternative route to Grünau. After another 65 km along the B4 is **Goageb**, a dusty village only noteworthy as the junction with the C14, which goes north to Bethanie, Helmeringhausen and on to Duwisib Castle (see page 324). The C14 is tarred for the first 28 km to **Bethanie**, another forgotten town that now serves the local community with a petrol station, takeaway, well-stocked shop, and the Rhenish Mission Church, which was inaugurated in 1899.

Aus → *Colour map 3, B2. Phone code: 063.*

Back on the B4, this small settlement 105 km west from the turn off to Bethanie is tucked between the folds of the Aus Mountains and is famous in Namibia for receiving occasional snowfalls during cold winters. After summer rains, the area is also renowned for the beauty of its wild flowers and hiking trails, particularly around **Klein-Aus Vista**, west of town. The name means 'out' in German, but may also be derived from a Khoisan word which means the 'place of the snakes'. The village consists of a recently refurbished hotel, guesthouse and campsite, now disused railway halt, police station, well-stocked shop and petrol station, and a line of old cottages.

Aus was established as a prisoner-of-war camp in 1915 following the surrender of the German colonial troops to the South African forces. The site was chosen for its strategic significance, situated as it is on the railway line between Keetmanshoop and the harbour at Lüderitz. This made it possible to ship food and equipment from Cape Town via Lüderitz to the camp.

By 15 August 1915, 1438 POWs and 600 guards were stationed here, initially living in tents. At one stage the camp held more than 1500 prisoners, many of these people were German nationals who had never been in the army but had been making their living as farmers and traders. The hot summer days and cold winter nights made life virtually unbearable, and in the face of South African apathy to improve the situation, the inmates themselves set about making bricks which they used to build their own houses. By the end of 1916 none of the prisoners were living in tents and they were even selling their surplus to their South African guards at 10 shillings per 1000 bricks. By 1916 the prisoners had built their own wood stoves on which to cook and the authorities had provided water for washing and laundry purposes. It seems as if the South African garrison was not so enterprising and continued living in tents until 1918 when barracks were finally constructed.

Following the signing of the Treaty of Versailles at the end of the First World War, the prisoners were gradually released, the last group leaving on 13 May 1919 after which the camp was closed. Little remains of the camp beyond a few weather-beaten walls and foundations.

The site of the old **POW Camp** can be visited and is indicated by a 'national monument' plaque on a rock. It really is a desolate place, and as you walk around, images of the place in its heyday are not hard to conjure. To get there, turn off the B4 into the village. Drive up the hill past the hotel and petrol station and continue for a further 3 km to the turn-off for Rosh Pinah. Ignore this, take the left fork, after 500 m the remains of the camp are to the right, drive slowly, the turning by the small trees can easily be missed.

Wild horses of the Namib

The legendary wild horses of the Namib are probably the only wild desert-dwelling horses in the world, and their origins are a source of much speculation. Romantics suggest that they are the descen-dants of the stud kept by 'Baron' von Wolf at Duwisib Castle 160 km away, or that they descend from thoroughbred horses shipwrecked on the coast. Other less fanciful suggestions are that they escaped from surrounding farms or that they originate from horses left behind by the German troops when they fled Aus in 1915. The latter is probably the truth, judging by a photograph on display at Klein-Aus Vista which shows Union soldiers and horses that were stationed at Garub for five weeks during the First World War. Allegedly there were 10,000 soldiers and 6000 horses, and during an aircraft battle over the base, some of the horses were dispersed.

These horses live in an area of about 350 sq km and are adapted to survive in their desert environment. They move slowly, sweat less and drink as infrequently as once every five days, their only source of water coming from a borehole at Garub sunk especially for them. A blind here allows visitors to observe the horses close up when they come to drink.

The numbers of horses are constantly fluctuating in response to the grazing conditions – only the toughest can survive the frequent droughts. It is estimated that the number has been anywhere from 50-280 during the 90 years of their existence, and it currently stands at about 150. Deaths of horses during drought periods are a necessary population control method. However, during good rainy seasons grass grows on the dunes and the horses are able to fatten themselves in preparation for the lean seasons ahead. They spend about three-quarters of their time grazing. The horses are now overseen by the **Namib Feral Horse Trust**, a collaboration between Klein-AusVista and the Lüderitz MET. Visit www.wild-horses-namibia.com or more information.

If you've ventured this far, then the chances are you're on the way to the coast. After leaving Aus, the B4 descends rapidly from the edge of the central highlands plateau to the desert floor, where it cuts a perfectly straight swathe through the sand dunes for a further 124 km until it reaches Lüderitz. The last stretch through the Namib Desert is one of the most stunning drives in Namibia, and along its length is a line of telegraph poles, occasionally studded with the nests of social weaver birds, and the sand laps the edge of the road in the wind. Allow yourself time to stop and to enjoy the calming silence, and stop off at the watering hole for the desert horses too (see box, above).

The railway that runs along the side of this road between Aus and Lüderitz runs from Seeheim where it branches off the Keetmanshoop main line. The Aus–Lüderitz section was originally constructed between 1905 and 1907 by the Germans. Just before Lüderitz, it crosses a moving dune belt over a distance of about 7 km, which historically has always been a challenge to the maintenance and operation of the line. It degraded over the years to such an extent that it had to close in 1999 pending total reconstruction. Since 2003, rebuilding the line, spanning a distance of 139 km, has been undertaken in parts but to date it has still not reopened. When and if it does, it will help the economy of Lüderitz considerably by linking the port to the interior by rail.

Gondwana Sperrgebiet Rand Park → Colour map 3, B2.

ⓘ *Klein-Aus Vista, well signposted 2 km west of the turning off the B4 for Aus, T063-258021, www.klein-aus-vista.com. Daily park/conservation fee N$40 per person when on activities. For accommodation see Where to stay, page 340.*

This 521-sq-km concession area around Aus was created by **Klein-Aus Vista** for tours from the 15,000-ha farm of Klein-Aus. Within the concession area is the Koichab dune belt, a region of high bright red dunes that are partially vegetated as well as many of Namibia's wild horses which migrate through the region. Also in the area are the remains of a heliograph station used by the Germans to maintain contact with Lüderitz from the hinterland.

As **Klein-Aus Vista** are the concessionaire of the Gondwana Sperrgebiet Rand Park, they are permitted to take people in their own vehicles into the park. Although day visitors are not permitted, there is accommodation here to suit all budgets in the **Desert Horse Inn**, **Eagle's Nest Chalets**, **Geisterschlucht Cabin** (bunkhouses) and **Desert Horse Campsite**. It's a wonderful spot, worth spending an extra day of your holiday here and, as it is only 124 km to Lüderitz, offers an alternative base to explore the region including the coast. On offer are sunrise and sunset drives (from N$290) and longer half- and full-day tours (from N$475) to see the wild horses and beautiful desert scenery. There are also six mapped hiking trails (free but daily conservation fee applies) in the hills from 4-17 km. You can also rent mountain bikes (N$$250 per day) and follow challenging trails from 23-28 km through the Aus Mountains, some of which are old Jeep tracks carved out by the Schutztruppe during the First World War. The best time to see the park is after the winter rains when the dunes are covered in a carpet of tiny flowers.

Garub Plain → Colour map 3, B2.

If you fail to catch a glimpse of the famous **desert horses** from the main road it is always worth making a short detour to the Garub Plain. Here you will find an artificial water point and a viewing shelter with information board and visitors book. The site is 1 km north of the B4, 11 km west of Aus. The horses are usually here in the winter, when there is little standing water elsewhere in the area. Back on the B4 it is another 114 km from here through the Sperrgebiet to Lüderitz where you are not allowed to leave the road.

For hotel and restaurant price codes and other relevant information, see pages 21-28.

⊕ Where to stay

Keetmanshoop *p331, maps p323 and p333*

There is plenty of adequate accommodation in town, but far better to push through Keetmanshoop in all directions and stay in the countryside.

$$ Bird's Mansions Hotel, 6th Av, T063-221711, www.birdsaccommodation. com. 23 rooms with a/c and DSTV, the rooms off the courtyard at the back are newer than in the main building, parking, pleasant beer/tea garden with thatched *lapa*, good restaurant and bar, a heated pool and internet café. Also has 10 rooms at **Bird's Nest Bed & Breakfast**, 16 Pastorie St, T063-222906, but these are a little overpriced for what you get; the hotel rooms are better value.

$$ Canyon Hotel, 5th Av, T063-223361, canyon@namibnet.com. Central 3-star hotel with 72 a/c rooms with DSTV, but built in 1975, refurbished in 1997 and well overdue for a revamp again. Worth mentioning though for the good restaurant (see Restaurants, page 341), and breakfast, included in rates, is decent and enough to tackle the next leg of your journey. There's Wi-Fi in the lobby and a bar by the swimming pool – a good place to escape from the summer heat of the south. Passers-by are welcome to drop in for a swim and a meal.

$$-$ Central Lodge, 5th Av, T063-225850, www.central-lodge.com. Comfortable and well priced with 19 a/c rooms with tea and coffee stations and DSTV, 3 with spa baths, also 1 self-catering unit sleeping 4, some

are in a very elegant refurbished 1910 building, swimming pool, bar, restaurant and Wi-Fi.

$$-$ Quivertree Forest Rest Camp, 13 km northeast of Keetmanshoop on the D29, T063-222835, www.quivertree forest.com. Well placed for morning or evening photography of the Quiver Tree Forest (see page 334), with 8 a/c guesthouse rooms with full board or B&B in the farmhouse, 8 fully equipped self-catering 'igloos' with 2-4 beds, or **camping** with electricity, lights and basic ablutions by the Quiver Tree Forest itself, 1 km from the farmhouse. Extras include a swimming pool, and pet warthogs and cheetah, which you can watch being fed in the afternoon, but unfortunately they live in a cage.

$ Pension Gessert, 138 13th St, Westdene, T063-223892, www.natron. net/gessert. A small, friendly, family-run guesthouse in a quiet residential area with 7 a/c rooms, 1 for families, lovely gardens and swimming pool, rates include a good-sized breakfast, slightly out of town in Westdene, follow signs.

West from Keetmanshoop *p335, map p323*

$$$$-$$$ Fish River Lodge, 28 km west of Seeheim turn left on to the D463 for 90 km, then follow signposts for 20 km over a rough farm track (high-clearance/4WD required) which involves passing through a number of farm gates, ensure you get a map, T063-683005, www.fishriverlodge-namibia.com. This luxury option lies in an astounding spot on the western rim of the Fish River Canyon, as the crow flies its opposite **Hobas** (see page 363). 20 thatch and stone chalets with fantastic views, modern and comfortably furnished and you can sleep out on the wooden verandas, cosy dining room with fireplace, terrace and good food, rim-flow pool. Offers guided day hikes and drives plus a 5-day assisted 65-km hike into the canyon. Has an airstrip for charter flights to get there which also give great views of the canyon.

$$$ Vogelstrausskluft Lodge, 28 km west of Seeheim turn left on to the D463 for 25 km, T063-683086, www. vogelstrausskluft.com. Set up on a hill with good views of the surrounding plains, this stylish thatched lodge has 24 tastefully decorated a/c rooms in earthy and natural colours with balconies, and a lovely **campsite ($)**, 5 mins' walk from the lodge, sitting picturesquely next to a dry pan and red dunes, with hot showers and thatched bar (campers can eat at the lodge). Small rim flow pool, lounge and library, bar and restaurant, and activities include guided hikes and game/nature drives to the rim of the northern section of the Fish River Canyon.

$$$-$$ Alte Kalkofen Lodge, 56 km west of Seeheim turn left on to the D462 for 2.5 km, T063-683415, www. altekalkofen.com. Peaceful spot with 10 spacious bungalows overlooking a dry riverbed and scenic valley, smart decor, freestanding baths and outdoor showers, facilities are at a restored farmhouse, bar, swimming pool and very good food in the restaurant where drivers can pull in for coffee or lunch. The name means 'limestone ovens' in Afrikaans and some historical ones can be seen on the farm. You can also visit the hothouse here to see lithops: a rare and unusual succulent that resembles a pebble and is commonly known as the 'flowering stone'.

$$-$ Seeheim Hotel, Seeheim, signposted off the C12, just south of the B4, T063-250503, www.seeheim.co.za.

Stone and thatch historic hotel in a quirky location at the bottom of a small canyon making it invisible from the road, though some of the 30 rooms can be both dark and hot as a consequence. Good facilities include swimming pool in nice open area with good sunset views across the plains, bar and restaurant, and packed lunches for the next day's drive are available. **Camping** facilities with ablutions, but there's only a small grassy spot.

Aus *p336, map p323*
Both **Klein-Aus Vista** and the **Bahnhof Hotel** offer excellent accommodation and it's a real contrast spending a night in the desert before hitting the coast at Lüderitz the following day.

$$$-$ Klein-Aus Vista, of the edge of the Gondwana Sperrgebiet Rand Park (see page 338), well signposted 2 km west of turning off the B4 for Aus, T063-258021, www.klein-aus-vista.com. There are 4 accommodation options here to suit all budgets and plenty of drives and hikes are on offer into the park. **Desert Horse Inn** has 24 large tastefully decorated rooms at the main house with patios or balconies. **Eagle's Nest Chalets** are 9 isolated self-catering cottages 6 km from the farmhouse, built into the rocks, and blessed with superb views across the desert. **Geisterschlucht Cabin** has 2 self-catering dorms with 5 bunks in each and is 5 km from the farmhouse in a valley of the Aus Mountains. **Desert Horse Campsite** is in a lovely spot in the hills, 2 km from the farmhouse, with 10 sites under camelthorn trees, with wind shelters, water but no electricity, though there is light in the excellent ablutions block. In the main building is the restaurant and **Wild Horse Bar**, with excellent food and lovely wooden decks to enjoy your meal with a view.

\$\$ Bahnhof Hotel, T063-258091, www. bahnhof-hotel-aus.com. First built in 1907, and rebuilt in 1948 after a fire, this rather quaint village-centre hotel was recently refurbished and offers 21 stylish rooms with pine floors and modern decor. There's an atmospheric historic bar, cosy lounge with fireplace, good restaurant, and sundeck at the front overlooking Aus's main street.

\$\$-\$ Namib Garage One-Stop B&B, T063-258029, namibaus@mweb.com.na. Reception is at the garage/shop where the entrepreneurial owner runs 7 simple self-catering units in the village and breakfast can be provided, shady but sandy campsite behind a wall with reasonable ablutions, as well as the well-stocked village shop which sells firewood, ice, meat and fresh produce and has a small café for light meals during the day.

❷ Restaurants

Keetmanshoop *p331, map p333*
Busy by day, Keetmanshoop becomes a dark and unwelcoming town once the sun goes down; you are best picking a dinner spot and settling in for the evening. Kitchens typically shut at 2100. There are plenty of takeaways at Keetmanshoop's supermarkets and very many petrol stations.

\$\$ Canyon Hotel (see Where to stay, above). Daily 0800-2200. The smartest restaurant in town offering Namibian game dishes as well as a wide variety of fish, pasta and other European dishes, with a decent selection of wines. There's also a poolside snack bar.

\$\$-\$ Bird's Mansions Restaurant, within the hotel (see Where to stay, above). Daily 1200-2200. Serves a good range of meat and fish with tasty sauces

in an airy dining room or at outside tables in a courtyard dotted with palms, good service and wide selection of drinks.

West from Keetmanshoop *p335, map p333*
\$\$-\$ Bahnhof Hotel, Aus (see Where to stay, above). Daily 0800-2100. A very good à la carte restaurant, that offers steaks from the interior farms and seafood from Lüderitz and some European dishes and South African wines, which is good for a lunch or coffee stop for its home-made bread and cakes and outside terrace.

\$\$-\$ Klein-Aus Vista, Aus (see Where to stay). Daily 0800-2100. With chunky wooden furniture and high wooden terraces overlooking the strewn boulders, the **Wild Horse Bar** offers light lunches and excellent freshly ground coffee for passing trade.

\$\$-\$ Seeheim Hotel, Seeheim (see Where to stay, above). Daily 0700-2100. Light lunches are served in a *lapa* next to the pool, and there are hearty meals including some game and South African dishes served in the main dining room, a well-stocked bar and curio shop.

\$ Kuibis Restaurant, about 9 km west of Seeheim, on the B4. Daily 0700-1700. This small restaurant, which is more like a farm stall, is known locally as the 'biltong farm'. Tea, coffee and cold drinks, toasted sandwiches and snacks, its shop sells excellent home-made jam, bottled fruit and cookies, biltong and basic provisions.

❍ Shopping

Keetmanshoop *p331, map p333*
There are plenty of shops in Keetmanshoop. The **Spar** supermarket is on Mittel St, Mon-Fri 0830-1830, Sat 0900-1300, and **Pick 'n' Pay** is 1 block

along, same times and also open Sun morning 0900-1200; both also have a bottle shop and takeaway counter.

Keetmanshoop Old Mutual Retail Centre, south of the **Canyon Hotel** along the Keetmanshoop–Lüderitz road (B4). At the time of writing, this new shopping mall (rather unimaginatively named after an insurance company) was about to open, featuring South African chain stores and fast-food restaurants.

Transport

Keetmanshoop *p331, map p333*
496 km to Windhoek, 337 km to Lüderitz, 303 km to Noordoewer (South African border).

Air

Keetmanshoop Airport is 5 km to the northwest of town. There are no scheduled flights but it's served by charter flights and is home to the Namibia Aviation Training Academy.

Bus

Intercape buses between **Windhoek**, and **Cape Town**, and **Upington**, stop at the 24-hr Lafenis Engen petrol station and Wimpy on the B1, 6 km southeast of town, which is a bit awkward as there's no transport into town; you may have to ask a hotel to arrange a taxi to pick you up but both services arrive/depart very late at night/early in the morning, see timetable on page 16. Shared minibus taxis (frequent service to **Windhoek**) collect in the car parks of the **Spar** and **Pick 'n' Pay** supermarkets on Mittel St.

Train

TransNamib Starline Passenger Service, central reservations T061-298 2032/2175, www.transnamib.com.na. The handsome railway station (built in 1908) is on the northern edge of town. The train departs **Windhoek** daily except Sat at 1940, and arrives in Keetmanshoop at 0700. In the other direction it leaves Keetmanshoop at 1850, and gets to Windhoek at 0700. The full journey between the 2 costs from N$95 but it takes a long time; the **Intercape** bus takes 5 hrs 45 mins in comparison. In Keetmanshoop there's an additional train service to **Karasburg** on Wed and Sat and in the opposite direction Sun and Thu; check with the stations for times and fares.

Directory

Keetmanshoop *p331, map p333*
Medical services State Hospital, T063-223388, off B1, 1 km north of town. A better option is you need to see a doctor is the private **Khabuser Medical Centre**, 4 Mittel St, T063-225687, which also has a pharmacy.

Lüderitz and around

With one road in and the same road out, the small harbour town of Lüderitz is built on rocks in a small enclave within the Sperrgebiet (restricted Diamond Area). It is one of Namibia's oddities: a faded, picturesque, German colonial town lying between the inhospitable dunes of the Namib Desert on one side, and the vast iciness of the South Atlantic on the other. It began life as a trading post, fishing and guano-harvesting town, and when diamonds were discovered in 1909 in nearby Kolmanskop, Lüderitz enjoyed a sudden surge of prosperity when thousands of prospectors arriving by land and sea. Nowadays diamonds are mostly found elsewhere and offshore, and the main thrust of the modern Namibian shipping industry is based in Walvis Bay, so Lüderitz has reverted to its former self as a sleepy, backwater coastal town. Its appeal lies in the fact that little has changed since the early 20th century – in terms of size and population it has hardly grown at all. It has a curious array of historical German-style buildings built during the diamond rush, with their gables, winding stairwells, verandas, turrets and bay and bow windows overlooking the sparkling bay. These buildings give Lüderitz a character that is quite different to any other parts of Namibia and the little town comes as quite a surprise when arriving on the long straight desert road from the interior. As does the climate – you'll notice a distinct cooling in temperature just within 10-20 km on the approach to the coast and will need something warm to put on even before you reach town.

Arriving in Lüderitz → *Colour map 3, B2. Phone code: 063.*

Tourist information
Lüderitz Safaris & Tours ⓘ *Bismarck St, T063-202719, ludsaf@africaonline.com.na, summer Mon-Fri 0800-1230 and 1330-1700, winter Mon-Fri 0730-1230 and 1330-1630, Sat 0830-1200, Sun 0830-1000*, can book accommodation, arrange taxis around town, and issue permits for Kolmanskop. The opening times correspond with the Kolmanskop tours and you need to book here, preferably on the previous day, and at least half an hour before the tours start so the office knows how many guides to send out. The office also sells books, postcards and a number of quality curios.

As you drive through the final dune belt just before entering town, there are some quirky triangle red warning road signs to pull over and have a photograph taken next to (perhaps while you're getting something warm to put on out of the car). One simply says just 'Sand', while the others have pictures of hyenas on them. The Lüderitz-based **Brown Hyena Project** (www.strandwolf.org) monitors these animals which prey on Cape fur seals around Lüderitz and have erected these signs to warn motorists to help to prevent them being run over.

Best time to visit
The climate in Lüderitz can be harsh and changeable. While most days are sunny, during September and February there are some severe storms and ferocious winds. The worst time to visit is between the end of December and mid-February, when the powerful winds enforce a 60 kph speed limit along the approach road for safety. The last 20 km of the main road pass through shifting sand dunes; if you hit a ridge of sand at speed it is like running into wet cement and can easily cause you to lose control – drive slowly.

Another significant aspect of the local climate is the absence of the thick fog that plagues Walvis Bay and Swakopmund. This is thanks to the town's position in a bay, thereby protecting it from this phenomenon. Quite often you can see the bank of fog off Diaz Point, but that is as close as it gets to town.

Background

Stone implements and skeletons found around Lüderitz area testify that Khoisan people were visiting the area long before the first Europeans arrived. The Portuguese explorer Bartholomeu Diaz was the first European to set eyes on Lüderitz Bay when he sought refuge from a South Atlantic storm on Christmas Day 1487. Upon his return from the Cape of Good Hope in July 1488 he erected a stone cross, in accordance with Portuguese seafaring traditions of the time.

The next European to show up was Cornelius Wobma, an employee of the Dutch East India Company, who was sent to investigate the possibility of establishing trading links with the local Nama communities. He failed and although the Dutch authorities at the Cape annexed the bay and surrounding islands in 1593, it was to be a further 200 years before further European influence arrived.

From 1842 onwards, European ships exploited the rich guano resources on the islands around the bay, with up to 450 ships anchored simultaneously. The cold seas of the South Atlantic also proved to be rich whaling grounds. Between 1842 and 1861, the British-ruled Cape Colony annexed all the islands along the coast.

In 1883, Heinrich Vogelsang negotiated a treaty with Nama chief Joseph Fredericks of Bethanie on behalf of the merchant Adolf Lüderitz. This treaty entitled Lüderitz to acquire all the land within a five mile radius of the harbour and cost £100 and 200 rifles. The following year Lüderitz persuaded Chancellor

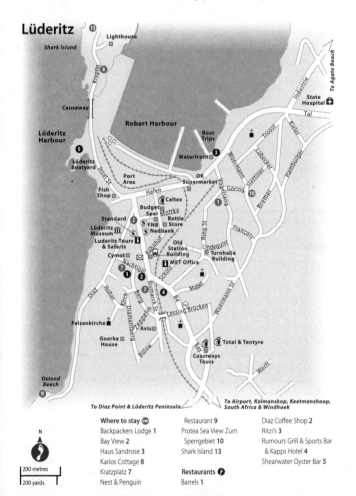

Lüderitz

Where to stay 🛏
Backpackers Lodge 1
Bay View 2
Haus Sandrose 3
Karios Cottage 8
Kratzplatz 7
Nest & Penguin

Restaurant 9
Protea Sea View Zum
  Sperrgebiet 10
Shark Island 13

Restaurants 🍴
Barrels 1

Diaz Coffee Shop 2
Ritzi's 3
Rumours Grill & Sports Bar
  & Kapps Hotel 4
Shearwater Oyster Bar 5

200 metres
200 yards

N

Bismarck to offer German protection to the area, and this event signalled the beginning of the development of the town itself. Unfortunately, Lüderitz himself did not live long enough to see the growth and development of his settlement, as he died in a boat accident whilst exploring the Orange River. The town was named in memory of him.

The main development of the town took place in the early 1900s during the period of German colonization, first as a base and supply point for the Shutztruppe during the 1904-1907 German-Nama War, and then as a Wild West-type boom town following the discovery of diamonds in the nearby desert in 1908. Lüderitz was officially declared a town in 1909 and enjoyed prosperous growth up to and during the inter-war years.

Lüderitz went into decline following the relocation of the Consolidated Diamond Mining Headquarters (CDM) to Oranjemund in 1938. Ironically, the stagnation of the economy prevented the development of the town and thus ensured the preservation of the original buildings, which gives the town its quaint turn-of-the-century feel. Today Lüderitz is popular as a tourist destination and the rock lobster and fishing industries keeps the little harbour busy with boats, while Lüderitz oysters are cultivated on the coastal flats and are exported to as far away as Cape Town. Currently the waterfront development around the harbour is being extended – an old power station has been demolished and there are plans to use the site as a campus for a new polytechnic (a student population will boost the local economy) as well as a maritime museum.

Places in Lüderitz → For listings, see pages 354-357.

Lüderitz has a number of fine old colonial buildings and a small museum, which can easily be explored in a couple of hours. A walk up Bismarck Street, the main thoroughfare, will take you past what was the **Deutsche-Afrika Bank** building, constructed in 1907 on the corner of Diaz Street, which today is home to **Nedbank**. Further up the street is the **Station Building**, commissioned in 1912 and finished two years later. The railway line from Lüderitz to Aus was completed in 1906 and became important as a means of transporting troops into the interior during the 1904-1907 German-Nama War. Following the discovery of diamonds in 1908 and the subsequent extension of the railway line to Keetmanshoop, the existing station became too small and the German colonial administration authorized the building of a new station.

The **Old Post Office**, found on Shintz Street, was completed in 1908, and originally had a clock in its tower, but this was removed in 1912 and transferred to the church. The building now functions as the local MET office. The **Turnhalle Building** on Ring Street dates from 1912-1913; originally a gymnasium, it now serves as a function room.

Two of the town's most impressive buildings, the **German Lutheran Church** ① daily winter 1600-1700, summer 1700-1800, entry by donation, or **Felsenkirche** (Church on the Rocks), and **Goerke House** (see below), are situated on top of neighbouring hillocks in the old part of town. Each has an excellent view of the

Namibia's diamonds

Diamonds have lured fortune seekers and enchanted mankind for centuries. The ancient Greeks believed they were splinters of stars that fell from the sky and these precious stones have been regarded with fascination and intrigue since they were first mined in India 2500 years ago. They are a pure mineral extracted from the earth's crust, the hardest of all natural substances in the world, and inarguably the most beautiful. A diamond is a crystal of pure carbon, formed by immense pressure 60-120 km beneath the earth's surface. Sixty million years ago, when today's southern continents began to divide, the earth discharged molten mass by way of volcanic eruptions known as Kimberlites (after which the famous South African diamond mine Kimberly is named). Diamonds are usually extracted from Kimberlites below the earth's surface by mining, but in Namibia these hardened masses eroded with time and weather causing them to emerge from the surface, and the debris was washed away and distributed through the deserts and rivers, which in turn washed them into the ocean too. Namibia's diamonds are largely mined by pushing back the desert's sand to expose ancient beaches rich in diamond-bearing gravel; at sea diamond divers sweep the ocean floor with suction hoses connected to pumps on small boats. Namibia extracts more than two million carats of diamonds per annum, and it is one of the world's largest producers of gem quality diamonds; about 98% of diamonds extracted are good enough to make jewellery. Once polished, 95% of these are sent to the major international diamond markets, such as Antwerp and Tel Aviv, whilst 5% are sold to local Namibian jewellers.

town centre and harbour area. The foundation stone for the church was laid in 1911 and the building was consecrated the following year. It is notable for its fine stained-glass windows and as with the Christuskirche in Windhoek, the altar window was donated by Kaiser Wilhelm II and the altar bible by his wife. Just below the church in Berg Street is an interesting collection of original townhouses. Unfortunately these can only be viewed from the outside. To get a better idea of what they would have looked like inside, visit Goerke House (see below).

One of the more modern attractions in town is the **waterfront,** below Hafen Street and next to the harbour. A wide promenade and pier offer views of the changing scenes at the harbour as boats come and go, and there is a playground for children and a tidal pool. The development is also home to coffee shops and restaurants and the active Lüderitz Yacht Club.

Goerke House

ⓘ *Diamantberg St, guided tours Mon-Fri 1400-1600, Sat-Sun 1600-1700, N$25, children (6-14) N$15.*
The house was named after its original owner Hans Goerke who had been a store inspector in the Shutztruppe and then became a successful local businessman.

The Sperrgebiet

Following the discovery of diamonds at Kolmanskop in 1908 and the ensuing diamond rush, the German colonial authorities declared a Sperrgebiet, or 'forbidden zone', along the Atlantic coast. It gave sole rights for mining in German South-West Africa to the Deutsche Diamantengesellschaft ('German Diamond Company'), and today the exclusive mining rights for this area are held by NAMDEB, owned jointly by the Namibian Government and De Beers. The Sperrgebiet extends from the Orange River in the south for 360 km to about 70 km north of Lüderitz and inland for 100 km, and covers 26,000 sq km; about 3% of Namibia's total land mass. However, mining only takes place in about 5% of the Sperrgebiet, with most of the area acting as a buffer zone. With the exception of the coastal area where the diamonds occur, where for over nearly a century has suffered considerable damage and scarring of the landscape from mining excavations, the inland habitat has been largely untouched making it one of Africa's last wilderness areas. Roughly 40% is desert, 30% is grassland, and 30% is rocky, and due to this lack of human intervention, the Sperrgebiet has a diverse range of flora and fauna. Despite the Orange River being the only permanent water supply in the area, there are nearly 800 species of succulent plants, of which 234 have been recorded as being endemic to southwest Namibia. It supports animals such as gemsbok, springbok and brown hyena, while rare bird species include the African oystercatcher, the black-headed canary, and the dune lark.

This untamed wilderness was granted extra protection when the Sperrgebiet National Park was gazetted in 2008, which now means that over 75% of the Namib Desert falls into protected areas. Then in 2012 it was renamed the Tsau //Khaeb National Park. The name derives from the local Nama language and means 'deep sandy soils' in reference to the park's most enduring feature. Given that these developments are still new,

CDM (Consolidated Diamond Mines) acquired the house in 1920, sold it to the government in 1944 when it became the town magistrate's official residence, and then repurchased the building in 1983. The house lay empty between 1980 and 1983 after the magistrate was recalled to Keetmanshoop (there not being enough crime in Lüderitz to warrant his presence).

From the outside, the house is an array of different architectural styles incorporating Roman and Egyptian, amongst others, and inside it is possible to imagine what many of the crumbling houses at nearby Kolmanskop must have looked like in their heyday. There is a fine stained-glass window above the staircase depicting a flock of flamingos on the beach, as well as an excellent view over the town and harbour from the balcony of the main bedroom.

it will be some time before names are correctly reflected and used, and diamond mining still goes on in selected areas, so it shouldn't come as too much of a surprise to learn that it's still inaccessible to visitors and it's forbidden to enter without a permit.

However, there is still the opportunity to explore the unexplored. The easiest is a visit to **Kolmanskop** (see page 350) which, although just off the main B4 road into Lüderitz, actually lies within the Sperrgebiet, which is why you need permits to visit, and the day trip to the **Bogenfels Rock Arch** (see page 356). For the more adventurous, there are other sandy (and windy) escapades into the 'forbidden zone' run by a selected number of tour operators along the stretch of coastline between Sylvia Hill northwards to Sandwich Harbour in the wilderness section of the Namib-Naukluft Park and as far as Walvis Bay. Participants drive in their own fully equipped self-sufficient 4WD vehicles and are accompanied throughout the trip by vehicles of the experienced guides, who will also teach drivers the skills necessary from what tyre pressure is needed for soft sand, to what gear you will need to shift into to descend a steep dune face. Most of these excursions start in Lüderitz and cover up to 450-650 km of remarkable desert, dune and beach scenery and take three to six days. Points of interest visited include **Saddle Hill**, **Koichab Pan**, **Sylvia Hill**, **Conception Bay**, **Langewand**, the wreck of the **Eduard Bohlen**, **Fischersbrunn** and **Sandwich Harbour**. Drivers should prepare themselves for deep sand, flying grit, fluctuating temperatures, savage gales, and most importantly of all – one hell of an adventure…

For more information contact the following companies: **Coastways Tours**, Lüderitz, T063-202002, www.coastways.com.na. **Faces of the Namib**, South Africa, T+27 (0)21-912 1411, www.facesofthe namib.com. **West Coast 4x4 Namibia**, Omaruru, T0817-752886, www. westcoast4x4.co.za.

Lüderitz Museum

ⓘ *Diaz St, T063-202582, Mon-Fri 1530-1700, phone and they may be able to open up at other times, N\$15 per person.*

This tiny museum was founded by Friederich Eberlanz who arrived in Lüderitz in 1914. Fascinated by the local flora, he started a private collection which grew to incorporate ancient stone tools, rocks and other items he discovered. This private collection attracted a wide interest and the existing museum was established in 1961. Today the museum also has displays of local history, the mining industry and an interesting collection of photos and artefacts of the indigenous peoples of the country. In the outdoor courtyard are some whale bones, wagons and colonial-era mining equipment.

Kolmanskop Ghost Town → *Colour map 3, B2.*

ⓘ *10 km inland of Lüderitz on the B4, clearly visible alongside the road, T063-204031, www.kolmanskuppe.com. Guided tours in English and German, Mon-Sat 0930 and 1100, Sun and public holidays 1000, N$75, children (6-14) N$40, under 6s free. Tickets can be purchased at the entrance or if you are already in Lüderitz purchase tickets beforehand from Lüderitz Safaris & Tours, on Bismarck St. These tickets allow you to go on the tour, visit the museum and spend some time exploring the houses and dunes after the tour until 1300. There is no access in the afternoon unless you obtain a special photo permit for N$220, which includes the 0930 tour and allows access between sunrise and sunset for photography.*

The former diamond boom town of Kolmanskop, finally deserted in 1956, is now a ghost town and lies crumbling in the desert 10 km inland from Lüderitz, gradually being weathered by the wind and buried by the sand. It is a fascinating place to visit, offering as it does a glimpse into an exciting part of Namibia's history.

In April 1908, Zacharias Lewala, a worker on the Lüderitz–Aus railway line, presented a shiny stone to his supervisor August Stauch, who was clever enough to obtain a prospecting licence before having it officially verified and thereby starting the diamond rush around the site of Kolmanskop. In the early days, in the nearby Itadel Valley, stones were so accessible that prospectors with no mining equipment would crawl on their hands and knees in full moonlight collecting the glittering stones.

In September 1908, the colonial government declared a Sperrgebiet or 'forbidden zone' extending 360 km northwards from the Orange River and 100 km inland from the coast in order to control the mining of the diamonds, and in February 1909, a central diamond market was established.

The First World War effectively stopped diamond production, by which time more than 5.4 million carats of very high-quality stones had been extracted from the region. The recession that followed the war hit the diamond industry badly. However, Sir Ernest Oppenheimer, the chairman of the Anglo-American Company, saw this as an opportunity to buy up all the small diamond companies operating in the Sperrgebiet, and combine them to form Consolidated Diamond Mines. CDM, as it became known, was to control all diamond mining in the area until entering into partnership with the Namibian government in 1995 under the new name of NAMDEB.

Kolmanskop enjoyed its heyday in the 1920s when it grew rapidly to service the diamond miners and eventually the families which followed. A hospital, gymnasium and concert hall, school, butchery, bakery and a number of fine houses were built in the middle of the desert, and at its peak there were as many as 300 German and 800 Oshiwambo adults living in the town. The hospital was ultra-modern and was equipped with the first X-ray machine in southern Africa (used principally for detecting swallowed gemstones, rather than broken bones!).

The sheer wealth generated at Kolmanskop (peak production was over 30,000 carats per day) is demonstrated by the way in which water was supplied to the town. Every month a ship left Cape Town carrying 1000 tonnes of water, and each resident was supplied with 20 litres per day for free. Those requiring additional water paid for it, at half the price of beer. The lack of fresh water to power steam engines also forced the building of a power station which supplied electricity, very advanced technology at the time, to power the mining machinery.

However, the boom years in Kolmanskop ended in 1928 when diamond reserves six times the size of those at Kolmanskop (although of lesser quality) were discovered at the mouth of the Orange River. The town of Oranjemund was built in 1936 to exploit these reserves and in 1938 most of the workers and equipment relocated from Kolmanskop to this new headquarters. Following this, the town went into steady decline, although the last people (including the 100 full-time labourers employed to remove the encroaching sand) only left Kolmanskop in 1956, abandoning this once-flourishing town to time and the forces of nature.

Kolmanskop was rescued from the desert in 1979 following a CDM-commissioned report to assess the tourist potential of this ghost town. In 1980, simple restoration began and the town was opened to tourism. At present the most carefully preserved/ restored buildings are the **Recreation Hall** and those adjacent to the **museum**, and the lavish **Manager's House**, complete with marble bath, grand piano and sun room.

The guided tour documents the history and stories about Kolmanskop, and afterwards you are left to your own devices to scramble through the dunes and explore all the deserted buildings. The **Ghost Town Tavern** is a pleasant café in what was the champagne bar of Kolmanskop's casino and is decorated with antique furniture found in the houses. It is open 0900-1400 for light lunches, coffee/tea and cakes, so you can visit here before the 1100 tour or after the 0930 tour. Next to it, the **Kolmanskop Diamond Room**, once the gentlemen's smoking room in the casino, has information boards with good photographs about today's diamond industry in Namibia. They follow the progression of diamonds from their valuation in rough form to their manufacture into finished stones for jewellery, and for the benefit of customers, the 'four Cs' are illustrated – cut, colour, clarity and carat. It also sells small single cut diamonds, which are cut and polished locally by the NamGem Diamond Manufacturing Company at their cutting factory in Okahanja, and each diamond is issued with a grading certificate so that the buyer knows exactly what the characteristics of the diamond is.

Lüderitz Peninsula → *Colour map 3, B1.*

Assuming you have your own vehicle and that the winds are not too strong, an interesting excursion can be made around the peninsula south of town. Follow the Keetmanshoop road out of town and look out for a signpost for Diaz Point just after the buildings end. From here a twisting gravel road heads south round the coast through a moonscape of rocky bays, mud flats, beaches and small islands. Shortly after passing the water tower, the Second Lagoon comes in to view. When the tide is out it is possible to cut the corner and cross the mud flats here, but you are better sticking to the road in a saloon car.

A few kilometres beyond the lagoon you have the choice of heading straight to the southernmost point of the peninsula, **Grosse Bucht** (6 km) via the D733, or continuing on the D701 to Griffith Bay, Sturmvogel Bucht and Diaz Point. Either way, the road loops round.

Most visitors head straight for Diaz Point and the viewpoint for Halifax Island. However, if it is late in the afternoon it is worth following the D734 as far as **Griffith Bay** where you can enjoy a distant view of Lüderitz bathed in the evening sunlight. Continuing along the D701, and after a further 5 km or so, look out for a turning to the right. This road leads to **Sturmvogel Bucht**, one of the best bathing beaches in

Lüderitz Peninsula

Dunes

Flamingo Island

Atlantic Ocean

Seal Island

□ Picnic Site

Agate Beach

■ Picnic Site

Penguin Island

■ Factories

Angra Point

Shark Island

Nautilus

Diaz Point

Diaz Cross

Lighthouse Radio Masts

Sturmvogel Bucht

Whaling Station

□ Picnic Site

Shearwater Bay

Lüderitz

Halifax Island

Guano Bay

Griffith Bay

Bathing Beach

□ Cemetery

Prison

B4

To Airport, Kolmanskop & Keetmanshoop

□ Picnic Site

Radford Bay

Angra Club ■

Essy Bay

□ Picnic Site

Swartberge

D734

□ Water Tower

D701

Second Lagoon

Eberlanz Höhle

Kleiner Fjord

□ Picnic Site

D702

Diamond Area No 1 (part of the Sperrgebiet: closed to the public)

Mud Flats

N

▲ *To Grosse Bucht*
▼ *To Grosse Bucht*

⊢ 1 km
⊢ 1 mile

Where to stay 🛏
Diaz Point Camping & Self-Catering
Accomodation & Coffee Shop **1**

the area. Also of interest are the rusty remains of a whaling station. It doesn't take much imagination to picture what used to occur here.

Just past the turning for **Shearwater Bay**, the road goes over a small ridge and presents a good view of Diaz Point. Take the next right to visit **Diaz Point**, 22 km from town. A large cross stands here, a replica of the original erected by Portuguese explorer Bartholomeu Diaz in 1487 on his way back to Portugal after sailing around the Cape of Good Hope. Access to the cross is via a wooden bridge and some steps up to an exposed position on a rocky headland. When the wind blows make sure everything is securely attached, it is easy to lose a hat or a pair of sunglasses. The nearby lighthouse was built in 1910 and the modern foghorn tower was added later. At the car park here are a few buildings which are the **Diaz Point Camping & Self-Catering Accommodation** (see Where to stay, page 354), which also has a simple but charming coffee shop (daily 0800-1800); in fact the sign says it all – "tea, cake and beer" – and this is well worth stopping at for a warming drink and piece of home-made chocolate cake.

As you follow the D702 towards Grosse Bucht there are plenty of tracks off to the right which lead up to a variety of vantage points along the coast including **Knochen Bay** and **Essy Bay** where there are *braai* sites and basic toilets. Finally the broad south-facing **Grosse Bucht** (Big Bay) comes into view, which is the furthest south you can travel along this part of the coast as this is where the Sperrgebiet (see box, page 348) begins. When you reach a junction, take a right and this will lead you to the western end of the bay and a *braai* site. The shortest route back to town is via the D733, about 40 minutes' drive.

All along this section of coast there is a profusion of wildlife; just offshore from the cross itself is a seal colony and further down the coast on **Halifax Island** there are large numbers of cormorants and African (jackass) penguins. Pink flamingos flock in the bays and also in small onshore lakes. The presence of so much wildlife is due to the cold, clean and abundantly fertile Benguela Current, which provides ideal conditions for catching their prey of fish, rock lobster and oyster. It's also not unusual to see brown hyena or jackal trotting along the shore, which in turn prey on seal pups.

Agate Beach → *Colour map 3, B1.*

A similarly rocky drive of about 6 km goes north out of Lüderitz alongside fenced-off areas of the Sperrgebiet. It leads to Agate Beach (follow the signs from Hafen Street), a fine, sandy stretch of coast on a calm bay suitable for surfing and swimming, for those willing to brave the cold sea. Small piles of stones and mini-trenches dot the beach, remnants from past diamond and agate diggings. In the late afternoon there is a good chance of seeing wild gemsbok and springbok. **Note** Most of the land on the inland side of the road is part of the NAMDEB concession area and thus closed to the public. It is not advisable to venture into these areas at any time.

For hotel and restaurant price codes and other relevant information, see pages 21-28.

🛏 Where to stay

Lüderitz *p343, map p345*
Lüderitz boasts an excellent selection of hospitable hotels and guesthouses. Heating rather than a/c is a priority here.
$$$-$$ Nest Hotel, Ostend Beach, T063-204000, www.nesthotel.com. The smartest option in town set on a peninsula with 73 modern rooms with DSTV, balcony and sea views (if you open the windows you can hear the waves lapping against the rocks), some of which are wheelchair-friendly and suitable for families. Very good restaurant, bar with open terrace where you can indulge yourself with oysters and champagne, plus a 'sunset bar' at the top of the hotel (residents only), swimming pool, sauna, Wi-Fi, the brave can swim off the beach at the front of the hotel. A perfect base for exploring Lüderitz.
$$ Bay View Hotel, Diaz St, T063-202288, www.luderitzhotels.com. Friendly, family-run place with small-town charm, in a blue-and-white art deco building with 22 rooms arranged around 2 courtyards, 1 with a swimming pool, old-fashioned decor but comfortable. Restaurant and bar, can arrange fishing trips and operates the 2 self-catering houses and campsite at **Diaz Point** (see below).
$$ Protea Sea View Hotel Zum Sperrgebiet, Woermann St, T063-203411/3, www.seaview-luderitz.com. Good-value mid-range hotel but in a modern block on a hill in a quiet residential area but lacks ambience compared to its competitors, 22 rooms

with DSTV and balconies overlooking the harbour, lovely indoor heated pool with sauna/steam room, and decent restaurant.
$$-$ Diaz Point, 22 km from town on the Lüderitz Peninsula beneath the cross (see page 353), T063-202288, www.diaz-point.com. 1 self-catering house sleeping up to 12 and a rather unusual campsite where you sleep outdoors on wooden slatted bunks with your own bedding in stone enclosures with fishing nets as a roof; a much better option than pitching a tent in the wind. Hot showers, flush loos but no electricity, the coffee shop, bar and kiosk here is open 0800-1800 where you can get breakfast, sandwiches, cakes and warming drinks.
$ Backpackers Lodge, 2 Ring St, T063-202000. Small, simple set-up in a colonial house with dorms and 2 doubles, shared bathrooms, kitchen, communal lounge with DSTV, *braai* area, small lawn for a few tents. An alternative for budget travellers to the exposed Shark Island campsite.
$ Haus Sandrose, 15 Bismarck St, T063-202630, www.haussandrose.com. Bright yellow house with hands-on owners and 4 lovely flats set back from the street in a plant filled courtyard, 1 sleeping a family of 5, self-catering available, but a better option is the breakfasts in the pretty dining room full of ceramics, *braai* area and Wi-Fi.
$ Karios Cottage, on the peninsula just before the boom gate to Shark Island, T0816-505598, christo.b@iway. na. Smart B&B in a modern house with 5 a/c rooms offering great views across the harbour, DSTV, Wi-Fi, mini-kitchen, *braais* on the terraces, handmade linen, breakfast packs can be ordered for early starts and light lunches can be taken

in the adjoining coffee shop. Run by a wonderful hospitable family who are very musical – you may be serenaded over breakfast.

$ Kratzplatz, 5 Nachtigal St, T063-202458, www.kratzplatz.info. Quirky and easy-going place in a central location in a bright pink converted church built in 1911 with high ceilings and interesting decor – a mixture of antiques and 'retro' fridges and TVs –12 large rooms, sleeping up to 4, with Wi-Fi, tea and coffee facilities and some have leafy patios. Very good food and atmosphere at the **Barrels** restaurant and pub (see Restaurants, below).

$ Shark Island, take a left at the end of Bismarck St and follow the road round the harbour and across the causeway onto Shark Island, reservations **Namibia Wildlife Resorts (NWR)**, Windhoek T061-285 7200, www.nwr.com.na. The NWR resort here is pretty rundown and basic of their properties but worth mentioning because of the location – Shark Island is the rocky peninsula that winds around the west of the harbour and is a windswept place with stormy ocean views that was in fact a concentration camp from 1904 to 1907 during the Herero and Nama genocide. Accommodation is in 3 poorly maintained self-catering chalets sleeping 4 and the much better option is the converted **lighthouse** with 2 bedrooms with the panoramic view from the top makes it totally unique but access is a little awkward via a ladder and a trapdoor. The rocky **campsite** has 20 sites with basic and weather-beaten ablution blocks. **Note** Tents have been known to blow away; make sure they are securely pegged down and it's strongly advised to put up your tent only when you're ready to get into it. If you want to go to the loo in the middle of the night, make sure someone stays in the tent or weigh it

down with rocks! For a swirl in the wind, day visitors are allowed on to Shark Island from 0800-1700; just ask nicely at the gate.

🍴 Restaurants

Lüderitz p343, map p345
Restaurants in Lüderitz serve the freshest seafood and platters are very good value. Some items, such as rock lobster (crayfish), are seasonal.

$$$ The Penguin, T063-204000, at the Nest Hotel (see Where to stay, above). Daily 1830-2200 for dinner; but light meals are available throughout the day. Smart and formal hotel restaurant offering good value buffets at the weekend plus an imaginative à la carte menu during the week. Ocean view and outside seating area (for when the wind stops blowing). On the expensive side but very good seafood, meat and vegetarian dishes and large choice of wines.

$$-$ Barrels, to one side of Kratzplatz, entrance from Berg St (see Where to stay, above). 1600-late. A popular local watering hole where residents occasionally bring out their guitars or rig up the karaoke machine. A short menu but good home-cooked food such as roast pork, *eisbein*, grilled fish, crayfish in season and *potjie* stews on winter days. Excellent cosy pub atmosphere with a roaring fire on cool evenings.

$$-$ Ritzi's, at the waterfront, Hafen St, T063-202818. Mon-Sat 0800-2200. Good location with tables on the wooden deck under umbrellas for great views of the harbour, decent choice including pizzas and specials such as fresh kingklip fish or oysters and reasonably priced South African wines, but reports of slow and indifferent service.

$ Diaz Coffee Shop, T063-203147, corner of Bismarck and Nachtigal Sts.

Mon-Fri 0700-1700, Sat 0800-1500, Sun 0900-1300. Excellent creamy cappuccinos, English breakfasts, lunchtime snacks, and the cakes, pastries and other goodies are baked daily, light and airy central venue with fat sofas to relax in and it also sells gifts.

$ Rumours Grill & Sports Bar, at the **Kapps Hotel**, Bay Rd, T063-202345, www.kappshotel.com. Daily 1800-late. Kapps is a historic hotel that dates back to the diamond boom days and was built in 1907, with 14 rooms grouped around the courtyard at the back of **Rumours**, but they are dark, dingy and can be noisy (ignore the fancy website). Far better to come eat and drink here; the bar is probably your best bet for 'action' in the evenings (not saying much in Lüderitz) and has a pool table and a menu of decent burgers and seafood.

$ Shearwater Oyster Bar, Lüderitz Boatyard, Insel St, T063-204031. Mon-Thu 1000-1800, Fri 1000-1900. On the way to Shark Island, a jaunty shed upstairs from the oyster farm decorated with nets and buoys. The drill is simple…a lunch of 2 dozen oysters washed down with a fine bottle of South African sauvignon blanc. Eat them raw or cooked with blue or parmesan cheese and they cost as little as N$5 each. Tapas are available as an alternative. Contact them to arrange a 30-min guided tour through the oyster processing factory.

O Shopping

Lüderitz *p343, map p345*
If you are self-catering, there is an **OK** on Hafen St and a **Spar** on Moltke St. Both have a bakery and a butcher's counter and are open Mon-Fri until 1800, Sat-Sun until 1300. The Portuguese supermarket in Bismarck St is also open Sat afternoons

1600-2000. The bottle store is just up from Haus Sandrose on Bismarck St, and the fishmonger is just outside the gate into the harbour. A branch of **Cymot** for fishing and camping gear and car accessories is on Nachtigal St, though it has limited stock.

O What to do

Lüderitz *p343, map p345*
**Bogenfels – 'Rock Arch' Tour
Coastways Tours**, office at the Total petrol station on Bay Rd, T063-202002, www.coastways.com.na. This is one of the most interesting tours in the Lüderitz region but it requires a certain degree of forward planning as most of the tour is within the Sperrgebiet and permits have to be processed in advance; visitors need to provide **Coastways** with clear scanned photocopies of their passports at least 10 days in advance. The tour lasts a full day; the 55-m-high rock arch lies 110 km south of Lüderitz. Most of the drive is across flat gravel plains, but to break the monotony there are also visits to another abandoned mining town, Pomona, and the Idatal Valley which famously yielded surface diamonds, gathered by crawling prospectors in the moonlight. This is an enjoyable trip and made that little bit special as it allows you to enter an area of the desert that has been closed to the public since 1908. Prices are from N$2500, children (under 12) N$812, minimum of 2; the cost goes down the more people in the group. **Coastways** also runs multi-day 4WD excursions into the Sperrgebiet (see box, page 348).

Diaz Point and Halifax Island
Boat trips depart every morning from the waterfront jetty, weather permitting. The route takes you between Shark Island

and Penguin Island, past Angra Point and on to Diaz Point. Under ideal conditions you will sail to Halifax Island to view the colony of African (jackass) penguins amongst the deserted structures of past guano mining. Cormorants, flamingos and oystercatchers are often seen on the island and you can also expect to see Heaviside dolphins and the colony of Cape fur seals. Dress warm, with windproofs. Both these boats depart every morning at 0800 and the trip returns at 1015 in time to get to and go on the 1100 tour of Kolmanskop; book the day before at the **Lüderitz Safaris & Tours** office (see page 344) when you can also get your Kolmanskop permit.
Sedina Boat Trips, T063-204030. The trip is by the schooner *Sedina* and if the wind is right the billowing red sails are hoisted for an exciting sail: N$350, children (6-14) N$175, under 6s free.
Zeppard Boat Trips, T0816-042805. The same trip is by a modern motorized catamaran (Zeppard means 'seahorse' in Dutch), which may appeal to those who want a little steadier time on the water if it's really windy: N$350, children (under 12) free. If there are enough takers they also offer a 1-hr sunset cruise that passes between Shark Island and Penguin Island and then heads towards Agate Beach for a view of the dune sea: N$150 per person.

Transport

Lüderitz *p343, map p345*
337 km to Keetmanshoop, 401 km to Fish River Canyon (Hobas), 563 km to Noordoewer (South African border).

Air
Lüderitz Airport, 9 km east of town off the B4 on the opposite side of the road to Kolmanskop, T063-202027; there is no public transport so ask your hotel to arrange a pick-up. **Air Namibia**, reservations Windhoek, T061-299 6111, www.airnamibia.com.na. There are flights Mon, Wed, Fri and Sun from **Windhoek** (Eros airport) to Lüderitz (1 hr) that continue on to **Oranjemund** (50 mins). From Lüderitz to Windhoek (1 hr 35 mins), you'll go via Oranjemund. Note that there can be delays if the wind is too strong, always allow an extra day if connecting with an international flight.

Car hire
Budget has an office at M&Z Motors, Bahnhof St, T063-202777, www.budget. co.za. **Avis**, 25 Bismarck St, T063-203968, www.avis.co.za. Ensure you reserve vehicles in advance.

Directory

Lüderitz *p343, map p345*
Mechanical breakdown Trentyre, 101 Bay Rd, near the Total petrol station, T063-202137, sells new tyres, and offers tyre repairs and breakdown services in and around Lüderitz.
Medical services State Hospital, Tal St, T063-202446.

The Far South and Fish River Canyon

The route south from Keetmanshoop is arguably the most desolate journey in Namibia, and if you have ever wondered what the surface of the moon looks like, this is the place to find out, albeit in blinding sunlight. But in defiance of the bareness of the arid, rocky landscape, a host of desert plants, cacti, succulents and quiver trees survive and even prosper. The B1 dissects this region on its long journey south to the border with South Africa, and there is little to interest the motorist – except for the service towns offering cold drinks and fuel along the way. But veer off to the east and you'll find the highlight of Namibia's deep south: the huge gash in the earth that is the spectacular Fish River Canyon. Its towering rock faces and deep ravines were formed by water erosion from the meandering Fish River, and today it is part of the |Ai-|Ais/Richtersveld Transfrontier Park which straddles the border of Namibia and South Africa. The best place to take in the jaw-dropping views is from the observation point at Hobas before dropping to the base of the canyon to the hot spring resort at |Ai-|Ais|. For many, the Fish River Canyon is the last or first place they visit in Namibia and it serves as a fitting example of the country's natural splendor.

Grünau → *Colour map 3, C3/4. Phone code: 063.*

Leaving Keetmanshoop, the B1 heads south for 163 km through the Karas Mountains to Grünau. This tiny settlement of no more than a few hundred people is strategically important as a crossroads and staging post to the two borders with South Africa and ultimately to Cape Town and Johannesburg (see Border crossing box, page 362). The B1 itself continues a further 142 km to the border at Noordoewer for the west coast of South Africa and eventually Cape Town, while the B3 heads towards Karasburg, 50 km away, and continues for another 112 km to the border at Ariamsvlei, for the South African town of Upington and the routes to Johannesburg. Grünau is also about a 100 km from the spectacular Fish River Canyon to the west. The name Grünau means 'green pastures' in German, but the plain that it lies on is the stony Gamchab Basin devoid of grass except after exceptionally heavy rains. The Grünau junction has a 24-hour petrol station, a supermarket, a garage with tow-in service, roadside craft stalls and there are some pleasant guest farms in the region which make a fine break from driving along the monotonous B1.

Karasburg → *Colour map 3, C4. Phone code: 063.*

From Grünau the route to and from South Africa via the B3 and the Ariamsvlei border goes through Karasburg, 50 km west of Grünau. Although it is the only relatively large town south of Keetmanshoop, Karasburg is no more than somewhere to stop en route to somewhere else and its main reason for existence is to support the large-scale sheep and game farms in the area. As such it has a number of services including 24-hour petrol stations, and **Spar** and **Shoprite** supermarkets, but otherwise is devoid of attractions for the visitor (even the town hotel has closed down). After refueling and stocking up, it's another 112 km to the border (see Border crossing box, page 362).

Warmbad → *Colour map 3, C4. Phone code: 063.*

Located 50 km south of Karasburg on the M21 road, Warmbad is a tiny settlement in the deep south of Namibia with a rich history. It is the site of the oldest mission station in Namibia, and in 1805 the Albrecht brothers, Abraham and Christian, attempted to convert the local Nama people and erected a church and a pastor's house. These two buildings were the first European-style buildings on Namibian soil, but both were destroyed in 1811 by the local community under leadership of Jager Afrikaner (father of the famous Jan Jonker Afrikaner). The Wesleyan missionary Edward Cook erected a new mission on the foundations of the destroyed buildings in 1834, baptizing 437 converts before being buried in a grave on the outskirts of the village that is today a national monument. The faith of the community was later taken up by the Rhenish Missionary Society, which built a school in 1868 and a church in 1877. The settlement livened up once again during the German colonial period when a Schutztruppe fort was built in 1905 to counter the Herero and Nama uprisings.

Some years later in 1922, Warmbad became the first sight in then South-West Africa to be bombed by the South African Air Force. The Nama had resisted

The |Ai-|Ais/Richtersveld Transfrontier Park

The |Ai-|Ais and Fish River Canyon Park was officially proclaimed in 1968, and not long after, the Huns Mountains to the west and several farms in the region were added. The Orange River formed the southern boundary of this protected area in Namibia, as well as the northern boundary of the Richtersveld National Park in South Africa. The similarity of geology, landscapes, flora and fauna of both resulted in the signing of a treaty in 2003 that amalgamated the |Ai-|Ais and Fish River Canyon Park and the Richtersveld National Park to form the |Ai-|Ais/Richtersveld Transfrontier Park. It covers 6045 sq km of the dramatic landscapes that sweep away inland from both the north and south banks of the Orange River (also known as the Gariep in South Africa), and is managed jointly by the Namibian Ministry of Environment and Tourism (MET) and South African National Parks (SANParks).

The Namibian side of the park is a vaguely defined area and there are no official boundaries, entry points or indeed entry fees (with the exception of the fees to Hobas and |Ai-|Ais and the odd conservation fee at some of the private lodges). In South Africa the whole of the Richtersveld section falls under the jurisdiction of SANParks and it does have boundaries, entry gates/offices and park entry fees do apply.

The Namibian and South African sections of the park have recently been connected by the **Sendelingsdrif border crossing** via a vehicle pontoon across the river. This is reached on the C13 and is 136 km northwest of the Vioolsdrift/Noordoewer border. To get there, the C13 turn-off on the B1 is at the Engen petrol station, and the 50 km section from Noordoewer to Aussenkehr is tarred and is a beautiful drive as the road meanders through the vineyards alongside the Orange River. Aussenkehr itself has a petrol station, a Spar supermarket with bottle shop, and if you want to stay, the **Norotshama**

a hunting-dog tax or alternatively changes to the borders of their reserve (depending on references used), and were bombed for their pains resulting in the loss of 115 souls.

Warmbad is also the site of some hot springs which give the place its name, and these were first harnessed as a swimming pool by the Germans in 1908. However, it was about this time that Warmbad lost its importance as a stopover from the Cape (it was bypassed by the railway and roads), and the original buildings were abandoned and fell into decay.

Today it's a rather lost village sprawling in the dust and the spring is surrounded by the crumbling ruins of the mission station and fort. Although some tourism development was started in 2006, including a new spa-like building and spring (which never opened), this decay still characterizes Warmbad, adding to the overall melancholic atmosphere shrouding the village. There was a community-run campsite that was also developed in 2006 but never really amounted to much and few people visited. If you want to stay, there's no reason why you can't ask in the

River Resort (see Where to stay, page 370). Beyond Aussenkehr the C13 is gravel, which can usually be driven without engaging 4WD, though there are narrow sections and sharp bends. If the river floods (December-April is flood season), this gravel section could be closed; check by phoning the lodge or SANParks at Sendelingsdrift.

The Sendelingsdrift pontoon operates daily 0800-1615 whenever there is a vehicle and is managed by SANParks. Again in flood season it is advisable to phone SANParks to find out if the pontoon is operating. It can carry two 4WD vehicles or one with a trailer; costs are R150-200 per vehicle depending on size, R100 for a motorbike, plus R100 per person. For details of vehicle requirements for border crossings between Namibia and South Africa, see Border crossing box, page 362.

Once across the river, Sendelingsdrift is where the park office and SANParks rest camp is, which has 10 self-catering chalets, a campsite, a small shop for basic provisions and petrol pump. Visitors also need to pay park fees here; R170, children (under 12) R85, per 24 hours. The rest of the Richtersveld is a rugged, hauntingly beautiful and virtually untouched corner of South Africa that is well worth exploring on the way to or from Namibia. But there are only basic rocky tracks and remote campsites, and away from Sendelingsdrift, SANParks stipulate that you need to be in a convoy of at least two fully equipped self-sufficient 4WDs. The route out of the park is via Alexander Bay and Port Nolloth on South Africa's West Coast, and eventually to Springbok on the N7, 330 km from Sendelingsdrift.

For more information on the |Ai-|Ais/Richtersveld Transfrontier Park and accommodation reservations, contact SANParks, Sendelingsdrift park office T+27(0)27-831 1506, head office and central reservations T+27(0)12-428 9111, www.sanparks.org.

village if you can still camp, and you should be able to enlist the services of a local guide to explain some of the ruins and the gravestones in the graveyard.

Noordoewer and Orange River → Colour map 3, C3/4. Phone code: 063.
The 163-km drive from Grünau to Noordoewer climbs steadily to a plateau, beyond which it is all downhill to the Orange River. Noordoewer is a small settlement on the banks of the river known for being one of the hottest places in Namibia, where summer temperatures can reach 50°C. It feels almost like entering hell's kitchen, but fortunately, there is an abundance of water, and the green riverbanks soon dispel that notion. The Orange River brings life to the surrounding arid lands, and as well as irrigating fruit, in particular grapes, mangoes and dates. With the water comes a varied birdlife, including red bishops, African darters and fish eagles.

The Orange, known as the Gariep in South Africa, was first explored by Europeans in 1760 and was named by Colonel Robert Gordon after the House of Orange. Another account of its naming suggests that it may have been called after the orangey colour

Border crossing

Ariamsvlei (Namibia)–Nakop (South Africa)

This border is 112 km west of Karasburg on the B3 and is open 24 hours, T063-280057. There's a Puma petrol station on the Namibian side with a shop and takeaway, as well as **Joliens Kitchen**, a small truck-stop and café where you can get a snack and cup of coffee. These are the final places to spend or swap over to rand any remaining Namibian dollars. Ensure you fill up here, as it's another 149 km on the N10 to Upington on the Gariep River (known as the Orange in Namibia). This is the largest town in this region of the Northern Cape and has numerous places to stay and other services, and accessible attractions include the **Augrabies Falls National Park** and the **Kgalagadi Transfrontier Park**. From Upington the most direct route to Johannesburg is 747 km via the N12 and N17. Consult the *Footprint South Africa Handbook* for options.

Noordoewer (Namibia)–Viooolsdrif (South Africa)

Again the border is open 24 hours, T063-209 9111, and here it involves crossing the bridge over the Orange River (also called the Gariep in South Africa) in no-man's land between the two border posts. The Engen petrol station on the Namibian side has a shop and takeaway and is the final place to spend or swap over to rand any remaining Namibian dollars. Ensure you have sufficient fuel to get to the next petrol stations, 119 km away at **Springbok**, which also has a choice of hotels and shops. This is the best border to cross for Cape Town which is 678 km south at the end of the N7, and alternative routes to the N7 include following South Africa's west coast, south from Port Nolloth. It's worth spending a day or two in Springbok itself if its wild flower season (usually August-September). Consult the *Footprint South Africa Handbook* for options.

Apart from over-busy holiday periods it should not take too long to complete formalities at either of these borders. Drivers will need to have a licence and vehicle registration documents, and police at the border may check your engine and chassis numbers, so it's helpful to know where these are on the vehicle. If you are in a hire car ensure you have written permission from the car hire company to take the vehicle into South Africa and make sure that your third-party insurance is valid in South Africa. **Note** Firewood cannot be taken from Namibia into South Africa and it will be confiscated on the South African side. Most nationalities do not need visas for South Africa and will be issued with a visitors permit for up to 90 days but your passport must be valid for six months from the date you leave South Africa. Namibia is on the same time zone as South Africa (GMT+2) during summer but reverts to one hour behind South Africa in winter – Namibia's daylight saving time is from the first Sunday of April to the first Sunday in September.

of its water thanks to its sandy banks. It rises in the Drakensberg Mountains along the border between South Africa and Lesotho at an altitude of over 3000 m and then runs some 2200 km westwards to sea level at the Atlantic where it forms the southern border of Namibia and South Africa's Northern Cape Province.

Noordoewer means 'north bank' in Afrikaans, and the village lies opposite the South African town of Vioolsdrif. By contrast, Vioolsdrif has a far lovelier meaning and is translated from the Afrikaans for 'the ford of the violin'. It is reportedly named after Jan Viool ('John Violin'), who is said to have played the fiddle in these parts in the 19th century. Some say he was a Nama man who used to guide ox wagons across the ford, and he would fiddle away merrily on the riverbank while waiting for wagons to arrive. Today Noordoewer and Vioolsdrif are connected by the road bridge at the border which forms the southern end of the Namibian B1 and the northern end of the South African N7. This is the principal border post and a crucial transport route between the two countries. The village consists of a post office, a bank, petrol stations and minimarkets with ATMs, and a couple of places to stay.

For those into canoeing, Noordoewer is the place to start an Orange River canoe safari. A few kilometres west of the border along the banks of the river are the basecamps for a number of **canoeing** companies (see What to do, page 372). Spending a few days floating down the river either in (winter) or submerged alongside (summer) your canoe is a fabulous way to unwind from the rigours of the road – throw yourself in (literally) and you'll have a wonderful time.

Noordoewer is also the access point to cross the border over the Orange River at Sendelingsdrift by pontoon and into the South African section of the |Ai-|Ais/ Richtersveld Transfrontier Park (4WD only); see box, page 360.

Fish River Canyon → For listings, see pages 369-373.

The Fish River Canyon is Namibia's biggest geological wonder and this gaping gash in the earth is approximately 160 km in length, up to 27 km in width, and 550 m deep. The towering rock faces and deep ravines were formed by water erosion from the meandering Fish River, as well as the collapse of the valley due to tectonic movements in the earth's crust. Although all the tourist literature boasts that the Fish River Canyon is second in size only to the Grand Canyon in Arizona, this is not actually the case. It remains unclear as to what criteria are used to measure the size of a canyon, but it is largely regarded as Africa's second largest after the Blue Nile Gorge in Ethiopia. Drive to the observation point at Hobas to witness the spectacular view and then head down into the depths of the canyon to enjoy the hot spring at |Ai|Ais. Alternatively, for the fit and the adventurous, there is a four-day, 85-km hike through the canyon.

Arriving in Fish River Canyon

There are several approaches to the Fish River Canyon depending where you are coming from. The two NWR resorts are **Hobas** which is 10 km from the canyon rim in the north, and **|Ai-|Ais Hot Springs Spa** which is by the riverbed, at the southern end. Most people go to both – either staying overnight or as day visitors. From

Fish River Canyon

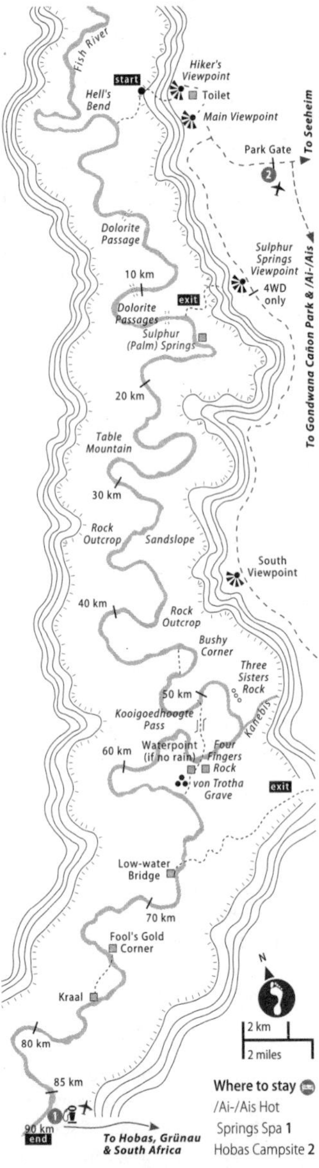
Fish River
start
Hell's Bend
Hiker's Viewpoint
Toilet
Main Viewpoint
Park Gate
To Seeheim
2
Dolorite Passage
Sulphur Springs Viewpoint
4WD only
10 km
exit
Dolorite Passages
Sulphur (Palm) Springs
To Gondwana Cañon Park & /Ai-/Ais
20 km
Table Mountain
30 km
Rock Outcrop
Sandslope
South Viewpoint
40 km
Rock Outcrop
Bushy Corner
Three Sisters Rock
50 km
Kooigoedhoogte Pass
Kanebis
60 km
Waterpoint (if no rain)
Four Fingers Rock
von Trotha Grave
exit
Low-water Bridge
70 km
Fool's Gold Corner
Kraal
N
80 km
2 km
2 miles
85 km
1
90 km
end
To Hobas, Grünau & South Africa
Where to stay
/Ai-/Ais Hot Springs Spa 1
Hobas Campsite 2

Keetmanshoop take the B4 for 46 km to Seehiem and the turn for the C12. From Lüderitz it's 292 km to Seehiem and the turn-off. From here follow the C12 south for 76 km to the turn-off for the D601 which leads 37 km to Hobas.

From Grünau, take the B1 south for 33 km, then turn onto the C10 which leads 73 km to |Ai-|Ais. If coming from South Africa, the C10 turning off the B1 is 113 km north of the Vioolsdrif border. Alternatively from the Vioolsdrif border, a shorter option is by turning west before the B1 reaches the C10, and instead follow the D316, which despite being a fairly minor road on the map, is usually in good condition and regularly graded. The D316 turn-off is 41 km from Vioolsdrif and then it's another 82 km to |Ai-|Ais.

To get between Hobas and |Ai-|Ais, go back along the D601 for 4 km and turn south on the C37 which takes you 42 km to the C10 junction after which it is another 22 km to |Ai-|Ais. It sounds very confusing but everything is clearly signposted on the ground – its 68 km or roughly just over one hour's drive between the two on the decent gravel C37.

Background

The history of the Fish River Canyon began roughly 1800 million years ago when sandstones, shales and lava were deposited along what are now the slopes of the canyon. Between 1300 and 1000 million years ago, extreme heat caused these deposits to become folded and change into gneiss and granites. About 800 million years ago, dolerite dykes intruded into these rocks and these are now visible inside the canyon.

Between 750 and 650 million years ago, the surface of these rocks was eroded to form the floor of a shallow sea which washed over southern Namibia.

The two final pieces in the jigsaw took place about 500 million years ago when tectonic movement caused a series of fractures which led to the formation of the Fish River Canyon. This early version of the canyon was deepened by the retreat southwards of glaciers during the Gondwana Ice Age some 300 million years ago.

However, this was not the end of the process. Within the main canyon a second or lower canyon was created by further movements of the earth's crust as it cooled. Initially a trough, this second canyon became the watercourse which is now the Fish River. The Fish is the longest river in Namibia and plays an important role in both watering and draining southern Namibia. In particular, it feeds the Hardap Dam near Mariental, Namibia's largest reservoir.

Early San (Bushmen) legends suggest an alternative origin to the canyon. Hunters were chasing a serpent called *Kouteign Kooru* across the veld; in order to escape, the snake slithered off into this deserted place and in so doing caused the massive gash that is the canyon. With a supply of water even during the dry winter months and food in the form of fish and game birds, archaeological evidence suggests that the San (Bushmen), or their ancestors, were here 50,000 years ago, so perhaps they witnessed something…

Hobas Campsite and Observation Point → *Colour map 3, C3.*

ⓘ *Day visitors sunrise-sunset, N$80, children (under 16) free, car N$10. Fees are for 24 hrs, if you are visiting Hobas and |Ai-|Ais in the same day, you do not need to pay another fee, just show your permit. Beside the entry gate to Hobas is a well-stocked shop for curios and refreshments.*

About halfway along the canyon at **Hell's Bend** is a series of tortuous curves in the river. Along this stretch, about 80 km north of |Ai-|Ais, are a number of observation points perched on the edge of the canyon where its awe-inspiring splendour can be fully appreciated. Driving out for 10 km from **Hobas Campsite** (see Where to stay, page 371), the first viewpoint you reach is known as **Main Viewpoint**. There is a smart new visitor centre here with several shaded picnic tables, information boards about the geology of the canyon, and toilets. As the viewpoint is westward facing, early morning rather than late afternoon is probably the best time to visit.

If you continue along the track from the car park, you reach **Hiker's Viewpoint**, the starting point for the 85-km trail. The view from here is equally rewarding and it is well worth visiting both sites if you have time. Returning to **Hobas Campsite** look out for a turning to the right. This is a track which follows the edge of the canyon southwards for about 15 km. The road to the **Sulphur Springs Viewpoint** is pretty good; beyond this it is only passable in a 4WD vehicle. There is a path into the canyon at Sulphur Springs, being one of the escape routes for hikers unwilling to continue the full four days to |Ai-|Ais; you are not permitted to enter here. In the past visitors were allowed to hike down to the bottom of the canyon and back up to Hiker's Viewpoint, but this is no longer permitted and the only method of exploring the bottom of the canyon is to go on the Fish River Hiking Trail.

Fish River Canyon Hiking Trail → *For listings, see pages 369-373.*

ⓘ *Reservations should be made well in advance through Namibia Wildlife Resorts (NWR) Windhoek, T061-285 7200, or their offices in Swakopmund (see page 228) or Cape Town (see page 24), www.nwr.com.na. Hiking Trail, N$250 per person, no children under 12.*

This 85-km, four-day trail starts from the main viewpoint near Hobas and ends at |Ai-|Ais and is reputed to be one of the toughest hiking trails in southern Africa. It is not suitable for beginners or the unfit. Although the trail is more or less flat, loose sand and large boulders make progress tiring and this, added to the fact that hikers have to carry all provisions with them, cause some to take the option of an early emergency 'escape' route from the canyon. For those who are fit and determined enough to complete the trail, it is a magical wilderness experience, offering opportunities for game and birdwatching as well as wonderment at the scale and power of nature.

Trail information

Due to extreme temperatures and the risk of flash flooding in summer, the trail is only open from 1 May to 15 September. Groups must consist of a minimum of three people and a maximum of 30. Medical certificates of physical fitness issued within the previous 40 days need to be shown to the ranger at Hobas before starting. Hikers are requested to spend at least one night at Hobas before the start of the trail and will need their own transport to get there, but you can leave your car at Hobas and transport can be arranged back from |Ai-|Ais at the end of the hike (about N$60 per person). If you are staying in one of the nearby lodges, then they should be able to arrange transport to and from the start/finish points. There are no designated campsites and hikers are free to camp where they wish, so you can take longer or shorter than the usual four days, it's up to you. Be sure to inform the ranger at Hobas if you are considering a five- or six-day hike.

The route

The route starts from **Hiker's Viewpoint**, 10 km from **Hobas Campsite**. From the rim, the path descends sharply to the canyon floor, losing 500 m in altitude on the way. Parts of the descent are very steep and it is advisable to make use of the chains. The route at the bottom follows the left-hand side of the river over boulders and soft, loose sand – one of the worst stretches of the walk. Most groups aim for a lunch stop on Day two at **Sulphur Springs**, also known as **Palm Springs**. According to legend, during the First World War two German soldiers sought refuge from internment in the canyon. One of them was suffering from skin cancer and the other from asthma. However, after bathing in the hot springs here these ailments were miraculously cured. Whether true or not, these springs, bubbling up from a depth of 2000 m at a rate of 30 litres per second, offer much-needed relief for sore feet and muscles.

Heading south of Palm Springs the shortest route crisscrosses the river as far as the Table Mountain landmark some 15 km on. This section of the trail is extremely tiring and not much fun as it involves struggling through deep sand and gravel. Further on, the canyon widens and the trail becomes firmer with more river crossings, more or less wet depending on the state of the river. If the rains have been good earlier in the year, trailists can expect to find a fair amount of water in the pools. Check with the rangers at Hobas regarding the availability of water.

Close to the 30-km point is **Table Mountain**, one of the more easily recognizable natural landmarks along the trail. After a further 18 km, you will reach the first of four possible short cuts. At this point the alternative path avoids an area of scrub vegetation known as **Bushy Corner**. Around the next corner of the canyon is the second short cut. Here the path climbs up to the **Kooigoedhoote Pass**. If you choose to take this short cut you will miss seeing the **Three Sisters Rock** and the point where the Kanbis River joins the Fish River. However, from the pass you will enjoy an excellent view of **Four Fingers Rock**. Along the third short cut you will pass the grave of Lieutenant von Trotha, a German soldier killed in 1905 during the German-Nama War and buried where he fell. A couple of kilometres beyond the grave, back in the main canyon, is the second 'emergency' exit path. From here it is a further 20 km to |Ai-|Ais, a cold drink, soft bed and no more walking for a few days.

Equipment

Hikers must take all their food with them – a camping stove is also needed as wood for fires is scarce during the first couple of days of the hike. Maps can be bought at the office in Hobas. Water is almost always available en route (from the river), but should be purified or boiled. It's worth taking a fishing line, provided the river/pools are deep enough; freshly grilled fish is a great luxury after a hot day's hike.

A tent is not necessary but a sleeping mat and sleeping bag is, as the temperature can fall dramatically at night. Tough walking boots, a hat, a comprehensive first-aid kit and plasters for blisters are all essential. Do not litter the canyon and carry all your rubbish out, including toilet paper. Recycling bins are provided at the viewpoints and campsites.

Bird and game viewing

Small mammals such as rock hyrax (dassies) and ground squirrels are a common sight in the canyon and, with luck, larger mammals such as klipspringer, steenbok and springbok may also be spotted. Kudu, gemsbok, mountain zebra and wild horses live in and around the canyon but are harder to spot and leopard is the hardest of all. The rock pools and reeds attract a large number of water birds, including the African fish eagle, grey herons and hammerkops; other birds such as bee-eaters, wagtails and rock pigeons are all common.

|Ai-|Ais Hot Springs Spa → *Colour map 3, C3.*

ⓘ *Day visitors sunrise-sunset, N$80, children (under 16) free, car N$10; additional fee for the indoor hot springs, N$20, children (under 16) N$10. Again fees are for 24 hrs, if you are visiting |Ai-|Ais and then Hobas in the same day, you do not need to pay another fee, just show your permit.*

|Ai-|Ais is a Nama name meaning 'fire-water', indicating the extreme heat of the springs here. Modern knowledge of the springs dates back to 1850 when a Nama

herder discovered the springs whilst searching for lost sheep. However, it is certain that Stone Age people inhabited the area thousands of years ago. During the 1904-1907 German-Nama War, the springs were used as a base camp by German forces. Following the First World War the site was partially developed but it was not until 1969 that the site was declared a conservation area. The present resort was opened in 1971, but was almost immediately destroyed by the Fish River coming down in flood. Since then flooding has occurred three more times, in 1974, 1988 and again in 2000, on each occasion forcing the closure of the resort for repairs.

Today's resort was last refurbished in 2009 and is in a beautiful and peaceful setting. It offers indoor and outdoor thermal pools and as with all springs the water is supposed to have natural curative properties and is especially beneficial for sufferers of rheumatism. In addition there is accommodation (see Where to stay, page 370), tennis courts, restaurant, bar, shop selling basic provisions and firewood, and a petrol station. For those feeling energetic there are some enjoyable walks into the canyon, especially pleasant in the late afternoon when the shadows are long and the heat off the rocks contrasts with the cool sand. Outside the school holidays, the tranquillity of the resort may lull you into a state of complete relaxation.

Gondwana Cañon Park → *Colour map 3, C4.*

Gondwana Cañon Park is a private operation that manages 1260 sq km of land to the east of the canyon, more or less the area between Hobas and |Ai-|Ais (access is off the C37 between the two; see page 364 for directions to the Fish River Canyon). After being over-grazed for many years by intensive sheep farming, the park was established in 1996 and game, reintroduced into the region, can roam freely now that the old farm fences have been removed. Species include small populations of kudu, gemsbok, springbok, mountain zebra, ostrich and a number of smaller antelope. Funding comes from the 5% tourism levy charged on accommodation at the four **Cañon** lodges in the area (see Where to stay, page 371), all of them situated no more 20 km from the main viewing point at Hobas. Visitors can explore the park on guided drives and hikes.

For hotel and restaurant price codes and other relevant information, see pages 21-28.

● Where to stay

Grünau *p359, map p323*

$ Grünau Country House, Main St, T063-262001, www.grunauch.iway.na. Hardly a country house but a simple small town hotel with 10 rooms and 4 cheaper bungalows that share bathrooms with the **campsite**. Bar, restaurant and small swimming pool. The whole place is surrounded by an electric fence and suffers from poor service and food but the only option in the village itself and adequate enough for a cheap overnight on the B1. Will pick up from **Intercape** buses by prior arrangement.

$ Grünau Lodge, behind the 24-hr Shell petrol station at the B1/B3 junction, T063-262026, www.grunaulodge. com. Reasonable roadside option with 6 small self-catering, a/c chalets and 4 rock-hard **camping sites** each with private ablutions, light, *braai* pit and electricity. The petrol station has a 24-hr shop for snacks and basic provisions and a small restaurant open until 1800. The **Intercape** buess between Windhoek, Cape Town and Upington stop here.

Guest farms

$$ Savanna Guest Farm, 1 km off the B1, 40 km north of Grünau, T063-683127, www.savanna-guestfarm.com. Set on a 22,000-ha working sheep farm and horse stud, a historical building (the busy German Shutztruppe again), with 5 a/c rooms, breakfast included and farm dinners with a good choice of wine by arrangement,

heated pool, hiking trails, horse riding, and children can feed the animals.

$$-$ Goibib Mountain Lodge, on the B1, 48 km north of Grünau, T063-683131, www.goibibmountainlodge.com. Well managed, set on a working cattle and sheep farm in the Great Karas Mountains, 8 modern rooms with DSTV, Wi-Fi, tea/coffee and minibar, campsite where you can hire tents which they will erect prior to your arrival if you book ahead. Swimming pool, bar/restaurant, on site butcher and *braai* areas, guided nature walks and drives.

$$-$ White House Guest Farm, on the B1, 11 km north of Grünau, T063-2622061, www.withuis.iway.na. The nicest farmstay in the region, in a beautifully restored historical white farmhouse (1912) with original oregan pine doors and floors, black-and-white photographs and antiques, 5 comfortable rooms in the main house, plus 3 self-catering chalets and a **campsite** (they can provide tents, mattresses and bedding for budget travellers). The welcoming and informative owners offer day and night game drives to see springbok and gemsbok and nocturnal creatures such as spring hares. *Braai* packs available, or they will cook for you if you book ahead using farm produce including lamb. There's a small rose quartz quarry on the farm which you can visit and jewellery is sold at reception.

$ Vastrap Guest Farm, 5 km down the B3 from Grünau, T063-262063, www. vastrapguestfarm.com. A useful stop en route to the Ariamsvlei border on a sheep farm with 6 pleasant rooms in the old farmstead buildings and 3 self-catering chalets with *braai* and freezer facilities, swimming pool, bar and great farm dinners on request; expect the likes of farm lamb, game pie and malva pudding.

Noordoewer and Orange River
p361, map p323

$$-$ Felix Unite Provenance Camp, 10 km from the border on the C13, T063-297161, www.felixunite.com. A great stopover close to the border with 17 lovely reed, thatch and stone a/c double and family cabanas with sliding doors out on to the springy green lawns, 10 permanent tents on wooden verandas and a neat **campsite**, with good shared bathrooms, plus swimming pool, bar, restaurant, shop for curios and basic foodstuffs, and all in a wonderful spot overlooking the Orange River. **Felix Unite** organizes 4-day canoe trips on the river, (see What to do, page 372).

$$-$ Norotshama River Resort, at Aussenkehr 50 km from the border on the C13, T063-297215, www.norotshama resort.com. On a grape farm on the banks of the Orange River with 30 neat tented or stone thatched chalets, 4 are for families and 2 are self-catering and all are river-facing, and a **campsite** with *braai* areas, electricity and ablution blocks. Restaurant and bar, and lovely swimming pool designed around piles of boulders, activities include mountain bike and 4WD trails, canoeing, fly-fishing, and hiking through the dramatic local canyons.

$ Amanzi River Camp, 16 km from the border on the C13, T063-297255, www.amanzitrails.co.za. Simple grassy campsite on the banks of the Orange River, hot showers, bar and kiosk at main *lapa*, ice, firewood and *braai* packs available, a, lovely spot with nice views. **Amanzi Trails** also organizes 4-day canoe trips on the river (see What to do, below).

$ Fiddler's Creek, 12 km east on a road from the Vioolsdrif border, South Africa, T+ 27 (0)27-761 8953, www. bushwhacked.co.za. In addition to the camps on the Namibian side, there's an excellent campsite on the South African side of the Orange/Gariep River accessible from the N7 (the continuation of the B1 in South Africa). Hot showers in reed huts, undercover kitchen area, great little rustic bar next to the river, meals with prior booking, and canoe trips from a few hours to 4 days.

$ Orange River Lodge, on the B1 3 km south of Noordoewer and 1 km before the border next to the BP petrol station, T063-297012, www.orlodge.iway.na. On the river but more of a motel-style stop on the B1 than a riverside retreat with 12 plain but functional rooms, 2 are self-catering, with a/c and TV, **campsite** with grassy sites, ablutions and firewood, *lapa* restaurant and bar and can arrange short canoe trips.

Fish River Canyon *p363, maps p323 and p364*

Both **Hobas** and |Ai-|Ais, are booked through Namibia Wildlife Resorts (NWR), in Windhoek T061-285 7200, or their offices in Swakopmund (see page 228) or Cape Town (see page 24), www.nwr. com.na. The **Fish River Lodge** is another option in the luxury bracket, but as it's on the western rim of the canyon (as the crow flies, opposite **Hobas**), it's accessed from the B4 near Seeheim (see page 335).

$$-$ |Ai-|Ais Hot Springs Spa, at the bottom of the canyon, for directions see page 367. Accommodation is in 7 family self-catering chalets, 16 river-view double/twin rooms, 20 mountain-view twin/double rooms and a spacious campsite with *braai* pit and light and communal ablutions. Facilities include a restaurant, bar, shop, kiosk, large outdoor swimming pool, classy indoor thermal pool, tennis courts, playground and petrol station. Overall a lovely place to stay and enjoy some short hikes into the base of the canyon and a splash around in the hot and cold pools, but like **Hobas** below, a 1-night stay is sufficient.

$ Hobas Campsite, 10 km from the main viewpoint and the starting point of the Fish River Canyon Hiking Trail, for directions see page 366, T063-266028. One of the better **NWR** campsites and a welcome oasis after the hot drive to get here. 14 shaded pitches with *braai* pit and light, communal ablutions, swimming pool, information office and shop selling frozen meat, cold drinks, beer and basic provisions, plus curios and T-shirts. Being smaller than most, and a popular stop for overland trucks, you are advised to book in advance. The usual drill is to arrive by mid-afternoon for a swim and to set up camp, before filling the cool box with cold beer or a bottle of wine and driving out to the viewpoint to watch the sunset. Again, in the morning there is the option of watching the canyon fill with light at sunrise. Allow sufficient time to drive the 10 km as the road is stony, and check with the office for times of sunset and sunrise.

Gondwana Cañon Park *p368, map p323*

Your sleeping arrangements, if not staying at **Hobas** or **|Ai-|Ais**, will probably be in the hands of the **Gondwana Collection**, which manages the 4 places to stay in this private concession to the east of the canyon. Book through central reservations, Windhoek T061-230066, www.gondwana-collection.com. For activities in the park, see What to do, page 372.

$$$ Cañon Lodge, off the C37, 2 km off the road, 12 km south of Hobas towards |Ai-|Ais. This is the smartest and most expensive in the collection in a beautiful setting with 25 well-designed and tastefully furnished stone and thatch a/c chalets built into the huge boulders, meals are served in the cool converted 1908 farmhouse, with a shaded terrace and swimming pool with views over the rocks and old farm implements and vehicles dotted around.

$$$ Cañon Village, see **Cañon Lodge** off the C37, 1.5 km off the road, 2 km before the turn-off to **Cañon Lodge** and 10 km south of Hobas towards |Ai-|Ais. Another attractive and peaceful setting set at the base of an impressive rock face and styled like a Cape Dutch hamlet with 24 comfortable chalets with veranda, the main thatched building houses a restaurant, bar, curio shop and a partly covered beer garden and there's a pool. The village is slightly cheaper than the lodge and is popular with tour groups.

$$$-$$ Cañon Roadhouse, on the D601 from the Keetmanshoop direction, 14 km before Hobas. This is the most characterful of the 4 properties because of the eclectic decor of old cars – you cannot drive around Namibia without noticing the abandoned rusty car shells in the desert. 24 a/c rooms arranged around pretty, shaded courtyards, (look for the unusual blinds made out of recycled air filters), the **campsite ($)** has *braai* pits and good ablutions but no light or electricity. Swimming pool, excellent restaurant, information centre about the flora and fauna of the canyon, and a petrol pump (not 24 hrs). Day visitors are welcome for coffee, lunch and a refreshing dip in the pool.

$ Cañon Mountain Camp, 6 km beyond **Cañon Lodge** on the same road (see above); guests must check in at the lodge on the way through. The cheapest option and self-catering in a U-shaped building surrounding a garden courtyard that used to be a sheep shearers hut, with 8 simple en suite rooms, communal kitchen and dining area, and shady terrace with *braai* facilities. Can sleep 16 in total and accommodates groups, but discuss with Gondwana (see above) if you have a smaller group; a couple of families/carloads could stay for example. You can eat, drink and swim at the **Cañon Lodge**.

🕐 What to do

Noordoewer and Orange River *p361, map p323*
Canoeing
Most of the lodges and campsites along the Orange River on both the Namibian and South African side offer relaxing canoeing during the morning or afternoon. Alternatively there are 4- to 6-day canoeing trips downstream and into the |Ai-|Ais/Richtersveld Transfrontier Park and the distance covered ranges from 60 km to 90 km depending on the water levels. They use 2-person inflatable or fibreglass canoes and clothes and sleeping bags are squashed into waterproof plastic drums which fit neatly into the boats. Every night is spent sleeping under the stars in a 'bush camp' by the banks of the river or even on sandbanks in the water. The guides take care of everything – navigating the river, choosing campsites and preparing all meals over an open fire, as well as pointing out the different species of birds and interesting rock formations along the river. These trips are not too physically challenging and children over the age of 6 can join; a wonderful experience and highly recommended. Expect to pay from N$3000 for a 4-day trip. You will need your passport regardless of which side of the border you start from, as you could be sleeping on either side of the river. If you're coming from Cape Town, ask about transfers.

Amanzi Trails, operates from **Amanzi River Camp**, see Where to stay, page 370, reservations Cape Town, T+27(0)21-559 1573, www.amanzitrails.co.za.

Felix Unite, operates from **Provenance Camp**, see Where to stay, page 370, reservations Cape Town, T+27 (0)873-540578, www.felixunite.com.

Umkulu, starts from their basecamp on the South African side near the Vioolsdrif border, where you can park and leave luggage in lockers and it has showers and a bar, reservations Cape Town, T+27 (0)21-853 7952, www.orangeriverrafting.com.

Gondwana Cañon Park *p368, map p323*
Activities on offer to all guests of the 4 lodges start from **Canyon Lodge** or **Canyon Village**. There are 1-hr sunrise guided walks to viewpoints around the lodges, N$125 pp; 3-hr (6-km) morning hikes through the park, N$255 pp; a 3-hr canyon drive to the Hobas viewpoints, N$650 pp; and 2-hr sundowner drives in the park with drinks, N$365 pp. They also operate the popular and enjoyable 3- to 5-day Mule Trails (Apr-Sep); guided hiking trails in the canyon area north of the main Hobas viewpoint, where mules carry all luggage and equipment and overnights are in pre-erected tented camps. Fully catered rates start from N$5000 pp for 3 days.

🚌 Transport

Grünau *p359, map p323*
163 km to Keetmanshoop, 50 km to Karasburg, 144 km to the South African border at Vioolsdrif.

Bus

Intercape buses between **Windhoek** and **Cape Town** and **Upington** in South Africa pick up and drop off at the 24-hr Shell petrol station at the B1/B3 junction. See timetable on page 16.

Train

The service between **Keetmanshoop** and **Karasburg** (see below for details) stops in Grünau very approximately 1 hr and 15 mins before and after Karasburg. The train stops at a siding near where the B1 crosses the railway.

Karasburg *p359*

212 km to Keetmanshoop, 112 km to the South African border at Ariamsvlei.

Bus

Intercape buses between **Windhoek** and **Upington** in South Africa pick up and drop off in front of the BP petrol station next to the Spar supermarket. See timetable on page 16.

Train

TransNamib Starline Passenger Service, central reservations T061-298 2032/2175, www.transnamib.com.na. The railway station is in the middle of town. In the unlikely event that you would like to get to Karasburg by train, there is a service between **Keetmanshoop** and Karasburg that departs Wed and Sat at 0850 and arrives at 1430, and then from Karasburg to Keetmanshoop that departs Sun and Thu at 1120 and arrives at 1630. It hooks up with the train between Keetmanshoop and **Windhoek**; confirm times and fares at the stations.

ⓘ Directory

Karasburg *p359*
Medical services State Hospital, T063-270167, signposted on southern outskirts of town.

Contents

376 History of Namibia
- 376 Pre-colonial Namibia
- 377 Oorlam migration
- 380 Missionaries and traders
- 383 The 1870 Peace Accord
- 384 Namibia becomes a colonial possession
- 385 The 1904-1907 German-Namibian War
- 387 Economic development
- 388 League of Nations mandate
- 389 Road to independence

391 Modern Namibia

393 Economy

395 Culture
- 395 People

397 Land and environment
- 397 Geography
- 397 Climate
- 398 Vegetation
- 399 Wildlife

Footprint features

- 378 Jonker Afrikaner
- 380 Charles John Andersson
- 396 The San (Bushmen)

Background

History of Namibia

Pre-colonial Namibia

Archaeological finds from southern Namibia suggest that humans have been wandering the vast plains, dense bush and harsh deserts of the country for around 45,000 years. Ancient cave paintings at the Apollo 11 shelter in the southern Huns Mountains have been estimated to be 27,000 years old and similar rock art of the same period has also been found at a number of sites around Damaraland in northwest Namibia. These are believed to have been the work of the **San** people, still referred to as **Bushmen** in most parts of Namibia. The San (Bushmen) are descendants of pre-historic people who had migrated from southern Africa into East and North Africa before subsequently returning to the tip of the continent.

The San were traditionally hunter-gatherers, extraordinarily successful at surviving in the bush and desert despite their limited technology and weapons. They lived in small bands of up to 50 people roaming across the veld in a continuous search for food and water, rarely coming into contact with other San groups. Rock art all around Namibia, clearly seen at sites such as Twyfelfontein and Brandberg, provides vivid evidence of the widespread distribution of San communities all over the country.

Around 2000 years ago the San (Bushmen) were joined by groups of **Khoe-khoe (Nama)** who had migrated from Botswana to the middle stretches of the Orange River. From here, it is believed that the group split into two, one group heading north and west into present-day Namibia, the other group moving south into the Cape Province area of South Africa. Unlike the San, the Khoe-khoe were both hunter-gatherers and livestock herders, living a semi-nomadic existence moving around the country with their herds of animals. Despite the differences in lifestyle, it appears as if Khoe-Khoe and San people co-existed peacefully. So much so, that the term 'Khoisan' is now used to collectively describe both peoples.

By the ninth century AD a third group was settled in Namibia living alongside the Khoisan; these were the **Damara** people. Sharing common cultural and linguistic ties with the Nama (rather than the Owambo, Herero or other Bantu-speaking tribes in Namibia), the exact origin and migration route of the Damara into Namibia remains a mystery. Some anthropologists argue that they must have originated in West Africa, whilst others maintain that they developed alongside the Khoe-khoe in Botswana and merely migrated later to Namibia.

By the early 19th century the Damara were living all over Namibia both alongside Nama and Herero communities as well as in their own settlements, which were reported to be more permanent than those of the Nama. They had also evolved a number of distinct characteristics; they practised communal hunting techniques, the cultivation of tobacco and *dagga* (marijuana), mined and smelted copper and manufactured soapstone pipes.

Bantu-speaking tribes started arriving in Namibia during the 16th and 17th centuries, having migrated south and west from the Great Lakes area of east and central Africa. These tribes settled in the northern parts of the country alongside or close to the perennial Kunene, Kavango and Zambezi rivers which more or less correspond to their distribution in present-day Namibia.

These peoples brought with them a variety of skills such as pottery and metal-working and lived by a mixture of farming, fishing and hunting. This influx of people looking for land to establish semi-permanent settlements inevitably put pressure on existing groups, and the Khoisan and Damara in particular were forced to move further south or into less hospitable parts of the country on the fringes of the Namib and Kalahari deserts.

The **Herero** people had arrived in Namibia from East and Central Africa during the 16th century and had originally settled in the Kaokoland area in the extreme northwest of the country. As cattle herders they required increasingly large areas of land to feed their growing herds and by the middle of the 18th century the marginal veld of the Kaokoland had become overgrazed and, suffering severe drought, was no longer able to support the Herero.

Gradually the majority of the Herero migrated southwards, and by around 1750 the first groups of Herero came into contact with groups of Khoisan in the Swakop River area. Pressure from the Herero pushing southward more or less coincided with the northwards migration of **Oorlam** groups from the Cape Province. These two opposing movements created enormous pressure, which was to erupt into almost a century of upheaval and at times open warfare in central Namibia. It was against this backdrop that the first European missionaries and traders came into the country, and their presence contributed significantly to the eventual establishment of the German colony of Southwest Africa.

Oorlam migration

The emergence of industrial capitalism in England during the second half of the 18th century drastically changed the economy of the satellite Cape Colony. Urban centres grew and **Boer** farmers moved progressively inland, claiming land and resources further and further away from the reach of the English authorities in the Cape Colony. The Boer farmers' freedoms were won largely at the expense of the local Khoisan population who lost their land, their hunting grounds and livestock, and even their liberty, as many became servants or even slaves of these European farmers.

In the wake of these developments a new group of frontiers people emerged. These were the Oorlams, a mixed bunch of Khoe-khoe, runaway slaves, and people of mixed race descent who worked for the Boer farmers and traders as hunters and guides. They were baptized, had access to guns and horses and had shed the traditional lifestyles of other Nama groups. Some of these formed themselves into commandos, autonomous groups living separate from the European farmers and traders, surviving by hunting, trading and raiding the cattle of the Nama tribes living over the Orange River into southern Namibia.

Early missionary reports at the time described the Nama tribes of southern Namibia to be living in highly organized communities numbering in some cases

Jonker Afrikaner

One of the key figures in Namibia during the first half of the 19th century was Jonker Afrikaner, an Oorlam from the Cape Province who established his authority over the central and southern part of Namibia, and who established the settlement at Windhoek, which was to eventually become Namibia's capital.

Jonker Afrikaner belonged to an Oorlam group who, around the turn of the century, crossed the Orange River and established a fortified village in the Karasburg District. The leader of the clan at the time was Jager Afrikaner, Jonker's father, who had killed his white employer in a dispute over wages and had subsequently fled over the Orange River beyond the reach of the Cape Province authorities. After his father's death in 1823, Jonker Afrikaner trekked north with a group of his followers and by the 1830s had established himself as leader of central and southern Namibia.

Due to the lack of accurate historical records during this period, there are differing accounts of how Jonker established himself as the senior Nama/Oorlam leader. One explanation is that by force of arms and constant cattle raids upon neighbouring Nama tribes, Jonker was able to establish his pre-dominance. Other theories suggest that Nama leaders, fearing the steady encroachment of the Herero on their grazing lands, called in Jonker to force the Herero back. The English explorer Sir James Alexander met Jonker in 1836 in the Rehoboth area and reported that the Afrikaners had defeated the Hereros in three decisive battles in 1835, allowing the Afrikaners to steal the Herero cattle and establish themselves as the dominant power in the area.

By the 1840s an informal but definite alliance between Jonker Afrikaner and other Nama chiefs, such as Oaseb and Swartbooi existed. The basis of the

more than 1000 individuals. They had large herds of cattle, sheep and goats, and were completely self-sufficient, producing all their own food and manufacturing the reed mats for their huts, as well as growing tobacco and *dagga*. The different Nama tribes co-existed peacefully, sharing and respecting each other's water and grazing rights.

Initial contact between the first Oorlam groups to cross the Orange River and the local Nama tribes was relatively peaceful, but as more and more Oorlams poured over the river, demanding watering and grazing rights, the level of conflict increased to open warfare. Although the Nama were superior in numbers to the Oorlams, they had far fewer guns and horses and with their large herds of livestock were less mobile than the Oorlams. Consequently the Oorlams were soon able to establish footholds in the region from where they continued to harry and raid the Nama tribes.

During a 40-year period up until the 1840s, southern Namibia – or Namaland as it became to be known – was in a virtually constant state of turmoil. Traditional patterns of living were disrupted, a new economy emerged and previously pastoral people started to settle in more permanent settlements.

alliance recognized Jonker Afrikaner as an equal of the Nama leaders, gave the Afrikaners sovereignty of the land between the Swakop and Kuiseb rivers and made Jonker Afrikaner overlord of the Herero lands north of the Swakop River. In this way the Afrikaners effectively acted as a buffer between the Hereros to the north and the Nama tribes of the south, ensuring greater security for the Nama lands to the south. This informal alliance was officially confirmed in 1858 in an agreement between Chief Oaseb and Jonker Afrikaner.

During the 1840s and 1850s, Jonker established relations with various Herero leaders, in particular Chief Tjamuaha and his son Kamaherero and Chief Kahitjene. The basis of these relations obliged the Herero to look after Afrikaner cattle and to pay regular tributes in the form of cattle, and in return the Herero leaders were generally spared cattle raids and were able to enrich themselves at the expense of their fellow Herero.

In 1840, Jonker had established the settlement of Windhoek in the Klein Windhoek Valley. In 1842, invited by Jonker, the first two missionaries Hahn and Kleinschmidt arrived to find a flourishing community, boasting a whitewashed stone church capable of seating up to 500 people. There were also well-established gardens where corn, tobacco and *dagga* (marijuana) were being cultivated in irrigated fields. For the next 20 years Windhoek was to flourish as a centre of commerce between the Hereros and the Oorlam/Namas.

Jonker Afrikaner died in 1861 and the years following his death were to see the gradual erosion of Afrikaner hegemony over central and southern Namibia, and the abandonment of the settlement at Windhoek.

In the 1840s Chief Oaseb, a paramount Nama chief, and **Jonker Afrikaner**, the foremost Oorlam leader, struck a deal that allowed Nama and Oorlam groups to live in peace. This deal was struck against the increasing realization that there was now little difference between the Oorlam and the Nama. The intense struggle for land and water had brought the two groups close together and intermarriage had become commonplace, so that making distinctions between the two groups was increasingly difficult. Furthermore, Herero-speaking groups who had been migrating southwards for almost 100 years were threatening the common interests of both Oorlam and Nama.

Oaseb and Afrikaner divided the land south of Windhoek amongst themselves and Afrikaner was declared overlord of the Herero lands north of the Swakop River up as far as the Waterberg Plateau. By force of arms, Afrikaner was able to maintain his hegemony over these Herero groups with their large herds of cattle, and in so doing was able to control loosely most of central and southern Namibia. Until his death in 1861, Jonker Afrikaner was probably the single most influential leader in this part of Namibia.

Charles John Andersson

Charles Andersson was born in Sweden in 1827 of a Swedish mother and English father. After a short spell at the University of Lund, in 1847 he abandoned his studies in order to hunt and trade with his father. In 1849 he left for England with the intention of pursuing a career of hunting and exploration in Iceland; he sailed for South Africa instead upon the invitation of an Englishman named Galton.

During the 1850s Andersson travelled and hunted for ivory all over southwestern Africa, visiting King Nangolo in Ondongo, exploring Lake Ngami and reaching the Okavango River. By 1860 he was in a position to buy up the assets of the defunct Walvis Bay Trading Company in Otjimbingwe and set up a trading company there. Andersson was interested in ivory and cattle for the Cape trade and was able to set up other hunters and traders to work for him. The fact that Andersson's trading post was permanent made it the first of its kind in Namibia. He could set up the best possible deals and, if required, travel to the Cape himself, leaving his trading partners to look after the business in Otjimbingwe.

The opening of the trading post at Otjimbingwe coincided with the outbreak of lung sickness in cattle in the region. This posed a serious threat to all the groups raising cattle – Nama, Herero and European alike. Determined to protect their herds and pastures from the deadly disease, Jonker Afrikaner and his allies were extremely reluctant to let Andersson drive his cattle south through their lands. Furthermore, by opening up Hereroland to trade, Andersson posed a threat to the hegemony of the Afrikaner clan.

In 1861, while Jonker Afrikaner was in Owamboland, Andersson set off with 1400 head of infected cattle for the Cape. Between Otjimbingwe and Rehoboth he was attacked by Hendrik Zes, a close ally of Jonker Afrikaner, who made off with 500 of the animals. Although Andersson and his traders were able to force Zes to return the cattle, the incident served as a serious warning to him. Thereafter, Andersson started to recruit and train mercenaries, mainly from the Cape, to protect his trading interests.

By January 1862, five months after Jonker Afrikaner's death, Andersson

Missionaries and traders

The first Europeans had appeared off the coast of Africa in the 15th century. In 1486, the Portuguese explorer **Diego Cao** erected a cross at Cape Cross, while **Bartholomeu Diaz** planted another at Angra Pequena near Lüderitz. However, the coast was barren and inhospitable, and the interior of the country at this time would have only been accessible to these explorers by crossing the Namib Desert. No other Europeans are believed to have visited Namibia until the late 18th century when a small number of Dutch settlers trekked north from the Cape Colony and established themselves as farmers. Following them a small number of traders also came to Namibia but without initially having any significant impact.

was established as a successful trader, organizing expeditions north into Hereroland, gradually changing the focus of his interest towards ivory and ostrich feathers. However, his position was not secure, as he noted in his diary on 26 January 1862: "The Hottentots [Namas] are fearfully jealous of me: they got a notion that I am the only person who benefits by my presence. I am not afraid of any Hottentot individually or collectively, but I may have to leave the country unless I resort to bloodshed."

The scene was then set for an escalation of the conflict between Andersson and his traders on the one hand and the Afrikaners and their allies on the other. A series of cattle raids and skirmishes took place during 1863, culinating in an attack on Otjimbingwe by the Afrikaners in June of that year. Andersson, his traders and mercenaries – the 'Otjimbingwe volunteers' as they had come to be known – routed the attackers, killing about a third of them including their commander Christian Afrikaner. However, the power of the Afrikaners was not broken, and guerrilla attacks on Andersson's cattle trains continued

In 1864 Andersson decided to seek an alliance with the Herero chiefs in an attempt to muster a big enough army to settle the conflict in one decisive battle. The Hereros had a long series of grievances going back many years against the Afrikaners and, after a series of negotiations and the election of Kamaherero as chief of all Herero speakers, a joint army of about 2500 men was put together. On 22 June 1864 the two armies met near Rehoboth in a battle that proved to be anything but conclusive. The Afrikaners retreated after a day's battle, neither having been defeated nor emerging victorious. Andersson's shin was shattered by a bullet, a wound he never fully recovered from. He sold his business interests to the Rhenish Mission and retired to the Cape to put together his bird book on Namibia.

He returned to Namibia in 1865 leaving his wife and two young children in Cape Town. However, he was never to return, and died in Owamboland in 1867 of a combination of diphtheria, dysentery and exhaustion.

The earliest missionaries, from the **London Mission Society**, began to operate in southern Namibia at the beginning of the 19th century and were soon joined by the German Rhenish and Finnish **Lutheran Mission Societies**. The appearance of the earliest missionaries coincided with increasing numbers of Oorlams crossing the Orange River, and the presence of these missionaries was crucial to the success of the Oorlam commando groups in establishing themselves in Namibia.

Missionaries were important in 19th-century Namibia as they fulfilled a number of different roles, in addition to their primary aim of preaching the gospel. Indeed one early missionary, Ebner, regretting that he was unable to provide the Nama leader Titus Afrikan with a supply of gunpowder as earlier preachers had done, was driven to write that "it seems to me that he is more interested in powder, lead and tobacco than in the teachings of the gospel".

Until the arrival of the missionaries, the Nama communities in the south of Namibia were semi-nomadic. The building of churches and the development of agriculture saw the establishment of the first stable settlements. The stone-walled churches fulfilled the role of mini-fortresses, and the brass bells that the missionaries provided were an effective warning system during raids. Many missionaries also introduced agriculture to the communities in which they lived, and the more stable food supply that followed allowed larger numbers of people to settle in an area. In turn, these larger settlements allowed for improved defence against raids through better organization.

Second, the missionaries acted as focal points for traders from the Cape, who were able to supply the missionaries and their families with the goods they needed. In this way the trade routes to the Cape were established and kept open, thus guaranteeing the Oorlam leaders continued supplies of the guns and ammunition upon which they depended for their supremacy. In the early years of the 19th century it seems as if some missionaries even supplied the guns themselves. Schmelen, who established a mission at Bethanie in southern Namibia, found it necessary to "furnish some of my people with arms". Even in later years when the export of guns and gunpowder from the Cape was prohibited, Kleinschmidt, who operated the mission at Rehoboth, provided Chief Swartbooi with gunpowder.

The almost constant conflict brought about the breaking down of social structures, although the missionaries armed with their Christian rules proved effective control mechanisms for tribal leaders. In 1815, referring to the Afrikaner clan, Ebner noted that "it is only the baptised who are allowed ... to use the gun." Blameless Christian behaviour was also a prerequisite to political positions in communities such as Bethanie, Rehoboth and Warmbad (behaviour defined, of course, by the missionaries). Missionaries also performed the roles of social worker and doctor, and Jonker Afrikaner once explained to Schonberg why he wanted a missionary at Otjimbingwe "... traders come and go, but the missionary stays, and consequently we know where to get our medicines from".

By the 1860s an extensive network of trading posts existed in Namibia, the most important being Otjimbingwe northwest of present-day Windhoek. Set up by the Anglo-Swede **Charles John Andersson**, Otjimbingwe was also a key mission station for the Herero-speaking peoples. Under Andersson's influence the European community of missionaries, traders and hunters were gradually sucked into the escalating Herero-Nama conflict (see box, page 378).

Following the death of Jonker Afrikaner in 1861 and the defeat of the Afrikaners and their allies at Otjonguere south of Windhoek in 1864, the years leading up to 1870 saw a virtual constant jockeying for position amongst the various Nama and Oorlam leaders. Once again the southern and central parts of Namibia were the scene of skirmishes and cattle raids. This infighting amongst the Oorlam/ Namas effectively allowed the Herero-speaking people under the leadership of Kamaherero to break free of Afrikaner dominance.

The 1870 Peace Accord

In 1870 Jan Jonker Afrikaner arrived at Okahandja with a large group of armed men with the intention of renewing the old alliance between Kamaherero and the Afrikaners. However, missionary Hahn intervened and when the treaty was concluded in September of that year the Afrikaners had lost their old rights over the Herero-speaking peoples. Furthermore, Hahn obtained permission for the Cape **Basters** to settle at Rehoboth. The Basters were a farming community of mixed Khoi-European descent who, having been forced from their lands in the Cape Province, had been looking for a place to settle. The Baster settlement at Rehoboth acted as an effective buffer between the Herero-speaking peoples and the Oorlam-Namas.

Peace was preserved between the Nama- and Herero-speaking peoples throughout the 1870s, and it was not until the beginning of the 1880s that conflict broke out once more. However, this period of relative peace amongst indigenous Namibians also saw the consolidation of the position of the missionaries and traders – particularly the latter. As the Nama leaders developed a taste for manufactured goods and alcohol, the economy of Namaland – virtually all the land south of Windhoek as far as the Orange River – became inextricably linked with that of the Cape. As a result the numbers of hunters, traders and explorers entering Namibia grew uncontrollably, and this in turn saw the over-exploitation of animal and natural resources in the central-southern part of Namibia.

The hunters and traders were chiefly interested in obtaining ivory and ostrich feathers to export to the Cape. At the same time they were selling guns, coffee, sugar, soap, gin and brandy to the local peoples. The only way the Nama chiefs could support their habit for western manufactured goods and alcohol was by granting licences to the hunters and traders, leading one explorer, A Anderson, to complain to the Cape government that "every petty kaptein claims a licence fee" for hunting, passing through and trading.

However, while the Oorlam/Namas of southern Namibia became caught up in this trading network, the Herero-speaking peoples living north of Windhoek remained largely aloof from this burgeoning trade. True, they were the main purchasers of guns, for they had learned during the middle part of the century of the importance of modern weapons, but for the rest, trade with Hereroland was tightly controlled.

Given the vast numbers of cattle which the Herero were breeding, it seems strange that the European traders were not more active in their contact with the Herero. The main reason for this it seems, was a lack of interest on the part of the Herero in exchanging their cattle for Western goods.

Unlike the inhabitants of Namaland who were experiencing a spiralling circle of dependency on imported manufactured goods together with the virtual invasion of their territory by Europeans of one description or another, the Herero-speaking peoples retained their traditional kinship-oriented pastoral way of life. In other words the Herero valued their cattle far more highly than any manufactured goods, and rather than exchanging cattle for goods, they actually increased the size of their herds.

Despite renewed raids during the early part of the 1880s by Oorlam/Namas who succeeded in stealing thousands of head of cattle, ex-missionary Hahn – now a full-time trader – remarked that the Herero "will in a few years make up for these losses. There is, perhaps, no people in the world who equals the Damaras (Hereros) as cattle breeders ...".

Namibia becomes a colonial possession

In 1880, after 10 years of relative peace, fierce fighting broke out once more in central Namibia. Once again the disputes were over cattle and grazing rights and they involved all the key players in central Namibia at the time. There were the Herero – led by **(Ka) Maherero** as he came to be known – the Nama Swartbois, the Afrikaners under Jan Jonker and the Rehoboth Basters (relative newcomers to the scene). All through 1880 and 1881 the fighting continued with a number of important leaders falling in battle, in particular Maherero's eldest son Willem in the fight for Okahandja in December 1880. Up until 1884 and the rise of **Hendrik Witbooi**, a bewildering series of shifting alliances, cattle raids and skirmishes characterized the scene in south and central Namibia.

However, it was the arrival of German representatives in 1884, the subsequent treaties with the Herero and the effective subduing of Hendrik Witbooi 10 years later that fundamentally changed the way in which Namibia was governed. Power steadily shifted away from traditional leaders, such as Witbooi and Maherero, into the hands of the German colonial administrators. Furthermore, over the next 25 years vast tracts of Namaland and Hereroland passed into the hands of the colonial government and individual settlers. This fundamental change culminated with the 1904-1907 German-Namibian war which saw the final consolidation of colonial authority over the country, and the subjugation of the Namibian peoples by Europeans.

Between 1883 and 1885, the German trader and businessman **Adolf Lüderitz** negotiated a series of agreements which saw him buy practically the entire coastal strip of Namibia between the Orange and Kunene rivers, extending as far as 150 km inland. A settlement was established at **Angra Pequena**, soon renamed as **Lüderitzbucht**, which helped open the country up to German political and economic interests. German policy in Namibia was that private initiative and capital would 'develop' the country, secured by German government protection.

In order to bring 'order' to Namibia, the German authorities pursued a policy of persuading local leaders to sign so-called protection treaties (Shuzverträge) with them. This they achieved by exploiting local conflicts to serve their own ends, and in the face of continuing conflict between Maherero and Hendrik Witbooi, were able to persuade Maherero to sign a protection treaty with the German authorities in 1885. In the same year Commissioner Göring wrote to Hendrik Witbooi ordering him to desist from continuing with his cattle raids against the Herero and threatening him with unspecified consequences.

However, these threats were empty gestures. During the period 1884-1889 the official German presence in Namibia consisted of three officials based in a classroom at the mission school in Otjimbingwe, plus a small number of business representatives who effected the protection treaties. It was not until 1889 that the first force of 21 soldiers (Schutztruppe) landed in Namibia, to be followed by another 40 the following year, and only after 1894, following the subduing of Hendrik Witbooi, that significant numbers of settlers were able to enter the country.

Between 1894 and 1904 the Witboois sold a third of their land to European settlers, and the treaties that Samuel Herero signed with the German colonial government in 1894 and 1895 ceded Herero land to them. Meanwhile, following the death of old Maherero in 1890, the German administration established its headquarters in Windhoek and during the confusion over the succession of the Herero leader was able to consolidate its position there. However, the greatest sale of Herero land took place in the years after 1896 – the result of the trade on credit systems in operation at the time, the rinderpest epidemic of 1897 and the fever epidemic of 1898.

With the further opening of Hereroland to trade following the treaties signed with the German colonial administration, there was a dramatic increase in the number of traders operating in the country. For Europeans without their own capital but prepared to put up with the hardships of living in the veld, this was a perfect opportunity to make money and acquire cattle and land. Large firms employed these traders to go out to Herero settlements in the veld and sell their goods there. Due to the risks involved, all parties attempted to maximize profit, often adding 70-100% onto the value of goods to achieve this. They were also quite happy to give the Hereros credit in order to encourage them to buy more and more, until the situation arrived whereby an individual or community's debt was greater than their assets.

In addition, following the rinderpest epidemic of 1897 in which up to 97% of unvaccinated cattle died, the only way in which the Hereros could pay for the goods they wanted or settle their debts was to sell land. An addiction to alcohol amongst many Hereros, not least their leader Samuel Maherero, also caused large debts which had to be settled through land sales. Although the colonial government attempted to put all business dealings between Europeans and Namibians on a cash basis, the protests of the traders brought about a suspension of this regulation almost immediately after its introduction.

Inevitably tension grew among the Herero as they saw their traditional lands gradually disappearing. The Rhenish Missionary Society petitioned the colonial government to consider creating reserves for the Herero where the land could not be sold, and despite initial resistance both within Namibia and from Germany, so-called paper reserves (because initially they only existed on paper) were created around Otjimbingwe at the end of 1902 and around Okahandja and Waterberg in 1903. However, there were many Herero leaders who were deeply dissatisfied with the land issue, and pressure was growing on Herero leader Samuel Maherero to take some action to recover lost lands – although he himself had been responsible for the sale of much of it.

The 1904-1907 German-Namibian War

The three years of fighting between the German colonial forces and various Namibian tribes ended with victory for the Germans and the consolidation of their colonial rule over Namibia. Thousands of Namibians died either as a result of the fighting or in the aftermath and the effect that this had was to put a stop to organized resistance to outside rule. The trauma of defeat and dislocation meant that 50-odd years were to pass before the emergence of the independence movements in the late 1950s.

The war began following a revolt of the Bondelswarts Namas in the extreme south of the country at the end of 1903. The majority of German soldiers were sent to the south to quell the uprising and in January 1904 Samuel Maherero, under intense pressure from other Herero leaders and fearing for his own position as paramount Herero leader, gave the order to the Herero nation to rise up against the German presence in Namibia. At the same time he also appealed to Hendrik Witbooi and other Namibian leaders to follow suit.

During the first months of the uprising the Herero were successful in capturing or isolating German fortified positions, however, following the appointment of **Lothar von Trotha** as German military commander, the Herero were gradually forced to retreat from around Okahandja and other strongholds in central Namibia. They made a final stand at the waterholes at Hamakari by the Waterberg Plateau south of Otjiwarongo in August of 1904. The German plan was to encircle the assembled Herero, defeat them, capture their leaders and pursue any splinter groups which might have escaped. The Herero objective was to hold onto the waterholes, for without these they and their cattle would either die or be obliged to surrender.

The German troops attacked the Herero forces on 11 August with the battle continuing on a number of fronts all day. By nightfall no clear picture had yet emerged, however, the following day it became apparent that although the Herero had not been defeated, their resistance was broken and Samuel Maherero and the entire Herero nation fled into the Omaheke sandveld in eastern Namibia en route for Botswana. Stories from those who eventually arrived in Bechuanaland (Botswana) tell horrific stories of men, women and children struggling through the desert, gradually dying of thirst.

A section of the German forces initially gave chase but by 14 August they had returned to the battle site, both soldiers and horses suffering from exhaustion, hunger and thirst. The chase was once again taken up on 16 August but finally abandoned at the end of September as it was impossible to provision both troops and horses in the inhospitable sandveld.

On 2 October Von Trotha issued a proclamation ordering all Herero-speaking people to leave German Southwest Africa or face extermination, and then turned his attention to subduing uprisings in the south of the country. Just over a month later, Von Trotha received orders from Berlin to spare all Herero except the leaders and those 'guilty'. Following the retreat of the Herero, three more years of sporadic resistance to German rule took place in the centre and south of Namibia as the Nama-speaking people continued the revolt.

Much has been written on the German-Namibian War, specifically of the deliberate intention of the German colonial administration to 'exterminate' the Herero nation. Until recently it was widely accepted that the Herero nation was reduced from a population of 60,000-80,000 people before the war, to between 16,000 and 18,000 people after the war. Similarly, the generally accepted view is that the population of the Nama-speaking peoples was also reduced by 35-50% to around 10,000 people.

It is impossible to obtain accurate figures to either confirm or refute the allegations of genocide. Nevertheless, some recent research, especially by the late Brigitte Lau, former head of the National Archives, challenges a number of popular conceptions of the war. In particular questions have now been raised on how the numbers were calculated and on the capacity of the German forces to actually set about the deliberate process of genocide.

The only figures available were based on missionary reports in the 1870s, but the missionaries only worked in a relatively small area of Hereroland. Furthermore, any accurate estimate of the numbers of Herero would have been near impossible, as the Herero were scattered across the veld. In addition, the effects of the rinderpest epidemic of 1897 and the fever epidemic of 1898 were also not taken into account. The suggestion is therefore that there were far fewer Herero than was originally believed.

As far as the capacity of German military to wipe out the Herero is concerned, medical records of the time show that the average military presence during the war was 11,000 men. Of these an average of 57% per year were sick from the effects of lack of water and sanitation, typhoid fever, malaria, jaundice and chronic dysentery. This information suggests that the German military presence was simply not capable of a concerted attempt to commit genocide – even if that had been the intention.

There is no question, however, that following the war both Herero and Nama prisoners of war died in concentration camps; there were executions of captured leaders and many survivors were forced into labour – working on the railroads and in the mines. By the end of the war, the German colonial administration was firmly in control of Namibia from the Tsumeb-Grootfontein area in the north down to the Orange River in the south. In 2004 Germany offered a formal apology for colonial-era killings of tens of thousands of ethnic Hereros, but ruled out compensation for victims' descendants.

Economic development

With the consolidation of German control of central and southern Namibia came rapid economic growth and infrastructural development. Land in the most productive areas in the country was parcelled up and given to settler families, forming the basis of much of the existing white agricultural wealth in the country today. The railway network, already in place between Lüderitz and Aus in the south and Swakopmund, Okahandja and Windhoek in the centre of the country, was expanded to reach the central-northern towns of Tsumeb and Otavi and Grootfontein, Gobabis in the east and Keetmanshoop in the south.

The discovery of diamonds at Kolmanskop near Lüderitz in the south in 1908 financed the economic boom in that part of the country – between 1908 and 1914, German mining companies cut a total of 5,145,000 carats of diamonds. The introduction of the **karakul** sheep (see box, page 334) to the south saw the start of the highly successful karakul wool and leather industry, which brought tremendous prosperity to white farmers in the ranchlands south of Windhoek. Finally, the development of the Tsumeb mines producing copper, zinc and lead brought wealth and development to the Tsumeb-Grootfontein-Otavi triangle in the central-northern areas.

While the wealth that accrued from this flurry of economic activity was concentrated in the hands of white settlers, the labour which built the railroads and worked the farms and mines was predominantly black. A vivid example of this was the estimated 10,000 Oshiwambo-speaking workers who came down from Owamboland in the far north (an area still outside German colonial control, although technically part of German Southwest Africa) to work on the railroads and in the mines. This was the start of migratory work patterns upon which the apartheid era contract labour system was built.

Self-government for the white population was granted by Germany in January 1909 and the following month the main towns including Windhoek, Swakopmund, Keetmanshoop, Lüderitz, Okahandja and Tsumeb were granted the status of municipalities. In Windhoek this period up to the beginning of the First World War in 1914 saw the building of many landmarks – in particular the **Christuskirche** (German Lutheran Church) and the **Tintenpalast** – now the seat of the Namibian Parliament. Self-government in German Southwest Africa lasted until the peaceful surrender of the territory to South African troops fighting on the side of the British in July 1915. This brought to an end the brief period of German colonial rule and ushered in the beginning of 75 years of South African rule.

League of Nations mandate

Following the end of the First World War and the signing of the Treaty of Versailles in 1919, the newly formed League of Nations gave the mandate for governing Namibia to Britain. The mandate, which was to be managed by South Africa on behalf of Britain, came into effect in 1921 and was the beginning of South African control of Namibia, which was to end only with independence in 1990.

The pattern of South African rule over Namibia was established from the start with the relentless expropriation of good farm land for white farmers and the removal of the black population, first to native reserves and later to the so-called homelands. When South Africa took over control of Namibia about 12,000,000 ha of land were in the hands of white (mainly German) farmers, however by 1925 a further 11,800,000 ha had been given to white settlers.

A great number of these new settlers were poor, illiterate Afrikaners who the Union government in South Africa did not want within their own borders. In this way Namibia effectively became a dumping ground for these unwanted farmers, who were given the most generous of terms. New farmers were not only given land for free, but also received credit in the form of cash, wire fences and government-built bore holes to help them get started.

In contrast, in 1923 the Native Reserves Commission proclaimed a mere 2,000,000 ha for the black population of the country who made up 90% of the total population. At the same time a series of laws and regulations governed where the black population was entitled to live and work, severely restricting their freedom of movement in the white-controlled areas. The most obvious consequence of these laws was the creation of a pool of readily available, cheap labour – the nascence of the contract labour system.

The bulk of the population of Namibia was forced to live in a narrow strip of land north of Etosha and south of the Angolan border, marked by the Kunene and Kavango rivers. The **Red Line**, a veterinary fence established by the Germans to prevent the spread of rinderpest and foot-and-mouth disease, effectively separated the communal grazing lands of the north from the commercial white-owned land of the centre and south of the country. This strip of land was far too small to support the number of people living there, obliging many to put themselves into the hands of the contract labour system by seeking work further south.

In 1925 two recruitment agencies were established to find workers for the mines in the centre and south of the country, and in 1943 these two original agencies were amalgamated into the South-West Africa Native Labour Association (SWANLA). Potential workers were sorted into three categories – those fit and able to work underground, those suitable for work above ground at the mines, and the rest only suitable for farm work. Workers themselves had no choice in this and a document of the time stated that "Only the servant is required to render to the master his service at all fit and reasonable times."

The period following the Second World War saw further land giveaways, mainly as rewards to Union soldiers who had served in the war. By the mid-1950s a further 7,000,000 ha of farmland had been put into white hands and the number of whites in Namibia had increased by 50% to around 75,000. The last viable farmland was given away in the 1960s to white conservatives who supported the South African regime's hard-line apartheid policies.

At the same time the Odendaal Commission of Inquiry formulated a plan for the creation of **bantustans**, or black homelands, around the country, involving the forced removal of the black population from all areas designated for whites. The commission also called for the even closer integration of Namibia into South Africa and stated explicitly that "the government of South Africa no longer regards the original (League of Nations) mandate as still existing as such".

Road to independence

Following the end of the Second World War, the newly formed United Nations (UN) assumed responsibility for the administration of the former German colonies, such as the Cameroons, Togo and Namibia. The UN set up a trusteeship system intended to lead to independence for these territories and in response the South African government sought to incorporate Namibia into South Africa. A series of 'consultations' with Namibian leaders during 1946 were intended to convince the UN that Namibians themselves sought to become part of South Africa. Although these efforts were unsuccessful, it was not until 1971 that the South African presence was deemed to be 'illegal'.

Organized resistance to South African rule took off in the 1950s and was initially led by Herero Chief **Hosea Kutako**, who initiated a long series of petitions to the

UN. In 1957 the Owamboland's People's Congress was founded in Cape Town by Namibian contract workers lead by **Andimba Toivo Ja Toivo**, its prime objective being to achieve the abolition of the hated contract labour system. In 1958 Toivo succeeded in smuggling a tape to the UN giving oral evidence of South African suppression and for his pains was immediately deported to Namibia. The same year the name of the organization was changed to the Owamboland People's Organization (OPO) and in 1959 Sam Nujoma and Jacob Kuhangu launched the organization in Windhoek.

The same year also saw the founding of Southwest Africa National Union (SWANU), initially an alliance between urban youth, intellectuals and the Herero Chief's Council. In September of that year the executive of the organization was broadened to include members of the OPO and other organizations, thereby widening its base and making it more representative of the Namibian population as a whole.

These new organizations were soon in conflict with the South African authorities and the December 1959 shootings at the **Old Location** in Windhoek effectively marked the start of concerted resistance to South African rule. 1n 1960 the OPO was reconstituted into the **South West Africa People's Organization** (**SWAPO**), with the central objective of liberating the Namibian people from colonial oppression and exploitation. SWAPO leader Sam Nujoma had managed to leave Namibia and was to lead the organization in exile until his return in 1989.

In 1966, SWAPO appealed to the International Court of Justice to declare South Africa's control of Namibia illegal. The court failed to deliver, even though the UN General Assembly voted to terminate South Africa's mandate. SWAPO's response was to launch the guerrilla war at Ongulumbashe in Owamboland on 26 August, with the declaration that the court's ruling 'would relieve Namibians once and for all from any illusions which they might have harboured about the United Nations as some kind of saviour in their plight'.

In the early stages, the bush war was by necessity a small-scale affair. SWAPO's bases were in Zambia, close only to the Eastern Caprivi Region, and it was only after the Portuguese withdrawal from Angola in 1975 that it became possible to wage a larger-scale campaign. In response to the launching of the guerrilla war, the South African government established military bases all across Namibia's northern borders, and as the scale of the fighting escalated during the 1980s, life became increasingly intolerable for the inhabitants of these areas.

On the political scene, SWAPO activists in Namibia were arrested, tried and sentenced to long prison terms. Among the first group to be sentenced in 1968 was Toivo Ja Toivo, at that time regional secretary for Owamboland. He was sentenced to 20 years imprisonment on Robben Island where he was to remain until 1984. Following the International Court of Justice ruling in 1971 that "the continued presence of South Africa in Namibia [was] illegal", a wave of strikes led by contract workers broke out around the country, precipitating a further round of arrests of strike leaders.

Although the South African government succeeded in quelling the strikes of late 1971 and early 1972, the rest of the decade saw growing resistance to South African rule of Namibia. Ordinary Namibians everywhere, but especially in the densely populated north, buoyed by the International Court of Justice ruling, became politicized, resisting South African attempts to push forward apartheid policies to create separate bantustans around the country.

In response to pressure from Western countries South Africa struggled to find an 'internal solution' to the deadlock in Namibia which would both satisfy the outside world and at the same time defend white minority interests in the country. In 1977 the **Turnhalle Conference** produced a draft constitution for an independent Namibia based on a three-tier system of government which would change little. Needless to say, no one was fooled and the war continued.

During the 1980s South Africa's position in Namibia became increasingly untenable. The bush war was expensive and never-ending and was seriously affecting the South African economy; at the same time attempts to find a political solution within Namibia that excluded SWAPO were proving impossible. Furthermore, opinion amongst the influential Western nations was swinging away from South Africa, making it inevitable that sooner or later Namibia would have to be granted independence with black majority rule.

The key to the solution was the withdrawal of Cuban troops from Angola in return for the withdrawal of South African soldiers from Namibia. At the same time a United National Transitional Government (UNTAG) was to oversee the transition to independence, with elections taking place in November 1989. The final months leading up to the elections saw the return of SWAPO President **Sam Nujoma** from 30 years in exile along with thousands of ordinary Namibians who had also fled into exile during the long years of the bush war.

The main political parties were SWAPO and the DTA, formed in the wake of the unsuccessful Turnhalle Conference. Support for SWAPO was almost universal in Owamboland where the majority of the population lived, while the DTA looked to the south and much of the white community for its support.

Following SWAPO successfully winning the elections, a new constitution was drafted by the various political parties, with the help of international advisers from a number of countries including the USA, France, Germany and the former Soviet Union. Widely viewed as a model of its kind, the new constitution guaranteed wide-ranging human rights and freedom of speech, as well as establishing a multi-party democracy governed by the rule of law. The final date for independence was set for 21 March 1990.

Modern Namibia

Since independence the SWAPO-dominated government has pursued a policy of national reconciliation designed to heal the wounds of 25 years of civil war and over a century of colonial rule. Strongly supported by the various UN agencies and major donors, the Namibian government has set about redressing the injustices of the past and rebuilding the economy, so badly damaged by the war. The mining sector, which is by far the largest sector of the economy, has been further developed and significant growth has also occurred in both the fishing and tourist industries. Nevertheless, Namibia is still largely dependent on South Africa for foodstuffs and manufactured products, and this is one of the weak links in the economy.

Elections in 1994 saw SWAPO win with a massive 68% of the vote, which effectively gave the party the right to change the constitution if it had wished to do so. Throughout 1998 a debate raged as to whether or not the constitution should be changed to allow the president to stand for a third term. On the one hand it was argued that allowing the generally popular Sam Nujoma to stand for a third term would contribute to stability and continuity in this young nation. On the other hand, some Namibians and external observers believe that changing the constitution would set a dangerous precedent and set Namibia on the path to becoming a one-party state.

The debate effectively ended in November 1998 when the Namibian Constitution Amendment Bill, allowing President Nujoma a third term in office, passed through the final parliamentary stage. General and presidential elections held at the end of 1999 saw another convincing SWAPO victory, and Sam Nujoma duly commenced his third term in office as president.

Around this time, the bizarre events in the Caprivi – which saw the governor of the region, prominent leaders and ordinary citizens flee to Botswana and apply for political asylum – were the first indications of serious unrest since independence in 1990. In addition, renewed fighting in the Angolan Civil War and Namibian government support for the MPLA government saw incursions by both UNITA and MPLA soldiers from Angola. At the same time well-publicized attacks on foreign tourists in 2000 damaged tourist confidence in the country.

An additional and unnecessary distraction from the serious business of creating economic growth was the country's involvement in the five-year conflict in the Democratic Republic of Congo, which ended in 2003 with a peace accord following the assassination of then-president of the DRC, Laurent Kabila. Despite the prime minister's explanations that Namibia was "fighting for peace" and "going every inch" for negotiations to end the conflict, the real reasons behind Namibia's involvement remained somewhat murky and were perhaps attached more to personal wealth than lofty ideals of freedom for the Congolese people.

Despite suggestions that another amendment to the constitution might be made to permit a fourth term of presidency, in April 2004, Nujoma announced that he would step down as the country's president at the end of his third term, though he continued to be the president of SWAPO until 2007. In the November 2004 elections, **Hifikepunye Pohamba**, the SWAPO candidate and Nujoma's handpicked successor (who uncannily looks just like him), won in a landslide victory and took over the presidency in March 2005, and SWAPO also retained a two-thirds majority parliament. In 2009, Pohamba and SWAPO were re-elected, each with over 75% of the vote. The next general election is due at the end of 2014, but Pohamba is unable to stand for re-election given that the current constitution only allows for two presidential terms. One of the present high-ranking ministers in the National Assembly of Namibia is expected to be nominated in his place.

Economy

Since the late 1990s, the Namibian economy has grown fairly steadily. Its mining sector is Africa's fifth largest, and currently contributes around 11-12% of GDP and provides about 50% of Namibia's foreign exchange earnings, while tourism and the fisheries sector make significant contributions. The country is an active member of the Southern African Development Community (SADC), which cements the government's commitment to increasing regional commerce and trade. In recent years there has been considerable development of the Walvis Bay port, as well as the completion of the Trans-Kalahari and Trans-Caprivi highways and the opening of the new road bridge across the Zambezi River between Namibia and Zambia. These routes through Namibia are now important (if not essential) trade routes linking the port with the land locked countries of Botswana, Zimbabwe and Zambia.

Namibia's per capita income in 2013 was estimated at US$8200, which is considered fairly high compared to other African countries, but disguises the great inequality in income distribution. Most of the productive farmland still lies in the hands of a minority of white farmers, while the majority of commerce and industry is controlled by a minority of whites and a small black middle class. The mass of the population earns a meagre living from subsistence farming, from the service industry and from the informal sector. Estimates in 2013 put almost 30% of the population living below the poverty line and of these over 50% live on just US$2 per day.

Agriculture

Agriculture is a very important sector in terms of the employment it provides. Despite the fragile environment and constant threat of drought, the sector regularly contributes about 8% to the GDP. The most important component is livestock, with beef and mutton production accounting for about 70-80% of the gross agricultural income. Cattle farming is concentrated in the northern and central parts of the country where a variety of breeds freely roam the nutritious grasslands. White farmers have developed Bonsmara and Afrikaner breeds as well as Brahman and Simmentaler to suit local conditions. About 70-80% of Namibia's beef is exported and most beef products are chilled and vacuum packed before being sent frozen to South Africa and the EU.

Namibia's low and erratic rainfall pattern, however, places severe limits on potential rain-fed agriculture and only 2% of the land is considered arable. It is only possible to grow a single rain-fed crop each year and this has to be in areas where the annual summer rainfall is more than 450 mm. The yields for rain-fed crops are also affected by poor soils, and many of the fertile areas in the north suffer from deficiencies of zinc, phosphorus and organic matter. Namibia remains a net importer of basic food crops and regularly imports up to 50% of its annual cereal requirements, mainly from neighbouring South Africa.

Fishing

The cold waters of the **Benguela Current** produce a nutrient-rich system which is very productive and typified by a low number of species being present but with large numbers of individuals per species. The Namibian fishing industry is generally subdivided into two sectors, white fish and pelagic. The **white fish** species – kingklip, hake, sole, monk and snoek – occur along the continental shelf which stretches from the Kunene River in the north to the Orange River in the south. The **pelagic** species – pilchard and mackerel – are found in more shallow waters which stretch from just south of Walvis Bay to Cape Frio in the north. Since independence the government has introduced legislation that promotes the conservation of the marine environment, and by introducing quotas, stocks of fish have not been overexploited. As such revenue from fishing grows steadily each year, and in the last few years the fishing industry has contributed between 4% and 7.5% to the GDP. A final positive point that will help ensure the future success of the industry is that all the fish come from one of the least-polluted coastal seas in the world. There are no perennial rivers polluted by industry and virtually no sewage flows into the ocean. As long as Namibia is careful in its management of its marine resources the sector will continue to be a valuable source of income.

Mining

Although mining is always vulnerable to demand and world-wide price fluctuations, in simple statistical terms Namibia is mineral rich and mining accounts for 11-12% of GDP. However, the mining and quarrying sectors employs only about 1.8% of the population. Namibia is the world's fourth largest producer of uranium and the country has the world's largest uranium mine at Rössing Uranium Mine near Swakopmund. Namibia is also the world's fifth biggest diamond producer and contributes some 30% of world output, of which 85% are gem quality. Marine diamond mining is becoming increasingly important as the terrestrial diamond supplies are dwindling. Namibia also produces large quantities of zinc and is a small producer of gold and other minerals.

Tourism

The **tourist** sector has been a bright beacon as the country has emerged as one of Africa's 'best-known secrets'. Many tourists from overseas are attracted to remote areas that are essentially 'unspoilt' and Namibia has an abundance of such areas. These are also the areas where the local communities have no employment opportunities and have suffered the most during periods of drought, and many are able to earn an alternative income and directly benefit from tourism. Currently the country receives about one million foreign visitors a year – one in three come from South Africa, and there are significant numbers from Germany and the United Kingdom. Namibia is consistently ranked as one of the world's best and fastest growing tourism destinations by the World Travel and Tourism Council (WTTC). Its popularity can be defined by observing that in 1989, when records were first started, just 100,000 tourists visited Namibia, compared to today's one million. Today the sector contributes more than US$7 billion to the GDP per year and provides tens of thousands of direct and indirect jobs.

Social conditions

Namibia's population of approximately 2.2 million has doubled in the past 30 years and grows at an average of 0.7% per year. Nevertheless, the population density of 2.7 people per sq km is one of the lowest in the world. While most Namibians still live in the rural areas, practising subsistence farming of one form or another, increasing mobility and a lack of employment opportunities in the rural areas are causing a rapid migration to the towns. As people lose touch with their homes and traditional ways of life and adopt a more urban, Western lifestyle, the levels of crime and unemployment experienced in many Western cities are unfortunately also becoming a fact of life in Namibia.

Life expectancy was 52 years in 2013, which although is low among the other more developed countries in Africa, has improved dramatically from just 44 years in 2000. This is mainly attributed to the successes in combatting the scourge of HIV/AIDS that plagued the country during that period (ant-viral drugs for example are now free to all).

Around 89% of the adult population is considered literate, and education is compulsory from ages six to 16. Namibia has placed a high priority on education and since independence the system has been rationalized and the quality and relevance of the education for all Namibian children has been improved. Today some 94% of children under 18 attend school.

Culture

People

Namibia is a blend of many different peoples and cultures, similar in some respects to the 'rainbow' nation next door. The population consists of 11 major ethnic groups scattered around the country, from semi-nomadic cattle herders and hunters to the sophisticated black and white urban elite. About 50% of the population are Ovambo, 9% Kavango, 7% Herero, 7% Damara, 5% Nama, 4% Caprivian, 3% San (Bushmen), 2% Baster and 0.5% Tswana. The remaining 12% are made up of communities of whites (of German and Afrikaner descent, with a small group of English speakers) and coloureds (people originally of mixed European and African descent).

Namibia's culture has absorbed both African and European elements and, unlike some other African countries, is largely free of hostility or conflict

Ethnic groups

The San (Bushmen)

The San, or Bushmen as they were previously known, are generally accepted to be the oldest indigenous inhabitants of southern Africa, and numerous examples of their rock art, dating back thousands of years, is to be found all over the sub-region.

Traditionally the San were skilled hunter-gatherers living in small independent bands with the family as the basic unit. Different bands had limited contact with each other, although individuals were free to come and go as they pleased, unhampered by possessions or fixed work responsibilities.

Although successful and well adapted to their environment, about 300 years ago the San started to come under pressure both from migrating **Bantu** tribes and early European settlers. Regarded as cattle thieves and considered as more or less sub-human by these groups, the San were hunted down and forced off their traditional lands, the majority seeking the relative safety of the Kalahari Desert in (now) Botswana and Namibia.

Today, the estimated 35,000 San living in Namibia live a marginalized existence on the fringes of mainstream society. The South African 'homeland' policy during the Apartheid years forced them to settle in remote 'Bushmanland', a desert-like area between the Khaudum National Park and Omaheke. Like aboriginal peoples in Australia and North America, the loss of their land and traditional way of life has seriously undermined the San people's culture and today only about 2000 still live by their traditional ways in the northeast of the country. They are unlikely to be granted significant tracts of land on which to return to their former way of life, and unless educational and employment opportunities can be provided for them, they will remain a poor and marginalized community.

between the ethnic groups. The government's stance on the issue was summarized by Prime Minister Hage Geingob shortly after independence at a 1993 conference on tribalism. "For too long we have thought of ourselves as Hereros, Namas, Afrikaners, Germans, Owambos. We must now start to think of ourselves as Namibians." These sentiments are still very much the case today, but in a predominantly rural country where many aspects of culture are closely linked with land ownership, unresolved land issues dating back to pre-colonial, colonial and apartheid days are still burning issues for many communities.

Land and environment

Geography

Namibia is located on the south west coast of Africa between the 17th and 29th latitudes. The territory stretches from Angola and Zambia in the north to South Africa in the south; most of the eastern border is with Botswana. The total surface area is 824,269 sq km, nearly four times the size of the UK, or twice the size of California.

Most of the country is either desert or semi-desert in appearance, and there are only five perennial rivers: the Cuando, Kunene, Okavango and Zambezi in the north and the Orange River in the south, which forms the border with South Africa. The country's dominant feature is the **Namib Desert**, which occupies almost a fifth of the total area. It varies between 80 and 120 km in width and stretches along the entire Atlantic coastline, a distance of approximately 1600 km. This whole region receives less than 100 mm of rain per year. The central portion of the desert is an impassable mass of giant sand dunes which are one of the major tourist attractions.

The centre of the country is a semi-arid mountainous plateau, where the capital Windhoek is located. Most of the annual rains fall during the summer months when the plateau is covered with green grasslands and the occasional flowering acacia tree. The average elevation is 1100 m, the highest mountains are the Brandberg (2573 m) and the Moltkeblick (2446 m) in the **Aus** range. Throughout the plateau are numerous dry, seasonal river courses that only flow for a few days each year if at all. Few ever drain into the ocean, the water disappearing in the sands of either the Namib or Kalahari deserts. The dramatic **Fish River Canyon** in the south of the country is evidence of the presence of a large body of water at some time in the distant past.

The southeastern area of the country is characterized by low-lying plains covered with scrub vegetation, typical of the Kalahari and Karoo regions of Botswana and South Africa.

The far north of the country is the only region which receives sufficient rainfall each year to sustain agriculture and a wooded environment. As you travel north of Etosha National Park the vegetation cover gradually increases and the overall landscape is more green than brown. The **Caprivi Strip** has some magnificent woodlands and lush riverine vegetation along with a wide variety of wild animals.

Climate

Namibia is blessed with a climate in which the sun shines for more than 300 days per year. Most of the year sees clear blue skies, and it is only during the height of the rainy season that days are cloudy. But Namibia, like so many countries in Africa, eagerly waits for the first rains to fall every year. The country lies within the dry latitudes and depends upon the unpredictable movements of the climatic zones for its rainfall. In general the rainy season lasts from November to March, although during this period it might not rain for several weeks. However, by February most parts of the country should have received a significant proportion of their annual rainfall. By April and May the country is far greener than most would imagine or expect. The southwest is the driest part and in a good year Lüderitz may receive only 20 mm of rain, while the Caprivi region receives the most rainfall with the annual average for Katima Mulilo being over 700 mm.

A quick glance at any map of Namibia will clearly show the entire coast to be desert. The three major coastal settlements – Lüderitz, Walvis Bay and Swakopmund – all depend upon water piped from the interior for their survival. The cold Benguela Current has a modifying influence on the weather, although one negative aspect of the coastal climate is the frequent sea fog which forms when the cool ocean air mixes with the hot Namib Desert air. It really can get very gloomy, but this fog is vital to the survival of plants and animals in the Namib Desert.

Vegetation

While much of the Namibian landscape is characterized by deserts and mountains, the country extends far enough north into the tropical latitudes to have a varied range of plant life. The most interesting ecological area is the Namib Desert where the diverse flora and fauna have had to adapt to a unique set of climatic conditions. Botanists from all over the world have visited the Namib to study some of the more unusual plants and the ways in which they cope with the hot and dry conditions. A good tour of the desert should include an introduction to some of these plants. This is also the only desert in the world where you can see elephant, lion and rhino; each of which have adapted to living in the harsh terrain.

Although a large proportion of the country is desert there are four distinct vegetation zones, which are loosely defined as follows: the mountainous escarpment regions such as Kaokoland and Damaraland; the tropical forests and wetlands along the banks of the perennial rivers in the Kavango and Caprivi regions; the savannah plains with occasional trees in the Kalahari; ; and the low altitude coastlands and Namib Desert.

Along the mountainous escarpment of Kaokoland and Damaraland most of the plants are either arborescent, succulents or semi-succulents. The most common species are the **quiver tree**, or kokerboom (*Aloë dichotoma*), the spiky tall cactus-like plants known as *Euphorbia* and the **paper bark tree**, or *Commiphora*. In the extreme north of Kaokoland, the Marienfluss and Hartmann's valleys are covered with open grasslands with very few trees and shrubs. Further to the south a few more trees start to appear in the savannah, notably the **mopane** (*Colophospermum mopane*) and **purple-pod terminalia** (*Terminalia prunioides*). Along the Kunene River the dominant trees are **leadwood** (*Combretum imberbe*), **jakkalsbessie** (*Diospyros mespiliformis*) and **sycamore fig** (*Ficus sycamorus*). After the rains look out for the magnificent pink flowers of the **Boesmangif** (*Andanium boehmianum*), a creeper which is found on many of the larger trees. The palm trees along the river are **makalani palms** (*Hyphaene petersana*), a common sight further east in Owamboland.

In areas where there is slightly more rainfall there are a variety of flowering annuals which will cover the land with a carpet of colour for a couple of months. Most of these annuals are of the *Brasicaceae* and *Asteraceae* families.

The Kavango and Caprivi regions are the only areas where you will see large stands of forest. Most of the trees are deciduous so, like the rest of the country, the area looks at its best after the rains. Along the riverbeds you can expect to see *mopane*, the **palm** (*Hyphaene ventricosa*) and a couple of **reed** species on the flood plains, *Phragmites australis* and *Typha latifolia*. The woodland areas of the game reserves are dominated by *Terminalia* shrubs, *Boscia albitrunca*, *Bauhinia macrantha* and *Grewia*.

Along the edge of the Kalahari Desert the sands gradually give way to trees and tall shrubs, although most of the vegetation is restricted to grasslands – *Stipagrotis* is the dominant grass. The most common flower is the **driedoring** (*Rhigozum trichotomum*).

As noted above, the Namib Desert has the most interesting mix of plants in Namibia. One of the most unusual of all plants is the *Welwitschia mirabilis*, a plant first seen by the white man in 1859. These plants are found in small groups inland from the coast at Swakopmund. Each plant has two long leaves which are often torn and discoloured. Using carbon dating they have been shown to live for over 1000 years in the harshest of conditions. After the welwitschia it is the lichens that attract the greatest attention in the desert. The lichens are found on west facing slopes and surfaces where they are able to draw moisture from the sea fogs. If it were not for the fog the plants would have no source of water. They are now recognized as a vital component of the Namib environment and most areas are protected. Many of the animals rely upon the lichen as an important source of water after the fog has condensed on the plants.

Wildlife

The Big Nine → *See African wildlife colour section in the middle of the guide.*

It is a reasonable assumption that anyone interested enough in wildlife to be travelling on safari in Africa is also able to identify the better-known and more spectacular African animals. It is indeed fortunate that many of the large animals are also on the whole fairly common, so you will have a very good chance of seeing them even on a fairly short safari. They are often known as the Big Five; a term originally coined by hunters who wanted to take home trophies of their safari, and thus it was that, in hunting parlance, the Big Five were elephant, black rhino, buffalo, lion and leopard. Nowadays the hippopotamus is usually considered one of the Big Five for those who shoot with their cameras, whereas the buffalo is far less of a 'trophy'. Equally photogenic and worthy to be included are the zebra, giraffe and cheetah.

But whether they are the Big Five or the Big Nine these are the animals that most people come to Namibia to see. With the possible exception of the leopard and the white rhino, you have an excellent chance of seeing all of these animals in Etosha National Park or in the parks along the Caprivi Strip. Namibia also has a number of privately owned guest farms and game ranches which also offer good game-viewing opportunities.

Lion The lion (*Panthera leo*), weighing in at around 250 kg for a male, is the second largest cat in the world after the tiger. Unusually for cats, they live in large prides consisting of related females and offspring and a small number of adult males. Groups of female lions typically hunt together for their pride; being smaller, swifter and more agile than the males, and unencumbered by the heavy and conspicuous mane, which causes overheating during exertion. They act as a coordinated group in order to stalk and bring down the prey successfully. Totally carnivorous, they prey mostly on large antelope or buffalo. Visually, coloration varies from light buff to yellowish, reddish, or dark brown, and the underparts are generally lighter and the tail tuft is black. Lion can be seen in most of Namibia's parks, especially Etosha, and there is also a small but rarely seen population of free-ranging lion in the northern region of Kaokoland.

Cheetah The cheetah (*Acinonyx jubatus*) is well known for its running speed. In short bursts it has been recorded at over 90 kph. But it is not as successful at hunting as you might expect with such a speed advantage. The cheetah has a very specialized build which is long and thin with a deep chest, long legs and a small head. But the forelimbs are restricted to a forward and backward motion which makes it very difficult for the cheetah to turn suddenly when in hot pursuit of a small antelope. They are often seen in family groups walking across the plains or resting in the shade. The black 'tear' mark on the face is usually obvious through binoculars. Any visit to a private game farm in Namibia should be rewarded with a sighting of cheetah as Namibia has the largest population of these animals in southern Africa not contained within national parks.

Leopard The leopard (*Panthera pardus*) is less likely to be seen as it is more nocturnal and secretive in its habits than the cheetah. It hunts at night and frequently rests during the heat of the day on the lower branches of trees. Well camouflaged, its spots – typically dark rosettes with a tawny-yellow middle – merge into foliage or blend well into less sparse grassland. Its habitat is extremely diverse and it can survive in high mountainous and coastal plains regions as well as rainforests and deserts. The excellent **Okonjima Private Nature Reserve**, 50 km from Otjiwarongo (see page 109), is home to the **Africat Foundation**; here guests are guaranteed to see cheetah and leopard in both natural and artificial surroundings.

Elephant Elephants (*Loxodonta africana*) are awe-inspiring by their very size and they are the largest land mammal weighing in at up to six tonnes with an average shoulder height of 3-4 m. Sociable by nature, elephants form groups of 10-20 led by a female matriarch, and it is wonderful to watch a herd at a waterhole. You will not be disappointed by the sight of them. Elephants are herbivores and are voracious and destructive feeders, sometimes pushing over a whole tree to get to the tender shoots at the top. They are readily seen in many of the game areas, but perhaps the most revered sighting in Namibia is that of the free-roaming desert elephants in Damaraland and Kaokoland (see box, page 182).

Rhino The **white rhino** (*Ceratotherium simum*) and the **black rhino** (*Diceros bicornis*) occur naturally in Namibia, although today you will find that in many of the reserves where you find them they have in fact been reintroduced after becoming extinct in previous years. Their names have no bearing on the colour of the animals as they are both a rather non-descript dark grey. The name white rhino is derived from the Dutch word 'weit' which means wide and refers to the shape of the animal's mouth. The white rhino has a large square muzzle and this reflects the fact that it is a grazer and feeds by cropping grass. The black rhino, on the other hand, is a browser, usually feeding on shrubs and bushes. It achieves this by using its long, prehensile upper lip which is well adapted to the purpose.

The horn of the rhino is not a true horn, but is made of a material called keratin, which is essentially the same as hair. If you are fortunate enough to see rhino with their young you will notice that the white rhino tends to herd its young in front of it, whereas the black rhino usually leads its young from the front. The white rhino is a more sociable animal, and they are likely to be seen in family groups of five or more. Their preferred habitat is grasslands and open savannah with mixed scrub vegetation. The black rhino lives in drier bush country and usually alone. They will browse on twigs, leaves and tree bark. Visitors to Etosha National Park have a good chance of seeing rhino with their young at one of the three floodlit waterholes in the evening. It is worth staying up late one night to see these magnificent ancient creatures. Namibia also has the privilege of being home to a population of free-roaming black rhino in Damaraland and Kaokoland (see box, page 185) which, like the desert elephant, have adapted their behavior to withstand the harsh environment that they live in.

Buffalo The buffalo (*Syncerus caffer*) was once revered by the hunter as the greatest challenge for a trophy; more hunters have lost their lives to this animal than to any other. This is an immensely strong animal with particularly acute senses. Left alone as a herd they pose no more of a threat than a herd of domestic cattle. The danger lies in the unpredictable behaviour of the lone bull. These animals, cut off from the herd, become bad-tempered and easily provoked. While you are more likely to see them on open plains they are equally at home in dense forest. To see a large herd peacefully grazing is a great privilege. Although they are not found in Namibia south of the so-called Red Line separating the communal grazing lands to the north from the commercial lands to the south, the parks in the Caprivi Strip have a good record for sightings of herds of buffalo.

Hippopotamus The most conspicuous animal of inland waters is the hippopotamus (*Hippopotamus amphibius*). A large beast with short stubby legs, but nevertheless quite agile on land. They can weigh up to four tonnes. During the day it rests in the water, rising every few minutes to snort and blow at the surface. At night they leave the water to graze. A single adult animal needs up to 60 kg of grass every day, and to manage this obviously has to forage far. They do not eat aquatic vegetation. The nearby banks of the waterhole with a resident hippo population will be very bare and denuded of grass. Should you meet a hippo on land by day or night keep well away. If you get between it and its escape route to the water, it may well attack. They are restricted to water not only because their skin would dry up if not kept damp but because their body temperature needs to be regulated. Again the rivers along the Caprivi Strip are the best place to see them and, if you are lucky, you may see them in the vicinity of Popa Falls if staying at the camp there (see page 154).

Giraffe The giraffe (*Giraffa camelopardalis*) may not be as magnificent as a full grown lion, nor as awe-inspiring as an elephant, but its elegance as a small party stroll across the plains is unsurpassed. Both male and female animals have horns, though in the female they may be smaller. A mature male can be over 5 m high. The lolloping gait of the giraffe is very distinctive and it produces this effect by the way it moves its legs at the gallop. A horse will move its diagonally opposite legs together when galloping, but the giraffe moves both hind legs together and both forelegs together. It achieves this by swinging both hind legs forward and outside the forelegs. They have excellent sight and acute hearing. They are browsers, and can eat the leaves and twigs of a large variety of tall trees, thorns presenting no problem. Their only natural threat are lions, which will attack young animals when they are drinking. Giraffe can be spotted both inside the parks and on the communal lands of Damaraland and Kaokoland.

Zebra The zebra is the last of the Big Nine and there are two common types in Namibia, **Burchell's zebra** (*Equus burchelli*) and **Hartmann's mountain zebra** (*Equus zebra hartmannae*). Burchell's zebra will often be seen in large herds, sometimes with antelope. You are most likely to see them in Etosha National Park. They stand 145-150 cm at the shoulder whereas Hartmann's mountain zebra are larger, standing 160 cm at the shoulder. Generally the latter only occur in mountainous areas close to the Namib Desert. They are found in three isolated pockets: in Kaokoland and as far south as the Brandberg, along the escarpment to the south of the Swakop River and in the Huns Mountains close to the Fish River Canyon. As the name suggests they live on hills and stony mountains. They are good climbers and can tolerate arid conditions, going without water for up to three days. During the heat of the day they seek shade and keep very still, making spotting them more difficult. They are closely related to the Cape mountain zebra, but stand about 25 cm taller than the southern sub-species.

Larger antelope
The first animals that you will see on safari will almost certainly be antelope. These occur on the open plains. Although there are many different species, it is not difficult to distinguish between them. For presentation purposes they have been divided into the larger antelopes, which stand about 120 cm or more at the shoulder, and the smaller ones, about 90 cm or less. They are all ruminant plains animals, herbivores like giraffe and the zebra, but they have keratin covered horns which makes them members of the family *Bovidae*. They vary greatly in appearance, from the small dik-diks to the large eland, and once you have learnt to recognize the different sets of horns, identification of species should not be too difficult.

The largest of all the antelopes is the **eland** (*Taurotragus oryx*) which stands 175-183 cm at the shoulder. It is cow-like in appearance, with a noticeable dewlap and shortish spiral horns present in both sexes. The general colour varies from greyish to fawn, sometimes with a rufous tinge, with narrow white stripes on the sides of the body. It occurs in herds of up to 30 in a wide variety of grassy and mountainous habitats. Even during the driest periods of the year the animals appear in excellent condition. Research has shown that they travel large distances in search of food and that they will eat all sorts of tough woody bushes and thorny plants.

Not quite as big, but still reaching 140-153 cm at the shoulder, is the **greater kudu** (*Tragelaphus strepsiceros*) which prefers fairly thick bush, sometimes in quite dry areas. You are most likely to see them in the northern areas of Etosha National Park and in the Caprivi Strip, although you have just as much chance of seeing one at dusk by the side of the road in central or northern Namibia. Although nearly as tall as the eland it is a much more slender and elegant animal altogether. Its general colour also varies from greyish to fawn and it has several white stripes running down the sides of the body. Only the male carries horns, which are very long and spreading, with only two or three twists along the length of the horn. A noticeable and distinctive feature is a thick fringe of hair which runs from the chin down the neck. Greater kudu usually live in family groups of not more than half a dozen individuals, but occasionally larger herds up to about 30 can be seen.

The **roan antelope** (*Hippoptragus equinus*) and **sable antelope** (*Hippotragus niger*) are similar in general shape, though the roan is somewhat bigger, being 140-145 cm at the shoulder, compared to the 127-137 cm of the sable. In both species, both sexes carry ringed horns which curve backwards, and these are particularly long in the sable. There is a horse-like mane present in both animals. The sable is usually glossy black with white markings on the face and a white belly. The female is often a reddish brown in colour. The roan can vary from dark rufous to a reddish fawn and also has white markings on the face. The black males of the sable are easily identified, but the brownish females can be mistaken for the roan. Look for the tufts of hair at the tips of the rather long ears of the roan (absent in the sable). The Roan generally is found in open grassland. Both the roan and the sable live in herds. Khaudum National Park is home to the largest roan population in Namibia. There are also small herds in Etosha which were originally transported from Khaudum. Sable can be seen in the Waterberg Plateau Park as well as Khaudum and the Caprivi Strip.

Another antelope with a black and white face is the **gemsbok** (*Oryx gazella*), which stands 122 cm at the shoulder. They are large creatures with a striking black line down the spine and a black stripe between the coloured body and the white underparts. The head is white with further black markings. This is not an animal you would confuse with another. Their horns are long, straight and sweep back behind their ears – from face-on they look V-shaped. The female also has horns but overall the animal is of a slightly lighter build. One of the lasting images of Namibia is a picture of a single gemsbok with the sand dunes of Sossusvlei as a backdrop. Visitors to Etosha will see large herds close to the waterholes, and you will also see gemsbok in the Namib-Naukluft Park, western Damaraland and the Skeleton Coast National Park.

The **wildebeest** or **gnu** (*Connochaetes taurinus*) is a large animal about 132 cm high at the shoulder, looking rather like an American bison in the distance. The impression is strengthened by its buffalo-like horns (in both sexes) and humped appearance. The general colour is blue grey with a few darker stripes down the side. It has a noticeable beard and long mane. They are often found grazing with herds of zebra and are often seen in Etosha and on privately owned game farms.

The **common waterbuck** (*Kobus ellipsiprymnus*) stands at about 122-137 cm at the shoulder, it has a shaggy grey-brown skin which is very distinctive. The males have long, gently curving horns which are heavily ringed. There are two species which can be distinguished by the white mark on their buttocks. On the common waterbuck there is a clear half ring on the rump and round the tail. In the other species, the Defassa waterbuck, the ring is a filled-in white patch on the rump. They occur in the eastern Caprivi Strip and on farmland in north-central Namibia.

There are three other species of antelope that you can expect to see in the wetlands of Caprivi: red lechwe, sitatunga and puku. The **red lechwe** (*Kobus leche leche*) is a medium-sized antelope standing at about 100 cm at the shoulder. It is bright chestnut in colour, with black markings on the legs. Only the males have horns which are relatively thin, rising upwards before curving outwards and backwards forming a double curve. They tend to feed on grass and water plants, favouring water meadows. As the river levels rise and fall so the herds migrate to the greenest pastures. They are unable to move fast on dry land, so when they feel threatened they will take refuge in shallow pools – if needs be, they are very good swimmers.

Puku (*Kobus adenota vardoni*) favour a similar habitat to the red lechwe, but you are only likely to see them in small numbers in Nkasa Rupara (formerly Mamili) National Park. They have a coat of golden yellow long hair and stand at about 100 cm at the shoulder. Only the males have horns which are thick and short with heavy rings. They usually live in small groups of five to 10 animals, but during the mating season the males gather in groups and will strongly defend their respective territories.

The chances of spotting the **sitatunga** (*Tragelaphus sekei*) are rare since this species of antelope favours swampy areas where there are thick reed beds to hide in. It is the largest of the aquatic antelope standing at 115 cm at the shoulder. If you only catch a glimpse of the animal you can be sure it was a sitatunga if the hindquarters were higher than the forequarters. Their coat is long and shaggy with a grey brown colour, and they have thin white stripes similar to those of the bushbuck. The horns are long, twisted and swept back. They have long hooves which are highly adapted to soft, marshy soils. When frightened they will enter the water and submerge entirely, with just their snout breaking the surface. This is a very shy antelope which few visitors will see, but if you spend some time at a quiet location by the river you may be rewarded with a sighting as they quietly move through the reedbeds. Again Nkasa Rupara (formerly Mamili) is the best location for spotting sitatunga.

The **red hartebeest** (*Alcelaphus caama*) stands about 127-132 cm at the shoulder. They have an overall rufous appearance with a conspicuous broad light patch on the lower rump. The back of their neck, chin and limbs has traces of black. The hartebeest has the habit of posting sentinels, which are solitary animals who stand on the top of termite mounds keeping a watch out for predators. If you see an animal on its 'knees' digging the earth with its horns then it is marking its territory – they are very territorial in behaviour. Their slightly odd appearance is caused by their sloping withers and a very long face. They have short horns which differ from any other animal as they are situated on a bony pedicel, a backward extension of the skull which forms a base. They are fairly common in central Namibia and the Kalahari regions.

Smaller antelope

The remaining common antelopes are a good deal smaller than those described above. The largest and most frequently seen of these is the **impala** (*Aepyceros melampus*) which stands 92-107 cm at the shoulder and is bright rufous in colour with a white abdomen. Only the male carries the long lyre-shaped horns. Just above the heels of the hind legs is a tuft of thick black bristles, which are surprisingly easy to see as the animal runs. This is unique to the impala. Also easy to see is the black mark on the side of the abdomen in front of the back leg. The impala are noted for their graceful leaps which they make as they are running after being startled. You are most likely to see them in herds in the grasslands but they also live in light woodlands. They are the most numerous of the smaller antelope and no matter what the state of the veld they always appear to be in immaculate condition. During the breeding season the males fight to protect, or gather, their own harem. It is great fun to come across such a herd and pause to watch the male trying to keep an eye on all the animals in the group. Young males may be seen in small groups until they are able to form their own harem. In parts of Etosha National Park you will see a distinct sub-species, the **black-faced impala**, which, as its name implies, has a black streak on the face (otherwise it is identical in appearance to the common impala).

Similar to the impala, the **springbok** (*Antidorcas marsupialis*), stands 76-84 cm to the shoulder. The upper part of the body is fawn and is separated from the white underparts by a dark brown lateral stripe. A distinguishing feature is a reddish-brown stripe which runs between the base of the horns and the mouth, passing through the eye. When startled they start to 'pronk'. The head is lowered almost to the feet, and the legs are fully extended with hoofs bunched together. Then the animal takes off, shooting straight up into the air for some 2-3 m, before dropping down and shooting up again as though it were on coiled springs.

The **common reedbuck** (*Redunca arundinum*), which is often seen in the Caprivi parks, stands 70-85 cm at the shoulder. The males have rigid horns that are sharply hooked forwards at the tip. Its general colour is described as dull grey-brown with white underparts, black forelegs and a short bushy tail. During the hottest time of day, it will seek out shelter in reed beds or long grasses, never far from water. Reedbuck are monogamous and live in pairs, though sometimes will gather in a herd if feel threatened.

Another tiny antelope is the **oribi** (*Ourebia ourebi*), which stands around 61 cm at the shoulder. Like the reedbuck it has a patch of bare skin just below each ear, but that's where the similarities end. The oribi is slender and delicate looking. Its colour tends to be sandy to brownish fawn, its ears are oval-shaped and its horns are short and straight with a few rings at the base. The oribi live in small groups or as a pair. As the day-time temperatures rise, so it seeks out its 'hide' in long grass or the bush. Like the reedbuck it never likes to venture far from water. Mudumu National Park has a few family groups.

The common **duiker** (*Cephalophus natalensis*) is a tiny, shy antelope that stands at about 50 cm at the shoulder with only the males having short horns. They have the ability to take off at high speed in a series of diving jumps when alarmed. The colour of the upper parts varies from a greyish to a reddish-yellow and considerable colour variation within populations has been observed in some areas. The underparts are usually white. Most have a black band on the lower part of the face near the nostrils. Duiker can be found all over Namibia, particularly in the Caprivi region, and they have been known to penetrate the coastal desert region by following dry riverbeds.

The last two of the common smaller antelopes are the bushbuck and the dik-dik. The **bushbuck** (*Tragelaphus scriptus*) is about 76-92 cm at the shoulder. The coat has a shaggy appearance and a variable pattern of white spots and stripes on the side and back. There are in addition two white crescent-shaped marks on the front of the neck. The horns, present in the male only, are short, almost straight and slightly spiral. The animal has a curious high rump which gives it a characteristic crouching appearance. The white underside of the tail is noticeable when it is running. The Bushbuck tends to occur in areas of thick bush especially near water. It lies up during the day in thickets, but is often seen bounding away when disturbed. Bushbuck are usually seen either in pairs or singly.

The **Damara dik-dik** (*Rhynchotragus kirki*) is so small it can hardly be mistaken for any other antelope; it only stands 36-41 cm high and weighs only 5 kg. In colour it is a greyish brown, often washed with rufous. The legs are noticeably thin and stick-like, giving the animal a very fragile appearance. The muzzle is slightly elongated which it wriggles from side to side, it has a conspicuous tuft of hair on the top of its head. Only the male carries the very small straight horns. Despite the name, they are not found in the Damaraland region of Namibia, but are found at Waterberg Plateau Park, Etosha National Park, Caprivi Strip and as far south as the Brukkaros Mountain.

Other mammals

Although the antelope are undoubtedly the most numerous animals to be seen on the plains, there are others worth keeping an eye open for. Some of these are scavengers which thrive on the kills of other animals. They include the dog-like jackals, two species of which you are likely to come across in Etosha National Park (both are about 41-46 cm at the shoulder). The **side-striped jackal** (*Canis adustus*) is greyish fawn and it has a rather variable and sometimes ill-defined stripe along the side. The **black-backed jackal** (*Canis mesomelas*) is more common and will often be seen near a lion kill. It is a rather foxy reddish fawn in colour with a noticeable black area on its back. This black part is sprinkled with a silvery white which can make the back look silver in some lights. They are timid creatures which can be seen by day or night.

The other well-known plains scavenger is the **spotted hyena** (*Crocuta crocuta*), a fairly large animal about 69-91 cm at the shoulder. Its high shoulders and low back give it a characteristic appearance. Brownish, with dark spots and a large head, it usually occurs singly or in pairs, but occasionally in small packs. When hungry they are aggressive creatures, they have been known to attack live animals and will occasionally try to steal a kill from lions. They always look dirty because of their habit of lying in muddy pools which may be to keep cool or alleviate the irritation of parasites. Both jackal and hyena are occasionally spotted along the coast of the Skeleton Coast National Park, where they scavenge for carrion, and they are common enough in Etosha and the other game parks.

Another aggressive scavenger is the **African wild dog** or **hunting dog** (*Lycaon pictus*), which are easy to identify since they have all the features of a large mongrel dog. Their coat is a mixed pattern of dark shapes and white and yellow patches, no two dogs are quite alike. The question is not what they look like, but whether you will be fortunate enough to see one as they are seriously threatened by extinction. In many areas of Namibia they have already been wiped out. The problem it seems is a conflict between the farmer and conservation. The dogs live and hunt in packs. They are particularly vicious when hunting their prey and will chase an animal until it is exhausted, and then start taking bites out of it while it is still alive. Unfortunately, these days the only chance you have of seeing wild dogs is in Khaudum National Park – one of the least accessible areas for the average visitor.

A favourite and common plains animal is the comical **warthog** (*Phacochoerus aethiopicus*). It is unmistakable, being almost hairless and grey in general colour with a very large head, tusks and wart-like growths on the face. These are thought to protect the eyes as it makes sweeps sideways into the earth with its tusks, digging up roots and tubers. Warthogs often kneel on their forelegs when eating. They frequently occur in family parties. When startled the adults will run at speed with their tails held straight up in the air followed by their young. Look out for them around the edges of waterholes as they love to cake themselves in thick mud to keep them both cool and free of ticks and flies.

In rocky areas, such as the Waterberg Plateau, look out for an animal that looks a bit like a large grey-brown guinea pig. This is the **dassie** or **rock hyrax** (*Heterohyrax brucei*), an engaging and fairly common animal. During the morning and afternoon you will see them sunning themselves on the rocks. Perhaps their strangest characteristic is their place in the evolution of mammals. The structure of the ear is similar to that found in whales, their molar teeth look like those of a rhinoceros, two pouches in the stomach resemble a condition found in birds, and the arrangement of the bones of the forelimb are like those of the elephant.

You are likely to see two types of primate in Namibia; the vervet monkey and the Chacma baboon. Both are widespread and you are just as likely to see them outside a game park than in one. The **vervet monkey** (*Cercopithecus.pygerythrus*) is of slim build and light in colour. Its feet are conspicuously black, so too is the tip of the tail. It lives in savannah and woodlands but has proved to be highly adaptable.

The adult male **Chacma baboon** (*Papio ursinus*) is slender and can weigh up to 40 kg. Its general colour is a dark olive green, with lighter undersides. It never roams far from a safe refuge, usually a tree, but rocks can provide sufficient protection from predators. The Chacma baboons occur in large family groups, known as troops, and have a reputation for being aggressive where they have become used to man's presence.

Birds

Over 630 bird species are present in Namibia, and of these approximately 500 breed locally whilst the others are migrants. There are several birds that are near-endemic to Namibia including the Rüppell's bustard, rosy-faced lovebird, Herero chat, and Monterio's hornbill, but the Damara tern is the only true endemic (see box, page 270). Regularly seen throughout the country are the extraordinary nests of the sociable weaver that hang in trees or off telephone poles. Some of these enormous nests are home to several hundred birds and have been in continual use for over 100 years.

Contents

410 Useful words and phrases

411 Index

415 Advertisers' index

416 Credits

Footnotes

Useful words and phrases

Afrikaans

Good morning	Goeie more
How's it going?	Hoe gaan dit?
Very well	Baie goed
Please	Asseblief
Thank you	Dankie
Goodbye	Totsies

Batswana

Hello	Dumela
How are you?	O kae?
Thank you	Ke a leboga
Goodbye	Sala sentle

Caprivi

I greet you	Ma lumele sha
Please	Na lapela
Thank you	Ni itumezi
Goodbye	Mu siale hande

Kavango

Hello	Morokeni
Thank you	Na pandura

Herero/Ovahimba

Are you well?	Perivi?
Yes, well	Nawa
Thank you	Okuhepa
Goodbye	Kara nawa

Nama/Damara

How are you?	Matisa?
Thank you	Ayo
Good morning	Moro
Goodbye	Gaiseha

Owambo

Did you sleep well?	Wa lelepo nawa?
Yes, well.	Nawa
Thank you	Iyaloo
Good bye	Kalapo nawa

San

How are you?	Am thai?
I am thirsty	Mem ari gu
I am hungry	Mem tlabe

Index → *Entries in bold refer to maps*

A

accidents 32
accommodation 21
  price codes 23
African wild dog 407
Africat Foundation 109, 400
Afrikaner, Jonker 51, 317, 379, 380, 382
Agate Beach 353
agriculture 393
Ai Aiba Farm 285
Ai-Ais Hot Springs Spa 367
|Ai-|Ais/Richtersveld Transfrontier Park 361
air travel 9, 13
  domestic 13
  international 9
Albrecht, Abraham and Christian 359
Ameib Ranch 283
Anabeb 195
Andersson, Charles 381, 382
Angola 175
  war 213
antelope 402, 405
Aranos 319
Arnhem Cave 97
Aus 336
  listings 340

B

Baaiweg, the 230
baboon 407
backpacker hostels 21
ballooning 4
  Sossusvlei 303
bars 28
Basters people 317, 383
Battle of Waterberg 111
beer 25
Benguela Current 243
Berlin Conference 153
Bethanie 336
Bird Island 245

birdwatching 5, 162, 175, 239, 318
  Naute Recreation Resort 335
black rhino 401
Bloedkoppie 296
Bogenfels, Lüderitz 356
Bohor reedbuck 405
border crossings 11
  Namibia–Angola
  Katwitwi 149
  Oshikango–Santa Clara 216
  Ruacana–Calueque 202
  Namibia–Botswana
  Buitepos–Mamuno 99
  Dobe 144
  Mohembo 158
  Ngoma Bridge 164
  Namibia–South Africa
  Ariamsvlei–Nakop 362
  Noordoewer–Vioolsdrif 362
  Sendelingsdrif 360
  Namibia–Zambia
  Kazungula 165
  Wenela–Sesheke 165
  Namibia–Zimbabwe
  Kazungula 164
Bosua Pass 280
braai 26
Brandberg 179
  listings 187
Brandberg Massif 180
Brukkaros Mountain 321
buffalo 401
Buitepos 99
  listings 101
Bull's Party 283
Büllsport 298
Burchell's zebra 402
Burnt Mountain 184
bushbuck 406
Bushmanland 142

Bushman's Paradise 179
Bushmen (San) 365, 376
  paintings 179
Bushy Corner 367
bus travel 11, 14
Bwabwata National Park 155, **161**

C

camping 21
canoeing 5
  Orange River 363, 372
Cao, Diego 380
Cape Cross Seal Reserve 270
Caprivi **146**, 152
  listings 166
Caprivi, East 159
Caprivi, West 154, **155**
caravan parks 21
car hire 15
  Windhoek 82
Carnet de Passages 11
car travel 11, 15
Chacma baboon 407
cheetah 400
Cheetah Conservation Fund 108
Chief Oaseb 379
children, travelling with 32
cinema 29
climate 4, 397
clubs 28
colonization 384
consulates 33
culture 395
currency 38
customs 32

D

Daan Viljoen Game Park 86
Damaraland 175, 176, **177**
Damara people 175, 376
Damara tern 270
dassie 407
desert elephants 182

Desert Express 84
desert flights 303
desert horses 337, 338
desert rhino 185
diamonds 29, 75
Diaz, Bartholomew 380
Diaz Point 353
dik-dik 406
dinosaur footprints 285
disabled travellers 33
Divundu 154
Dordabis 97
Dorob National Park 268
drink 25
    tap water 25
driving 18
Dune 45 302
duneboarding 7
dunes 302
Durissa Bay North 274
Düsternbrook 87
duty free 32
Duwisib Castle 324
    listings 328

E

economy 393
eland 403
electricity 33
elephant 400
embassies 33
    Windhoek 85
emergencies 32
entertainment 28
Epupa Camp 205
Epupa Falls 175, 201
    listings 205
Erongo Mountains 283
Essy Bay 353
ethnic groups 395
Etosha National Park
    119, **120**
    listings 124
exchange rate 38

F

fauna 399
fishing 6, 175, 259, 393

Fish River Canyon 358, **364**
    equipment 367
    Hobas Campsite 365
    listings 370
flora 398
food 25
football 76
Four Fingers Rock 367

G

game farms 22
Gamsberg Pass 282
Ganab 295
Garub Plain 338
gay and lesbian travellers 33
gemsbok 403
geography 397
German-Namibian War
    1904-1907 385
Giant's Playground 334
Gibeon Meteorites 54
giraffe 402
gnu 404
Goageb 336
Gobabis 97
    listings 100
Gochas 319
golf 259
Gondwana Cañon Park 368
Gondwana Sperrgebiet
    Rand Park 338
Griffith Bay 352
Grootfontein 135, **136**
Groot Tinkas 296
Grosse Bucht 353
Gross Nabas 321
Gross Spitzkoppe 178
Grünau 359
guest farms 22
guesthouses 23
Guinas, Lake 134

H

Halali 127
Halifax Island 353
Hamilton Mountains 296
hartebeest 404

Hartmann's mountain zebra
    402
Hartmann's Valley 199, 204
health 33
Helmeringhausen 325
Henties Bay 268
Herero people 377
Heroes' Acre 64
hiking 6
    Brukkaros Mountain 322
    Fish River Canyon 366
    Naukluft Park 300
Himba people 175, 197
    etiquette 197
    visiting the Himba 197
Hinterland 280, **281**
hippopotamus 401
history 376
hitchhiking 20
Hoba Meteorite 137
Hobas 363
Hobas Campsite and
    Observation Point 365
holidays 36
Homeb 295
horse riding 6, 259
    Namib Feral Trail 338
hostels 21
hot-air ballooning 4
hotels 24
    price codes 23
hyena 406

I

Ibenstein Weavers 97
immigration 43
impala 405
Impalila Island 166
Independence 389, 391
inselbergs 178
insurance 37
Intercape timetable 17
internet 37

J

jackal 406
Jakkalsputz Trail 269

Jonker, Jan 230, 244, 383, 384
Joubert Pass 195

K

Kalkfeld 285
Kalk Kegel 186
Kalkrand 318
Kamanjab 186, 202
Kaokoland 175, 192, **193**
karakul sheep 334, 387
Karasburg 359
Karibib 283
Katima Mulilo 148, 163
Katutura 64
Katwitwi border 149
Kavango **146**, 147
Keetmanshoop 331, **333**
    listings 339
Kgalagadi Transfrontier Park 320
Khaudum National Park 403
Khomas Hochland 87
Khorixas 181, 191
    listings 187
Khowarib 194
    listings 203
Klein Aub 298
Klein Spitzkoppe 178
Knochen Bay 353
Kolmanskop Ghost Town 350
Kongola 160
Königstein 180
Kooigoedhoote Pass 367
Kriess-se-Rus 295
Kristall Kellerei vineyard 285
kudu 403
Kuiseb Canyon 294
Kunene River 175
Kutako, Hosea 389
Kwando River 159

L

Lake Guianas 134
Lake Oanob Resort 318
Lake Otjikoto 134

language 37
    useful words and phrases 410
Lappiesdorp 232
League of Nations mandate 388
leopard 400
Lianshulu Lodge 160
Liebig House 280
lion 400
lodges 24
London Mission Society 381
Lüderitz 343, **345**
    Agate Beach 353
    climate 344
    Goerke House 347
    Halifax Island 353
    history 344
    listings 354
    museum 349
Lüderitz, Adolf 384
Lüderitz Peninsula 351, **352**
Luther, Martin 239

M

Mahango Game Reserve 148
Maherero 384
Maherero Day 90
makalani palm 208
malaria 33, 35
Maltahöhe 324
    listings 327, 328
Mamili National Park
    see Nkasa Rupara National Park 162
maps 21
Marienfluss Valley 199
    listings 204
Mariental 319
    listings 326
Martin, Henno 294
Mashi Craft Market 160
media 37
Mirabib 295
missionaries 380
mobile phones 40
Mondesa 240

money 38
    exchange rate 38
monkey 407
motorbiking 20
mountain biking 20
Mudumu National Park 160, **161**

N

Nakambale Museum 211
Nama people 376
Namibia Tourism Board (NTB), Windhoek 51
Namibia Wildlife Resorts (NWR) 51
Namib-Naukluft Park 291
NamibRand Nature Reserve 304
Namib Section 293
Namutoni 128
Nara melons 294
national parks
    accommodation 24
National West Coast
    Recreation Area 268
    see Dorob National Park 268
Naukluft Hiking Trail 296, 300
Naukluft Mountains 297
    history 297
Naukluft Park 296
    hiking 300
Naute Dam 335
Naute Recreation Resort 335
Navachab Gold Mine 284
newspapers 37
Nkasa Rupara National Park **161**, 162
Nkurenkuru 149
Noordoewer 361
    listings 370
Nyae Nyae Conservancy 143

O

Oanob Lake Resort 318
Odendaal Commission 178
offroad driving 20

Ogongo Canal 201
Okahandja 88, **89**
  listings 92
Okaukuejo 120
  listings 125
Okavango River 148
Okongwati 199
Okonjima Private Nature
  Reserve 109
Olive Trail 300
Omaruru 284
Ombalantu Baobab Tree 215
Ondangwa 210
  listings 217
Ongulumbashe 215
Ongwediva 214
Oorlam migration 377
Oorlam people 377
opening hours 39
Opuwo 198
  listings 204
Orange River 361
Organ Pipes 184
oribi 405
Orupembe 197
Oshakati 214
  listings 217
Oshikango 212
Oshikuku 215
Otavi 131
Otjihaenamaperero Farm
  286
Otjiwarongo 107, **107, 109**
  listings 115
Outapi 215
Outjo 113, **113**
overland trucks 12
Owamboland 175

P
packing 5
Palm Springs 366
Peace Accord 1870 383
penguins 353
people 395
performing arts 29
Petrified Forest 183
Phillip's Cave 283

Pohamba, Hifikepunye 392
Pondok Mountain 178
Popa Falls 154
post 39
price codes 23
public holidays 36
puku 404
Puros 195
  listings 204

Q
quad biking 6
  Sossusvlei 260
Quiver Tree Forest 334

R
radio 37
rail travel 14
  luxury trains 14, 83
Red Drum 197
red lechwe 404
Red Line 132, 147, 195, 389
Rehoboth 317
responsible travel 30
restaurants 28
  price codes 23
rhino 185, 401
Rietoog 298
roan antelope 403
rock art 175, 179
  Omaruru 285
  Spitzkoppe 179
  Twyfelfontein 183
rock hyrax 407
Rössing Uranium Mine 240
Ruacana 202
Ruacana Falls 201
  listings 206
Rundu 148, **148**

S
sable antelope 403
safari 7
safety 39
San (Bushmen) people
  376, 396
sandboarding 7
Sandwich Harbour 246
scenic flights 7

sea kayaking 6
Seal Beach 276
seals 270
Seeheim 335
Seeis 96
Sesfontein 195
  listings 203
Sesriem Canyon **299, 302,**
  304
Shearwater Bay 353
shopping 29
sitatunga 404
Skeleton Coast 267, **273**
Skeleton Coast National Park
  268, 272
Skeleton Coast wilderness
  276
skydiving 7
Solitaire **299,** 301
Sossusvlei 301, **302**
  desert flights 303
  hot-air balloon trips 303
Spitzkoppe 178
  listings 187
Springbokwasser 272
springbuck 405
Stampriet 319
Stone Elephant Head 283
Sturmvogel Bucht 352
Sturmvogel Bücht 352
Swakopmund 224, **225, 226**
  Alte Gefängnis 233
  Bismarck Street 236
  Daniel Tjongarero Avenue
    234
  history 228
  listings 247
  Living Desert Snake Park
    235
  museum 231
  Theo-Ben Gurirab Avenue
    234
  tourist information 227
  transport 225
Swakopmund Saltworks
  238
SWAPO 390, 392

T

Table Mountain 366
tax 40
taxis 20
telephone 40
Terrace Bay 276
Three Passes 280
Three Sisters Rock 367
time zone 41
tipping 41
Torra Bay 275
tourist information 42
tour operators 41
traders 380
train travel 14
TransNamib 14
transport 9–21
Triangle 130
Trockenposten 280
Tsarishoogte Pass 302
Tsaris Mountains 302
Tsumeb 132, **133**
Tsumkwe 143
Turnhalle Conference 391
Twyfelfontein 183

U

Ugab River 274
Uis 180
   listings 187
Uniab River Delta 275
Uri-Ais 183
Usakos 282
Ushoogte Pass 282

V

vaccinations 33
Van Zyl's Pass 199
VAT refunds 40
vegetation 398
vervet monkey 407
Vingerklip 185
visas 43
Vogelfedeberg 296
volunteering 44
Von Bach Dam Resort 87, 91
Von François Fort 280
von Trotha, Lothar 386

W

Walvis Bay **225**, 241, **242**
Walvis Bay Lagoon 245
War in the Naukluft
   Mountains 297
Warmbad 359
Warmquelle 194
   listings 203
warthog 407
Waterberg Plateau Park 110
   hiking 112
   listings 116
   wildlife 112, 123
waterbuck 404
Waterkloof Trail 300
weights and measures 43
Welwitschia Drive 240
White Lady 179
white rhino 401
wildebeest 404
wild horses of the Namib 337
wildlife 399

Windhoek 48, **49**, **55**, **57**, **59**
   accommodation 66
   airports 48
   Alte Fest (Old Fort) 58
   Bahnhof Street 63
   bars and clubs 72
   Christuskirche 56
   climate 50
   clock tower 53
   directory 84
   eating 69
   embassies and consulates
      85
   entertainment 73
   festivals 73
   Fidel Castro Street 56
   Heinitzburg Castle 60
   history 51
   Post Street 54
   Robert Mugabe Avenue
      61
   safety 51
   Sanderburg Castle 60
   Schwerinburg Castle 60
   shopping 74
   suburbs 64
   tourist information 51
   tour operators 77
   townships 64
   transport 48, 80
   Zoo Park 53
Witbooi, Hendrik 384
Witvlei 96
women travellers 44
Wondergat 184
working 44

Z

Zebra Pan 295

Advertisers' index

Credits

Footprint credits

Editor: Nicola Gibbs
Production and layout: Emma Bryers
Maps: Kevin Feeney
Colour section: Angus Dawson

Publisher: Patrick Dawson
Managing Editor: Felicity Laughton
Advertising: Elizabeth Taylor
Sales and marketing: Kirsty Holmes

Photography credits

Front cover: Superstock/Hermes Images
Back cover: Superstock/Hermes Images

Colour section

Page i: superstock: Lizzie Williams. **Page ii**: superstock: Dave Stamboulis/age fotostock. **Page v**: dreamstime: Grobler Du Preez/Dreamstime.com. **Page vi**: superstock: Roger de la Harpe/Roger de la Harpe; Radius/Radius. **Page vii**: Lizzie: Lizzie Williams. dreamstime: Bevanward/Dreamstime.com. **Page viii**: Lizzie: Lizzie Williams. **Page ix**: superstock: Gallo Images/Gallo Images; Ingram Publishing/Ingram Publishing

Wildlife section

Page i: superstock: Gallo Images/Gallo Images. **Page ii**: dreamstime: Mogens Trolle/Dreamstime.com. **Page iii**: dreamstime: Johannes Gerhardus Swanepoel. superstock: NaturePL/NaturePL. **Page iv**: dreamstime: Pytyczech/Dreamstime.com. superstock: Kim Walker/Robert Harding Picture Library. **Page v**: superstock: Minden Pictures/Minden Pictures. **Page vi**: superstock: Mint Images/Mint Images; Tibor Bognár/age fotostock; Prisma/Prisma. **Page vii**: dreamstime: Johan63/Dreamstime.com. **Page viii**: dreamstime: Anke Van Wyk/Dreamstime.com. superstock: age fotostock/age fotostock; Mint Images/Mint Images. **Page iv**: superstock: imageBROKER/imageBROKER; Minden Pictures/Minden Pictures; Radius/Radius. **Page x**: superstock: age fotostock/age fotostock; imageBROKER/imageBROKER; Mint Images/Mint Images. **Page xi**: superstock: Biosphoto/Biosphoto; imageBROKER/imageBROKER; Westend61/Westend61. **Page xii**: superstock: Minden Pictures / Minden Pictures. dreamstime: Steven Prorak/Dreamstime.com Andries Alberts/Dreamstime.com. **Page xiii**: dreamstime: Mogens Trolle/Dreamstime.com. **Page xiv**: superstock: Kerstin Layer/Mauritius; NaturePL/NaturePL. **Page xv**: superstock: age fotostock/age fotostock; Bill Gozansky/age fotostock. dreamstime: Smellme/Dreamstime.com; Anke Van Wyk/Dreamstime.com. **Page xvi**: superstock: Cusp/Cusp.

Printed in India by Thomson Press Ltd, Faridabad, Haryana

Publishing information

Footprint Namibia
7th edition
© Footprint Handbooks Ltd
January 2015

ISBN: 978 1 910120 071
CIP DATA: A catalogue record for this book is available from the British Library

® Footprint Handbooks and the Footprint mark are a registered trademark of Footprint Handbooks Ltd

Published by Footprint
6 Riverside Court
Lower Bristol Road
Bath BA2 3DZ, UK
T +44 (0)1225 469141
F +44 (0)1225 469461
footprinttravelguides.com

Distributed in the USA by National Book Network, Inc.

Every effort has been made to ensure that the facts in this guidebook are accurate. However, travellers should still obtain advice from consulates, airlines, etc about travel and visa requirements before travelling. The authors and publishers cannot accept responsibility for any loss, injury or inconvenience however caused.

Footprint Mini Atlas
Namibia

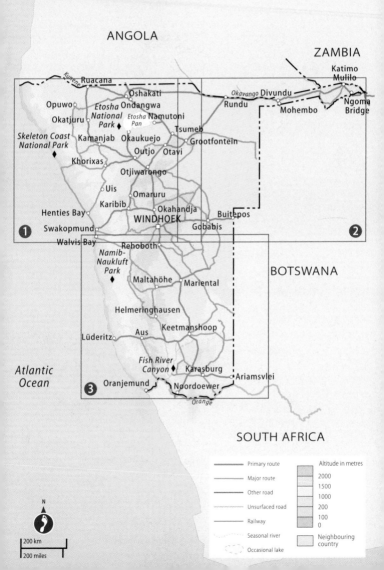

ANGOLA

ZAMBIA

Katimo
Mulilo

Kunene   Ruacana

Opuwo   Oshakati   Ondangwa
                                          Okavango Divundu
Okatjuru   Etosha   Rundu   Ngoma
            National   Etosha Namutoni   Mohembo   Bridge
Skeleton Coast Park   Pan
National   Kamanjab Okaukuejo   Tsumeb
  Park   Khorixas   Outjo Otavi Grootfontein

                        Otjiwarongo

               Uis   Omaruru

           Karibib
Henties Bay   Okahandja   Buitepos
Swakopmund   WINDHOEK   Gobabis
Walvis Bay

            Rehoboth
         Namib-   BOTSWANA
         Naukluft
          Park   Maltahöhe   Mariental

              Helmeringhausen

Lüderitz   Aus   Keetmanshoop

Atlantic   Fish River
Ocean   Canyon   Karasburg
         Oranjemund   Noordoewer   Ariamsvlei
                             Orange

                    SOUTH AFRICA

	Primary route		Altitude in metres
	Major route		2000
	Other road		1500
	Unsurfaced road		1000
	Railway		200
	Seasonal river		100
	Occasional lake		0
			Neighbouring country

N

200 km
200 miles

Map 1

ANGOLA

KAOKOLAND

NORTHERN DAMARALAND

SOUTHERN DAMARALAND

Atlantic Ocean

Skeleton Coast National Park

N

30 km
30 miles

Distance chart

	Ariamsvlei	Buitepos	Gobabis	Grootfontein	Henties Bay	Kamanjab	Keetmanshoop	Lüderitz	Mariental	Namutoni	Noordoewer	Okaukuejo	Ondangwa	Otjiwarongo	Ruacana	Rundu	Swakopmund	Tsumeb
Buitepos	1118																	
Gobabis	1003	115																
Grootfontein	1250	772	657															
Henties Bay	1223	745	630	645														
Kamanjab	1261	783	668	425	345													
Keetmanshoop	333	802	687	934	907	945												
Lüderitz	579	1136	1021	1268	923	1279	334											
Mariental	537	581	466	713	686	724	221	555										
Namutoni	1331	853	738	167	677	506	1015	1349	794									
Noordoewer	306	1106	991	1238	1211	1249	304	609	525	1319								
Okaukuejo	1233	755	640	397	579	262	917	1253	696	123	1221							
Ondangwa	1471	993	878	307	817	646	1155	1489	934	210	1459	333						
Otjiwarongo	1043	565	450	207	389	218	727	1061	506	288	1031	190	428					
Ruacana	1658	1180	1065	494	1143	272	1342	1676	1121	469	1646	534	187	615				
Rundu	1498	1020	905	248	893	645	1182	1516	961	415	1486	617	555	455	742			
Swakopmund	1156	678	563	578	67	412	840	731	619	659	1144	561	799	371	684	826		
Tsumeb	1224	746	631	60	570	399	907	1242	687	107	1241	345	247	181	434	308	552	
Windhoek	798	320	205	452	466	463	482	816	261	533	786	435	673	245	860	700	356	426

Distances in kilometres   1 kilometre = 0.62 miles

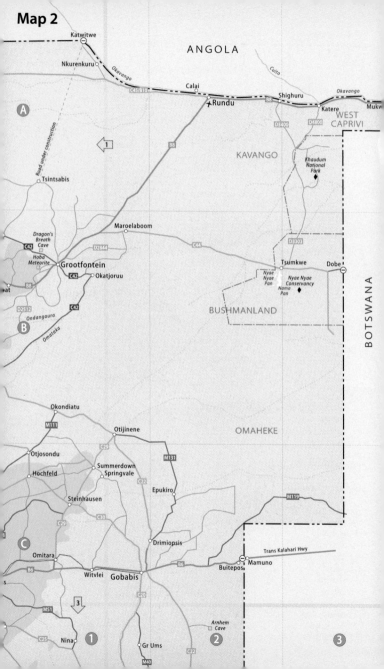